THOMAS E. HILL, Ph.D. University of Edin-
burgh, and B.D. Union Theological Seminary,
Virginia, is Professor of Philosophy at Macalester
College. He carried on postdoctoral research at
Harvard University, Oxford University and Tüb-
ingen University, Germany, and previously taught
at the University of Georgia, and King College
and Southwestern College, both in Tennessee.

CONTEMPORARY
THEORIES
OF
KNOWLEDGE

THOMAS ENGLISH HILL

PROFESSOR OF PHILOSOPHY
MACALESTER COLLEGE

THE RONALD PRESS COMPANY • NEW YORK

2V

Library of Congress Catalog Card Number: 61-5658

PRINTED IN THE UNITED STATES OF AMERICA

Preface

THE purpose of this book is to summarize, compare, and evaluate the most significant trends of British and American epistemological thought during the present century, to orient the reader in the current epistemological scene, and to help him come to grips with the central problems raised by present conflicting views.

The book is designed to aid and encourage at every level the sort of critical and reflective thought required for clarification in the presently confused but always crucial area of theory of knowledge. It is intended to help advanced undergraduates and graduate students broaden their grasp of epistemology, to review for experienced teachers and scholars crucial phases of epistemological works they have previously read, and to introduce students of other aspects of philosophy to current epistemological inquiries that may prove relevant to their own special interests. The book should also serve as a suitable basis for courses and seminars in epistemology and contemporary philosophy.

The theories presented here are classified according to major types and subtypes. Insofar as possible, each subtype is presented in terms of the thought of a single selected representative, or at most two or three. Other writers are introduced for the most part only very briefly, as their views supplement or differ from those of the chosen representatives, though with reference to some more recent types of thought, more than two or three selected representatives are deemed necessary.

Each chapter begins with a brief introduction to the type of epistemology to be considered; then each philosopher's work is presented as far as possible in its own terms, the author's remarks being confined to the introductions and comments at the beginnings and endings respectively of each chapter. The comments with which each chapter closes are largely directed toward the work of the major representatives of the theory under consideration. They attempt to offer some suggestions concerning generally recognized achievements and conspicuous deficiencies of each type of theory in such manner as to facilitate comparison of theories and to focus attention upon major issues.

The book is largely confined to British and American epistemological thought, and indeed to what may be called the "main stream" of such thought. This involves the omission of such interesting epistemological suggestions as some of those of recent neo-Thomists, Marxists, phenomenologists, and existentialists. But an additional volume would have been required to include satisfactory expositions of all these theories, and most of the crucial issues arise in one place or another within the pattern of theories that are considered here. The views of a few continental writers whose influence upon British and American thought has been particularly strong are explicitly presented in this volume.

Although I have been sustained in the writing of this book by the kindness of more persons than I can name here, I wish to express special gratitude to the Fund for the Advancement of Education and to Mr. DeWitt Wallace for grants for research at Harvard and Oxford, to Macalester College for arranging reduced teaching loads and leaves of absence, and to Professors C. I. Lewis of Harvard and Brand Blanshard of Yale for their generous advice and encouragement.

Thomas English Hill

Saint Paul, Minnesota
    January, 1961

Contents

Part III
MEDIATING THEORIES

Part IV
PRAGMATIST THEORIES

Part V
ANALYTIC THEORIES

CONTEMPORARY
THEORIES
OF
KNOWLEDGE

CHAPTER 1

Introduction

PROBLEMS of theory of knowledge already implicit in ancient and medieval philosophy have set the major themes of modern philosophy and, despite some shifts in emphasis, continue to play vital roles in contemporary philosophy. Epistemological inquiry is in constant and fruitful interaction with metaphysics, ethics, and every other branch of philosophy as well as with scientific methodology and esthetic criticism. It helps to render inquiry in every other field self-conscious, and it is itself enriched by the procedures and findings of every other type of inquiry. Although men commonly acquire their knowledge without benefit of specific epistemological inquiry, whenever they encounter contrasting ways of knowing, approach boundaries of knowledge, or attempt to relate such different kinds of knowledge as scientific, moral, esthetic, and religious knowledge, they are compelled to re-examine the basic presuppositions and prospects of knowledge; and no end of such re-examining seems to be in sight. The more knowledge advances in the mastery of its objects, the more varied and complex it becomes; hence the more urgent becomes the demand that it turn from time to time upon itself to see whence it comes and whither it leads.

While theory of knowledge embraces a considerable variety of questions, most of the issues that have been discussed in connection with it fall under one or the other of three problems: the nature of knowledge or the meaning of epistemic terms, the validation of cognition or the criteria of knowledge, and the relation between cognitive experience and its object. Although the seeds of major conflict concerning each of these problems were already present in the philosophy of the ancient and medieval periods and occasionally came fully to light in those periods, there remained a broad tendency among the philosophers who set the course of the thought of those periods to agree in their main assumptions on the problem in question. On the whole, these philosophers were inclined to regard knowledge as apprehension of truth, its principal criterion as rational certainty, and the relation involved in it as one between an objective reality on the one hand and a conforming experience on the other. Accordingly, it has for the most part remained for philosophers of the modern period to bring to focus those basic differences that have produced the epistemological controversies of the contemporary period.

Until about the beginning of the present century, most modern philosophers were inclined to concur in the assumptions of their philosophical forebears that knowing was apprehension of truth, and its principal criterion, rational certainty. But they soon became aware of a possible conflict between these two assumptions and the assumption that the relation between cognitive experience and its object was one between objective reality and conforming experience. Accordingly, although the earlier philosophers of the modern era endeavored to hold on to the traditional view of the cognitive relation, they were aware of difficulties in this view, and their successors developed some quite different views. Thus, at the outset of the modern period, Hobbes, following the lead of the long-neglected Greek atomists, interpreted perceptual knowledge in terms of brain events and associated phantasms caused by external events, and in so doing raised, without resolving, the question of how cognitive experience, being mediate, could be assumed to conform to objective reality. Descartes was deeply troubled by this difficulty as well as by those posed by the facts of error and illusion, and in the end he was able to save the traditional idea of the cognitive relation only by invoking divine intervention. Spinoza and Leibnitz were scarcely much more successful in defending the traditional view, and Locke was obliged to confess that, while agreement among ideas could be established, the substance which cognition sought to grasp was a something he knew not what. In the light of this impasse Berkeley abandoned the traditional view that the object of knowledge need be objective to all cognition and laid the foundations of a new idealist epistemology. Hume's thought undermined this view by showing skeptical implications involved in its presuppositions. Kant tried to restore a modified version of the traditional view by joining sensations with fixed forms of experience. However, nineteenth-century successors of Kant revitalized the Berkelean idealism and, reinterpreting it in terms of Kantian categories, developed a type of absolute idealism emphasizing system and embracing in a single unity both cognitive experience and its object. It was this idealism that, despite some rumblings of realism in Germany and Austria, was dominant in Great Britain and America as the twentieth century opened.

However, idealism is somewhat too far removed from common sense and science to remain long unchallenged, and just at the turn of the century there began to emerge in England and America a new realism whose conflict with idealism was the major theme of the philosophy of the first part of the present century. Meanwhile, it occurred to other philosophers that the difficulties in which modern epistemology had landed might be attributable to wrong assumptions on issues other than that of the character of the relation of cognitive experience and object. Hence the American pragmatists reopened the question of the validation of cognition and challenged both idealism and realism with the contention that both were mistaken in accepting outmoded assumptions concerning the criteria of knowledge. Soon afterward analytic philosophers, reopening what they considered the even more basic issue of the meaning of epistemic terms, began to challenge all previous epistemologies on the ground that they were based on naïve and outmoded assumptions on this issue and that perhaps knowing was not a relation at all.

It is, accordingly, scarcely surprising that the contemporary period, being one in which there is fundamental conflict not only concerning the basic answers in epistemology but also concerning what the crucial questions are, should be, despite the misgivings of some critics, at the same time one of the most fruitful and one of the most bewildering periods in epistemological thought. Our task in the pages that follow will be to endeavor to sketch the leading epistemological ideas of the period in terms of a frame of references that will disclose an intelligible order in the literature and facilitate comparison and evaluation.

Perhaps it will be helpful to indicate at the outset the sort of classification of theories that is to be developed. Since answers are scarcely likely to be illuminating apart from the questions to which they reply and since the questions principally raised by various contemporary theories are very different, our major classification of theories will hinge upon which of the major epistemological problems is emphasized in the case of each type of theory. Although all contemporary epistemologies are in one way or another concerned with all of the major epistemological questions, on the whole those considered in Parts I–III, the idealist theories, the realist ones, and the mediating ones, are theories that have been primarily concerned with the problem of the relation of cognitive experience and its object; those considered in Part IV, the pragmatic theories, are theories that have been primarily concerned with the problem of the criteria of valid cognition; and those in Part V, the analytic theories, are theories that have been primarily concerned with the problem of the meanings of epistemic terms. Subclassifications are to be developed for each of these larger classes of theories, in terms of issues that are foremost within each.

Part I

IDEALIST THEORIES

CHAPTER 2

Earlier Expressions of Contemporary Idealism

At the beginning of the nineteenth century the dominant epistemological trend, at any rate in university circles in Great Britain and America, was absolute idealism. It was accordingly inevitable that the rise of new epistemological trends should have been oriented in one way or another to the claims of this type of idealism. Idealists of this type were inclined to take epistemological problems very seriously, and while their primary epistemological concern was with the traditional problem of the relation of the knower and the known, they also devoted careful attention to the problems of the validity of knowledge and of the nature of truth, and they were by no means unmindful of the problem of the nature of knowledge. Accordingly, one of the best procedures for working one's way into various aspects of contemporary epistemological thought, both as to its leading schools and as to its crucial issues, is to begin with a careful examination of the thought of one of the major idealistic writers of the close of the past century and the beginning of the present one.

1. The Nature and Background of Contemporary Idealism

Traditionally, epistemological idealism has been taken to be the view that the object of knowledge depends upon the experiencing or knowing process. That view may, however, be interpreted in a num-

7

ber of different ways. It may mean that the finite knower creates or
conditions the finite object, or in any case that some knowing process
creates or conditions those objects. It may mean that all reality is
essentially experiential in character, or it may mean, as it does for
most of the writers now to be considered, that all of reality, embracing both objects and knowings, belongs to a single interdependent
and coherent system.

The philosophical roots of idealistic epistemology are very ancient.
Idealistic notions are already suggested, for example, in the thinking
of the Pythagoreans, who, though in no sense disposed to make knowledge subjective, saw in the intelligible order of number the root of
reality. The idealist tendencies implicit in Pythagoreanism were
more fully developed in the thought of Plato, for whom reality was
an intelligible realm of rational Ideas. This strain of thought, by no
means entirely abandoned by Aristotle, continued to exercise a powerful influence throughout the Middle Ages. The conception of a
complete order of necessary truth and reality also dominated the
thought of Spinoza, as well as that of Hegel and many other modern
philosophers.

The subjective side of idealism that makes the object not only
intelligible but also dependent upon the activity of intelligence received a powerful impetus from Augustine, and in Descartes' *Cogito
ergo sum* it became a cornerstone of modern epistemology. Berkeley
was unable to believe that anything that was neither mind nor a
product of mind was thinkable, and Kant pointed out an impassable
chasm between our intuitions and categories on the one hand and
the thing-in-itself on the other. From Hegel's time onward German
idealists found in the categories of mind the root of all reality, and
even as the idealist tradition was declining in Germany, it was being
successfully revived in Great Britain and America under the leadership of Bradley, Bosanquet, and Royce. Of these three, perhaps the
most influential was F. H. Bradley (1846–1924). By way of describing
the kinds of questions and answers that set the stage for contemporary
epistemology, we shall in this chapter sketch the thought of Bradley
fairly fully and touch much more briefly on that of some other significant idealists of the same period.

The world of the philosophical thought of Bradley and his idealist
contemporaries is so radically different from that of more recent
philosophical thought that philosophers brought up upon Russell,
Moore, Carnap, and the earlier and later Wittgenstein may find it
strange and at first even unintelligible. It is a world in which while
religion and philosophy have been officially separated, philosophical
discussions are still oriented to religious issues. It is a world where

there is none of the recent timidity with reference to the metaphysical terms and questions, in which "entity," "reality," "self," "object," "world," "universe," and even "absolute" are not only spoken of but often capitalized, hypostatized, and dealt with in utmost confidence. It is a world in which subsequent opposition to "psychologisms" has not yet made itself felt and upon which the new logistic and the current demand for logical rigor and clarity of meaning has not yet had its impact, a world accordingly in which thought moves all too easily and loosely. It is a world in which science is not yet supreme or even for that matter the equal partner of other modes of insight, a world in which feeling and intuitions play prominent roles and in which reason is expected to be no mere guide to conduct but an organ of insight into the nature of things. It is a world to which the rigid dichotomy of analytic and empirical that has dominated most recent thought is as yet largely foreign, and in which the metaphysical ideal of discerning the character of existing fact by means of sheer logical thought is still cherished. It is a world in which truth is fundamentally necessary truth to be tested by, built out by, and even in the end reduced to, coherence. Nevertheless it is a world in which perennial problems of epistemology are raised and seriously wrestled with, a world in which many of the roots of current issues are to be found, and oddly enough a world including some significant ideas to which the most recent thought tends to return, a world into which the serious student of contemporary thought can and should enter.

2. Bradley's View of the Structure of Knowing

Bradley's first significant work, *Ethical Studies*, appeared in 1876 and, although it was mainly concerned with a different subject, suggested already the idealistic trend of his epistemology. His *Principles of Logic*, published in 1883, was much more than logic in the traditional sense, and contained the essential concepts of his theory of knowledge. His *Appearance and Reality*, first printed in 1893, is specifically concerned with metaphysics, but a fully developed idealistic epistemology is worked out in it. Bradley's *Essays on Truth and Reality* (1914), a collection of articles written for the most part in the early years of the twentieth century, is in considerable part directly concerned with epistemological problems. These essays, together with the appendices added to *Appearance and Reality*, the "Terminal Essays" published with the more recent editions of the *Logic*, the copious footnotes in the latter, and a few selections in his *Collected Essays* (1935), represent Bradley's defense and modification of his earlier views. Without troubling the reader with specific changes in

Bradley's epistemological conceptions, we shall endeavor to present as systematically as possible the conclusions that seem to be most characteristic of Bradley's mature reflection.

The part of theory of knowledge with which Bradley initiates, in his *Principles of Logic,* his inquiry into epistemological issues concerns the logical and psychological structure of knowing, and it is with Bradley's account of this part that we begin. Included in this part are Bradley's accounts of immediate experience, meaning, judgment, and inference.

A. The knowing process arises from and, in a sense to be explained, culminates in, immediate experience or feeling. By feeling Bradley does not mean, as is sometimes meant by the term, simply emotional response. Rather, he means any full and direct experience as it is enjoyed in the moment of experiencing before reflection has altered it; he means what is commonly meant by a given. "Immediate experience," he says, is "that which is comprised wholly within a single state of undivided awareness or feeling." [1] Perhaps such experience is rarely if ever to be found in complete purity, for "a state of feeling may have details, which though felt, are internally far beyond being merely felt"; but this restriction in no sense rules out the existence or the importance of immediate experience.[2]

Although immediate experience is fully unified and contains no breaks or relations, it is not undiversified. It binds together rich variety in unbroken unity and never contains "either qualities without relations or relations without qualities." [3] It is a kind of feeling which "being more than merely simple, holds many in one, and contains a diversity within a unity which itself is not relational." [4]

Similarly, although it does not illuminate all reality, it involves no sharp break with that which is beyond it,[5] and in this sense it is continuous with all reality. In a suggestive passage Bradley compares its focus with an illuminated spot upon a dark river, shading off by imperceptible degrees into a larger setting.[6]

Immediate experience is basic to all knowledge in the sense that all that we become aware of has its origin and unity here.[7] A segment of immediate experience is the initial subject of our elementary judgments. Immediate experience is the sole area in which we

---

[1] F. H. Bradley, *Essays on Truth and Reality* (Oxford: Clarendon Press, 1914), p. 173.

[2] Bradley, *Collected Essays* (Oxford: University Press, 1935), II, 632 f.

[3] Bradley, *The Principles of Logic* (2d ed., corrected impression; New York &

London: Oxford University Press, Humphrey Milford, 1928), I, 2, 9.

[4] *Collected Essays,* II, 633.

[5] *The Principles of Logic,* II, 482.

[6] *Ibid.,* I, pp. 54 ff.

[7] Cf., e.g., *ibid.,* II, 695 f.

directly apprehend reality.[8] With some qualifications, it must also be taken as the final test of truth.[9]

But despite its cardinal role in knowledge, immediate experience or feeling is not knowing. "For for us to remain everywhere within the stage and the limits of feeling is impossible. If we are to know, we must understand."[10] Clearly a single given experience cannot be by itself an instance of knowing, for knowing involves an application of ideal content to datum that is far more complex than any such experience. Some thinkers hold that there are given *complexes* that yield infallible knowledge. But no such complexes can be given at all, and even if they could they would, by conjoining factors that reveal no inner connection, involve self-contradiction.[11]

B. All knowing requires, over and above immediate experience, ideas, but ideas in turn involve three quite different elements which must be clearly distinguished if confusion is to be avoided. First, there is the vast variety of minute and often irrelevant psychological detail that fluctuates rapidly as each mental event gives way to its successor.[12] Second, there is that for which the idea stands, its extension; for example, if one is thinking of a horse, the actual horse to which the thought refers.[13] But third, and most important for rational knowledge, there is the meaning of the idea, the universal, which beyond the variety of psychological coloring is its basic intension or content.

Although the universal in which intension consists is not as such a psychological event, it is everywhere present in the knowing process. Thus every term used in significant discourse has intension as well as extension. This is true even of proper names, which are commonly thought to *stand for* something but not to *mean* anything. If this were not so there would be no reason for the repeated use of the same name, and, instead of using such a sentence as "John is asleep," one might as well simply point at John and pronounce the word "asleep."[14] The universal is present even at the elementary levels of infant and of animal thought; for example, the dog takes the cat to be his enemy, not a particular cat.[15] "From the very first beginnings of soul-life universals are used."[16]

It would, however, be a serious mistake to think with traditional logic that intension and extension vary inversely in such fashion

[8] Cf. *ibid.*, I, 44.
[9] *Collected Essays*, II, 650.
[10] *The Principles of Logic*, II, 653.
[11] Bradley, *Appearance and Reality* (2d ed., 9th impression, corrected; Oxford: Clarendon Press, 1930), pp. 501 ff.

[12] Cf. *The Principles of Logic*, I, 8 ff.
[13] *Ibid.*, pp. 168 f.
[14] *Ibid.*, p. 59.
[15] *Ibid.*, p. 36.
[16] *Ibid.*, p. 34

that "the less you happen to have of the one, the more you therefore must have of the other." [17] This is obviously not the case where extensions are individuals, and it is trivial where only adjectival words are in question.[18] Besides, it is by no means clear that ideas are less concrete as they become more inclusive, for example, that "the idea of a state has less content than the idea of any one of its citizens" or that "the idea of God [is] assuredly less full than the idea of a molecule." [19] Actually, extention and intension tend to vary together, so that further knowledge of facts tends to enrich the meanings attached to them. "As the extension is increased, so also is the meaning." [20]

This connection is a proper reminder of the necessarily concrete character of the universals in which genuine meaning consists. Abstract universals, or meanings thought of in isolation from the actuality in which they are embedded, are mere "mental creations, . . . distinctions within a whole, hardened into units that stand by themselves." [21] Even these abstract universals are always rooted in reality, as in the continued recurrence of an individual through a period of time. The relative concrete universal is the identity in diversity of the finite individual. But finite individuality itself is not real or self-sufficient individuality, so that in the end the absolute concrete universal is perhaps to be found only in the one whole individual.[22]

C. As the source and end of knowing is immediate experience, and the principal vehicle, meaning, the basic manifestation of knowing is judgment. Indeed, one may go on to say that to think at all is to judge.[23] Judgment is present wherever truth and falsehood are in question.

The processes of judgment begin at that presumably prehuman, and accordingly prelinguistic, level [24] at which "the ideal content which is also fact, and the ideal content which is nothing beyond itself" [25] are first distinguished. Neither mechanical association of ideas [26] or practical operation on the one hand nor inclusion and exclusion or identity of subject and predicate on the other correctly represents the essential character of judgment. The one, however, does indicate the unity and practical basis of judgment, and the other, its necessary complexity. The essential fact about the structure of judgment is that every judgment selects from reality a single idea,

[17] *Ibid.*, p. 170.
[18] *Ibid.*, p. 172.
[19] *Ibid.*, p. 173.
[20] *Ibid.*, p. 184.
[21] *Ibid.*, p. 189.

[22] *Ibid.*, p. 190.
[23] Cf. *Appearance and Reality*, p. 324.
[24] *The Principles of Logic*, I, 32.
[25] *Ibid.*, pp. 33 f.
[26] *Ibid.*, pp. 34 f., 299 ff

which may involve a considerable complexity in its unity, and applies this idea to reality. This fact has, as will be seen, two sides.

From the standpoint of the ideal content every judgment must be regarded as universal.[27] This applies even to an analytic judgment of sense, such as "I have a toothache," [28] —which entails both recurrence through time and the exemplification of universals applicable to any toothache. This means that ultimately all judgments are in an important sense only hypothetical, for universals never fully formulate the nature of an individual, and every judgment is mediated by conditions which it cannot include.

Nevertheless, from the standpoint of their subjects and their purposes, judgments must be taken to be more than hypothetical; indeed, in varying degrees and for practical purposes, they may be taken as attaining categorical standing. Every judgment has as its subject not only an idea but reality.[29] This remains true regardless of the character of the logical operations involved in the judgment. In negative judgments the rejection involved is rooted in what is given of reality, and in disjunctive judgments the pattern of the alternatives is set by the reality apprehended. Even the necessities and possibilities of modal judgments are determined by the nature of reality.[30] "To hold a thought, so to speak in the air, without a relation of any kind to the Real, . . . we should find in the end to be impossible." [31] There are no "floating ideas." [32]

The proximate subject of most judgments is some limited segment of reality, such as a datum or an individual, concerning which the judging process endeavors to determine whether or not it is qualified by a certain ideal content. Every datum and every finite individual is an abstraction from the whole.

D. Judgment never stands in isolation from other mental processes. While it is to be distinguished from inference in that it does not, like the latter, consist in the specific drawing of conclusions from premises, it always rests upon and constitutes a final phase of inference.[33]

All reasoning proceeds from something known through an internal process to something not previously known.[34] The basic principle of this process is *identity*. Not only are inferences obviously involving identities grounded in the end in identities but so also are inferences

[27] Cf. *ibid.*, pp. 106, 295.
[28] *Ibid.*, p. 49.
[29] Cf. *ibid.*, pp. 50, 56; *Appearance and Reality*, p. 324; *Essays on Truth and Reality*, p. 42.
[30] Cf. *The Principles of Logic*, I, chaps. iii, iv, vii.

[31] *Appearance and Reality*, p. 324.
[32] Cf. *The Principles of Logic*, I, 11; II, 665 ff.; also *Essays on Truth and Reality*, pp. 28 ff.
[33] *The Principles of Logic*, II, 437 ff.
[34] Cf. *ibid.*, pp. 245 ff.

apparently depending on similarities.[35] Identities are discoverable because thought proceeds primarily not through particular ideas or associations of ideas but through universals. Connections can be established because the principle of the identity of indiscernibles, the principle that contents between which no difference is discoverable are the same, is inevitably accepted in inference.[36] The special task of logic as such is so to arrange the contents of thought that the underlying identities may be readily recognized.

Although the types of inference vary considerably, the essential structure of inference remains constant. Perhaps the most frequently employed type of inference is that which connects two terms by means of a third with which each has something in common. Very different types are comparisons and mathematical reasonings, in each of which new terms not included in the premises appear.[37] Induction in general, and Mill's methods in particular, while useful for certain practical purposes, are in the end confused and self-contradictory procedures.[38] In all types of acceptable reasoning, a pattern of ideas drawn from reality is applied to reality. Thus the essential structure of inference may best be expressed by saying: "Inference then . . . is an ideal experiment which procures a result from a given basis. This result is a judgment in which the new product is predicated of the given." [39]

Inference demands both analysis and synthesis, which turn out in the end to be simply different sides of the same process; but the essential requirement of inference is that the thread of identity should be maintained, that transitions never be mere external connections but only necessary internal implications. "Not only does inference preserve an identity throughout the whole process, but in the actual experiment itself we rest upon a central sameness." [40] The very essence of contradiction is external connection without recognizable internal involvement.

Since inference passes from the known through inward recognition of identities to that which was not previously known, it may be regarded as a "self-development" of an object.[41] No isolated piece of inference can be valid in itself. In every inference there must be operating a perfect rational whole in which every part implies every other. Only thus can the further extension of the fragment of the whole that is the subject of the inference be achieved. What fully

[35] *Appearance and Reality*, p. 533.
[36] *Ibid.*, p. 288.
[37] *Ibid.*, Bk. III, Pt. 1, chap. i.
[38] *Ibid.*, Bk. II, Pt. 2, chaps. ii, iii.
[39] *The Principles of Logic* (II, London: Humphrey Milford, Second Edition, Corrected Impression of 1928) p. 446.
[40] *Ibid.*, p. 466.
[41] *Ibid.*, p. 493.

satisfactory inference would require is "a way of thinking in which the whole of reality was a system of its differences immanent in each difference." [42]

In this requirement a character of inference already implicit in other features of inference is clearly indicated, namely, the incapacity of inference to achieve its goal. As we have seen, inference progresses through universals; but, since none of our universals can fully formulate the rich character of any part of given reality, inference is caught in the hopeless dilemma of either not satisfactorily representing reality or else of being unable to proceed by its own principles. In this situation we must prefer given reality to the laws of inference.[43] Similarly, when we ask, concerning each of the modes of inference, whether or not it fulfills the requirements of the ideal self-development of an object, we discover that each involves such obvious gaps that the answer must be in the negative.[44]

Fortunately, however, thought is not confined to the analyses and syntheses of formal logic. Beyond these lies another method which, though also incapable in the end of full apprehension of reality, takes us much further toward the individual in which the real consists and involves substantially more of that genuine self-development which true thought must be. This method, which is the essential one of Bradley's metaphysics, consists in large part in passage from unopposed possibility to reality.[45] It begins with actual experience, and, relying on the fact that belief is natural while doubt is a difficult acquisition, is favorably inclined toward the given. When contradictions are encountered, whatever involves them must be ruled out. But when thought, turning its natural curiosity upon the given, arrives at that which contains no contradictions, it tends to find satisfaction. Such intellectual satisfaction in the noncontradictory is the central feature of knowing and, as we shall see, the final test of truth.

3. BRADLEY'S VIEW OF THE OBJECTS OF KNOWLEDGE

If the structure of knowledge is essentially as indicated, what is the general character of the objects upon which this process is directed? We shall consider first Bradley's idea of the proximate objects of knowledge, then his account of the manner in which the true object comes to light, and finally his interpretation of the nature of the true object.

[42] *Ibid.*, p. 489.
[43] *Ibid.*, pp. 588 ff.
[44] *Ibid.*, pp. 597 ff.

[45] *Ibid.*, p. 453, pp. 486 ff.; cf. also *Appearance and Reality*, p. 173.

A. The proximate or apparent objects of our common observation and thought are in the first instance, given data, and then things, selves, and perhaps nature as a whole. Any of these may be the subject of a judgment or of an inference and to any the ideal experiment of thinking may be applied. But none of these can constitute the true object of genuine knowledge. Each is but a broken fragment of reality, an illuminated spot on the vast stream of reality. None can stand alone; each is only an appearance, never reality as such.

This is evident from the outset with regard to immediate experience, which is by its nature so fleeting and indefinite that thought persistently endeavors to transcend it. Similarly, things and selves are readily seen to be unstable constructions, unable to subsist alone. While the concept of nature is useful for many practical purposes, "nature by itself is but an indefensible division in the whole of experience"—built upon the "poor fiction of primary qualities." [1] It excludes most of that which makes life meaningful.

As a matter of fact, the very character of the concepts employed in human thought is such as to involve all endeavors to know limited objects in hopeless self-contradictions. Whatever parts of our alleged knowledge we take up, the result is the same. "They offer that is, a complex of diversities joined in a way which does not satisfy my intellect, a way which it feels is not its way and which it cannot repeat as its own, a way which for it results in mere collision." [2] For example, both primary and secondary qualities are misleading abstractions such that, while recognizing their presence under given circumstances, we are unable to determine anything about them in the absence of these conditions. [3] In like manner, the affirmation of the inherence of qualities in a substance involves either the false assumption of the independence of the substance and its qualities or the meaningless assumption of their identity. [4] Moreover, with regard to quality and relation, while each depends on the other for its meaning, neither can be established unless the other has independent meaning. [5] Relations themselves are mere abstractions that are not properly either internal or external, and "any relational view involves self-contradiction in its essence." [6] Similar considerations ruin our common concepts of time, space, cause, change, self, and everything else other than the whole.

B. Although no finite object can in itself be the object of genuine knowledge, inquiry into each phase of the knowing process points at least indirectly toward an ultimate object of such knowledge, which

---

[1] *Appearance and Reality*, p. 434.
[2] *Ibid.*, p. 509.
[3] *Ibid.*, chap. i.
[4] *Ibid.*, chap. ii.
[5] *Ibid.*, chap. iii.
[6] *Collected Essays*, II, 630 ff.

is, as has already been suggested, to be found in the perfect whole of Reality.

This is the suggestion implicit, for example, in the proceeding analysis of meaning. Meanings are, as we saw, universals, and the only universal that is in the end self-subsistent is the absolute concrete universal, which constitutes the individual totality of Reality. This absolute concrete universal may be approached in either of two ways. On the one hand, as we expand the scope of our universals, we approach in thought nearer to the whole: "In becoming more abstract, we gradually reach a wider realm of ideas; which is thus not sensibly but intellectually concrete." [7] On the other hand, as we concentrate universals about a focus we reach a relative concrete individual, which in its individuality resembles the whole but in its relativity points beyond itself to the absolute concrete universal; for "there is nothing which, to speak properly, is individual or perfect, except only the Absolute." [8] This duality of approach may well be formulated in terms of the conception of increasing possibility: "That which is more possible is either internally more harmonious and inclusive; it is, in other words nearer to a complete totality of content, such as would involve passage into and unity with, the Real. Or the more possible is, on the other hand, partly realized in a larger number of ideal groups. Every contact, even with a point in the temporal series, means ideal connexion with a concrete group of relations." [9]

Investigation of the process and structure of judgment points in the same direction. As we have seen, judgments can attain the categorical form which basically they intend only when their real subject, the whole of Reality, is in view. "All judgment . . . predicates its idea of ultimate Reality." [10] No matter how self-evident finite judgment may be, it is always mediated by Reality and says in effect not merely "S is P," but "R is such that S is P," or that Reality is such that the predicate may be attributed to the subject. The finite or "mere judgment" which ignores this consideration "is no more than an abstraction, which lives solely in and through our one-sided emphasis and our failure to observe." [11]

Inquiry into the nature of the expansion of judgment in inference has in like manner revealed that all of the usual types of inference are too much broken by impassable gaps to permit their disclosing genuine objects of full knowledge, and that only as a perfect implicative whole operates through them do they have validity at all. Conclu-

---

[7] *The Principles of Logic*, II, 474.
[8] *Appearance and Reality*, p. 217.
[9] *Ibid.*, p. 449.
[10] *Essays on Truth and Reality*, p. 253.
[11] *The Principles of Logic*, II, 624 f.

sive inference would have, on the one hand, to be true to the original object and, on the other, to extend the object in organic self-development. But this is possible only as "the object not only is itself, but is also contained as an element in a whole; and *is* itself, we must add, only as being so contained." [12]

Immediate experience or feeling points more satisfactorily than does inference toward the true object of knowledge. Despite its unstable, fleeting character, feeling affords genuine insight into reality and leads thought to an understanding concerning the Absolute that, though fragmentary, is yet secure. Whereas our reasonings entail ruinous contradictions, feeling immerses us in a diversity in unity that is continuous with the whole and, because it contains no relations, meets the crucial test of avoidance of all contradictions. In feeling, we confront a whole that "contains diversity" and yet "is not parted by relations." [13] From this fact we gain the idea of "an absolute experience in which phenomenal distinctions are merged, a whole become immediate at a higher stage without losing any of its richness." [14] Thus, beginning with feeling, does thought "form the idea of an apprehension, something like feeling in directness, which contains all the character sought by its relational efforts." [15] But in the end both nonrelational feeling and relational thought prove insufficient, and "it is only in what is super-relational that we can find a reality which is ultimate and absolute." [16]

The Absolute is necessarily a single whole. On the one hand, the unity of the Absolute is required by thought, which cannot endure contradiction, and finding such contradiction wherever there is connection without unity, avoids contradiction only in terms of the idea of a single comprehensive totality. Thus for thought, "reality is one in this sense that it has a positive nature exclusive of discord, a nature which must hold throughout everything that is to be real." [17] On the other hand, feeling equally requires unity in the Absolute. "A mode of togetherness such as we can verify in feeling destroys the independence of our reals. And we discover in feeling and at a stage where relations do not exist, that diversity is never found except as one integral character of an undivided whole." [18] Thus, the plurality then sinks to become merely an integral aspect in a single substantial unity, and the reals have vanished.[19]

Being one, the Absolute transcends time; it is eternal. By its inconsistency time itself "diverts us beyond itself. It points to some-

[12] *Ibid.,* p. 600.
[13] *Appearance and Reality,* p. 141.
[14] *Ibid.*
[15] *Ibid.,* p. 160.

[16] *Collected Essays,* II, 650.
[17] *Appearance and Reality,* p. 123.
[18] *Ibid.,* p. 125.
[19] *Ibid.,* p. 126.

thing higher in which it is included and transcended. Change demands some permanence within which succession happens." [20] Thus, although growth and decay are possible within the relative, they are excluded from the real as such. "There is of course progress in the world, and there is also retrogression, but we cannot think that the whole either moves on or backward. . . . For nothing perfect, nothing genuinely real, can move." [21]

The Absolute is not a self or a soul, for self and soul are, as will become clearer later, finite constructions that are in the end unstable. Rather, the Absolute is all that the soul longs for, "the complete realization of our desires for truth, beauty, emotion, sensation, and activity." [22] Clearly such perfection cannot but include intelligibility. For although the universe can not "throughout be understood, one can scarcely reasonably doubt that every single element in the world is intelligible, because it is taken up into and absorbed in a whole." [23]

The fact about the absolute object that is most important for knowledge is that the Absolute is pure experience. Adequate thought inevitably brings us to this conclusion. "We perceive, on reflection, that to be real, or even barely to exist, must be to fall within sentience. Sentient experience, in short, is reality, and what is not this is not real. . . . Feeling, thought, and volition . . . are all the material of existence, and there is no other material, actual or even possible." [24] Nor can any fact be discovered that conflicts with this. "Find any piece of existence, take up anything that anyone could possibly call a fact, or could in any sense assent to have being, and then judge if it does not consist in sentient experience. Try to discover any sense in which you can still continue to speak of it, when all perception and feeling have been removed; or point out any fragment of its matter, any aspect of it being, which is not derived from and is not still relative to this source." [25] The truth is, "you cannot find fact unless in unity with sentience, and one cannot in the end be divided from the other." [26] Although the experience that is the Absolute is vastly more than merely "*my* experience, . . . it cannot be a unity of experience and also of something beside; for the something beside, when we examine it, turns out always to be experience." [27] Indeed, "anything, in no sense felt or perceived, becomes for me quite unmeaning. . . . Experience is the same as reality. The fact that falls elsewhere . . . is a vicious abstraction whose existence is meaningless nonsense, and therefore not possible." [28]

[20] *Ibid.*, p. 183.
[21] *Ibid.*, p. 442.
[22] *Collected Essays*, pp. 630 f.
[23] *Appearance and Reality*, p. 427.
[24] *Ibid.*, p. 127.

[25] *Ibid.*, pp. 127 f.
[26] *Ibid.*, p. 129.
[27] *Ibid.*, p. 469.
[28] *Ibid.*, p. 128.

The foregoing account of the absolute object of true knowledge might suggest the assumption that the Absolute is quite distinct from those appearances which constitute the limited objects of our ordinary knowledge, or even that the latter are mere illusions. This would be extremely misleading. The Absolute contains, or is in some degree present in, all its appearances. In this sense "the Absolute *is* its appearances." [29] Thought, feeling, will, nature, self, and ideas are all a part of the Absolute, and "in the Absolute no appearance can be lost." [30] The term *appearance* should not suggest illusion but simply "looseness of content from existence." [31] The degree of worth and reality in a particular appearance varies according to the extent to which the whole is present in the appearance and the extent to which the appearance requires readjustment for harmonious reception into the whole.

The Absolute is each appearance, and is all, but it is not any one as such. And it is not all equally, but one appearance is more real than another. In short the doctrine of degrees of reality and truth is the fundamental answer to our problem. Everything is essential and yet one thing is worthless in comparison with others. [32]

4. Bradley's Account of the Knower and the Relation of Knower and Known

A. As analysis of the structure of knowing has already amply disclosed, knowing occurs on a variety of levels such as would lead one to expect that no simple account either of the knower or of the relation of knower and known is possible. This expectation is strongly supported in Bradley's account of the knower, for this account involves at least three more or less distinct levels.

(*1*) Experience in its first or immediate form always takes place, for reasons that "we cannot explain," in "finite centers." [1] These centers "while they last" are not "directly pervious to one another." Yet every one of them affords a genuine insight into Reality and "qualifies the Whole," which, "as a substantive, is present in each of these its adjectives." [2] The experience involved in every finite center is prior to the distinction of self and not self, and the center with which my self is associated represents far more than simply my feeling. Of each finite center one may say that both self and universe "are contained in it but partially . . . and a finite experience already *is* partially the universe." [3]

[29] *Ibid.,* p. 431.
[30] *Ibid.,* p. 404.
[31] *Ibid.,* p. 430.
[32] *Ibid.,* p. 431.

[1] *Ibid.,* p. 200; see also *Essays on Truth and Reality,* pp. 189 f.
[2] *Appearance and Reality,* p. 464.
[3] *Ibid.,* p. 465.

In such a finite center the knower is in a fundamental sense to be found. It is here, at any rate, that that immediate experience, which affords our only direct access to Reality unbroken by relations, takes place; and it is here only that the knowing subject directly apprehends its object. Nevertheless, the finite center with its immediate experiencing is not *the* knower, and indeed in one sense it is not even *a* knower; for the insights of immediate experience, direct as they are, are always limited and in need of further expansion and testing before they can count as knowledge in any full sense.

(2) Such is the fleeting character of the immediate experience of a finite center that "feeling is compelled to pass off into relational consciousness." [4] It is here that the self begins to appear. First, since single experiences are unable to sustain practical adjustments, the soul emerges, as moments are added together and past and present are connected by threads of memory.[5] Then within the soul the self is distinguished from the not-self: "Self and Ego, on one side, are produced by this development, and, on the other side, appear other selves and the world and God." [6]

The self that thus emerges cannot be assigned any perfectly specific extension or independent status. It is neither "total present contents" nor "average contents" nor "personal identity" nor present "interests" nor physical "residue," [7] and certainly it is neither an "independent substantive" [8] nor a given fact.[9] It is rather simply an "ideal construction" formed within the soul when the self is distinguished from the not-self. Nevertheless, the self remains in an important sense real, and "the highest form of experience which we have." [10]

Although Bradley does not discuss the point specifically, it is probably correct to say that, for him, the self is to be regarded as the knower in knowing as it occurs in judgment and inference. Not only is the self aware of its own present experiences, and, in a measure, of its own self,[11] but also, through inference, it can apprehend its past and even the nature of things and other selves.[12]

(3) However, because the self is neither definable content nor substance nor given fact, and because the knowing which it attains is shot through with relativity and contradictions, the self is clearly not to be thought of as the knower in any ultimate sense. Indeed, it is fortunate that this is not the case, for if a self with determinate limits were the ultimate knower, knowing would have no means of reaching out beyond its own boundaries save through the ruined

[4] *Ibid.*, p. 407.
[5] Cf. *ibid.*, p. 268.
[6] *Ibid.*, p. 465.
[7] *Ibid.*, pp. 87 f.
[8] *Essays on Truth and Reality*, p. 248.
[9] *Ibid.*, pp. 246 f.
[10] *Appearance and Reality*, p. 103.
[11] *Essays on Truth and Reality*, p. 166.
[12] *Appearance and Reality*, pp. 225 ff.

forms of judgment and inference, and hence it would be caught in a stifling solipsism. Since the self passes on one side over into the immediacy of finite centers from which the divisiveness of relations is excluded and on the other side tends to transcend itself in a kind of organic metaphysical thinking that suggests a comprehensive harmonious whole, the net of solipsism can be avoided.[13] Thus in the end the knower is not either the finite center or the self but, like the ultimate object of knowledge, is the experience of the Absolute.

B. Turning now specifically to the problem of the relation of the knower and the known, at least four crucial questions must be considered, and the answer to each is complicated by the variety in the levels of knowing.

(*1*) In what sense is the object of knowledge present to the knower? In general Bradley's answer is that the actual object and not merely its representation must be present to the knower and contained in his experience. With respect to immediate experience this is clearly the case. To such experience "other and the world and God . . . all appear as contents of one finite experience, and they really are genuinely and actually contained in it, . . . partially [but in] their very being and reality." [14] On the level of conceptual thinking a distinction must, as we have seen, be made between the meaning that is directly present to the mind and the object referred to in meaning; but the distinction must in the end be transcended if genuine knowing is to occur, for "there surely can be no knowledge of anything except what is real, nor about anything which itself falls outside our knowledge." [15] This basic directness characterizes knowledge of objects belonging to the distant past as well as those belonging to the present. "If . . . I am to know anything whatever about Caesar, then the real Caesar beyond doubt must himself enter into my judgments and be a constituent of my knowledge;" [16] and this the real Caesar may be seen to do when one remembers that "though ideal, the past and future are also real." [17]

(*2*) Does knowing make a difference to its object? At the level of logical thinking the answer must be essentially negative, for "in logic we are forced to assume that some processes do not modify their consequence" [18] and that "some operations do but change our power of perceiving the subject, and leave the subject itself unaltered." [19] Indeed, quite generally one must insist that from the ordinary human point of view it is not "possible that any knowledge should alter its

[13] Cf. *ibid.*, pp. 464 ff.; *Essays on Truth and Reality*, p. 42.
[14] *Appearance and Reality*, p. 465.
[15] *Essays on Truth and Reality*, p. 425.
[16] *Ibid.*, p. 409.
[17] *Ibid.*, p. 426.
[18] *The Principles of Logic*, II, 559.
[19] *Ibid.*, pp. 570 f.

object." [20] But this is at best only a "partial truth." Knowing may leave the particular object as such unaffected, but being itself a part of Reality, it belongs to the context of the object, and no object is fully definite apart from its context.[21] In the end the Absolute is the object of knowledge, and every finite center, as well as every aspect of knowing, "makes a difference to our Absolute." [22]

(3) Is the knower himself an object of knowledge? In general the answer must be in the affirmative. Since finite centers are a part of the Absolute, they are a part of the ultimate object. Experience, itself, may also become an object to itself.[23] Moreover, at the level of the ideal construction of self, the self can, as we have seen, know itself at least in part. As on the one hand the knower may be said to confront and even to embrace all Reality, so, on the other hand, the object, being ultimately the Absolute, may be said to embrace the knower. Even the finite object, though insufficient in itself, necessarily expands in the knowing process until it embraces the knower; [24] and all the ideas through which knowing takes place are integral parts of Reality. Neither objects without subjects nor "floating ideas" can exist.[25]

(4) What is the character of the tie that binds knower and known together? For any theory which draws an ultimate distinction between knower and known, this problem is difficult and indeed insoluble.[26] For Bradley, the matter is much simpler. Both at the basic level of immediate experience and at the advanced level of rational insight concerning the Absolute, experiencer and experienced tend to coincide. In the middle region, in which knowing in the usual sense takes place, the distinction of knower and known is of course fairly sharp, but even here an underlying unity remains alongside the diversity. The essential character of this unity is that of immediate experience still present and active even when subject and object have been distinguished. "At every moment my state, whatever else it is, is a whole of which I am immediately aware. It is an experienced nonrelational unity of many in one. And object and subject and every possible relation and term, to be experienced at all, must fall within and depend vitally on such a felt unity." [27]

5. Bradley's Interpretation of Truth and Error

Knowing is always knowing truth, and this inevitably raises the difficult questions of the character and tests of truth. We begin with Bradley's account of two widely accepted views, coming afterward to

[20] *Essays on Truth and Reality*, p. 336.
[21] Cf. *Appearance and Reality*, pp. 518 ff.
[22] *Ibid.*, p. 200.
[23] *Essays on Truth and Reality*, vi.
[24] Cf. *ibid.*, p. 161.
[25] Cf. e.g., *ibid.*, chap. iii; p. 301.
[26] *Ibid.*, p. 198.
[27] *Ibid.*, pp. 175 f.

his positive interpretations first of the nature of truth and then of
its criteria.

A. (*1*) A natural and popular opinion is that "truth consists in
copying reality." [1] "From a lower point of view" this opinion represents in several ways a "convenient" manner of speaking and contains
a certain amount of validity. "In the first place the individual in
truth-seeking must subject himself. He . . . must suppress ideas,
wishes and fancies. . . . Secondly, in truth-seeking the individual
. . . must follow the object, . . . [His ideas] in a sense must conform to it. In the third place reflection . . . must take up sensible
qualities as given matter, and it must accept also more or less brute
conjunctions of fact. . . . And finally, to some extent language and
truth must seem even to copy perceived facts, and, . . . to convey
them faithfully." [2]

Nevertheless as an ultimate account of truth the copy theory is
completely wrong. To begin with, there is nothing for perception to
copy. The alleged facts or *data* which are to be copied have already
for the most part been worked over by the mind; [3] and if feeling
itself be offered as that which is copied one must remember that
feeling can really be copied only by feeling.[4] Again, reflective attainment of truth does not merely copy perception, for clearly "disjunctive, negative, and hypothetical judgments" yield some truth without
copying anything. Finally, the truth which in the end we seek is
"general truth about the Universe," and "it seems impossible to
regard this as transcribed from the given Universe." [5] Even if the
whole could be given, no idea could copy it, for the idea would itself
belong to the whole which it sought to copy. Thus one may properly
insist quite generally that the copy definition of truth is circular, that
"apart from knowledge and truth, there can be no original object
before you to copy." [6]

(2) A more recent interpretation of truth is the pragmatist one
that truth is what "serves" or "works." [7] Bradley quite agrees with
the pragmatist that in knowing something is made or done, that the
knowing process is usually initiated in practical conflicts, and that
truth must in the last analysis be tested by the total satisfaction of
the knower. But none of this implies that true knowledge is merely
what works. After all, in any activity whatever, something has to be
done; and while truth is in fact ultimately made, to say that a finite
creature makes it in knowing it violates the basic conviction that a

---

[1] *Ibid.,* p. 107.
[2] *Ibid.,* pp. 118 f.
[3] *Ibid.,* p. 108.
[4] *Ibid.,* p. 345.

[5] *Ibid.,* p. 109.
[6] *Ibid.,* p. 345.
[7] *Ibid.,* p. 110.

clearly defined statement once true is always so.[8] Moreover, origin in practical conflict does not entail termination in practice, and many kinds of efforts to know that were originally mainly practical, come in time to be predominantly theoretical. In any case, a definition of truth as working would become in the end circular since recourse must finally be had to the idea of truly working,[9] and the kind of satisfaction sought in knowing as such is not simply any kind of satisfaction but a comprehensive intellectual satisfaction.

The root error of both of the two preceding views consists in "the division of truth from knowledge and of knowledge from reality." [10] The one view fails to see that what is to be copied must be already true and known, and the other neglects to observe that an idea can be seen to "work" only relatively to what is real and known.[11] In these neglected aspects of knowledge and reality are central clues to the problem of the nature and criteria of truth.

B. (1) The most important fact about truth is its essential oneness with reality: This unity "must be taken as necessary and fundamental" [12] although it is not to be thought of as implying that truth and reality are altogether identical. Truth is attained by ideal experiment and may be regarded as the ideal aspect of which reality is the substantive. It is the perfect system of reality on which all judgment and reference must be based. "Truth is reality taken as ideal, and that must mean reality taken as an intelligible system; and every judgment and inference therefore must be understood as directed and aimed at such reality." [13] The ultimate objective of truth "is to be and to possess reality in an ideal form." [14] This objective "is not satisfied . . . until it is all-containing and one." [15] Its realization "must include without residue the entirety of what is in any sense given, and . . . is bound to include this intelligibly." [16] Obviously such an objective can never be completely attained, both because of the limitations of our thought and because truth that fully achieves its end by passing over into reality is no longer truth. This limitation of truth by reality gives us the key to the distinction between truth and reality, for "those aspects in which truth for itself is defective, are precisely those which make the difference between truth and reality." [17]

From the fact that truth is the ideal aspect of the whole of Reality, it follows that there can be no simple or infallible truth. No idea can

[8] Cf. The Principles of Logic, II, p. 727; Essays on Truth and Reality, pp. 336, 340.
[9] Cf. Essays on Truth and Reality, p. 111.
[10] Ibid., p. 110.
[11] Ibid.
[12] Ibid., p. 113.
[13] The Principles of Logic, p. 620.
[14] Essays on Truth and Reality, p. 114.
[15] Ibid.
[16] Ibid.
[17] Essays on Truth and Reality, p. 116.

exist in isolation from judgment; "an idea apart from a judgment
. . . is no more than an abstraction." [18] But neither can any judgment maintain itself apart from inference. "Our simple judgment
. . . is an abstraction, the mere creature of a false theory." [19] "Judgments are conditional in this sense, that what they affirm is incomplete. It cannot be attributed to Reality, as such, and before its necessary complement is added." [20] Any alleged truth depends upon a
larger context and this in turn upon a still larger one; no statement
can in itself be fully true. Even so seemingly obvious a statement as
"Caesar crossed the Rubicon" cannot without qualification be true,
for there may be other worlds in which "Caesar never saw the Rubicon nor indeed existed at all." [21] Only if one knew all Reality could
the truth about Caesar become final.

The fact that the objective of truth is the whole of reality explains
another fact about truth that otherwise would appear quite paradoxical, the fact of degrees of truth. Just as there are degrees of reality,
so, contrary to prevailing opinion, there are degrees of truth. As
might be expected, these degrees vary according to the degree of
approximation to the end of truth in the attainment of reality. Thus,
"the degree in which the various types each succeed and fail in reaching their common end, gives to each of them its respective place and
rank in the whole body," [22] and "the amount of either wideness or
consistency gives the degree of reality and also of truth." [23] One may,
however, estimate the degree of truth from the other side; he may
measure the truth of a statement indirectly "by the relative amount
of transformation, which would be required if its defects were made
good." [24]

The ideas of the limitation of truth or reality and of degrees of
truth help to clarify the character of error. Error is not, like appearance, simply loosened content "related to some fact which accepts its
qualification." [25] Rather, "error . . . is content made loose from its
own reality, and related to a reality with which it is discrepant." [26]
This does not mean that even errors contain no truth, or that they
are excluded from the Absolute. Just as "there will be no truth
which is entirely true" [27] so also "there will be no error which is
totally false." [28] Errors are only relatively further from the Absolute
as such than are beliefs commonly called truths; they are never entirely outside it. "A total error would mean the attribution of a

---

[18] *The Principles of Logic*, p. 713.
[19] *Ibid.*, p. 632.
[20] *Appearance and Reality*, p. 320.
[21] *Essays on Truth and Reality*, p. 262.
[22] *The Principles of Logic*, p. 620.
[23] *Appearance and Reality*, p. 332.

[24] *Ibid.*
[25] *Ibid.*, p. 166.
[26] *Ibid.*
[27] *Ibid.*, p. 321.
[28] *Ibid.*

content to Reality, which, even when redistributed and dissolved, could still not be assimilated," [29] and there can be no such thing.

(2) In the light of the foregoing account of the nature of truth the criteria of truth may be formulated in a number of different ways. The point of origin of all tests of truth, and indeed in a sense of Bradley's whole philosophy, is the quest for intellectual satisfaction. Bradley, himself, makes this quite plain in answer to the charge that he erroneously builds his thought either upon mere feeling or upon the assumption of bare identity: "Since I have been taken to build on assumptions which I am unable to recognize, I will here repeat what it is that I have assumed. I have assumed first that truth has to satisfy the intellect, and that what does not do this is neither true nor real." [30] In assigning to intellectual satisfaction the central role, no exclusion of other satisfactions, such as aesthetic and religious ones, is intended. Indeed, in some measure one must assume that "reality satisfies our whole being," [31] including our desires "for truth and life, and for beauty and goodness." [32] In particular, our practical needs must be met and "in proportion as a truth is idle it is less true." [33] But no nonintellectual satisfaction is entitled to set up a truth claim in its own right. Every such satisfaction has a "voice but no vote." Its claims are to be heard only through, and not in independence of, intellect, which in matters of truth and falsity remains supreme. If other sides of our nature remain unsatisfied "they will manifest themselves so in idea." [34] The ultimate criterion includes all aspects of our nature and even so is never fully realizable by us. "It is feeling, will, sense, and understanding in one. And though from any one side it can be approached and enjoyed, it cannot be fully there except from all sides at once in a way which, in and for finite beings, is not possible." [35]

The ground on which the criterion of intellectual satisfaction is insisted upon is that this criterion is simply unavoidable and indispensable even to discussion of its own validity: "This is a doctrine which, so far as I can see, can neither be proved nor questioned. The proof or the question, it seems to me, must imply the truth of the doctrine, and, if that is not assumed, both vanish." [36] "This assumption, I can defend only by showing that any would-be objector assumes it also." [37]

The criterion of intellectual satisfaction operates at every level of knowledge. For example, when we feel uneasiness toward another

[29] *Ibid.*, p. 332.
[30] *Ibid.*, p. 509.
[31] *Ibid.*, p. 140.
[32] *Ibid.*
[33] *Essays on Truth and Reality*, p. 122.

[34] *Ibid.*, p. 222.
[35] *Collected Essays*, II, 653 f.
[36] *Appearance and Reality*, pp. 491 f.
[37] *Ibid.*, p. 509.

person and presently objectify this feeling as a quality of that person, the qualification "may satisfy us because it is that qualification which answers to what we felt and still feel." [38] The operation of intellectual satisfaction that especially concerns us, however, is at a higher level. Here such satisfaction regularly attaches itself to thinking that has certain characteristics that may themselves be regarded as criteria of truth. The principal question remaining then concerns the nature of these characteristics.

Approaching the matter from an apparently negative side, Bradley finds that any sound thinking must operate "as if the self-contradictory could not be real." [39] Only the noncontradictory can be such that "in a calm moment the mere intellect is incapable of doubting," and it is only of what is thus indubitable that "thought must assert in attempting to deny." [40] Ultimate reality is such that it does not contradict itself and herein is an absolute criterion of reality and truth. A closely related way of formulating the criterion is to say that a statement is true in proportion as its "opposite is inconceivable." [41]

Although the criterion of noncontradiction appears to be negative, one must remember that negation must be built on positive knowledge [42] and that the denial of inconsistency "asserts consistency." [43] The principle of noncontradiction points to a formulation of standards that are clearly positive, for "truth is an ideal expression of the Universe, at once coherent and comprehensive." [44] These standards of coherence and comprehensiveness may at first seem to be at variance with one another. But this cannot be the case, for "the whole reality is so immanent and so active in every partial element, that you have only to make an object of anything short of the whole, in order to see the object beyond itself." [45] Thus both in principle and by examination of normal procedure in quest of truth, one may affirm that "our actual criterion is the body of our knowledge, made both as wide and as coherent as is possible, and so expressing more and more the genuine nature of reality. And the measure of the truth and importance of any one judgment or conclusion lies in its contribution to, and its place in, our intelligible system." [46] "The more our ideas are coherent and wide—the more fully they realize the idea of system—so much the more at once they are real and true." [47] Such a standard is in principle essentially the same as that of noncontradiction, for "the order to express yourself in such a way

[38] *Essays on Truth and Reality*, p. 181.
[39] *Appearance and Reality*, p. 120.
[40] *Ibid.*, p. 133.
[41] *Ibid.*, p. 477.
[42] *Ibid.*, p. 122.

[43] *Ibid.*, p. 123.
[44] *Essays on Truth and Reality*, p. 223.
[45] *Ibid.*
[46] *The Principles of Logic*, p. 620.
[47] *Appearance and Reality*, p. 477.

as to avoid contradiction, may be said in the end to contain the whole criterion." [48]

If one considers what it is that is ultimately comprehensive, coherent, and real, another formulation of the standard becomes plausible. Only individuality meets these requirements, and in this sense itself becomes a standard of truth: "Our standard is Reality in the form of self-existence; and this, given plurality and relations, means an individual system." [49] This standard becomes more explicit when we recall the doctrine of degrees of truth and reality: "Whatever is individual is more real and true; for it contains within its own limits a wider region of the Absolute, and it possesses more intensely the type of self-sufficiency. . . . We should require less alteration, less destruction of its own special nature, in order to make this higher element completely real." [50]

6. OTHER ABSOLUTE IDEALISTS OF THE EARLY TWENTIETH CENTURY

The absolute idealism of which we have taken the thought of Bradley to be representative included among its advocates a number of other able thinkers. Almost equally as well as Bradley, either of two of these philosophers might have been considered representative of the movement. One of these was Bradley's friend and compatriot, Bernard Bosanquet (1848–1923), in whose work nearly all of the familiar Bradley themes reappear, though often in an altered light.

A. Knowledge, according to Bosanquet, must be rooted not in abstractions but in living experience.[1] Meaning consists of universals, of which the true type is not the abstract universal of barely repeated identity but the concrete universal [2] involving an identity recognizable despite differences and being fully achieved only in the individual whole. Judgment is the application of ideal content to reality [3] and is continuous with inference.[4] Inference is vastly richer than mere formal logic through fixed types.[5] The object of our knowledge is directly some segment of reality but ultimately only the individual comprehensive whole.[6] Although being known does not create the object, it does alter the "mode of being of the object." [7] Truth ap-

[48] *Essays on Truth and Reality*, p. 223.
[49] *Appearance and Reality*, p. 332.
[50] *Ibid.*, p. 338.
[1] Bernard Bosanquet, *The Principle of Individuality and Value* (London: Macmillan & Co., Ltd., 1912), pp. 44 ff.
[2] *Ibid.*, chap. ii.
[3] Bosanquet, *The Essentials of Logic* (London: Macmillan & Co., Ltd., 1895), p. 79.
[4] Bosanquet, *Logic* (Oxford: Clarendon Press, 1888), II, 1.
[5] Bosanquet, *Implication and Linear Inference* (London: Macmillan & Co., Ltd., 1920), chap. i.
[6] Cf. *ibid.*, pp. 150 ff., 168 ff.
[7] *The Essentials of Logic*, pp. 8 ff.

proximates reality in varying degrees [8] and satisfies intellect,[9] and even error does not fall outside reality.[10]

In at least three important respects the absolute idealist epistemology of Bosanquet differs from that of Bradley. First, Bosanquet is on the whole much more systematic and somewhat more consistent, although perhaps correspondingly somewhat less penetrating. In the later editions of his *Principles of Logic*, Bradley himself repeatedly praises and adopts Bosanquet's more orderly formulations; and, with respect to his own early inclination to separate the ideas *by* which we judge from the reality *of* which we judge, he credits Bosanquet with having helped him to return to consistent idealism by rejecting "floating ideas." Second, Bosanquet tones down considerably some of the more extreme phases of Bradley's system. For example, while he never specifically repudiates Bradley's doctrine that the object of knowledge is in the end solely experience, and indeed sometimes seems to approve it, he often writes in another vein. Sometimes he writes almost as though he accepted physical objects in a common-sense way, and he offers at times to abandon the term "idealism" in favor of a less "mentalistic" term.[11] "This type of qualification is accompanied by a corresponding modification of the idea of truth. Truth is no longer a paradoxical striving to *be* reality, in the attaining of which truth would cease to exist. Rather, truth is simple *approximation* to reality, the apprehension in idea of as much of reality as the idea can contain.[12] Even more important, Bradley's insistence on the presence of contradictions throughout the best forms of our thought and his consequent tendency to retreat from intellect to feeling is largely abandoned by Bosanquet, who, while deploring mere abstractions, regards intellect as far more capable of genuine insight into the nature of the Absolute than Bradley would have admitted. Third, Bosanquet develops certain constructive lines of thought not explicitly worked out by Bradley. These include special doctrines of internal relations, the concrete universal, and the operation of system or of a "spirit of the whole" in all cognitive activity. The third and most important of these doctrines involves the claim that neither in daily life nor in science does thought ordinarily proceed in "linear" fashion, by placing atoms of thought alongside one another as both the older syllogistic logic and modern formal logics are disposed to do,[13] but that thought operates nearly always in terms of the systematic relations of the subject under consideration and

[8] *Implication and Linear Inference*, pp. 150 ff.

[9] *Ibid.*, p. 96.

[10] *Ibid.*, p. 154 f.

[11] See *The Meeting of Extremes in Con-* temporary Philosophy (London: Macmillan & Co., Ltd., 1924), vii.

[12] *Implication and Linear Inference*, p. 151.

[13] *Ibid.*, chaps. ii, iii.

ultimately of the whole of reality. It is thus, Bosanquet insists, that the common man proceeds in simple matters who reasons that if a ton of coal costs thirty, this half ton costs fifteen; [14] and it is thus that the scientist reasons in more complex matters when out of a vast store of ordered knowledge of his subject he formulates a new hypothesis for subsequent verification.[15]

B. The second of the two most influential absolute idealist contemporaries of Bradley was the American philosopher Josiah Royce (1855–1916). Royce's idealism, though in essential harmony with that of his British contemporaries, differs from theirs in at least two important respects. First, it places a relatively greater emphasis upon the volitional element in knowledge. And second, it largely abandons the coherence theory of truth, which usually accompanies idealism, in favor of a correspondence theory.[16] One may also add that Royce gives a greater positive significance to the finite human knower than do his English contemporaries.[17]

The key to a correct theory of knowledge, Royce contends, lies in a proper conception of the relation of the idea and its object. Realism, one of the three basic theories of knowledge that opposes idealism, rightly recognizes the integrity of the object, but renders genuine knowledge impossible by insisting upon an independence of idea and object that, if carried to its logical conclusion, would mean that the extinction of the object would make no difference to the idea.[18] From the opposite side, mysticism, while correctly apprehending the need for immediacy in the relation of idea and object, destroys the possibility of knowledge by "quenching" the idea itself. The third theory, critical rationalism, properly recognizes the integrity of the idea and the requirement of validity among such ideas as those of mathematics and morals, but, confining itself largely to inner meanings, fails to disclose the nature of objective reality.[19] Indeed, objective reality can never be disclosed by a mere coherence among ideas, but always requires an appropriate correspondence of idea to fact.

On the constructive side, a sound idealism manages to avoid all the difficulties of the other three theories and so arrives at a genuinely tenable account of the knowing relation. Such an idealism recognizes at the outset that every idea has both an internal meaning or purpose and an external meaning or reference. But an idea as a purpose

---

[14] Ibid., p. 25.
[15] See ibid., especially chaps. iv, v.
[16] This was first clearly pointed out to me by Professor C. I. Lewis.
[17] See G. Watts Cunningham, The Idealistic Argument in Recent British and American Philosophy (New York: The Century Co., 1933), pp. 256 f.
[18] Josiah Royce, The World and the Individual (New York & London: The Macmillan Co., & Mamillan & Co., Ltd., 1900), 1st series, p. 266.
[19] Ibid., p. 267.

selects both the object to which it refers and the mode of correspondence appropriate to its relation to that object. Hence we may expect to find the requisite correspondence not in the artificial, and indeed impossible, picturing of a wholly independent object,[20] but in a vital teleological relation in which the idea is a partly volitional fragment of the object, and the object, a fulfillment of the intention of the idea.[21] Similarly, since the idea is a genuine purpose, it retains its integrity. And finally, since the object is the satisfying realization of the idea's purpose in living individual experience, knowing is never confined to arbitrary abstraction or senseless tautology.[22] Indeed, knowing becomes the very kind of fulfillment of purpose that men actually find it to be, and a human self as a whole is among other things an excellent example of the sort of realized idea that becomes an object of knowledge.

In that no human mind can fully apprehend its whole self, or indeed the whole of any other significant object, the complete realization of idea implies the existence of an Absolute for whom each idea appears in its objective completeness. This infinite Absolute is no mere negation of the finite. Rather He is a Self such that in Him all finite selves are preserved intact and all limited human insights remain valid. The manner in which the integrity of the individual can be preserved in the infinite is suggested by the relations among infinite series and by spans of consciousness. For example, as the infinite series 2 4 6 8 is included in the infinite series 1 2 3 4 . . .[23] without losing its own character, a shorter span of consciousness may be comprehended without loss in longer ones.[24]

C. Among the several competent absolute idealists writing near the turn of the century, at least two others in addition to Bradley, Bosanquet, and Royce should at any rate be mentioned in passing. One is the English statesman and philosopher, Richard B. Haldane (1856–1928), who contended that the Kantian and Spencerian idea of an Unknown was meaningless and that abstraction should work upward in reason and valuation as well as downward in science.[25] The other is James E. Creighton (1861–1924), founder of the American Philosophical Association and the most influential of the Cornell philosophers. While unable quite to accept Bosanquet's recommendation for the abandonment of the term "idealism," Creighton insists that the term has misleadingly been used to cover two entirely different and by no means equally sound types of philosophy. One is a

[20] Ibid., pp. 300 ff.
[21] Ibid., pp. 306 ff.
[22] Ibid., pp. 316 ff.
[23] Ibid., p. 518.
[24] Ibid., II, 418 ff.

[25] See R. B. Haldane, "The Function of Metaphysics in Scientific Method," in J. H. Muirhead, Contemporary British Philosophy (London & New York: George Allen & Unwin, 1924), pp. 129 ff.

"mentalism" rooted in Berkeley and worked out in such epistemological experientialism as that of Bradley. The other, the true idealism,
is a "speculative philosophy" that insists on the organic wholeness of
reality and experience but "repudiates all allegiance with" the
"philosophical doctrines" of "the good Berkeley." [26] The Absolute,
believed in only because of the insistent demand of experience, "must
come, not to destroy but to fulfill the program and promises of ordinary experience." [27] The Absolute involves both existence and value
and is apprehended not, as Bradley's language would sometimes suggest, immediately, but *"in the whole course of experience."* [28]

7. Some Personal Idealists of the Early
Twentieth Century

Alongside the absolute idealism which set the stage for the epistemological inquiry of the present century and with which we are
principally concerned here, there emerged in the latter part of the
past century and the beginning of the present one a different kind
of idealism, sometimes referred to as "personal idealism" or simply
"personalism"; and although the special contributions of personalism
lie more in the field of ontology than in that of epistemology, some
characteristic ideas of a few early personalists must now be briefly
referred to. Deeply influenced by Kant and Lotze and much more
sensitive than was absolute idealism to the demands of common
sense, religion, and democratic individualism, personal idealism represents in part a defense of the views of absolute idealism and in part
a protest against these views. Remaining at base idealistic in their
epistemological assumptions, personalists often make considerable
concessions to basic realism and so help to forge connecting links
between idealism and realism. For these thinkers, both the finite self
and the object are more independent than for the absolute idealists,
and the connection of knower and known becomes a more acute
problem.

Perhaps the most influential of all the personal idealists was the
American philosopher Borden Parker Bowne (1847–1910), in whom
idealism was developed against a strongly Kantian background.
Bowne is on the whole willing to accept our ordinary experience
of world, self, and others, when rendered consistent by science, as
knowing; but he proposes also to seek out the underlying implications
involved in this experience. Even the simplest kinds of experience

---

[26] J. E. Creighton, "Two Types of Idealism," *Philosophical Review*, XXVI (1918),
515.

[27] *Ibid.*, pp. 524 f.

[28] *Ibid.*, p. 529; see also Frank Thilly,
"The Philosophy of James Edwin Creighton," *Philosophical Review*, XXXIV (1926),
211–29.

already involve interpretation through the categorizing activity of the mind, he thinks, which constructs a world for each of us.[1] The community of our experiences tends to confirm our individual constructions, and only that which fails to be so confirmed need be regarded as illusory. The very idea of a reality that transcends the community of minds is an absurdity. Selves and their experiences are the only realities.[2] Categories cannot operate in a vacuum. That alone upon which the category of being can operate is a self, for only a self combines the essential requirements of activity and continuous existence, and intelligence is the only instance in which the category of causality is directly encountered. However, our human selves are not their own causes, nor is there in us alone any sufficient ground for the unity of our common world or for any reality that may lie beyond the reach of human selves. Thus, analysis of knowledge points to the existence of the infinite Self, who, being activity or agent rather than substance, creates and sustains us without absorbing our individuality in His or rendering our partial knowledge untrue.

George H. Howison (1843–1916), like his contemporary Bowne, uses Kantian categories to discomfort the opponents of personal idealism. These opponents are not primarily mechanistic materialists as such but agnostic evolutionary philosophers on the one hand and pantheistic idealists on the other. The categories of "Time, Space, Causation, Logical Unity, and Ideality" are necessary to that generalizing activity of mind by which evolution itself is apprehended. Hence these categories cannot without circularity be attributed to evolution.[3] The minds to which these categories belong are human minds which have their origin not in time but in a metaphysical Absolute and find their perfection as a "Republic of Spirits," in a "Supreme Reality."

On the British side of the Atlantic, personal idealism becomes, in the writings of James Ward (1843–1925), somewhat more subjectivistic than on the American side. Ward takes his stand upon the basis of a unity of experience that is prior to the distinction of mind and matter but in which the duality of subject and object is always present, "a duality in the unity of experience."[4] That which is known in experience is basically not the Absolute, for unless knowledge begins with the finite Many it will never discover the Many in the infinite One. Nor is the known those physical objects that physi-

---

[1] Borden P. Bowne, *Personalism* (Boston: Houghton Mifflin Co., 1908), pp. 62 ff.

[2] See *ibid.*, pp. 107 ff.

[3] G. H. Howison, *The Limits of Evolution and Other Essays* (New York & London: The Macmillan Co., & Macmillan & Co., Ltd., 1904 & 1905), pp. 30 ff.

[4] James Ward, *The Realm of Ends* (3d ed.; Cambridge: Cambridge University Press, 1920), p. 10.

cal realism pretends to disclose in terms of mechanistic science. Such objects are only convenient "ejects" of an experience which has forgotten the original practical objectives of the subject [5] and mistaken intersubjectivity of concepts for transsubjectivity of objects.[6] When we begin from the side of the subject rather than from that of the object, no such sundering of subject and object can take place, and we gain a sympathetic understanding which reveals, as the true objects of knowledge, finite spiritual existences in varying degrees of self-preserving activity. In its quest for a ground for finite existences, reason seems to require the existence of a God, who in creating the world limits himself to permit freedom to his creatures; but only in faith can this conclusion be confirmed.

Among British philosophers who were inclined toward personal idealism, some, however, while remaining ontological idealists, moved, as personal idealism readily does, toward realism in theory of knowledge. Such thinkers include Andrew Seth Pringle-Pattison (1852–1922) and J. E. M. McTaggart (1860–1925). Pringle-Pattison, a theistic ontological idealist, adopted a realist epistemology to the extent that he distinguished sharply between the realms of nature and of human consciousness. But holding that man was organic to nature, being that through which "the universe beholds and enjoys itself," [7] he also retained an element of idealism. McTaggart, an atheist, pluralistic, ontological idealist, was epistemologically realistic to the extent of regarding the knowing relation as primarily one of noncopying correspondence.[8] At the same time he remained ontologically idealistic in insisting that only related spirits are real. His philosophical method outreaches even the most thoroughgoing idealistic epistemology in its virtually completely aprioristic character.

8. COMMENTS CONCERNING EARLY TWENTIETH-CENTURY IDEALISM

Some very important features of Bradley's epistemological thought, including his emphasis upon immediate experience and his belief that concepts entail the ruin of the quest for truth, are by no means peculiarly idealist, and since these notions will in any case recur as important features of the intuitionist epistemology of Bergson, critical evaluations of them can await the presentation of Bergson's

---

[5] *Ibid.*, pp. 430 f.
[6] *Ibid.*, pp. 10 f.
[7] Andrew Seth Pringle-Pattison, *The Idea of God in the Light of Recent Philosophy* (New York: Oxford University Press, 1920), p. 111.

[8] See J. E. M. McTaggart, "On Ontological Idealism," in *Contemporary British Philosophy* (London & New York: George Allen & Unwin, & the Macmillan Co., 1924), 1st series, p. 251.

thought. Most of the other significant features of the epistemology of Bradley and the other early twentieth-century idealists such, for example, as their doctrines of universals, ideas, necessity, truth, and systems, are more clearly developed by later twentieth-century idealists, especially by Blanshard; and critical comments upon them may appropriately await the presentation of Blanshard's thought. There is, however, one feature of Bradley's thought that is prominent both in his work and in that of most idealists up to his time but less prominent in the work of subsequent idealists, namely the tendency to reduce all knowledge and reality to experience. There is also a related doctrine that is especially characteristic of Bradley's thought, and present only in more carefully guarded fashion in the thought of his idealist successors, namely the contention that intellectual satisfaction is the criterion of truth. It is upon these two features of Bradleian epistemology that the following critical remarks will be focused.

A. At least one basic claim that the idealist reduction of both cognition and its object to experience was designed to emphasize, i.e., the claim that cognition, instead of being merely passive, always involves active experiencing at some point, seems sound and significant; and indeed the success of the early twentieth-century idealists in impressing this claim upon a very large segment of contemporary epistemology is perhaps the major achievement of the early contemporary idealists. This claim represents a considerable advance, for example, not only over a naïve realism that construes perception on the model of the wax's reception of the imprint of the seal and a Lockean empiricism that construes perception after the fashion of the blank paper's reception of the ink marks, but also over a scholastic realism that takes even apprehension of the most comprehensive truths to be, despite the use of the term "*active* intellect," a matter of essentially receptive contemplation. The influence of the idealists' insistence upon this claim is to be seen in the modern pragmatists' idea of the creativity of intellect, in the constructionists' notion of the building out of percepts, in the critical realists' emphasis on selection and symbolization, in the new realists' tendency to identify aspects of external events with aspects of human experience, and in the analytic philosophers' inclination to tie facts to linguistic forms.

That this insistence upon a place for active experiencing in cognition is essentially sound, is amply indicated by a number of considerations, most of which early twentieth-century idealists have themselves stressed and most of which will also come up again in other connections. One such consideration is the invariable presence of some sort of recognition in every instance of knowledge; for whatever be the character of sensing as such, recognition represents an additional achievement, and where recognition is not at all achievable, knowledge can scarcely be said to be present. A second consideration, emphasized by Bradley along with the pragmatists, is the practical function of intellect; for intellect serves not only its own ends but also the ends of the whole individual, and its function is oriented to all of its ends. A more specific consideration is the selective role of attention, for observations subsequent to those of the moment of a given observation tend to show that one has noticed mainly those aspects of the situation that were relevant to his present purposes and has left out of account much that might have been observed. A fourth consideration is the creative character of perception as evidenced by its indirectness; for since perceiving evidently involves intervening physical events as well as nerve impulses not themselves percepts, the emergence of percepts would seem to require some sort of creative activity even if that activity achieves no more than a kind of recreation of what is already in the external world. A fifth consideration is the experimental character of inquiry; and this character seems to be found not only in the obviously experimental processes of scientific and common-sense investigations but even, in view of the selective and creative character of perception, in perception itself. A final consideration consists of familiar facts of error and illusion that remain unintelligible apart from contributions of active experiencing to cognitive processes.

However, neither Bradley nor any of the idealists with whom we are here concerned was content simply to say that active experiencing was always involved in cognition. Each, especially Bradley and Royce, went on to contend that experience is itself the only possible *object* of knowledge, and each meant by experience some sort of sentient experience. Bradley's principal argument for this view of the object of knowledge is that we are never able to find any "piece of existence . . . [or] fact" that is not experience,[1] and what has principally disturbed nearly all those who have had doubts about the possibility of objects of knowledge independent of experience has been the very sort of inability he had in mind.

Many objections, from Moore's distinction between acts and objects to Perry's protest against the exploitation of the egocentric predicament, to the latest polemics of physicalists and ordinary language philosophers, have been directed against this type of argument; and while none of these objections constitutes a complete refutation of the argument—perhaps none can—some of them reveal basic weak-

[1] *Appearance and Reality*, p. 127.

nesses in the argument. Each of the more significant of these objections will be presented in due time.

For the present, we shall be content to call attention to a distinction, now more or less familiar, confusion concerning which tends to render the argument that we can never find anything not an experience plausible, and clarity concerning which tends to render the argument implausible. The distinction is that between experience in the broad sense in which it consists of complexes embracing both sentient experiences and what such experiences are experiences of, on the one hand, and experience in the more restricted sense in which it consists of sentient experiences as such, on the other. In the first sense, taking a trip, playing a game, looking at the stars, listening to a symphony, and watching the road are experiences; each is a complex involving both sentient experiences and what these experiences are experiences of. In the second sense, suffering, daydreaming, planning, and remembering, apart from the external objects and events involved in each case, are experience; each is a sentient experience taken in isolation from that of which it is an experience.

Now, if we are concerned with experience in the broader sense, it would seem that all that we ever encounter belongs to experience. Our sensations, feelings, volitions, mental images, and thoughts do, for if they are themselves sentient experiences they also belong to larger complexes containing such experiences. In this sense, houses and trees, rivers and mountains, the sun and the stars also belong to experience, for they too belong to complexes including sentient experiences. Moreover, since referring can be construed as a variety of sentient experience and since our references may be made general enough to embrace everything whatever, it may indeed be said that everything whatever belongs to experience in the broad sense. To this extent Bradley's claim that we can never find anything not an experience is persuasive. Accordingly, in that the term "experience" is used both of complexes embracing sentient experiences and other things and of sentient experience as such, and in that sentient experience is essential to experience in either sense, one may be inclined, by assimilating the first sense of "experience" to the second, to concede that Bradley's claim is correct with reference to the sense of "experience" that is pertinent to his type of idealism, and to say without qualification that we cannot find anything not a sentient experience. A great deal of the plausibility of Bradley's argument rests upon this sort of procedure.

However, such a procedure plainly involves fundamental mistakes. To begin with, the fact that something belongs to a complex properly called an experience does not mean that that thing itself is, or is properly called, an experience, any more than the fact that something, e.g. a hand or a foot or an ear, belongs to a man means that it is or is properly called a man. Thus, that houses, trees, stars, and mountains belong to complexes properly called experiences by no means implies that they are or are properly called experiences even in the broad sense of that term. But even if, by some queer twist of fact or language, such physical objects were rightly called experiences in the broad sense, this would by no means involve their being experiences in the narrow sense that is relevant to Bradley's claim. The assumption that they would is a tempting but completely erroneous confusion fostered in substantial part by the ambiguity of the term "experience." Indeed, if we attend to the complex manner in which, in experience in the broad sense, physical objects actually present themselves in sentient experiences, we can readily see that they must be given definitive characteristics so radically different from those of the very sentient experiences through which they are presented as to place them upon a different logical level.

B. The second of the two aspects of Bradley's thought to be discussed here, his conception of the ultimate criterion of truth as intellectual satisfaction, is related to the first in this sense, that if experience alone is real or can be known, there can scarcely be any other way of determining truth than through the fulfillment or satisfaction of that aspect of experience that is primarily concerned with truth, namely intellect. But, even on the assumption that reality is not confined to experience, the notion of intellectual satisfaction as an ultimate criterion of truth has something to commend it.

If the idea of a criterion of truth can be stretched to cover the psychical conditions likely to be attained with the apprehension of truth, then intellectual satisfaction can in a certain sense be regarded as an ultimate criterion of truth. At any rate there seems to be no other psychical condition that can be regarded as superior to it, and in fact everything else that may be said to be a mark of apprehension of truth at all must in the end be measured by its conformity to this one. Thus, for example, emotional satisfaction, sensation, intuition, and even logical insight are all more limited in scope than intellectual satisfaction, and whatever contributions they make toward the attainment of truth must be judged in the light of their place in a more comprehensive satisfaction of intellect. Indeed, their status as marks of the attainment of truth at all must in the end be sustained, if it is to be sustained, in the light of the extent to which their presence can satisfy intellect. Insofar, then, as a criterion of truth can mean a condition of mind attained in apprehending truth, Bradley's intellectual satisfaction can be said to be an ultimate criterion.

Nevertheless, the doctrine of satisfaction of intellect as the ultimate criterion of truth involves at least three serious difficulties. In the first place, unless one accepts without qualification the implausible doctrine that experience alone is real, there is something very odd about regarding satisfaction of intellect, or for that matter any other mental condition, as a *criterion* of truth at all. Prima facie, at any rate, a criterion would seem to be not a mental condition acquired with the attainment of truth but a set of test conditions requisite to a mind's attainment of truth, not a feeling present when truth is duly apprehended but a set of procedures properly justifying such a feeling. Such a criterion would seem to be analogous not to the state of mind of the jurors at the end of the trial or even to their unanimous vote, but rather to the law in terms of which the jurors determine guilt or innocence. Satisfaction of intellect may represent the ultimate court of appeal of truth but it can hardly be strictly construed as the law of truth. A second difficulty of a more practical nature is that when the concept of a criterion of truth is so expanded as to make satisfaction of intellect in the previously indicated loose sense a criterion of truth, the temptation is strong to treat intellectual satisfaction as though it were also a criterion in the literal sense and hence to accept its presence as a substitute for painstaking detailed application of the kinds of tests that actually seem to be pertinent to the practical effort to separate truths from falsehoods. To be sure, this has by no means always been done by idealists. Idealists, including Bradley, have repeatedly urged the importance of the criteria of coherence and system; but these criteria are themselves none too definite, and idealists have sometimes been willing to accept notions that scarcely have much more to commend them than that they are in some way satisfying to the intellects of their advocates. However essential in the end intellectual satisfaction may be, no appeal to such satisfaction can ever take the place of careful inductive and deductive tests applied in terms of procedures and methods patiently worked out through the centuries.

In the third place, insistence that intellectual satisfaction is the ultimate criterion of truths tends mistakenly to suggest that what is really intellectually satisfying cannot be in error. Moreover, that Bradley himself, despite his doctrine of degrees of truth, sometimes tends to lean toward this view would seem to be indicated not only by the general manner in which he presses his doctrine but also by his insistence upon the even stronger claim that "an idea [that] does not contradict itself, either as it is or as taken with other things . . . is at once true and real." [2] However, there seems to be no reason in

[2] *Appearance and Reality*, p. 455.

principle why, despite the fact that they have no higher capacity to appeal to, human beings should not be, and even indefinitely remain, intellectually satisfied as to the truth of many propositions that are not in fact true. Certainly they have been intellectually satisfied for many centuries concerning some propositions subsequently found to be false, and no convincing reason can be given why with reference to some false propositions now entertained their intellectual satisfaction in such propositions may not continue as long as the race endures.

CHAPTER 3

Recent Idealism

THUS far our concern with epistemological idealism has been largely with the work of the early idealists in introducing some of the issues on which contemporary theories of knowledge have been focused. If, however, we are fully to appreciate either the character of the issues introduced or the conclusions insisted upon by the idealists, we must move on to consider idealism in the work of more recent idealists. We have selected for primary consideration Brand Blanshard's *The Nature of Thought,* which is the clearest and most fully developed of recent presentations of the kind of idealism we are concerned with. This book gathers in much of the best of the thought of each of the older absolute idealists, avoids some of their extravagances, and formulates the idealist thesis in terms of more recent philosophical and psychological inquiry. Subsequently we shall consider very briefly the work of a few other recent idealists, some of whom have thought along different lines from those chosen by Blanshard.

1. PERCEPTION AND IDEAS IN BLANSHARD'S THOUGHT

Like most other contemporary epistemologists, Blanshard is unwilling to apply the term "knowledge" to any experience that does not have sufficient cognitive content to involve the possibility of error.[1] Such content is, however, to be found far down in the scale of experi-

[1] Brand Blanshard, *The Nature of Thought* (London: George Allen & Unwin, 1939), I, 94.

ence, even in elementary forms of perception. It is with these elementary forms of perception that Blanshard's account of knowledge begins.

There is, to be sure, for Blanshard as for Bradley, an ingredient in knowing that lies even below the level of elementary perception, namely, a given or immediate experience. Such immediate experience, however, plays no such cardinal role in Blanshard's epistemology as in Bradley's. It affords no favored insight which a self-contradicting relational thought distorts; nor is it required to bind the parts of otherwise invalid inferences together; nor indeed is it needed, in the defeat of reason, as a final resource for the discovery of the Absolute. Immediate experience is indeed a necessary element [2] in knowing, and upon it reason builds; but it claims no special priority, never occurs alone, and must be discerned, if at all, by analysis and reconstruction.

Perception itself lies between given sensation on the one hand and explicit judgment on the other. It is a minimal interpretation of sensation. "With the barest and vaguest apprehension of anything given in sense *as* anything, it is already present." It may be defined as "that experience in which, on the warrant of something given in sensation at the time, we unreflectingly take some object to be before us." [3] Thus from the very beginning there is in perception, alongside the given, a repeatable or universal element. If animals and infants perceive, this repeatable element is present in their experience also, for, if universals were not present at the very beginning of cognitive experience, they could not be injected into it later. For all thought, the fact is that "unless there are universals there are no identities; and unless there are such identities a false report must be rendered by every perception, judgment, and inference." [4]

The range of purposive intelligence in perception is not, however, sufficiently suggested simply by saying that a universal is ascribed to a given. The choice of the universal is itself significant and calls for explanation. For example, when, upon seeing a tiny cross in the sky and hearing a pervasive hum, one says that he perceives an airplane, the transition from the scant data that sense gives to the perception is substantial and complex. Such transitions cannot be accounted for either as mere reflex actions or as psychical associations, for either type of process would, in many instances in which in fact we perceive correctly, lead us astray. Indeed, the ascription of universals in perception can be adequately understood in terms of noth-

[2] *Ibid.*, p. 118.   [4] *Ibid.*, p. 580.
[3] *Ibid.*, pp. 51 ff.

ing short of "implicit inference," in which purposive mentality is seeking its goal of truth.

The purposive character of perception is further indicated by analysis of the structure of a thing,[5] which, contrary to commonly accepted belief, is by no means a fixed and passively encountered entity. The unity of the thing depends upon such active and non-material factors as the joint prominence of qualities, movement together, utility, and the tendency of the mind to organize the elements of experience as simply as possible. The qualities attributed to the thing depend upon the choice of one perspective out of many possible ones, as for example the roundness of the coin depends upon viewing it from the perpendicular. Similarly, the externality of the thing depends on its relation to one's body. The substantiality of the thing depends on a special emphasis on the quality of hardness, together with a kind of animistic attribution of selfhood to the thing. Even the independence of the thing hinges upon such psychological factors as the defeat of expectations and the convergence of the testimony of the senses.

Still further insight into the purposive character of perception may be gained by considering the manner of influence of the meanings accumulated through earlier perceptive experiences upon later perceptions. Ordinarily accumulated meanings lie hidden out of sight, but in the act of recognition they become vital parts of the experience of perception. For example, the meanings that permit an expert mechanic to locate the difficulty in a motor car by the sound of the motor are previously nowhere to be seen, but at the right moment they come usefully into play to resolve his problem.[6] To suppose that the retained meanings involved here are merely physical or mechanical completely fails to explain their activation in so suitable a manner, and any behaviorist account of them overlooks the fact that they are either true or false. Such meanings can be intelligibly explained only as purposive "physical dispositions." Their remarkable activity for example in focusing attention, sharpening discrimination, increasing speed of reaction,—and resolving without deliberation such problems as some of those involved in operating an automobile, is nothing short of a kind of "perceptual thought." That they sometimes involve us in errors which sensation alone could not produce is additional evidence of their purposive cognitive character.

Turning now to the *ideas* involved in perception and the liberation of ideas from the perceptive context, Blanshard finds within perception itself at least three kinds of ideas.[7] These include (1)

[5] *Ibid.*, pp. 121 ff.
[6] *Ibid.*, pp. 161 ff.
[7] *Ibid.*, pp. 522 ff.

"ideas of sensible complements of the given," such as "the other side of an apple or the inside of a box"; (2) "ideas of undiscriminated features of the given," such as its spatial and temporal aspect; and (3) "dispositions" [8] such as stored knowledge of the scholar. At best such ideas, tied as they are to perception, are limited in their range; they are dependent on what is present at the moment, incapable of abstraction, and thus unable to cope successfully with that which is novel.

Although the ideas that are first detached from dependence upon perceptual contexts are, in contrast to some tied ideas, weak in explicitness and poor in detail,[9] the freedom of these detached ideas permits a vast increase in scope and versatility. Their actual liberation is achieved partly through the presence of theoretic interest and partly through a complex process involving the remembering of successful ideas and the forgetting of futile ones. It is also greatly facilitated by the development of language, which is to free ideas what sensation is to tied ones, although free ideas do not therefore depend upon language or occur only after its emergence. Images also serve as vehicles of ideas and, Bradley to the contrary notwithstanding, often coincide with them.

Far above the level of our first vague free ideas are the general ideas in terms of which the more advanced phases of reflective thinking operate. These general ideas are true universals and no mere syntheses of particulars. This is shown alike by their logical character and by the psychological process of their emergence, for logically all general ideas must be universals and in psychological fact the general is often grasped before the particular. The special process that most facilitates the clear emergence of general ideas is that of comparison in which, under the prodding of both theoretical and practical interests, the mind ferrets out identities and differences.

Concentration upon the generality of general ideas often leads to the view that such ideas are abstract attributes or intensions determining classes.[10] However, while the notion of an abstract idea, a genus as distinguished from its various species, has some value as a scientific fiction, no genus can exist either in nature or in thought, or even as implicit generalization, apart from its species.[11] The absurdity of endeavoring to conceive any genus apart from its species becomes apparent in the effort to think, for example, of color apart from colors or of triangularity apart from triangles. Moreover, the increased control over instances involved in general knowledge is quite unintelligible if species are separated from their genera, and

8 *Ibid.*, p. 31.   10 *Ibid.*, p. 582.
9 *Ibid.*, pp. 530 ff.   11 *Ibid.*, pp. 592 ff.

the traditional theory, implicit in the notion of abstract ideas, that the wider the experience the poorer the concept, is plainly false.[12] But what general ideas really are can be seen only when the relation of the idea to its object has been developed.

2. Ideas and Their Objects, Knowing and the Known

The crucial question concerning ideas is not what they are or how they emerge but what their relation to their objects is. The answer to this question is also the key to the problem of the relation of knowing and the known.

The correct view of the relation of the idea and its object is "at violent odds with common sense and is to be accepted only from necessity." [1] Accordingly, one may well begin with a consideration of alternative views.

One view, suggested by the classical British empiricists, is that the idea is an image resembling its object; but, while some sort of resemblance is involved in ideation, ideas and images often vary independently of one another, and of general ideas there can be no images.[2] Another view, presented by Russell and others, is that an idea is a cause of an effect similar to the one that would have been caused by its object, but this view is vitiated by the fact that meaning is often attached to an idea prior to any significant effect and that changes in effect sometimes leave meaning unaffected.[3] The behaviorist doctrine is that ideas can be reduced to silent speech-movements; but language and thought do not always operate together, and any attempt to make thought *mean* bodily movements undermines its own intellectual basis.[4] The pragmatist view, which takes ideas to be plans of action, properly recognizes purposive aspects in ideas but obscures their cognitive objectives and is hopelessly confused in its endeavor to reduce the facts of the past to considerations about the future.[5] Such realists as G. E. Moore and Samuel Alexander attempt to substitute mental acts for ideas in the hope that in this manner the directness of knowing and the independence of objects may be preserved. But their alleged mental acts can be discerned neither by introspection nor by inference, and even if such acts could be discovered by introspection or by inference, the implied theory of knowledge would apparently involve an incredible attribution of reality to all manner of dreams and fictions.[6] The critical realists' claim, that

[12] *Ibid.*, p. 586.
[1] *Ibid.*, p. 414.
[2] *Ibid.*, chap. vii.
[3] *Ibid.*, chap. viii.

[4] *Ibid.*, chap. ix.
[5] *Ibid.*, chap. x.
[6] *Ibid.*, chap. xi.

subjective experience and objective fact are linked by essences, is more plausible, but essences turn out upon analysis to be unstable inventions having contradictory characteristics and requiring their inventors to choose in the end between idealism and a more naïve realism.[7]

The only account of the relation of the idea and its object capable both of satisfying the insights of the various theories considered, without falling prey to their fallacies, and of meeting the other requisites of a theory of this relation, is one that has been present all the while in the thought of idealists from Plato to Bradley and Bosanquet, and especially in that of Josiah Royce. It is the view that the idea is the partially realized object, and the object, the fully realized idea. "The relation between idea and object must be conceived teleologically, as the relation of that which is partially realized."[8] Thus "when we say that an idea is *of* an object, we are saying that the idea is a purpose which the object alone would fulfill, that it is a potentiality which this object alone would fulfill, that it is a potentiality which this object alone would actualize, a content informed by an impulse to become this object."[9] To use Royce's language, "the object is for us simply the completely embodied will of the idea."[10]

The character of this theory may be illustrated by reference, for example, to Othello's remorse.[11] The idea of Othello's utter dismay is neither an "image," nor a "set of words," nor a "bit of physical behavior," nor the "character of that despair divorced from its existence in Othello or his creator." It is rather "the mind's effort to realize that passion," and it "becomes adequate to its object just so far as this effort succeeds."[12] Falling short of full success, it remains a partially realized purpose, a fragment of the object.

In this view the values of the image theory are conserved and its weaknesses avoided, for the idea is here both like and unlike the object. Again, the theory shares with critical realism the correct claim that "the object of knowledge transcends experience," but it shows, as critical realism cannot, how "the *character* of the object is presented in experience directly."[13] The theory rightly agrees with new realism that the object itself is presented in experience, but it refuses to be misled with that view into supposing that the object is therefore sufficiently presented in experience at the outset.[14] With behaviorism the theory recognizes that the thought is the potentiality

[7] *Ibid.*, chap. xii.
[8] *Ibid.*, p. 473.
[9] *Ibid.*
[10] *Ibid.*, quoted in *ibid.*, p. 519, from Josiah Royce, *The World and the Individ-* ual (New York & London: The Macmillan Co., & Macmillan & Co., Ltd., 1900), I, 315.
[11] *Ibid.*, p. 550.
[12] *Ibid.*
[13] *Ibid.*, p. 495.
[14] *Ibid.*, pp. 496 f.

of the thing, but, unlike behaviorism, it demands an adequate potentiality. Finally, with pragmatism, it sees thought as a means to an end, but it also goes on to show what the end is and how it may be realized.

In addition to meeting the specific requirements emerging from analysis of the alternative theories, the view of the idea as an unfulfilled purpose satisfies also the more general requirements, often overlooked, involved in the teleological character of the mind. The mind grows not by accretion but by maturing purpose. Its choices are made in terms of desires under the direction of the good. Its inferences are accomplished not by mere association but by perceived necessity. Now when the object is taken to be the fulfillment of the purpose partially embodied in the idea, these facts are duly accounted for; otherwise, they remain quite unintelligible. If the objection is raised at this point that the theory fails to reckon with the fact that physical objects often thwart or disappoint us rather than satisfy us, the reply is that the objection is largely a result of mistakenly identifying the real will with empirical desires and that when real will is properly seen in its larger scope the conflict disappears.[15]

The theory of the idea now under consideration also explains the riddle, previously encountered, of the nature of general ideas. As has been seen, such ideas are not mere abstractions in which the genus is isolated from the species. What then are they? One may now reply "that the generic universal *is* the partial realization of its more specific forms . . . that it exists only as the *thought* of these."[16] Unlike the view that the general idea is abstract, this account explains the advance of knowledge from the generic to the specific, the greater command over instances attained by the person who grasps the particulars in the general, and the distinction between the kind of thinking that indicates a genus, such as *man*, having many unknown details and the kind that refers to a definite quality, such as whiteness. In terms of this view one may see the value of generality without losing sight of the importance of detail.

The interpretation of the idea as a partially realized object is the only view that accords with the nature of knowledge. Knowing embraces all sorts of cognitive activities, such as "perceiving, judging, inferring, doubting, conjecturing and wondering."[17] Its aim is twofold. The transcendent aim is "seeing things as they are,"[18] "the direct revelation in experience of what is also beyond it."[19] The immanent end is "to achieve a state of insight that will bring the

---

[15] *Ibid.*, pp. 507 ff.
[16] *Ibid.*, p. 609.
[17] *Ibid.*, p. 486.

[18] *Ibid.*, p. 488.
[19] *Ibid.*, p. 489.

theoretic impulse to rest," [20] to find an order that yields intellectual satisfaction. If these two ends are independent, that is to say, if the knowing that satisfies our inner demand is independent of the object which knowing seeks to apprehend, then knowledge is either a miracle or a fraud. In like manner, if the two are identical, knowledge is also impossible, for we are then compelled either to embrace a solipsism or to swallow the monstrous errors which experience sometimes suggests. But if, as is indicated by the theory of the idea as partially realized object, the inner satisfaction of the mind is neither identical with nor independent of the object, a genuine connection between the two ends is established without involving a stultifying confusion of the two. *"If thought can be seen as a stage on the way to its transcendent end or object, as that end itself in the course of becoming actual, the paradox of knowledge is in principle solved.* The idea can then be *both* the same as its object *and* different; the same because it *is* the object *in posse;* different because that object, which is its end, is as yet incompletely realized." [21]

In the light of the foregoing considerations, further understanding of the objects of knowledge as universals is possible. As has been seen, objects of knowledge are not to be construed as abstract universals; but neither are they to be taken as particulars for those "individual things in which the generic universal would be realized may themselves be resolved away into specific universals." [22] A thing consists of "characters grouped together for special causes or ends," the idea of a "featureless substratum" being sheer myth based on "primitive anthropomorphism." [23] Even the appeal to space and time coordinates cannot rescue the particular, for these coordinates also are universals.[24] All universals belong to a single system and constitute together an individual Absolute, which is the ultimate object of knowledge. But, since a given idea may have as its proximate object some finite focus in which its special purpose is realized, even a finite object may be regarded as relatively individual and an object of restricted knowledge. Knowledge of such an object needs only to be matured within the larger system to which it belongs, not, as Bradley thought, radically transformed, in order to become fuller knowledge.

3. BLANSHARD'S VIEW OF INFERENCE

We come next to Blanshard's account of those phases of the "movement of thought" that lie beyond simple perception and judgment and may in a broad sense be referred to as inference. What is pre-

[20] *Ibid.*
[21] *Ibid.,* p. 494.
[22] *Ibid.,* p. 625.

[23] *Ibid.,* p. 633.
[24] *Ibid.,* p. 636.

sented here is neither merely psychological description, which would remain incomplete without reference to the objects of thought, nor a bare list of logical forms, which would be no more than a skeleton of thought. It is rather a more comprehensive effort to represent the manner in which fully developed thought actually moves, and from the point of view of this larger perspective the fact becomes clear from the outset that the immanent end that all the while operates in thought is an ideal of system.

That in which the thought process begins is always a certain tension between the ideal system and a confused state of affairs that cannot for the moment be accommodated to such a system. It is as though an island appeared over against a mainland and the mainland were ill at ease until the island were linked with it.[1] For example, while the details of a proposed trip remain undecided, there is a tension between the ideal of the completed journey and the incompleted plan that sets thought moving. Again, if a traveler encounters a conspicuous but unfamiliar part of the ship on which he sails, there emerges a tension between his total ordered and accepted conception of the ship and this strange part that caused him to wonder and to inquire.[2]

Once begun, reflection proceeds through a more or less orderly sequence of steps. The first step consists of "specifying the problem," or, to return to the analogy of the island, of bringing the island into proximity with the mainland.[3] Merely to consider a topic is not to reflect; one must formulate a specific question. One needs to see just what circle of thought it is that needs to be closed and what the requirements for closing it are. This preliminary organization of materials is a necessary part of thought and will be seen to have taken place even when solutions of problems seem to have been achieved by chance or accident.

The second step is a resumption of the process of observation guided by theory. For example, confronted by an illness the nature of which is not immediately apparent, the doctor proceeds to search for further data, such as temperature, pulse, blood count, and so on. In general, observation itself is reliable; theory may lead it astray in all manner of bypaths such as noticing the irrelevant, focusing attention at the wrong point, overlooking what is relevant, or failing to see exceptions. But theory is quite as necessary to successful observation as observation is to satisfactory theory, for such is the multitude and complexity of data that observation without a guiding principle is hopelessly lost.

[1] *Ibid.*, II, 48.
[2] *Ibid.*, p. 47.
[3] *Ibid.*, pp. 64 ff.

The third and most dramatic step in the movement of thought is invention, the occurrence of an hypothesis or proposed solution,[4] "the leap of suggestion." [5] At this point the associationist principle, still present in considerable degree in psychological theory, attempts a mechanical explanation. If association of particulars is meant, one must observe with Bradley that once an experience is finished it is no longer present to be associated. But even if association of universals is intended, neither *similarity* nor any of the other modes of connection on which associationists commonly rely has the requisite explanatory power. Multitudes of associations other than the one relevant to the solution of a given problem are suggested by the similarity factor; and that factor actually explains neither the emergence of the right suggestion nor exclusion of wrong ones. *Recency,* *intensity,* and *spatiotemporal continuity* are scarcely more helpful. They mislead as often as correctly lead, and thought in terms of them has little in common with what actually occurs in satisfactory problem-solving. For example, in Plato's famous account of the boy who gradually resolves a geometrical problem, every step in the process is a step away from association and toward a logical or teleological necessity.[6]

As a matter of fact, merely descriptive factual psychology can never render a correct account of the higher levels of reflective thinking for the reason that it leaves out of account the central feature of thought, the operation of the system of values at which thought aims. Psychologists resort in vain to all sorts of devices in the effort to avoid bringing value into the picture. The behaviorist denies the existence of value; the structuralist admits it but leaves it out "when speaking professionally." Others attempt to give it a place in psychology but exclude any recognition of its validity.[7] The simple fact is that thinking is a quest for truth and that truth cannot be apart from an impersonal logical system of value. The goal of thought is the discovering not of the structure or function of the individual thinker's mind but of the laws of the material in hand. Even when we think of our own thought we do so in terms of an ideal system that also transcends our thought. An adequate psychology will never say of a piece of sound thinking merely that "an element appeared in someone's mind because *his notion of logic* suggested it." Such a psychology will rather also go on to say that the appropriate element appeared because *logic really did* require it." [8] Thinking always has reference to and is guided by "an ideal order," [9] and what the thinker

[4] *Ibid.,* pp. 98 ff.
[5] *Ibid.,* pp. 98.
[6] *Ibid.,* pp. 112 ff.

[7] *Ibid.,* p. 126.
[8] *Ibid.,* p. 122.
[9] *Ibid.,* pp. 124 ff.

intends to do is to subject his thinking to this order.[10] Blanshard's contention is then "that in the mind of the successful thinker the spirit of logic itself is at work leavening the unformed mass, and that in the mind of the creative artist the spirit of beauty is at work, supplying both ends and means." [11] This explains why the better mind is able to understand the movements of the poorer one, but not the other way around.

As William James suggested, the most important specific capacity required for successful problem-solving is probably sagacity, or the ability to select those characteristics of a situation that are crucial. But the essential feature of such sagacity is by no means, as James thought, simply fertility in the discovery of analogy, for multitudes of analogies may be seen by a madman.[12] Much more important is "control of analogy by the conditions of the problem," [13] and this can be successfully achieved only by a kind of a priori reasoning. Such reasoning applies the principles implicit in the whole problem to the crucial phase of it. It is a *"power to extend a partially given whole."*

To endeavor to confine the a priori, as is frequently done, to formal reasoning, is to sink into skepticism with reference to facts.[14] An a priori element, limited only by our lack of knowledge of the whole system under consideration, is present in every type of thinking. It is in terms of a priori thinking, for example, that Shakespeare brings his *Othello* to a close in the only possible way; and only in terms of the power of such thinking to apply the principles of the whole to the parts are we ever able to fill in those gaps in thought in which all our problems in the end consist.

Since invention is thus in large part an a priori cognizing in "surrender of the will to an order whose structure is quite independent of it," [15] much of invention may take place, as many a genius has testified, beneath the level of clear consciousness.[16] Indeed, the reasoning in which the subconscious element is most notably present is not after all in principle very different from deliberate thought, in which in any case "much goes on behind the scenes." [17] The basis of the distinction between the two varieties lies simply in the proportion of conscious labor involved. In both cases it is the "spirit of the whole" that directs the process.

At least four methods are known for aiding the work of the subconscious: the accumulation of data, the direction of attention to

[10] *Ibid.*
[11] *Ibid.*, p. 129.
[12] *Ibid.*, p. 133.
[13] *Ibid.*
[14] *Ibid.*, p. 142.

[15] *Ibid.*, p. 166.
[16] *Ibid.*, pp. 166 ff.; see also Blanshard, "The Nature of Mind," *Journal of Philosophy*, XXXVIII (1941), 207 ff.
[17] *Ibid.*, p. 214.

special problems, the cultivation of feeling for sound form of thought, and the alternation of work and rest. But neither these methods nor any set of rules can reduce to formal procedures the movement of the whole of thought, whose laws transcend all our efforts to formulate them.

In addition to the three steps in reasoning already indicated, two others, the elaboration of implications and the comparison of these with facts, are also commonly distinguished.[18] But many of the essential features of these have already been considered, and both are resolvable into *coherence,* whose essential role in verification is now to be examined.

4. BLANSHARD'S CONCEPTION OF TRUTH AND ERROR

That coherence is the test of truth is perhaps not at first plausible, but the fact that coherence must be the proper test becomes increasingly apparent as inquiry reveals the eventual inadequacy of the other tests that have been proposed and the manner in which each of these rests, insofar as it is at all valid, upon coherence itself. "The person who rejects coherence can be shown, in such fashion as to convince him if he is unbiased, that he is doing one or other of two things: either resorting to coherence without knowing it, or else applying a standard that he himself would reject as soon as its nature was made explicit." [1]

Of proposed tests other than coherence, five are worthy of serious consideration. The pragmatist test has already by implication been found wanting in what has been said concerning the pragmatist account of the idea. It is obviously incapable of testing truths about the past, and, where other kinds of truth are in question, it wavers helplessly between individual and social criteria, and between intellectual and motor-affective criteria.[2]

The test in terms of authority yields, when thought out, either a self-contradictory irrationalism, which no one would care to endorse, or a veiled appeal through other tests to coherence.[3] The test in terms of mystical insight makes little advance over that in terms of authority. While its advocates correctly observe that many aspects of reality cannot be caught in the net of words, they continue to argue without realizing that argument is in the end appeal to coherence.

The tests to which common sense most often appeals are those of correspondence to fact and self-evidence.[4] The first of these is quite

18 *The Nature of Thought,* II, 212.
1 *Ibid.,* pp. 215 ff.
2 *Ibid.,* I, chap. x.
3 *Ibid.,* II, 216 ff.
4 *Ibid.,* pp. 226 ff.

inapplicable in cases of moral judgment, where there is nothing to which judgment may correspond. It is only partially applicable to judgments of the past, where the judged is no longer present. Even to perceptive judgment the test of correspondence is really scarcely applicable; for we never are actually confronted with "brute facts" unmixed with mental elements, and science is unwilling to accept as fact anything that cannot be placed in an ordered system. The test of self-evidence, often appealed to in the past by mathematicians, is scarcely stronger than that of correspondence. Reliance on self-evidence often yields conflicting judgments and has long since been abandoned by mathematicians and logicians, who should be the experts concerning it. The appeals that are legitimately made in the name of self-evidence to basic principles of logic, such as the law of contradiction, are in fact applications of the principles of coherence. Correspondence tests and self-evidence tests as such "can validate nothing, and are compelled, like the others, to fall back upon coherence." [5]

The manner of the failure of all other tests of truth entails the vindication of the coherence test, for in the end all the others must rely on this one. The coherence test is also ultimately the one demanded by mathematics, the physical and social sciences, and even common sense. "Coherence *is* our test, the final and invariable test, when our beliefs are under pressure." [6]

Coherence is not only the test of truth, it is also the nature of truth. That this is so is already implicit in what has been said about the relation of thought and reality, for it is precisely in the relation of these two that truth is on any theory to be found. Now, as has been seen, "thought in its very nature is the attempt to bring something unknown or imperfectly known into a subsystem of knowledge, and thus into that larger system that forms the world of accepted beliefs. . . . To think . . . is to have that within us which if *it were developed and completed,* would identify itself with the object." [7] Thus, "thought is related to reality as the partial to the perfect fulfillment of purpose," [8] and truth becomes "approximation of thought to reality, . . . thought on its way home." [9] But such bringing into system, such approximating fulfillment, is precisely what is meant by coherence. Hence, in terms of the relation established between thought and reality, truth can be nothing else than coherence; "the degree of truth in our experience as a whole is the degree of system it has achieved." [10]

[5] *Ibid.,* p. 259.
[6] *Ibid.,* p. 215.
[7] *Ibid.,* pp. 261 f.
[8] *Ibid.,* p. 262.
[9] *Ibid.,* p. 264.
[10] *Ibid.*

Whether or not truth exists or is attainable, that is, whether or not a coincidence of the processes of internal satisfaction and apprehension of object exists and can be ascertained, is another question that cannot be answered with certainty.[11] But that there is such a coincidence is the assumption not only of science but of "every act of thinking whatever." [12] Moreover, one can, if he will take the trouble to do so, find sufficient vindication of this assumption in "the impressive fact of the advance of knowledge." [13] Indeed, the coincidence of thought and reality is the metaphysical key to "the structure of the real." [14]

The coherence in which truth consists is perhaps not amenable to precise definition, but its character becomes sufficiently clear by noting the progressive degrees of system, interdependence, and mutual implication, for example, in a junk heap, a stone pile, a machine, an organic body, and a mathematical system. Thus, a completely satisfactory system "would be such that no proposition would be arbitrary, every proposition would be entailed by the others jointly and even singly, and no proposition would stand outside the system. The integration would be so complete that no part could be seen for what it was without seeing its relation to the whole, and the whole itself could be understood only through the contribution of every part." [15]

The view that coherence as now described is the nature of truth as well as its test was really implicit not only in the relation established between thought and object but also in the acceptance of coherence itself as a test. "To say that the nature of things may be *in*coherent, but we shall approach the truth about it precisely so far as our thoughts become coherent, sounds very much like nonsense." [16] How indeed could a theory that held any other view of the nature of truth test truth by coherence? For example, if one holds that truth is correspondence of idea to independent object, the discovery of coherence does not help him to test this correspondence. Nor in fact can he test it any other way. To do so he would have to know the object independently, but if he knows it thus no truth is involved, and if he does not, no independent knowledge is present. Similar difficulties vitiate all other attempts to test by coherence a truth that is not coherence. Hence, "assume coherence as the test, and you will be driven by the incoherence of your alternatives to the conclusion that it is also the nature of truth." [17]

[11] See Blanshard, "The Heritage of Idealism," in Dixon Wecter and Others, *Changing Patterns in American Civilization* (Philadelphia: University of Pennsylvania Press, 1949), pp. 82 ff.
[12] *The Nature of Thought*, II, 263.
[13] *Ibid.*, p. 263.
[14] *Ibid.*
[15] *Ibid.*, pp. 265 f.
[16] *Ibid.*, p. 267.
[17] *Ibid.*, p. 269.

Since the coherence view of truth makes truth relative to "approximation to an absolute system,"[18] it implies a doctrine of degrees of truth similar to that of Bradley. No proposition is completely true and none completely false; each contains some truth and some falsehood. This doctrine does not rest upon the misleading supposition that propositions contain fragmentary propositions, some of which may be true, as for example the mistaken judgment "that is Colonel Bailey yonder" contains the truth that "that is a man." Nor does the doctrine draw upon the analogy of approximation of accuracy in measurement. Rather, its kind of approximation is that of growth from fragmentary and general to full and specific knowledge. This may be illustrated by the advance of the boy's apprehension of the bare fact that Napoleon was defeated at Waterloo to the mature historian's understanding of this event.[19]

The psychological ground of the claim that knowledge manifests such degrees of maturity and truth is that meaning in judgment is always partly determined by context in reality. The logical ground consists in the consideration that concepts can be determined only by reference to a system to which they belong. This consideration is obviously applicable to mathematical concepts, but it is also applicable to concepts of parts of organisms and even to ideas of inanimate objects. Every concept involves relations to what is beyond it, and at the very least some of these relations are essential to the adequacy of the concept; but, since all the essential relations are never grasped at once, "adequacy is a matter of degree."[20]

If truth is coherence it is to be expected that error will be a kind of incoherence, and this is so. Error is not, of course, absolute incoherence, nor any absolute error. Absolute incoherence would break the connection between idea and object and so rule out the possibility of a proposition. What occurs in erroneous judgment is "discrepancy between the end of thought and a premature formulation of that end, between what we really mean and what we take ourselves to mean; or perhaps better between what we mean to mean, and what, in ignorance and precipitancy, we do mean."[21] For example, if one speaks of the Persian victory over the Greeks at Platea, his thought intends a certain battle but can be fully realized only along somewhat different lines in which the order of victory is reversed.[22] The major source of error is not observation as such but theory, which however useful and necessary often blinds us to what we should see, and may "alter what we do perceive" and even cause us to see what is not before us.[23]

<hr/>

[18] *Ibid.*, p. 272.
[19] *Ibid.*, pp. 307 ff.
[20] *Ibid.*, p. 319.

[21] *Ibid.*, I, 512.
[22] *Ibid.*, p. 511.
[23] *Ibid.*, pp. 211 ff.; *ibid.*, II, 83 ff.

5. Blanshard's Account of the Nature of Necessity

The system at which the knowing process aims, in which alone the mind can be satisfied, must be one in which every proposition not only finds its appropriate place but also entails and is entailed by every other proposition of the system. It must be "a system . . . whose parts are bound together by intelligible necessity." [1] Accordingly, no account of knowledge can be complete without asking what *we mean by necessity.* [2]

In general three types of mistaken accounts of necessity have claimed acceptance; the empiricist, the formalist, and the positivist. The empiricist view is that what is commonly thought to be necessity is really "nothing whatever but habituation" [3] or invariable association, either in individual experience or in that of the race. But such a view is false to the actual manner of our recognition of necessity, and so prejudicial to logic as to undermine, along with all other truth, its own truth-claim. [4] The formalist view attaches necessity solely to general nonsensible patterns such as those found in symbolic logic and mathematics. [5] But this view ignores the very considerable material element involved in much of our reasoning, and furnishes no satisfactory account of many of the connections that thought actually establishes. The logical propositions become tautologies rooted only in the structure of language and essentially irrelevant to fact. [6] Such a view can be held, however, only if one irrationally ignores intensional meaning and the claim of all judgment to refer to reality and if one is willing to accept the implied vitiation of the truth-claims of his own theory.

Over against these mistaken views may be placed the correct conception of "concrete necessity." Such necessity is in our experience never absolute, but always relative to some system having a limited degree of comprehensiveness. It cannot attach to a single proposition or to the relation between several propositions, for propositions are always relative to conditions that lie outside themselves. It yields no single definition linking all its varieties, but itself varies in its intellectual, esthetic, and moral manifestations. Like truth, it has degrees depending upon the completeness of the system in which it is found, and the fact of its degrees precludes any attempt to distinguish sharply, as rival views do, between analytic and synthetic judgments. [7]

[1] *Ibid.*, p. 331.
[2] *Ibid.*
[3] *Ibid.*, p. 336.
[4] *Ibid.*, pp. 338 ff.
[5] *Ibid.*, pp. 358 ff.

[6] *Ibid.*, pp. 99 ff.
[7] Cf. *ibid.*, pp. 319 ff.; see also, Blanshard, "Current Strictures on Reason," Philosophical Review, LIV (1945), 345–68.

At this point an objection emerges that requires consideration of the problem of relations. Relations, it is said, are external or quite independent of their terms, so that their addition to or withdrawal from a term can make no difference to that term.[8] If this claim were true it would of course preclude both necessary connections and, with them, that coincidence of thought and reality on which truth and knowledge depend. But the doctrine of external relations cannot be sustained. On the one hand, the empirical argument for external relations builds in large part upon ignorance of internal relations and tends to ignore the implications of the extremely limited scope of its own inductions. On the other hand, the a priori argument for external relations relies upon presupposed logical atoms and abstract numbers that in fact could never exist in isolation,[9] and if they did, would bring thought to a standstill.

In contrast to the weakness of the case for the externality of relations, the case for the internality of at least many relations, that is, for the claim that these relations are such that without them their terms would be different, remains strong. That properties generated by relations, such as *being a brother of John, being similar to another thing* or *being like another thing* are internal, would seem to be almost self-evident. Difference is, however, quite as relational as likeness, for since "a thing is as truly characterized *by not* being *x* as by being *y*, . . . a change in its relations of difference would mean a change in itself." [10] Moreover, it is difficult to see how any thing could remain the same if certain of its relations were changed, and even universals, when properly considered in relation to their species, are quite dependent on these relations.

None of this proves, of course, that all relations are internal, but each part of it contributes to the plausibility of that thesis. Meanwhile, the thesis is rendered still more plausible by the consideration that in the end the causality that seems to link all things really involves logical necessity. This coalescence of logical and causal necessity can readily be seen in cases in which logical necessity is a cause of the making of an inference. For example, when the *abbé* stated that his first penitent was a murderer and the squire subsequently announced that he was the *abbé's* first penitent, the auditors of the two statements immediately concluded that the squire was a murderer.[11] In cases in which physical connections are the only ones apparent, the logical necessity involved in causality is by no means so obvious. But the mind cannot avoid belief that such necessity is involved here also, and the opposing view that physical causality is

---

[8] *The Nature of Thought,* II, 451.   [10] *Ibid.,* pp. 478.
[9] *Ibid.,* pp. 463 ff.   [11] *Ibid.,* pp. 495 f.

merely invariable sequence involves a multitude of paradoxes, such as the implication that no unique event is caused and that no human action springs from a motive. Besides, the relation between cause and effect inevitably presents itself as an intrinsic connection of a kind that cannot but be also a necessary one.[12]

6. OTHER RECENT IDEALIST THINKERS

Although Blanshard's book represents perhaps the most satisfactory formulation of idealistic epistemology to date, and the only full current expression of that absolute or objective idealistic epistemology with which we are primarily concerned; idealism, both in the form of absolute idealism and in other forms, has continued to find a considerable variety of significant advocates. We shall distinguish here four main groups of writers. The first consists of writers who, like Blanshard, have continued the absolute idealist tradition; the second, of personalists similar to Ward and Bowne; the third, of critical idealists; and the fourth, of writers who, while making substantial concessions to realism, continue to hold on to what they consider essential features of idealism.

A. An interesting member of the absolute idealist group who has followed Royce and apparently been followed by Blanshard but who differs significantly from both, is the Harvard philosopher, W. E. Hocking (b. 1873). Contending, along with Royce and Blanshard, that infinity is confronted by the knowing mind from the beginning [1] and that each particular idea is a purpose on its way to completion in its object,[2] Hocking nevertheless accepts nature in a less qualified way than Royce or Blanshard, and finds in knowing more pronounced social and mystical elements.

Initially man is confronted by nature, which, though he apprehends it in some measure *creatively* [3] through his whole idea, he cannot but accept in general as he finds it.[4] To experience nature objectively is, however, invariably to experience it as experience of other minds also.[5] If it be asked how we know other minds, the answer is that, since minds consist in part of their objects, in knowing objects we literally have partial knowledge of minds.[6] Moreover, in having ideas of other minds at all, we also experience these minds.[7]

[12] *Ibid.,* pp. 511 ff.
[1] W. E. Hocking, *The Meaning of God in Human Experience* (New Haven, Conn.: Yale University Press, 1912), pp. 93 ff.
[2] *Ibid.,* pp. 68 ff.
[3] Cf. Hocking, *Types of Philosophy* (New York: Charles Scribner's Sons, 1929), pp. 273 ff.; and "Some Second Principles," in G. P. Adams and W. P. Montague, *Contemporary American Philosophy* (New York: The Macmillan Co., 1930), I, p. 292.
[4] *Ibid.,* pp. 484 ff.
[5] *The Meaning of God in Human Experience,* pp. 287 ff.
[6] *Ibid.,* pp. 260 ff.
[7] *Ibid.,* p. 274.

But the objectivity of nature is not fully sustained by the fluctuating force of our own and other finite minds. Both nature and minds must rest in the end upon an Absolute Mind, which, in sustaining the world, also sustains finite minds, and upon which our knowledge is from the beginning dependent.[8] The reality of this Absolute Mind is established by an ontological argument that finds experience of God in the idea of God[9] and especially by a specifically religious experience that illuminates all human experience.[10]

Similar to the idealism of Hocking is that of Mary Whiton Calkins (1863–1930) of Wellesley. Calkins grounded her epistemology squarely upon what she took to be Berkeley's basic position, "the insistence that what any man unchallengeably knows—what he knows in other words, without any element of hypothesis—is himself and his experiencing, clearly a mental reality.[11] This foundation she finds unshaken by Moore's famous "Refutation of Idealism" or by any other realist challenge.[12] From this initial position, Calkins finds herself driven, in order to account for the encounter within one's own experience with that which is not himself, to the recognition of an Absolute Self, who embraces all finite selves in whom alone the experience of another becomes intelligible.[13] Putting this claim in a different way, Calkins contends that experienced relations can be neither "internal" nor "external" but become understandable only as relations "of whole and part," so that all finite beings are parts of "some including entity and are thus related to each other only indirectly."[14] Such an idealism she finds not only unavoidable but at the same time more in accord with science, empiricism, and even common sense than any opposing realism.[15]

B. The type of personalistic and theistic idealism that we have previously encountered in Ward and Pringle Pattison has found fresh expression in W. R. Sorley's attempt, in his *Moral Values and the Idea of God,* to bring to light the indispensable role of the apprehension of values in the knowing process. Although the objects of knowledge, including both things and values, have distinguishable existence recognizable in knowledge,[16] they are not isolated entities

[8] *Ibid.,* p. 297.
[9] *Ibid.,* pp. 306 ff.
[10] *Ibid.,* pp. 341 ff.
[11] M. W. Calkins "The Philosophical Credo of an Absolute Personalist," in *Contemporary American Philosophy,* p. 205.
[12] See Calkins "The Idealist to the Realist," *Journal of Philosophy, Psychology, and Scientific Method,* VIII (1911), 452 ff.
[13] *Ibid.,* pp. 207 ff.; and Calkins *The Persistent Problems of Philosophy* (5th. ed.; New York: The Macmillan Co., 1936),

pp. 452 ff.; see also Calkins, "The Personalistic Conception of Nature," *Philosophical Review,* XXVIII (1919), 115–46.
[14] "The Philosophical Credo of an Absolute Personalist," p. 211.
[15] Calkins, "Unjustified Claims for Neo-Realism," *Philosophical Review,* XXII (1913), pp. 53–56.
[16] W. R. Sorley, *Moral Values and the Idea of God* (Cambridge: University Press, 1930), pp. 194 ff.

but parts of a coherent whole in which alone they are fully apprehended.[17] The roots of our knowledge of the causal order lie both in
sense experiences and in experiences of the moral order in value
intuitions.[18] But attempts to discover the coherent whole by either
analysis or synthesis end in hopeless dualism.[19] What is needed is a
synoptic view that apprehends the whole, however vaguely to start
with,[20] and then proceeds to interpret it in terms of better-known
specific experiences.[21] At this point the causal order is of little help,
for no logical path leads from it to the valuational order. The
valuational order itself affords a much better clue to the interpretation of the whole, for values, being incapable of existence apart from
the personal experiences in which they inhere, have a claim upon
existence or "ought to be."[22] Since persons intuit not only values but
an order of values in which their personalities may find fulfillment,
and since the causal and valuational orders are seen to fall into
coherent wholeness, it is reasonable to assume that the order of values
has its existence in a Divine Reason who is the ground of both
orders.[23]

Similar in its conclusion to Sorley's book is A. E. Taylor's *The
Faith of a Moralist*, which insists upon a valuational element in all
knowledge and suggests that our knowledge of God may be the most
real knowledge we have.[24] In the work of another British contemporary of Sorley and Taylor, H. W. Carr, personal idealism takes the
form of a monadism in which the theistic element, if present at all,
is subordinated to subjectivistic and individualistic ones: "The
world consists of active, living, individual subjects of experience.
. . . Material objects . . . are appearances or phenomena and exist
only in the perceptions of the monads. . . . I know my own existence. . . . The world is only our own activity reflected to us. . . .
Only living things are."[25]

On the American side of the Atlantic, the personalist tradition of
Bowne and Howison is ably resumed in the thought of Edgar Sheffield
Brightman (1884–1952) of Boston University, who concedes more to
realism than does either Sorley or Taylor. From the beginning
Brightman deliberately advocates a dualistic theory of knowledge in

[17] Cf. *ibid.*, pp. 196 f. See also Sorley,
"Value and Reality," in *Contemporary
British Philosophy*, ed. J. H. Muirhead
(London: George Allen & Unwin, 1925),
pp. 245–67.
[18] Cf. *Moral Values and the Idea of God*,
pp. 88 ff.
[19] *Ibid.*, pp. 241 ff.
[20] *Ibid.*, pp. 249 ff.
[21] *Ibid.*, pp. 271 ff.

[22] Cf. *Ibid.*, pp. 76, 285.
[23] *Ibid.*, pp. 347 ff., chaps. xiv ff.
[24] A. E. Taylor, *The Faith of a Moralist*
(London: Macmillan & Co., Ltd., 1930),
chap. ii, sec. 3.
[25] H. W. Carr, *Cogitons Cogitats* (Los
Angeles: University of Southern California
Press, 1930) pp. ix–xi. See also Carr, *A
Theory of Monads* (London: Macmillan &
Co., Ltd., 1922).

which idea and object are kept distinct. The opposing identification of idea and object he regards as an unfortunate misunderstanding of the nature of knowledge.[26] It leads all too easily to an impossible pan-objectivism on the one hand or to an illegitimate absolutism on the other. Brightman even accepts a realistically slanted correspondence *definition* of truth: "A true proposition is one that describes or refers to a state of affairs that is as described, . . . one that corresponds to a real state of affairs." [27] But since we possess no independent facts, correspondence cannot be the criterion of truth. The only criterion that can adequately test truth and do justice to the valid elements in other proposed tests is a coherence test that involves both consistency and comprehensiveness. Thus, "any proposition is true if it is both self-consistent and coherently connected with our system of propositions as a whole." [28] Because conscious experiences, including values, afford an explanation of experience of a physical world, whereas the converse is not true, persistent application of the test of coherence to the total experiences of the self [29] leads away from belief in "nonexperiential reality," which is "purely hypothetical," [30] and toward an idealist belief that "the whole universe is a society of intercommunicating selves or persons, of which God is the creative center." [31] The physical world is neither material nor monadic in structure; it is God's activity meant always for good.[32] However, the God who thus acts is neither the Absolute of Bradley, Royce, and Blanshard, nor the omnipotent and self-limiting deity of Ward and Sorley. He is rather a personal God, who, though infinately good, nevertheless has to overcome the limits of a *given* within himself.[33]

Other American expressions of personal idealism are similar to the work of Brightman in essential features, but each has its special emphases. Thus H. B. Alexander (1873–1939) accepts the personalistic perspective as basic but stresses the importance of esthetic sensibility [34] in apprehending the character of the world, finds that "things

[26] E. S. Brightman, *An Introduction to Philosophy* (rev. ed.; New York: Henry Holt & Co., Inc., 1951), pp. 80 ff.; Brightman, "The Finite Self," in C. Barrett, *Contemporary Idealism in America* (New York: The Macmillan Co., 1932), pp. 179 ff.; Brightman, "Personalism," in Vergilius Ferm, *A History of Philosophical Systems* (New York: Philosophical Library, 1950), p. 345; see also Brightman, *Person and Reality* (New York: The Ronald Press Co., 1958).

[27] *An Introduction to Philosophy*, p. 47. See also *ibid.*, p. 60.

[28] *Ibid.*, p. 69; see also Brightman, *A Philosophy of Religion* (New York: Prentice-Hall, Inc., 1946), pp. 122 ff.

[29] "Personalism," *op. cit.*, p. 245.

[30] *An Introduction to Philosophy*, p. 307.

[31] *Ibid.*, p. 293.

[32] *Ibid.*, p. 178.

[33] *A Philosophy of Religion*, chaps. ix and x; Brightman, *The Problem of God* (New York: Abingdon Press, 1930).

[34] See W. H. Werkmeister, *A History of Philosophical Ideas in America* (New York: The Ronald Press Co., 1949), pp. 308–16.

and moments are but the hieroglyphs of reality," [35] and defines reality as "the significant." [36]

A. C. Knudson (b. 1873) draws upon the same personalistic sources as Brightman, especially the work of Bowne, and develops a similar dualistic and rationalistic epistemology, but in his account of the ultimate object of knowledge, Knudson is more inclined than Brightman toward a monistic type of theism.[37] R. T. Flewelling, like Brightman and Knudson, finds in personality and value basic keys to the apprehension of reality, but also stresses the importance of faith in reason. In the thought of W. H. Werkmeister (b. 1901) emphasis upon the focal character of personal experience of the individual is combined with renewed stress upon system somewhat like that of Bradley and Blanshard. The ideal of knowledge is "one comprehensive system of logically interdependent propositions;" [38] and while the connections involved in such a system are in principle independent of being known, they are formulated only by the ordering of individual experiences. Truth is adequately tested only by coherence, and knowledge of it is achieved through "a systemic integration of first-person experience." [39] Reality transcends the material, and requires, in order to be brought into comprehensive understanding, a metaphysical perspective that embraces "social living, art, morals, and religion" as well as the physical and biological sciences.[40]

C. The members of the third group of recent idealists to be considered here, who may be somewhat loosely referred to as critical idealists, differ from both the absolute idealists and the personal idealists in that they are disposed to distrust metaphysical claims and to identify the object of knowledge with the fruits of cultural development. This type of philosophy, which traces its roots through Hegel back to Kant, was launched in Germany around the turn of the century by the Marburg philosophers, Herman Cohen (1842–1918), who endeavored to eliminate the Kantian thing-in-itself and identify reality with the findings of the sciences; Paul Natorp (1854–1924), who sought the basic object of knowledge in the products of philosophical psychology; and Wilhelm Windelband (1848–1915), Heinrich Rickert (1863–1936), and Wilhelm Dilthey, all of whom were inclined to find

[35] H. B. Alexander, "The Great Art Which Is Philosophy," in *Contemporary American Philosophy*, I, p. 100.

[36] *Ibid.*, p. 98. See also Alexander, *Nature and Human Nature* (Chicago: The Open Court Publishing Co., 1923); Alexander, *Truth and Faith* (New York: Henry Holt & Co., Inc., 1929); and Alexander, *God and Man's Destiny* (New York: Henry Holt & Co., Inc., 1936).

[37] A. C. Knudson, *The Philosophy of Personalism* (New York: Abingdon Press, 1927), chap. ii.

[38] W. H. Werkmeister, *The Basis and Structure of Knowledge* (New York: Harper & Bros., 1948), p. 155.

[39] *Ibid.*, p. 155.

[40] *Ibid.*, p. 417.

the primary objects of knowledge in cultural history and human evaluations. We shall illustrate the type of thought in question by brief references to an Italian philosopher, a German philosopher, and a British philosopher. As might have been expected, each was deeply interested in problems of cultural history as well as in philosophy as such.

The Italian philosopher Benedetto Croce (1866–1953) holds that the manifestations of the Spirit, which embrace both knowing and the known, occur upon the distinct levels of art, thought, utility and morality. Each higher level depends upon and includes the lower, and oppositions are encountered only within, never between levels.[41] Intuition, which occurs at the level of art, yields genuine insight, that can be independent of conceptual thought [42] though it is often influenced by such thought.[43] At the level of thought, pure concepts, such as those "of *quality*, of *development*, of *beauty*," are universal in their applicability [44] and at the same time fully concrete in being necessarily united with intuitions. Pseudoconcepts, including most of the concepts of common sense and science, such as "*house, cat, rose, . . . triangle . . . , free motion*," [45] are of considerable practical value but, being merely substitutes for images, are theoretically negligible. As concepts presuppose and embrace intuitions, so individual judgments presuppose and embrace definitive judgments. Individual judgment having as their subjects particular intuitions are synthetic a priori.[46] But the manifestation of the Spirit which they apprehend is by no means a changeless eternity. As living, changing history, it is apprehended only by changing concepts that preclude any general system of philosophy, for philosophy would be empty apart from history as definitive judgments would be without individual ones.[47] Judgments of utility may for certain purposes be considered in abstraction from those of ethics, but the full life of the Spirit requires that the judgments of utility be qualified by the judgments of ethics.

The German critical idealist, Ernst Cassirer (1874–1945), repudiates as hopelessly inadequate oversimplification both "that naïve realism which regards the reality of objects as something directly and unequivocally given," [48] and that Baconian method that assumes that the facts themselves constitute a self-contained whole which is only

[41] D. Ainslee (trans.), Benedetto Croce's *Logic* (London: Macmillan & Co., Ltd., 1917), pp. 92 f.

[42] D. Ainslee (trans.), Croce's *Aesthetics* (2d ed.; London: Macmillan & Co., Ltd., 1929), pp. 1 ff.

[43] *Ibid.*, p. 22.

[44] *Logic*, p. 20.

[45] *Ibid.*, p. 23.

[46] *Ibid.*, pp. 218 ff.

[47] Cf. *ibid.*, pp. 310 ff.

[48] Susanne K. Langer (trans.), Ernst Cassirer's *Language and Myth* (New York: Harper & Bros., 1946), p. 6.

later subjected to theoretical treatment and interpretation.[49] Everywhere our knowing involves activity, and although there is a given,[50] it is in all that we confront already in some measure intellectualized. Since man cannot examine things directly but can only organize his experience "in language, in religion, in art, in science," [51] that which knowledge discloses is not finished science only but, as Windelband and Dilthey contended, the cultural history.[52] Within every branch of science itself one finds a constant interaction between actual experimental procedures and fundamental conceptual and methodological revision, and in this interaction science must be treated not as pure description of particular facts but as the organization of experience in terms of a whole conceptual scheme.[53] Our basic concepts themselves are formed, however, at a level far below that of science and often neglected by philosophy, namely, at the level of the making of myths and language. Not only does the form of our experience prevent direct apprehension of an independent reality, but the form of our mythological and linguistic activity prevents the inspection of pure experience. Hence the only course is, at the level of symbols as well as at that of experience, "to accept in all seriousness Kant's 'Copernican revolution,' " and to see that "the special symbolic forms are not imitations but *organs* of reality." [54] Only by the agency of symbolic forms does anything real "become an object for intellectual apprehension." [55] The forms of myth and language may of course be progressively refined by critical and scientific inquiry, and, if we wish to understand the process of the formation of categories and concepts, we must study them with care; but always our new findings must themselves take linguistic, and in some degree also mythological, forms.[56] Many of Cassirer's best insights with reference to symbolism are supported and developed along with related ideas of her own by Susanne K. Langer,[57] who is especially interested in the relation of basic types of symbols and rational discourse.

The British historian-philosopher, R. G. Collingwood (1889–1943), whose philosophy has been deeply influenced both by Croce and by the German critical idealists as well as by his own historical studies, was, throughout his philosophical career, opposed to the claim that knowledge could ever be had directly by simple intuitions and in-

[49] W. H. Woglom and C. H. Hendel (trans.), Cassirer's *The Problem of Knowledge* (New Haven, Conn.: Yale University Press, 1950), p. 254.

[50] Cassirer, *An Essay on Man* (New Haven, Conn.: Yale University Press, 1944), pp. 218 ff.

[51] *An Essay on Man*, p. 221.

[52] Cf. *The Problem of Knowledge*, p. 324.

[53] *Ibid.*, pp. 52 f., 113 f.

[54] *Language and Myth*, p. 8.

[55] *Ibid.*

[56] Susanne K. Langer, *Philosophy in a New Key* (Cambridge: Harvard University Press, 1942); Langer, *Feeling and Form* (New York: Charles Scribner's Sons, 1953).

[57] *Ibid.*

sistent that reflective thought was required before the knowledge process could even begin.[58] In his earlier writings he held that the kind of reflection which at any given point must be considered final was philosophical criticism. Such criticism must not be rigidly confined within traditional philosophical categories, for all classes tend to overlap; [59] it must rather be like literature in the freedom with which it approaches its task.[60] As time went on, however, Collingwood became increasingly convinced that the final mode of reflection was historical. Thus in *The Idea of History* he became critical of the theory of knowledge of the Greeks, which was oriented to mathematics, of that of the Middle Ages, which was oriented to theology, and of that of the Renaissance, which was oriented to physical science. None of these he thought, could "touch on the special problems of historical knowledge." [61] In *The Idea of Nature*, Collingwood went on to insist that current cosmologies, such as those of Alexander and Whitehead, must inevitably fail for the reason that they take as their starting point natural science rather than history; for "natural science as a form of thought exists and always has existed in a context of history, and depends on historical thought for its existence." [62] Indeed, metaphysics itself comes in the end to be a mode of history, and this may be seen in the following manner. In the thought of Aristotle what came to be called metaphysics consisted of an inquiry into being and into basic presuppositions, and since no science of being is possible, metaphysics is really concerned with basic or absolute presuppositions.[63] But absolute presuppositions, being without grounds, are neither true nor false and hence can be intelligently inquired into only historically.[64] Hence the business of the metaphysician is not to inquire whether or not certain absolute presuppositions are true or valid, but only to ask what the absolute presuppositions of certain men and certain types of thought were.

D. The last group of writers to be considered in presenting current idealism consists of a number of American philosophers, who, like Creighton and others among the earlier idealists, make such substantial concessions to realism that their title to the term idealism

---

[58] Cf. R. G. Collingwood, "Can the New Idealism Dispense with Mysticism," *Aristotelian Society, Supplementary* Vol. III (1923), pp. 161–75; Collingwood, "Sensation and Thought," *Proceedings of the Aristotelian Society*, XXIV (1923–24), 55–76; Collingwood, *Principles of Art* (Oxford: Clarendon Press, 1938), pp. 149–51; Collingwood, *Autobiography* (London: Oxford University Press, 1939), pp. 44 ff.

[59] Collingwood, *An Essay on Philosophi-*

cal Method (Oxford: Clarendon Press, 1933), chap. ii.

[60] *Ibid.*, chap. x.

[61] Collingwood, *The Idea of History* (Oxford: Clarendon Press, 1946), p. 5.

[62] Collingwood, *The Idea of Nature* (Oxford: Clarendon Press, 1945), p. 177.

[63] Collingwood, *An Essay on Metaphysics* (Oxford: Clarendon Press, 1940), chaps. i-iv.

[64] *Ibid.*, chaps. v-vii.

becomes doubtful. However, these philosophers tenaciously adhere to certain emphases of idealism, and their affinities are on the whole more with idealism than with any other school of thought. They are accordingly presented here rather than later, although their resemblances to a group of mediating writers subsequently to be considered will naturally be quite noticeable.

G. Watts Cunningham (b. 1881) has undertaken a careful exposition and criticism of the older types of idealism, in which he finds and evaluates three principal types of argument. The epistemological argument to the effect that "to be is to be known" [65] unduly neglects the self-transcending reference in experience [66] and must be rejected. The opposing ontological or a priori argument neglects experience itself and so is of little use.[67] A sound argument for a satisfactory idealism properly insists upon the inseparability of experience and transcendent reality. Thus, "the object is more than it is known as, but this 'more' is apparently inextricably involved in conceptual construction." [68] An idealism thus correctly grounded will reject absolutism (especially that variety of it which finds the Absolute unintelligible),[69] as involving a false denial of time [70] and as violating the facts of experience which it is designed to explain. But a sound idealism will also be critical of a personalism that attempts to make individual will ultimate or neglects the content of experience in the interest of the unity of its center.[71]

With the realists, George Plimpton Adams (b. 1882) holds that the knowing process refers beyond itself and that apart from such self-transcendence there can be no knowing.[72] "There are vast stretches of existence lying beyond experience"; [73] and if reality is to be known, certain aspects of it must be accepted as given or as data.[74] Attempts like that of A. N. Whitehead to assimilate the world beyond con-

[65] G. Watts Cunningham, *The Idealistic Argument in Recent British and American Philosophy* (New York: The Century Co., 1933), pp. 339 f.

[66] *Ibid.*, pp. 376 f.

[67] *Ibid.*, pp. 458 ff.

[68] *Ibid.*, p. 543; see also pp. 451 ff., pp. 515 ff.

[69] *Ibid.*, pp. 534 ff.

[70] *Ibid.*, pp. 526 f.; see also Cunningham, "A Search for System," in *Contemporary American Philosophy*, I, 258 ff.

[71] Cunningham, "The Meaning Situation," in *Contemporary Idealism in America*, pp. 67–100; see also Cunningham, "Perspective and Context in the Meaning Situation," *University of California Publications in Philosophy*, XVI, 29–52; Cun-

ningham, "Meaning, Reference and Significance," *Philosophical Review*, XLVIII; Cunningham, "On the Linguistic Meaning Situation," *Philosophy and Phenomenological Research*, IV; Cunningham, "On the Meaningfulness of Vague Language," *Philosophical Review*, LVIII, 541–62.

[72] Cf. G. P. Adams, "The Mind and Knowledge of Reality," *Journal of Philosophy*, XII (1915), 63; Adams, *Idealism and the Modern Age* (New Haven, Conn.: Yale University Press, 1919), p. 163; Adams, "Naturalism or Idealism," in *Contemporary American Philosophy*, I, 71.

[73] Adams, *Man and Metaphysics* (New York: Columbia University Press, 1948), p. 50.

[74] *Ibid.*, pp. 55 ff.

sciousness to consciousness itself are seriously misleading; [75] and the history of modern thought has exhibited too strong an animistic tendency to make "all objects . . . into literal possessions of the mind." [76] Nevertheless, in keeping with traditional idealist thought, Adams stresses the importance of the "accessibility" of being to mind,[77] the folly of isolation of experience from reality,[78] and the "vital concourse [of] self and world." [79] If reality must in part be given, it still cannot be intelligibly apprehended apart from meanings and categories which belong primarily in the province of mind.[80] But nature itself, if it is to be adequately accessible to mind, must involve an intelligible system; [81] and an intelligible system may transcend both nature and mind. Mind involves "intimations of a dimension of being other than nature," [82] and, while human knowledge emerges within nature and often serves other interests, it properly claims sovereign rights to judge nature, to evaluate other interests, and to observe reality as a spectator.[83]

Throughout his long career Wilbur M. Urban (1873–1952) persistently contended that knowledge depended upon value. Like Adams, he came to believe that the uncompromising conflict of idealism and realism is now an anachronism, and a needless waste of the energy that should be going into constructive speculative philosophy.[84] What was needed was neither acrimonious debate nor futile attempt to reconcile contradictions, but sane dialectic that seeks out the irrefutable minima of the conflicting epistemologies and attempts with sympathetic insight to bring both under a higher principle.[85] The irreducible minimum that must be conceded to realism is that the object of knowledge is independent and that "reality in some way transcends my present knowledge of it," [86] but it cannot be conceded to realism that space and time are independently real lest mind and all its scientific works be unduly depreciated.[87] The irreducible minimum that must be conceded to idealism is that reality is intelligible and can be known only in relativity to mind, and "that truth is an ideal and not a thing." [88] These essential minima of realism and idealism are, however, not to be established either by logical proof or by empirical observation—here positivism is right. They are

[75] Ibid., pp. 117 ff.
[76] Ibid., p. 89.
[77] Ibid., p. 67 ff.
[78] "Naturalism or Idealism," p. 72.
[79] Ibid., p. 72.
[80] See Idealism and the Modern Age, p. 167; Man and Metaphysics, chap. iv.
[81] Idealism and the Modern Age, chaps. iv, vii, ix.
[82] Man and Metaphysics, p. v.

[83] Ibid., chap. i.
[84] Cf. W. M. Urban, The Intelligible World (London: George Allen & Unwin, 1929), pp. 220 ff.; and Urban, Beyond Realism and Idealism (London: George Allen & Unwin, 1949), pp. 5 ff., 18 ff., 339 ff.
[85] Ibid., pp. 123 ff.
[86] Ibid., p. 139.
[87] Ibid., pp. 216 ff.
[88] Ibid., p. 141.

rather to be established, if at all, as in the end is every fragment of knowledge, on the basis of the appeal to the rational value of validity.[89] Indeed, "thought and thing, fact and value are inseparable, . . . and this relation is the condition of philosophical intelligibility." [90] Thus the best in realism and the best in idealism come to supplement and sustain one another under the guidance of a higher order of value in which both share.[91]

The thought of W. H. Sheldon of Yale (b. 1875) is like that of Urban in its intent to reconcile realism and idealism but unlike that of Urban in its refusal to make the value categories more basic than ontological ones.[92] Sheldon is, however, much more impressed than Urban with the roles of action, experiment, and mystical experience in knowing.[93]

7. Comments Concerning Later Twentieth-Century Idealism

Since the epistemological thought of Blanshard, to which most of the ensuing remarks are directed, resumes and develops themes already prominent in earlier twentieth-century idealism, much of what is to be said here may be taken to be applicable also to corresponding features of those earlier idealisms. In the main, four themes characteristic of Blanshard's thought need to be considered. With respect to each, the kind of idealism in question has made substantial contributions to current epistemological thought, and with respect to each, such idealism has apparently indulged in some excesses.

A. The first of these themes concerns universals. One of the major contentions common to most idealists is one taken over from the classical tradition through Kant by nineteenth-century idealists and quite explicit in the thought of Bradley as well as Blanshard, that all knowing involves apprehension of universals.

Whether or not this contention is correct depends, of course, upon what is meant by "knowledge" and by "universals," and both terms remain under dispute. However, upon any intelligible interpretation of the terms, this much seems to be plain: that we can scarcely properly be said to know anything unless we can attribute to subjects,

[89] *Ibid.*, 116 ff.
[90] Urban, "Metaphysics and Value," in *Contemporary American Philosophy*, II, 375.
[91] *Beyond Realism and Idealism*, pp. 136 f., 143 f.; cf. also *The Intellectual World*, chap. iii.
[92] See *Beyond Realism and Idealism*, p.

115 n.; *The Intelligible World*, pp. 384, 165 ff.; W. H. Sheldon, *The Strife of Systems and Productive Duality.*
[93] See Sheldon, "What is Intellect?" *Philosophy East and West*, II, 4–19, 129–43; Sheldon, "The Criterion of Reality," *Review of Metaphysics*, I (1947), 3–37.

predicates connected with repeatable and recognizable aspects of experiences. Moreover, if either the language of common sense or that of science and mathematics affords any reliable clues, it would seem to be quite possible to say some significant things concerning many of the predicates we so employ. That responsible philosophers have specifically denied such minimal claims as these concerning universals may be doubted, but that some have strongly resisted them is evident. Insofar as idealists may be regarded as defending these minimal claims and demanding further inquiry into the whole problem of universals, their contentions may be said to constitute a genuine contribution to contemporary thought.

However, idealists of the type under consideration have never been willing to stop here. Blanshard has, for example, gone on to make a characteristic idealist claim that universals are in the end the sole objects of our knowledge. But whatever other valid or invalid claims about universals idealists may have made, this claim surely represents a needless and extravagant leap beyond the *prima facie* indications. We may indeed have some knowledge of universals, and when we assert what we know of things we may predicate universals of things; but what in such assertions we claim to have knowledge about surely seem to be things themselves rather than universals. This seems to be so not only of the knowledge of the common man but of that of the scientist as well, for scientists and philosophers of science are increasingly disposed to insist that it is about a real world that they are speaking, and to distinguish increasingly sharply between those notions that serve only as convenient vehicles of thought and those that are to be taken as representations of actual entities. The principal motives for the claim that we know only universals seem to be desire to avoid the paradoxical notion of a featureless substratum and a feeling that what is known must somehow enter into and become a part of experience. But in order to avoid the featureless substratum, one may, instead of holding that what we know consists solely of universals, hold that what we know often consists of individual things having sufficient known characteristics to make reference possible. And in order to bring the object of knowledge sufficiently into touch with experience, it is enough that some features of the object be discernible by experience; to ask that some features of the object become a part of the experience is to ask the impossible—even universals are at best exemplified, never literally present, in experience. If all we knew were universals, our knowledge would be confined to such matters as logic and mathematics, and could never embrace existing things, and neither Blanshard nor any other modern idealist wishes to say that. Most idealists attempt to avoid such an unwelcome consequence by suggesting that sufficiently complex universals become also concrete existents; but this is to misconstrue the character of universals, for if universals there be, they are surely such that no matter how complex they become they remain universals and never become individual things. Moreover, if all we know is universals, then all that we know, or ever can know, consists of tautologies; and no satisfactory way of avoiding this unpalatable and unlikely consequence has yet been, or is likely to be, proposed.

B. A second major theme of Blanshard's thought, closely related to the first, is his theory of ideas. One aspect of this theory is the claim that the most significant ideas are never baldly abstract ones but those that entail the greatest wealth of specific detail. This claim comes near the core of what most idealists have been driving at in their concept of the concrete universal. And while it must not be construed so as to preclude the development of abstract systems that may turn out to be far more fruitful than anticipated, it does call attention to the important considerations that ideas tend to be fruitful roughly in proportion to the experienceable details that can be satisfactorily connected with them and that those persons have the most significant ideas who can best see what is involved in their ideas in many varied situations. Whether or not this sort of consideration has ever been specifically denied, it has often been in practice virtually ignored. For example, some scholastic systems have adopted, as cornerstones, concepts from which few, if any, significant details could be inferred, and even some more-recent formal systems, not to speak of some idealistic ones, have been constructed in essentially the same manner. In bringing a demand for concreteness of ideas to focus, philosophers of Blanshard's type have, unintentionally perhaps, but significantly, helped to pave the way for much that is best in current empiricism.

Another aspect of the theory of ideas common to most absolute idealists and developed with exceptional clarity by Blanshard, is the thesis that an idea is an as yet undeveloped thing, and a thing, a developed idea. The problem for which this thesis is offered as a solution, namely how an idea being mental and abstract can apply to a thing which is material and concrete, is indeed a puzzling one; and the solution offered is illuminating insofar as it calls attention to the fact that the more specific an idea becomes, the more it may approximate a description constituting the sense of an adequate idea of a thing or event. However, the solution appears to be quite erroneous insofar as it suggests that as an idea becomes increasingly specific it tends increasingly to become identical with the thing referred to. The schoolboy's idea of the battle of Waterloo more nearly approximates the description of the battle as the boy matures into a competent historian, but the idea does not thereby come in the least nearer to being identical with the battle itself. The supposition that it does is an unfortunate instance of neglect of the distinction between sense and reference, and it may be doubted whether either the supposition in question or the more general efforts of idealists to reduce reality to experiences or to universals would have been developed had this distinction been adequately attended to all the while.

C. A third characteristic idealist theme developed with special clarity by Blanshard is that a single system is working in all cognition and that all truth is necessary truth. Now, that necessary systems are in fact extensively operative in science is at present much more generally acknowledged by nonidealist philosophers than in the days of the early idealists and far more than at the time at which Blanshard wrote *The Nature of Thought,* and it may fairly be claimed that the newer insights concerning the role of system in knowing are in part due to the groundwork laid by idealist philosophers. Thus, for example, almost all philosophers will now recognize not only that mathematical statements are nonempirical and necessary but that most other sciences as well, instead of being merely inductive as was formerly thought, are hypothetico-deductive. Indeed, most highly developed sciences are now often thought of largely as conceptual schemes oriented to observations, but bound together by deductive relations in such fashion that one part being known, others may be deduced and that even though the facts may seldom or never follow with entire precision, the deductive relations hold unless and until the conceptual scheme is altered. Actually, the scope of necessary system is wider yet; for even in common-sense inferences, both elementary logic and multitudes of necessary relations implicit in the forms of our language are at work.

Nevertheless, the claim of Blanshard and the other idealists that a single complete necessary system is at work in all cognition and that all truth is necessary goes too far both with respect to singleness of system and with respect to universality of necessity. Surely the fact that necessary system is at work in a very large part of knowledge does not imply that the system at work is a single system, nor would any such implication be present even if it could be shown that necessary system was at work in all knowledge whatever. In any case, no such *single* system is apparent in the knowledge we have. Even the prospect of joining mathematics and logic in a single system, that seemed so bright in the days immediately after the publication of *Principia Mathematica,* are now somewhat dimmed, and it becomes increasingly evident that, at any rate for the present, not only do logic and mathematics have to be treated as in part distinct but that each of a variety of branches of logic and each of a variety of branches of mathematics requires its own postulates and its own rules of inference. Each of the empirical sciences must also, insofar as it can be reduced to deductive system, adopt its own postulates, and many significant sciences apparently cannot for practical purposes be reduced to postulational systems at all. Not only is there in prospect no satisfactory way of reducing all the different sciences and all systems of language to anything even remotely resembling a single deductive system, but far-reaching efforts to achieve such unity invariably tend to obscure insights gained by various separate modes of inquiry.

We turn now to the other excessive claim in the idealists' notion of necessary system, the claim that all truth is necessary truth. Certainly the validity of this claim does not follow from the fact that necessary systems are at work in knowing. As we have seen, the scope of such systems is far from universal, and in any case the manner in which facts conform to such systems is only one of rough approximation. If all truth is to be shown to be necessary truth, all events will have to be shown to be governed by causal relations and these relations will have to be shown, as Blanshard acknowledges, to be necessary. Actually, attempted demonstrations of the universality of causality invariably break down far short of their goal, and this principle can justly lay claim to be little more than a valuable methodological postulate of some of the sciences. But even a proof of the universal reign of causality would help all too little toward the required proof that all truth is necessary truth, for it is extremely doubtful if causal relations among facts *ever* are necessary, let alone *always* being necessary. However deductive scientific systems may be, observed facts are connected with them only by probability relations of varying kinds, and theoretical physicists who inquire into submicroscopic events are increasingly disposed to limit themselves to probability and statistical statements.

D. The fourth characteristic idealist theme most clearly developed by Blanshard is the claim that comprehensive coherence is ultimately the sole criterion of truth and also the very nature or meaning of truth. If coherence may be thought of as embracing both formal consistency and a variety of implicative principles, one may plausibly accept Blanshard's view that coherence is the criterion of truth, at least insofar as it applies to logical and mathematical truths. If, in addition to consistency and implicative relations, coherence is thought of as including principles of probability and other more loosely defined principles in terms of which hypotheses are regarded as reasonable when they bring available data together into ordered patterns, and if ample data are initially given, coherence may also be thought of as the criterion of empirical truths. After all, the range of truths that can be directly ascertained by observation is at best very limited, and even such truths as are so ascertained are subject to further coherence tests. Most truths concerning facts of nature, history, and even psychology are not directly observational at all and must be ascertained in terms of the manner in which our hypotheses coordinate given data and previously ascertained facts. The body of scientific knowledge grows by progressive coordination of conceptual schemes and expanding bodies of accepted facts and new data, and even when drastic changes are made in scientific systems they are made in accord with the demands of comprehensive coherence. All this is far better recognized by present-day philosophers of science than by those of a generation ago.

Nevertheless, the view that coherence is even the criterion of truth is misleading and perhaps mistaken in at least two important respects. In the first place, no one has ever given, or is ever likely to give, an account of coherence that is at all precise. At very best, coherence is scarcely more than a general term for an assemblage of those methods, other than observations, for testing truth that are most effective in discriminating it, and presumably one will do as well or better to focus attention directly upon these methods rather than to insist upon the general coherence criterion. Indeed, the insistence upon such a general criterion often proves harmful to inquiry in that, as in the instance of concentration on the general idea of intellectual satisfaction, it tends to obscure the need for inquiry into and application of the more specific tests that are required in the actual quest for truths. The other major difficulty in the coherence criterion of truth is even more serious, namely that while such a criterion may be quite reliable given initially plausible observational data, apart from such data it may yield no plausibility at all and so can surely not be taken by itself to be an adequate criterion. As C. I. Lewis has pointed out, one might develop in an extensive novel a completely coherent story containing no word of truth; and, having collected a vast and perfect coherent system of truths, one might negate each and so construct a perfectly coherent system containing no truth at all. Nor can the idealists' insistence upon comprehensiveness answer the implied challenge, for the coherent system containing all truths might be negated in each of its propositions so as to remain completely coherent and completely false. Unless some of the propositions involved have at least some initial plausibility the whole system is without plausibility.

Blanshard's claim that coherence is the nature of truth is largely based on the claim that coherence is the ultimate criterion of truth and if the latter doctrine is untenable so is the former. But even if the doctrine of coherence as the ultimate criterion of truth could be accepted, it could by no means bear the weight of the doctrine that coherence is the nature or meaning of truth. However truth may be *ascertained*, all our ways of speaking and thinking seem amply to indicate that what we *mean* by truth is not merely coherence but some sort of conformity to fact, and in the end even Blanshard seems to concede something of this sort in demanding as a condition of knowledge, faith in an eventual conformity of the inner world of coherence and intellectual satisfaction and an outer world of objects.

Part II

REALISTIC THEORIES

CHAPTER 4

American New Realism

1. THE NATURE AND ANCESTRY OF CONTEMPORARY REALISM

ALREADY in the period of its dominance in the last decade of the nineteenth century and the first decade of the twentieth, epistemological idealism had been compelled to make substantial concessions to realism. Even within the movement some idealists eventually so qualified their claims as almost to become realists. Far more devastating for idealism was the determined attack from the outside, early in the twentieth century, by a strong realist movement that deliberately denied nearly all of the basic tenets of idealism. Over against the idealist contention that the object of knowledge depends upon its being known, either for its existence or for its character, the realists placed their claim that the object of knowledge is independent of the knower and the knowing process with respect both to its existence and to its character, and over against the idealist doctrines of system and coherence many realists placed opposing doctrines of contingent pluralism and correspondence.

The occurrence of realist theories of knowledge was, however, no new phenomenon. The sources of this kind of epistemology are even older than those of idealism, for realism requires no such sophistication as is demanded by even the more elemental types of idealism. Indeed some form of realism seems to be the epistemology of ordinary man, and the roots of realism lie within phases of common sense that are as old as the human race.

In philosophy proper, the pre-Socratic Greeks were nearly all genuine, though not always explicit, realists, and the post-Socratic atomists were uncompromising realists. Plato, despite his disdain for the notion of a fully real material world, took the Ideas, with which he identified the ultimately real objects of our knowledge, to be quite independent of our knowledge of them. Aristotle also found universals to have an existence in things independently of being known and, unlike Plato, regarded things themselves as being independently real. Platonic realism was in some measure kept alive throughout the Middle Ages, and, in the philosophy of St. Thomas, the realism of Aristotle was launched upon a new and extremely influential career.

Although Descartes and Locke, who set the major themes of modern epistemology, were both fundamentally realists, they brought to focus the peculiarly difficult realistic problem of representation—how subjective ideas can represent objective realities—and so gave some aid and comfort to the enemies of realism. While both believed in the existence of independent objects and made the apprehension of these the objective of the knowing process, both acknowledged that all that we can know directly consists of ideas that are neither individuals nor known to be like individuals.

Fresh realistic beginnings were made, along intuitional lines, by Thomas Reid (1710–1796) and his common-sense school in Scotland and, along critical lines, by J. F. Herbart (1776–1841) in Germany. A little later the Aristotelian realism of St. Thomas began to gain new impetus through the famous encyclical of 1879 of Pope Leo XII commending the study of the philosophy of St. Thomas to all Catholic schools. It was in this type of thought that Franz Brentano, who furnished to the founders of recent realism some of their initial suggestions, began his philosophical career.

Steeped alike in the Aristotelian-Thomistic and British empiricist traditions, Franz Brentano (1838–1917) revolted against the rigidity of the one and the subjectivism of the other. Nevertheless, he drew from the Thomistic tradition the central idea of his own realism. Ideas, he taught, are always *of* something, whether real or unreal. That is to say they have what the scholastics called intentionality. It is of the nature of mental acts to refer, and in our representations, judgments, and evaluations is to be found a self-evidence that gives us valid assurance concerning realities that lie beyond us.

On foundations laid by Brentano, and in the light of new logical insights that were emerging at the time, Alexius von Meinong (1853–1920) proceeded to build what he called a "theory of objects." This theory distinguishes sharply between mental acts, such as believing and judging, and the objects to which such acts refer. Objects may exist, as in the case of material things, or subsist, as in that of relations, or do neither, as in the case of such self-contradictories as round squares, which are nevertheless there to be thought of. The theory also distinguishes between mental content, which is "existent, present, . . . psychical," and *"in* the mind," and object, which may be non-existent, past or future, physical, and "is only *before* the mind." [1] A little later Edmund Husserl (1859–1938) gave to the thought of Brentano a phenomenalistic turn that encouraged some realists to examine the structure of experienced content with great care. The logical studies of the Oxford scholar and teacher John Cook Wilson (1894–1915) also helped to prepare an atmosphere in England and America favorable to realism.

Within the first four years of the present century, R. B. Perry and W. P. Montague in America had launched vigorous attacks upon Royce's attempted refutation of realism,[2] and G. E. Moore in England had made significant use of Meinong's distinction between act and object in his celebrated "Refutation of Idealism." Within a few years Bertrand Russell, who was to give classic expression to the newer logical tendencies, together with other writers in England and America, joined the attack, and a new realist movement was well on its way.

By the end of the second decade of the present century a rather sharp cleavage had developed within the ranks of current realists. One group, made up principally of American new realists, were for the most part epistemologically monistic in refusing to make a distinction between the object and that through which the object is known. Stressing the independence of the object, they were at the same time impressed with the idealistic refutation of representative realism. Accordingly, though stoutly realistic, they conceded to idealists that the object is often identical with that by which it is known, that reality involves considerable logical system, and that truth is somewhat more than correspondence. A second group, made up principally of American critical realists, were largely epistemologically dualistic in distinguishing between the object and that in terms of which the object is known. More thoroughgoing even than the new realists in insisting upon the independence of the object, they revived the idea of independent substances, and found little place for system in reality or for much besides correspondence in truth. Meanwhile, the members of a third group, made up of British realists, though often leaning to one side or the other concerning the issues that

[1] R. B. Perry, *The Philosophy of the Recent Past* (New York: Charles Scribner's Sons, 1926), p. 207.

[2] Perry, "Professor Royce's Refutation of Realism and Pluralism," *Monist,* XII (1901–02), 446–58; W. P. Montague, "Professor Royce's Refutation of Realism," *Philosophical Review,* II (1902), 43–55.

divided their American colleagues, also differed among themselves on other important issues, so as not to be simply classifiable in terms of the broad criteria that separated the two American groups. In this and the following chapter, by way of developing the major cleavage in contemporary realism, we shall present the views of American new realists and American critical realists; and in the next chapter, by way of bringing to light some more-subtle distinctions within current realism, we shall present the views of leading British realists.

2. Polemical New Realism: Ralph Barton Perry

The controversial element is naturally pronounced in the thought of all the early American new realists, for these thinkers had to gain a hearing in face of a firmly entrenched idealism. This controversial element is especially prominent in the thought of R. B. Perry who, however, also contributed some interesting constructive suggestions toward the building of the relatively novel type of epistemologically monistic realism that came to be called new realism. We shall consider here first his polemic and then the more constructive aspects of his thought.

A. The principal errors of idealism are not for the most part rooted, Perry thinks, in special inventions of idealist philosophers, but in fallacies to which philosophers generally have always been liable. To point out these fallacies is therefore not to accuse the idealists of peculiarly pernicious confusion, but it is to destroy the foundations upon which the idealist system is built, to reveal the major reasons for the mistakes of that system, and to lay suitable foundations for a new realist system.

The cardinal error of the idealists, and the source of many of their other mistakes, is an unjustifiable exploitation of the "egocentric predicament" in which every knower necessarily finds himself. To this theme Perry's essays and books repeatedly return,[1] and it is for Perry's persistent attack upon the exploitation of the egocentric predicament that his epistemological work is best known.

Since to encounter or even to think about something is already in some sense to know it, and since to be a known object is already to be accompanied by a knower, one will never encounter an object that is not in some sense known or that is not accompanied by a knower. This fact constitutes the egocentric predicament. Wherever

[1] See Perry, "The Ego-Centric Predicament," *Journal of Philosophy*, VII (1910), 5–14; Perry, "Realism as a Polemic and Program of Reform," *ibid.*, pp. 337–53; Perry, "Some Disputed Points in Neo-Realism," *ibid.*, X (1913), 449–63; Perry, *Present Philosophical Tendencies*, (New York: Longmans, Green & Co., Inc., 1912), esp. pp. 129 ff., 271, 317 ff.

a known object is, a knower is at the center of the field, and no complete escape from this predicament is even conceivable. Idealists have almost invariably, either explicitly or implicitly, made this situation a basis for their characteristic epistemological doctrine that the object of knowledge depends upon the knower. But no such conclusion follows from the egocentric predicament as a premise. The only conclusion that can plausibly be drawn from "the impossibility of finding anything that is not known" is either the foolish redundancy that "all known things are known" or the false claim that "all things are known." [2] When the idealist goes on to use the egocentric predicament to show that every object depends upon a knower, he illegitimately employs the inductive method of agreement in circumstances that involve special reasons for the agreement and, finding the safeguarding check of the method of difference inapplicable, leaps to a conclusion that is without foundations. His argument is as if one should say that because all the people with whom I am personally acquainted speak English, therefore all people speak English.[3] To be sure, all known objects are accompanied by a knowing process, but the very fact that they are known is a special circumstance that should lead one to expect just such an accompaniment, without in any way suggesting a dependence of the object itself upon such an accompaniment. Moreover, the fact that the method of difference cannot be applied in this sort of instance is a mere accident that in no sense renders idealism plausible or indicates that being known is anything other than an incidental relation into which objects are occasionally brought.

The mistake of the idealist's inference from the egocentric predicament is a special instance of the common error of "definition by initial predication," which consists in "regarding some early, familiar or otherwise accidental characterization of a thing as definitive." [4] The idealist's reasoning on the issue in question makes the blunder of treating the merely familiar relation of being known as though it were a definitive element in the constitution of the object.

Another common philosophical error is that of "exclusive particularity." This fallacy consists in supposing "that a particular term of any system belongs to such a system exclusively." [5] When idealists suppose that the idea, belonging to the system of the mind, cannot also belong to an external order, they are flagrantly guilty of this error. Actually many entities, such as for example a point on two

---

[2] "Realism as a Polemic and Program of Reform," p. 339.

[3] *Present Philosophical Tendencies*, pp. 130 ff.

[4] *Present Philosophical Tendencies*, p. 128.

[5] *Ibid.*, p. 351.

intersecting lines, or a man who is both a Republican and a captain of industry, belong to more than one system. There is no reason why this sort of dual membership should not characterize objects in their relations to minds on the one hand and to the world of independent realities on the other. A third common philosophical error, also committed by at least some idealists, is that of "pseudosimplicity." To commit this error is "to assume the simplicity of that which is only familiar or stereotyped." This is just what those idealists do who assume the simplicity of the mind, for, however familiar the mind may be, analysis reveals in it a vast complex not only of cognitive but also of volitional phases.

The foregoing fallacies represent major errors of that subjective idealism which Perry takes to be basic to all idealism; absolute idealism is peculiarly liable to at least three further closely related errors. One is the fallacy of verbal suggestion, which consists in being misled by rhethoric and the ambiguity of words into the invention of "utterly fictitious concepts simply by combining words." [6] A second is the fallacy of "speculative dogma," the assumption for philosophical purposes that there is an "all-sufficient all-general principle . . . that adequately determines or explains everything." [7] The third fallacy is an appeal to the unity of apperception which, however plausible initially, can scarcely be legitimate; for while some cohesion of consciousness is an encountered fact, such ultimate unity of consciousness as absolute idealism requires is a doubtful and misleading assumption.

The ultimate objective of Perry's attack upon idealism is not simply the overthrow of idealism but the establishment of realism, which Perry considers the only plausible alternative. "Idealism and realism are so related that if idealism is false, realism is true." [8] Nevertheless, the refutation of idealism does not yet completely clear the way for a fully satisfactory realism. At least one type of realism, the representative or dualistic type of Descartes and Locke, is so formulated as to be indefensible against idealistic attack. If our ideas are basically what are known, it is impossible ever to know objects, for we can never be sure that our ideas adequately represent objects or even establish any basis of comparison between our ideas and the objects they are supposed to represent. [9] Against representative realism, the idealists themselves have often provided the best antidote. For example, what Berkeley says about the impossibility of knowing matter

[6] *Ibid.*, p. 351.
[7] *Ibid.*, p. 348.
[8] "Some Disputed Points in Neo-Realism," p. 459.

[9] *The Philosophy of the Recent Past,* pp. 197 ff.

through ideas refutes representative realism although it does not, as he thinks, establish idealism. Representative realists, along with opposing idealists, are in fact victims of some of the common errors to which philosophers are predisposed. Especially notable among these errors is the already mentioned one of "exclusive particularity." As idealists commit this error in assuming that what is in the mind cannot also be a part of the external world, so the representative realists commit it in assuming that what is in the material world cannot also be mental. Representative realists also commit the error of "transcendent implication." This is "the supposition that one can by means of inference or implication somehow get a footing outside content, it being self-evident, on the contrary, that if the inference or implication is followed through it cannot but terminate in an object, which, like the initial object, is exhibited to the mind." [10]

B. As a sound realism will, on its destructive side, repudiate both the idealist doctrine of the dependence of the object on knowing and the representationist doctrine of the inaccessibility of the object, so it will, on its constructive side, champion both the independence of the object and the immediacy of the apprehension of the object. To establish these constructive doctrines, the new realism will need to give adequate answers to questions that arise in each of four branches of epistemology; it will have to furnish satisfactory realist theories of consciousness, ideas, objects, and truth.[11]

(1) Since realists, like everyone else, must operate within the egocentric predicament, they are no more able than anyone else to examine the object in isolation from the knowing mind. But they can do what others have in fact for the most part failed to do; they can examine the character of the knowing mind so as "to discover precisely in what respects consciousness is determinative of its object—so that when present it may be credited with what it is really responsible for and no more." [12] The methods of such inquiry include the traditional introspective one of examination of the contents of one's own consciousness. This method has the initial advantage that each mind is more directly accessible to itself than to any other. But this is not necessarily the best method of examination of mind.[13] It is quite possible to be familiar with a thing without knowing much about it, for example, some farmers daily perform the chores of the farm knowing comparatively little about farming. Also available is the method of observation of behavior, which more than makes up

10 "Realism as a Polemic and Program of Reform," p. 343.
11 See *ibid.*, pp. 375 f.; Perry, "A Division of the Problems of Epistemology," *Journal of Philosophy,* VI (1909), 709 ff.

12 "Some Disputed Points in Neo-Realism," p. 454; see also *Present Philosophical Tendencies,* p. 273.
13 *Ibid.*, pp. 281 ff.

in objectivity what it lacks in directness. This method may determine the character of desires, and even to some extent of memory and thought, by observing the activity of body and brain. The elements of conscious experience are in fact sufficiently neutral and interchangeable to permit me to have an adequate apprehension of your idea through observation and verbal report and to know you from the outside as you cannot know yourself.

When the methods of inquiry into the nature of consciousness are properly applied, there is nothing to indicate that mind makes or constitutes objects, and much to show that its role is that of a more passive apprehension. The method of behavioral observation discloses mind as an observable pattern of things, and therefore not the creator of things, and "mental action" as "a property of the physical organism." [14] The mode of the mind's operation is selective rather than constitutive, and its "action is a property of the physical organism." [15] The mind may thus be regarded as "an organization possessing as distinguishable, but complementary, aspects, *interest, nervous system, and contents.*" [16] It is in short "relativity and exclusion within a world of reals, . . . selection within the realm of things." [17] To be sure, it apprehends things in terms of categories, but these categories give every evidence of belonging to the realm of things rather than to that of the mind, and their cognitive value would be very little if this were not so. The mind's selective and essentially passive character does not, however, imply that mind is no more than the elements that enter into it; for, in terms of the modern concept of *pattern,* the organizational structure of mind lifts the mind above its separate ingredients and may render it an irreducible complex.[18] Nor does the organic character of the mind confine mind to the level of mere materiality, or even to that of animality, for the modern concept of *emergence* discloses how old laws may produce new systems, which, once attained, may in turn evolve new laws of their own.[19]

(2) So long as an *idea* is regarded as a sort of a second entity standing between the object and the knower, knowledge is, as has been suggested, impossible. The new realist alternative to this representative realist interpretation of the idea may be formulated as follows: "Ideas are only things in a certain relation; or things, in respect of being known, are ideas." [20] Thus new realism, though dualistic with

[14] *Ibid.,* p. 298.
[15] *Ibid.,* p. 298.
[16] *Ibid.,* p. 304.
[17] Perry, "Conceptions and Misconceptions of Consciousness," *Psychological Review,* XI (1904), 296.

[18] Perry, "Peace Without Victory in Philosophy," *Journal of Philosophical Studies,* III (1928), 300.
[19] *Ibid.,* pp. 307 ff.
[20] *Present Philosophical Tendencies,* p. 308.

reference to the relation of the knower and the known, is monistic with reference to the relation of the object and that by which the object is known. "When things are known they are ideas of the mind," [21] and "mental content consists of portions of the surrounding environment illuminated by the action of the organism." [22] Objections to this doctrine are rooted in large part in the false prejudice, already mentioned, against regarding an entity as a member of more than one system, but such multiple memberships are extremely common. Just as the same man may be both a member of the Democratic party and a member of the proletariat, [23] or both "my grandfather and the man you met on the street," [24] so what I call my ideas may belong both to the series of my conscious experience and to "the series of reality." [25]

(3) The crucial aspect of the new realism as over against idealism is its theory of objects as independent of the knowing process. This phase of realist theory Perry carefully develops and defends in detail in his contribution to the cooperative volume *The New Realism* under the title "A Realistic Theory of Independence."

Independence means with reference to object and knowing, as elsewhere, nondependence. But what specifically is the dependence that is denied? It could be interpreted as either *relation, whole-part, exclusive causality, implying,* or *being exclusively implied.*[26] Idealists such as Royce attempt to force upon realists the first interpretation and to say that the realist is in effect denying the existence of any relation between the object and knowing. But clearly no sane realist could mean any such thing; for unless there were some relation between object and knowing, the connection implied by knowing would be completely excluded and knowledge would be impossible. Actually the object may enter both the relation of being known and many other relations. What the realist wishes to say at this point is not that the object is unrelated but simply that, from the standpoint of the object, the relation of being known is incidental.

What then is the dependence which the realist conception of independence denies? It includes in a word all the kinds of dependence listed above except the neutral one of mere *relation.* That is, the object is neither a whole of which consciousness is a part, nor the exclusive cause or effect of consciousness, nor something which

---

[21] *Ibid.,* p. 308.
[22] *Ibid.,* p. 300.
[23] *Ibid.,* p. 309.
[24] "A Division of the Problems of Epistemology," p. 712.
[25] Perry, "A Review of Pragmatism as a Theory of Knowledge," *Journal of Philos-*

ophy, *Psychology and Scientific Method,* p. 374.
[26] Perry, "A Realistic Theory of Independence," in E. B. Holt and Others, *The New Realism* (New York; The Macmillan Co., 1922), p. 117.

implies consciousness or which is exclusively implied by consciousness. If the object were any of these, it would be dependent on consciousness in the sense that the nonexistence of consciousness would entail the nonexistence of the object, and in this sense, the realist is especially concerned to deny.

What is the independence of the object and consciousness that the realist affirms? The above analysis of dependence does not, it must be observed, include either *being implied* or *causing* (in the nonexclusive sense), and in fact while the converse of each of these relations is a relation of dependence, the relations themselves are basically relations of independence. That is to say, while that which implies depends upon the implied, the implied may be independent of that which implies it, and while effect depends upon a cause, a cause need not depend upon a particular effect. This sort of one-way independence associated with a converse dependence is precisely the kind of relation that the realist finds in knowing, for while consciousness depends upon the object, the object need not depend upon consciousness. Thus, just as that which is implied by, or causes, something else may exist apart from the existence of that thing, so the object of knowledge, which is implied by, and is a partial cause of, consciousness, may exist apart from consciousness into which it occasionally enters.

That the object of knowledge is in general independent of consciousness does not mean that everything related to consciousness is independent of it. One must note some important distinctions here. All epistemologically simple entities are independent of consciousness; so are all complexes with respect to their simple elements. The laws of logic and mathematics are independent of consciousness. So also are physical complexes. That which is independent of consciousness includes secondary qualities as well as primary ones, and the categories in terms of which physical complexes are conceived. However, the various parts of consciousness are dependent upon consciousness and to some extent upon each other. The inclusion of some factors rather than others in consciousness, and the manner of combining elements in consciousness, are also in some measure dependent on consciousness. The existence of subjective complexes and of value is also dependent upon consciousness although the existence of neither need depend on reflection or judgment.[27] Works of art, as well as history, society, and effective thought are all also partly dependent on consciousness.

---

[27] Cf. *Present Philosophical Tendencies,*   (New York: Longmans, Green & Co., Inc.,
pp. 331 ff.; Perry, *General Theory of Value*   1926).

While an adequate definition of the independence of the object tends on the whole to constitute a sufficiently convincing defense of this independence, some further considerations in favor of the doctrine are worthy of note. One is the fact of the progressive advance of knowledge, which suggests the presence of a virtually limitless expanse of objects lying beyond the present attainments of our science. Another is the discovery in science of increasingly complex causal systems that seem to operate quite independently of our consciousness of them. A third consideration in support of the independence of objects is the success of logical, mathematical, and all other varieties of analysis. All such analysis depends for its accomplishments upon an externality of relations in which terms are independent of relations in general and especially of the relation of being known.[28] A final consideration of the sort in question is the evident dependence of consciousness itself upon a previously existing environment, which accordingly cannot in turn depend upon it.[29]

(4) With regard to the concept of truth, Perry does not so much furnish us with a fully developed theory as indicate some of the conditions he thinks such a theory would have to meet. Since the notion of a representation linking knower and known is excluded by Perry's aspect theory of ideas, that with which the object is related in truth can be neither subsisting term nor existing idea. It is rather simply the attitude of belief in the knower. Hence, the only sense of the word "truth" that is relevant to epistemology, the only one in which truth is properly contrasted with error, is one in which truth involves in addition to objective factors "the specific additional factor of an intending mind." [30] That is to say, "truth is always relative to particular intention." [31] This subjective side of truth must never be allowed to obscure the objective side, for truth never involves less than "harmony between thought and things." The pragmatists correctly point out "that truth when sought and found is satisfying," but this is no justification for the claim that "the satisfaction element is identical with the truth element." [32] "My thinking is true so far as true or false is in terms of the object itself." [33] The term "true knowledge" is marked by its being the term in which the series of consciousness intersects the series of reality.[34] Truth may properly be said to include: (1) commitment or a motor set of readiness for action, (2) an objective or a content believed, and (3)

[28] *Present Philosophical Tendencies*, p. 320.

[29] *Ibid.*, pp. 321 ff.

[30] Perry, "The Truth Problem," *Journal of Philosophy*, XIII (1916), 567.

[31] "A Review of Pragmatism as a Theory of Knowledge," p. 368.

[32] *Ibid.*, p. 371.

[33] *Ibid.*, p. 373.

[34] "The Truth Problem," II, 567.

an objective reference. When truth rather than error is present these three are in harmony. When error is present they are not.[35]

The existence of error poses a serious problem for Perry's type of realism in that "it seems impossible to define a situation that shall be cognitive without providing that the cognition shall be true." But this difficulty is adequately met, Perry thinks, by the consideration that, "although the object of belief must be, it need not be as it is believed." [36] Consciousness does not create its objects but may arrange them and in doing so it may foreshorten them, or place them in arrangements that do not correspond to nature.[37]

Among the tests of truth that have been proposed, those of fulfillment of expectation and of coherence are valid and useful. That of successful operation is only a modification of these. The test of emotional satisfaction is not correct nor is any test which includes this one as an essential part.[38]

In two chapters of his *Realms of Value* (chapters 17 and 22) written nearly a half century after most of Perry's writings in the field of epistemology, Perry restates his major epistemological conclusions, but also includes some newer ideas and different emphases. A very significant role is now assigned to the concept of expectation, which had been prominent in Perry's *General Theory of Value* but not particularly so in his writings on epistemology as such. Perry now contends "that cognition is expectation, that knowledge is *qualified expectation,* and that science is *highly qualified expectation."* [39] Knowledge in contrast to bare cognition demands truth, proof, and certainty.[40] "A judgment . . . is true when that which is expected agrees with that which is going to happen." That is to say, "two series—an unfolding series of attitudes and acts, and an unfolding series of events in the environment—are convergent." [41] Proof calls for "evidence that a given expectation is destined to fulfillment rather than to surprise." It "will look to the sequel, rather than to its internal structure." [42] Certitude can be withdrawn but is demanded at the moment of judgment if action and the development of further judgment is to be facilitated. "Qualities such as colors, and structural characteristics, such as number, are not mental or bodily, but may be either or both." [43] Each such quality, being neutral, is such that "if the appropriate mode of experiencing were present it would retain its antecedent identity in acquiring the new

[35] *Ibid.,* p. 566 ff.
[36] *Ibid.,* p. 571.
[37] *Present Philosophical Tendencies,* pp. 323 ff.
[38] *Ibid.,* pp. 206 ff.

[39] Perry, *Realms of Value* (Cambridge: Harvard University Press, 1954), pp. 297 f.
[40] *Ibid.,* pp. 300 ff.
[41] *Ibid.,* p. 301.
[42] *Ibid.,* p. 302.
[43] *Ibid.,* p. 444.

status of being experienced." [44] The object remains independent. "What is truly known owes nothing to that fact except that fact itself," [45] and one must never confuse the "statement that 'everything which is known, is *known*' with the statement that 'everything which *is*, is known.'" [46] Even logic and mathematics remain as firmly rooted as ever in an independent nature. "If the logical and mathematical structures of knowledge are to be true of nature they must be abstracted from nature, and verified by nature; if so, they must be *in* nature." [47]

3. RADICAL NEW REALISM: E. B. HOLT

As a pioneer of new realism preoccupied with the general statement and defense of the position, Perry did not undertake to work out all aspects of the theory, and many of his suggestions were so formulated as to be capable of being developed in either a more radical direction, in disregard of the claims of common sense and realistic tradition, or in a more conservative one, in which these claims are honored. This is especially true of his doctrines of ideas and of mind. One can stress the unity of the thing and the apprehension of it, and the objective and behavioral aspect of mind, as is done by the radical wing of new realism. Or one may concede significant differences between the thing and the apprehension, and give substantial recognition to the subjective and conscious aspects of mind, as is done by the more conservative or moderate wing of new realism. The most significant representative of the radical type of realism is E. B. Holt (b. 1873) in whose thought one may see whither some of the more distinctive doctrines of the new realism lead.

A. Apparently convinced from the outset of the essential correctness of the central new realist doctrines, Holt begins his principal epistemological work, *The Concept of Consciousness,* with an attempt to lay adequate logical and metaphysical foundations for his account of these doctrines. The first requirement of such a foundation is the discovery of the basic category in terms of which, and toward the explication of which, logical inquiry proceeds.

This category must, in the nature of the case, be one which denotes everything and connotes nothing. Accordingly the basic category cannot be, as the idealists suppose, that of *"being real," "being willed,"* or *"being thought by the Absolute."* [1] Categories of this sort

[44] *Ibid.,* p. 445.
[45] *Ibid.,* p. 446.
[46] *Ibid.,* p. 447.
[47] *Ibid.,* p. 454.

[1] E. B. Holt, *The Concept of Consciousness* (London: George Allen & Co., 1914), pp. 20 ff.

connote and hence cannot denote everything. The fact is, the requisite category can be nothing less than that of *being*, for "being" alone connotes nothing and denotes all that in any sense *is*. *Being* is then, as the new logic has shown more plainly than ever, the sole objective of logical inquiry.[2]

Philosophers of opposite schools have frequently endeavored to confine being solely to either mental substance on the one hand or material substance on the other. But all such efforts are doomed to failure by their own narrowness. To attempt to make mind the sole substance, as idealists have done, is to ignore the fact that while the complex can be explained in terms of the simple, the converse of this is not true.[3] Consciousness is complex and mental but the elements that make it up need not be mental at all.[4] The order which these elements manifest is their own and not impressed upon them by mind; for not only numbers and primary qualities, but also colors and even emotions form independent series.[5] Moreover, in reducing the whole universe to mind alone, the idealist excludes any sufficiently distinctive account of the part of the universe that unmistakably is mental, namely, hallucinations, dreams, and the like.[6] The attempt of materialists to make matter the sole substance is also futile. What the physicist deals with is not material particles but "stresses, tensions, straight and curvilinear motions, positive and negative oscillations," and equations which, though conceptual, are no more tractable than matter itself. The difficulty common to the contending views is that if either mind or matter is taken as a name for a single basic substance of which all being consists, the one so chosen will then have, like being itself, to be regarded as so devoid of particular qualities as to lose altogether such explanatory power as idealists on the one hand or materialists on the other hand wish to attribute to their favored entities. This gives a clue to what must be said concerning ultimate being.

Fundamental being consists of simples which constitute all the complexes that experience encounters. These simples are neither minds nor material things but neutral entities having neither mental nor material properties. As logic, which is the science of being, would suggest,[7] they are of the order of concepts and could be referred to as concepts except for the fact that this term inappropriately suggests subjectivity to some minds. They are identifiable with what are sometimes called essences and are native neither to mind nor to matter.

[2] *Ibid.,* p. 3.
[3] *Ibid.,* p. 95.
[4] *Ibid.,* pp. 92 f.

[5] *Ibid.,* pp. 106 ff.
[6] *Ibid.,* pp. 93 ff.
[7] Cf. *ibid.,* p. 103.

These simple neutral entities arrange themselves in a hierarchy of complexes, each higher type being deducible from the lower ones. Thus the entire universe may form a single deductive system. The simplest entities we know are those "of identity, of difference, of number, and of the negative." [8] Beyond these are in order other "logical and mathematical entities," "innumerable algebras," " 'secondary' qualities," "geometry," "higher mathematics," "extension" in space and time, "mass," "physics entire," "*concrete* physical objects," "larger aggregates," "life," "consciousness or mind," the subject matter of "psychology, anthropology, political economy, government, ethnology, history and archaeology," and "the realm of values." [9]

B. This logico-metaphysical doctrine of neutral entities provides for Holt the foundation both for an uncompromising realism and for a striking development of some of the more distinctive doctrines of new realism. Thus, to begin with he sets forth a rigorous doctrine of the independence of objects that nevertheless avoids Royce's criticism concerning two-way independence. Being neutral and having the restrictive qualities of neither mind nor matter, basic entities may enter equally freely into either the physical series or the mental series without losing their own character; they retain their *distinct self-identity* whatever their context. A logical entity is what it is regardless of its spatiotemporal or any other setting. The whiteness of the cloud yesterday, insofar as it is not discernibly different from that of the snow today, is essentially the same [10] as that of the snow today, and whiteness experienced is the same as whiteness not experienced.

The realism associated with the metaphysics of neutral entities also avoids, Holt believes, the mistakes of the sort of representational epistemology in which entities are thought to represent others of a basically different kind. Locke, for example, and the traditional representative realists, denied objectivity to the secondary qualities but treated them as signs or representatives of totally different primary ones. The impossibility of this sort of dualism was revealed by Berkeley who demonstrated the fact that precisely the same kind of consideration that called for rejection of the objectivity of the secondary qualities could be brought against the objectivity of the primary ones. Nevertheless, Berkeley himself continued to hold to a theory of knowledge that was in an important respect a representational dualism. For him, "secondary and primary qualities alike . . . are 'known' by means of entities which have neither extension, shape,

[8] *Ibid.*, p. 154.   [10] *Ibid.*, p. 106.
[9] *Ibid.*, pp. 154–60.

size, motion, colour, sound, odour, taste nor touch"; [11] and for him
these entities "constitute consciousness." [12] All such dualistic representational theories are misled by a complete misunderstanding of
representation; for while representation has its proper place in
knowledge, representation is not a reference from a certain entity
to a totally different kind of entity. Genuine representation of the
kind that occurs in knowing is rather such a partial identity as the
doctrine of neutral entities renders possible by showing the basic
similarity in kind of all entities. "A representation is always partly
identical with that which it represents, and completely identical in
all those features and respects in which it is a representation." [13] A
photograph represents a landscape only insofar as it is in certain
respects identical with it, and the representational relation is much
the same in the case of a sample and a piece of cloth. Hence, "ideas
of space are spatial ideas," [14] "the adequate 'idea' of a minute or of
an hour is just a minute or an hour," and an "adequate idea of a
year," if anybody ever had one, "would be just a year long." [15] "What
symbol or other device . . . could represent a color or a sound
except just that color or that sound?" [16] Similarly for all other
qualities.

C. What, in the kind of world thus far described, can the complex
of consciousness be? Something of a clue is given in the concept of
a cross section. A plane passing through a tree is a cross section
of a tree. The prime numbers are a cross section of the system of
numbers. A searchlight on a moving ship at night reveals a cross
section of wind and wave. In short, *"when a part of any object is
defined by some law that is independent of the laws that define the
whole object, the part usually intersects the whole in such a way as
to reveal the essentially neutral constitution of that object,"* [17] and
this intersection is a cross section of the object.

The particular kind of cross section that constitutes consciousness
is indicated by the presence of nervous response. Thus consciousness
is "a cross-section of the infinite realm of being and a cross-section
that is defined by the responses of a nervous organism." [18] Nervous
response becomes the searchlight that chooses out the cross section of
being in which consciousness consists. Such nervous response is
found all the way down the scale of living organisms, and is present
in human beings [19] at levels far deeper than those amenable to ordinary introspective analysis. Thus the basic unit of consciousness is

[11] *Ibid.,* p. 141.
[12] *Ibid.*
[13] *Ibid.,* p. 143.
[14] *Ibid.,* p. 145.
[15] *Ibid.,* p. 147.

[16] *Ibid.,* p. 148.
[17] *Ibid.,* p. 169.
[18] *Ibid.,* p. 208.
[19] *Ibid.,* p. 173.

not the introspectively discovered idea but the reflex or stimulus-response arc in which no intervention of soul is needed,[20] and one must beware of confusing that bare nervous response which defines consciousness with reflection upon the contents of consciousness.[21]

That the cross section of being in which consciousness consists is defined by reference to nervous response does not, however, mean that the object of knowledge is in any sense in the skull or in any part of the nervous system. Nervous response can never itself be described without reference to what is responded to. The object of knowledge is genuinely and objectively "out there." This is not only true of physical objects of perception, but also of objects remembered and correctly thought of. It is equally true of objects imagined, of pleasures and pains and even of emotions. The business of the poet is to "create situations which in all their objectivity are blythe or the reverse," and a place envisioned by a poet may be "a gladsome mask on the face of the earth" which he has "the perception to see." [22]

The theory of consciousness set forth here must explain rather than explain away the facts ordinarily recognized with reference to consciousness, and Holt undertakes to use the theory to this end. Especially important in this connection are the facts of perception and sensation. The theory accords very well indeed with the long-observed dependence of sensation and perception upon the sense organs, for it is of course obvious that sight, for example, depends upon having the eyes open.[23] The entry, maintenance, and exit of sensations and perceptions poses no difficult problem for the theory, for "the conscious cross-section is a manifold that moves in time and space as would the contents of a township if its boundaries were defined anew from moment to moment, or as the collection of all particles on which the sun casts shadows, or as the objects that a search-light illuminates." [24] Sensations themselves do not change; rather, they succeed one another in their presence in the experience of a given organism. The theory also accounts for the recognized difference between sensation and perception, regarding the former as a less, and the latter as a more, organized cross section.[25] No intervening introspection is needed in either case. The need for recognized correspondence does not in this theory, as in others, raise an impassable barrier to knowledge, for in this theory "sensation and perception are the objects" [26] just as really as are any objects to which they seem to refer. "If, as Aristotle said, 'thought and its object are one,' so are sensations and perceptions one with their 'objects.' " [27]

[20] Ibid., pp. 176 ff.
[21] Ibid., pp. 191 ff.
[22] Ibid., p. 111.
[23] Ibid., p. 185.

[24] Ibid., p. 210.
[25] Ibid., p. 210.
[26] Ibid., p. 222
[27] Ibid., p. 219.

The phenomena of memory and imagination do present something of a problem for the theory of consciousness as a cross section. If space and time were absolute, so that a given position could be fixed without reference to any other, it would indeed be difficult to see how memory and imagination could be accounted for. But space and time are not thus absolute. Rather, they are altogether relational, and no position is definable save by its place in a system.[28] Thus an event in a distant location must be defined by spatial relations to many observers. Essentially the same is true of an event in the past.[29] An event has position both in the spatiotemporal system of any given knower and in systems of many other knowers, and remains the same event in all such systems.[30] Hence knowledge of the distant past may, like knowledge of the near and present, be cross-sectional. Knowledge of the future is similar to knowledge of the past.[31] Indeed, in all cases of memory or of "knowledge of distant space and remote time, . . . knowledge is a cross-section of the realm of *being* and so far as it *is* at all, is identical with the so-called 'object' of knowledge."[32] Imagination, fancy, reverie, and dreams involve additional problems relating especially to error, presently to be considered; but, in general, "their position in consciousness, entrance into the specious presence and exit therefrom, is determined by the responses of the nervous system precisely as in the case of perception of any entities." The objects of these apparently unrealistic functions belong as truly as any others to the realm of being,[33] and are as truly "out there" as are any others.[34]

D. Since knowledge is for Holt not merely consciousness of an object but veridical consciousness of it, the cross-section theory, like any other, must furnish a satisfactory account of truth. With Perry, Holt is obliged to reject an unqualified correspondence theory, but the kind of theory he does adopt is rather nearer the coherence theory than is that of Perry. Although correspondence is a fact in the universe, consisting of the partial identity of a more abstract and less comprehensive system with a less abstract and more comprehensive one, correspondence cannot, as Joachim has shown, as such be the character of truth.[35] Rather, truth is consistency or noncontradiction.[36] There is, indeed, a truth of correspondence when one system is correctly said to correspond with another, and this occurs when "there is no feature of one system that contradicts any feature of the

---

[28] *Ibid.*, p. 224 ff.
[29] *Ibid.*, pp. 229 ff.
[30] *Ibid.*, p. 236.
[31] *Ibid.*, p. 252.
[32] *Ibid.*, p. 254.
[33] *Ibid.*, p. 257.

[34] "The Place of Illusory Experience in a Realistic World," in *The New Realism,* p. 354.
[35] *The Concept of Consciousness,* pp. 31 ff.
[36] *Ibid.*, p. 31.

other." [37] But such truth is consistency within a larger system that embraces both,[38] and veridical consciousness is a consistent cross section of being selected by nervous response. Moreover, even beyond veridical consciousness is "truth as a whole," which is both consistent and involves "more determinants . . . than enter consciousness." [39]

When the unity of apprehension and object is stressed the problem of error becomes acute. The usual solution, which relegates error to the realm of the subjective, would be as destructive of knowledge as of error.[40] Error is inconsistent or contradictory fact in the cross section of being that constitutes consciousness. It is thus both within consciousness and in the external fact. It is not present either in mere images, for no contradiction is involved here, or in systems in which one "sees around" seemingly inconsistent propositions, for apparent contradictions are overruled here. It is present in groups of propositions that contain genuine unreconciled contradictions. A single term has nothing to contradict and the words "contradictory system of terms" are meaningless.[41] That contradictory propositions are encountered in thought and even in perception need occasion no surprise. In discourse one often goes far in developing the implications of propositions before their contradictory character shows up, and in physical systems contradictions may occur quite apart from any human consciousness whatever, for example, when oppositely directed bodies meet or one animal kills another.[42]

E. The writings upon which the foregoing account of Holt's new realism has been based were produced in the early days of new realism, and in the years that followed, Holt wrote little to reveal the direction of his subsequent epistemological thought. However, nearly thirty years later, toward the close of his life, he did publish an article which affords some insight into later developments. Here, for purposes of the article in question at any rate, the perspective is rather drastically altered, and although some of the changes are developments of trends already present in the earlier work, most of the more radical new-realist doctrines have almost disappeared. Here, for example, the term "consciousness" is reserved for a reflective awareness that applies to only a small part of that to which we respond, so that much of the "cross-section" selected by nervous response is now excluded from consciousness. The knowing process becomes much less direct and more subject to distortion by nervous response. The emphasis on nervous response has become a more fully developed behaviorism,

[37] *Ibid.*
[38] *Ibid.*, p. 70.
[39] *Ibid.*, p. 339.
[40] *Ibid.*, p. 259.

[41] *Ibid.*, p. 263.
[42] *Ibid.*, pp. 264 ff.; also "The Place of Illusory Experience in a Realistic World," pp. 360 ff.

and neutral monism is abandoned in favor of avowed materialism. Thus, within man "all causation is strictly in the physiological mechanism," [43] and "motor response is the only genuine criterion of the psychic." [44] Matter itself is now identified with a vaguely known but consistently interpreted Kantian "thing-in-itself." [45]

4. CONSERVATIVE NEW REALISM: W. P. MONTAGUE

Although W. P. Montague (b. 1873) was one of the founders and most forceful supporters of the new realism in its earlier years, he has always been unwilling to go along with the more extreme developments of the movement, and his work may properly be regarded as representative of the more conservative branch of the movement. His moderation is apparent alike in his accounts of the process of knowing, of the subject-object relation, and of truth and error.

A. Although Montague is perhaps more generous than either Holt or Perry in the recognition he gives to mysticism, pragmatism, and even to authoritarianism and skepticism, as ways of knowing,[1] he is nevertheless convinced that an integrated rational way of knowing is the only fundamental one.[2] Unlike Holt and the idealists, who seem to think the universe a deductive system, Montague contends that empiricism is quite as essential as rationalism and in fact that the two methods are inseparably interdependent. On the one hand, every attempt of the rationalist to explain the universe solely in terms of a priori connections of universals comes to grief upon the fact of contingency, for "logical and mathematical systems may be wholly irrelevant to the facts of existence." [3] On the other hand, every attempt of the empiricist to explain the world in terms of sense experience alone is embarrassed by the dependence of its hypothetical propositions upon universal ones, as for instance the hypothetical proposition "if 2 things be added to 3 things the result must be 5 presupposes the universal proposition '2 + 3 = 5.' " [4] Any satisfactory attainment of knowledge requires that empiricism and rationalism unite in integrated effort [5] and, beginning with perceptual facts and universals, proceed through contingent and necessary judgments to reliable beliefs. Indivisible in fact, the rational and empirical phases of knowing may, however, be separated for inquiry.

[43] "Materialism and the Criterion of the Psychic," *Psychological Review,* XLV (1937), 49.

[44] *Ibid.,* p. 53.

[45] *Ibid.,* pp. 33–53.

[1] W. P. Montague, *The Ways of Knowing* (London & New York: George Allen & Unwin, & The Macmillan Co., 1925), pp. 224 ff.

[2] *Ibid.,* pp. 69, 126 ff.

[3] *Ibid.,* p. 127.

[4] *Ibid.,* p. 122.

[5] *Ibid.,* p. 128.

Universals are not, as the nominalists say, mere names for characters of things, nor are they, as the Platonists claim, independent existences of peculiarly comprehensive kinds.[6] Nor again are they, as Holt seems to think, the sole constituents of things. Rather, they are generic qualities such as roundness, redness, beauty, and the like, found in things.[7] While particulars precede them in the order of knowledge, universals are always prior in the "logical *order of being*," [8] as for example "man" is prior to "earthly poet." Traditional empiricism and rationalism are both mistaken in thinking that universals are not in the objective order of things, the one in eliminating them altogether and the other in supposing that the mind introduces them.[9] Universals are found in things not imposed upon things, and the method of finding them is not that of withdrawing the elements of a composite picture, but simply that of focusing attention upon the generic aspects of things.[10] They do not, however, include space and time, for spatiotemporal position is the prime root of particularity.[11]

All propositions are relational and the relations involved in them "may be resolved into the basic relation, complete or partial, of identity." [12] The gist of the identity relation is "single denotation combined with diverse connotations." [13] For example, to say "this smooth thing is black" means that the diverse connotations *smooth* and *black* have one denotation.[14] When the fact is recognized that a thing can belong to more than one order, as a point may belong to different lines, the major objections of both Hegelian logicians and most symbolic logicians to the essential features of the Aristotelian logic of identity are in principle answered, although of course Aristotle's version of that logic needs considerable expansion.[15]

What then of universal propositions with which the rational thought in general and science in particular are especially concerned? Whether a proposition is universal or particular depends upon whether its subject term is universal or particular.[16] Among those that are universal some are necessary and some are merely contingent.

Universal and necessary judgments are arrived at simply by a selective seeing of the identity of the connotations involved in objects. For example one *sees* . . . the identity of $7 + 5$ as such with 12 as such when one focuses attention upon the numerical aspects of objects having these properties. By an extension of the same sort of process the whole of mathematics is derivable. "In the

[6] *Ibid.*, p. 354.
[7] *Ibid.*, p. 107.
[8] *Ibid.*, pp. 73 f.
[9] *Ibid.*, p. 77.
[10] *Ibid.*, p. 72.
[11] *Ibid.*, p. 78.

[12] *Ibid.*, p. 78.
[13] *Ibid.*, p. 79.
[14] *Ibid.*, pp. 79 f.
[15] *Ibid.*, pp. 83 ff.
[16] *Ibid.*, p. 85.

sphere of mathematics, then, it may be said that we can derive universal propositions from particular cases, in exactly the same way as we derive universal terms from particular terms by abstracting the nature of a thing from the particular space and time in which it figures." [17] Proof of all such insights is to be found in the ultimately contradictory character of their contradictories.[18]

The truth of a universal contingent proposition, or a proposition the truth of which is not to be seen solely in the nature of the universals involved, such as "all bodies gravitate," must be arrived at by more indirect methods.[19] Here one must begin with a disjunctive major premise which lists the possible causes or effects of the type of phenomenon under consideration. One may then, through observation and the usual canons of induction, establish particular propositions which contradict each of these possible causes or effects but one, and so, by disjunctive syllogism, arrive at the required contingent proposition.

B. Although indications of an interpretation of new-realist principles that is considerably more moderate than that of Holt or even that of Perry are already apparent in Montague's account of the *process* of knowing, it is in his discussion of the knower and the known that this difference becomes most apparent.

(*1*) With Perry and Holt and all other realists, Montague contends that *the object cannot be dependent upon the knower.* Idealism rests in considerable part upon fallacious confusion of the subjective psychological side of such words as "belief" and "experience" with their objective logical side.[20] Its reliance upon the egocentric predicament is of no more avail than would be the attempt to support astrology on the ground that the stars cannot be observed in isolation from facts of human destiny.[21] Against all who so confuse the ontological and the psychological, and illegitimately exploit the egocentric predicament, the realist insists that nothing could become an object of knowledge at all unless it were independent of being known. And, if Royce and other idealists complain that this is to make the reality of the object depend upon its independence, the realist replies that "the independence of an object is not what makes it real, it is what makes us aware of its reality." [22] Sufficient evidence for the independence of objects is present in the manner in

[17] *Ibid.,* pp. 86 f.
[18] *Ibid.,* pp. 89 ff.
[19] *Ibid.,* pp. 89 f.; pp. 93 ff.
[20] Montague, "A Realistic Theory of Truth and Error," in *The New Realism,* pp. 256 ff.

[21] Montague, "The Story of American Realism," *Philosophy,* XII (1937), 140–50, 155–61.
[22] Montague, "Professor Royce's Refutation of Realism," *Philosophical Review,* XI (1902), 43.

which mind and its objects may be independently varied, and in the character of the probabilities concerning the order of nature.

Regarding the question of what objects there are that are thus independent of being known, Montague is also in partial agreement with Perry and Holt. That which is includes vastly more than is commonly recognized. Every object of awareness, including universals and even the most fantastic illusions, has possible existence. Such objects as do not actually exist at least subsist, and the island of actual existence is surrounded by a vast sea of subsistent entities. All manner of thinkable universals including even fantastic ones have their place in the realm of the subsistent, and untrue propositions are in this sense quite as objective as are true ones.

Nevertheless Montague is not willing with Holt to make all entities ultimately neutral. However objective the realm of the subsistent may be, its ontological status remains quite different from that of the existent, the term "possibility" being appropriate to the one and "actuality" to the other. Nor can Montague accept, with Holt and Perry, the notion that all manner of illusory objects exist and are perceived, though in a manner that distorts and misplaces them. To assume that they do is not only absurdly to ascribe existence to the objects of dreams and illusions,[23] but also to attribute contrary properties to the same space and to distort the meanings of the terms "physical" and "existence." [24] It is, moreover, to give to mere subsistents, including errors, a causal efficiency which they cannot have.[25] A proper recognition of the category of substance together with due allowance for the causal contexts of errors and illusions is adequate to explain such errors and illusions in fully realistic terms without resorting to the doubtful expedient of ascribing objective reality to them.[26]

(2) Montague's account of *the knowing mind* is in substantial agreement with that of Perry and Holt on two important points. The first of these is an anti-idealistic recognition of a dependence of the functioning of mind upon matter, "a pathetic dependence of consciousness upon the very objects which it is supposed to create." [27] In its higher manifestations a mind is inseparably connected with a particular *brain*, and the attempt to explain *"my brain"* in terms of *"your mind"* is palpably absurd.[28] The second point of agreement

[23] *The Ways of Knowing*, pp. 294 ff.
[24] "Confessions of an Animistic Materialist," in G. P. Adams and W. P. Montague, *Contemporary American Philosophy* (London & New York: George Allen & Unwin, & The Macmillan Co.,

1930), II, 147.
[25] *The New Realism*, p. 481.
[26] *Ibid.*, pp. 322 ff.
[27] "A Realistic Theory of Truth and Error," p. 252.
[28] *Ibid.*, pp. 274 f.

between Montague's theory of mind and the theories of Holt and Perry is the contention that the role of consciousness in the apprehension of objects is largely only "selective" and "relational" rather than constitutive or creative.[29] Had the selective functions of consciousness been duly recognized all the while, the whole process of the degeneration that has marked the history of modern philosophy from natural realism through dualism to subjectivism might have been avoided; [30] a proper acknowledgement of the relational character of consciousness would have been sufficient to assure appropriate recognition that "the objects of consciousness must be real independently of their standing in that relation." [31]

Nevertheless, Montague is unable to think of mind as essentially passive, and he certainly cannot agree with Holt that consciousness is only a by-product of the more complex nervous structures.[32] Rather, consciousness is an intensive capacity, inhering even in the smallest particles of matter, to store up and reissue essentially unchanged the course of events.[33] It is the hidden force of causality for which physics searches in vain; its actuality is "the potentiality of the physical, . . . the potential or implicative presence of a thing at a space or time in which the thing is not actually present." [34] It is present in all things but attains its greatest versatility in connection with the intricate organization of the brain through which the selective activity of our knowing takes place.[35]

(3) Montague agrees with Perry and Holt that the object is often immediately present to the knower, or that what is immediately apprehended in knowledge is often identical with the object. "What I perceive in the visual field may be identical in every respect with what exists in the physical world outside my body." [36] Thus, Montague takes his stand against the contention of most critical realists and all epistemological dualists that idea and object are always distinct. Dualism, he acknowledges, is not necessarily vulnerable in holding the idea to be a copy of which the original remains unknowable, for the character of the original might be aimed at by probability inference from the copy.[37] Nor is dualism necessarily an

[29] "The Relational Theory of Conciousness," *Journal of Philosophy*, II (1905), 309–16; see also "Contemporary Realism and the Problems of Perception," *Journal of Philosophy*, IV (1907), 374–83.

[30] *The Ways of Knowing*, chap. IX.

[31] "The Relational Theory of Consciousness and Its Realistic Implications," *Journal of Philosophy*, II (1905), 313.

[32] "Note on Professor Holt's Essay," in *The New Realism*.

[33] "Confessions of an Animistic Materialist," pp. 150 ff.

[34] "A Realistic Theory of Truth and Error," p. 281.

[35] *The Ways of Knowing*, p. 309.

[36] *The Ways of Knowing*, p. 308; see also Montague, "Current Misconceptions of Realism," *Journal of Philosophy*, IV (1907), pp. 100–105.

[37] *The Ways of Knowing*, pp. 258 ff., 332 f.

artificial dissociation of primary and secondary qualities, for although such dissociation is always untenable, not all dualists are guilty of it.[38] Rather, the fatal mistake of epistemological dualism lies in its denial of the numerical unity of space and time,[39] its attempt to locate ideas and things in totally different frames of reference. Such a view is self-contradictory and yields only confusion. The fact is that there is identity of thing and apprehension in shared substance, in reflected quality, and frequently in identical location.[40]

But Montague is unable to accept the view, sometimes suggested by Perry and Holt, that in all instances the mind's apprehension of the object is direct.[41] Indeed, in the case of error direct apprehension is just what does not happen; either mind or some distorting medium intervenes. But even in cases of true judgment, truth is arrived at only after corrections of distortions have been duly made. Thus there may be a subjective realm involved in knowing any object, and experiences may vary independently of the object.[42] Indeed, there are for Montague four distinct realms to which an object may belong; namely, the objective and externally existent realm of "actualized truth," the subjective but not existent realm of "actualized error," the externally existent but nonsubjective realm of "potential truth," and the nonexistent and nonsubjective realm of "*potential error.*"[43] Such recognition of subjective realms alongside objective ones involves, of course, concessions to dualism that neither Holt nor Perry could very well accept.

Montague has formulated his own summary of his view of the relation of the knower and the known by comparison with competing theories, including those of other new realists, in three couples of propositions which he thinks constitute an essential reconciliation of the three major types of epistemology. Within each couple, the first proposition states the truth involved in the theory, and the second, the error. Thus, concerning objectivism, or new realism in less moderate forms Montague writes: "(1) All experienced objects have an independent meaning or essence that gives them a status of *possible* physical existence. (2) All perceptually experienced objects (sense-data) enjoy a status of *actual* physical existence."[44] Concerning subjective idealism, Montague continues: "(1) All entities are selectively [relative] to a self and possible objects of experience. (2) All entities are [constitutively] relative to, or dependent upon, a self, and cannot exist except as actual objects of its experience."[45] And

[38] *Ibid.*, pp. 260 ff.
[39] *Ibid.*, p. 261 f.
[40] Montague, "Contemporary Realism and the Problems of Perception," *Journal of Philosophy*, IV (1907), 374–83.

[41] *The Ways of Knowing*, pp. 307 ff.
[42] *Ibid.*, pp. 297–306.
[43] *Ibid.*, p. 394.
[44] *Ibid.*, p. 292.
[45] *Ibid.*, p. 297.

finally, concerning dualism, or representative realism, Montague concludes: "(1) *The system of objects experienced by a self and the system of objects existing externally to that self and causing its experience can vary independently of each other.* (2) *The experienced objects and the existent objects, because they vary independently of one another, are never coincident or identical, but constitute two mutually exclusive systems of metaphysical entities."* [46]

C. Although a number of features of Montague's theory of truth and error have already been alluded to, some require further consideration. In general, Montague's account of truth does not, like Holt's, interpret truth in terms of consistency or, like Perry's, treat truth as a relation of belief and fact. Rather it takes truth to refer to the reality of what propositions state and so approximates the traditional correspondence theory of truth much more closely than do either of the other two accounts.

All propositions are objective, Montague thinks, and since every proposition has a contradictory proposition, this consideration applies to false and illusory propositions as well as to true ones.[47] Not all propositions are true. The ones that are true are the ones that either refer to existents in space and time or are real in the sense of being included in "that which is logically presupposed or implied by the totality of what is experienced." [48] In that the term "truth" has not only a primary sense denoting what is aimed at or believed but also a secondary one referring to the aiming or believing,[49] essentially the same idea may be expressed by defining the real and the true, as "that which would appear to an absolute mind who experienced each object in the light of the totality of objects." [50]

The propositions in which truth is expressed always state a whole or partial identity. Hence true propositions must formulate identities that belong to "fact or reality." Such identity is achieved when the whole complex of essences involved in the proposition refer to a single denotation or position in an ordered series. In the case of contingent propositions this is accomplished when the complex of qualities occupies a single "position in the spatio-temporal system." [51] In the case of necessary propositions, such as "7 plus 5 equals 12" or "black is the opposite of white," [52] the series in which a single position may be occupied "is as real as spatio-temporal position," but it is a logical series and the identity achieved is not "caused by external circumstances" but is necessary and inseparable from the essences which participate in it.[53]

[46] *Ibid.*, pp. 306 ff.
[47] Cf. *ibid.*, pp. 337, 355.
[48] *Ibid.*, p. 401.
[49] *The Ways of Knowing*, p. 399.

[50] *Ibid.*, p. 401.
[51] *Ibid.*, p. 339.
[52] *Ibid.*
[53] *Ibid.*, p. 340.

Although beliefs change from generation to generation, truth in the objective sense does not change. "Once true always true." [54] Moreover, while known truths are often partial and incomplete in that the recognized is less comprehensive than the real, there can be no degrees of truth as such.[55]

As the foregoing account of truth would suggest, Montague's views of falsity and error steer a middle course between the subjectivism of representative realism and the extreme objectivism of such new realists as Holt. On the one hand, false propositions are fully objective, for "to say that a true proposition is objective and independent of an apprehension or belief, but that its false contradictory is subjective as dependent on consciousness, would be as absurd as to say that the convex aspect of a curve was objective, but that the concavity, correlated with it and determined by it, was subjective." [56] But on the other hand, false propositions are no part of the external world and the attempt to place them there confuses essences and the implicates of experience, ascribing an impossible causal efficiency to the former. Error is even less a part of the external world; it is the judgmental assertion of false propositions. It is "that relation of a conscious individual to his objective environment in which a false proposition is made an object of belief or the content of a judgment." [57]

Error may come about either through a distorting influence in the medium through which an object is apprehended, as in the case of the bent stick, or may be produced by a distorted interpretation.[58] In either case, the causes of error may be recognized and offset so that the error no longer exists although the tendency to produce it does. In the light of this account of error and of the natural tendency of consciousness to accept what is presented to it, truth can now be spoken of as apprehension in which no distortion is present.

D. In the years subsequent to the publication of *The Ways of Knowing*, Montague has moved farther than ever from the extreme position of Holt and in the direction of representative realism. Thus for example in a conversation with the author in 1953, he singled out such a shift as the major change in his epistemological outlook. And in his book *Great Visions of Philosophy*, while still finding some difficulties in the dualist's notion of the transcendence of the object, Montague defends the possibility and even plausibility of some sort of copy theory of ideas.

---

[54] *Ibid.*, p. 400.
[55] Cf. "A Realistic Theory of Truth and Error," pp. 299 f.
[56] *The Ways of Knowing*, p. 338.

[57] *Ibid.*, p. 338.
[58] *Ibid.*; "A Realistic Theory of Truth and Error," p. 291.

5. Other First Generation New Realists

In addition to the writers whom we have considered as representatives of new realism, at least three groups of other new realists require mention here. The first consists of the contributors to *The New Realism* not yet considered. The second includes other first-generation new realists not represented in that volume, and the third is made up of new realists of the second generation. The first two of these groups will be considered in this section and the third in the succeeding one.

A. (*1*) The author of the first essay in *The New Realism*, W. T. Marvin, undertakes in that essay to undermine the claim of idealists and others that epistemology occupies a position of logical priority among all intellectual disciplines. Epistemology is not, Marvin insists, "logically fundamental" but "posterior to many of the special sciences such as physics and biology." [1] It "does not enable us to show . . . either what knowledge is possible or how it is possible, or again what are the limits of human knowledge." [2] For the most part, epistemology throws no light "upon the nature of the existent world or upon the fundamental postulates and generalizations of science." [3] It neither "gives us a theory of reality" nor "solves metaphysical problems." On the contrary, it is only "one of the special sciences." It "assumes the formulae of logic and the results of the special sciences," which along with "logic and metaphysics" are "logically prior" to it.[4] When epistemology is thus reduced to its proper place, the way is clear for a wholesome realism.

Another aspect of Marvin's endeavor to remove initial obstacles to realism is presented in an article entitled "Existential Propositions," which is intended to yield a definition of existence sufficiently neutral to avoid prejudging the basic philosophical issues. The type of definition that identifies existence with the occupation of spatio-temporal position has from the outset closed the question whether or not there can be nontemporal existents. In like manner the type of definition that identifies the existent with the particular prejudges the issue of the existence of universals. These and other difficulties are avoided by the following definitions: "The existent is the asserted sufficient condition of any true proposition." A term "is said to exist when it is a member of a proposition that is the asserted sufficient condition of some true proposition." [5] On the basis of such neutral

<hr/>

[1] W. T. Marvin, "The Emancipation of Metaphysics from Epistemology," in *The New Realism*, p. 49.
[2] *Ibid.*, pp. 49 f.

[3] *Ibid.*, p. 50.
[4] *Ibid.*
[5] Marvin, "Existential Propositions," *Journal of Philosophy*, VIII (1911), 49.

definitions one can proceed without initial antirealistic presuppositions to discuss the problem of the existence of anything conceivable.

(2) The author of the final essay in *The New Realism,* Walter B. Pitkin, is especially concerned to show that the objections commonly raised against any sort of direct realism on the ground of the intervention of the biological organism cannot be sustained.[6] "Ordinary methods of analysis and research pursued by natural scientists," [7] he thinks, yield an account of life and mind that shows the content of experience to be far less dependent on the activity of the organism than has been commonly supposed, and suggests that this content is sometimes quite independent of the organism. Thus, for example, whereas John Dewey takes the character of "seen light" to be a product of the interaction of the organism and the environment, experiments in which the source of the light is increased without noticeable increase in seen light conclusively disprove this contention.[8] In like manner, "geometrical, mathematical and other relations can be shown to be genuine stimuli and not products of the cognitive reaction." [9] Even when it is fully admitted that narcotics may sometimes play the role normally played by external objects in stimulating belief, no suggestion is involved that "the objects believed in depend for their . . . existence upon the conscious activity of believing." [10] Not even the most extreme error is properly attributable to the activity of the organism. "Error is not a product of the nervous system, but the nervous system is a contrivance to deal with a physical state of affairs of which error is only a very intricate instance." [11] Moreover, so fully is the independence of the object, which biological analysis sustains, accepted by "the man on the street" that a heavy burden of proof must rest on the idealist who denies it, for of any thesis it is true that *"the evidence necessary to refute it must be commensurate with the strangeness and heterodoxy of the proposition set up in its stead."* [12]

(3) The most significant of the three contributors to *The New Realism* now under consideration is E. G. Spaulding (1873–1940). While sharing the new-realist doctrine of the independence of the object and the immediacy of knowledge, Spaulding is not nearly so much impressed with the naturalistic implications of these positions

[6] Walter B. Pitkin, "Some Realistic Implications of Biology," in *The New Realism*, p. 377.

[7] *Ibid.*

[8] *Ibid.*, pp. 416 ff.

[9] *Ibid.*, p. 415; see also Pitkin, "The Empirical Status of Geometrical Entities," *Journal of Philosophy*, X (1913), 393.

[10] "The Relation Between the Act and the Object of Belief," *Journal of Philosophy*, III (1906), 311.

[11] "The New Realist and the Man on the Street," *Philosophical Review*, XXII (1913), 191.

[12] *Ibid.*

as are most of the other members of the school. Much of his effort is devoted to discovering in independent objects something of the same rational order which the idealists found in the whole of reality.

In a series of articles entitled "The Ground of the Validity of Knowledge," [13] which antedated the publication of *The New Realism* by six years, Spaulding insisted that the *need* which knowledge meets can be satisfied only if the object is both transcendent and immanent. Knowing becomes here a kind of biological inference, an "act of a-logical inference to which the implied transcendent stands in the relation of a simultaneous 'in' and 'beyond.'" Logic itself is an abstraction from this more basic type of inference.

Subsequently in his monograph *The New Rationalism*, Spaulding attributes most of the subjectivism of modern philosophy to its allegiance to an antiquated Aristotelean logic, and, on the basis of a new logic, sounds most of the characteristic neorealist notes. The basic mistake of the older logic was that of attempting to construct its forms on the analogy of the physical thing, so that its central concepts became those of qualities inhering in substance.[14] Such a logic tends not only to locate error in a substantive consciousness but ultimately also to imprison all sensations and thought within consciousness so as to render knowledge impossible. Fortunately, however, alongside the older logic, there has developed in and out of science a different relational logic which must now become a foundation for all philosophical inquiry. Such a relational logic facilitates the realist insights that consciousness is relational [15] and that knowing is an external relation into which entities may enter without thereby being altered in their basic character. Thus, *"the knowing process neither causally affects, modifies, or creates that which is known, nor demands an underlying entity to mediate the relationship between knowing and its object."* To be sure, "'things' are known and *are related* to the knowing," but they "are known as if they were not known." [16]

If things are thus known as if they were not known, analyses in which the parts of wholes are singled out must be possible and capable of vindication with respect to each possible type of object. Critics of analysis almost invariably fail to take account of actual connecting relations. Analysis of aggregates requires no infinite regress of intervening entities between its terms, nor does it need any single basic ground. Similarly, despite the protests of Henri Bergson

---

[13] E. G. Spaulding, "The Ground of the Validity of Knowledge," *Journal of Philosophy*, III (1906), 197–208.
[14] Spaulding, *The New Rationalism*

(New York: Henry Holt & Co., Inc., 1918), pp. 29 ff.
[15] *Ibid.*, p. 42.
[16] *Ibid.*, p. 86.

and others, analysis of spatial and temporal continuities and of movement is satisfactorily achieved in terms of the modern concepts of rational and irrational numbers.[17] Even analysis of organic unities, the properties of which are not fully predictable in terms of knowledge of their ingredients, is sound as far as it goes.[18]

Spaulding's special emphasis upon the rationality of the universe is early apparent in his essay on "The Ground of the Validity of Knowledge." Here his claim is that if the quest for knowledge is to be successful, the object must be " 'a transcendent' which is itself order and regularity, causal agent, persistent and permanent." [19] This emphasis is continued in *The New Rationalism,* a central purpose of which is to vindicate the sound rationalistic claims of idealism within the framework of a realism which is in the end implicit in every philosophy.

As this emphasis upon cosmic rationality might lead one to expect, Spaulding is like Montague in giving to consciousness a somewhat more significant role than do most other new realists. "Knowing and the known are numerically distinct" [20] and also qualitatively distinct. Mental occurrences are genuinely "processes or events that occur at a certain specific time." [21] The nervous system conditions but "does not cause them." [22] They themselves are, however, not "limited temporally, as are their conditions." [23] Moreover, the consciousness of which they are aspects is an emergent whole which is "nontemporal and non-spatial." [24] Error, however, for Spaulding, as for Holt and most new realists, does not belong to a special subjective realm but is a misplacement of objective entities.[25]

B. (*1*) Although, F. J. E. Woodbridge (1867–1940) deliberately declined the opportunity to contribute to *The New Realism* and was in fact not especially interested in epistemology as such, his influence in shaping new-realist epistemology has been very considerable. His contribution has been largely in terms of the development of one aspect of new-realist thought, namely the relational theory of consciousness. While this theory has been frequently encountered in the thought of other new realists, Woodbridge's influence perhaps more than any other is responsible for its place in new realism.

Consciousness is not, as Locke, Kant, and others have supposed, a mere receptacle into which experiences come. Such a view even

[17] *Ibid.,* pp. 169 ff.
[18] *Ibid.,* pp. 237 ff.
[19] "The Ground of the Validity of Knowledge," p. 208.
[20] *Ibid.,* p. 372.
[21] *Ibid.,* p. 491.
[22] *Ibid.*
[23] *Ibid.*
[24] *Ibid.,* p. 492.
[25] *The New Rationalism,* chaps. xlii, xliv.

if it were true could never be verified, for consciousness and objects are never encountered separately.[26] In this respect, consciousness, which "each can identify and analyze for himself as readily as he would a plant or a rock," [27] is like space or time which, invariably present with things, are not such as to lead anyone to ask how things got into them. Consciousness is, as James showed, simply a certain kind of relation, "an instance of the existence of different things together." [28] It is "a kind of continuum of objects." [29] When we search for minds it is only bodies in certain relations that we discover.

This does not mean that consciousness is the same thing as body. Consciousness was not said to be just any sort of relation or continuum, and it may even be that "the relation of soul and body is not something to which an eventual metaphysics ought to conform." [30] The particular kind of relation that consciousness is, is best described as representation or meaning. Hence, consciousness "cannot be identified with the objects of experience, but is to be identified with a relation between them, and that relation is the relation of meaning or implication, in short the logical relation." [31] It is not mentalistically-conceived ideas that in consciousness represent things, but rather things that represent things, as bread represents nourishment. Thus, in its proper interpretation "an idea is an object in its logical connections." [32]

Since consciousness, on which the existence of knowledge depends, is a kind of relation among objects, the objects that enter into knowledge are in no way dependent upon their being known for their existence or character.[33] Nor can consciousness set any limits in advance to what can be known. However, by the same token, the things that enter into consciousness must have some order of their own, else they could never give rise to the representational relation that constitutes consciousness. Hence, there is in the logic of things that which can give rise to consciousness, what Woodbridge calls a "natural teleology." One can even speak of the realm of discourse as a realm of objective mind which is essentially coextensive with being itself.[34]

It is the order of things that in the end gives rise to our individual minds for "we have minds because our bodies are in contact with

[26] E. J. E. Woodbridge, "The Nature of Consciousness," *Journal of Philosophy*, II (1905), 119.

[27] *Ibid.*

[28] *Ibid.*, p.120.

[29] *Ibid.*, p. 121.

[30] Woodbridge, *The Realm of Mind* (New York: Columbia University Press,

1926), p. 114.

[31] Woodbridge, "Consciousness, the Sense Organs, and the Nervous System," *Journal of Philosophy*, VI (1909), 449–55.

[32] *The Realm of Mind*, p. 85.

[33] *The Nature of Consciousness*, p. 123.

[34] *The Realm of Mind*, p. 33.

other bodies which jointly with it are in order enmeshed."[35] These individual minds contain no sensations, for there is in fact no evidence that sensations exist.[36] Not even alleged errors lend credibility to sensations, for what is known to be error is not error and what is not known to be error is of no use in this connection.[37] The so-called secondary qualities differ from the primary ones only in that they seem to require a specific type of sense organ and not like the primary ones *any one* of several.[38]

(2) Somewhat more conservative than the thought of Woodbridge is that of E. B. McGilvary (b. 1861), who adopts new-realist doctrines only with substantial qualifications. Consciousness is, for McGilvary as for James and Woodbridge, thoroughly relational.[39] The object is not a state of consciousness, is often quite independent of the knowing process, and may be "the real thing,"[40] a "dandum" which exists prior to its becoming datum. It may consist of "sensibilia" that only occasionally become "sensa." Moreover, apprehension of the object is direct, as must be admitted at least of the brain and nervous system even by those who claim that the brain and nervous system always intervene between known and knowing.[41]

But simply to say that consciousness is a relation among objects or even a meaning relation is by no means a sufficient characterization of consciousness. Before anything can be meant it must be experienced and "to be experienced is an ultimate fact not to be identified with anything else."[42] Moreover, consciousness has a "centered character," which is not adequately recognized in the relational theory as such.[43] This should remind us of another fact not sufficiently emphasized in the relational view, that in its capacity to span space and time, consciousness has a limited ubiquity and eternity radiating from here and now.[44]

These qualifications of the James-Woodbridge relational view of consciousness are quite naturally accompanied, in McGilvary's

[35] "Confessions" in G. P. Adams and W. P. Montague, *Contemporary American Philosophy*, II, 431.

[36] Woodbridge, "The Belief in Sensations," *Journal of Philosophy*, X (1913), 599–608.

[37] C. F. Woodbridge, "The Deception of the Senses," *Journal of Philosophy*, X (1913), 5–15.

[38] Woodbridge, "Consciousness, the Sense Organs, and the Nervous System," *Journal of Philosophy*, IV (1907), 225–35.

[39] Cf. McGilvary, "The Stream of Consciousness," "Experience and Its Inner Duplicity," *Journal of Philosophy*, VI (1909), 225–32; "The Relation of Con-

sciousness and Object in Sense Perceptions," *Philosophical Review*, XXI (1912), 152–73.

[40] McGilvary, "Prolegonomena to a Tentative Realism," *Journal of Philosophy*, IV (1907), 453.

[41] McGilvary, "Physiological Argument Against Realism," *Journal of Philosophy*, IV (1907), 591.

[42] McGilvary, "Experience as Pure and Consciousness as Meaning," *Journal of Philosophy*, VI (1909), 525.

[43] McGilvary, "The Relation of Consciousness and Objects in Sense Perception," p. 165.

[44] *Ibid.*, pp. 203 ff.

thought, by qualifications of some new-realist ideas concerning the object in relation to the knower. For one thing awareness need not, McGilvary holds, be directed solely to objects as such but may sometimes be directed toward awareness itself. There is, to be sure, no consciousness of a consciousness without objects, but awareness of awareness of objects is a frequently encountered experience.[45] Implicit in this fact is a further qualification of radical new realism, to the effect that while the object of knowledge is often independently real this is by no means always so. Hence, "some of the 'qualities perceived' are numerically identical with and some numerically different from the 'actual qualities,' "[46] and "perceived objects are sometimes real and sometimes not real."[47] It should, of course, be noted that for McGilvary the object is in neither case a physical object but a complex of qualities. Otherwise, McGilvary would feel compelled to adopt epistemological dualism rather than the monism to which he adheres.

6. Some Second-Generation New Realists

In the changing philosophical climate of the decades following the first impact of the new realism, discussion has shifted away from the problems that gave birth to this movement and, regardless of the merits or deficiencies of the movement, many philosophers have lost interest in the kind of epistemology represented by it. Nevertheless, the new realism has left a permanent impact upon virtually all types of epistemology and still numbers very able men in its own ranks. Naturally the altered philosophical atmosphere is reflected in the writings of these men, but the essential tenets of the movement remain. The following sketches will afford some indication of the character of new realism in its recent setting.

A. One of the foremost of the second-generation new realists is Donald C. Williams (b. 1899) of Harvard. Williams' epistemology involves a polemic, an argument for realism, a realist account of meaning and confirmation, and a discussion, within the realist setting, of the character of data and of objects.

Williams' realist polemic is directed not entirely or even mainly against the traditional type of idealists, whom he considers no longer a serious threat, but against a wide variety of contemporary prag-

---

[45] Cf. "The Stream of Consciousness," p. 234; "Prolegonomena to a Tentative Realism," p. 449; "The Relation of Consciousness and Object in Sense Perception," pp. 172, 204.

[46] McGilvary, "Realism and the Physical World," *Journal of Philosophy*, IV (1907), 684.

[47] "The Relation of Consciousness and Object in Sense Perception," p. 152.

matists, operationalists, positivists,[1] and others who sustain their positions by taking advantage of the egocentric predicament. Such writers are, in Williams' judgment, the underminers both of sound philosophy in general and of the best in the American tradition in particular. To those who attempt to build an antirealist subjectivism upon a priori grounds, Williams replies that while their subjectivism cannot be disproved, it is completely without rational basis.[2] More damaging to realism than any a priori arguments are inductive arguments for subjectivism, and these Williams endeavors to overcome as follows.[3] The prevalence of perceptual error would be effective evidence only against an extreme sort of monism, and if the mind can create occasional errors this in no sense tends to prove that it creates all objects. The method of agreement, often used to show the dependence of the object on mind, is at best an inadequate method apart from the method of difference. In any case it requires that the agreement apply to a single circumstance, whereas the occurrence of objects is invariably accompanied by other factors than mind, including, for example, space and time. While subjectivism cannot be disproved, neither can many another extremely doubtful hypothesis, and disproof of this one is prevented only by the introduction of subordinate hypotheses specifically designed for the purpose. The only aspect in which subjectivism can claim to be simpler or more parsimonious than realism is in terms of gross tonnage. The explanatory power of subjectivism is actually less than that of realism, and the "as if" which subjectivism must add to the realist account makes it in this important matter more complex than realism. At best inductive arguments for subjectivism would support only a solipsistic variety of subjectivism such as almost no one cares to defend and, when solipsism is abandoned, these same arguments begin to count against subjectivism.

Williams' positive argument on behalf of realism rejects as inadequate all such attempts as have been made to establish realism on a priori grounds, and rests solely upon positive inductive grounds.[4] All manner of common-sense observations and scientific predictions have come to constitute powerful evidence for the existence of an independent reality upon which they depend. The realist hypothesis is free from contradictions within itself or with the data, and it yields all manner of fruitful subordinate hypotheses, which its rivals merely

[1] D. C. Williams, "The *A Priori* Argument for Subjectivism," *The Monist*, XLIII (1933), 173–202.

[2] Williams, "The *A Priori* Argument for Subjectivism," *The Monist*, XLIII (1933), 201.

[3] Williams, "The Inductive Argument for Subjectivism," *The Monist*, XLIV (1934), 80–107.

[4] Williams, "The Argument for Realism," *The Monist*, XLIV (1934), 186–209.

assume. It stands or falls with the inductive method on which science relies, and it could be sustained even by the organismic logic of the idealists or the experimental one of the pragmatists.

The theory of meaning on which Williams builds his realist epistemology is the antithesis of the prevalent verification or confirmation theory. "One finds properties in experience, and by connoting these properties, *and* universals, i.e. as determining similarity sets, one can *denote* unobserved instances of them. . . . There is no reason why we can't refer to utterly unobservable things-in-themselves, just describing them by analogy . . . with observed things; there is no reason why we can't, in the same way, refer to things whose existence is not even indirectly confirmable—that is, we may entertain conjectures about them, though by hypothesis we can't infer them." [5]

If meanings then are connotations ascertained through experience but not limited in denotation to experience, how does knowledge formulated in propositions made up of such connotations come to be confirmed?

In the case of one of the two pillars of knowledge, analytic or logical propositions, the answer is fairly simple. Such propositions neither are true by definition nor are they synthetic. Rather, their truth is implicit in the meanings of the terms involved.[6] This applies alike to tautologies such as "all rectangles are rectangular" and "all equilateral rectangles are rectangular," to such obviously true propositions as "all squares are rectangular" and "all horses are animals" and even to somewhat less obviously true propositions such as "being red entails being colored" and "43×56 equals 2048." [7] In all such instances "immediate inspection of certain intrinsic relations among properties or 'universals' " is in the end all that is required. Moreover, the assumption that propositions of this sort rule nothing out is a mere bogus; for truth tables clearly reveal that they rule out the impossible, and it is only among possibles that they exclude nothing.[8]

In the case of the other pillar of knowledge, empirical propositions, the process of confirmation is more complex. It consists in part of observations of the causal nexus where analysis of meaning reveals nothing. These observations are expressed in protocol sentences, which though not in themselves knowledge are "infallible" and in no need of further confirmation.[9] These protocols enter into

[5] From a letter to the author, April 25, 1953.

[6] Williams, "The Nature and Variety of the *A Priori*," *Analysis*, V (1938), 85–94.

[7] *Ibid.*, pp. 90 ff.

[8] *Ibid.*, p. 89.

[9] Letter to the author.

the structure of knowledge through inductive procedures, common sense, and science. The validity of induction itself rests upon no mere animal faith, shrewd guess, practical postulate, or customary procedure of the scientists of our time.[10] Nor does it rest upon any such impossible infinite "collective" of instances as is required by some contemporary frequency theories of probability.[11] The ground of induction lies rather in a kind of logic which, while quite as genuinely analytic as any other, yields only probable rather than conclusive results. Prejudice against the recognition of such a ground springs from failure to see that there are genuine logical relations that lie between strict entailment and exclusion.[12] The mode of operation of such logic is in general not the indirect one advocated by Carnap and others in terms of which one calculates the probability of p on q from that of q on p but rather the direct one of calculating the probability of p from the evidence for p.[13] Induction requires no foreknowledge of equiprobability of possibilities but only the classifiability of possibilities, and such classifiability is always within reach. There is no reason in principle or in fact why such inductive logic may not be applied to the future as well as to the present and to the most recondite metaphysical entities as well as to the most commonplace experiences.[14]

Thus far, Williams thinks, virtually all realists should be able to agree. There remain, however, the related problems of the location of data and of the ultimate constitution of objects. Difference here, Williams considers realistically unimportant—family quarrels within the household of realism.

Concerning the first of these problems, Williams contends that the opposing views of strict monistic realists, who think the given to be at the place of the object, and the dualistic ones, who locate the datum either in the mind or in the brain of the knower, are predicated upon the false assumption of equivalence between knowledge and the given.[15] When, however, it is shown, as Williams undertakes to do, that the given is in itself "innocent" of knowledge claims and neutral in this family quarrel, the sharp edge of each type is turned, and either view is seen to be possible and even

---

[10] Cf. "Probability, Induction and the Provident Man," in Marvin Faber (ed.), *Philosophic Thought in France and the United States* (Buffalo, N.Y.: University of Buffalo, 1950), pp. 525–43.

[11] Williams, "On the Deviation of Probabilities from Frequencies," *Philosophy and Phenomialogical Research,* V (1945), 449–83.

[12] *The Ground of Induction* (Cambridge: Cambridge University Press, 1947), Bk. II.

[13] Cf. *ibid.,* chap. viii.

[14] *The Grounds of Induction,* chap. vii.

[15] Cf. "The Argument for Realism," pp. 207 f.

plausible.[16] As for Williams himself, he is inclined to depreciate the mentalistic form of epistemological realism and to prefer either the monistic view or the dualistic one that places data in the brain. Of these last two, he favors the monistic view.[17]

Upon the question how data can be at the same time in an experience and in an object, light is thrown by the suggestion that the ultimate constituents of the universals are "tropes." Entities divide themselves logically not merely into "abstract universals" such as "triangle" and "concrete particulars" or "whole chunks" in space-time but include also "concrete universals," or lowest species, and "abstract particulars," such as "grin" or "sneeze." [18] The latter constitute the basis of the trope which is the occurrence of an essence, "a particular entity either abstract or consisting of one or more concreta in combination with an abstraction." [19] It is these tropes that are the basic constituents of the universe and the elements out of which our knowledge is built.[20] Thus the claim that knowledge has its origin in abstract universals and the contention that knowledge starts with concrete particulars, are equally mistaken.[21]

B. Charles Baylis (b. 1902) is like Williams in defending universals against current nominalistic trends and in finding in inductive processes a principal ground of assurance concerning objects not directly experienced. Baylis is, however, very different from Williams both in his philosophical ancestry and in his apparent metaphysical presuppositions. Instead of learning primarily from early new realists and English realists themselves, Baylis has looked primarily to the American conceptual pragmatist C. I. Lewis and the English phenomenalist H. H. Price; and instead of adopting such a metaphysical platform as Williams' materialism, Baylis tends, in metaphysics, to remain somewhat more open to a variety of possibilities.

All knowledge, for Baylis, is achieved through meanings, and meanings in their basic connotative sense are universals. Any view which "denies that there are meanings" or universals precludes the possibility of knowledge and is in fact "a silly view" in the sense

[16] Williams "The Innocence of the Given," *Journal of Philosophy*, XXX (1933), 617–28, and "Truth, Error, and the Location of the Datum," *ibid.* XXX (1934), 428–38.

[17] Williams "On Having Ideas in the Head," *Journal of Philosophy*, XIX (1932), 617–31; see also "Naturalism" and "The Nature of Things," *Philosophical Review*, LIII (1944), 417–43.

[18] Williams "The Nature of Universals and Abstractions," *The Monist*, LI (1951), 583–93.

[19] Williams "On the Elements of Being," *Review of Metaphysics*, VII (1953), 7.

[20] *Ibid.*, pp. 10 ff.

[21] *Ibid.*, pp. 15 ff.

that "only an extremely able man would attempt to hold it." [22] In contrast to any such skeptical nominalism, Baylis writes: "Some people, at least, mean meanings. These meanings are independent of exemplification. They are also independent of being meant, and are eternal and unchangeable in the sense that at any time, they might be meant, and given certain conditions will be meant, and in the sense that they have certain relations to other meanings, which latter also might be meant." [23] Baylis subsequently puts the matter thus: "There are unchanging characters or universals at least in the sense that the same characters can be thought of again and again, that they can be exemplified repeatedly and that certain relations obtain among these characters whether they are exemplified or not and whether they are thought of or not." [24]

Baylis distinguishes more sharply between a priori or analytic knowledge and empirical or synthetic knowledge than did the earlier new realists, for whom the laws of logic were interwoven in the constitution of the universe. For Baylis, as for Williams and many others, a priori or analytic knowledge is entirely dependent upon perceived relations among meanings or universals. Thus "*a priori* knowledge is possible because there are meanings which are chooseable, unchangeable, independent of exemplification, and which have relations such as logical inclusion, to other meanings." [25]

Empirical knowledge, which depends both on meanings and on an experiential given is, however, another matter. Here Baylis takes the character of the given to be of crucial importance. If the given is entirely private and without depth it cannot serve as a basis for objective knowledge, and one must use extreme care to avoid presupposing such privacy and lack of depth in any initial definition of the given. An initial account of the requisite sort is indicated by saying that "anything of which we are immediately aware is 'given'." [26] Beginning with such an empirical, noncommittal usage of the term "given," careful inquiry will reveal that the given can "have qualities other than . . . those which are noted," [27] and that we can also "make mistakes about the given." More important, it also shows that sensa are sometimes "three-dimensional" [28] and that

[22] Charles Baylis, "Meanings and Their Exemplification," *Journal of Philosophy*, XXVII (1930), 173; and "Universals, Communicable Knowledge and Metaphysics," *Journal of Philosophy*, XLVIII (1951), 637 ff.

[23] "Meanings and Their Exemplifications," p. 173.

[24] "Universals, Communicable Knowledge and Metaphysics," p. 644.

[25] "Meanings and Their Exemplifications," p. 173.

[26] Baylis, "The Given and Perceptual Knowledge," in *Philosophic Thought in France and the United States* (1950), p. 451.

[27] *Ibid.*

[28] *Ibid.*, pp. 453 ff.

being accordingly capable of solidity they are also sometimes public.[29] The proof of these claims is to be found in direct examination of data and in the application of the process of extrapolation to them. Baylis is thus committed to belief in the existence of "unsensed sensibilia" as basic constituents of knowledge and reality.

All the rest of our empirical knowledge, and in particular our knowledge of causation, is built up by the use of inductive procedures. These procedures establish not merely invariable association but also real connections or what Lewis has called "necessary connections of matters of fact." Such real connections in contrast to accidental associations can be confirmed by refined use of such already established procedures as "Mill's Methods of Agreement, Difference, and Concomitant Variations." [30]

Unlike Williams, Baylis has devoted considerable attention to the problem of truth, which has always been an especially difficult one for new realists. His solution is a complete rejection of every sort of verification theory [31] and an attempt, by using the polar concepts of "characterization" and "exemplification," to establish, within the framework of a basically monistic epistemology, a satisfactory correspondence theory. Defining "facts" as "entities in relation," [32] and treating propositions as strictly analogous to universals, Baylis asserts that "a propositional expression and the proposition it signifies is true of precisely those facts which exemplify it." [33] Such a theory is compatible with monism in that the exemplification and characterization in terms of which it operates are distinctions of aspects rather than existences. At the same time, according to Baylis, the theory avoids both of the two major difficulties attaching to the older correspondence theories. "Both the proposition and its verifying fact . . . are open to observation and examination." And the nature of the correspondence under consideration is sufficiently plain, for "it is specified as the relation of exemplification whose converse is characterization."

7. Comments Concerning American New Realism

In view of the rich variety of detailed suggestions offered by new realists and the limitations upon the space available for the ensuing remarks, we shall have to pass by a great many interesting questions

[29] *Ibid.,* p. 455.
[30] *Ibid.,* p. 459.
[31] "Critical Comments on the 'Symposium on Meaning and Truth,'" *Philoso-*
phy and Phonomenological Research, V (1944), 88 ff.
[32] "Facts, Propositions and Truth," *Mind,* LVII (1948), p. 462.
[33] *Ibid.*

arising out of the views of the new realists and concentrate upon their major theses concerning the issue that was foremost in their thought and in the epistemologies of most philosophers during the first quarter of the century, namely, the issue concerning the relation of cognitive experience and its objects. Presumably the principal task of epistemologists with reference to this issue is, insofar as possible, to give an intelligible account of that relation in accord with the manner in which it is encountered in common-sense and scientific inquiry.

A. If this be so, one may perhaps say that the principal contribution of the new realists to contemporary epistemological thought consists in their effective insistence upon three now relatively noncontroversial claims the current acceptance of which is in considerable part due to the efforts of the new realists themselves. The first is the claim that all cognitive experiences intend objects other than themselves. The second is that it is reasonable to believe that there are such objects. And the third is that such objects are in fact sometimes known. A good deal has already been said in these pages that bears upon these three claims; much more remains to be said. For the present we shall be content to call special attention to a few lines of thought, in most (but not all) instances developed by the new realists themselves, tending to show the essential plausibility of each of these three claims and providing an important point of departure from the idealist views dominant in the last century.

(1) The soundness of the claim that cognitive experiences intend objects independent of themselves, though often obscured by philosophical theories, would seem to be evident almost as soon as the question concerning what such experiences intend is unambiguously raised. To claim to know is to claim to know about something, and even when what one claims to know is itself a sentient experience, the experience said to be known presents itself as distinct from the experience in which it is known. For the most part what cognitive experiences claim to apprehend are not experiences at all but logical or mathematical truths or physical objects or events, and by their very nature neither logical or mathematical truths nor physical objects or events can themselves be just experiences. The force of this intention in cognitive experiences to refer to objects beyond themselves is reflected not only in the character of such experiences and in the structure of our sciences but also in the elementary forms of our language. Thus, for example, when we say that we believe, or take for granted, or know something, we are saying, not that we believe or take for granted or know our believing or taking for granted or knowing experiences, but that we believe, take for

granted, or know some true proposition, fact, or possible fact independent of these attitudes.

(2) The claim that there are independent objects answering to
the referential aspects of our cognitive experiences raises again the
classic controversies about the Kantian thing-in-itself. In the nature
of the case proof concerning the issue is out of the question. But
on the whole the new realists and others who have supported them
seem pretty well to have established at least the reasonableness of
the claim. To begin with, the fact that cognitive experience is
incurably referential is itself a *prima facie* reason for believing in
the existence of independent objects, a reason such as places the
burden of proof entirely on those who deny the existence of independent objects. In the second place, as the new realists have urged,
there is no reason in principle why an object experienced should
have to depend for its existence or its significant characteristics upon
its being experienced, for being experienced is a relation into which
or out of which objects may pass without being affected in any way
that is epistemologically significant. In the third place, the fact that
knowing mind is always present when active cognition occurs implies
nothing whatever about the existence or nonexistence or the character of objects or events in the absence of mind, and candid
recognition of this fact robs the objection to the notion of the independence of the object of most of its force and leaves the natural
force of that notion intact. Finally, it seems clear that we should
scarcely be able to adjust at all satisfactorily to our environment let
alone offer any satisfactory account of our experiences apart from
an assumption of the existence of independent objects, and the most
satisfactory explanation of the fact that the assumption of the
existence of independent objects works as well as it does is that it is
correct.

(3) The claim that independent objects are themselves known is
the most difficult of the three claims now under consideration to
establish. Many philosophers, notably representative realists and
Kantians, believe that cognitive experiences intend objects independent of themselves and that such objects in fact exist, but hold
that cognitive experiences never succeed in apprehending anything
beyond phenomena that *represent* the objects ultimately intended.
The question just *how* knowledge of independent objects can be
achieved will be perhaps the major issue discussed in the five succeeding chapters, but even at this stage it may be worth-while to
indicate some considerations tending to support the claim of new
realists and others *that* such knowledge is attainable. In the first
place, if cognitive experiences always intend objects independent of

themselves and objects answering to these intentions are reasonably believed to exist, these considerations are themselves strong *prima facie* reasons for believing knowledge of objects independent of cognitive experience possible; indeed, a rudimentary knowledge may even be said to have been already attained. In the second place, our cognitive experiences have many reliable features that are evi-dently not contingent upon our purposes and are most plausibly explained as effects of the objects to which our cognitive experiences refer. If such explanations are at all trustworthy they, in conjunc-tion with the experiences they explain and the predictions they facilitate, may be said to constitute at least a kind of knowledge of probabilities concerning independent objects. In the third place, our cognitive experiences are from beginning to end so shot through with assurance that they apprehend independent objects that to deny that these experiences ever apprehend such objects would be not only to render such experiences false but to show them to be basically misguided and even absurd. This latter, few philosophers seriously wish to do, and the common man cannot do. Finally, the language in which we express our cognitive experiences is so per-meated with presuppositions concerning things as actually known that to deny that things ever are known would be not merely legiti-mately to reject some of our statements about what we know as untrue, but to reduce nearly all of our talk about what we know to virtual nonsense, and that too is something that most philosophers and all common men wish to avoid.

B. The most distinctive feature of new realism is much more controversial than the three claims we have been considering. This feature is that combination of realism and epistemological monism in terms of which the new realists attempt to explain *how* inde-pendent objects can be known, or more specifically, their doctrine that in being known the independent object and a cognitive experi-ence become momentarily identical.

Whatever may be the other merits or defects of this doctrine, it represents, on the one hand, a clearer understanding than had ever previously been achieved of the requirement that any satisfactory theory of knowledge be so formulated as to conserve both the inde-pendence of the object and the genuineness of knowledge and, on the other hand, an honest attempt to present a clear reconstruction of the cognitive situation that would achieve these ends. In that it does not altogether succeed, it suffers the fate of most bold philo-sophical hypotheses but, like some other bold hypotheses, it is more instructive even in its failures than some more timid hypotheses are in their successes.

The major weakness of new realism consists in its inability to sustain the doctrine of epistemological monism to which it has attached most of its other epistemological claims. Among the reasons that this docrtine cannot be accepted at face value are the following, some of which will be encountered again in subsequent chapters.

(1) The monistic claim that knowledge consists in the temporary identification of a thing or set of things with a phase of an experience tends to compromise that very idea of the independence of the object of knowledge that the new realists strove so hard in their initial efforts to maintain. Having complained that the idealists' assimilation of objects to experience undermined the independence of objects, the new realists proceeded to assimilate experiences to objects, with surprisingly similar results. Whichever way the assimilation operates, it tends to destroy the integrity of both involved factors. How easy it is to pass from new realism to idealist theses can readily be seen in the new realism of E. B. Holt who, like almost any absolute idealist, takes all objects of knowledge to be universals and indeed adopts a whole system very similar in many ways to that of absolute idealism. No matter how much the new realist writes of the independence of the object, he cannot be quite convincing while making objects and experiences even temporarily identical, or aspects of one another.

(2) In identifying objects and experiences even momentarily, the epistemological monism of the new realists either ignores or insufficiently recognizes certain basic differences between objects and experiences. For example, objects can be pushed, pulled, kicked, cut, looked at, listened to, exploded, and placed side by side; none of these things can be done to experiences. Experiences can be immediately felt and introspectively examined, and these things cannot be done to objects. Objects are open to public inspection, never given all at once, and subject to re-examination by renewed observation. Experiences are private, given all at once, and not subject to re-examination save by being remembered. Objects are confined to a fairly rigid order in time and space; experiences are bound by no such rigidity in these respects.

(3) In regarding experiences as arrangements of objects and, as a corollary, mind, as a continuously developing pattern of objects, new realism adopts a theory of mind that seems to be hopelessly inadequate both to the specific character of minds and to complexity of minds. To begin with, it may be doubted that minds and the physical objects they refer to should be thought of as entities of the same order at all, to say nothing of becoming momentarily identical. Their capacities, their relations to space and time and almost every-

thing else about them seem to be far too different to permit their even being placed on the same logical level, let alone being treated as sometimes identical. But even granting the conceivability of the new realists' account of the intersection of minds and physical objects, the implied account of minds is far too simple to constitute a sufficient description of the character of such mental processes. Not only are intending, remembering, believing, reflecting, predicting, trusting, fearing, hoping, expecting, sympathizing, desiring and wishing highly complex and radically different from the physical objects to which they refer but each has its distinctive features; and no mere arranging of objects, however cleverly conceived, can be adequate to the intricacies and interrelations of such functions of minds.

(4) The most often cited objection to the epistemological monism of the new realists remains one of the most powerful, namely, that the theory cannot be reconciled with certain facts concerning error and illusion. In dreams and hallucinations we seem to see what is not occurring at all. In illusions and double vision we see things differently from the way they are. In all manner of mistaken judgments, we take to be facts what are not facts at all. Since in all such instances there are cognitive experiences closely resembling the cognitive experiences of veridical knowledge and since experiences are, for new realists, patterns of objects, consistent new realists would seem obliged to recognize the existence not only of objects that present themselves in veridical perception and judgment but also of those that seem to present themselves in illusion and even in the wildest fancies. Most new realists accept this odd consequence and offer some special explanation of the objects involved in error, but the explanations are strained and tend to obscure, or even obliterate, an indispensable distinction implicit both in common sense and in science between that which is objectively real and that which is not. To say that erroneous objects are misplaced objects or that errors can be corrected is in any case of little help, for in either case the impossible task remains of finding a suitable locus for erroneous objects. However, if the new realist declines to accept erroneous objects, he seems driven at once toward the dualistic views he opposes.

(5) The attempt to construe the cognitive relation as a momentary identity of objects and experiences is inadequate not only to the central facts of erroneous cognition but also to certain elemental features of veridical cognition. Recent analysis emphasizes the fact that cognition is not confined to active perceptions and judgments and that the term knowledge is most characteristically used of *dis-*

positions to make certain judgments or to behave in certain ways on appropriate occasions. Epistemological monism is inadequate with respect both to active and dispositional cognition. With respect to the first, it fails sufficiently to recognize that whatever arrangements of objects may be involved in cognitive situations, such situations also involve in addition active processes without which their character would be drastically altered so as to be no longer active cognitions, namely such processes as perceiving, judging, and reasoning. With regard to dispositional cognition, it has little to say at all, and one can scarcely see what could be said to account of such cognition in terms of momentary identity of object and experience. A further fact about veridical knowing which those who hold that knowing is a momentary identity of object and experience have never, despite valiant efforts, been able to fit into their system is the fact of the physical, physiological, and cultural indirectness of knowing. Cognitive experiences are mediated through such physical processes as the passage of light, such physiological ones as the functioning of sense organs, nerves, and brains, and such social factors as language and other symbolic forms, and, being so mediated, can scarcely plausibly be held to be numerically or even qualitatively identical with those arrangements of independent objects intended in them. Apparently the new realists, like their opponents, the idealists, were so fearful of the inroads of the skeptic, once the smallest gap between object and experience was allowed, that, like the idealists, they forgot or refused to see that an experience may refer to an object without being that object, but in any case, the union of cognitive experiences and objects that they sought to achieve, however laudable its aims, could not be consummated.

CHAPTER 5

American Critical Realism

AGAINST the idealists' conception of the dependence of the object the new realists pressed their doctrine of the independence of the object, but in their effort to avoid the idealists' criticisms of representative realism, they conceded to the idealists that the idea could be an aspect of the object, and found themselves unable to sustain a clear correspondence theory of truth. It is scarcely surprising that this situation was not acceptable to all realists or that a different kind of realism should have sprung up in protest. Thus *critical realists,* many of whom contributed to the cooperative volume *Essays in Critical Realism,* while supporting the realist doctrine of the independence of the object, replaced the new realists' epistemologically monistic theory of the relation of the object and that by which the object is known with a dualistic account of this relation in terms of which the idea could no longer literally participate in the object and truth could be unambiguously construed as correspondence. In so doing, however, they did not concede to the earlier representative realists that we really know only our own ideas; instead they contended that we know objects themselves *through* our ideas.

Differences among critical realists depend upon what aspect of that through which the object is known is emphasized. Three major types may be distinguished. The first stresses the ideational aspect of the representative ingredient of knowing and is referred to here as "mentalistic critical realism." The second stresses the universals or essences involved in the representative ingredient and is referred to here as "platonistic critical realism." The third stresses the neural or physiological aspect of the representative ingredient and is referred to here as "materialistic critical realism." The work of a significant advocate of each of these three varieties of critical realism will be considered in each of the three succeeding sections of this chapter, and the work of some advocates of certain more or less intermediate varieties of critical realism will be touched upon in the fourth section.

1. The Polemical and Mentalistic Critical Realism of A. O. Lovejoy

The most significant of the critical realists' attacks upon epistemological monism, and one of the clearest formulations of what we have called mentalistic critical realism, is to be found in A. O. Lovejoy's *The Revolt Against Dualism*. Included in Lovejoy's argument are an outline of a natural dualistic realism, an endeavor to show that such a realism is really implicit in the views of its monistic opponents, and a discussion of some problematic aspects of dualistic realism.

A. Lovejoy contends that there is a dualistic realism so natural to man that it is capable of supplying its own evidence, needing only to be freed from the misinterpretations of misguided philosophical friends and from the artificial strictures of philosophical opponents. It is rather through careful examination of the character and implications of this natural realism than through any radical Cartesian doubt that a sound epistemology is to be attained,[1] for we must begin with world and consciousness, not with consciousness alone, if knowledge is ever to get started.

Natural realism must be clearly distinguished from the dualistic representative realism of such seventeenth- and eighteenth-century writers as Descartes and Locke. This earlier realism ambiguously places *sense-data* "in the mind," and erroneously denies that they have extension. Moreover, it fails properly to distinguish "between the terms 'sensation,' 'perception' and 'thought' as signifying the event, function or act of sensing, perceiving, thinking, etc., and the same terms as signifying the items sensed, perceived or thought." [2] For these reasons the earlier representative realism is obliged to make the gap between idea and object so wide as to be virtually unbridgeable, and so must renounce any claim to be a natural epistemology. But natural realism is also to be distinguished from contemporary new realism, in which there is no distinct break at all between idea and thing, in that this monistic realism fails alto-

---

[1] A. O. Lovejoy, *The Revolt Against Dualism* (La Salle, Ill.: The Open Court Publishing Co., 1930), pp. 16 f.

[2] *Ibid.*, p. 6.

gether to do justice to that duality that common sense finds in the knowing process.

The kind of realism that Lovejoy wishes to present in contrast both to monistic realism and to seventeenth-century dualistic realism has its origin in five assumptions that "men naturally make" with reference to "things-to-be-known-if-possible": [3] (1) some of the things to be known are "at places in space external to the body of the percipient," (2) many of them are "things that are not, because they are by-gone or have not yet come into being," (3) some of them are "as they would be if unknown," (4) one's apprehension of things to be known includes "experience of others of his kind," and (5) one's apprehension of things to be known is "capable of verification in experience other than the one experience in which, at a given moment, they are in some sense before him." Such a natural realism involves not merely a dualistic reference from one part of experience to another, but "an existential distinctness of datum and cognoscendum" or object.[4]

Substantial grounds for insisting upon a basic duality of sense-datum and object are readily to be found by reference to certain aspects of experience in which apparently "the object of our knowing must be different in time, place or mode of existence, or in its character, from the perceptual or other content which is present to us at the moment when we are commonly said to be apprehending that object, and without which we should never apprehend it at all." [5] The grounds in question are as follows: [6] (1) "Intertemporal cognition, the knowing at one time of things which exist or events which occur at another time, seems a patent example of a mode of knowledge which we are under the necessity of regarding as potentially genuine and yet as mediate." (2) "The temporal sundering, and therefore existential duality of the content given and the reality made known through that content" is everywhere apparent in the physical lag in the transmission of the impulses on which sensation depends. (3) "The qualities sensibly presented vary with changes which appear to occur, not in the place where *the* object is supposed to exist, but in regions between it and the body itself, and, in particular, in the very organs of perception." (4) "While many knowers are . . . dealing with what is said to be one and the same object . . . they notoriously are not experiencing the same sensible appearances." (5) "The experience of error and illusion . . . seems to have at least one direct and obvious implication: namely, that the thing which at any moment we err about . . . cannot be a thing

[3] *Ibid.,* pp. 12–15.
[4] *Ibid.,* p. 16.
[5] *Ibid.,* p. 17.
[6] *Ibid.,* pp. 17–24.

which is immediately present to us at that moment, since about the latter there can be no error." [7]

Recognition of such considerations as these seems to Lovejoy to be sufficient to establish an epistemological dualism in which datum and object differ, but the natural realism which he wishes to defend includes also a psychophysical dualism in which the datum is mental even when the object is physical. While these two dualisms have no necessary connection and the supposition that they have has led to many irrelevant attempts to refute the one by disproving the other, they are related in an important respect. The discovery that men sooner or later almost invariably make, that perceptual and other data cannot be fitted into the physical order of things, requires that such data be placed somewhere else, and psychophysical dualism provides the natural locus in its psychical side.

But what is it about the physical that prevents the psychical from finding a place in it? The following are the distinctive marks of the physical: "(1) It is spatial as well as temporal; (2) some or all parts of it continue to exist during the interperceptual intervals of any and all percipients, and no part belongs to it solely by virtue of the occurrence of a perception; (3) the extended things, or groups of characters, existing in it go through that sort of uniformly correlated change usually called causal interaction, the laws of these inter-actions being in some degree determinable; (4) these causal processes continue their regular sequences when not attended to by any per-cipient; (5) this order is a common factor in or behind the expe-rience of all percipients." [8] These are plainly not characteristics that the sense-data have or can have, and therefore natural realism has always been compelled to assign to sense-data some sort of non-physical status.

B. We turn now from Lovejoy's constructive account of natural dualistic realism to his refutation of those monistic theories in which he finds a misguided "revolt against dualism." Lovejoy divides the monistic revolt against dualism into three phases, and his answer to opponents in each phase consists of an effort to show that the theories concerned either presuppose dualism or are nonsense. Before con-sidering his treatment of the first two opposing theories, however, we pause to say a word about his attitude toward absolute idealism, which involves an older and different kind of monism.

In brief Lovejoy holds that absolute idealism is ruled out on the following counts. In the first place, idealism in general rejects that physical world which common sense and philosophical analysis both

---

[7] *Ibid.,* p. 23.
[8] *The Revolt Against Dualism* (La Salle, Ill.: Open Court Publishing Co., 1930),

p. 27. Reproduced by permission of the publisher.

require. In the second place, absolute idealism in particular attempts, in self-contradictory fashion, to disclose in the same experiences both temporality and eternity, and is in any case for the most part irrelevant to the issues of the finite universe.[9] But in the third place, even if the central theses of idealism were sound, they would in the end lead to some kind of natural dualism, for even idealism acknowledges the validity of meaning, which in turn implies a distinction between object and mental content.

The earliest phase of current monistic realism's revolt against dualism consisted in the attempts of James's "Does Consciousness Exist?" and G. E. Moore's "Refutation of Idealism" to discount the role of consciousness in knowing. The one attempted to show that consciousness was either nonexistent or an estate of "pure diaphaneity," and the other, to show that consciousness is entirely distinct from and without effect upon that which is before it. But these attempts were, from the point of view of the essential features of dualism, almost completely misdirected. They were effective only against the earlier Cartesian and Lockean dualism which confused experiencing and the experienced.[10] When it is clear that the real issue does not concern the relation of consciousness or experiencing to the object in experience but rather that of sense-data to thing, the "independence" of immediate data versus their identity with parts of the "physical world," it is evident that the issue can never be settled merely by examination of consciousness but requires criteria of the physical and comparison of sense-data with these criteria.[11]

The second phase of monistic realism's attack upon dualistic realism, the first really significant phase, consisted of attempts by American new realists and others to overthrow dualism to establish an impregnable panobjectivism in which nothing is mind-generated and everything is quite independent of cognitive activity. Lovejoy's refutation of this phase involves rebuttal of three major objections to dualism, the rejection of a positive argument for panobjectivism, and the presentation of two fatal objections to epistemological monism.

One group of the arguments of the second phase of the monistic attack upon dualism is, like those of the earlier phase, irrelevant in refuting positions that no epistemological dualist ever should have held. Such arguments include for example the contention of Holt

[9] A. O. Lovejoy, "A Temporalistic Realism," in G. P. Adams and W. P. Montague, *Contemporary American Philosophy* (London & New York: George Allen & Unwin, & The Macmillan Co., 1930), II, pp. 91 f.; see also *The Revolt Against Dualism*, pp. 30 ff.
[10] *Ibid.*, pp. 7 ff.
[11] *Ibid.*, p. 10.

and others that it is a mistake to say that sense-data have no qualities,[12] the claim of Woodbridge and others that mind does not consist of qualities only,[13] and the claim of most new realists that mental contents are not parts of the subject as such.[14]

Other monistic arguments of the second phase are more pertinent but incapable of being carried through. These include for example the contention that a camera can do the essential part of what mind is alleged to do in perception, an argument which ignores the fact that a camera cannot, like a mind, project the object back without the use of light waves into the place from which it is supposed to have come. Also included are various unsuccessful attempts to show how all illusions could be explained in terms of physical laws. The effort to exclude dualistic realism in terms of the analogy of the meeting lines on a single point, ignore the fact that the real issue is not whether the coalescence of two things is ever possible but whether the two things in question in knowing are sufficiently compatible for such coalescence to occur.[15]

A third group of arguments of the second phase of the current revolt against dualism is more telling than either of the others but still ineffective. One such argument is that sense-data may be only *instruments* through which knowing can take place. Such in fact they may be, but the crucial question is whether or not they *are*, and they never do seem to be. Another argument of this group accuses dualistic realism of the fallacy of "transcendent implication," but then it is difficult to see how one can be a realist at all and not believe that the object in some sense transcends the knowing of it.[16] Even the monistic claim that the dualist cannot know the copy that lies behind the thing need not disturb the dualist if he keeps the grounds of his claims clearly before him. Finally, the monistic suggestion that epistemological dualism, having once degenerated into phenomenalism, is sure to do so again, also turns out to be impotent, for that "physical realism is incompatible with the hypothesis of the immediacy of knowledge" is not answered by saying that this "places realism itself in a perilous position." [17]

The attempt of some panobjectivists to substantiate their positive thesis by transforming most of what were formerly considered to be mental contents into subsistent entities is interesting and ingenious but completely fails to accomplish its end. Certainly no such attempt can be reconciled with the claim of the new realists to be a naïve realism.[18] When, on the one hand, the subsistence theory is so

---

[12] *Ibid.*, p. 39.
[13] *Ibid.*, p. 38.
[14] *Ibid.*, p. 39.
[15] *Ibid.*, pp. 45 ff.

[16] *Ibid.*, pp. 49 f.
[17] *Ibid.*, p. 54.
[18] *Ibid.*, p. 56.

interpreted as to make the universe mathematical, its extravagant Platonism yields an unwarranted and even absurd elimination of the physical world,[19] but when, on the other hand, it is so interpreted that the fully real is spatiotemporal, a fundamental dualism remains. In any case, even if the subsistent as such is objective and independent of mind, the psychological existence of the subsistent has to be explained, and this may still be "dependent upon the occurrence of a percipient act and limited to the time during which, and the context in which the percept is by an individual being experienced." [20]

Whatever arguments may be set forth in favor of epistemological monism, at least two insuperable difficulties remain as permanent barriers to the acceptance of such monism. One is the finite velocity of light. If it be acknowledged that time is consumed in the passage of light from the place of the object to that of the percipient, then the object and the percept cannot but be numerically distinct, and any alternative to this acknowledgment leads to impossible paradoxes.[21] The other insurmountable obstacle is the existence of illusions and errors, which epistemological monism remains unable to explain. It is difficult to believe that those who say that illusions and errors are merely displacements really mean what they say, and those who do really mean this sort of thing, create a mass of confused entities that spoils any prospect of maintaining order in science.[22]

Since Lovejoy's refutation of the third and final phase of the revolt against dualism deals almost exclusively with types of thought which we have yet to consider, we shall for the most part pass it by here. However, one phase of this refutation is especially significant in revealing Lovejoy's relation both to monistic realists and other dualistic realists, namely, his contention that whether or not qualities can be universals, they cannot enter into either sensations or objective facts without being dated and so losing their eternal character. Hence, whatever eternal essential status qualities may possess, they are particulars in the aspects that concern knowing, and this being true, they must, as data, be mental if the universe is not to be hopelessly confused.

C. If, as man cannot help believing, there is knowledge of a real and independent physical world; and if, as has been shown, all plausible attempts to account for this knowledge without recognizing a dualism of physical world and psychical ideas fail, the essential correctness of the epistemological and psychophysical dualism of natural realism would seem to be sufficiently established.[23]

[19] *Ibid.*, p. 58.
[20] *Ibid.*, p. 60.
[21] *Ibid.*, pp. 62 ff.
[22] *Ibid.*, pp. 70 ff.
[23] *Ibid.*, pp. 257 ff.

Nevertheless, two special questions that are repeatedly directed to dualistic realism require further consideration. One is this: Must belief in the reality of the physical world remain simply a conviction natural to man but unsupportable by argument, and if not, what grounds support it? The other is the question whether or not the sort of representational knowledge involved in dualism is really possible, and if so, why.

Lovejoy begins with the question about the physical world. Through the centuries scientific and philosophical inquiry has increasingly and almost uninterruptedly led to belief in a world "independent and common, i.e., not variant with diversities of its relations to various percipients, . . . operative in a universal causal order," and distinct from "a great part of visual, auditory, and other content." [24] The major ground of this belief is not, however, "the assumed necessity of postulating external causal objects to account for our percepts." [25] An even stronger ground is an irrepressible belief in the continuity and interconnected order of things of which what is perceived is only a part, a conviction of *the persistence of something which is in some manner connected with what is perceived, during the interperceptual intervals.*" [26] This belief is no mere "blank act of faith." Rather, it represents the simplest, most intelligent hypothesis that can be offered in explanation of what is in fact perceived. In comparison with this, such an alternative as the phenomenalists' claim that things happen only *as if* there were a real world, are "plainly arbitrary and far-fetched; they multiply types of causal agency beyond necessity." [27] Moreover, the claim that other hypotheses may explain the facts equally well, overlooks the fact that the hypothesis that there are real objects is not one suddenly adopted as a whole but rather one that has been built up a little at a time out of a vast amount of mutually confirmatory evidence; the spaces and times and total experiences of multitudes of people over many centuries have been put together in the common world of science.

This world is not, of course, as naïve realists suppose, a world of color and sounds and other secondary qualities, for there are ample evidences of "concomitant variation of sense-data with differences in the perceptible natures or states of the percipients." [28] But it is a world in which there is in the object that which causes the sense-data of secondary qualities and in which "extension, shape, relative positions, temporal succession, and motion" are reliable guides to

[24] *Ibid.,* p. 263.
[25] *Ibid.,* p. 267.
[26] *Ibid.,* p. 268.

[27] *Ibid.,* p. 269.
[28] *Ibid.,* pp. 269 f.

the actual frame of the physical world. Moreover, recent science discloses nothing contrary to this realistic claim. The phases of modern science that have been used in support of subjectivity, such as the relativity principle, the persistence of contrasting undulatory and corpuscular theories or light, and the Heisenberg principle of uncertainty, are not literal or final descriptions of the physical universe but simply ways of helping us to do our cosmic bookkeeping in a physical universe involving much of which we are still ignorant.[29]

Turning now to the second question, the often reiterated difficulty in mediate or representational knowledge is this: being mediate, such knowledge seems to imply that the *thing* is not directly known, but being knowledge and requiring a basis of comparison of thing and representation, such knowledge seems also to imply, in self-contradictory fashion, that the thing is directly known.[30] In short, mediate knowledge seems to imply that the object both is not and is before the mind. Actually, no such absurd implication is involved in mediate knowledge, as reflection upon the temporal situation readily reveals. One can apprehend yesterday today. In doing so, while the pattern of yesterday's experience is in today's, yesterday's experience itself is not. In remembering, what is before the mind is not the past *"in propria persona"* but only "a particular concrete datum . . . and the conception of a mode of relatedness." [31] Knowledge of physical objects is a fact of the same order as knowledge of the past to the extent that in both we refer data to a date different from that in which the data occur. In knowing physical objects we not only project into the present data furnished by events already past, but we also ascribe to objects spatial characteristics different from the data and an existence that is not reducible to data at all. But the referential process involved in all this differs in no essential respect from the referential process involved in memory, and the one process is no more paradoxical than the other.

In the light of the foregoing considerations it is possible to indicate "the distinctive character and the role of knowledge in the economy of nature. Essentially, knowing is a phenomenon in which the simple location of things is circumvented without being annulled." [32] It is a way in which things "get reported" at places at which they do not actually exist. For this getting reported at such places, physiological and sensory functions are required; but in addition to these, "two further functions are required: (a) a power to conceive of some realm or order of interrelated existents which includes but extends beyond the organism itself and the sense and images which are

[29] *Ibid.*, pp. 277 ff.   [31] *Ibid.*, p. 312.
[30] *Ibid.*, pp. 309 ff.   [32] *Ibid.*, p. 315.

immediately present to it; and (b) a propensity of the organism to think some of the characters of the immediately given as actually or potentially belonging to external situations in that order." [33] Knowledge of the physical world is thus in part faith, but it is rational faith; it is in part instinctive but it is "capable of extensive modification and control through experience and reflection." [34]

2. THE PLATONISTIC CRITICAL REALISM OF GEORGE SANTAYANA

The most comprehensive positive formulation of the principles of critical realism that has yet appeared is the one presented in *Skepticism and Animal Faith, Realms of Being,* and various essays by George Santayana (1863–1952). The aspect of the mediating ingredients in knowing that Santayana emphasizes is not their being partially produced by mental activity, but their exemplifying eternal essences.

Unlike Lovejoy, Santayana begins with a skepticism far more radical than the Cartesian doubt that Lovejoy thinks already too radical. In the framework of such skepticism Santayana proceeds to examine the essences that even the most radical skeptics must acknowledge. He also traces successive steps in which knowing may go beyond skepticism and delineates the character of the knowing relation. Finally, he deals at length with the problem, somewhat neglected by Lovejoy, of the nature of truth. Accordingly, we shall consider successively Santayana's accounts of skepticism, essences, the knowing process, the relation of knowing and the known, and truth.

A. Radical skepticism neither helps nor interests the common man,[1] but constitutes an indispensable instrument of the philosopher's effort to avoid illusion.[2] Though often attempted, it is rarely and only with difficulty achieved. Those who suppose with Descartes that a solipsism of an enduring self remaining when the material world is ruled out is the limit of skepticism are seriously mistaken.[3] With the elimination of the material world, memory and expectation as well as self-consciousness itself become groundless and must also be excluded. Indeed even change, presumably the most indubitable of facts, fails at times to be represented in experience and

---

[33] *Ibid.,* p. 319.
[34] *Ibid.*
[1] George Santayana, *Realms of Being* (New York: Charles Scribner's Sons, 1942), p. 25.

[2] Santayana, *Skepticism and Animal Faith* (New York: Charles Scribner's Sons, 1923), pp. 10, 72.
[3] *Ibid.,* pp. 13 ff.

must, as the mystics remind us, also be called in question.[4] Only the data of experience remain.

But these data, when properly distinguished from the intuitions in which they are given, are seen to have no existence. To be sure, like everything mentionable, including illusions, they have *being* or reality,[5] but existence, in the nature of the case, they cannot have. The reason is this: "Existence involves external relations and actual . . . flux whereas, however complex a datum may be it must be embraced in a single apperception." [6] An existence can change, be obliterated, or be placed in a different context, but a datum "can neither suffer mutation nor acquire new relations." [7] A datum is by definition an appearance, but it does not imply a substance that appears,[8] and if it is assumed to have existence, it no longer has the luminosity of an appearance. What does exist in connection with the datum is its occurrence or the *intuition* in which it is present. The sense of existence connected with this intuition is often surreptitiously transferred to the datum itself; but when memory and expectation are ruled out, the grounds for any such transfer vanish. With the removal of belief in the *existence* of immediate data, and then only, skepticism attains completion.

This complete skepticism—difficult both to attain and to abandon —affords a rare vantage point from which one may survey constructive epistemological possibilities; and constructive epistemology must be one's objective, for to rest in an unmitigated skepticism is a hypocritical betrayal of a human nature that commits us to inevitable quest for knowledge. This quest follows certain natural steps that lead, if not to certain knowledge, at least to reasonable belief.

B. The immediate data to which skepticism is driven back, together with all else that is intuitable, whether actually intuited or not, constitute the realm of essence. All those characteristics, forms, or qualities that experience apprehends, or could conceivably apprehend, are essences, but essences need not be apprehended at all, and when they are, they should not be thought of as parts or qualities of things.[9] The ideal types and geometrical forms constituting Plato's ideas are essences but so also are "all the qualities of sensation" and "all types of change or relation." All such comparatively simple qualities as specific shades of blue are essences, and so also are the enormously complicated patterns of quality and form required to describe any particular existing or nonexisting thing. In a word "anything that might be found, every quality of being" is an

[4] *Ibid.*, p. 27.
[5] *Ibid.*, p. 33.
[6] *Ibid.*, p. 34.

[7] *Ibid.*, p. 48.
[8] *Ibid.*, p. 39.
[9] *Realms of Being*, pp. 18, 25, 43.

essence.[10] Essences are perfectly clear and transparent, all upon the surface like clothes without persons inside them.[11] About them "I cannot be mistaken." [12] An essence is an "aspect which anything can wear, determining its nature and revealing it to an attentive mind." [13] Essences are universals in the sense that they need not figure in any particular place or time, may be encountered over and over again, and are easily recovered when lost sight of.[14] But this does not prevent their being completely individual and concrete. Although essences "may be considered recurrently, on separate occasions and by separate minds," no essence may be repeated. For "two essences, if not different will be one essence; if different they will be two essences and not repetitions of the same essence." An essence is eternal, not in the sense that it endures through time, but in the sense that it is "the quality which it inherently, logically, and inalienably is." [15] The eternity of essence "has nothing to do with . . . mortal hazards. It is merely the self-identity proper to each of the forms which existence may put on or off, illustrate somewhere or perhaps illustrate always, or very likely never illustrate at all." [16]

Although essences do not exist, they are encountered in existence in two ways. On the one hand, they may be either intuited or, as often happens in practical experience, merely intended. They may even come to be in terms of possibility of entering experience, as that which may be directly given. On the other hand they may be enacted in physical objects and events. In such cases their embodiments are perfect. Even the essences of complex objects are just the essences of these objects and not mere combinations of the essences of the constituents of these objects. It is the exemplification of essences in things that gives meaning to the notion of change, for while an essence never changes, things may exchange some essences for others.[17] Thus, "essence is just that character which any existence means insofar as it remains identical with itself and so long as it does so; the very character which it throws overboard by changing, and loses altogether when it becomes something else." [18]

But whether or not essences are experienced or exemplified in things, they always retain their own independence and have no existence or influence upon that which they enter. No essence is a mere idea,[19] but no essence by receiving the "local and temporary"

[10] *Skepticism and Animal Faith*, p. 78.
[11] *Ibid.*, pp. 70 ff.
[12] *Ibid.*, p. 74.
[13] *Realms of Being*, p. 40.
[14] *Ibid.*, p. 42.
[15] *Skepticism and Animal Faith*, p. 74.
[16] *Realms of Being*, p. 25.
[17] *Ibid.*, p. 5.
[18] *Ibid.*, p. 23.
[19] *Ibid.*, p. 40.

realization of embodiment in a thing ceases to be part of the "different and non-existent realm" [20] of eternal essence. Plato was right in recognizing essences but wrong in supposing they existed or could alter the actual world. An essence is purely passive, "an inert theme, something which cannot bring itself forward." It neither chooses anything nor affects what chooses it. It enters reality only as men and things select it. "There accordingly it stands waiting to be embodied or noticed, if nature or attention ever choose to halt at that point or to traverse it." [21]

Although men and things select the essences that are exemplified in existence, the realm of essence itself gives no preferential status to any of its members and the choice is from its standpoint entirely arbitrary. Essence has no family tree. No basis of logic excludes one essence in favor of another. Inconsistent essences such as those of round squares and the like may subsist and be entertained quite as well as consistent essences, for the former may easily be essences of those confused oscillations of thought that we call contradictions.[22] No goodness or beauty affords any basis for preference, for "these chosen types are surrounded in the realm of essence by every monster, every unexamined being, and every vice; no more vicious there, no more anomalous or monstrous than any other nature." [23]

C. Apprehension of essences as such, however delightful, leaves us in complete ignorance of the actual world.[24] The steps by which this ignorance is overcome are, in their evidential order, as follows.

(1) Although, in order of occurrence, recognition of requirements of action precedes recognition of the existence of intuitions, the latter takes precedence in the order of evidence. "The first existence, then, of which a skeptic who finds himself in the presence of random essences may gather reasonable proof is the existence of the intuition to which those essences are manifest." [25] The existence of intuitions of essences in no way alters the basically nonexistential status of essences as such, for an intuition is "an utterly different thing from the essence intuited;" [26] but recognition of intuitions is apprehension of a mode of *existence,* the only mode in which essences appear or in which we choose or make "arbitrary assault" upon them.[27]

(2) A step beyond recognition of the existence of intuition—one that in fact often occurs even prior to such recognition—is belief in identity and duration. Such belief, innocent as it apparently is,

[20] *Ibid.,* p. 22.
[21] *Ibid.,* p. 19.
[22] *Ibid.,* p. 27 f.
[23] *Skepticism and Animal Faith,* p. 80.
[24] *Ibid.,* p. 110.
[25] *Ibid.,* p. 133.
[26] *Ibid.,* p. 130.
[27] *Ibid.,* p. 132.

involves a very substantial advance beyond the sheer skepticism of merely beholding essences, for it presupposes not only belief that something can be the same as itself but also belief in time and the ability of thought to traverse time.[28]

(3) Since none of the essences which intuition encounters is likely to be simple, the identification of essences would seem in most instances to require something more than intuition, namely some facility "in identifying terms in isolation with the same terms in relation." [29] Such identifying takes place in discourse or dialectic, and marks a further advance over sheer skepticism. That such a process exists is evident, not only in the fact that we are constantly engaged in it and repeatedly confronted in logical and mathematical systems with its results, but also in the existence of error. Neither pure essence nor fact can by itself be defective, and a special realm of discourse must for this reason, if for no other, be posited as a locus for our mistakes.

Dialectic, as "an analysis or construction of ideal forms which . . . traces . . . the inherent patterns or logical relations of . . . forms as intuition reveals them . . . ," is the basis of all logic and mathematics. Since valid logical and mathematical formulae represent only what is already implicit in meanings or essences, they are fully necessary. They are also, over the whole realm of essence, definite in that "their nature and their eternal intrinsic relations to other comparable natures are perfectly determinate." [30] This means that dialecticians are in effect "exploring" the realm of essence,[31] and that insofar as they are successful, various explorers "will help to fill in the same map, and the science of essence, in that region, will be enriched and consolidated." [32]

The applicability of dialectic is, however, far more limited than is commonly supposed. As we have previously observed, the realm of essence contains no basis of logical preference and is infinite. Accordingly, no science of essence can ever indicate where, with regard to matters of fact, one should start or which of the many possible turns at each point one should take. If indeed we do make profitable beginnings and choose suitable turns, it is really under the guidance of matter rather than sheer logic. Only after the essences exemplified in facts are apprehended can logical analysis relate these complex essences to the constituent essences.[33] The most that can be expected of applied dialectic is that if "any essence falls within the sphere of truth, all its essential relations do so too" and

---

[28] *Ibid.*, p. 72.
[29] *Ibid.*, p. 119.
[30] *Realms of Being*, p. 5.

[31] *Ibid.*, p. 4.
[32] *Ibid.*, p. 408.
[33] Cf. *Realms of Being*, p. 85.

thereby form "a complement to a proposition that happens to be true." [34]

(4) The remaining steps beyond skepticism need be only mentioned here since we shall have subsequent occasion to refer to most of them in another connection. Events that involve at least mild shock or surprise tend to interrupt discourse and thus to make one aware of that fact of *experience* of which discourse is a part.[35] But experience on the human level does not exist entirely unorganized, and its basic character soon leads to the recognition of a *self* which is able to say "that I existed before, that I am a principle of steady life, welcoming or rejecting events, that I am a nucleus of active interests and passions." [36] Memory is a special aspect of experience, the acknowledgement of which evidently involves a significant transitive element.[37] Recognition of self is prior to that of matter in the evidential order though not in the chronological one. Truth and spirit are higher realms, the evidence for which is somewhat more subtle than the evidence for matter and essence, although these higher realms are encountered whenever there is fact and awareness.

D. From Santayana's account of the principal steps from skepticism to knowledge, we turn to his account of the known, the knower, and the cognitive relation.

The object that is known is not, as the seventeenth-century realists supposed, a mere idea, for the known in order to be a known must lie outside the act or state of mind by which it is apprehended. Basic to all knowing is the presupposition that "there is some real object or event to be known or reported, prior or subsequent to the report that reaches us." [38]

The object of knowledge is always a substance or "a thing or event subsisting in its own plane, and waiting for the light of knowledge to explore it." As a substance, it *"has parts . . . external to one another, . . . is unequally distributed,* [and] *. . . composes a relative cosmos."* [39] Substance *"sometimes takes the form of animals in whom there are feelings, images and thoughts."* [40] It remains continuous in quantity, and is *"predetermined in its place and quality"* by its antecedents.[41] It may include intuitions and whatever else exists. [42] But primarily it is material substance, for all mental or spiritual phenomena are merely modes of manifestation of matter; and matter is the dynamic flowing matrix of all that does not merely subsist but exists.[43]

[34] *Ibid.*, p. 409.
[35] *Ibid.*, chap. xv.
[36] *Ibid.*, p. 149.
[37] *Ibid.*, chap. xvii.
[38] *Realms of Being*, p. 831.
[39] *Ibid.*, pp. 202 f.
[40] *Ibid.*, p. 233.
[41] *Ibid.*, pp. 233 ff.
[42] *Ibid.*, p. 205.
[43] *Ibid.*, p. 234.

The substances that are the objects of knowledge must of course have form, and accordingly embody certain patterns of essence. They are never, however, *composed* of essences. Nor do they, strictly speaking, even "have" those qualities which the observer seems to see in them, though they may be loosely said to have these qualities relative to the observer.[44] The primary qualities that we seem to see are no more in the substance than are secondary ones.[45] In attempting to identify objects with their perceived qualities the new realists fail to do justice either to brute material fact or to the meanderings of mental images.[46] The knowing mind is not a separate kind of entity but a special organization of matter, characterized by what Santayana calls *tropes,* and functioning in a way that he calls spiritual. "The essence of any event, as distinguished from that event itself," is a *trope;*[47] and a psyche is "a system of tropes, inherited or acquired, displayed by living bodies in their growth and behavior, the specific form of physical life, present and potential, asserting itself in any plant or animal."[48] It is these special phases of matter confronting other matter under favorable circumstances that give rise to knowledge. But knowledge as such is not, as some new realists would have us believe, a mere state of the psyche. When the psyche undertakes to trace things out it gives rise to that pure but ineffectual illumination known as spirit or consciousness. It is in the consciousness produced by the psyche, but itself spiritual, that knowing takes place. Only when there is "the actual light of consciousness falling upon anything"[49] can there be that reaching beyond the here and now that is knowing; however the functional base always remains an organic process. "Consciousness is a spiritual synthesis of organic movements; and were it not this, no spirit and no consciousness would ever have any transcendent significance."[50]

If the knower is then spirit in conjunction with an animal psyche, what is the character of the relation by which such a knower apprehends substantial objects? From the outset it must be clear that this relation cannot be that of intuition, for knowing is a transitive relation and nothing given exists or is substance. Knowing is not, as common sense commonly takes it to be, the passage of essence from thing to minds; for, being universals, essences can never be so transmitted. Knowing is no mere copying nor even resemblance; for "discourse is language and not a mirror,"[51] and there is no

[44] *Ibid.,* p. 44.

[45] *Skepticism and Animal Faith,* pp. 82 ff.

[46] Cf. Santayana, "The Coming Philosophy," *Journal of Philosophy,* XI (1914), 449–63.

[47] *Ibid.,* p. 293.

[48] *Ibid.,* p. 331.

[49] *Ibid.*

[50] *Ibid.,* p. 349.

[51] *Skepticism and Animal Faith,* p. 179.

evidence that copying exists or that, even if it did, it would be of any use.

Knowing rests rather upon the psyche's imaginative reconstruction under favorable circumstances, its choice of essences in the realm of spirit. The psyche must invent or work up, without visible or other precise patterns by which to work, configurations of essence appropriate to that which it encounters, for "the essences given in intuition are fetched from no original." [52] Knowing is therefore at best symbolical and almost never literal. The psyche produces symbols that are appropriate to that which it encounters in view of the demands of action, and it is primarily in terms of these practical representations that knowing takes place. To demand more literal or directly intuitive knowledge is to mistake the nature of knowledge and invite hopeless skepticism.[53] Science is as much limited to symbolic knowing as is common sense, and differs from the latter for the most part only in being more systematic and thorough.[54] The best that one can possibly hope to do is to surround the object with appropriate symbols and then, perhaps by a fortunate sympathetic imagination that nevertheless remains uncertain, to apprehend the essence of the object as one sometimes ascertains the thoughts of other minds.[55]

The symbolic character of knowledge of course leads to the question of the evidence that supports our knowledge of substantial objects. How do we know that there is substance behind our symbols or that the symbols appropriately represent the substances? The answer is to be found neither in intuition nor in logical inference nor even, as many would suppose, in probable inference.[56] It is rather to be found in an *animal faith* that, though natural and unavoidable, can never be proved or even rendered strictly probable. All attempted proofs concerning substances depend upon such faith, and even probability depends upon belief in the fruits of such faith.[57]

Animal faith is not, however, completely blind, and acceptance of it, far from being unreasonable, rests upon grounds that, though scarcely rigorously implicative, are quite reasonable. Animal faith is indeed a kind of "rational instinct or instinctive reason." Its demands are "irresistible" [58] and the attempt to rule them out is itself an "affectation of disbelief where life and action render belief inevitable and perpetually renew it." [59]

[52] *Ibid.*, p. 86.
[53] Santayana, *Obiter Scripta* (New York: Charles Scribner's Sons, 1936), pp. 108 ff.
[54] *Realms of Being*, pp. 829, 241.
[55] *Skepticism and Animal Faith*, pp. 106 f.
[56] *Realms of Being*, p. 303.
[57] *Skepticism and Animal Faith*, pp. 308 f.
[58] *Realms of Being*, p. 453.
[59] *Ibid.*, p. 831.

That behind our symbols there is substance is indicated in many ways. Such grounding of our symbols in substance is indicated by the very existence of a claim to know.[60] An ego must exist before being posited and so must a world; experience implies both. "Experience at its very inception, is a revelation of things." [61] "To grope, to blink, to dodge a blow or return it" [62] is perhaps to feel substance without specific sense-data. Even phenomenalists recognize transitive substance in intuition, memory, and the mind; and if they allow this much transcendence, why should they balk at the further admission of other substances? [63] Even apprehended essences imply transitivity, and surely if one accepts this fact, there should be no objection to a substance transcending all experience.[64]

That our symbols not only refer to substances, but do so with a degree of accuracy appropriate to their purpose is also not difficult to see. The baby points to the moon, and to see that he and some other observer point to the same object requires only a little elementary triangulation.[65] If the symbols of knowing were not suitable, most knowers would long since have ceased to be. "The mind affords a true expression of the world, rendered in vital perspectives and in human terms, since this mind arises and changes symptomatically at certain foci of animal life, foci which are a part of nature in dynamic correspondence with other parts, diffused widely about them." [66] Moreover, "ideas apply to their occasions because they arise out of them, mark them, and are a part of the total natural event which controls their development." [67] The same stimuli set events in motion and also cause our intuitions.

E. Although truth, like essence, is completely devoid of existence, it is in its own realm as completely objective as essence. Truth as such is never relative to what any individual may think. It is never merely partial or transient or dependent on persons or spirits. It is not even a matter of correct opinion; for opinions are dated as truth is not, and when opinions are true or false they owe this to their "repeating or contradicting some part of the truth about the facts which they envisage." [68] Apprehension of the nature of truth can be readily achieved, and denial of the possibility of truth rests for the most part on confusion between truth and knowledge. Thus,

[60] *Skepticism and Animal Faith*, p. 185.
[61] *Ibid.*, p. 189.
[62] *Ibid.*, p. 190.
[63] *Ibid.*, pp. 183 ff. See also Santayana, "Three Proofs of Realism," in Durant Drake and Others, *Essays in Critical Realism* (New York: Henry Holt & Co., Inc., 1921, pp. 173 ff.

[64] *Ibid.*, pp. 178 ff.
[65] See *Essays in Critical Realism*, pp. 169 ff.; *Skepticism and Animal Faith*, pp. 172 ff.
[66] *Skepticism and Animal Faith*, p. 98.
[67] *Realms of Being*, p. 242.
[68] *Ibid.*, pp. 403 f.

"we join mankind in positing a comprehensive and inviolate truth hanging above us, and making our falsehoods false and our truths true." [69]

As substance consists of active events and essence of passive characteristics, truth is "a luminous shadow or penumbra which substance, by its existence and movements, casts on the field of essence."[70] In other terms it is "that segment of the realm of essence which happens to be illustrated in existence" [71] or "the whole ideal system of qualities and relations which the world has exemplified or will exemplify." [72] Perhaps a better definition is that truth is "the standard comprehensive description of any fact" [73] in all its relations. In speaking of such description, it should be remembered that what is meant is not simply "the essence of any fact present within the limits of time and space which that fact occupies" but also "all the radiations of that fact . . . all that perspective of the world of facts and of the realm of essence which is obtained by taking this fact as a center and viewing everything else only in relation with it." [74] Thus, truth may appropriately be said to be "what omniscience would assert." [75]

Truth is an absolute eternal whole in the sense that "truth displays the whole eternal labyrinth of real relations;" [76] and in the sense that "if views can be more or less correct and complementary to one another, it is because they refer to the same system of nature, the complete description of which, covering the whole past and the whole future, would be the absolute truth." [77] The eternity of truth is not mere endurance through time or even such potentiality of recurrence at any time as is possessed by the laws of nature. In terms of such interpretations "an eternal truth would mean an everlasting fact," [78] which could conceivably be rendered false, so that eternal truths would be "presumptive" only. Rather, the eternity of truth means complete supratemporality. "Though everything in the panorama of history be temporal, the panorama itself is dateless, for evidently the sum and system of events cannot be one of them. It cannot occur after anything else or before anything else." [79] This eternity of truth must not be obscured by the changing tenses of verbs, which depend merely upon "the sentimental colour of our temporal perspectives." [80] Nor does the contingency of the future constitute a legitimate objection to the eternity of truth, for whether

---

[69] *Ibid.*, p. 528.
[70] *Skepticism and Animal Faith*, p. 227.
[71] *Realms of Being*, p. 403.
[72] *Ibid.*, p. 402.
[73] *Skepticism and Animal Faith*, p. 266.
[74] *Ibid.*, p. 267.

[75] *Realms of Being*, p. 402.
[76] *Ibid.*, p. 805.
[77] *Ibid.*, p. xv.
[78] *Ibid.*, p. 505.
[79] *Ibid.*, p. 485.
[80] *Ibid.*, p. 489.

or not the future is predetermined, it is determinate and so also is its truth.[81]

However, since truth follows the meanderings of matter, which is by its very nature contingent, there are no necessary truths. While mathematical propositions are indeed formally necessary, they deal directly with essences and merely incidentally and indirectly with those material facts which truth describes. Causal and other factual propositions are not necessary at all.[82] To be sure, certain logical propositions may be said to be true in the sense that they involve fidelity to one's presuppositions, but this is at best only a figurative sense of the word "true."[83]

The quest for truth has tremendous human significance. Consciousness would never have emerged "had not essence and truth overarched existence from all eternity and summed it up with all its perspectives ready, for spirit to perceive."[84] Moreover, even if consciousness be assumed, apart from the quest for truth recognition of the existence of the flux of matter would have been impossible, for "it is only in the realm of truth that events can be unified or divided."[85] Truth as such merits our respect, and when distractions are in some measure eliminated, genuine love of truth for its own sake becomes possible.[86] Whatever else man's objective may include, "the first step toward union with the Good is to have settled one's accounts with the world and with the truth."[87]

Nevertheless all that man can hope for is "glimpses"[88] of the truth, and even these are severely limited in a variety of ways. For one thing, "all knowledge of truth, by virtue of its seat and function, must be relative and subjectively colored."[89] "Both sense and science are relatively and virtually true, being appropriate to the organ employed and to the depth to which this organ may penetrate into the structure of things or may trace their movement."[90] Not only is truth as apprehended by us relative, it also falls far short of literalness and is at best dramatic and symbolical. Instead of actually describing the course of events, it can only suggest and symbolize. "Facts must be recast selectively on a grand scale,"[91] and a pronounced mythological element remains. This means of course that in all our alleged truth there is an admixture of error, and that "to be partly wrong is a condition of being partly right."[92]

---

[81] *Realms of Being*, pp. 500 f.
[82] *Ibid.*, pp. 408 ff.
[83] *Ibid.*, pp. 426 ff.
[84] *Ibid.*, p. 633.
[85] *Ibid.*, p. 487.
[86] Cf. *Skepticism and Animal Faith*, p. 307; *Realms of Being*, pp. 516 ff.

[87] *Realms of Being*, p. 821.
[88] *Ibid.*, p. 486.
[89] *Ibid.*, p. 526.
[90] *Ibid.*, p. 829.
[91] *Ibid.*, p. 467.
[92] *Ibid.*, p. 469.

Although it would be foolish to deplore or try to avoid the kind of error that must remain in all that we call truth, what we commonly call error is a more radical departure from full and literal truth and ought to be deplored and avoided. Error, broadly speaking, should be construed as imperfect realization of essence, in which thought imposes upon things essences that do not properly belong to them; it is assigning "to anything an essence which is not its essence." But only a certain type of instance of such misassignment is error in the usual, narrower sense. As we have seen, the essences selected by the psyche to guide thought and action need not literally copy things. Error in the usual sense does not occur until and unless we affirm that which misdirects us. Assignment of essences that are not literally there may accordingly often be justified, and the justification is not that the essence given in discourse repeats the essence embodied in material events—a repetition which would be in any case unlikely, superfluous, and incongruous with the primary function of sensation. . . . The justification is rather "such a vital harmony between the life of thought and that of things as may render discourse appropriate and adorning."[93] This need for harmony is the key to the character of error in the usual narrower sense; for such error occurs when "maladaptation exists in the respective movement and rates of change between psyche and her environment, so that the essences revealed imaginatively to that psyche are late or early or out of key with the march of events." [94] When this maladaptation exists, the psyche "will impose on things that which she adds, and deny that which she leaves out; and this hypostasis of her fancies or of her ignorance will become infathomable error." [95]

3. THE MATERIALISTIC CRITICAL REALISM OF R. W. SELLARS

While Lovejoy does not deny significance in the knowing process either to essences or to brain physiology, the aspect of that through which knowing occurs that most interests him is the ideational or psychical aspect. While Santayana does not reject the psychical aspect he makes that aspect wholly dependent upon a physiological one, and the aspect that interests him most is that of the essences illustrated. While R. W. Sellars (b. 1873) agrees with Santayana that the psychical is wholly dependent upon the physiological, he has no place at all in his epistemology for essences. Rather, he

93 Ibid., p. 125.
94 Ibid.
95 Ibid.

attempts to build on a nominalistic basis an epistemology in which
the mediating ingredient in knowing is principally brain impulses.
In considering Sellars' epistemology we shall first indicate briefly in
what sense in general he thinks knowledge possible, and then refer
to three significant differences between his thought and that of most
other critical realists including not only those already considered
but also others to be mentioned in the next section.

Whereas seventeenth-century realism erroneously attributed full
knowledge only to our ideas, thereby giving rise to an even more
mistaken subjectivistic idealism,[1] and the new realism took objects
to be directly sensed, thereby filling the universe with strange objects
and virtually ignoring the epistemological function of the "percipient organism," [2] a sound realism will, Sellars contends, recognize
that "the total act of perceiving with its beliefs, categories, and dis-
criminations is the most elementary unit of knowing the external
world." [3] One may, instead of being enclosed in a world of data,
take perception to be "a judgmental act directed outward" [4] toward
genuinely independent physical objects which are its causes. If what
is immediately grasped is not in all respects like the independent
object, it can at any rate be like that object in structure, and one can
see that "the reproduction of order is the basis of knowing." [5] The
accuracy of knowledge may accordingly be said to vary with its level.
Insights upon a given level are valid there but partially illusory
from the standpoint of higher levels. Thus, for example, at the level
of perception, the apple is red and the water is cold although, at
higher scientific levels, such statements must be corrected in terms
of knowledge of atoms and electrons, which rule out secondary
qualities.[6]

Unlike most other critical realists, Sellars deliberately rejects the
concept of essences. Neither the content of the knowing mind nor
the known object involves any such universal as most other critical
realists insist upon. Sense-data are invariably particulars and so are
the characters of things. The only sense in which universals exist is
a fictional one based on the fact that various data are often so similar
to one another that differences can for practical purposes be ignored,
which fact detracts not at all from the particularity of each thing.[7]

[1] R. W. Sellars, "Knowledge and Its
Categories," in *Essays in Critical Realism* (New York: The Macmillan Co., 1921),
p. 192; Sellars, *The Philosophy of Physical
Realism* (New York: The Macmillan Co.,
1932), pp. 26 ff.

[2] *Ibid.*, p. 54.

[3] Sellars, "Realism, Naturalism and
Humanism," in *Contemporary American
Philosophy,* II, 269.

[4] *The Philosophy of Physical Realism,*
p. 32.

[5] *Ibid.*, p. 86.

[6] *Ibid.*, pp. 95 ff.

[7] See *Ibid.*, chap. viii.

Unlike most other critical realists, Sellars also excludes all mental entities that are more than aspects of brain. He does recognize consciousness and mental aspects of nerve processes, but in both instances the mental aspect is entirely secondary and derivative. For Sellars, the self is a brain-mind and accordingly involves an awareness that cannot be reduced to mere bodily events, but this consciousness is purely a product of its bodily conditions and has no initiative force of its own. Similarly, sense-data and other mental events, though genuinely real, are in no sense independent entities but only qualitative aspects of brain events. Thus "consciousness . . . is an event adjectival to the brain." [8] However, since *data are intrinsic to the brain*," [9] they yield a knowledge of brain events supplementary to and far richer than that afforded by anatomical observation of the brain. The categories, which are essential to knowledge, are not peculiar mental forms. Rather, they "arise in us as expressions of ourselves as operationally immersed in the sea of being." [10] As we use them "we are conscious organisms thinking the things around us in accordance with our nature and theirs." [11]

Unlike most other critical realists, Sellars makes truth a function of knowledge rather than knowledge a function of truth. "Knowledge is disclosure of the characteristics of existence," [12] and as such it implies that correspondence which is truth. Thus correspondence becomes an implicate of knowledge rather than a characteristic of it, and "trueness as a property of an idea depends upon the content of the idea as agreeing with, and capable of disclosing, the object selected in the act of cognition." [13] The tests of truth are also the tests of knowledge. These tests are "insight into the constitution of the universe, . . . greater power of adjustment to it if we allow ourselves to be guided by knowledge, . . . ability to predict events," and especially being "founded on or demanded by empirical data." [14]

4. Other Versions of Critical Realism

The remaining four contributors to *Essays in Critical Realism* adopt positions somewhat nearer to those of Lovejoy and Santayana than to that of Sellars, and in general nearer to that of Lovejoy than to that of Santayana. All four hold views of the nature and the epistemological function of essence somewhat similar to those of Santayana, but each in his own way repudiates the materialistic slant

[8] *Philosophy of Physical Realism*, p. 408.
[9] *Ibid.*, p. 410.
[10] *Ibid.*, p. 216.
[11] *Ibid.*, p. 217.

[12] *Ibid.*, p. 106.
[13] *Ibid.*, p. 117.
[14] *Philosophy of Physical Realism*, p. 120.

of Santayana and Sellars and assigns a more active role in knowing
to a distinctive psychic factor. The first two of the writers under
consideration combine epistemological dualism with panpsychism,
and the other two continue, with Lovejoy, to insist upon the distinction between material entities and the mental ones through which
the material ones are known.

A. The thought of Durant Drake (1878–1933) takes issue at the
outset both with that of the new realists and Lovejoy. The typical
panobjectivism of new realism, which assigns independent external
status to every datum, hopelessly clutters up the world of common
sense and science with an utterly unmanageable conflicting mass of
primary and secondary qualities, and if logically carried out, even
absurdly invites such tertiary qualities as sullenness and gaiety into
the external world.[1] That modification of new realism which
assumes that we really project qualities into the external world is
scarcely in any better position; for there is no evidence for any such
projection, and in any case, knowing claims to apprehend reality
as it was before the knowing occurred.[2] The attempt of Lovejoy to
explain knowing by placing a realm of subjective existents over
against the objective realm obscures the true character of knowing
in another way. Perception purports to apprehend not merely our
own inner states but aspects of objects themselves; and the placing
of a mental existent between the physical object and the knower
multiplies entities beyond necessity, revives the difficulties of the
older representationalism, and renders knowing virtually impossible.[3]

A sound theory will steer between the Scylla of panobjectivism
and the Charybdis of extreme dualism.[4] Data, which Lovejoy takes
to be mental objects, really do not for the most part exist but are
suppositious objects. Except when they happen to coincide with
the real characteristics of observed objects, they are no more than
nonexisting "essences, characters, logical entities, . . . possibilities
of existence, and possibilities of discourse." [5] The only existents involved in perceiving are the external physical object, the mental
event, and the brain event. The reality of mental events must be
acknowledged; such facts as illusions, the time lag between objective
event and apprehension, memory, and anticipation cannot be satisfactorily accounted for without them.[6] But careful analysis reveals
that brain events and mind events are really only two different

[1] Durant Drake, "The Approach to
Critical Realism," in *Essays in Critical
Realism* (New York: The Macmillan Co.,
1921), p. 11; *Mind and Its Place in Nature*
(New York: The Macmillan Co., 1925),
pp. 14 ff.

[2] *Ibid.*, pp. 17 ff.
[3] *Ibid.*, pp. 179 ff.
[4] *Ibid.*, p. 160.
[5] *Ibid.*, p. 198.
[6] *Ibid.*, chap. vi.

aspects of the same thing.[7] Moreover, the most plausible interpretation of the whole physical world is in terms of a panpsychism that finds a mindlike aspect in every existent.

While the data of illusions, hallucinations, dreams, secondary qualities, and some primary ones are nonexistent, those involved in veridical knowledge do exist. Indeed, "in so far as perception is veridical, the outer existent *is* the very existent affecting our organisms," and "the very things we know, or some of their characteristics are present to our consciousness, data of our experience." [8] Knowledge itself "consists in the relation of identity between datum and object cognized." [9]

It is however at best only qualities or characteristics of the object that are thus apprehended even in veridical knowledge; the "substance or inner nature" of the object "remains private." [10] Although data are simple essences, the physical and mental events that produce them are extremely complex, and introspection is never able fully to penetrate to them. For this reason, even primary qualities must be treated as "fusions" of actual events, and secondary qualities must be regarded as symbolic representations which, though not literally found in objects, may nevertheless be extremely useful practical guides. That which sustains our faith in the validity of our knowledge both of the character and of the existence of the external world is in substantial measure success in action.

B. A more penetrating presentation of an epistemology essentially similar to that of Drake is to be found in the writings of C. A. Strong (1862–1940), who not only influenced Drake but also collaborated with him in the writing of *Mind and Its Place in Nature.*

Strong held that any satisfactory theory of knowledge in the present day and age must be one which, unlike most of those currently offered, was compatible with natural accounts of the relations of mind and body and of the origin of mind.[11] For this reason he believed that the epistemologist should accept in outline the findings of physiology concerning the nervous system and should seek here the essential key to the problems of cognition.[12]

Following this method one discovers that elemental nervous responses, which in their inner nature consist of sensations or "sentience," are basic to all cognitive processes, the stuff of which cognition is made. Sentience consists of minute tendencies to psychical response that may in a broad sense be referred to as feelings.

---

[7] *Ibid.,* chap. vii.
[8] *Ibid.,* p. 32.
[9] *Ibid.,* p. 50.
[10] *Ibid.,* p. 72.

[11] C. A. Strong, *Essays on the Natural Origin of the Mind* (London: Macmillan & Co., Ltd., 1930), p. 1.
[12] *Ibid.,* pp. 4 ff.

These atoms of sentience are not ordinarily themselves objects of awareness. They are rather factors through which we perceive, remember, and imagine without our noticing them.[13] They do, however, sometimes become objects of awareness as when for example, through excess light, the sensations of seeing become painful, or when, in esthetic experience, sensations themselves are enjoyed.[14]

Atoms of sentience turn out in fact to be the basic elements not only of knowing but also of reality itself. Contrary to prevalent philosophical notions, some of them constitute substantial selves spread out in space and time. If this were not so, neither apprehension of spatial and temporal position nor the efficient mind would be comprehensible.[15] Atoms of sentience are also the fundamental stuff of that external nature out of which mind arises. If this were not so, the origin of mind would be an insoluble mystery. Nervous structure and function constitute the outward or perceived aspect of which sentience or feeling is the inner or introspected aspect.[16] Awareness is, however, a function or use of sentience rather than sentience itself; it is accordingly not knowable.

From sentience the basic types of knowledge emerge along two distinct but parallel lines. One of these is perception and the other is introspection. So long as there is no demand for action, sentience may continue indefinitely without the occurrence of perception, but when such a demand intervenes, a process of simplification begins, in which segments of the vast chaotic mass of sensations are fused and organized in terms of unified qualitative sense-data. These data are in turn projected outward toward the place of the object as useful *phantasms*.[17] Since atomic sensations themselves occur in a spatial self, the phantasms are also seen in space and since they have been projected outward, they have the natural order of things rather than the reversed one that the lens of the eye directs inward.[18] This production and projection of phantasms or sense-data is the first or intuitive phase of perception.

A second phase of perception is intention, which is to be clearly distinguished from intuition. By "intention" is meant "reference to an object." [19] More specifically it is "the inevitable implication of the active side of our nature, by which, when an object produces an impression on us, we are moved to behave with reference not to the impression, but to the object which is its cause." [20] Intuition never in fact occurs in ordinary life without intention, and these

[13] *Ibid.*, pp. 8 ff.
[14] *Ibid.*, pp. 37 f.
[15] *Ibid.*, pp. 115 ff.
[16] *Ibid.*, pp. 124 f.; chap. viii.
[17] *Ibid.*, pp. 29 ff.

[18] *Ibid.*, pp. 57 ff.
[19] *Ibid.*, p. 92.
[20] Strong, "Nature and Mind," in *Contemporary American Philosophy*, II, 318.

two together yield the apparent object or "the thing as present to the mind." [21] The process of perception is completed by an animal faith that affirms the existence and nature of the object. Such faith normally accompanies intuition and intention, for belief is natural and doubt intervenes only upon the occurrence of special reasons for doubt.[22]

The sense-data or phantasms in terms of which we perceive are neither physically real things nor psychological entities.[23] Indeed, they do not exist at all, at any rate in the sense of continuing independently of the knowing process.[24] They are rather basically logical natures or essences.[25]

When the apparent objects that occur when such essences are intuited and intended are believed in but do not correspond with existing objects, perceptual error, which is quite different from error of interpretation, occurs. When the apparent object does coincide with the real one, correct illusions are in a sense projected upon the real objects; but since the essences projected are in such cases those of the real objects, one is then properly said to be veridically perceiving the objects. Indeed, it is only objects themselves and never merely data that we are ever correctly said to perceive at all. Thus the new realists are right in saying that "the apparent thing and the real thing coincide where or in so far as cognition is truthful." [26] Although coincidence of essences, apparent objects, and real objects does in fact occur with reference to shape and position, it generally remains incomplete even here, and with reference to the secondary qualities it can scarcely be said to occur at all. The secondary qualities accordingly constitute persistent and highly useful perceptual errors, and most of our perceptual knowledge is at best symbolical rather than literal.[27]

The second basic variety of knowledge, introspection, is often thought to be, unlike perception, immediate. Actually it is a mediate process strictly analogous to perception. The sensation is never quite directly known. Rather, the apprehension of such a sensation is mediated by introspective data, which, though they may resemble the sensation more closely than the qualities of perception resemble their object, are still simplifications of the chaotic complexity of the atoms of sentience.[28]

[21] *Essays on the Natural Origin of the Mind*, p. 94.

[22] Cf. *ibid.*, pp. 101 f.

[23] Strong, "The Nature of the Datum," in *Essays in Critical Realism*, pp. 224 ff.

[24] Cf. Strong, "The Missing Link in Epistemology," *Journal of Philosophy*, XXIX (1932), 673 ff.

[25] "On the Nature of the Datum," p. 237.

[26] *Essays on the Natural Origin of the Mind*, p. 29.

[27] *Ibid.*

[28] *Ibid.*, pp. 177 ff.

C. The thought of J. B. Pratt (1875–1944) is like that of San-tayana, Drake, and Strong in assigning an important epistemological role to essences, but it is unlike that of Drake and Strong and like that of Lovejoy in maintaining a sharp distinction between the physical and the mental. It perhaps goes beyond the thought of any of these writers in stressing the activity of the self in the knowing process.

Knowledge, Pratt contends, must begin with our actual experi-ence. This experience involves relations, to be sure, but it also involves "intrinsic qualities," without which "there could be neither things, relations, relational characters, nor patterns." [29] It is also not a mere collection of universals but an actual existing fact. The nature of existence itself is not definable, for existence is not a nature or essence at all, but pure givenness. The recognition of the irreduci-bility of experience to rationality is basic to any empirical phi-losophy.[30]

The facts about existing experience that especially require epis-temological explanation include "the fact that experiences pop into our minds . . . quite unexpectedly," the fact that "we are somehow compelled to hear and see and feel the same things . . . at the same moment," and the facts of "the orderly nature of much that we all experience, and the apparent continuance of this order during periods of time when, so far as we know, the order and the things it orders are being experienced by no one." [31] Of these facts of experience neither solipsism, nor pragmatism, nor so-called specu-lative or objective idealism seriously attempts an explanation.[32] Pan-psychism offers us a possible explanation but has on the whole little to commend it. The only really plausible answers are those of abso-lute idealism, personal idealism, and realism; [33] and of these, realism is much the simplest and most probable.[34]

The explanation common to all realists is that the facts of expe-rience demanding explanation are to be accounted for mainly by phys-ical objects that are existent substances, independent of experience and capable of making a difference to experience.[35] But for critical realists, this is only the beginning. Any satisfactory explanation of the character of our actual experience will have to include, in addi-tion to the physical object and experience of this object, at least two other factors, namely, meaning, or epistemological object, and the self. The content of consciousness is virtually always shot through

[29] J. B. Pratt, *Personal Realism* (New York: The Macmillan Co., 1937), p. 38.
[30] *Ibid.*, chap. v.
[31] *Ibid.*, pp. 142 ff.
[32] *Ibid.*, pp. 218 ff.
[33] *Ibid.*, p. 216.
[34] *Ibid.*, p. 217.
[35] *Ibid.*, pp. 148 ff., 165.

with reference to that which is thought to be independent of consciousness. While the physical object itself is one aspect of what is so referred to, another aspect is "the character complex or definable nature or group of definable natures, which one is thinking about." This latter aspect is "an epistemological object," "*definable nature*," or "essence." Being universal, it can be shared with other persons, despite the fact that two persons can never have the same experience.[36] In knowing physical things, we ascribe such character complexes to existing things. Our doing so accurately and upon good evidence constitutes knowledge and our doing so inaccurately constitutes error.

But ideas or essences entertained, do not refer themselves; it is we who must refer them. Apart from an active substantial self, who assimilates, organizes, refers, composes, and evaluates, there could be no knowing.[37]

If it be asked how, if epistemological objects are distinct from ontological ones, we can know the latter, the answer is, as has been suggested, that the assumption of ontological objects is the only plausible explanation of our experience. If it be asked how we know the characters of things, the reply is that while we do not know the intrinsic nature of things, we know at least some of their relational qualities with a fair degree of probability by the character and order of our experience. This does not mean that we do not know the objects themselves; for while experiences of definable natures are all that is directly given, through these experiences we do apprehend objects themselves. When you conceive of Niagara Falls, you think directly of it; that is as direct as your thought of anything can conceivably be.[38] If anyone objects to the transcendence involved here he must remember that any nonsolipsist theory, that is, any theory in which knowledge is possible at all, will inevitably involve transcendence.[39]

D. The critical realism of A. K. Rogers (b. 1868) is much like that of Pratt in its insistence upon the nonexistential character of essences. It involves, however, a somewhat sharper distinction between mental content and mental act, and has much less to say of a knowing self. It also acquires special interest by its sustained inquiry into the problem of truth, which has not been extensively discussed by other critical realists with the exception of Santayana.

[36] *Ibid.,* pp. 200 ff.
[37] *Ibid.,* pp. 203 ff.; chap. xix.
[38] *Ibid.,* p. 208; see also J. B. Pratt, "The Confessions of an Old Realist," *Journal of Philosophy,* XIII (1916), 687–93.

[39] *Ibid.,* pp. 87 ff.; and Pratt, "Critical Realism and the Possibility of Knowledge," in *Essays in Critical Realism,* pp. 111 ff.

Knowledge is for Rogers a natural fact in no sense dependent for its existence upon justification of it by epistemology.[40] The business of epistemology is not the creation of knowledge but the analysis and criticism of knowledge. Such analysis reveals four basic elements in the knowing process.[41] The first is "the object perceived, the real thing with its status in the world of reality independent of the knowledge relations." The second is the idea or "the state of consciousness." The third is the "meaning," "character," "nature," or "essence." The fourth is the "mental act." [42]

When we perceive something we refer a character that belongs to our mental state to an object that lies beyond it.[43] Attention is ordinarily focused not so much upon the mental state as upon the reference to the object, but reflection reveals that a sensation having the character referred is necessary to the process.[44] The mental activity is not a "metaphysical category" but a succession of concrete mental states attended by a sense of direction, of intent or purpose, such as is rendered possible through the process of an "idea" of some future end or event to which the process is felt as leading.[45] Neither consciousness nor its object consists merely either of relations or of any other logical entities. Both consciousness and its object actually exist. Neither is apprehended as an essence only; each is confronted in its existence.[46]

Truth is "a correspondence between ideas and reality," [47] and an idea enables us to think the character of an object truly, only insofar as it has itself the characteristics of the thing to which it professes to refer.[48] It is of course true that symbols can for practical purposes differ widely from what they represent, and even for theoretical purposes, considerable deviation is permissible. Essentially, however, "we have no proper imaginative realization of the meaning of the symbol unless we are capable of translating it back into the concrete fact of which it is the sign." Thus "in true knowledge the essence of the object and the essence of the mental state are potentially identical." [49] A satisfactory account of the nature of error, which proves an unanswerable difficulty for objective idealism and new realism, accords fully with the foregoing kind of account of truth, for error becomes simply "the ascribing of an ideal character to what

[40] A. K. Rogers, *What Is Truth?* (New Haven, Conn. Yale University Press, 1923), p. 160.
[41] Rogers, "A Statement of Epistemological Dualism," *Journal of Philosophy*, XIII (1916), 169; *What Is Truth?* pp. 66 ff.
[42] *Ibid.*
[43] *Ibid.*, p. 59.
[44] *Ibid.*, pp. 63 f.
[45] *Ibid.*, pp. 85 f.
[46] *Ibid.*, pp. 75 ff.
[47] *Ibid.*, p. 55.
[48] *Ibid.*, p. 72; see also "A Statement of Epistemological Dualism," p. 174.
[49] *What Is Truth?* p. 75.

we are mistaken in supposing to be real, or the ascribing to a reality of a wrong character instead of a right one." [50]

Essences and relations do not, as in Santayana's system, constitute an independent realm of subsistences.[51] Essences may be present in existing experiences or in existing things; they are abstractions from experiences and things and have no independent being.[52] To ascribe to them any sort of existence whatever, as Strong seems sometimes to do, is an epistemologically fatal mistake.[53] Similarly, relations may be found between aspects or between things, but "relations have no being in any sense apart from particulars that presuppose an existing world," [54] and they belong to the conceptual world only insofar as we "*put*" them there.[55] The fact that "every character which we can assign to the real world must first be found within experience" suggests that "the world of nature is . . . in its substance akin to the world of feeling." [56] But this is a metaphysical speculation concerning the nature of the object of which we can never be at all sure.

5. Comments Concerning Critical Realism

In critical realism the main lines of thought of the present century concerning the relation of cognitive experience and its objects tend to converge. Hence the principal issues requiring comment with reference to critical realism concern the question whether or not and in what ways critical realists have been able successfully to combine these lines of thought.

A. The central thesis common to most critical realists brings together the claims that idealists and new realists have most successfully urged against one another and the claim that both have urged against representative realists. With idealists against new realists, critical realists have properly claimed that knowledge involves at one stage or another an active experiencing that cannot be assimilated to objects. With new realists against idealists, critical realists have rightly claimed that knowledge involves objects that are independent of being known. And with both against representative realists, critical realists have recognized that knowledge is apprehension not merely of one's own cognitive experiences but of the objects themselves intended in such experiences. To this extent

---

[50] A. K. Rogers, "The Problem of Error," in *Essays in Critical Realism*, pp. 117 f.

[51] Cf. *What Is Truth?* p. 131.

[52] *Ibid.*, p. 62.

[53] Rogers, "Professor Strong's Theory and Essence," *Journal of Philosophy*, XVI

(1920), 61 ff.; see also "Essence and Existence," *Philosophical Review*, XXVIII (1919), 234.

[54] *What Is Truth?*, p. 137.

[55] *Ibid.*, p. 132.

[56] *Ibid.*, pp. 163 f.

critical realists seem to have combined what might be regarded as the basic requirements of an account of the relation of knowing and known that conforms to the claims implicit in our actual cognitive experiences. Whether or not they have sufficiently showed how the combination can be structured and sustained is of course another matter.

Arguments in support of the correctness of the three claims in question have already been sketched in the exposition of idealism and new realism, in the critical remarks concerning these theories, and in the exposition of critical realism itself, and need not be further developed here. What does seem to be worth pointing out now is that with respect to each of the first two of the three claims, the position of the critical realists is more forthright and unequivocal than that of either idealism or new realism. On the one hand, whereas idealists insist that knowledge involves an active experiencing that cannot be assimilated to objects, but by assimilating objects to experience compromise the integrity of the experience on which knowledge depends; critical realists keep their objects distinct from their sentient experiences and hence their sentient experiences distinct from their objects. On the other hand, whereas new realists insist that knowledge is of objects quite independent of experiences, but by assimilating experiences to objects compromise the independence of objects; critical realists avoid making objects even momentarily identical with experiences and so are able to maintain an unequivocal independence for objects. Regarding the third of the three claims under consideration, the claim that the object itself is known, it may be doubted that the assertions of critical realists are quite as convincing as those of the advocates of either of the other two views; for while critical realists do insist that the object itself is known, the link between object and experience is none too easy to establish in view of their insistence on separation of experience and object.

B. In addition to bringing together the claims that cognition involves distinct experiences and objects neither of which can be assimilated to the other and the claim that our knowledge is nevertheless apprehension of objects themselves, critical realists have offered a number of interesting and illuminating suggestions concerning *how* these claims can be reconciled and integrated. Two such suggestions that will be considered here are designed to point out modes of connection between experiences and independent objects. Three other suggestions, that can only be noted in passing, are designed to meet specific objections to the claim that such connections can be established.

One suggestion, which is most dramatically—though hardly most adequately—formulated in Santayana's doctrine of animal faith, is that man's experience is from the beginning oriented to the nature in which it originates and that the acceptance of the reference of that experience to a material world beyond it is natural and virtually inevitable. This seems surely in fact to be the case. So much a part of us is the natural tendency to accept the most vivid and best ordered of our experiences as presentations of a material world that no philosophical objection is able to overcome or even long to diminish its force. The untutored man rarely, if ever, doubts the essential soundness of the references in his experience. The thoughtful man recognizes that *most* of his cognitive experiences guide him concerning the nature of things, and he soon learns to ascribe to the illusory, appropriate illusory characters. If he becomes a scientist, he may be somewhat hesitant about assigning directly experienced characters to things, and he may find that some properties not directly apprehended are better guides to predictions than some directly apprehended ones; but still he recognizes the existence of objective things to which in one way or another he ascribes characters found in his experience. If he becomes a philosopher, he may even doubt that there are things reliably connected with his experiences or indeed that reality can be apprehended at all. But, as Hume admitted, such moods of extreme skepticism are rare and of brief duration; immediately following them, the skeptical philosopher returns to the world of ordinary things, and even in his moments of deepest skepticism, he is never able to sustain doubt of all things at once. His disease, of realistic reference, if disease it be, seems in fact to be unavoidable and incurable.

A second significant suggestion of the critical realists designed to reconcile distinctness of experiences and objects and the genuine knowability of objects is that only upon the assumption that independent objects are under favorable circumstances apprehended in experiences, can a degree of order be achieved among experiences that renders them intelligible and facilitates the progress of science. This suggestion also is sound and illuminating. If, on the one hand, we reject the presupposition that experiences can yield apprehensions of an external world, our experiences themselves tend to fall apart in chaotic disorder, and scientific inquiry to lose its point. If, on the other hand, we accept this presupposition, plausible explanations are at hand concerning how experiences are collected together in ordered bunches, how such bunches of experience change together in regular ways, why such bunches of experiences appear, disappear, and reappear as they do, and how they are related to one another. This presupposition also lends itself readily to the organization of vast systems of knowledge within which even those disappointments and unexpected arrangements of experience that produce illusions and errors are rendered intelligible. Far from being an *ad hoc* device for explaining special features of experience, this presupposition supplies, as Lovejoy reminds us, not only an amazing coordination of existing data but an admirable foundation of an ever expanding growth of common-sense and scientific knowledge.

A third phase of the critical realists' attempt to show how independent objects can be apprehended through experiences distinct from them, and one designed especially to meet the objections that if objects and experiences are distinct there is nothing common to them through which the one may be grasped by the other, is the suggestion implicit in the thought of nearly all the critical realists, with the notable exception of Sellars, that physical objects and experiences may involve in one way or another the same universals. Just what universals are, remains, of course, a moot question, and that the same universals are directly attributable both to physical objects and the experiences in which they are disclosed is very doubtful. But that often in speaking of physical objects we do at some points employ the same predicates that we employ in speaking of certain of our experiences and that indeed we sometimes speak about these predicates in ways that justify our calling them universals seem to be plain. At very least the suggestions of the critical realists concerning universals may be said significantly to call attention to such facts as these and so to supply one possible way of speaking of an important aspect of the connection between physical objects and experiences, that does not either reduce such objects to experiences or experiences to objects or either to universals.

A fourth suggestion intended to show how independent objects can be apprehended by distinct experiences, and also especially designed to answer the objection that experiences distinct from objects may not even be *like* the objects they are supposed to apprehend, is the suggestion of Santayana that our experiences at least symbolize things sufficiently for practical purposes. This suggestion must of course be taken analogically, for experiences are not literally symbols of things; but in any case the suggestion properly indicates that the relation of things and experiences in veridical cognition involves a practical adjustment that does not depend upon a high degree of likeness of object and experience.

A final suggestion is that of Sellars, designed especially to meet the objection that experiences, being of a totally different order from things, can never grasp things, to the effect that conscious experiences are aspects of brain events that are in turn caused by things. Whatever may be the drawbacks of this suggestion, it has the advantage of calling attention to the significant considerations that things that are independent of that through which they are known can still be causally connected with that through which they are known, and that through which things are known may be inseparable from cognitive experience itself. In this fashion it proposes at least one not implausible way of overcoming one aspect of the alleged isolation of experience.

Whether or not any or all of the suggestions of the critical realists concerning how independent objects can be apprehended in experiences distinct from them can be regarded as sufficient answers to questions concerning such apprehension depends on how severe a standard is set with respect to what is to count as sufficient. If what is demanded is simply some considerations that tend to show that independent objects can in fact be apprehended in distinct experiences of them, then the critical realists have surely succeeded, though one may of course question the extent to which such considerations are required at all. But if what is demanded is a generally acceptable description of the structure of the relation between independent objects and distinct apprehending experiences, a plausible model of this relation, or what would now be called a satisfactory logic of the relation, the critical realists have furnished no such thing. Indeed, it may be doubted if, apart from some vague and rather poetic than precise notions of Santayana, they have seriously tried to furnish such a model or logic, and the suggestions they have offered remain quite inadequate. Thus, while the suggestions that belief in independent objects to which our experiences are coordinated is natural and that apart from the acceptance of such beliefs no satisfactorily coherent account of our experiences seems achievable are to be sure significant and tend to render plausible the notion of a genuine apprehension of real objects, neither suggestion does much to sketch a specific structure or logic for the relation between object and experience. The notion that the same universals may be involved in physical objects and experiences may tend to establish one sort of tie between physical objects and experiences; but, quite apart from serious questions concerning universals themselves and the modes of their involvement in objects and experience, this suggestion leaves unresolved the crucial issues concerning the existential ties between physical objects and experiences. The notion that experiences symbolize facts points at best analogically to a link between physical objects and experiences that is only vaguely set forth. Sellars' double aspect theory of brain events represents an interesting speculation concerning the causes of sentient experiences, but tells us all too little concerning the logic of the relations between such experiences and the objects in which they originate. Whether or not other types of thinkers, whose philosophical procedures are somewhat more refined than those of the critical realists, have been able to work out a model or logic or the relation of object and experience that is more satisfactory than any implicit in the suggestions of the critical realists, who while recognizing the elements of a satisfactory theory never satisfactorily structured them, remains to be seen.

CHAPTER 6

English Realism

THE realism that emerged in England at the beginning of the present century more or less simultaneously with that in America was, as one might have expected, more directly influenced by the continental realisms of Brentano and Meinong than was its American counterpart. This English realism involves the same cleavage between direct and indirect realism that we encountered in discussing American new realism and critical realism, but it also involves other significant distinctions that cannot be neatly typed in terms of this sort of distinction. Each of the two writers to be considered in the first two sections of this chapter is a significant contributor both to English realism and to the analytic movement, and while it seems best to present the views of each in connection with realism, each is as much concerned with problems of method and meaning as with traditional epistemological problems. While the contrasts between direct and indirect realism is present in their works, the major cleavages between them concern rather the kinds of knowledge inquired into and the methods employed in the inquiry. In the thought of the three writers considered in the third section, the contrast between direct and indirest realism again becomes prominent, but an interesting kind of compromise is also suggested. The writers considered in the fourth section are united by no basic similarities save their generally realist principles, but each offers hypotheses that are distinctive and significant.

1. THE COMMON-SENSE REALISM OF G. E. MOORE

In his epistemological conclusions G. E. Moore (b. 1873) is stoutly realistic and in his procedures he is incisively analytic. The kind of knowledge that Moore is concerned to discuss is mainly that of ordinary experience, and the terms of his analysis are mainly those of ordinary language. In these respects the thought of Moore tends to be in marked contrast to that of Bertrand Russell, which is to be considered in the next section. Moore's epistemological thought is directed to a variety of questions and does not always proceed in the same ways. Its contribution is mainly along three lines to be successively considered, namely, criticism of idealism, defense of common sense, and application of analytic method to the problem of the status of sense-data. In its frequent insistence upon the certainty of our awareness of objects themselves, Moore's thought resembles that of the American new realists, upon whom it exercised a very substantial influence; but in its maintenance of a strict dualism of mental act and object, and in its analysis of sense-data, it is often closer to that of the American critical realists.

A. In his famous "Refutation of Idealism," first published in 1903, Moore located the distinctive feature of epistemological idealism in the claim that *esse* is *percipi*. If this claim is to be true, it can only mean that the properties, other than that of being perceived, which constitute anything cannot exist without also being perceived.[1] So interpreted and regarded as a necessary and therefore nonsynthetic and ungrounded proposition, this claim cannot be refuted. But the fact is that idealists have never been content to regard *esse* is *percipi* as an ungrounded proposition. Instead they have supported it with an argument apart from which they would never have held it at all, and the argument can be shown to be mistaken.

The argument in question treats the claim that the object of experience is inconceivable apart from the subject as an analytic proposition, one the opposite of which would be self-contradictory. [2] But this treatment is plausible only because of a failure to see that "object and subject," e.g. yellow and the sensation of yellow, are quite distinct. If the idealist could see this distinction he would become aware that *esse* is *percipi* is not only not analytic but is self-contradictory; for that doctrine implies both the claim that experience and its object are the same and the counterclaim that they are different, e.g. that yellow and the sensation of yellow are analytically connected and essentially identical and at the same time that, being significantly related, they are different.[3]

That subject or consciousness and objects are in fact quite distinct is evident in the fact that we are aware both of awareness and of the objects of our awareness, that is to say, both of what is common to

[1] G. E. Moore, "The Refutation of Idealism," (first published in *Mind*, 1903) Moore, *Philosophical Studies* (London: Kegan Paul, Ltd., 1922).

[2] *Ibid.*, pp. 12 f.
[3] *Ibid.*, p. 14.

blue and green and of blue and green themselves. Philosophers have universally failed to notice this distinction partly because language has no common name for such objects as blue, green, and sweet, and partly because we tend to see *through,* rather than to *see,* consciousness.[4]

Even when the distinction between consciousness and its object begins to emerge, idealists tend to obscure this distinction by making the object a mere "content" of consciousness. But obviously blue is not a content of consciousness in the sense in which blue is a content of a blue flower or in that in which a quality is a part of the content of a substance, and these are the only intelligible senses of the term content. Blue stands rather to consciousness in the unique relation of *knowing.* In terms of this relation, even if blue were a part of the content of consciousness, it would have also to be more than this, for consciousness is by its very nature consciousness *of* something.[5] Moreover, if awareness applied only to its own contents, there could be no such knowledge, even of other minds, as idealists themselves are eager to defend. Actually, since awareness always reaches beyond itself, we are never confined to our own mental contents in isolation from other human beings, and we are in fact just as aware of material objects as we are of our own awareness or of other persons.[6]

Having become doubtful of some of the arguments of his "Refutation of Idealism," Moore subsequently returns to the attack upon idealism in more modest fashion in the middle section of his essay on "The Status of Sense Data." [7] Moore insists that the denial that *esse* is *percipi* is certainly not, as Berkeley thought, self-contradictory and that he at any rate cannot see that the principle is true at all. He also holds that human beings have a "strong propensity" to believe at least that sensibles which are not at a given time observed would be observed if a certain body were in a suitable position to observe them. The only plausible argument against this sort of belief is, he holds, that changes in the nervous system change the object; but such changes, he finds, really alter only the experience; and in the absence of any convincing argument to the contrary, the instinctive belief that objects endure beyond perception cannot be abandoned.

Again in section II of the "Defense of Common Sense," [8] Moore challenges idealism, this time with specific reference to the view that

---

4 *Ibid.,* pp. 17–20; see also Moore, *Some Main Problems of Philosophy* (London & New York: George Allen & Unwin, & The Macmillan Co., 1953), pp. 31 ff.

5 *Ibid.,* p. 72.

6 "The Refutation of Idealism," p. 30.

7 *Philosophical Studies,* pp. 180 ff.

8 Moore, "A Defense of Common Sense," in J. H. Muirhead (ed.), *Contemporary British Philosophy* (London: George Allen & Unwin, 1925), 2d series, pp. 208–23.

physical facts depend either logically or causally upon mental ones. On the one hand, it seems sufficiently plain that no physical fact is ever logically dependent upon a mental one. For example, "there is no good reason to suppose that there is any mental fact whatever, such that the fact that that mantel-piece is at present nearer to my body than that bookcase could not have been a fact, unless the mental fact in question had also been a fact." [9] On the other hand, while some physical facts, such as those caused by human intentions, may depend causally upon mental facts, other physical facts are not even causally dependent upon mental ones. For instance, "There is no reason to suppose that there is any mental fact of which it could be truly said: unless this fact had been a fact, the earth would not have existed for many years past." [10]

B. Turning now from the negative side of Moore's epistemology, we consider the part of its positive side of which Moore seems most certain, his defense of common sense or of knowledge of other people and especially of physical objects.

In his early essay, "The Nature and Reality of Objects of Perception," first published in 1905–06, Moore is principally concerned with our knowledge of other persons and of their perceptions. Here he contends that almost everyone "believes that *something* other than himself and what he directly perceives *exists* or is *real*," and that "among the real things, other than himself and what he directly perceives, are other persons who have thoughts and perceptions in some respects similar to his own." [11] Good grounds for such belief, Moore asserts, are such facts as that Moore in reading his paper to his audience has perceptions which he would probably not have unless they were hearing his voice, and that the members of the audience in turn have perceptions which they would probably not have if he were not seeing the words on his paper.[12] The reason that such experiences as these are said to be good grounds for the belief in other persons is not, as is usually supposed, that one is entitled by his perceptions of his own perceptions to transfer the property of perceptiveness by analogy to other persons. The reason is rather that in his perception of other peoples' bodies, his mind has a link with them which is entirely missing in his usual perceptions of his own mind or body.[13]

In *Some Main Problems of Philosophy*, Moore holds that "we *know* that there are and have been in the Universe . . . material objects and acts of consciousness . . . —huge numbers of both— . . . [and] that many material objects exist when we are not conscious of

[9] *Ibid.*, p. 214.
[10] *Ibid.*, p. 216.
[11] Moore, "The Nature and Reality of Objects of Perception," in *Philosophical Studies*, p. 31.
[12] *Ibid.*, pp. 45 f.
[13] *Ibid.*, pp. 82 ff.

them." [14] Subsequently in "A Defense of Common Sense" Moore lists a substantial number of specific things that most people "know with certainty." For example, one knows with certainty that his body exists, was born, has grown, and is in contact with the earth, that many bodies have died, that many are alive now, and that the earth has existed for some time. In his essay on "The Status of Sense-Data," in discussing a situation in which he observes a half crown and a florin so placed that both appear elliptical and the larger half crown is sufficiently farther away to appear smaller than the smaller florin, Moore lists even more specific propositions that he knows to be true, for example, that "I am *really seeing two coins*," "that the upper sides of the coins are *really* approximately circular, . . . that the coins have another side, . . . that the upper side of the half crown is really larger than that of the florin, . . . and that both coins continue to exist, even when I turn away my head or shut my eyes." [15]

To the question how one knows that the more general of the propositions in the foregoing lists are true, for example, how one knows that he and other people and physical objects exist, Moore's reply in "A Defense of Common Sense" is essentially that the truth of these propositions is implicit in our whole manner of thinking, that they are presupposed by many things that we all admit we know.[16] If any philosopher denies such propositions as these, the admission of his own existence implicit in his denial shows him to be mistaken.[17] Besides, any philosopher who denies such propositions holds other views in line with common sense that are incompatible with such denials. And if any philosopher declares that while the claims of common sense that people and material things exist may be true, they cannot be known to be so, he contradicts himself in that the very existence of common sense implies these very truths.

In his "Proof of an External World," Moore goes on to offer a formal demonstration of the existence of an external world on the basis of known facts. The expression "external to our minds" is here taken to mean approximately "to be met with in space," in the sense in which houses, animals, human bodies, and even shadows are met with in space but sense-data are not. In the existence of any object that is external in this sense, the existence of an external world is implied.[18] Thus, any instance of knowledge of an encounter with

---

[14] *Some Main Problems of Philosophy*, p. 12.

[15] Moore, "The Status of Sense-Data," in *Philosophical Studies*, p. 186.

[16] "A Defense of Common Sense," pp. 204 ff.

[17] See also Moore, "Hume's Philosophy," in *Philosophical Studies*, p. 158.

[18] "Proof of an External World," *Proceedings of the British Academy*, XXV (1939), 294.

an object in space can be said to yield a proof of the existence of an external world. For example, "by holding up my two hands, and saying, as I make a certain gesture with my right hand, 'Here's a hand,' and adding, as I make a certain gesture with the left, 'and here is another,' I have in accord with what has been said of the implications of such statements, proved that there are external objects." [19] This argument, Moore claims, meets all the requirements of proof; for the premises and conclusion are different, the conclusion strictly follows from the premises, and the premises are known to be true.

In answer to the question how he knows the truth of the premises of his argument, e.g. that here's a hand, and indeed how he knows the truth of any of the more specific propositions in the foregoing lists, Moore's reply is in general that he does not have to know *how* he knows these truths but that in simple fact he does know them. To deny them is either absurdly to reject obvious facts or else to use language in odd and misleading ways. Indeed, particular pieces of knowledge of the kind in question are so much more certain than any arguments that can be marshaled either against or for them that they are both impervious to attack and not in need of defense.[20]

In his lectures in 1910–11, Moore goes so far as to suggest that such a proposition as "this pencil exists" is "known by me immediately." [21] This claim does not imply that the pencil is "immediately apprehended" in the manner in which sense-data are apprehended, or indeed that the pencil could be known at all apart from data or its existence verified apart from evidence. It does not even mean that we know the analysis of the proposition that the pencil exists, for we understand and know the truths of many statements of which we do not know the analysis. If indeed, in the effort to know the existence of a physical object, we were confined to sense-data and the manner in which we apprehend them, we should never know such objects at all. The fact that we do immediately know many physical objects is evidence that knowing involves more than data, though just what the more is is difficult to say. Memory gives us a clue in that here an act of mind proceeds beyond the given image to the assurance that the image refers to something.[22] But whatever one's ignorance of the evidences, analyses, or processes of such knowledge as one has that the hand or pencil before him exists, that on some occasions he has such knowledge is certain and is a fact with which epistemological inquiry may begin, not one at which it has to arrive.

---

[19] *Ibid.*, p. 295.
[20] See *Some Main Problems of Philosophy*, chaps. v–ix.

[21] *Ibid.*, p. 125.
[22] *Ibid.*, chap. xiii.

C. The third aspect of Moore's epistemological thought to be considered here, his account of the relation of sense-data and physical objects, is one to which he has devoted a great deal of attention without being able to arrive at conclusions that satisfy him. This much is clear, that there are sense-data or, as he calls them, "sensibles," and that these sometimes exist apart from corresponding physical objects. Moore's favorite example of a pure sense-datum is the afterimage such as one may, for example, see on looking away after staring for some time at an illuminated electric light bulb. The question that most interests Moore in connection with sense-data is whether or not in the perception of physical objects sense-data may be regarded as parts of the surfaces of these objects, and on this question Moore is especially hesitant between conflicting views.

In the closing paragraphs of his early essay, "The Nature and Reality of the Objects of Perception," Moore undertakes to show that it is at least possible "that *some* of the sensible qualities (including secondary ones as well as primary) which we perceive as being in certain places, really exist in the places in which we perceive them to be." [23] This he holds to be the case for the reasons that on the one hand we have a strong natural disposition to believe it and that on the other the only plausible objection to it breaks down under examination. The objection in question is that conflicting properties may seem to exist at the same place, as when the same object appears to have one color when seen directly and another when seen under the microscope, or to be hot to one hand and cold to the other. But the whole of an object may well have one color while the parts have another; and, as Berkeley himself admits, the apparent presence of two conflicting properties in a given place, instead of proving "that *neither* exists there," only shows that we are unable to tell which exists there.[24]

In his lectures of 1910–11 Moore puts forward the following three propositions as representing the views concerning sense-data most commonly held by philosophers: "(1) that absolutely every sense-datum that any person ever directly apprehends exists only so long as he apprehends it, (2) that no sense-datum which any one person directly apprehends ever is directly apprehended by any other person, and (3) that no sense-datum that is directly apprehended by one person can be in *the same space with* any sense-datum apprehended by any other person—that no sense-datum that is seen or heard or felt by me can possibly be either in the same place or at any distance

[23] "The Nature and Reality of the Objects of Perception," p. 95. Parenthetical phrase mine.

[24] *Ibid.,* p. 93.

from any that is seen or heard or felt by anyone else." [25] At the time
Moore thought that the first of the three propositions was certainly
not self-evident and possibly not true, but on the whole he seems to
have been inclined to accept all three propositions and to have regarded sense-data as reliable signs of objects rather than as either
parts or surfaces of them.

Three years later (1913) in his essay on "The Status of Sense-
Data," Moore outlines four possible views of the relation of sense-data
to physical objects, but indicates serious objections to each. The first
is the view that the connection between the directly perceived sensible
and the object intended, for example, in such a proposition as "I
really see *coins*" is that *"if* certain conditions were fulfilled, I or some
other person, *should* directly apprehend certain other sensibles." [26]
This view has the advantage of showing "how our knowledge of
physical propositions can be based on our experience of sensibles," [27]
but it involves the very serious objection of attributing existence,
roundness, etc. to coins in only a Pickwickian sense that outrages a
"strong propensity to believe" in their reality in the usual sense. The
second view is that the object is both the cause and the source of the
sense-datum. Such a view attributes genuine existence to the object
but the properties of the object (e.g. the roundness of the coin) are
still attributable to it in an only Pickwickian sense that leaves us
dissatisfied. A third view affirms the objective reality of all of the
conflicting sense-data that may be attached to the object, but this view
does not permit us to attribute any property to a thing in a straightforward manner. The fourth view, that of Locke, which Moore seems
still to prefer, is that the object really exists and really has *some*
such properties as it seems to have. This view involves the difficulty
of showing how these properties could be known to be in the object,
but then that such things cannot be known immediately may be only
a prejudice.

After four more years, in "Some Judgments of Perception," [28]
Moore points out in objection to the view that sense-data belong to
the surfaces of objects the fact that sensibles change, for example with
changes in distance, but he immediately counters this objection with
the proposal that perhaps the sensibles only seem to change and do
not really do so. If this counterproposal should be unacceptable he
feels that he would have to fall back upon the first of the four above-
named views, which interprets objects as permanent possibilities of
perception. In "A Defense of Common Sense," Moore returns to the

[25] *Some Main Problems of Philosophy,*
p. 43.
[26] "The Status of Sense-Data," p. 189.

[27] *Ibid.,* p. 190.
[28] *Philosophical Studies,* pp. 220–52.

problem but with no more conclusive result. Like Socrates, however, while convinced that no philosopher has ever arrived at a satisfactory answer,[29] unable to arrive at one himself, and candidly admitting that he is strongly drawn toward each of contradictory conclusions,[30] he is confident that an answer can be found, not indeed by empirical inquiry, since the problem is not of a suitable kind for that purpose, but by reflective analysis.

2. The Causal Realism of Bertrand Russell

One of the most lucidly suggestive of all contemporary writers on epistemology is Bertrand Russell (b. 1872). Like Moore, who deeply influenced the earliest phase of his realism, Russell combines analytic procedures with realistic conclusions, and his interest in the procedures is often as significant as his interest in the conclusions. While Russell, like Moore, is sometimes concerned with common-sense knowledge, the subject matter of his epistemological inquiry is more often scientific knowledge. The methods in terms of which the inquiry proceeds are intended rather to resemble the technical procedures of science than to conform to the more fluid ones of common sense or of ordinary language. The methods and conclusions of Russell's present epistemological thought have emerged through an extensive series of stages.[1] These stages will be briefly sketched in the first part of this section and the thought of the latest stage, which is our major concern, will be presented in the second section.

A. Before he began to launch out upon his own in philosophy Russell was an idealist of the type of Berkeley. However, under the influence of Moore and in the conviction that mathematical knowledge could not be adequately supported unless its objects were independent of mind, Russell turned in his *Principles of Mathematics* to the opposite extreme of a realism, akin to that of Meinong, in which anything in any way thinkable, including even such things as round squares, was an independent object. This latter view, however, he soon came to see was self-contradictory; for in saying for example that a round square did not exist, one would by mentioning the object be implicitly affirming the existence of the object in the

[29] "A Defense of Common Sense," p. 215; *The Philosophy of G. E. Moore,* pp. 647 ff., 659 f.

[30] *The Philosophy of G. E. Moore,* pp. 658 f.

[1] An excellent account of the development of Russell's thought, from which a number of significant points in the present account of that development are drawn,

is to be found in Morris Weitz, "Analysis and Unity of Russell's Philosophy" in P. A. Schilpp, *The Philosophy of Bertrand Russell* (Evanston and Chicago: Northwestern University Press, 1944). A more recent account is Charles Fritz, *Bertrand Russell's Construction of the External World* (London: Routledge & Kegan Paul, Ltd., 1952).

subject of the sentence while denying it in the predicate.[2] It was in substantial part in the effort to meet this sort of difficulty without reverting to idealism that Russell developed the distinctive analytic methods first presented in early essays, more rigorously presented in *Principia Mathematica*,[3] and applied to various epistemological and other philosophical problems in subsequent books and essays.

The principal method of Russell's analytic procedure insofar as it bears upon epistemology is often referred to as the method of constructions. It consists of reformulating statements seeming to refer to puzzling entities in such fashion that this reference disappears. The rule of construction is accordingly: "Whenever possible substitute constructions out of known entities for inferences to unknown entities." [4] Applying this method to numbers, Russell was able to substitute for statements concerning numbers other statements concerning classes. Subsequently he was able to substitute for statements about classes other statements referring only to values of variables in propositional functions. The aspect of the method of constructions that applies most specifically to the problems of general epistemology is, however, Russell's celebrated theory of descriptions which was first presented in the essay "On Denoting." [5]

The essential features of the theory are as follows. Since sentences that mention such nonentities as round squares, unicorns, and the present King of France seem wrongly to presuppose the existence of these nonentities, what is needed is a way of reformulating all such misleading sentences, as well as other innocent sentences about complex objects, in such fashion that reference is made only to that with which one is, or could be, acquainted. Thus "the author of *Waverley* was Scotch" could be reformulated in three propositions such as "(1) At least one person wrote *Waverley;* (2) at most one person wrote *Waverley;* (3) whoever wrote *Waverley* was Scotch." [6] The complex terms involved here could in turn be further resolved until not only the original possibly misleading terms but all the introduced terms that might be misleading would be eliminated.

In the writing of Russell's first systematic study of epistemology, *The Problems of Philosophy,* the theory of descriptions was projected into general epistemology so as to facilitate the grounding of knowledge of unexperienced objects in experience or acquaintance. Thus,

[2] See Morris Weitz, "Analysis and the Unity of Russell's Philosophy," p. 93.

[3] A. N. Whitehead and Bertrand Russell, *Principia Mathematica* (Cambridge: Cambridge University Press, 1910).

[4] Russell, "Logical Atomism," in *Contemporary British Philosophy,* (London &

New York: George Allen & Unwin, & The Macmillan Co., 1924), 1st series, p. 363.

[5] *Mind,* 1905, pp. 479–93.

[6] Russell, *Introduction to Mathematical Philosophy* (2d ed.; London: George Allen & Unwin, 1920), p. 177.

"in spite of the fact that we can only know truths which are wholly composed of terms which we have experienced in acquaintance, we can yet have knowledge by description of things which we have never experienced." [7] We are directly acquainted with sense-data, thoughts, feelings, desires, memories, subsisting universals, and ourselves.[8] By the use of intuited a priori principles of logic together with assumed inductive principles we are able to infer from sense-data and memories a descriptive knowledge of probabilities concerning material objects that transcend and are causes of sense experience. The inductive principle in this process of inference rests partly on instinct and partly on the fact that it furnishes the most plausible explanation of sense-data.[9] Idealists, who deny the existence of independent objects, are misled, as Moore has shown, by failure to distinguish between the act and the object of knowledge.[10] Matter, space, and time are probably similar in *structure* to our experiences of them, but more than this can scarcely be affirmed of them. Truth consists in correspondence of the structure of a belief to that of a fact.[11]

Two years after the publication of *The Problems of Philosophy,* Russell carried his method of constructions a bold step farther in *Our Knowledge of the External World.* He now undertakes to get rid of the notion of material objects altogether and to reconstruct sentences about these objects in such a way as to make the reconstructions refer only to sense-data and primary memories, i.e. to data that because of their irreducibility may properly be called "hard data." [12] He retains, however, the distinctions between mental act and object of knowledge as an encountered fact and safeguard to realism.[13]

Soon after the publication of *Our Knowledge of the External World,* Russell began to doubt the possibility of constructing apprehension of physical objects in terms of actual sense-data. Thus in "The Ultimate Constituents of Matter" (1915) he writes of constructions whose constituents are not merely actual data but "such evanescent particulars as may, when an observer happens to be present, become data of sense to that observer." [14] Subsequently in his "Sense-Data and Physics" Russell writes of "appearances" which include not only actual sense-data but also "those 'sensibilia,' if any, which, on grounds of continuity and resemblance, are to be regarded

[7] Russell, *The Problems of Philosophy* (New York: Henry Holt & Co., Inc., 1912), p. 92.
    [8] *Ibid.,* pp. 80 f.
    [9] *Ibid.,* pp. 34 ff.
    [10] *Ibid.,* pp. 65 ff.
    [11] *Ibid.,* pp. 188 ff.

[12] Russell, *Our Knowledge of the External World* (London: George Allen & Unwin, 1914).
    [13] *Ibid.,* p. 76.
    [14] Russell, *Mysticism and Logic* (London: George Allen & Unwin, 1917), p. 137.

as belonging to the same system of appearances, although there happen to be no observers to whom they are data." [15] Indeed construction in terms of actual immediate data is now regarded merely as a rather remote ideal and in practice we must admit both data supplied by other persons and supported by testimony and "sensibilia" which never become data at all.[16] In commenting later on upon this broadening of his epistemological base, Russell confesses having previously confined himself too narrowly to the "verifiables," [17] and suggests that the attempt to construct knowledge solely in terms of percepts was after all only the attempt to work out a "technical hypothesis." [18]

In 1918 in "The Philosophy of Logical Atomism," Russell gives favorable consideration to a neutral monism in which "the distinction between the mental and the physical is entirely a matter of arrangement," but is prevented from thus abandoning his earlier distinction between mental act and object by the psychical character of belief and the difficulty of interpreting such "emphatic particulars" as "this," "now," and "here" in neutralistic terms.[19] However, in 1921 in *The Analysis of Mind,* he adopts in the main the previously considered neutral monism and specifically rejects the distinction between mental act and object, so that mind like matter now becomes for the most part a logical construction grounded in sensible particulars. Sense-data are now simply aspects of objects and whether sensations are to be regarded as belonging to the life of a mind or to the physical objects that are constituted by them is a matter of arrangement. Thus for example when one looks at the stars, the mental aspect consists of "all the appearances of a given star in different places," or better, "the collection of all those correlated particulars which would be regarded by common sense as its effects or its appearances in different places." [20] Images and memories, however, cannot quite satisfactorily be treated as aspects of material things,[21] and indeed psychology, which deals with the nonmaterial mode of organization, may be "nearer to what actually exists" than is physics which deals with the material mode.[22]

In *The Analysis of Matter,* in which the method of constructions is applied to the interpretation of modern physics and the emphasis is more on philosophy of science than on epistemology, mind and

[15] *Ibid.,* p. 154.
[16] *Ibid.,* pp. 157 f.
[17] *The Philosophy of Bertrand Russell,* p. 707.
[18] *Ibid.,* p. 718.
[19] Russell, "The Philosophy of Logical Atomism" (Minneapolis: Department of Philosophy of the University of Minnesota, from *Monist,* 1918–19), pp. 60 f.
[20] Bertrand Russell, *The Analysis of Mind* (London & New York: George Allen & Unwin, & The Macmillan Co., 1921), pp. 100 f.
[21] *Ibid.,* pp. 290 ff.
[22] *Ibid.,* p. 308.

matter remain constructions, but the basic constituents of the universe seem to be neither actual nor potential appearances but basic events. Though percepts themselves are events of a kind, events of a different kind occur where no observer is present [23] and percepts themselves are caused by and compounded from simpler events. Although we infer the existence of basic events from percepts and probably correctly surmise that the two kinds of events are similar in structure, basic events as well as the physical objects constituted by them presumably have aspects of which we know nothing. The place of a percept is now the brain of the perceiver, and in knowing the aspect of his brain involved in his percepts, the perceiver knows his own brain better than does the physiologist who externally examines his brain.[24]

B. In the books that best represent the present stage of Russell's thought, and on which we are to focus our attention (i.e. *An Inquiry into Meaning and Truth* and *Human Knowledge*), the epistemological point of view again comes to the fore, and the emphasis is again upon the percepts and possible percepts that are constituents of events and objects, but alongside and indeed underlying sensed and sensible qualities are other intrinsic physical qualities of which we can have no knowledge. The epistemology of the books in question, which returns to a point of view similar in some important respects to that of the *Problems of Philosophy*, includes significant accounts of belief and meaning, the object of knowledge and its relation to knowing, the character of evidence with special reference to the assumptions implicit in inductive inference, and the nature of truth.

(1) The lower levels of belief lie somewhat deeper than is commonly supposed, in elemental attitudes far below the threshold of linguistic response. Common to such elemental belief attitudes and verbally formulated beliefs is reference to something beyond the attitudes or beliefs. The cat believes that the mouse is in the hole and the scholar that his book is on the shelf.[25] Indeed belief may be defined as a "collection of states of an organism bound together by all having in whole or in part the same external reference." [26] When a belief is more complex than can be shown by action as such, it often involves an ideal element and may be said to consist of "an idea or image combined with a yes-feeling." [27] Since the beliefs that human knowing confirms are in substantial part of the verbal variety, and since, for Russell, the structure of language remains, as in his

---

[23] Cf. Russell, *The Analysis of Matter* (New York & London: Harcourt, Brace & Co., & Kegan Paul, Trench, Trubner & Co., Ltd., 1927), p. 216.

[24] *Ibid.*, pp. 382 f.

[25] Russell, *Human Knowledge* (New York: Simon & Schuster, Inc., 1948), pp. 95 ff.

[26] *Ibid.*, p. 145.

[27] *Ibid.*, p. 148.

earlier writings, an important key to that of reality,[28] analysis of the *language* of beliefs is of crucial importance.

Words, which are the elements of linguistic expression, involve three distinct levels including instances of written or spoken signs, classes of such signs, and meanings.[29] Meanings are what words express or refer to. They depend on association with sounds, so that "words have meaning when there is an association or conditioned reflex connecting them with something other than themselves." [30] Words are understood when they are caused by the appropriate objects or lead to behavior of the kind that would be elicited by such objects. The meanings of words rest ultimately on ostension or pointing to what is intended, but when some words have been thus acquired, others may be built upon them by verbal definition.[31]

Words include a variety of kinds, of which names are the simplest. The latter are distinguished from other types of words in several ways. They are term words only, never relations words, and they can accordingly enter into any sort of sentence regardless of the degree of its relations. They are meaningful even when they stand alone, and they never enter into sentences save as subjects.[32] Ordinarily we apply names to considerable slabs of space-time, such as Socrates or Napoleon. Because of our ignorance, such proper names are useful, but ideally from the point of view of science, it is simpler to apply names only to specific qualities, such as certain shades of red or blue, certain varieties of hardness and softness, and specific positions in "visual space and remembered time." [33] When names are so applied, everything that we need to define can be defined, and the confusing notion of an instance of a quality is replaced by that of a complex in which the quality is present.[34] Thus a complex can be verbally defined by means of the ostensively defined qualities present in it.

A second type of word required even in a minimum vocabulary consists of what Russell calls, in the *Inquiry into Meaning and Truth*, true universals, i.e. relation words. These include words for such spatial relations as "right-and-left in one visual field," and "earlier-and-later in one specious present." To what extent Russell now takes these and other relation words to signify universals is not entirely clear. In the *Inquiry into Meaning and Truth* he argues that since the universal intended by the word "similar" has in any case to be retained, there should be no objection to retaining some other universals as well. Whether he would now adhere to this or

---

[28] Russell, *An Inquiry into Meaning and Truth* (New York: W. W. Norton & Co., Inc., 1940), pp. 437 ff.

[29] *An Inquiry into Meaning and Truth*, pp. 26 ff.

[30] *Human Knowledge*, p. 113.

[31] *Ibid.*, pp. 63 ff.

[32] *Ibid.*, p. 73.

[33] *Inquiry into Meaning and Truth*, p. 117; *Human Knowledge*, pp. 262 ff.

[34] *Ibid.*, p. 265.

not, it is quite clear that the vast role assigned to universals in *The Problems of Philosophy* is now drastically reduced.

The foregoing types of words, being a minimum vocabulary for "what we experience," constitute also a minimum vocabulary in terms of which "all our knowledge" could be expressed. However, when we wish to give manageable expression not to facts themselves but to certain "attitudes" toward the sentences in which we refer to them, we need certain other terms commonly called logical terms.[35] These include such words as "and," "or," "not," "all," and "some." Thus for example, "not" represents a kind of disbelief and "or" stands for an attitude of hesitancy.

Another class of words required, if not to express the content of our knowledge, then at least to indicate its psychology, consists of "egocentric particulars" such as "this," "I," "here," and "now." All such words involve relativity to the observer and are for this reason undesirable from the point of view of science. By defining "I" as the "person attending to this," "now" as "the time attending to this," and "here" as "the place of attending to this," all egocentric particulars can be reduced to "this." "This" can in some degree be relieved of its particularity; for, as terms become more abstract, "this" tends to become the same for different individuals. But the process of reduction can never be completed, and "in all empirical knowledge liberation from sense can be only partial." [36]

Although in an appropriate context a single word can sometimes express the content of verbal belief, it is ordinarily a sentence composed of several words that expresses such a belief. Just as important as the words that make up a sentence is the order of the words as determined by the rules of syntax and the character of the belief expressed. For this reason, we say that whereas words have meaning, sentences have significance and intention. It is by reason of the compound character of a sentence as involving both words and structure that the intention of a sentence is not bound by the meanings of its words *alone*. So long as the words refer to existing things, the sentence as a whole does not have to do so. Failure to note this fact, that is to say, confusion of the meanings of words and the significance of sentences, prompts some positivists mistakenly to deny meaning to everything that does not refer to an empirical fact. It is in virtue of the order involved in it that a sentence may have or lack structural properties akin to those of reality. The simplest kind of sentence is an atomic one; a sentence consisting of a single relation and the number of ostensively defined terms that are appropriate to the relation.[37] Other sentences are built upon atomic ones.

[35] *Ibid.*, pp. 95 ff.
[36] *Ibid.*, p. 93.
[37] *Inquiry into Meaning and Truth,* chap. ii.

In an instance in which the content of a belief consists primarily of an idea rather than of a verbalized pattern or bodily attitudes, the relation of the ideas to the impression whence the idea springs is similar to the relation of an atomic sentence to the fact to which the sentence corresponds. That is to say, the idea is caused by the impression, resembles the impression, and yields somewhat the same effects as the impression.[38]

(2) The objects of knowledge are not sense-data or percepts; for, indispensable as data are to knowing, they are only mediating criteria and by no means either initial or eventual objects. Indeed, unlike sense-data, the objects of knowledge are quite independent of the knowing process. That this is so is indicated by the concurrence of different senses, the same sense at different times, and the senses of different persons; also by the fact that sense-data themselves are caused compounds and that if they are regarded as arising spontaneously, they seem completely erratic and unaccountable.[39] That the object of knowledge is external and independent does not, however, mean that it is a substance having, rather than being constituted by, qualities. Substance theories rest on the following of a false lead of the subject-predicate sentence structure. They make the object of knowledge indefinable and inject into epistemology the useless and misleading concept of an unknowable.

When needless assumptions are duly eliminated an object of knowledge at a certain place is to be regarded as "a collection of qualities existing at the place in question." [40] If space and time themselves are defined in qualitative terms, an object may be regarded simply as a complex of qualities. The minimum conceivable object of which space-time and all objects are composed is the point-instant, which may be defined as "a complete complex of compresence." Compresence refers to the overlapping of qualities in space-time, so that a complete complex of compresence is a group of qualities such that "(a) all of them are compresent and (b) nothing outside the group is compresent with every member of the group." [41] An event, the kind of object toward which our actual knowing is most often directed, is an "incomplete complex" that "occupies a continuous region in space-time" in that in it, given any two space-time points of which it is a part, there is a continuous route from one to the other, consisting wholly of points of which the incomplete complex is part.[42] Particles are "strings of events interconnected by the law of inertia." [43] For example, a certain shade of color is "a complex

---

[38] *Human Knowledge*, p. 109.
[39] Cf. *Human Knowledge*, p. 226.
[40] *An Inquiry into Meaning and Truth*, p. 122.
[41] *Human Knowledge*, p. 304.
[42] *Ibid.*, p. 305.
[43] *Ibid.*, p. 299.

of which that shade is a constituent." [44]   What we commonly call things are somewhat differently organized complexes. For example such names "as 'Socrates,' 'France,' and 'the sun' apply to continuous portions of space-time which happen to interest us." [45]   They are distinguishable by the continuity of their causal lines.[46]

One of the principal advantages of treating the objects of knowledge as complexes of qualities is that, adhering as it does to the principle of the identity of indiscernibles, this procedure renders individuals definable. Such definability of individuals in terms of distinguishables involves a serious difficulty; for if an individual can be so defined, all of the properties of the individual presumably follow analytically from the definition, for example, all that Caesar did, from the definition of Caesar. However, we can often perceive a complex of compresent qualities without necessarily perceiving all of the constituent qualities.[47] When we do become aware that the complex has some hitherto unnoticed quality, the new insight is indeed a product of analysis of the whole, but it is by no means an analytic judgment. Thus I may refer either to Caesar or to myself, by calling to mind enough to identify the quality complex in question, and then go on in an empirical way to discover aspects of the complex not previously noticed.[48]

That the ultimate objects of our knowledge are complexes of qualities certainly does not mean that these objects are the same as that with which we are immediately acquainted, our percepts; nor does it mean that objects closely resemble our percepts. These facts are abundantly apparent when we compare our percepts with the entities with which physics deals, such as atoms, electrons, and protons.[49] Our percepts are essentially private, noninferential, and virtually certain, whereas the constructs of physics are public, inferred, and at best only probable. Even our perceptual space is in many respects quite different from physical space.[50]

What then do percepts and objects have in common and how are they related? What they have in common is some sort of structure such that, generally speaking, for each distinction within a percept there is a corresponding distinction of some kind within the object. This can only be the case if our percepts represent the terminal points, or at any rate the last points before action is taken by us, of uninterrupted causal lines that reach us from the object. This means that, for Russell now, as in *The Analysis of Matter*, the location of

---

[44] *Ibid.*, p. 303.
[45] *Ibid.*
[46] Cf. *ibid.*, pp. 316, 453 ff.
[47] *Ibid.*, p. 302.

[48] *Ibid.*, pp. 301 f.; *An Inquiry into Meaning and Truth*, p. 160.
[49] Cf. *Human Knowledge*, pp. 7, 203 f., 225 ff.
[50] *Ibid.*, pp. 202, 219 ff.

our percepts is in our heads.[51] If the objection is raised that our percepts appear quite different from the fibers of our brain, it must be noted that we do not ever really *see* our brains, so that our brains may in fact resemble our percepts more than they seem to.[52]

Indeed in general: "While mental events and their qualities can be known by inference, physical events are known only as regards their space-time structure. The qualities that compose such events are . . . so completely unknown that we cannot say either that they are or that they are not different from the generalities that we know as belonging to mental events." [53]

(3) Because Russell now regards objects of knowledge as distinct and different from percepts and as known only by inference from percepts, the problem of how we can legitimately pass from immediately apprehended percepts to inferred objects, from private data to confirmed beliefs about objects, has again become acute for him. That a pure empiricism, which accepts only the evidence of the senses plus the laws of formal logic, can never furnish a sufficient evidential basis for our knowledge is apparent in the inability of empiricists as such to justify their reliance on nonempirical principles of induction.[54] A rationalism that relies, as Hegel, Dewey, and some recent analytic philosophers have done, upon coherence is equally inadequate, in that unless a system contains some initially credible propositions it cannot by its internal structure acquire credibility with reference to fact.[55] By its very nature the evidential process can yield with reference to facts only probabilities; and while probabilities are indeed achieved through interlocking and mutually supporting propositions, they are never achieved save on foundations of initially credible propositions which coherence cannot create. Sources for the initially credible propositions on which knowledge of matters of fact must in the end rest are the following: first, basic beliefs causally connected with actual occurrences, second, "principles of logical inference," and third, "principles of extra-logical inference." [56]

What Russell calls a basic belief is a reliable belief caused by and expressing direct experience. A basic proposition is "a proposition which arises on occasion of a perception, which is the evidence for its truth, and has a form such that no two propositions having this form can be mutually inconsistent if derived from different percepts." [57]

---

[51] Cf. *ibid.*, pp. 296 ff., 202 ff.; and *An Inquiry into Meaning and Truth*, p. 428.

[52] *Human Knowledge*, p. 229.

[53] *Ibid.*, p. 231.

[54] Cf. *An Inquiry into Meaning and Truth*, pp. 383 f.; and *Human Knowledge*, pp. 496 ff.

[55] Cf. *An Inquiry into Meaning and Truth*, pp. 174 ff.; and *Human Knowledge*, pp. 157 f.

[56] *An Inquiry into Meaning and Truth*, p. 283.

[57] *Ibid.*, p. 174.

The principles of formal inference are those of deductive logic and those of mathematics, the latter being wholly derivable from the former. All such principles are, as the *Principia Mathematica* has shown, analytic and formal though they are selected in view of psychological needs. While these principles are not sufficient, as was supposed in some of Russell's earlier works, to implement an adequate construction of common-sense and scientific knowledge upon the basis of sense-data, they continue indispensable to the adequate formulation and manipulation of the propositions in which scientific hypotheses and conclusions are formulated.

However, if evidential foundations included basic propositions expressing sense experiences and the principles of logic and mathematics, and only these, most of what we call knowledge would still be impossible. We should be able to make very little progress, even within the area of our own experience, beyond the here-now to which solipsism is confined.[58] Even in the subjective realm, some reliance on memory is required if we are to put our experiences together;[59] and if our attempts to achieve probabilities concerning something beyond our experience are not to be swallowed up in an infinity of indeterminate possibilities, a reliable principle of induction will also be needed. The difficulty of any attempt to prove a general principle of induction is that any such principle depends upon actual inductions that in turn depend upon it. Instead of attempting to establish or of even assuming such a general principle, Russell undertakes in the last part of his *Human Knowledge* to set forth a minimal list of nonempirical and nonlogical postulates that have to be made in order to sustain the knowledge of matters of fact that we seem to have. The postulates are as follows:

(a) "The postulate of quasi-permanence": *"Given any event A, it happens very frequently that, at any neighboring time, there is at some neighboring place an event very similar to A."* [60] This postulate helps to establish a basis on which we may intelligibly think of a material object. (b) "The postulate of separable causal lines": *"It is frequently possible to form a series of events such that from one or two members of the series something can be inferred as to the other members."* [61] This postulate affords the basis for distinguishing a thing, such as a drop of ocean water, from its neighbors, and it connects our percepts with external things or events, for example, our impressions of a star with the star to which it applies. (c) "The postulate of spatio-temporal continuity," which denies "action at a distance" and serves as a basis of many of our "inferences to unobserved occurrences, both in science and in common sense." [62] (d) "The structural postulate": *"When a number of structurally similar complex events are ranged about a center in regions not widely separated, it is usually the case that all belong to causal lines having their origin in an event of the same structure at the center."* [63] (e) "The postulate of analogy": *"Given two classes of events A and B, and given that, whenever both A and B can be observed, there is reason to believe that A causes B, then if, in a given case, A is observed, but there is no way of observing whether B occurs or not, it is probable that B occurs; and similarly if B is observed, but the presence or absence of A cannot be observed."* [64] This postulate enables us to extend inference to what is not observed and is thus especially useful in enabling us to infer the existence of other minds.

Apart from some such principles as these, neither universal propositions involving prediction nor unexemplified existence propositions, both of which are in fact in many cases known and needed by science, would be possible.[65] Man has an initial "propensity" to make inferences of the kinds justified by such principles, and all the verifiable consequences of adopting these principles "are such as experience will confirm," but this sort of fact cannot "make the principles even probable." [66] The real ground for adopting the principles is simply the fact that "they seem indispensable in reaching conclusions that we all accept." [67]

(*4*) Truth is not, as Hegelians and some modern positivists seem to suppose, mere coherence; the quest for truth is never simply a verbal quest but remains, as these writers tend to forget, always responsible to empirical fact.[68] True beliefs are not, as the pragmatists tend to think, to be identified with "beliefs that promote success," for success itself can hardly be defined without reference to knowledge and so indirectly to truth.[69] The concept of truth is clearly wider than that of knowledge, and the latter must be defined in terms of the former and not conversely.[70] "Truth is a property of beliefs, and derivatively of sentences which express beliefs, . . . a certain relation between a belief and one or more facts other than the belief." [71] The term may also apply to what "if it were believed . . . would be true." [72] In general the truth relation is one of corre-

[62] *Ibid.,* pp. 490 f.
[63] *Ibid.,* pp. 491 f.
[64] *Ibid.,* p. 493.
[65] *Ibid.,* pp. 504 ff.
[66] *Ibid.,* p. 507.
[67] *Ibid.,* p. 156.
[68] Cf. *An Inquiry into Meaning and Truth,* pp. 175 ff.
[69] Cf. *Human Knowledge,* p. 157; and

Bertrand Russell, *A History of Western Philosophy* (New York, Simon & Schuster, Inc., 1945), pp. 819 ff.
[70] *An Inquiry into Meaning and Truth,* pp. 23, 295 ff.; and *Human Knowledge,* p. 154.
[71] *Ibid.,* p. 148.
[72] *Ibid.*

pondence, correspondence being regarded as structural similarity. Remembering that, in view of the principles of continuity, causes are structurally similar to their effects, a simple belief that can be expressed in a word may be said to be true if the word is caused by what it means. "This is A is called 'true' when it is caused by what A' means." [73] In other cases the formulation is more complex, but he principle is much the same: "Every belief which is not merely an impulse to action is in the nature of a picture, combined with a yes-feeling or a no-feeling; in the case of a yes-feeling it is 'true' if there is a fact having to the picture the kind of similarity that a prototype has to an image; in the case of a no-feeling it is 'true' if there is no such fact." [74] The relation of prototype to image includes similarity, partial causation, and causation of some of the same effects. Truth is then correspondence of a belief or possible belief to a fact, or more specifically, a relation of a belief or possible belief to a fact in such fashion that the belief is similar to, partially caused by, and has effects in common with the fact.

3. THE CONTRASTING REALISMS OF SAMUEL ALEXANDER, C. D. BROAD, AND G. DAWES HICKS

In the thought of the three thinkers now to be successively considered, interesting contrasts are to be found, on the one hand between a position similar to that of the American new realists and one similar to that of the American critical realists, and on the other hand between positions of both of these kinds and a type of realism that though akin both to new realism and critical realism differs decisively from both.

A. Probably the most comprehensive and incisive of all attempts to formulate the type of realism that we have encountered in new realism and in the middle phase of Russell's thought, is Samuel Alexander's *Space, Time and Deity*. Attaching central importance to Moore's distinction of act and object and sharing Russell's concern to ground epistemological theses in findings of recent science, Alexander also retains the idealists' devotion to coherence and to systematic metaphysical construction; his epistemology represents a brilliant effort to do justice to all varieties of the objects of knowledge within a single objective framework of space-time. We shall begin by observing the general character of his metaphysics with special reference to minds and then pass on, in the order suggested by his book, to consider his accounts of the relation of minds to objects, the ways of apprehending objects, and the character of truth.

---

[73] *Ibid.,* p. 118.   [74] *Human Knowledge,* p. 154.

(*1*) Reality consists fundamentally of space-time. Space and time though distinguishable and forever operating upon one another, are inseparable.[1] Things begin with space and time and continue always to be configurations of space and time.[2] Those characteristics of space-time that remain constant amid changes, its permanent features are known as categories. They include identity, universality and particularity, relation, order, substance, quantity and intensity, whole and parts, and motion. In the course of the operation of time upon space, there emerge more and more complex configurations some of which give rise to qualitative distinctions.[3] Thus reality comes to include a variety of levels, each of which is dependent upon and expressible in the terms of the one below it but none of which is predictable on the basis of knowledge of the one below it. Above elementary space-time and its accompanying motion is matter. Matter presently gives rise to the secondary qualities, and matter so qualified gives rise to life. Subsequently, the configurations of space-time that constitute life, especially in the brain, produce mind, which is not reducible to, though dependent upon, the levels from which it emerges. In the course of its development mind in turn sometimes yields a higher quality which may appropriately be called deity.

Mind is, in one of its two major aspects, simply consciousness, but the understanding of the experiences that enter into consciousness requires at the outset a distinction closely related to Moore's distinction between the act and the object of knowing, namely the distinction between enjoyment and contemplation.[4] Enjoyment refers to the inward process of an experience, and contemplation to the outward reference. Every experience has these two sides: "The mind enjoys itself and contemplates its objects." [5] For every thing, image, concept, or inference contemplated there is a corresponding perceiving, imagining, thinking, or inferring enjoyed.

In experiences enjoyed or lived through, one essential aspect of mind consists, but mind has another equally important aspect. Enjoyed experiences are commonly acknowledged to be at least accompanied by neural processes, and such processes can scarcely be related to consciousness either as mere parallels or as independent forces interacting with consciousness.[6] They constitute rather the other essential aspect of mind, apart from which mind could not exist. Thus, "that which as experienced from the inside or enjoyed is a conscious process, is as experienced from the outside or contemplated

[1] Samuel Alexander, *Space, Time and Deity* (London: Macmillan & Co., Ltd., 1920), I, 44 ff.

[2] *Ibid.*, p. 180.

[3] *Ibid.*, II, 45 ff.
[4] *Ibid.*, I, 11.
[5] *Ibid.*, p. 12.
[6] *Ibid.*, II, 9 ff.

a neural one," [7] and "consciousness is in fact the enjoyed innervation of the appropriate neural process." [8]

(2) What is the relation of mind, so interpreted, to the objects of its knowledge? Instead of occupying a privileged position, as it is commonly supposed to do, the knowing relation is an instance of the simplest of all relations, that of the togetherness or compresence of configuration in space-time. It is "strictly comparable with the relation of two comparable physical finites, like the floor and the table." [9] It differs from other such relations not in its character as a relation but only in the character of its terms, in that one of these is a mind. The table is compresent with the floor and reveals itself to the latter as far as can be; the table may be compresent with a living mind in the same way but the mind happens to be susceptible to the self-revelation of the table as the floor is not.[10]

The conception of compresence gives rise in Alexander's thought to two basic convictions concerning the cognitive relation. The first of these is that the objects of knowledge are nonmental and independent of mind. Since the mind, which is of a higher order, is together in space-time with objects, which are of a lower order, and since the higher is dependent on the lower, the mind is dependent on objects rather than they dependent upon it.[11] "All that they owe to mind is their being known." [12] This independent, nonmental character of objects holds alike of the space-time configurations called things, of the primary and secondary qualities of things,[13] memory objects, universals, images, and even the elements of illusion. Introspection yields no exception, for introspection is not contemplation of objects but only enjoyment of experiences. When the prejudice that the object owes its qualities to a subject is removed, "experience itself declares the distinct existence of the object as something nonmental." [14]

The second of the two convictions mentioned above is that the object, instead of being inferred from mediating representations, is directly apprehended by the knowing mind. To be sure the whole of a thing is not always, or even commonly, immediately before the mind in perception; rather, a perspective of the thing is before the mind.[15] What is true of perception in this respect is true also of memory and even of imagination. If I remember a man, a perspective of the configuration of space-time that constitutes him is directly before my mind; and if I think of a tree, a perspective of the tree is

---

[7] *Ibid.,* p. 5.
[8] *Ibid.,* p. 107.
[9] *Ibid.,* p. 83.
[10] *Ibid.,* pp. 102 f.
[11] *Ibid.,* pp. 105 f.

[12] *Ibid.,* p. 106.
[13] *Ibid.,* pp. 138 f.
[14] *Ibid.,* I, 16; also II, 87.
[15] Cf. *Ibid.,* pp. 92 ff.

before me. When an object seems to grow smaller or less intensely hot as I move away from it, this fact is no indication that my perception of the object is only indirect; it is simply an instance of the mind's selecting for attention under given circumstances only relevant aspects of the object. Indeed always selection, not creation, is the proper function of mind with respect to its objects.[16] The relatively passive role of mind in knowledge does not, however, justify the so-called searchlight theory of Holt and others, to the effect that knowing consists only of an illumination of objects, for this theory fails to recognize that the objects in question are in an important sense *my* objects.[17]

(3) In the observation that at least an aspect of the object is directly before the knowing mind, the essential character of the process of knowledge is already evident. The space-time patterns of the object are sufficiently compresent with the mind when the mind enjoys itself in contemplating them or when they confront appropriate selective neural structures. However, the modes of the requisite contemplation differ according to the character of the object confronted. Hence, the process of knowing involves a variety of "ways of apprehending."

Space-time, the permanent features or categories of space-time, and the so-called primary qualities, are apprehended by what may appropriately be called *intuition*.[18] This intuition is a priori [19] in the sense that it underlies and is a condition of all sensation [20] and that no experience whatever, either of matter or of mind, is possible apart from it.[21] But it is empirical in that it always occurs along with other features of experience, and especially in that, instead of importing something into experience, it simply discovers what is already there,[22] for space-time and its categorical features are prior to mind. That despite our intuitions concerning space and time we are sometimes deceived concerning space and time is the penalty we pay for receiving our intuitions in invariable association with sense experiences.[23]

Materiality is apprehended by the sense of resistance, which, while lacking any special prerogative for informing us about reality in general, does successfully reveal the material aspect of reality.[24] The secondary qualities, which also belong directly to segments of space-time rather than being creations of the mind, are apprehended by our specific senses. At the next higher level, "the quality of life is

---

[16] *Ibid.*, p. 95.
[17] *Ibid.*, pp. 109 ff.
[18] *Ibid.*, pp. 148, 158.
[19] *Ibid.*, I, 185 f.
[20] *Ibid.*, II, 148.

[21] *Ibid.*, I, 185.
[22] *Ibid.*, pp. 166 ff.
[23] *Ibid.*, p. 202.
[24] *Ibid.*, p. 160.

apprehended in ourselves by the organic and kinesthetic sensations" and is extended to others by natural inference.[25] Apprehension of mind is achieved with reference to ourselves by immediate enjoyment [26] and, with reference to others, through the social intercourse of daily life [27] "supplemented by sympathetic imagination." [28]

(4) Truth, though never merely subjective, is also not altogether objective. It must be interpreted in terms of a "subject-object theory" [29] in which each side is essential to the whole. Beliefs by themselves do not constitute truths but neither do facts by themselves. The beliefs to which truth applies are built upon universally particular propositions which bring together various aspects of the real world in terms of perspectives. These perspectives may be merely entertained or supposed.[30] They become beliefs only when to them is added "the fiat of the speculative will"; [31] only then do proper questions concerning their truth and error arise. Beliefs about particulars may attribute certain qualities to certain segments of space-time, and it is not necessary to know all truth in order to know the truth of these beliefs. But in the sense that in a belief about a particular object we are aware that that object's "space-time is a part of the whole," Bradley is right in contending that every belief is about the whole of reality.[32]

That which makes a belief true is not, as realists commonly suppose, correspondence to external reality, for "if reality is something other than what appears to us . . . it cannot be appealed to." [33] Neither is what makes truth true, as the pragmatists claim, that which "works," for while truth does work, truth without responsibility to reality "is not truth at all." [34] The substance of that which makes a belief true may be formulated thus: "In the intercourse of minds the truth is created as truth at the guidance of reality, by mutual confirmation or exclusion of belief." [35] At one level that which makes truth true is reference to the standard mind, the coherence of the truth is created as truth at the guidance of reality, by mutual collective judging. But at a higher level the standard mind itself must be under constant control by reality or the totality of space-time itself. Such a view of truth does not imply degrees of truth, but it does suggest progress of truth in which a given belief can have been true for those who held it but not for their more enlightened descendants.[36]

---

[25] *Ibid.*, pp. 170 ff.
[26] *Ibid.*, pp. 176 f.
[27] *Ibid.*, pp. 31 ff.
[28] *Ibid.*, p. 177.
[29] *Ibid.*, p. 271.
[30] *Ibid.*, p. 222.

[31] *Ibid.*, II, 248.
[32] *Ibid.*
[33] *Ibid.*, p. 252.
[34] *Ibid.*, p. 266.
[35] *Ibid.*, p. 261.
[36] *Ibid.*, pp. 263 ff.

Error is of course most easily explained as mental, but this sort of explanation is not open to a view in which all objects of knowledge are nonmental. The illusory experiences which give rise to error are instances of reality misplaced either through the interference of other objects such as mirrors and misty atmospheres or through that of the mind. In illusory experiences the mind as it were "squints at things" so as to place their elements in relations that space-time cannot accept. Mere illusory experience without belief is, however, not by itself error, and when commitment to propositions based on illusory experience does occur, it is generally in large part due either to custom or to the interest of the moment.[37]

B. In contrast to the thought of Alexander and the new realists, who tend to identify the object and that through which the object is known and to regard the knowing process as directly confronted by the object, the thought of C. D. Broad (b. 1887) resembles that of the American critical realists in placing intermediaries—referred to by Broad as "sensa"—between the object and the knowing process. However, Broad, whose analytic methods resemble those of Russell and Moore, differs from the American critical realists in focusing attention mainly upon the sensa.

At the outset Broad adopts Moore's distinction between act and object of knowing.[38] This distinction is at any rate obviously applicable to visual sensations and possibly applicable to all sensations.[39] It does not, however, justify the refutation of idealism that Moore bases upon it, for by no means all idealists have built upon blindness to it, and the objects that are distinguished from mental acts may themselves conceivably be mental.[40] Both acts and their immediately sensed objects are included in sensation; but immediately sensed objects, or sensa, though real, are only intermediaries and by no means to be identified with the objects of the physical world with which science is primarily concerned.

With regard to the character of our knowledge of the physical world, Broad's approach is very different from the common-sense approach of Moore. Such evidence for belief in physical objects as Moore develops in his formal proofs of the existence of the external world is, he thinks, quite inadequate to its purpose. The sensa which we experience are real and "the existence of sensa is absolutely certain," [41] but an "observer who thinks he perceives a certain physi-

---

[37] Ibid., p. 212.

[38] Cf. C. D. Broad, Perception, Physics and Reality (Cambridge: Cambridge University Press, 1914), p. viii; and Scientific Thought (New York: Harcourt, Brace & Co., 1923), pp. 251 ff, 521.

[39] Ibid., chap. viii; p. 521.

[40] Cf. Perception, Physics and Reality, p. viii.

[41] Scientific Thought, p. 390.

cal event may be mistaken." [42] Indeed, although we cannot help believing in an external world, apart from some initial probability in its favor we lack even any probable grounds for any such belief. Accordingly, the best we can do in this matter is to discover such corroborative coherence among sense-data as would support belief in a physical world if there were some initial probability in its favor.[43] The suggestion implicit in common sense and in certain phases of the thought of Moore and Russell that sense-data are parts of the surface of the object is hardly helpful in furnishing evidence for physical objects. Any such view is precluded by the facts of erroneous perception, mirror images, and the like; and these facts, instead of being mere abnormalities, belong as much as any other fact to the given, of which so-called normal data are only special cases. Indeed there is not "the faintest chance of rehabilitating" common sense, and Broad suggests that that way of thinking should "go out and hang itself." [44]

Of the three most plausible alternatives to common sense, one, developed by Alexander and Whitehead and called by Broad the *multiple inherence* theory, interprets the physical inherence of a property in a physical object to mean that from every place occupied by a normal human organism, a certain property will sensibly inhere in that object, such inherence being a unique relation.[45] Contrary to the criticisms of some of its opponents, this theory works quite as satisfactorily for sizes and shapes as for colors. A second alternative to the common-sense view that the *sensum* is a part of the surface of the object is a view suggested by Moore, Hicks, and others and called by Broad the *multiple relation theory of appearing*.[46] According to this theory, which has much to commend it, that a physical object has a certain property means that it stands in the unique relation of appearing in such and such ways to such and such observers.[47] Both of these alternatives, however, suffer from the defect of presupposing an untenable idea of absolute space. Over against both must be placed the empirically more satisfactory *sensum theory*. Such a theory, while recognizing in sensa objectively real and uniquely related parts of physical objects, will show that sensa "cannot be spatio-temporal parts of physical objects." [48]

Sensa are in some respects like physical objects and in others like mental states. "They are not physical," for the degree of their cer-

[42] *Ibid.*

[43] *Ibid.*, pp. 266 ff.

[44] Broad, *The Mind and Its Place in Nature* (London & New York: Kegan Paul, Ltd., and Harcourt, Brace & Co., 1929), pp. 185 f.

[45] *Ibid.*, pp. 161 ff.

[46] *Ibid.*, p. 178; see also *Scientific Thought*, p. 237.

[47] *Ibid.*; *The Mind and Its Place in Nature*, pp. 178 ff.

[48] *Ibid.*, p. 181.

tainty and manner of their variation are quite different from those of physical objects; but neither are they "states of mind or existentially mind-dependent." [49] They are like physical objects in their extension, size, shape, color, hardness, etc.; but in being dependent on body and possibly even on mind for some of their characteristics and in failing to fit into physical space in any literal sense, they are like mental states.[50]

How then do sensa come to be? Generally speaking, they are joint products of external physical objects and our own bodies.[51] Their emergence depends upon three different sets of conditions, i.e. those respectively of their origination, their transmission, and their actual production.[52] The primary condition of the origination of sensa is the presence of a physical object. The external conditions of the transmission of sensa include the presence of air and other media. The principal internal condition of this transmission is the presence of a nervous system.[53] Some of these conditions are active occurrences. Others, often erroneously overlooked, are merely "continuant" in the sense that while they are not active, they must be present if sensa are to occur.[54] Being awake and being free from psychic blindness are instances of continuant conditions. Since at least visual sensa may sometimes originate apart from the presence of external objects, a distinction must be drawn between conditions that are independently necessary to sensa, as for example certain brain states usually are, and those that are only dependently necessary, as for example external physical objects in the case of vision.[55]

The really crucial conditions of the emergence of the sensa are those of their actual production, that is, those of the passage from purely physical brain states to quasi-mental sensa. Is this actual production of sensa simply a selection of some aspects of the world in preference to others or is it a generation of something new? [56] On the one hand, purely selective theories, as advocated by Alexander and the new realists, have the ontological advantage of giving to the sensa an objective status in reality and the epistemological advantage of bridging the gap between perceptual situations and the unperceived part of the physical world; but they are thrown into confusion by the facts of illusion and error. On the other hand, while purely generative theories avoid this difficulty, they make sensa more peculiar than necessary and knowledge virtually impossible.

If the production of the sensa is acknowledged to be in some *part*

[49] *Ibid.*
[50] *Ibid.;* see also *Scientific Thought,* chap. viii.
[51] *Ibid.*, p. 488.
[52] *Ibid.*, pp. 490 f.
[53] *Ibid.*, p. 491.
[54] *Ibid.*, pp. 510 ff.
[55] *Ibid.*, pp. 499 ff.
[56] *Ibid.*, pp. 573 ff.

generative, the question arises whether this generation is merely causative or actually creative. Conditions may be said to be causative if and only if "the event which is determined by them *joins up with* one or others of the continuant conditions, and becomes part of *its* history." [57] Since the sensa, which are in the nature of the case different from their physical conditions, can scarcely be said to join up with these conditions, the production of the sensa can scarcely be said to be causative. The production of the sensa must then be in some measure creative although it is by no means an unrelated occurrence. It is surely a production of particulars and is quite different from physical causation, but its precise relations to physical causation have still to be worked out. [58]

The physical object is not, as Russell and others have thought, a mere class of sensa, or, as Berkeley would say, "God's habits of volition," or, as Leibnitz would have it, "a colony of unintelligent monads." [59] The physical object in its relation to the sensa must be characterized, rather, in the way that critical examination of the presuppositions of science suggests,[60] in terms of some such "critical scientific theory" as follows. "Perceptual objects" are actual correlations of sensa in the specious present of the observer.[61] Such objects are slices of larger perceptual life histories. The visual space of an observer is built up out of correlations of the visual fields of which his visual sensa are accented parts. The spaces of other sensa are instituted in corresponding fashion. But none of these spaces is literally physical space, nor does any sensum literally occur in physical space. Our apprehensions of physical objects are arrived at by correlation of the sensa connected with movement of our own and other bodies, not indeed by inference, but in terms of the "category" of physical objects.[62] Out of these apprehensions and on the analogy of visual space, we construct our concept of the physical space of bodies in motion.[63] Physical objects are literally in physical space and have size, shape, and motion in it just as visual sensa do in their fields. Physical objects do not, however, literally have color, temperature, and the like,[64] and although these properties consist of real sensa that genuinely inhere in perceptual situations, they are better correlated with certain physical shapes than with anything more closely analogous to themselves in physical objects.[65] Physical objects

[57] *Ibid.*, p. 535.
[58] *Ibid.*, pp. 539 ff.
[59] *The Mind and Its Place in Nature*, pp. 200 f.
[60] *Ibid.*, p. 183; *Scientific Thought*, pp. 273 ff.

[61] *The Mind and Its Place in Nature*, pp. 330 ff.
[62] *The Mind and Its Place in Nature*, p. 217.
[63] *Ibid.*, pp. 203 ff.
[64] *Ibid.*, pp. 204 ff.
[65] *Scientific Thought*, pp. 279 f.

may be said to be quasi-permanent, public, and literally extended, but not colored, loud, warm, and so on.[66] They have, as science for the most part assumes, primary qualities but not secondary ones.

So far we have been mainly concerned with the sensa and their relation to physical objects. We must now consider the relation of sensa to minds, with special reference to such beliefs as, when sufficiently supported, constitute knowledge of things. Every such belief, according to Broad, includes, as its principal ingredients, "certain sensible qualities," "a mass of bodily feeling, emotion, etc.," intuitive "apprehension by the percipient," and reference.[67] The first of these has been amply discussed in what has been said of the sensa, and the second hardly needs discussion here. Mention of the third ingredient suggests the question how the sensa are apprehended, and since sensa may quite well exist unapprehended,[68] this question comes to be a rather important one. The answer attempted by Russell in *The Analysis of Mind* and by the new realists is to the effect that to be sensed is simply to become a part of a sensory field. But this answer is surely wrong. In the first place, "no one would admit that a sensum which was a part of a sense-field which is not intuitively apprehended would itself be intuitively apprehended." [69] In the second place, sensa from various fields can be apprehended at the same time. Finally, the unity of apprehension is a unity of center and not, as the answer in question tends to suggest, of system.[70] The correct answer seems rather to be that to be sensed is to come into the relation of sensible simultaneity in the specious present with some part of a "somatic sense-history," such a sense-history consisting of certain "unanalysable mental states," [71] i.e., "the mass of general bodily feeling of the percipient at the time." [72] The fourth or reference factor in the perceptual situation, "the non-inferential beliefs . . . which go beyond anything that is intuitively apprehended in the situation," [73] seems clearly to consist of "certain emotions, and certain feelings of expectation . . . causally dependent on the traces left by past experience" and aroused by the apprehension of the present sensum.[74]

In closing this account of Broad's epistemology we must touch very briefly upon his views on two other subjects, our knowledge of entities other than physical objects and the nature and criteria of truth. With reference to the first of these topics, Broad accepts the

---

[66] *The Mind and Its Place in Nature,* pp. 195 ff.

[67] *Ibid.,* p. 209.

[68] *Scientific Thought,* pp. 519 f.

[69] *The Mind and Its Place in Nature,* p. 211.

[70] *Ibid.,* p. 213.

[71] *Ibid.,* pp. 522 f.

[72] *Ibid.,* p. 215.

[73] *Ibid.,* p. 209.

[74] *Ibid.,* p. 215.

genuineness of introspective knowledge of one's own mind but contends that this knowledge requires no apprehension of a "pure ego" and consists primarily of awareness of "objective situations, such as perceptual and memory situations, the sensing of sensa, the feeling of toothaches, and so on." [75] There is no reason to doubt the validity of careful introspection as far as it goes, but neither is there any reason to believe in its exhaustiveness.[76] Broad regards knowledge of other minds as genuine and on the whole reliable. Such knowledge is built noninferentially upon ingredients present to the knower consisting primarily of sensa connected with the intelligently behaving body of the mind that is known, and also partly perhaps of a "telegnostic factor" in which the mentality of the other is more directly revealed.[77]

Some interesting aspects of the correspondence view of truth adopted by Broad are involved in the following suggestion from his *Scientific Thought*. A judgment "is true, if it has the peculiar relation of concordance to the fact to which it refers." The "discordance" which characterizes falsity "is not mere absence of concordance." [78] There can be intelligible statements which are neither true nor false. Notable instances of such statements are those of judgments about the future, which, although they are about certain characteristics that will or will not obtain in the future, do not refer to any now existing fact.[79] The facts referred to by any judgment may be positive, but they may quite as well be negative.

C. The realism of G. Dawes Hicks, which unfortunately was presented only in a series of essays and never systematically developed, strikes out in a new direction different in important respects from that of any of the forms of realism thus far specifically considered. With Broad and the American critical realists Hicks agrees against Alexander and the American new realists that the role of mind in knowing is far more than that of a selective relation among objects or even than that of enjoyment and contemplation of objects; but with Alexander and new realists Hicks agrees against Broad and the critical realists that the mind immediately confronts its objects so as to require no intermediate entities. The positive conception in which these seemingly conflicting trends are reconciled is a theory of *appearing*. We shall consider first Hicks's criticism of opposing types of realism and then his own constructive suggestions.

The representative realism of Locke rests, Hicks thinks, upon the assumption of a "violent . . . antithesis between the process of

[75] *Ibid.*, p. 315.
[76] *Ibid.*
[77] *Ibid.*, p. 331.

[78] *Scientific Thought*, p. 70.
[79] *Ibid.*, p. 73.

sense-apprehension, on the one hand, and that of thinking or judging on the other," [80] and for that reason among others cannot be sustained. The new realists are correct in contending that knowledge is not mere "mental 're-action,' " [81] for such a view merely transports into the mind "the very mechanisms . . . shown to be unavailing in the domain of matter." [82] But in obscuring the distinctions of subject and object, knower and known, and act and object, the new realists, like the idealists whom they resemble far more than they care to admit, really render knowledge impossible.[83] Broad is correct in distinguishing between mental act and object of knowledge, in regarding the object as an independent extended object, in beginning his account of knowledge with a perceptual situation in which a thing appears to an observer, and in much else besides. But Broad and others like him are badly mistaken in "regarding an 'appearance' as an existent entity, a *tertium quid*, between the real object and the perceiving mind." [84] Broad himself admits that his sensa are of a very peculiar character, neither physical nor mental and very different from things, and most people find themselves quite unable to locate any such odd entities. As a matter of fact, the qualities with which sensa tend to be identified are in themselves mere abstracta too remote from experience to be of much use in the knowing process.[85] Even supposing sensa to exist they could scarcely be appearances of physical objects, for "it is the sensa alone that are colored or hot or cold or hard or soft" and "there is not the slightest reason for believing that sensa disclose to us the shapes, sizes and positions of physical entities." [86] It is difficult to see how the sensa "could so much as indicate to us the bare existence of physical entities," [87] but if indeed sensa did exist, they would, like the "sense presentations" of Stace and other phenomenalists, constitute an "impenetrable wall" [88] that would forever preclude the apprehension of any object.

On its constructive side Hicks's theory is an exposition of the relation of appearing. Basic to any realistic theory of knowledge is "the distinction between the act of knowing and the object known." [89] The object, in the case of perception, is always unequivocally the independent physical object and not in any sense a state of consciousness.[90] "Sense appearances presuppose, as the condition of their pos-

[80] G. Dawes Hicks, *Critical Realism* (London: Macmillan & Co., Ltd., 1958), pp. 71, 121.

[81] *Ibid.*, p. 33.

[82] *Ibid.*

[83] *Ibid.*, pp. 32 ff.

[84] *Ibid*, p. vi.

[85] *Ibid.*, p. 77.

[86] *Ibid.*, p. 54.

[87] *Ibid.*, p. 55.

[88] *Ibid.*, p. 263.

[89] *Ibid.*, p. 40.

[90] *Ibid.*, p. 30.

sibility, real existing things which appear. The appearances are dependent upon the actually real objects, and not the objects upon the appearances." [91] Moreover, "if we start from a subjectivism . . . there is no mode of effecting a transition to a knowledge of objective reality." [92]

What appears to us in knowing is never a mere isolated fragment of an object such as a patch of color or a feeling of hardness. There is, to be sure, much in the object that does not appear, and an appearance may be erroneous. But that which appears, instead of being a mere sensory quality, is a full-bodied object such as a tree or a table.[93] If things are presented to different observers differently it is not because they produce different sensa, but only because they appear in different ways according to the processes by which they came to appear or the relations in which they stand to the observer.[94] Such a view does not require, as Broad thinks, a concept of absolute space, for no space is really empty.[95]

It is quite impossible to reduce secondary qualities to primary ones, and such qualities probably inhere in physical objects alongside the primary ones.[96] Certainly there is no contradiction in affirming such inherence, and since physical objects must have some qualities other than primary ones, this affirmation, which is strangely suggested by perceptual experience, is quite plausible.[97]

The role of the mind in the knowing process is neither the constitutive one assigned by the idealists nor the passive one assigned by the new realists. It consists rather of processes of discriminating, comparing, and relating what is found in nature. These processes do not color nature because they themselves have no color.[98] Through them we do indeed bring past experiences to bear upon present sensations and in this way form images, but this process may be only a progressive discrimination that, far from distorting what it finds, clarifies and reveals the object with increasing economy of effort.[99] Provided care is taken to remember that there is no separate entity represented by the term appearance, it is useful for some purposes to distinguish mental act, totality of appearances, and object appearing. The content of the mental act is awareness of something, and mental acts vary as their objects do.[100]

Discrimination is in the process of knowing, both in the most elementary perception and in the most advanced conceptual reasoning. Any effort to sunder these manifestations of discrimination is

[91] *Ibid.*, p. 259.
[92] *Ibid.*, p. 262.
[93] *Ibid.*, p. 49.
[94] *Ibid.*, pp. 46, 70 ff.
[95] *Ibid.*, p. 52.

[96] *Ibid.*, pp. 30 ff., 178.
[97] *Ibid.*, p. 83.
[98] *Ibid.*, pp. 15 ff.
[99] *Ibid.*, chap. iv.
[100] *Ibid.*, pp. 60 ff.

disastrous for knowledge. However, it is plausible for purposes of special inquiry to concentrate attention upon conceptual thought. As in perception we may distinguish act, mind, totality appearing to mind, and object, so in conceptual thought we may distinguish act of conceiving, concept, and universal referred to.[101] The act is a "concrete occurrence," the concept is "a way in which a universal is conceived." The universal is "a quality characterizing a number of particulars." [102] Universals do not exist but they do subsist. On no theory can such universals as "similarity" be avoided, and it seems plain enough that other universals are conditions "which we find or discover *in rerum natura*." [103] That conceptual thought is reflective is not prejudicial to its objectivity, for its concepts and processes have come to light in the actual world.[104]

4. OTHER BRITISH REALISTS

Alongside the major British realists whose epistemologies have now been considered must be placed a number of other realists, brief notices of whose thought will bring to light some new suggestions and reinforce some old ones.

One of the most influential of these realists, especially in the early days of contemporary realism, was G. F. Stout (1860–1944). Beginning with "what we actually or immediately experience, as we experience pains or pleasure . . . or a sensum," [1] Stout finds experiences not isolated from one another or from the world but parts of a "sensory continuum," which is in turn an aspect of reality. There are visual, tactual, auditory, and other continua, each representing a determinable for which the specific colors, tactual sensations, and sounds are determinants. All of these continua are united into a common sensory whole by their common connection with bodily feeling or "organic sentience." [2] But our sensible experiences can scarcely exist without being recognized as part of what lies beyond them. If this inevitable extension is legitimate, the sensory continuum may properly be further extended into the physical world and regarded as an aspect of it that can be grasped by sentient creatures.[3] The qualities so extended must be taken to include not merely the so-called primary ones of size, shape, and the like, but also the secondary ones of color and sound; for while the former can no doubt be more precisely and coherently ordered, the latter

---

[101] *Ibid.*, pp. 134 f.
[102] *Ibid.*, p. 135.
[103] *Ibid.*, p. 138.
[104] *Ibid.*, pp. 53 ff.
[1] G. F. Stout, *Mind and Matter* (Cam-

bridge: Cambridge University Press, 1931), p. 161.
[2] *Ibid.*, pp. 246 ff.
[3] *Ibid.*, pp. 249 ff.

are given in essentially the same way and are inseparable from the former.[4]

Even the projected sensory continuum is, however, not by itself sufficient to account for our knowledge. Cooperating with it is an activity factor or a tendency in our striving that, being incomplete in itself, points beyond itself.[5] Our knowledge of other minds, unlike our knowledge of the world is, however, primarily inferential, being grounded in recognition of "responsive behavior" and vindicated in "intersubjective intercourse."[6]

Similar to the epistemological thought of Russell in its middle period is that of T. P. Nunn (1870–1944). A thoroughgoing realist, Nunn finds "that in perception the object announces itself as having a certain priority to and independence of our act and that this announcement is itself the sufficient certificate of the object's extramental status."[7] Nunn begins with the psychical monad and a universe of objects. Realism has, for him, no need for intervening representative "mental" data.[8] Thus for him, "the existence of unperceived sense-data" is fundamental.[9] Secondary qualities are just as much in objects as are primary ones, for it would be quite impossible to conceive anything having primary qualities without secondary ones. Indeed, secondary qualities like primary ones tend to "exist as they are perceived"[10] although either kind of quality can be misplaced as in mirror images and illusions.[11] A thing consists of "nothing but senses and their forms of associations,"[12] it is "a structure embracing and actually consisting of all the 'sense-data,' 'sensibles' 'sensa' or 'sense-objects' which common sense regards as appearances or qualities of the thing and which are 'presented' to any percipient at any time or place."[13] One is sometimes tempted to suppose that scientific objects such as atoms and electrons are more fully real than the sensibles that constitute common-sense objects; but this supposition is completely in error, for "there is in the physical world nothing but sensa and their modes of connection,"[14] and "the real achievement of science is not to have disclosed any reality behind the veil of sensible things, but to have greatly

[4] *Ibid.*, Bk. IV, chap. v.
[5] *Ibid.*, Bk. IV, chap. vi.
[6] *Ibid.*, pp. 303 ff.
[7] T. P. Nunn, "Are Secondary Qualities Independent of Perception?" *Proceedings of the Aristotelian Society*, X (1909–10), 201.
[8] "Are Secondary Qualities Independent of Perception?" pp. 191–218.
[9] Nunn, "Sense-Data and Physical Objects," in *op. cit.*, XVI (1915–16), 157.

[10] "Are Secondary Qualities Independent of Perception?" p. 193.
[11] *Ibid.*, pp. 207 ff.
[12] Nunn, "Scientific Objects and Common Sense Things," in *op. cit.*, XXIV (1923–24), 13.
[13] *Ibid.*, p. 7.
[14] Nunn, "Anthropomorphism and Physics," *Proceedings of the British Academy* (London: Oxford University Press, 1927), p. 45.

extended and deepened and rationalized the scheme of the world revealed in perceptions." [15]

Closer to the realism of Alexander than to that of Russell is the realism of John Laird (1887–1946) who undertakes, in *A Study in Realism,* to supplement the work of Alexander. Like Alexander he believes that we perceive objects directly or, as he has it, that our percepts are "glimpses" of objects.[16] Even in the case of memory one apprehends "the very thing that he perceived" and no mere image of it. This is clearly so during the specious present and the rest of memory is only a prolongation of the memory involved in such internals.

Perhaps more than Alexander, Laird acknowledges an activity of minds that, for example in the biological and social sciences, builds very considerable constructs, the knowledge of which may be more important than the knowledge of events.[17] But these constructs themselves must be observed, and in the end, in knowing as such, mind is essentially passive.[18] Universals subsist but are in things as well; and principles, though a priori, come to light with their instances.[19] The functioning of mind involves an "enormous risk of error," but error is for the most part avoidable and "anything is precisely what it appears to be when sufficient precautions have been taken to avoid confusion between the actual genuine appearance and spurious, though very plausible, glosses upon it.[20]

The principal contribution of the incisive epistemological thought of H. A. Prichard (1871–1947) is an analysis of such terms as "see" and "perceive" that, if correct, discloses serious defects in the epistemologically monistic analysis of Laird and Alexander and the new realists on the one hand, and in the dualistic one of the critical realists on the other.[21] With the monists Prichard contends that perception is not judgmental in character but purports to disclose directly, not merely patches of color and the like, but full-bodied objects. With the dualists he acknowledges that no such direct perception of objects is possible. Then against both, he argues that, since perception is by its nature direct, the facts of error and illusion preclude all perception of objects themselves whether direct or indirect. Concerning what we do perceive he adopts a view reminis-

---

[15] "Scientific Objects and Common Sense Things," p. 18.

[16] *How Our Minds Go Beyond Themselves in Knowing,* J. H. Muithead (ed.), *Contemporary British Philosophy* (London: George Allen & Unwin, 1924), 1st series, pp. 213 ff.

[17] John Laird, *A Study in Realism* (Cambridge: Cambridge University Press, 1920), pp. 185 f.

[18] *Ibid.,* chap. viii.

[19] *Ibid.,* p. 108.

[20] *Ibid.,* pp. 8 f.

[21] H. A. Prichard, *Knowledge and Perception* (Oxford: Clarendon Press, 1950), chaps. iv, vi.

cent of Locke that we perceive only such subjectively oriented fragments as sounds and color extended. This means that virtually all
perception is to some extent illusory. Just how the illusion is to be
overcome Prichard seems not especially concerned to show, though
that it can be overcome, his assurance concerning its illusory character seems to indicate.

5. Comments Concerning English Realism

At the close of the preceding chapter we remarked that, in holding
that independent objects are genuinely apprehended by experiences
that are distinct from them, critical realists seemed to have brought
together the essential ingredients of a satisfactory account of the
relation between cognitive experience and the eventual objects of
knowledge, but that they had neither succeeded in showing how
these ingredients could be held together nor seriously attempted to
do so. In the present chapter we have considered some writers whose
penetrating analyses do constitute such an attempt. Leaving aside
a number of other interesting features of the works of these writers,
we shall focus the following comments on three features of their
thought that may throw some light on the issue in question. The
first is Moore's endeavor to point out that whatever may be the
analysis of our knowledge, we do in fact know with certainty many
facts about material objects. The second is the attempt of Moore,
Russell, and others to establish the needed link between cognitive
experience and its eventual objects in terms of sense-data. And the
third is the renewal, especially by Russell, of a causal theory of
perception.

A. Moore's contention that he knew certainly many facts, such as
that he was born, that the world had existed for a very long time,
and that there were other people, was not, as is sometimes supposed,
intended as an instance of a general paradigm argument to the effect
that only if a term has some standard application can it have any
meaning; and had it been so intended, it would have been, for
reasons that will subsequently appear, almost certainly mistaken.
It was also not an argument depending upon the inconceivability
of our being mistaken about the kind of knowledge claims in question, for concerning the falsity of most such claims there is no such
inconceivability. The fact is, it was really not an argument at all,
for while Moore did at times use arguments in connection with it,
he always took his stand in the end upon some instance of knowledge of which he was certain but for which he was able to furnish
neither analysis nor adequate evidence. What his contention really

amounted to would seem then to have been a recognition, by a philosopher with a keen eye for the essential features of a problem, that so certainly are some things in the ordinary sense known, that the knowledge of them may be regarded as an accepted datum for epistemological inquiry rather than as something to be established by such inquiry.

In this contention, Moore would seem almost certainly to have been correct. It is not the case that every term has to have an application in order to have a meaning, but it is the case that we do ordinarily use the term "know" in such a way that it would be absurd to say that we did not know many matters of fact. If we discover what we said we knew to have been mistaken we withdraw the statement that we knew it, but concerning most of what we say we know no withdrawal is necessary and none would be appropriate. In calling attention to this basic consideration concerning knowledge, Moore advances beyond the position of the critical realists, for whereas they took genuine knowledge of independent objects to be possible, they were never so clear as he about the fact that epistemological inquiry is entitled to treat many facts about the material world as known regardless of its ability or inability to show how they are known.

This is not, however, by any means the end of the story. Even the ordinary use of the word "know" has the roots of some philosophical puzzles in it. While to know is commonly taken to include being certain, we are often obliged to retract our claims to know. Moreover, the falsity of many of our justifiable knowledge claims is not inconceivable in the way in which that of some logical and mathematical truths is, and their truth is not indubitable in the way that that of some truths about sensory experience is. Such considerations as these have led some philosophers to place alongside the ordinary sense of "know" another sense for whose applicability some sort of inconceivability of the opposite or some sort of indubitability is demanded, and then to ask in what ways what is known in the second sense contributes to knowledge in the first sense. This philosophers are entitled to do provided they keep their records straight concerning the senses they are using and do not try to persuade people that they do not know in the ordinary sense many ordinary facts. In any case philosophers may properly inquire, as Moore himself did without success, what the analysis and grounds of knowledge in the ordinary sense are in terms of the sensory, logical, and other ingredients that enter into the structure of knowledge. For this sort of inquiry Moore's insistence upon the certainty of some knowledge is only a beginning point and not a conclusion.

B. If English realists, especially Moore, Russell, and Broad, have shown that sense-data such as they described are in fact media of perceptual knowledge, they have taken a considerable step toward solving the sort of problem encountered in American critical realism concerning how independent objects can be genuinely known through experiences that are distinct from them. Such a step would not be entirely original, for something like it was suggested in some phases of ancient and medieval philosophy and especially in the writings of the earlier British empiricists; but it would mark a distinct advance, for the English realists under consideration were the first to introduce and develop an explicit sense-datum terminology.

However, whether or not Moore, Russell, and Broad have in fact succeeded in establishing sense-data as media of perceptual knowledge should, at least tentatively, be regarded as questionable, for in recent years the whole notion of sense-data has come to be widely considered very dubious. Such arguments as the following, for example, have been urged against sense-datum theories. Sense-datum statements have no such certainty as they were once said to have and for the sake of which they were invented. The argument from illusion that was supposed to sustain them falls to the ground for the reason that most supposedly illusory experiences are sufficiently different from veridical experiences to be distinguishable from veridical ones. In any case, first to divide all experiences into veridical and nonveridical ones and then on the basis of the unreliable references of the latter to insist that both must be really only apprehensions of sense-data would be absurd.[1] Differences among appearances of objects are readily explainable by laws of perspective without recourse to such queer entities as sense-data. The language of sense-data is highly artificial and misleading. It becomes peculiarly misleading when it is used to suggest that sense-data are separate entities or that we really perceive only our own sense-data and must infer all the rest that we know. Altogether mistaken is the almost inevitable suggestion of sense-datum language that sense-data create some sort of insurmountable barrier between knowing and the known so that we can never really know objects or facts themselves at all. Gestalt psychologists insist that our experiences contain no isolated sense-data but are always complete perceptive patterns. Finally, the language of appearing is far more natural than sense-datum language and can say all that can be said in the latter language without ensnaring us in the traps that inevitably await the unwary user of sense-datum language.

[1] Such arguments as the foregoing have been urged with exceptional cogency in J. L. Austin's lectures.

Now, it is quite clear that a number of these objections are in fact applicable to what the English realists under consideration have said about sense-data. These writers did often overemphasize the facts of illusion and underemphasize those of perspective. They did sometimes write as though sense-data were a barrier between minds and things, and they surely often represented sense-data as distinctly separable entities of a queer sort. One of the major difficulties was that they were never quite clear concerning just what sense-data were. Sometimes they represented sense-data as parts of the surfaces of objects, sometimes as mental entities, sometimes as universals, and sometimes as intermediate entities exactly or nearly like experiences but not necessarily experiences. No single clear-cut theory was ever developed, and any composite theory that one might try to draw from their various claims that were made concerning sense-data would be either incoherent or innocuous. Nevertheless, there appear to have been some genuine insights involved in what Moore, Russell, and others said about sense-data.

One such insight is that sensory experiences lie at the base of all our perceptual knowledge. Sometimes such experiences are reasonably clearly separable from the associational and interpretative factors involved in our percepts. Sometimes they are so intricately interwoven with such factors as to be inseparable from them, and properly considered as indistinguishable aspects of whole percepts. Sometimes they themselves constitute the wholes of our percepts. But whether or not sensory experiences are separable from other ingredients in percepts, it is difficult to see how there could possibly be a percept in the entire absence of sensory experience. Not only does recognition of the indispensability of sensory experience to perception seem to be demanded by the facts but it entails none of the more damaging paradoxes commonly attributed to sense-datum theories. It in no way depends upon or suggests that we know only our own experiences. It requires no claim either that illusion always deceives us or that our experiential statements are infallible. It makes no demands concerning the isolation or isolability of sense-data and it need ignore no referential claim implicit in sensory experience.

A second significant insight in what the writers under consideration have said about sense-data is the recognition that we are more certain of our sensory experiences than of their references and that when we are in doubt about the latter we sometimes focus attention upon the former in order to question or gain greater assurance concerning the latter. For example, in approaching a mountain region, one may for a long time remain uncertain whether what appears in the distance is snow-capped mountains or low clouds or a figment of his own imagination, but he may have no doubt at all of his experience of seeing whitish forms. Similarly, a desert traveler may be uncertain of the proper reference of the image before him but certain that the image is there, and the field commander may be unsure of what to make of his experience of a mustard-like smell but be sure that he smells such a smell. The astronomer may be in doubt about the actual size of the star at which he looks without being at all in doubt about how the star appears to him.

For the most part we take objects to be pretty much as they normally present themselves to us in our perceptual apprehensions. But occasionally when significant doubt arises concerning the natural reference in our perceptual apprehensions we may in fact even for practical purposes, abstract for the moment from the natural references in these apprehensions and re-examine the pattern of our *sensory* experiences in order to achieve more reliable references. Thus for example the traveler may suspend his thought that it is a mountain he sees and focus upon the elements of the sensory pattern in the quest for a more reliable judgment concerning what is really before him. Similarly, the astronomer may put aside both his natural feeling that a tiny star is twinkling before him and his hasty judgment that a star of a certain magnitude is there in order to note more carefully the color and brightness of what he senses as a guide to correct interpretation. Philosophers find it more difficult in their philosophical moments to take things as presented in perception than do most persons, and they sometimes explicitly ask what kinds of things there could be to which their sensory experiences refer, indeed whether or not there are any such things. These questions, however odd, seem to be perfectly legitimate questions that grow directly out of questions asked by common sense, and they are in the end perhaps inevitable. Yet apparently they can not be adequately formulated apart from some such terminology as that of sense-data.[2]

A third significant insight involved in what the writers under consideration have said about sense-data is their recognition that it is reasonable to believe that between the eventual objects of our perception and our sensory experiences are more or less continuous ordered series of events similar in structure to the objects and capable of yielding sensory experiences. This insight is unfortunately linked with a serious confusion, for the philosophers in question,

[2] See Roderick Firth, "Phenomenalism," in American Philosophical Association, *Science, Language and Human Values* (Philadelphia: University of Pennsylvania Press, 1952), pp. 1–20.

especially Russell, sometimes wrote as though the events intervening between objects and sensory experiences were exactly like sensory experiences except for not being experienced. Actually while it is quite intelligible to talk of events capable of yielding sensory experiences, it is difficult to know what could be meant by anything being exactly like a sensory experience but not experienced. Light waves and sound waves there may be throughout many spaces but surely these spaces are not crowded with unseen images and unheard sounds. It was in part this sort of confusion that brought the sense-datum theory into bad repute. Nevertheless the notion of ordered series of events resembling the objects of our knowledge remains plausible, and assuming the existence of these objects, is supported by almost the entire body of physical science. This notion does not of course establish the reality of physical objects, for it presupposes that. Nor does it bridge the gap between such objects and experiences, for these two remain in important respects radically different. It does, however, do a great deal toward bridging the gap between the physical origin of our percepts and the states of our sense organs and brains in perception; for if patterns capable of yielding such states and structurally correlated with our percepts are to be found between the objects and percepts, they significantly link these diverse factors. Moreover, since the gap between object and brain is a part of the gap between physical object and experience, the suggestion does at least a little toward bridging the latter gap as well as the former.

One may of course grant the essential validity of all such considerations as these and still claim that most of what is involved in them may be put in a language of appearing that is much closer to ordinary language than is that of sense-data; and provided such a language really permits us to sustain these insights and to say what we wish to say it should be regarded as satisfactory. However, a language of appearing seems at any rate to fall short of what is required in at least the following respects. For one thing, such language does not bring sufficiently into focus the distinction between the object or event and the experience in which it is apprehended; for such language involves rejection of talk even of "appearances" save in highly fictitious senses. For another thing, a language of appearing is able to handle such phenomena as rainbows and mirages only in somewhat clumsy and inadequate fashion, and it can scarcely deal adequately at all with such phenomena as hallucinations and double vision. In many doubtful cases, including some of the kinds mentioned above, it tends to ignore questions that can be of considerable practical as well as theoretical importance, and it tends to beg fundamental philosophical questions about the existence of a physical world. Presumably the genuine issue of the truth or falsity of phenomenalism cannot adequately be even stated in terms of it.[3]

C. If English realism has, especially in Russell's thought, been able to furnish a defensible causal theory of perception, it has contributed further to the solution of the central problem remaining unresolved in the thought of the critical realists, for if sensory experiences are caused by physical objects and the characters of objects can in some sense be inferred from sensory experiences, an answer to the question how independent objects can be known through distinct experiences is in sight. However, causal theories of perception, like sense-datum theories, having been heavily under fire in recent years not only by philosophers who reject sense-data but by some who accept them, are not easy to defend.

Among the principal objections urged against causal theories of perception are the following: first, that since material object-statements and sense-experience statements neither entail nor are entailed by one another and valid inductive inference depends upon the presupposition of an unprovable principle of induction, no causal inference from sensory experiences to material objects is possible; second, that since the concept of cause is designed to establish relations among physical objects, the extension of that concept beyond the range of physical objects is illegitimate; third, that we do not in fact infer our knowledge of physical objects from sensory experience; and finally, that the existence of physical objects is already presupposed in talk about inferring them from sensory experience. Whether or not such objections are conclusive against the sort of causal account of perception that Russell presented in his *Problems of Philosophy* and later in more sophisticated form in his *Human Knowledge,* is a question requiring fuller analysis than can be undertaken here, but *prima facie* the answer seems to be in the negative.

Regarding the objection concerning induction, Russell claimed, even in *Problems of Philosophy,* not that physical-object statements could be validly inferred from sense-datum statements but only that belief in the former could be reasonably supported by the latter; and in his *Human Knowledge,* he made this claim more specific by pointing out a series of assumptions upon which rational support of physical-object statements in terms of sense-datum statements would have to depend. Since neither entailment nor strict inductive inference is involved, the objection is scarcely applicable to Russell's position; and as for the broad type of inductive inference that

[3] *Ibid.*

Russell does adopt, almost no nonskeptical philosopher can afford to refuse to accept something of this sort.

With regard to the objection concerning the illegitimate extension of the concept of causality, it may be doubted that this objection is conclusive against *any* sort of causal theory of perception, for when different levels of reality must somehow be connected, we have to proceed in terms of some concept, and there is in principle no reason why a concept, such as causality, that has been developed at one level of discourse should not in duly qualified form be illuminatingly used to link different levels with one another. Moreover, in the instance of Russell's *Human Knowledge,* it may be questioned whether different levels are involved at all, since things are here said to be made up of bundles of qualities.

With reference to the objection that we do not employ inference in our perceptual apprehensions, Russell seems entitled to a still useful twofold answer. First, we do sometimes seem in a broad sense to make inferences to the existence of what we perceive, as for example when being puzzled by a novel pattern of sensory experiences we project hypotheses concerning probable causes and test them by the character of the sensory patterns before us. Second, even when we do not directly employ causal inference, our perceptual assurances seem sometimes to rest upon causal inferences at least implicitly formed in previous situations.

With regard to the final objection, that causal theories of perception presuppose physical objects, Russell is entitled to reply that if one asks simply what explanations of his sensory experiences are most reasonable, no such *presupposition* is needed and that a broadly conceived *inference* to the agency of physical objects on the ground that that affords the best available explanation of our experiences has in its favor the only sort of consideration that in such matters can be appealed to, namely that of rendering the realms of discourse under consideration more intelligible than would otherwise be possible. Accordingly, it would appear that the moderate sort of causal theory advocated by Russell is not entirely ruled out by the usual objections against causal theories and that some parts of it may survive as useful aspects of an adequate interpretation of the relation between cognitive experience and its objects.

In summary then, we may say that while English realists have by no means resolved the central epistemological problem left unresolved by the critical realists, how independent objects can be genuinely known through experiences distinct from them, they have at very least made some ponderable contributions toward the solution of that problem, first, in Moore's insight that some facts are in the ordinary sense known regardless of what the analysis of such knowledge may be; second, in the recognition by several of the English realists that sensory experience has a special sort of certainty, is epistemologically significant, and seems to be linked with objects through events structurally resembling those objects; and finally, in Russell's presentation of a causal theory sufficiently cautious and adequately defended to withstand at any rate the more obvious attacks upon it. We turn now to a group of theories that are not realist or idealist but attempt to occupy intermediate ground, and we shall endeavor to see whether or not they have been able to advance beyond these modest accomplishments.

Part III
MEDIATING THEORIES

CHAPTER 7

Constructionist Theories

LIKE the epistemologies considered in the two preceding parts those to be considered in this part are primarily concerned with the traditional epistemological problem of the relation of the knower and the known. Unlike the theories of the two preceding parts, the theories now to be considered are uncommitted in the controversy between realism and idealism. They are also persistent in the effort to preserve the merits and avoid the deficiencies of those conflicting systems. There is, however, no sharp break between the mediating theories now to be considered, on the one hand, and idealism and realism, on the other; for, as we have previously observed, a number of important advocates of each of the older systems already made significant concessions to their opponents, and as we shall presently see, some advocates of mediating theories lean considerably toward one or the other of the older conflicting systems.

The group of mediating epistemologists to be considered in the present chapter consists of writers who, like most realists and some idealists, tend to consider the problems of knowledge in minute detail, and who effect their compromise for the most part by endeavoring to select out what is and what is not independent of the knower. A second group, which is to be considered in the next chapter, consists of writers who seek to mediate the conflict between realism and idealism by disclosing a level of experience below that of the conflict. A third group, which is to be considered in Chapter 9, consists of writers who attempt to embrace in a comprehensive whole the best insights of members of both sides of the conflict as well of other intermediate groups. The epistemologies of these three groups are referred to in the order indicated as constructionist theories, intuitional theories, and organismic theories.

Advocates of the type of theory referred to here as constructionism do not for the most part deny the existence of an object independent of the knowing process, but their attention is focused largely upon the manner in which the complex object-as-known is built up or constructed of simpler ingredients. One version of the type of theory in question has already been encountered in our sketch of Russell's *Our Knowledge of the External World;* other versions are now to be considered.

Perhaps the most carefully and suggestively formulated of all versions of this type of theory is that of H. H. Price, and to this version of constructionism the major portion of this chapter will be devoted. The work of a number of other writers, whose views vary between positions very close to idealism and positions quite close to realism, will, however, also be considered. In presenting Price's thought, we shall begin with his account of perception, which after detailed structural analysis arrives at a position resembling Russell's later realism. We shall then go on to his conception of thinking, which carefully examines the function of symbols and of universals in the knowing process.

1. H. H. Price's Account of Perception

Basic to all knowing for Price are the sense-data that are immediately given in experience. Any attempt to get behind data, whether by reference to brains, sense organs, physical objects, or anything else, is doomed to certain failure for the reason that any such attempt is bound to appeal to the sense-data which it seeks to explain. Sense-data are the source of our apprehension of material things. They have the peculiar character of sensuousness.[1] They are intuited and indubitable. When I think I see a tomato, for example, there is much involved that may be doubted, but "that something is red and round then and there I cannot doubt." [2] With our sense-data we are directly acquainted, and neither their occurrence as aspects of facts nor their being often imbedded in descriptive or interpretative contexts in any way detracts from their basic character. Without them there would be nothing for facts to be about, or for associations to associate, or for descriptions to describe, or for interpretations to interpret.[3] Analysis of them and knowledge about them may vary the settings of sense-data but cannot destroy sense-data. In believing that there are sense-data, however, we are in no sense committed to the view that such data persist when they are not sensed, or to the

---

[1] H. H. Price, *Perception* (2d ed.; London: Methuen & Co., Ltd., 1950), p. 4.

[2] *Ibid.,* p. 3.

[3] *Ibid.,* pp. 4 ff.

view that other minds sense such data, or to any particular view of the origin or nature of sense-data.[4]

Since sense-data actually occur, they are particulars or instances of universals rather than universals.[5] They are not substances; for, unlike substances, they come and go at a stroke. They cannot even be said to be *in* bodies. Neither are they properly to be said to be cerebral; our brains do not take on either the expansiveness or the other properties attributed to sense-data.[6] Nor, finally, are sense-data properly said to be products of a compound of mind and brain, for this would absurdly require them to be in two places at one time. Sense-data may be said to be *in* minds in the sense that they do not have to be sought out, but this should not carry spatial implications. They may also be said to be *for* minds in the sense that they involve presentation which is only for minds.

The mere occurrence of sense-data is, however, a long way from perceptive knowledge either of things or of facts. Unlike material things, sense-data are private and noncausal.[7] If sense-data belong to material things at all, they present at best only fragmentary aspects of things. Many aspects of things are not sensed at all; and in any case, not all aspects are sensed at any one time. When we pass from one sensed aspect of a thing to another, we are often no longer aware of the first, and we cannot even be sure we are observing the same thing. Moreover our apprehension of the sense-data that seem to belong to anything is not at all continuous.[8] If then we may properly be said to have any perceptive knowledge, we must be able to overcome some very considerable gaps in our sense-data or to develop and justify what Price calls "gap-indifference" with reference to certain series of sense-data.[9]

The suggestion comes readily to mind, of course, that the belief that things exist despite vast gaps in our sense-data rests primarily upon inference from sense-data to their material causes;[10] but even if such an explanation could be carried through, it is contrary to the phenomenology of the knowing process. Actually, we are aware of no inference in our perceptive knowledge. The fully developed material object, including back, inside, and causal properties, none of which given in sense, as well as front surface, which does seem to be so given, appears to be there for us in perceptual consciousness all at once and without any reasoning process. The primary question concerning the process of knowing comes then to be, by what succes-

---

[4] *Ibid.*, pp. 18 f.
[5] *Ibid.*, p. 103.
[6] *Ibid.*, pp. 134 ff.
[7] *Ibid.*, pp. 145 f.
[8] *Ibid.*

[9] Price, *Hume's Theory of the External World* (Oxford: Clarendon Press, 1940), pp. 60 ff.
[10] *Perception*, pp. 66 ff.

sive steps such perceptual consciousness, whether illusory or not, comes into being and how if at all it can be justified.

The first real step beyond the sense-datum is not then, as is often supposed, an inference. Nor is it either a conviction or a problem. It certainly is not indubitable knowledge. Rather, it is simply an acceptance somewhat akin to what has been called *"being under an impression that."* [11] In terms of it one accepts an object as having besides present sense-data many properties not now being observed. "What the perceptually conscious subject takes for granted when he senses a particular visual or tactual sense-datum is that there now exists a material thing to which this sense-datum belongs; and that this thing has a front surface of a certain general character, to be more exactly determined by subsequent perceptual acts." [12]

Unlike sense-data, that which is accepted in perceptual consciousness has a wide range of degrees of definiteness. Although sense-data themselves are never vague or indefinite, they sometimes yield "a vague or indefinite perceptual act," and sometimes a clear and definite one. Thus, for example, whereas one pattern of colors perfectly definite in itself may enable us to make out only a dim landscape, another pattern no more definite in itself may permit us to see just what is there.

The content of perceptual acceptance is also unlike the sense-data on which it depends in being subject to all manner of errors either in detail or in general. A man may be perceptually conscious of a pink rat that is not there, and all of us are conscious of a blue sky that does not exist. Indeed the whole notion of material things that seems to be assumed in perceptual acceptance may be a gigantic error.

But, whatever possibilities of error may be revealed in reflection upon perceptual acceptance, doubt is no part of this mode of consciousness itself. Perceptual acceptance, though obviously not intuition, has rather the baffling character of being very much like intuition in its apparently immediate and unhesitant mode of presentation. This pseudo-intuitive character of perceptual acceptance is not to be explained away either as mere inference or as association. As a matter of fact we do not appear to be *thinking* at all in perceptual consciousness; the whole object seems to be presented to us at once rather than being pieced together from past experiences. However much past experiences may be necessary conditions of perceptual acceptance, they can scarcely be its present ingredients or constituents.[13] Again, the apparently intuitive character of perceptual acceptance cannot be accounted for in terms of bodily adjustment; for

[11] *Ibid.,* p. 140.
[12] *Perception,* p. 145.
[13] *Ibid.,* pp. 153 ff.

"if all so-called perceptual consciousness is only bodily behavior, how should we know or even conjecture that we have bodies at all?" [14] Emotion also affords no adequate account of the apparently intuitive character of perceptual acceptance; for emotions alone can never yield beliefs but are always directed toward something which must be believed in prior to emotion.[15]

The explanation of the apparently intuitive character of our perceptual consciousness is to be found in the fact that perceptual acceptance lies on this side of judgment. That is to say, we only judge of what is already accepted. "The act of perceptual acceptance, then, owes its undoubting, non-active, and non-transitional or totalistic character . . . to the fact that what is accepted in it always stands on the side of the subject thought about;" [16] for "how can we judge about a thing unless we already have it before the mind to judge about?" [17] When green grass is before us we do not make such judgments as "this grass is green" but rather such as "this grass has a heavy dew on it." [18] If anyone is surprised that we should so accept what is not certain, it must be recognized that such acceptance, however much we might like it to be otherwise, is simply "an ultimate fact about human nature." [19] Thus, basic to all our knowing is a kind of *primitive credulity;* and this is after all on the whole fortunate, for if our consciousness were confined to what Russell has called the "hard data" of sense, it is doubtful if we should have the courage to act with decision in our kind of world.[20]

The second step beyond sense-data toward perceptual knowledge is the achievement of what Price calls "perceptual assurance." This phase of perceptual consciousness is "above the level of doubting and questioning whereas the primary acceptance is below." [21]

How is this higher level attained? No mere speculation can yield a correct answer; the answer must be determined rather by examining closely the nature of the perceptual consciousness itself. The way that perceptual assurance is in fact achieved is by supplementing original vague acceptances through other acceptances in such fashion that the whole patterns of acceptances fit together and mutually sustain one another. This process can, of course, be justified only if each acceptance has some validity of its own, for a coherence in which nothing at all is credible in any degree by itself will not advance credibility at all. But, as when several witnesses each of whose testimony has some credibility agree with one another, the testimony of

---

[14] *Ibid.,* p. 158.
[15] *Ibid.,* p. 160.
[16] *Ibid.,* p. 166.
[17] *Ibid.,* p. 164.
[18] *Ibid.,* p. 163.
[19] *Ibid.,* p. 168.
[20] *Ibid.,* p. 169.
[21] *Ibid.,* p. 172.

each tends to add confirmation to that of the others, so each percep
tual acceptance, though insufficient in itself, tends when coherent
with others to become a part of a mutual confirmation series.[22] The
principle of confirmability on which perceptual assurance must rest
may be formulated as follows: "The existence of a particular visual
or tactual sense-datum is *prima facie* evidence (1) for the existence
of a material thing such that this sense-datum belongs to it, (2) for
the possession by this thing of a front surface of a certain sort." [23]

If it be asked why such a principle should hold, no answer can be
given either in terms of self-evidence, logical deduction, or empirical
evidence. Whether we like it or not, it is simply an ultimate fact
about human nature that perceptual acceptances that fit together
tend to yield assurance about material objects. "It seems to me
indubitable that we do often advance by way of a further specification series to something quite different from the mere acceptance
with which we began. It simply is the case that the existence of the
material thing (merely accepted at first) becomes *more and more
probable* as we specify further. I cannot prove this, but I think it is
just evident." [24] Accordingly, "any attempt to demonstrate that what
we are perceptually assured of does not or may not exist, or that it
does not or may not have the characteristics which we are assured that
it has, is bound to use arguments which are beyond all comparison
less certain than that which they set out to overthrow." [25]

What one is *assured of* in perceptual assurance is that *there exists*
a material thing of such and such a shape, etc.; but what one *knows*
in such assurance is only that "there is *strong evidence* for the existence of such a material thing," not that the thing exists. Even this
evidence is sometimes said not to be *known;* for since the object is
absolutely determinate, nothing short of complete specification of its
characteristics would seem to suffice. But for most purposes approximate determination of evidence suffices and approximation can be
achieved in ever increasing degree. It remains true at best that, in
view of the infinite series of confirmations required and of the frequent gaps in our evidence, we can never be entirely certain of the
existence of the material object; new evidence may at any time overthrow the evidence already accumulated. Nevertheless the evidence
may be sufficiently well-grounded and strong to lead from acceptance
through confidence to an ample practical assurance. "This assurance
is a rational conviction of the existence of a material thing having a
certain determinable character . . . : that the thing does exist is
then *almost* certain, though no specification-series of finite length can

---

[22] *Ibid.,* pp. 182 f.
[23] *Ibid.,* p. 185.

[24] *Perception,* p. 188.
[25] *Ibid.,* p. 189.

make it completely certain. Thus perceptual assurance, though it cannot strictly be called *knowledge* of the material world, is quite sufficient for all the purposes of Science and of daily life." [26]

In producing that perceptual acceptance and subsequent assurance in which they are transcended in perceptual consciousness, sense-data tend to fit together in certain ways and are said to *belong to* material things. If then we are to understand the structure of perception, we must examine both the interrelations of various sense-data and, especially, the nature of *belonging to* a material thing.

One interpretation of *belonging to* a material thing identifies this relation with belonging to certain classes of resembling sense-data, as, for example, the colors attaching to a given object tend to belong to a class of resembling colors.[27] But this account by no means always works out. Different sides of an object may, for instance, manifest contrasting colors. A much more plausible suggestion is that the sense-data *belonging to* a given object display a relation of gradual transition.[28] Thus, when one moves around an object the various shape patterns change only gradually, and the same is often true of colors and sensations of touch. Even when such distorting factors as colored glasses are involved one can by gradual transitions approach what might be regarded as standard qualities of the object. Actually this view seems to be quite correct as far as *nonspatial* characteristics of the sense-data belonging to an object are concerned, but it will not suffice concerning some spatial relations. While the various sizes and shapes of the data belonging to a single object may form gradual transition series, so also may various data belonging to similar but different objects in different parts of the world.

Accordingly the gradual transition series must be supplemented, as in our actual perceptual experience it certainly is, by a kind of spatial synthesis, which operates in approximately the following manner. All visual sense-data have—despite the protests of some philosophers—the given characteristic of *"depth* or 'outness,'* " [29] and the objects to which all such data belong fall within one or the other of three zones of stereoscopic vision. In the first zone, that of perfect stereoscopy (ranging from six inches to a few feet), the object sensibly faces in different directions in such fashion that, by putting together the presented data along with other data that can be found, perfect solids or three-dimensional figures can be constructed. In the second zone (ranging from a few feet to very considerable depths depending upon light, contrasting shadows, familiarity and other conditions), surfaces still sensibly face in different directions but not in such a

[26] *Ibid.*, p. 203.
[27] *Ibid.*, pp. 206 ff.
[28] *Ibid.*, pp. 208 ff.
[29] *Ibid.*, p. 218.

manner that the solid could be perfectly constructed without over-lapping. In the third zone, sensible directions still differ but now so little that "spatial synthesis is no longer possible at all." Seeing a matchbox from a distance of two feet exemplifies the first zone; seeing a tower from a distance of fifty feet, the second; and seeing a mountain a mile or so away, the third. Beginning now with the perfectly con-structible stereoscopic data of the first zone we can construct what may be called a *nuclear solid*. The imperfectly constructible data of the second zone can then be arranged in order of imperfection, beginning with the datum which is just not perfectly constructible. Even the nonconstructible data of the third zone can be arranged in series of *increasing distortedness* beginning with a just constructible datum. The whole process yields then a *"perspectival* distortion series," including "nuclear datum, imperfectly constructible data in order of imperfection, [and] non-constructible data in order of im-perfection." [30] Fortunately such a series can be sustained and supple-mented by a converse series depending on differentiation of specific detail. As one approaches a distant object and the distortedness diminishes, specific detail increases, and although microscopic views, not being stereoscopic, are not constructible, even they may be re-garded as revealing more specific details of the surface of the nuclear solid than unaided vision.

The nuclear solid constructed from perfectly stereoscopic data and supplemented by the maximum specificity of microscopic data now becomes a *standard solid* that limits and unites the distortion and differentiation series; and "a collection of sense-data so unified, con-sisting of a standard solid together with a set of distortion series and a set of differentiation series," may now be said to constitute a *"family of sense-data."* [31] Even an *illusory* sense-datum belongs to a family of sense-data, but it "does not have that place or rank in the family which we perceptually take it to have." [32] An *hallucinatory* sense-datum, however, is completely "wild" in that though taken to belong to a family, it does not in fact belong to one. The par-ticular data before an observer in any perceptive experience are relative to the observer's position and to other conditions, for it is the changes in these factors that yield the distortion and differentia-tion series. The family itself is not relative in this fashion and often remains essentially constant through many changes as does the stand-ard solid. Sense-data are not in physical space and even nuclear solids are not in the strictest sense in such space, for it is they that make physical space possible.

[30] *Ibid.*, p. 222.
[31] *Ibid.*, p. 227.

[32] *Ibid.*, p. 228.

While Price's concern is, as we indicated at the outset, primarily with the structure of knowing rather than with the nature of the object, he does give some attention to the latter problem; and before going on to complete his account of the structure of knowledge, we pause to note what he has to say on this related problem. Essentially naïve realists hold that the object of perceptual knowledge is a material object of the surface of which our visual and tactual sense-data are parts; but no such theory can be maintained in face of the facts of illusion and distortion of perspective.[33] Various modifications of naïve realism such as Whitehead's multiple location theory and Dawes Hicks's theory of appearing are little more satisfactory; for while they sufficiently account for illusions, they either require incredible assumptions or are unable to account for hallucinations and other "wild" data.[34] The attempt to interpret the object of perceptual knowledge as an inferred cause of our sense-data is belied both by the phenomenology of knowing and by the logic of causal inference.[35] One is aware in perception of no inferential process, and one confirms the reality of the objects which sense seems to present by examining sensory contexts rather than by causal inference. Moreover, to say that sense-data have a cause is already to place them in a material world and thus to assume what has to be shown; it is by reference to sense-data that objects are to be explained rather than the other way around. In his book *Hume's Theory of the External World,* Price suggests without finally either approving or disapproving, two other views.[36] One is that material objects are convenient fictions in that sense-data occur *as if* they were parts of material objects. The other view is that our reference to material objects can be reduced to rules governing the use of language. But Price seems here to be only exploring possibilities; he does not find either view very satisfactory.

What then is Price's own view of the nature of perceptual objects? An answer that might be suggested by what Price says about solid objects and families of sense-data is that the objects of perception are sensibilia or existing particulars like sense-data except that they need not be sensed. This view however, Price specifically rejects on the ground that it ignores important causal factors and obscures the fact that our perceptual dispositions are in part dependent on the actual occurrence of sense-data. What is properly suggested by the doctrine of families of sense-data is, Price thinks, the similar but different view that a family consists of "an ordered system of *possible* sense-

[33] *Ibid.,* p. 26.
[34] *Ibid.,* pp. 55 ff.
[35] *Ibid.,* pp. 66 ff.

[36] *Hume's Theory of the External World,* chaps. v, vi.

data," [37] and accordingly that material objects may be thought of as constituted in part at least by possible or "obtainable" sense-data. To put this a little more precisely, the sensible aspect of a material object consists in actual sense data together with an indefinitely large series of facts to the effect that "if an observer were at such and such a point of view . . . such and such a datum would exist." [38]

The directly sensible aspect of a perceptive object is not, however, the only one; nor indeed is it sufficient by itself to guarantee that a physical object is under consideration. There may indeed be standard solids and families of sense-data to which no physical object answers, and phenomenalists are inclined to believe that all so-called material objects are of this sort. In order that there should be a physical object, "the place where the standard solid (and therefore the family) is situated must also be *physically occupied*, i.e. certain causal characteristics must be manifested there." [39] Such causal characteristics are manifested most significantly in terms of impenetrability, and impenetrability in turn is revealed not primarily by the sense of touch but by the observation of one standard solid moving toward another and then altering its course.[40] The causal characteristics or powers that constitute physical existence are quite different from the unsensed parts of families of sense-data in that, instead of being inoperative universals, they actually exist and are operative all the while. It is they that give stability to the thing with reference to the many times and places at which there are no observers. We have reason to believe that these characteristics existed before man and will persist after man is extinct. We apprehend them through sense-data in that when a foreign family of sense-data projects itself to the vicinity of a physical object it may be seen to change directions. Physical objects have, however, other characteristics besides causal ones, for relational characteristics must depend on intrinsic ones. But these other characteristics remain hidden from us: even the causal characteristics that are known to us may be only a fraction of causal characteristics that there are, and these latter may in turn be only a small fraction of the total characteristics of the object.[41]

A material thing, or what may now be called a *complete thing*, is then an entity of which a family of sense-data with its standard solid constitutes one aspect, physical or causative factors another, and unknown characteristics still others. Secondary qualities as well as primary ones, though in one sense not *in* the thing, belong to the thing in being part of the family which constitutes the thing. The

[37] *Ibid.*, p. 264. Italics mine.
[38] *Ibid.*, p. 284.
[39] *Ibid.*, p. 301.

[40] *Ibid.*, pp. 275 ff.
[41] *Ibid.*, pp. 296 ff.

concept of a complete thing in the sense indicated is basically an a priori concept, not indeed in being given as a whole prior to experience, but in the sense that we constantly expect to find things having the sort of spatiotemporal and causal characters indicated. In passing, it may be noted that while perceptual consciousness cannot be dependent upon knowledge of material things, knowledge of material things may help to explain the existence of sense-data.[42]

2. PRICE'S ACCOUNT OF THINKING

The part of the knowing process that consists in perceiving is by no means the whole of cognition; and while the remaining part depends upon perception, it also extends far beyond perception. Hence Price has added to his book on perception two more recent books on the nature of thinking. For the most part these latter books are critical reviews of three major theories of thinking. In each theory Price finds some significant insights but with none of them is he entirely satisfied.

A. The first theory regards thinking as a process of recognizing instinctively learned signs such as the clouds that signify rain. This view may appropriately be referred to as the sign theory of thinking.

Signification, according to this view, is a process by which something that is absent is in some degree indicated or brought to mind by something else that is present. Obviously such a process involves perception in that one perceives the sign and has previously perceived either the significate (i.e. the thing signified) or something like it. But signification transcends perception in that its object lies beyond that which is perceived.

The most elemental form of signification is what may appropriately be called secondary recognition. In such recognition the sign is *coinherent* with the significate in the same substance, as, for example, the gray color which is a sign of lead is coinherent in a piece of lead with the "softness, ductility and heaviness which are signified." [1] In more complex cases of signification, for instance the bell's signifying someone's presence at the door, no such coinherence is involved. But even in the most elemental kinds of signification, thinking is already present. This may be inferred, first, from the possibility of error, which exists only where thought is present (the grey substance may turn out not to be lead after all); second, in the fact that even elemental sign cognition is not of the present but of the absent; and, third, in a certain abstractness or generality of sign cognition (e.g.

[42] *Ibid.*, pp. 309 ff.
[1] Price, *Thinking and Experience* (London: Hutchinson's University Library, 1953), p. 88.

while the ice looks cold it does not do so in any specific degree) .[2]

Almost anything perceived, whether an individual thing or a characteristic, can serve as a sign. That which is signified (the significate) may also be either a thing or a characteristic. It may be quite simple, but it also may be very complex. It may include implicit logical relations even when the signifying process is fairly elemental. Thus, wherever dispositions to recognize instances are sufficiently developed to bring about expectations, negation may be implicit in the significate in terms of the possibility of disappointment. Similarly, when a sign produces bodily readiness to perform either of two actions, disjunction is implicit in the significate. Further, if there is uncertainty about an outcome contingent upon unknown conditions, an *if then* is involved in the significate.[3] The tie that binds the sign to the significate is never, as is often supposed, merely one of similarity. For example, an object that is similar to a lion does not signify that a lion is in the neighborhood. In this sense there are no natural signs. All sign connections whether in nature or at more conventional levels have to be learned by inductive processes. The actual functioning of the sign sometimes fully activates the significate by bringing the subject to encounter an instance of the significate. More often the sign subactivates the significate by making the subject ready in one way or another to encounter an instance of the significate. Sometimes the readiness in question takes the form of images, sometimes, that of bodily sets, and sometimes, that of overt behavior.

The sign theory of thinking undertakes to show that not only our recognition of the signs we observe in natural phenomena and in other people's overt behavior but also our understanding of the linguistic expressions of others and our own use of symbols in our own thinking can be explained in terms of sign functions. No symbols, the theory holds, are basically different from signs, for all symbols are inductively learned indications of publicly observable facts. Linguistic symbols are like thermometers and other scientific instruments in openly revealing publicly observable characteristics of persons.

Undoubtedly, according to Price, this sign theory explains a great deal about thinking. It properly calls attention to the fact that many of our concepts pass directly into words and need no intervening images. It correctly notices that we often think aloud, referring, in so doing, to objects and not merely talking without thinking. Furthermore, it accords with the use of the word "sign" in the sense of that word in which, even concerning deliberately invented symbols, we often speak of "making signs." Especially it gives proper expres-

[2] *Ibid.,* pp. 94 ff.   [3] *Ibid.,* pp. 123 ff.

sion to the evident facts that the meanings of all complex terms tend to rest in the end upon ostensive definitions of simple terms, and that these meanings have always to be learned by inductive processes in listening to people talk and in reading.[4] Indeed as a description of the first phase of human learning, in which terms are mastered, and as a description of what thinking is from the point of view of the "looker-on or the listener," the sign theory seems on the whole to be fairly adequate.[5]

This is, however, by no means the whole story. The active side of thinking, or what thinking is from the viewpoint of "the speaker, the writer, the gesticulator, the one who draws diagrams," is here barely dealt with at all.[6] Besides, the thinking involved in sign cognition is almost exclusively tied thinking in that it does not occur save in the actual presence of some sensible sign whereas actually much of the most significant thinking depends on no such present sign. While one often thinks aloud, what one then says is not ordinarily a sign for him save in automatic speaking or writing. Moreover, many of the symbols in terms of which a person thinks are images and quite clearly these images are by no means merely inductively acquired signs.[7] Even understanding of what another says is not simply a matter of inductive association, for one scarcely treats in the same way that which he regards as originating in intelligent beings and that which he does not so regard.[8]

B. The side of thinking that is neglected by the sign theory is duly recognized by the image theory. This theory, which begins at the other end of the thinking process,[9] was characteristic of the British empiricists Locke, Berkeley, and Hume, and remains for the most part the view of common sense. It is, however, at present largely either ignored or specifically repudiated by most philosophers and psychologists.

This theory emphasizes the undeniable fact that images do occur and that they are likely to be much closer to the objects to which thought refers than are words. Indeed upon this theory words are only substitutes for images, and unless we are to use meaningless words we must repeatedly "cash" our words in terms of the images for which they are substitutes. Thinking in images makes possible a freedom from sensible presentations which can never be attained at the level of sign recognition,[10] and by means of diagrammatic and pictorial representation, it often circumvents the necessity of using many words. This kind of thinking requires no impossible perma-

[4] *Ibid.*, pp. 198 ff.
[5] *Ibid.*, p. 198.
[6] *Ibid.*
[7] *Ibid.*, p. 140.

[8] *Ibid.*, pp. 203 ff.
[9] *Ibid.*, pp. 234 ff.
[10] *Ibid.*, p. 238.

nent retention of images as such but can be quite adequately carried on with the more modest proviso that images can be produced, as in fact in the main they can be, when needed. It also for the most part avoids the confusion resulting from taking signs intended to symbolize determinate objects to represent higher determinables under which these objects fall. Even the fact that a specific image must often represent facts that are much more general is no insuperable obstacle to the use of images in thought; for an image may have a kind of composite character, and a specific image may readily bring to mind a whole cluster of associated images.[11]

Nevertheless, the image theory remains weak where the sign theory is strong. Failing to trust memory sufficiently it erroneously insists upon "cashing" all verbal symbols in terms of images. Actually we often pass directly from words or conceptual dispositions to objects without intervening images, as when being asked to draw a triangle we do so directly without first imagining one. In addition, the image theory is quite unable to give any satisfactory account of logical terms, and any attempt to reduce all logical and mathematical thinking to images would lead to preposterously cumbersome, if not quite impossible, procedures.[12]

C. In the classical theory of thinking, conceptual thinking is supposed to consist of looking through symbols to universals.[13] On behalf of this view one may point out that thinking does often go far beyond the symbols it employs, that we often find ourselves in the predicament of looking for a symbol for a concept we already have, and that consciousness is too narrow to contain all of the names that would be needed if thought were altogether in symbols. Such considerations as these properly suggest that much more is indeed involved in the concepts of our thought than is present either in symbols or in images, but these considerations scarcely justify the claim that universals are either discerned in things or conceived in thought. In actual psychological fact, we find no such entities as existing concepts. What we do find is *dispositions* to recognize characteristics that are repeated. These characteristics may be either specific determinants or more general determinables. In terms of dispositions all of the actually discoverable functions attributed by the classical theory to intuitions of universals can be adequately explained in more empirical fashion, for concepts seem to operate in us rather than being presented to us.

Regarding the traditional problem of the existence of universals as objects of knowledge, Price's view is essentially as follows. The

[11] *Ibid.*, pp. 287 ff.   [13] *Ibid.*, pp. 298 ff.
[12] *Ibid.*, p. 297.

realist-Platonist doctrine that universals exist *ante rem* may well be left aside, not indeed because it is uninteresting or altogether implausible, but rather because it is scarcely likely to receive serious consideration by contemporary philosophers and because most of what is most valuable in it is sufficiently retained in the milder Aristotelian doctrine that universals subsist *in rebus*. This more moderate realism involves nothing impossible or implausible, and it accounts satisfactorily for the empirical fact of "recognizing the same again." The most serious objection to it, that it seems unable to account for instances in which a thing only partially embodies a given universal, can readily be answered by calling attention to the fact that the universal in a thing need not be a specific determinate but may be a more general determinable.[14]

A promising alternative to all realist theories of universals is the modern nominalist theory of resemblances. In terms of this theory, that a thing has a certain characteristic means not that it is an instance of a certain universal, but simply that it resembles one of several standard objects at least as much as they resemble one another. Thus, for example, if a certain tomato and a certain blushing cheek are taken as the standard objects for the term "red," then if an object, such as an apple, resembles these as much as they resemble one another, that object is correctly said to be red. This theory seems capable of explaining the fact of recognition, in terms of fewer entities than are required by realist theories. Moreover, the usual objections to this theory, that one must specify in terms of a universal the respect in which objects resemble one another, and that resemblance itself is a universal,[15] may be met by insisting that the respect of resemblance is simply approximation to the standard object, and that resemblance itself is an approximation of a higher order.

In view of these considerations, instead of attempting to choose between moderate realism and the theory of resemblances, one may well recognize in these theories alternative languages suited to different purposes.[16] In his lecture entitled *Thinking and Representation,* Price seems to have preferred moderate realism on the ground that one cannot very well define a class in terms of similarities without already having in mind the defining universal.[17] But in his subsequent *Thinking and Experience,* Price seems to have become doubtful of the literal correctness of any references to universals, though he still seems to consider the language of universals useful.

Concerning our knowledge of other minds, Price regards as hope-

---

[14] *Ibid.,* pp. 26 ff.
[15] *Ibid.,* pp. 19 ff.
[16] *Ibid.,* pp. 30 ff.

[17] Price, *Thinking and Representation* (Oxford: Clarendon Press, 1946), pp. 31 f.

lessly one-sided dualistic arguments from analogy, behavioristic explanations in terms of signs, and intuitivist theories of direct meeting of minds. His own theory begins with the apprehending of linguistic symbols taken, not indeed merely as publicly observable events, but as cases of *thinking* aloud, and goes on to fill in the inner side of the character of other minds on the basis of one's own private image thinking. Thus the apprehension of other minds, though operating through matter, moves, not from "matter to mind, but from public mind to private mind, from public and overt mental processes to inward and private ones." [18]

3. W. T. STACE AND LEDGER WOOD

From a larger number of writers any of whom might have been chosen to represent a significant aspect of the type of epistemology now before us, we have chosen seven for brief consideration in the remaining sections of this chapter. The two writers to be considered in the present section are Princeton philosophers whose findings lean away from realism in the direction of phenomenalism. The two to be considered in the next section are British thinkers whose initial orientations and metaphysical convictions associate them with idealism but whose epistemological writings lean strongly in the direction of realism. The three writers to be considered in the fourth section approach their subject in considerable part from the modern analytic point of view but retain sufficient interest in traditional epistemological problems as such to be thought of as constructionists rather than as primarily analytic philosophers.

A. In his suggestive book *The Theory of Knowledge and Existence* W. T. Stace (b. 1886) rejects the idea that there are unsensed sensibilia and attempts to reduce his basic epistemological realities to the level of the phenomenally given. The given is for Stace that which is "necessarily taken as given or granted, as logically ultimate . . . ; that which we cannot doubt because we cannot go behind it; that which possesses primitive and absolute certainty, and which is therefore the necessary logical beginning of argument." [1] Included in the given are (1) "sense presentations, colours, sounds, odours, tastes, smells, muscular sensations, etc."; (2) "images of hallucination, dream, illusion, or memory"; [2] (3) "relations of position in extension-spread, such as 'to the left of,' 'between,' and the like"; (4) "relations of position in the duration-spread such as 'before,' and 'after' "; (5)

---

[18] *Thinking and Experience*, p. 243.
[1] W. T. Stace, *The Theory of Knowl-* edge and Existence (Oxford: Clarendon Press, 1932), p. 33.
[2] *Ibid.*, p. 24.

"resemblance and its opposite"; [3] and (6) *"acts* of . . . the empirical mind." [4] Extension-spread as given includes breadth but not, as Price thinks, depth. Data consist of particulars, and consciousness consists of universals; [5] but consciousness and data are inseparably linked and can be divided only in abstraction. In the lower levels of consciousness, universals remain largely submerged in particulars, and only at higher levels of thought are they clearly distinguished.[6]

Although simple concepts of the given, such as the concept "red," can be arrived at through comparison by the solitary mind, every step beyond the given and concepts of the given depends upon *"communication with other minds."* [7] Our belief in other minds depends for its logical justification upon an "argument by analogy from bodily behavior" that yields a "genuine inference" to such minds, not mere constructions or convenient fictions.[8]

Through reflection in communication with other minds, we proceed to build upon the given a knowledge of a common world whose objects are quite different from data and from other minds. These objects are neither given nor inferred objects but rest upon constructions or convenient fictions, and so are neither independent nor factual.[9] Underlying one's conception of every so-called physical object are five general constructions upon which the mind builds but to which it does not commit itself. They are as follows: (1) *"that the presentations of one mind bear to the corresponding presentations of other minds the relation of resemblance";* (2) *"that the corresponding presentations of different minds are identical";* (3) *"that the presentations of a mind may continue in existence unperceived by that mind";* (4) *that presentations may exist when no mind is aware of them";* and (5) *"that there exist 'things' or 'objects,' which are not identical with presentations and that the presentations are 'qualities' and that the 'qualities' may change while the 'things' remain the same,"* and *"that with different senses we may perceive the 'same' objects."* [10]

Every one of these constructions is useful and indeed indispensable to that common sense by which we live. The realists ask us also to take each of them as literal fact and indeed to go beyond common sense to the extent of believing in physical objects whose characteristics we cannot even imagine. For neither part of this realist program can we find any logical basis. We cannot use induction concerning that

---

[3] *Ibid.,* p. 39.
[4] *Ibid.,* p. 41.
[5] *Ibid.,* pp. 168, 443; Stace, *The Nature of the World* (Princeton, N.J.: Princeton University Press, 1940), pp. 139 ff.
[6] *Ibid.,* chap. v.

[7] *The Theory of Knowledge and Existence,* p. 100.
[8] *Ibid.,* pp. 196 f.
[9] *The Nature of the World,* p. 93.
[10] *Ibid.,* pp. 101–42.

of which we have no experience, and deduction is precluded by the fact that data apart from physical objects involve no inconsistency.[11] Moreover, an alleged instinctive belief in physical objects represents only a long-standing prejudice affording no basis for rational belief. Thus, although there could of course be physical objects, all that the evidence for physical objects, or our language about them, properly entitles us to affirm is that if minds were in certain situations, certain data would occur.

Although constructions are never literally true and justifications of them must depend upon pragmatic considerations, some of them may be regarded in a sort of metaphysical way as having more truth than others. The requirements of this sort of truth in a construction are that *"it involves no implications which are contradicted by the given,"* and that it *"is required or necessary for the practical or theoretical purposes of knowledge.*[12]

The point of view of all Stace's books prior to 1952 was essentially naturalistic. Indeed, he says of his convictions prior to that date that if he had been asked, "Is religion, or is anything in religion, true?" he would "until recently have replied with an unqualified no." [13] Nevertheless, even in his *Nature of the World,* Stace kept open the possibility of mystical knowledge, writing that he could not see "any reason for discrediting the mystic's evidence except prejudice." [14] In his recent books *Religion and the Modern Mind, Time and Eternity,* and *Mysticism and Human Reason,*[15] Stace develops and amplifies this suggested mysticism, saying that he would now answer the question about truth in religion with a "qualified yes." His position concerning mystical insight at present is in general that while naturalistic conclusions are completely justified within their frame of reference, the conclusions of the mystics are equally justified within their frame of reference, that man lives in fact in both temporal and eternal orders and that in man's mystical experiences, these orders interact.

B. The thought of Stace's Princeton colleague Ledger Wood is similar to that of Stace both in the manner of its structural analysis of knowing and in its refusal to adopt realist conclusions concerning objects of knowledge. However, Wood, whose approach to epistemological problems is primarily psychological, injects into his account

[11] Stace, "The Refutations of Realism," in H. Feigl and Wilfrid Sellars, *Readings in Philosophical Analysis* (New York: Appleton-Century-Crofts, Inc., 1949), pp. 364–72.

[12] *The Theory of Knowledge and Existence,* p. 436.

[13] Stace, *Religion and the Modern Mind* (Philadelphia and New York: J. B. Lippincott Co., 1952), p. 213.

[14] *The Nature of the World,* p. 250.

[15] Stace, *Time and Eternity* (Princeton, N.J.: Princeton University Press, 1952); *Mysticism and Human Reason* (Tucson: University of Arizona Press, 1955).

of the structure of the knowing process an emphasis upon *reference* that suggests a much stronger inclination toward realism than is to be found in any of Stace's writings.

Basic to all knowing are data, which though rarely, if ever encountered alone, must be taken for granted. Nearly always intimately associated with data in consciousness is a reference factor which never merely copies the data but *intends* an object.[16] Traditional realist theories have taken the object in question to be the existing ontological object, to which they have added, as the other ingredients in the knowledge situation, the subject and the content of consciousness. However, recent thought properly assimilates the subject to the content, and it is not in fact the existing ontological object but the cognitive or epistemic object (i.e. "the 'meaning' or . . . 'objective' constituted by the intentional process") which the reference in the knowing process intends; the ontological object "belongs to the domain of metaphysics," not epistemology.[17]

All knowing is referential in character. Perception, which is the basic kind of knowing, "may be defined as the apprehension of a phenomenal object on the occasion of sensory stimulation."[18] It involves at least four phases including "the carving of qualitative 'blocks' out of the continuum of experience, . . . the discovery of *de facto* correspondence between the 'sensory blocks' or patterns derived from different senses, . . . the *synthesis* . . . whereby the diverse data are synthesized into the unity of a thing or object, and *external projection*." The last of these phases is the characteristically referential or intentional one and it reveals in the intentional process a natural belief in both "the externality" and "the continued existence of the perceived object."[19] Perceptual memory refers to its object somewhat less directly than does perception. It may be defined as *"the primary or non-inferential cognition of the object of a past perception in the absence of direct sensory stimulation."* Introspective knowledge, which is defined as *knowledge by a subject of his own states and processes and of the self considered as the unity of its several states,"*[20] is not, as commonly supposed, immediate but, like memory, involves reference beyond a present given to a former state. Knowledge of other selves is primarily a referential knowledge by analogy.[21] The objects to which conceptual knowledge refers are not subsisting universals but classes of resembling things,[22] and formal

---

[16] Ledger Wood, *The Analysis of Knowledge* (Princeton, N.J.: Princeton University Press, 1942), pp. 9 ff.

[17] *Ibid.,* pp. 22 f.

[18] *Ibid.,* p. 30.

[19] *Ibid.,* p. 67.

[20] *Ibid.,* p. 88.

[21] *Ibid.,* pp. 103 ff.

[22] *Ibid.,* pp. 130 ff.

and valuational knowledge, instead of being intuitional, as they are often thought to be, are postulational in character.[23]

Truth, according to Professor Wood, is neither self-evidence nor coherence, but *"congruence . . . between the meaning of a proposition and a factual situation."* [24] The *congruence* in question can hardly be defined but must be felt in the situation. The fact by reference to which truth is determined is neither material fact nor bare sensation; it is rather "a fact . . . suffused with meaning." Hence the congruence involved in truth is a congruence "between a propositional meaning and a non-propositional, usually a perceptual meaning." [25] The direct verification of a proposition is achieved by "exhibiting in experience actual objects which exemplify the concepts specified by the proposition." All indirect verification depends ultimately upon such direct verification.[26] A "meaningful proposition" is "the description of a factual state of affairs by a set of concepts each of which is empirically definable or exemplifiable," and a concept is empirically meaningful provided it is "resolvable into concepts and operations which are exemplified or exemplifiable." [27]

4. NORMAN KEMP SMITH AND A. C. EWING

Each of the two writers now to be considered is essentially idealist in his metaphysics and in some phases of his epistemology, and each retains a reference to idealism in the title of his principal epistemological work. However, in epistemology as such, each is more realist than any of the writers considered in the other sections of this chapter and perhaps as much so as some of the writers considered in the chapters on realism.

A. The first of the two writers in question, Norman Kemp Smith (b. 1872), arrives at his epistemological results by giving to Kantian intuitions of space and time his own realist slant and building upon these intuitions a system of knowledge. Smith's avowed purpose, and the reason for calling his book *Prolegomena to an Idealist Theory of Knowledge,* is to build upon an essentially realist theory of knowledge a solid foundation for the metaphysically idealist claim that "spiritual values have a determining voice in the ordering of the Universe." [1] His conclusions present interesting suggestions for compromising, not only the differences between realists and idealists, but also the differences between monistic realists, such as the American new real-

---

[23] *Ibid.,* chaps. ix, x.
[24] *Ibid.,* p. 239.
[25] *Ibid.,* pp. 242 ff.
[26] *Ibid.,* p. 243.

[27] *Ibid.,* p. 244.
[1] Norman Kemp Smith, *Prolegomena to an Idealist Theory of Knowledge* (London: Macmillan & Co., Ltd., 1924), p. 1.

ists and Alexander, and dualistic realists, such as the American critical realists and Broad.

The sensa, including colors, sounds, and the like, are, Kemp Smith suggests, now generally recognized to be ultimate data. They are not, and cannot be, literally parts of the surfaces of physical objects; and they are private rather than public. The sensa are also "transitory" events "capable of happening only once." [2] They are by no means selections from an independently existing world but are rather in all probability generated on the occasion of their appearance and belong to the history of that which generates them.[3] Thus far, Kemp Smith's views are in harmony not only with the metaphysical idealism which he advocates but also with the subjective idealism which in general he repudiates; but from here on the realist emphasis of his epistemology begins to break away from the idealist setting.

Although the sensa are transitory and private they are not merely subjective but are objective in the sense that they are more than merely psychical or mental events. The conditions upon which they are contingent are largely physical and physiological rather than psychical; [4] and if one has to place them either in the category of the psychical or in that of the physical, it seems plain that they are somewhat nearer the latter. Moreover, we do not merely apprehend or contemplate things through them; we rather apprehend and contemplate them. "They are objects to the subject." [5] Although from the point of view of the quest for literal description of the real world, the sensa are inadequate and even somewhat deceptive,[6] and have always been so regarded by modern science, they are better suited to our practical needs than literal presentations, for example of atomic and molecular facts, could possibly be. It must, however, be noted that "none of them in and by themselves, possess spatial extensity." [7] Being produced by extended objects, they can scarcely be extended qualities of those same objects; their own extensity would only be an implausible duplication of objectively real space; and the complexity of space seems to be far beyond the grasp of mere sensation.[8]

The lack of extensity in the sensa leads to the presupposition of the inseparable association of some other factor with the sensa in our experience, for we never seem to encounter sensa without extensity both spatial and temporal. The requisite factor consists of intuitions of space and time distinguishable from the sensa but invariably present with them. Sensa never in fact occur apart from intuitions

[2] *Ibid.*, p. 70.
[3] *Ibid.*, pp. 89 ff.
[4] *Ibid.*, p. 71.
[5] *Ibid.*, p. 69.

[6] *Ibid.*, p. 180.
[7] *Ibid.*, p. 86.
[8] *Ibid.*, pp. 178 f.

of space and time, and such intuitions never manifest themselves apart from sensa. We should avoid saying that space and time are apprehended *through* the sensa and should say rather that they are apprehended *in terms of* the sensa. However, whereas the sensa are partially misleading, our intuitions of space and time are direct disclosures of essential aspects of reality. "Real independent space, in its own person, is here making entry into the 'conscious field.'" [9]

Much more however is involved in our intuitions of space and time than the bare apprehension of elementary spatial and temporal relations. Whereas sensa are relatively discrete, space and time involve a continuity and possible complexity that facilitate enormous extension of knowledge and "demand for their 'adequate' apprehension vaster labours than the mathematicians from Pythagoras to Einstein have yet accomplished." [10] Indeed involved in our intuitions of space and time is the whole system of categories including not only such obviously extensional categories as *whole* and *part* but also such less obviously extensional ones as *causality* and *substance*. Although the categories are purely formal so that the application of them, what we are to learn through them, depends upon experience, they serve as instruments through which experience may correct its own errors and extend its scope indefinitely. Not only has nature led us through the sensa to practical means of adjustment, but she has also, through the intuitions presupposed in the sensa and through the categories in turn presupposed by these, enabled us to apprehend directly the spatial and temporal aspects of her character, to infer other aspects, and even to use initially misleading sensa to extend our knowledge.[11]

B. A. C. Ewing of Cambridge (b. 1889) takes as the essential common characteristic of idealism not the broad metaphysical thesis referred to by Kemp Smith, that spiritual values play a dominant role in the ordering of the universe, but a more restricted epistemological argument to the effect that "there can be no physical objects existing apart from some experience." [12] On the whole, Ewing retains in his thought even more that is characteristically idealist than does Kemp Smith. Ewing manages to preserve the major portion of the idealist doctrine of internal relations.[13] He contends that there is synthetic a priori knowledge and that the causal relation involves a kind of entailment.[14] Ewing also holds not only that truth is tested by coherence [15] but that reality itself is coherent.[16] He contends that the ideal-

---

[9] *Ibid.*, p. 180.
[10] *Ibid.*, p. 157.
[11] Cf. *ibid.*, pp. 224 ff.
[12] A. C. Ewing, *Idealism; A Critical Survey* (New York: Humanities Press, 1933), p. 2.

[13] *Ibid.*, chap. iv; see also Ewing, "The Relation Between Knowing and Its Object," *Mind*, XXXIV (1925) 137–53, 300–10.
[14] *Idealism*, pp. 173–74.
[15] *Ibid.*, pp. 236 ff.
[16] *Ibid.*, pp. 228 ff.

ists were right in thinking "that we cannot 'get beyond' sensa," [17] and that cognition "always involves thinking facts as they would be for a mind." [18]

However, while these considerations support idealist metaphysics and demand qualification of extreme realist epistemologies, they are, in Ewing's opinion, entirely insufficient to sustain idealist episte-mology. The doctrine of internal relations in any but the most extreme forms is quite compatible with the epistemological inde-pendence of the object, for while being known or being about to be known does in fact change the object in the sense of placing the object in a new relation, it does not change the object in the sense of causing a change in the object.[19] Causal entailment is *discovered* rather than invented and synthetic a priori knowing is a mode of finding facts rather than of projecting ideas.[20] The coherence involved in reality and in the testing of truth has no tendency to show that truth *is* in fact coherence,[21] and even the consideration that nothing but minds and sensa in the end exist fails to show that all sensa depend upon minds.

The kind of epistemology that should replace the now discredited idealist one is surely not a phenomenalist one that forbids us to say anything about physical objects "except that they produce such and such . . . sensa . . . when we observe them," [22] for among other things, such a theory is quite incompatible with our ordinary state-ments about physical objects and would forbid our saying that we knew the properties of anything.[23] What is needed is rather a realism in which knowing is "a finding of reality independent of the cognition of it" [24] and "physical objects can exist independently of being per-ceived." [25]

Such a realism explicitly recognizes the existence of mind and of mental acts, not only because of abundant direct evidence, but also because failure to do so blurs the distinction between experiencing and experienced and, by inclining one to think of sensa as mental, tends to create an impassable gap between experiences and things.[26] Such a realism need not, however, with the new realists, assert that the object is directly perceived or even, with Kemp Smith, claim that the spatiotemporal aspects of the object are immediately intuited.[27]

---

[17] Ibid., p. 366.
[18] Ibid., p. 59.
[19] "The Relation Between Knowing and Its Object," Pt. I; see also Idealism, chap. iv.
[20] Ibid., pp. 173–74, 251–58.
[21] Ibid., p. 201.
[22] Ibid., p. 290.
[23] Ibid., pp. 293 ff.
[24] Ibid., p. 59.
[25] Ibid., p. 366.
[26] See Ibid., pp. 14, 23 ff.; and Ewing, "Mental Acts," Mind, LVII (1948), 201–20.
[27] Cf. "Knowledge of Physical Objects," Mind, LII (1943), 97–121.

The existence of errors and illusion precludes any such views.[28] Once the facts are admitted, as in the end they must, that the sensa are more akin to the physical than to the mental, that—Kemp Smith to the contrary notwithstanding—the sensa are extended,[29] and that physical objects consist of collections of unsensed sensa,[30] there is no reason why the existence and character of independent physical objects, consisting of groups of unsensed sensa that cause our sensed sensa, should not be validly inferred from sensed sensa that are numerically distinct from physical objects and indeed partially dependent upon our minds. Indeed only in terms of this sort of inference can the data presented to us be coherently organized. The grounds of such inference give us no warrant, however, for belief in physical objects that are different in kind from the sensa; and if physical objects were not like sensa, we could have no knowledge of them at all.[31] In all probability the collections of sensa that we call physical objects include secondary qualities as well as primary ones.[32] All this means, of course, that perception is in an important sense representative rather than direct, but since normal perception apprehends the actual character of physical objects such preception may also be said in a significant sense to "cognize" such objects "directly." [33]

Truth, though tested in part by coherence, is to be defined in line with the correspondence theory as "accord with reality." [34] Even as a test of truth the coherence principle must be qualified; for a set of propositions such as those found in a novel can be quite coherent without being true and in any case the coherence of any given proposition with a set of propositions must ultimately be recognized by intuition.[35]

That part of our knowing which builds upon and goes beyond perception may in general be thought of as reasoning; but if so, reasoning must be thought of as including intuition.[36] Were it not that intuition affords a general insight into a situation, reason could scarcely set up the mediating steps on which proofs depend, and—what is more important—the validity of each step must be seen by intuition.[37] Intuition sometimes also transcends a previous process of reasoning and enables us to apprehend a complex matter directly. To be sure, intuitions can be mistaken, but they are not to be ex-

[28] *Idealism*, pp. 274 ff.
[29] *Ibid.*, pp. 336 ff.
[30] *Ibid.*, pp. 355 ff.
[31] *Ibid.*, pp. 360 f.
[32] *Ibid.*, p. 339.
[33] *Ibid.*, pp. 288 ff., 318 f.
[34] *Ibid.*, p. 208; see also Ewing, *The*

Fundamental Questions of Philosophy (London: Routledge & Kegan Paul, Ltd., 1951), chap. iii.
[35] Ewing, *Reason and Intuition* (London: Humphrey Milford, 1941), p. 24.
[36] *Ibid.*, pp. 18 ff.
[37] *Ibid.*, pp. 12 f.

plained away either as empirical generalizations or as linguistic conventions; the one kind of explanation leads to the absurd consequence that $2 + 2$ might $= 5$, and the other, to the equally absurd view that "a majority" could alter the laws of logic.

5. C. J. DUCASSE, R. M. CHISHOLM, AND RODERICK FIRTH

The writers whose epistemological views are now to be sketched have all been deeply influenced by the analytic movement and some phases of the work of each belong to that movement. This analytic influence has no doubt had a good deal to do with the fact that these writers are considerably more concerned than are most philosophers to discover the precise meaning, for example, of statements referring to sensory experiences. However, the analytic influence has not been permitted by these writers to exclude direct epistemological inquiry or the development of epistemological conclusions that tend to mediate the dispute between realists and idealists.

A. C. J. Ducasse (b. 1881) of Brown University has combined in ingenious and somewhat novel fashion, ingredients of monistic realism, idealism, and dualistic realism. With monistic realists, he denies the existence of intermediaries between knower and known; and with idealists, he assigns to cognitive activity an essential role in knowing, grounding knowing in modification of such activity. But with dualistic realists he denies the possibility of direct knowledge of physical objects and seeks foundations for knowledge of such objects in causal inference.

That in knowing the knower at times apprehends that which is object over against himself and is independent of him, Ducasse regards as sufficiently evident to require no proof. Thus, we all at times seem clearly enough to apprehend such independent objects as coins, bells, and quinine.[1] Even more evident to Ducasse is the fact that in the knowing process the mind is active and that knowledge is in substantial part dependent upon the activity of mind. Indeed, Ducasse's insistence upon this point seems to have had considerable influence in bringing even such a staunch realist as Moore to reverse an earlier claim and to recognize that in the instance of some sensory aspects of knowing *esse* is *percipi*.[2] However, when Ducasse begins to look for distinguishable entities intervening between cognitive activ-

---

[1] C. J. Ducasse, *Nature, Mind and Death* (La Salle, Ill.: The Open Court Publishing Co., 1951), chap. xiii, sec. 5.

[2] Ducasse, "Moore's Refutation of Idealism," and G. E. Moore, "A Reply to My Critics," in P. A. Schilpp, *The Philosophy of G. E. Moore* (Evanston and Chicago: Northwestern University Press, 1942), p. 653.

ity and known object, such as sense-data or sensibilia, he is unable to discern any such distinguishable entities. What he does find is not entities in addition to cognitive activity at all but modifications of that activity itself. What are commonly called sense-data are then really only ways of apprehending or "species of awareness." [3]

The key to the meaning of this observation lies in a basic distinction that Ducasse insists upon between the "alien accusative" and the "connate accusative." On the one hand, the alien accusative represents an object that stands over against the activity represented by the verb, as when one is said to jump a fence or to see a coin. On the other hand, the connate accusative represents a mode or modification of the activity represented by the verb, as when one jumps a jump or when something tastes bitter. Now, the facts referred to when people talk about sense-data are really instances of connate accusatives. Thus, whereas seeing a coin or hearing a bell or tasting quinine are instances of the occurrence of alien accusatives, seeing brown, hearing middle C, and tasting bitterness in the purely sensory way are instances of the occurrence of connate accusatives. In these latter instances the relation of what is sensed to the sensing is not that of being an object at all but that of being a modification or mode. This means of course that in sensing as such one no more encounters an independent datum than in jumping a jump he encounters an independent jump or in dancing a waltz he encounters an independent waltz.[4] Moreover, since the mind is nonspatial, it would scarcely make sense to say that a datum was *before* the mind.[5] Thus just as in the case of dancing it would be literally more accurate, instead of saying that one dances a waltz, to say that one dances waltzily, so in using the language of the senses it would be more accurate, instead of saying that one senses blue, to say that one senses bluely.[6]

Sensing is elemental and indubitable knowing. That apprehension in sensing is in fact indubitable is implicit in the connate character of sensory qualities, for since blue, hard, warm, and the like are not objects but species of sensing, to doubt their presence in sensing is simply absurd.[7] Some writers, including John Dewey, C. I. Lewis, and a good many others, nevertheless refuse to apply the term knowledge to sensory experience on the grounds that such experience involves no objective reference, but this restriction does violence to common English usage, in terms of which for example one speaks of "knowing pain." [8] Indeed, sensory experiences are properly spoken

---

[3] *Nature, Mind and Death,* p. 265.

[4] *Ibid.,* chap. xiii.

[5] See *ibid.,* p. 273; and Ducasse, "On the Attributes of Material Things," *Journal of Philosophy,* XXXI (1934), 57–72.

[6] *Nature, Mind and Death,* pp. 246–90.

[7] *Ibid.,* pp. 308 ff.

[8] *Ibid.,* pp. 242 ff.; and "Facts, Truth and Knowledge," *Philosophy and Phenomenological Research,* V (1945), 328.

of as "knowing by intuition," and were it not for knowing by intuition there could be no knowing at all.[9]

All knowledge that transcends the elementary sensory variety depends for its justification upon causal inference. Every event, we are compelled to think, rests upon a sufficient cause, not indeed necessarily as a transfer of energy or an exemplification of an invariable sequence, but at least as a specific change introduced into the situation and followed by the event.[10] Thus when various qualities of awareness occur, we infer beyond them to causal events; and reliable capacities to cause such qualities we call *physicopsychical* properties of objects.[11] Material objects themselves or, if we prefer, "substances" consist of combinations of properties or capacities to produce qualities in the experience of an observer. The property of being red, for example, consists in the fact that if observers should be placed in various positions they would see various shades of color depending on lighting and organic conditions. Thus to perceive a red object is implicitly at least to infer an object having the property red as the cause of one's present sensations.

The boundaries of an object are determined by the reach of its causal efficiency and may vary from one aspect to another. For example the visual aspects of a stone are much more extensive than the tactual ones.[12] Objects can of course be causally related to one another as well as to conscious beings, and it is in these relations that physical science is primarily interested.[13] Nevertheless, the resulting properties of malleability, fusibility, and the like, which may be called physicophysical properties in contrast to the physicopsychical ones just now considered, are in the end apprehended solely through such physicopsychical properties as tangibility and visibility. That is to say, we know for example, that one moving object can cause another to move only as each object produces certain experiences in our awareness. If then it be asked what a physical object is over and above that which causes in an observer certain types of awareness, no answer can be given, for in no other way can the concept of a physical object be rendered intelligible save by reference to it as a cause of experiences.

Minds can be substances in precisely the same sense that material objects can—in being compounds of various empirically discerned properties.[14] Moreover, minds are known in essentially the same way that material objects are, namely, by at least implicit inference to the causes of certain aspects of immediate awareness—in this case the stream of intuitions that constitutes consciousness itself. While we

[9] *Ibid.,* pp. 329 f.
[10] See *Nature, Mind and Death,* Pt. II, esp. pp. 147 ff.
[11] Cf. *ibid.,* pp. 333 f.
[12] Cf. *ibid.,* pp. 135ff.
[13] *Ibid.,* pp. 333 f.
[14] *Ibid.,* pp. 401 f.

do not directly intuit the substantiality of minds, our knowledge of minds is in one sense more direct than our knowledge of material objects, for the immediate experiences through which we know both physical objects and minds are mental rather than physical. Although minds seem for the most part to be associated with bodies, no convincing reason can be found to show that they must be.[15]

With reference to that part of knowing that lies beyond perceptual apprehension, Ducasse presents a theory of meaning which is essentially as follows. Signs are representations that involve causal relation, belief, and interpretations.[16] Symbols in contrast to signs refer to objects without involving belief. They become discursive entities when they become reliably recognizable parts of human utterance.[17] Concepts are verbal symbols with corresponding interpretants.[18] The clarification of concepts and the determination of their relations in terms of analytic judgments is not, as C. I. Lewis and others suppose, in terms of examination of criteria in mind, but rather in terms of examination of the facts that the concepts are designed to deal with.[19] Moreover the allegation that we are directly acquainted with universals is false, for if we were we should know, as we obviously do not, all the properties of silver by "direct scrutiny" of a universal.[20] A proposition consists of an existing locus or *where* plus a descriptive *element* or *what*. A proposition is meaningful if and only if it is verifiable or falsifiable in terms of "moderate extrapolations in degree and in kind from assertions already verified and from the processes by which they were verified." [21] But statements commonly taken to be mere nonsense can often be shown to be simply false. A fact is a true proposition and the truth of a proposition consists not, as is commonly supposed, in the correspondence of a proposition to an external entity, but in the agreement of the locational *where* of the subject of the proposition and the descriptive *what* of the *predicate*.[22]

B. Although R. M. Chisholm (b. 1916) of Brown University approves and for the most part employs the methods of recent analytic philosophy, he also undertakes to show the untenability of some frequently encountered attempts by the use of these methods to avoid what he considers basic philosophical issues. Thus for example, with

[15] *Ibid.*, chap. xix.
[16] *Ibid.*, pp. 365 ff.
[17] *Ibid.*, pp. 372 f.
[18] *Ibid.*, p. 389.
[19] See "C. I. Lewis's Analysis of Knowledge and Valuation," *Philosophical Review*, LVII (1948), 270 ff.
[20] *Nature, Mind and Death*, p. 301.

[21] "Verification, Verifiability and Meaningfulness," *Journal of Philosophy*, XXXII (1936), 235.
[22] "Propositions, Truth and the Ultimate Criterion of Truth," *Philosophy and Phenomenological Research*, IV (1944), 334.

reference to the view that philosophical propositions are *proposals,* Chisholm protests that philosophers do and have every right to appeal to facts, that "no one has yet succeeded in formulating a criterion of verifiability which will allow us to say *both* that the statements of science and common sense are verifiable and that those of philosophy or metaphysics are *not* verifiable," [23] and that no reasonable criterion of the descriptive is available by which philosophical statements can be shown to be nondescriptive.[24] The effort of some analytic philosophers to ground their logical systems in material implications, he suggests, ignores genuine logical connections between some antecedents and their consequents; [25] and the current tendency to substitute sentences for propositions leaves out of account, among other things, the facts that when philosophers "use words differently, it does not at all follow that they have different *beliefs* concerning which use is more nearly correct," [26] and that such characteristics as "certainty and uncertainty" seem to be "characteristics, not of *sentences,* but of beliefs." [27] At the same time, while the insistence of current advocates of ordinary language that "many apparently important philosophical statements 'violate' ordinary language, and that such statements are misleading" is correct and helpful, those advocates of ordinary language who go on to claim that "any philosophical statement that violates ordinary languages is false" are surely mistaken,[28] for the philosopher is as fully entitled as anyone to attach special meanings to the words he uses.

Chisholm's important contributions to epistemological thought prior to 1957 consisted of brief analytic studies concerning cognition at three different levels, namely those of sensation, perception, and scientific law. At each level the analytic study contains, in addition to pure analysis, an indication of a need to pass beyond analysis of language into epistemological and metaphysical inquiry as such.

(1) At the level of sensory experience one of the most acute of current analytical issues concerns the choice of the language in terms of which such experience is to be spoken of. Advocates of a sense-datum language, such as Russell, Broad, Price, and others, hold that sense-data "must be found in any perceptual experience; . . . are essential to the perception of physical things; and, . . . are, in an

[23] R. M. Chisholm, "Comments on the 'Proposal Theory' of Philosophy," *Journal of Philosophy,* XLIX (1952), 304.

[24] *Ibid.,* pp. 301–6.

[25] Cf. Chisholm, "Sextus Empiricus and Modern Empiricism," *Philosophy of Science,* VIII (1941), 382 f.

[26] Chisholm, "Philosophers and Ordi-

nary Language," *Philosophical Review,* LX (1951), 323.

[27] Chisholm, "Some Theses on Empirical Certainty," *The Review of Metaphysics,* V (1952), 625.

[28] "Philosophers and Ordinary Language," p. 317.

important aspect, independent of the physical things in the perception in which they are involved." [29] Advocates of a language of appearing, such as G. Dawes Hicks and Arthur Murphy, reply that the sense-datum language is "metaphysically changed" in such fashion as to lead to all manner of needless puzzles and that if, instead of speaking of sense-data as intervening between object and subject, we speak simply of the object as appearing to the subject "we escape the puzzles."[30] In attempting to adjudicate this dispute, one must at the outset distinguish clearly between the "epistemic" sense of such terms as "appear," in which the term is used to "express an inclination-to-believe," and the "phenomenological sense," in which the term refers to a "phenomenal variation" or the way something looks regardless of belief; [31] and one must keep the fact clear that in this issue it is the latter sense, not the former, that is primarily involved.

Now there can be little doubt, Chisholm maintains, that the language of appearing is closer to the language of common sense than is the sense-datum language. The language of appearing also helps to avoid awkward questions about the locus of sense-data,[32] weakens the grip of the fallacy of supposing that one can infer from descriptions and conditions of appearances that physical things are not perceived,[33] and hinders the unfortunate tendency of philosophers to think that demonstratives apply to appearances when they really apply to things.[34] However, basic epistemological and metaphysical problems are neither removed nor resolved by the language of appearing. For example, one must still ask about the status of the object when no one apprehends it, for in terms of the language of appearing one would seem paradoxically obliged to infer from the fact that "nothing is appeared to" that "nothing appears." [35] Dreams, hallucinations, and afterimages seem to be facts for which the language of appearing can offer no satisfactory explanation.[36] Indeed, while sense-data may not be fully isolable entities, refusal to use the sense-datum language would seem to be a retreat from analysis somewhat akin to the insistence of absolute idealists that all finite things "are but aspects of the Whole." [37]

[29] Chisholm, "The Theory of Appearing," in M. Black, *Philosophical Analysis* (Ithaca, N.Y.: Cornell University Press, 1950), pp. 102 f.

[30] *Ibid.*, p. 105.

[31] *Ibid.*; see also Chisholm, "Verification and Perception," *Revue International de Philosophie*, V (1951), 263; and Review of G. E. Moore's "Some Main Problems of Philosophy," in *Philosophy and Phenomenological Research*, XV (1955), 572.

[32] *Ibid.*, pp. 104 ff.

[33] Chisholm, "Sellars' Critical Realism," *Philosophy and Phenomenological Research*, XV (1954), 34 f.

[34] Chisholm, "Verification and Perception," *Revue International de Philosophie*, V (1951), 263–64.

[35] "The Theory of Appearing," p. 109.

[36] *Ibid.*, pp. 116–17.

[37] *Ibid.*, p. 117. It should be noted that this position has subsequently been revised. See pp. 336 f. below.

While the language of appearing has its special advantages and the sense-datum language has other advantages, less misleading than either is Ducasse's language of qualities of intuiting, in terms of which, for example, one says not that "the object appears . . . in a bluish manner" or that "the object takes on a bluish appearance," but that "the observer intuits in a bluish manner with reference to the object." [38] While no linguistic formulation can settle the basic issues, this one avoids most of the misconceptions fostered by the other two and provides for Ducasse's important distinction between "sensible qualities" and "perceptible properties of physical things." [39] Chisholm would probably hold that in addition it accords with the fact, upon which he insists, that one is never entirely certain of all the characteristics even of what one intuits.[40]

(2) Turning now to Chisholm's suggestions concerning cognition at the level of perception, we find him pressing two claims. One is that the intentionality involved in perception is essentially psychological rather than physical in character; the other is that in veridical perception, it is the object and not merely a state of the perceiving mind that is apprehended.

Concerning the intentionality involved in perception, Chisholm's position is indicated by his criticism of Reichenbach's claim that the problem of the "apparent intentional character of perception" can be avoided by reformulating statements concerning perceiving in terms of physicalistic statements concerning observing, in the sense of being "sensibly stimulated by." [41] Chisholm's contention is that the proposed reformulation cannot be carried through for the reason that, while such a reformulation "would allow us to say that, on a certain occasion, a man may observe a fox and yet perceive a dog, it would forbid us to say that, on this occasion, the man does *not* perceive a fox." [42] Other similar attempts to get rid of the intentionality involved, for example, in speaking of perceiving a dog would, Chisholm thinks always leave on our hands some such intentional expression as "take (something) to be a dog." [43] Subsequently, defining "Brentano's thesis" concerning intentionality, of which he takes perceiving to be an instance, as the view that *"intentionality* is peculiar to psychical phenomena," Chisholm undertakes to defend Brentano's

[38] Chisholm, "Ducasse's Theory of Properties and Qualities," *Philosophy and Phenomenological Research,* XIII (1952), 53.

[39] *Ibid.,* p. 42.

[40] Chisholm, "The Problem of the Speckled Hen," *Mind* LI (1942), 368–73; and "Verification and Perception," *Revue International de Philosophie,* V, 262 f.

[41] Chisholm, "Reichenbach on Observing and Perceiving," *Philosophical Studies,* II (1951), 45 f.

[42] Chisholm, "Reichenbach on Perceiving," *op. cit.,* III (1952), 82.

[43] *Ibid.,* p. 83.

thesis against all more physicalistic accounts of sign situations.[44] Accordingly, with specific reference to perceptual intentionality, Chisholm insists that "the organism, rather than be merely stimulated by the referent, must *perceive* it, or *recognize* it, or have it *manifested* to him, or take *something to be* it." [45]

Chisholm's statement and defense of his claim that the object of veridical perception is a physical object and not a mere datum is presented mainly in the form of a restatement and revision of some leading ideas of R. W. Sellars. The *"sense-datum fallacy"* consists in believing that "merely from statements describing how things appear and statements describing the causal conditions of appearing, one can infer that appearances are perceived or that no physical things are perceived." Chisholm finds this fallacy committed in inferring from such statements as "he perceives a boat which appears green [or] . . . which takes on a green appearance for him," such further statements as "he perceives a green appearance [or] . . . he does not perceive a boat." [46] The appropriateness of the appearance or datum to the thing which renders a perception veridical may consist either in the fact that the appearance is "a reliable index" of some property of the thing or in the fact that a significant "structural similarity" obtains between the appearance and the thing.[47]

(3) With reference to scientific laws, Chisholm holds that all efforts to distinguish between lawlike statements and statements referring to accidental conjunctions without using either "modal terms," such as "causal necessity," or metaphysical terms, such as "real connections between matters of fact," or counterfactual inferences, such as "if that metal were gold it would be malleable," have so far failed.[48] He further suggests that, since logic cannot deal altogether successfully with counterfactual statements, it is doubtful that we can in the end "say all the things we want to say in our serious moments" without reference to "ontological" connections.[49]

In 1957 Chisholm published a volume entitled *Perceiving*, in which his major epistemological contentions are presented systematically, some earlier suggestions are revised, and some new suggestions are added. Among the leading ideas of this book are the following. That

[44] Chisholm, "Intentionality and the Theory of Signs," *Philosophical Studies,* III (1952), 56–63; see also "Sellars' Critical Realism," pp. 44 ff.

[45] "Intentionality and the Theory of Signs," p. 62.

[46] "Sellars' Critical Realism," p. 34.

[47] *Ibid.,* pp. 40 ff.; see also Chisholm, "Psychophysics and Structural Similarity,"

Revista Brasileira Felosofia, I (1951), 31–35.

[48] Chisholm, "Law Statements and Counterfactual Inference," *Analysis,* XV (1955), 97–105.

[49] Chisholm, "The Contrary to Fact Conditional," in Herbert Feigl and Wilfrid Sellars, *Readings in Philosophical Analysis* (New York: Appleton-Century-Crofts, Inc., 1949), p. 496.

someone perceives something to have a certain characteristic means that there "is" something which has that characteristic and "appears" to him in some way, that he "takes" the thing to have that characteristic, and that he has "adequate evidence" for the proposition that the thing has that characteristic.[50] The *truth* involved in a perceptual proposition would have to be determined by an absolute evidence with which the practical evidence that actually concerns us is connected by "animal faith." [51] Marks of adequate evidence must be clearly distinguished from adequate evidence itself. Since the relation of marks of adequate evidence to adequate evidence depends upon what is in fact taken to be adequate evidence, one's justification of a set of marks of evidence would seem in the end to depend, like one's justification of "right-making" characteristics, upon acceptance of a synthetic a priori.[52] One basic mark of evidence is what Chisholm calls being appeared to in a noncomparative way, i.e. in a way that does not involve assumptions about normal ways of appearing; but to infer [53] from the fact that one is appeared to the fact that one "sees an appearance" and hence does not see a physical object would be an instance of the "sense-datum fallacy." [54] The empiricist assumes that some sort of appearing is the only mark of adequate evidence, but here he is mistaken.[55] What may properly be called *"sensible takings"* are further marks that are commonly needed for the justification of physical object statements. These takings consist primarily in taking something to have such characteristics or relations as *"red, blue, . . . hard, . . . rough . . . sounding, . . .* being the *same,* or *different."* [56] Their tendency to be both correct and self-correcting is supported by induction in general and may be more rigorously justified by a logic of confirmation.[57] Phenomenalistic reduction of physical object statements is impossible, and one can in fact in interpreting physical object statements never avoid reference to conditions that cannot be stated in the language of appearing or of sensing.[58] The accepting involved in perceiving as well as in all other intentional attitudes are, as Brentano maintained, distinctively mental.[59]

C. The published writings of Professor Roderick Firth (b. 1917) of Harvard University have thus far been devoted to three main contentions. The first is that the usual conception of the sense-datum is too restricted and should be enlarged. The second is that sense-datum language, properly broadened, is essential to adequate discus-

[50] Chisholm, *Perceiving* (Ithaca, N.Y.: Cornell University Press, 1957), p. 3.
[51] *Ibid.,* pp. 7 f., 14, 38 f.
[52] *Ibid.,* p. 112.
[53] *Ibid.,* pp. 58 ff.
[54] *Ibid.,* pp. 151 ff.
[55] *Ibid.,* pp. 67 f.
[56] *Ibid.,* p. 83.
[57] *Ibid.,* pp. 89 ff.
[58] *Ibid.,* pp. 189–97.
[59] *Ibid.,* pp. 168–85.

sion of the problems of epistemology. And the third is that phenomenalism is a tenable position.

(1) Advocates of the traditional sense-datum theory to the effect
that we immediately sense such data as patches of color agree, Firth
observes, upon at least two basic points: (1) "that the sense-data directly observable by any *one* *s*ense are quite limited in their qualities," and (2) "that we are never directly aware of physical objects." [60]
The inquiries of James, Husserl, Dewey, the Gestalt psychologists, and
others have, however, revealed the essential untenability of this view.
It is impossible to isolate in experience such simple qualities as the
traditional sense-datum theorists intended. Experience seems actually
to involve, for example, along with extent and color, such additional
qualities as "simplicity," "gracefulness," reptilian quality, and feline
quality. Accordingly, "the qualities belonging to objects of direct
awareness cannot be thought of as limited, in the manner traditionally
assumed, by the use of one or another particular organ of sense . . . ,
[and] the experience of a man looking at a distant mountain from a
warm room comprises both whiteness and coldness each in precisely
the same manner." [61] Moreover, "the qualities of which we are conscious in perception are almost always presented to us, in some obvious
sense, as qualities *of physical objects*," for "we are not conscious of
liquidity, coldness, and solidity, but of the liquidity of water, the
coldness of ice and the solidity of rocks." [62] Those who cling to the
traditional sense-datum theory are misled by such fallacious assumptions as that there must be in experience some exact counterpart of
the physiological processes involved in perception,[63] and that when
one has pared away all that is involved in an experience that does not
fit the sense-datum theory, what remains is essentially the same as the
original experience.[64] Actually, that with which we are confronted
in experience is not a mere sense-datum but what, following a
terminology suggested by Price, may be called an "ostensible physical
object," a "content of perceptual consciousness"—not a fragmentary
datum but a fully formed percept.[65]

An interpretative element consisting of "a tendency to bodily behavior" or "a tendency to have certain kinds of conscious experience"
may indeed accompany ostensible physical objects; [66] but it would
be a serious mistake to suppose that the ostensible physical object and
the interpretative element could vary separately. An even more serious mistake would be to assume that ostensible physical objects are

[60] Roderick Firth, "Sense-data and the
Percept Theory," *Mind,* LVIII (1949),
438 f.

[61] *Ibid.,* p. 448.

[62] *Ibid.,* p. 449.

[63] *Ibid.,* pp. 452 f.

[64] *Ibid.,* pp. 458 ff.

[65] *Ibid.,* p. 451.

[66] *Ibid., op. cit.,* LIX (1950), 36.

physical objects, for "a physical object is at the very *least* a thing which transcends any one of the states which might be called a perception *of* it," and "the properties of ostensible physical objects can be discovered by direct inspection of a single state of perceptual consciousness, whereas properties of physical objects cannot." [67] The role that the ostensible physical object or percept does play in the cognitive process is essentially that which was played in the traditional sense-datum theory by the sense-datum itself, for the ostensible physical object not only constitutes a kind of given but also functions both as a sign of other experiences and a datum for the verification of physical object statements.

(2) The foregoing considerations suggest that the ostensible physical object or percept may properly be regarded as a sense-datum in a somewhat enlarged sense of the term; and when the term "sense-datum" is thus revised, sense-datum language may be seen to be indispensable to adequate epistemological inquiry. It is, to be sure, true that the now favored language of appearing has certain advantages of simplicity, and can satisfactorily express not only what occurs in veridical perception but also what occurs in illusory experience. Such language can even—despite the misgivings of Broad and Price—express what occurs in visual displacement and double vision. Thus, for example, if the candle appears double, one can say that the candle "appears the way two candles would appear under more normal vision." [68] But what the theory of appearing can never adequately express is what takes place in hallucinations. The difficulty is that in such cases there is nothing to appear and that all efforts to fill the gap lead to confusion.[69] For reasons of a similar sort, the theory of appearing is incapable of even formulating the hypothesis of phenomenalism,[70] which seems surely to be a discussible possibility.

Indeed, Firth contends, not only is phenomenalism discussible, it can, whether literally true or not, be consistently carried through. Defining phenomenalism or as he sometimes calls it, "radical empiricism," as the view that "the meaning of any statement about the material world can be expressed, at least in theory, by a combination of hypothetical statements which refer only to sense-data," [71] Firth finds the major obstacle to such a view in a consideration pointed out by Chisholm in discussing C. I. Lewis's views, namely, that *"if P is a statement about the physical world, there are some conceivable . . . conditions of observation under which any statement which refers*

---

[67] *Ibid.,* p. 42.
[68] Firth, "Symposium: Phenomenalism," *American Philosophical Association* (Philadelphia: University of Pennsylvania Press, 1952), p. 13.

[69] *Ibid.,* pp. 5 ff.
[70] *Ibid.,* p. 6.
[71] *Ibid.,* p. 6; see also Firth, "Radical Empiricism and Perceptual Relativity," *Philosophical Review,* LIX (1950), 164.

only to sense-data would be false even though P were true." [72] This objection can, however, be met, not indeed along the lines suggested by Lewis, by making the premise relative, but rather by insisting that when the expected sense-datum fails, although the original physical object statement has to be withdrawn, a similar revised physical object statement which may even in some instances be expressed in the same words, remains true.[73]

6. Comments Concerning Constructionist Theories

The most significant of the achievements of the theories considered in this chapter and one of the very significant achievements of contemporary epistemology, is the account of the phenomenology of perception in Price's book *Perception*. The value of this achievement is independent of the question whether or not Price or any of the other writers considered here have successfully mediated the dispute between idealists and realists. Actually, Price and these other writers have offered some interesting and useful suggestions for the mediation of that dispute and in so doing have shed significant light on the problem of the relation of knowing and the known even though each of the suggestions proves in the end to be inadequate.

A. Price's account of the phenomenology of perception is to be sure not without its defects. Written as it was, before the findings of Gestalt psychologists had had their full impact, it perhaps overemphasizes the distinctness of sense-data from one another and from the perceptual acceptance and perceptual assurance that enter into perceptual experience. It also tends to make more of a break between perception and causal expectation with reference to the interactions of objects than is commonly to be found in actual experience, for to perceive an object is already to have begun to anticipate what it will do in interaction with other things. In addition, it underestimates the role of what may in a broad sense be called inferences from sense experiences to objects and events felt to be their causes, in the growth of perceptual experience. To be sure, fully developed causal inference of the usual kind is achieved only where there are fully developed concepts of physical objects. But in the fumbling efforts of the child to make something of his sensory experience there is already a rudimentary sort of inference to objective causes that binds together bundles of experiences, and at times even in adult life of the most sophisticated kind there occur, as we have previously tried to show, causal inferences specifically from sensory experiences to supposedly objective causes. It may well be doubted that apart

[72] *Ibid.*, p. 166.   [73] *Ibid.*, II, 319–31.

from multitudes of rudimentary causal inferences from sensory experiences and occasional deliberate ones the sort of perceptual experience enjoyed by normal adults could be achieved. Another difficulty in Price's phenomenology of perception is its overestimate of the possibility of determining an optimum perspective for the defining of a standard object and his failure sufficiently to appreciate the possibilities of definition through a variety of perspectives each under prescribed conditions.

However, despite those and other defects, Price's account of perception, considered as phenomenology of adult perception, remains a landmark in its field, a point of departure from which most subsequent discussions of the subject take their initial cues. Among its most significant insights are the following. It properly recognizes the occasional occurrence of a mode of experience in which the question of objectivity has not yet arisen and the fact that the potential distinguishability of such a mode of experience affords a method of checking some dubious perceptual beliefs; for sometimes we do sense without interpreting and when we doubt our perceptions of objects we can always discern in them or beneath them elements of experience of which we are surer than we are of our perceptual takings. It appropriately insists that for the most part our perceptual experiences include not only elemental data but also assumptions regarding associated data and the objectivity of what we perceive. It correctly points out that such perceptual acceptances do not in the main have the phenomenological character of causal inferences. Especially significant is Price's delineation of the distortion and differentiation series; for while we can hardly properly be said to take just one perspective to be standard, we do certainly tend to regard some perspectives as superior to others in indicating the character of what is perceived, and Price's account of the orders of preferences in this matter corresponds rather closely to the order of the values that we tend to attach to our sensory experiences in disclosing the characters of their objects. Price's accounts of illusion and hallucination are also revealing with reference to the way we are inclined to take such experiences when we have discerned their misleading nature. Finally, Price's emphasis upon impenetrability and reliable effects on other families of sense-data is surely in accord with the criteria in terms of which we distinguish physical objects.

B. With reference to the relation of cognitive experience and its object, idealists claim that the object, if not itself an experiencing, is at any rate of the order of sentient experience; and realists claim that the object is certainly no mere product of experiencing and that perhaps it is not of the order of sentient experience at all. The theories considered in this chapter endeavor to mediate these conflicting views in part by recognizing a perceptual consciousness that tends to meet the more moderate requirements of both idealists and realists in being of the order of experience but no mere product of experience.

Price's perceptual consciousness is not only experiential but contains in itself ingredient sense-data that come unbidden into experience and belong to material objects. Similarly the perceptual consciousness acknowledged by Wood and Firth is both experiential and a possible product of external objects. Kemp Smith's perceptual consciousness is compounded of sense-data that are experiential responses to an external world and intuitive insights into that world itself. Even Ducasse and Chisholm, who dislike the drawing of too sharp a distinction between perceptual consciousness and eventual object, nevertheless recognize patterns of experience produced by something beyond experience.

Moreover, the recognition of a perceptual consciousness as an actual occurrence consisting of sentient experience yet no mere product of experiencing is, for reasons already sketched, quite plausible. While one must avoid hypostatizing such consciousness to make it a perceived object in its own right standing as a barrier between the perceiver and the eventual object—the sense-datum fallacy against which Chisholm warns—to see that perceptual consciousness does occur and may indeed not only be inferred but also in some sense noticed seems to be both phenomenalogically sound and foundational for any adequate analysis of knowledge. Always in some sense we carry with us as we look and listen patterns of impressions of which we can be surer than we can of objects we see and hear; and while we ordinarily look through these patterns rather than at them, still when the references involved in our perceivings go wrong, we sometimes notice the patterns themselves and use them for the guidance of new references.

C. Because none of the writers under consideration can confine his inquiry to perceptual consciousness and each is obliged to raise questions about eventual objects beyond such consciousness, none can at best be regarded as having successfully mediated the dispute between realists and idealists or resolved the problem of knowing and the known simply by virtue of recognizing a perceptual consciousness that is both experiential and not altogether created by experience. The crux of the issue is encountered only when the question is raised concerning the relation between perceptual consciousness and whatever eventual objects may be involved in perception. Upon this issue we may distinguish among the suggestions offered by the writers under consideration five main views, which, for convenience, we shall call respectively fictional, compositional, causal, evidential, and linguistic.

The view that is nearest idealism is the fictional one, according to which we treat the contents of perceptual consciousness *as if* they were real objects. This is the "as-if" view sketched by Price in his book *Hume's Theory of the External World*. It is also in the main the view of Stayce and Wood, and Firth seems to regard it as at least a possible view. However, such a view cannot really satisfy even idealists; for it leaves open the possibility that the eventual object is something remote from and perhaps alien to experience. It certainly cannot satisfy realists, for it leaves open the possibility that perceptual consciousness is all that there is. Moreover, instead of honestly endeavoring to solve the problem of the relation between cognitive experience and object, it in effect renounces the problem before the attempt to solve it has fairly begun.

The view nearest to new realism is the compositional one, according to which elements of perceptual consciousness belong to the eventual object itself. One version of this view is to be found in Price's claim that sense-data entering into perceptual consciousness are members of families of data that together with physical objects make up material objects. Such a claim will, however, leave even many realists dissatisfied in that it includes something so insubstantial as sense-data in its material objects, and it will certainly leave idealists dissatisfied by its contention that physical objects independent of experience are parts of the eventual objects of perception. Moreover, it can scarcely represent any adequate solution of the general problem of the relation of cognitive experiences and their objects, for the reason, among others, that the two sides of its material objects, namely, its families of sense-data and its physical objects, are developed more or less in isolation from one another with only the sketchiest indication of what their relations to one another are or of how they can constitute unified objects.

Another version of the compositional view is to be found in the claim of Kemp Smith that while one aspect of perceptual consciousness is a joint product of eventual object and the experiencing organism, another aspect is intuition into the spatiotemporal character of the object itself. This view is extremely attractive in preserving the contrast between primary and secondary qualities that is presupposed in most of modern science and in combining the prospect of some real insight into the nature of things with a candid recognition of the indirectness of some of our clues to their characters. However, the recognition of a wholly independent order is sure to leave idealists dissatisfied, and the allegation of a quasi-experential origin of the more conspicuous aspects of objects will leave many realists discontented. In any case Kemp Smith's grounds for giving preferred status to intuitions of space and time can hardly be considered sufficient; and in these days of non-Euclidean geometries, relativity theories, and quantum mechanics, the objective validity of intuitions of space and time is very difficult to establish.

The view closest to critical realism is the causal view present in the suggestions of Ewing and Ducasse to the effect that material objects are known by causal inference from our perceptual experiences. In referring to nonexperiential existents as the causes of perceptual consciousness and the eventual objects of knowledge, this view leaves idealists dissatisfied, and in excluding direct apprehension of objects, it fails to meet the demands of nonrealists. In emphasizing causal inference, it touches upon a factor that doubtless underlies much of our perceptual experience, but fails to do justice to the noncausal phenomenology of much of our perceptual experience or to explain how causal inference from sense-data is possible. Ewing's version of the theory takes on the added difficulty of explaining how unsensed sensibilia can exist or even be intelligibly spoken of. That of Ducasse has the special merit of careful avoidance of the sense-datum fallacy and of preservation of maximal intimacy between object and perceptual consciousness within the framework of a causal theory, by means of its concept of appearing. However, it leaves the character of causal inference to the object somewhat vague and by no means explains adequately how a causal theory can be combined with a theory of appearing.

The most subtle and perhaps the most promising of the views under consideration is that of Chisholm, to which we have referred as the evidential theory. The substance of the theory is somewhat as follows. In veridical perception the object appears to the perceiver; but the appearing can be treated as knowledge only if the perceiver has adequate evidence, the marks of such evidence being ordered appearing and perceptual takings backed by inductions which themselves involve perceptual takings. Such a view has the merits of avoiding some of the usual sense-datum troubles by its language of appearing; of advancing beyond a strict empiricism in recognizing, as we seem in fact to do, at least a quasi-evidential value in perceptual takings; of calling attention to inductive support for these takings; of distinguishing between adequate evidence and marks of such evidence; and of requiring a less rigid sort of inference than is commonly demanded by causal theories. However, these various promising features of Chisholm's view are thus far very loosely tied together in his thought, and a great deal remains to be done, even assuming the theory operates along sound lines. Moreover, the procedure of assigning to perceptual takings what amounts to a key role in perceptual knowledge cannot but give rise, protests to the contrary not withstanding, to at least some suspicion of circularity in this account of perceptual knowledge.

What we have called the linguistic view is the view, suggested in Price's book on Hume's theory, that whether or not our perceptual consciousness adequately represents a real world in which the gaps in our experience are filled in, the most convenient form of language may be one in which it is assumed that our perceptual consciousness does represent such a world. That such a language is in fact the most convenient one seems on the whole to be beyond dispute, though to stop with saying this, appears to be to avoid rather than to resolve the problem of the relation of cognitive experiences and their objects. However, we shall have occasion subsequently to discuss views of this sort at some length.

In view of the fact that the theories of the relation of cognitive experiences and their objects considered here, as well as those considered earlier, turn out to have such unsatisfactory features as they seem to have, one may perhaps suspect that the problem concerning such a relation has no solution or perhaps that it has been improperly formulated or is not really a proper problem at all, hence that what needs to be examined is not the possible solutions but the problem. However, before turning to theories that develop this line of thought, we shall look briefly at two other types of proposed solutions of the idealist-realist controversy. One is an attempt to solve the problem by penetrating to a level of reality below that at which the problem emerges, and the other, an attempt to place the problem in a larger metaphysical perspective.

CHAPTER 8

Intuitional Theories

THE type of theory we are now to consider undertakes to settle the dispute between idealists and realists in a way that is very different from that of the theories with which we were concerned in the preceding chapter. Instead of trying to piece together the various ingredients of the cognitive process in such a way as to represent adequately the respective contributions of subject and object, it endeavors to ground knowledge in a level of experience more basic than the distinction between subject and object. It takes the most fundamental knowledge to be achieved by a pure intuition, which is neither a presentation of object nor an activity of subject but is logically and chronologically prior to either. The relation between subject and object, so central to the views previously discussed, here recedes from the forefront of epistemological theory.

The earlier sources of this type of epistemology are to be found in the works of long lines of mystical thinkers both in the East and in the West. More immediate sources are the writings of the French spiritualists from Main de Biran (1766–1824) to Felix Ravaisson-Mollien (1813–1900). A source of a very different kind is the immediate empiricism of such writers as Avenarius, Mach, and James. Yet another kind of influence is the evolutionary philosophy of Herbert Spencer. By all odds the most significant representative of this type of epistemology among contemporary philosophers is Henri Bergson, and to such an extent does the work of Bergson (1859–1941) overshadow that of all other recent thinkers of this type that we shall be content to focus attention solely upon his work in the present connection.

1. Bergson's Intuitional Account of the Process of Knowing

The roots of knowing, according to Bergson, lie deep within the evolutionary process in which a creative life force continuously bursts forth in ever new manifestations. The very existence of life requires on the one hand the "accumulation of potential energy from matter" and on the other hand the expending of such energy "in a discontinuous and explosive way in movements." [1] In the earliest organisms these primitive tendencies are combined in fairly even balance, and as more highly specialized tendencies appear in the process of evolution, each *tries to preserve and develop everything in the primitive tendency that is not incompatible with the work for which it is specialized.* [2] Of the two primitive tendencies, the first, storing up of energy, has been concentrated in the plants. Here life remains in a deep sleep, as it does also in some animals. One of two major branches of the energy-storing plants consists of nitrogen-fixing bacteria, and the other, of more complex plants. [3] The second primitive tendency, that of expending energy, is mainly a function of animals. Apart from some relatively unsuccessful experiments in heavy armor, [4] animals are diversified along two main lines. [5] One line consists of insects, and in insects a wide variety of highly specialized appendages is accompanied by instincts that perform specific functions with a high degree of efficiency. The other line consists of higher vertebrates. Here the appearance of much more adaptable appendages is accompanied by an intelligence capable of performing a far wider range of functions somewhat less efficiently. [6] Intelligence is inferior to instinct in being costly in effort and in lacking precision, but intelligence is vastly superior to instinct in versatility and wealth of organization. Indeed, "it lays open to activity an unlimited field into which it is driven further and further, and made more and more free." [7] Intelligence is never entirely absent from the insects, nor instinct from the higher vertebrates; but the insects specialize in the one and the higher vertebrates in the other. Intelligence and instinct and their various combinations lie at the roots not only of scientific knowledge but of everything that can in any sense be called knowing. We must now examine each more closely.

Being limited to two pairs of limbs and, apart from intelligence, to a generally rather meager native equipment, man is obliged to resort

[1] Arthur Mitchell (trans.), Henri Bergson's *Creative Evolution* (New York: Henry Holt & Co., Inc., 1913), pp. 115 f.

[2] *Ibid.*, p. 119.

[3] *Ibid.*, p. 117.

[4] *Ibid.*, pp. 130 f.

[5] *Ibid.*, pp. 131 ff.

[6] *Ibid.*, pp. 139 ff.

[7] *Ibid.*, p. 141.

to inorganic or merely material instruments for his defense and the fulfillment of his needs. Hence, it is upon matter that intelligence is from the beginning oriented. As *"instinct perfected is a faculty of using . . . organized instruments,"* so *"intelligence* perfected is the faculty of making and using *unorganized instruments."* [8] Indeed, "intellect and matter have progressively adapted themselves one to the other in order to attain at last a common form." [9]

Since intelligence is throughout oriented to matter, it "spacializes," breaks up and divides reality in ways which suit its own practical purposes without regard to other considerations. Thus, for example, it sets the qualities found in experience over against one another as quite separate and distinct without recognizing their inseparable interpenetration of one another.[10] In like manner it marks out within the continuous flux definite objects, which it thinks of as remaining the same amid changes.[11] It also marks out a system of discrete numbers and, in terms of this system, undertakes to subdivide its objects for purposes of measurement without regard to natural joints. Its characteristic mode of expression is geometrical, and even the logic from which in due time it deduces its formal geometry is at bottom geometrical.[12]

The abstractive character of intelligence in general and in particular of the science in which intelligence attains its fullest expression is especially evident in the manner in which intelligence treats the temporal dimension. Since the primary objective of intelligence is to predict the state of affairs at some future moment, intelligence need not concern itself with what takes place in the intervals between observed states, and for the most part it ignores these intervals. If, in order to make its predictions, it requires to know some intervening states, it may make its divisions finer while still remaining indifferent to what happens between the new divisions. And if, as is the case in modern science in contradistinction to Greek science, it seeks to ascertain the character of *any possible* state, it still only cuts its intervals shorter and shorter without ever grasping the flow of things.[13] No mere multiplying of states of rest can enable it ever to grasp movement. Time has a place in modern science, but rather as *"time-length"* than as *"time-invention,"* as measured mechanical time, not as actually elapsing time.[14] Scientific intelligence spreads time out as it were like points upon a line, so that even an infinite acceleration

[8] *Ibid.,* p. 140.
[9] *Ibid.,* p. 206.
[10] F. L. Pogson (trans.), Bergson's *Time and Freedom of Will* (London and New York: George Allen & Co., & The Macmillan Co., 1912), chap. i.

[11] Cf. *Creative Evolution,* pp. 247 ff., 299 ff.
[12] *Ibid.,* pp. 161, 212.
[13] *Ibid.,* pp. 329 ff.
[14] *Ibid.,* p. 342.

of time would neither disturb scientific calculations nor direct attention to the actual passage of time upon which events really hinge.

That which "fills the intervals between what is done and what might be done" [15] is consciousness, but while consciousness involves instinctive and intuitive as well as intelligent aspects, its more prominent manifestations have the practical and abstractive character of intellect. Thus sensation already involves a practical selection from the extremely rapid vibrations with which events confront us and ignores all the rest.[16] Similarly, perception brings selections from the past to bear upon presently proposed action.[17] Memory differs in kind from perception, for no one mistakes a weak perception for a strong memory or vice versa.[18] Moreover, in pure memory the past is preserved without need of the action of brain. Nevertheless, in most efforts of memory, intelligence exercises through brain a selective activity upon the total past for practical ends.[19]

Intelligence, especially in its scientific form, is fairly successful in its practical endeavor. It achieves many of the correct predictions necessary to the preservation and enhancement of life; it warns us of pitfalls and points out to us opportunities. Indeed, in its own material sphere, it not only yields practical results of utmost importance but also helps to overcome mistaken implications of common linguistic expressions, gradually surmounts many of its own initial limitations, and may even in its material sphere "reach an absolute." [20]

But one must never forget that the objectives and capacities of intellect are largely limited to the material sphere and to the achievement of practical results. When intellect attempts, as it all too often does, to attain theoretical apprehension of reality or to plumb "the depth of mind," confusion and eventual self-contradiction invariably result. Among the most barren of human responses is the kind of dialectic that merely takes over the common expressions of ordinary language and attempts to draw out their metaphysical implications. The concepts involved are merely pragmatically achieved for purposes of conversation and action without regard to real distinctions in nature.[21] Man the doer and man the knower may be respected but not man the talker, and mere "reflection upon his talk" has little cognitive value.[22] The concepts of science itself are grounded in our

[15] *Creative Evolution*, p. 179.

[16] Cf. N. M. Paul and W. S. Palmer (trans.), Bergson's *Matter and Memory* (London & New York: George Allen & Co., & The Macmillan Co., 1913), pp. 8, 24, 170; and Mabelle Andison (trans.), Bergson's *The Creative Mind* (New York: Philosophical Library, Inc., 1946), pp. 111 f.

[17] Cf. *Matter and Memory*, p. 177.

[18] *Ibid.*, pp. 72 f.

[19] *Ibid.*, pp. 233 f.

[20] *The Creative Mind*, p. 45.

[21] *Ibid.*, pp. 91 ff.

[22] *Ibid.*, p. 100.

common-sense linguistic concepts; and while science does indeed grasp reality at the material level, it can do nothing to disclose the nature of mind or of the whole of reality.

Philosophical refinement of common-sense and scientific concepts only brings to light the basic contradictions likely to be involved in the attempt to embrace all reality in these concepts. This fact is illustrated for example in the paradoxes of the Eleatics.[23] Movement marks out a path in space; but, assuming in terms of the ordinary concept of movement, that movement, like its path, could be infinitely divided, Zeno was at a loss to determine how movement could ever take place. He failed to see that movement must be intuitively grasped as a whole. Another striking illustration of the speculative failure of common sense and science in the theoretical realm is the skepticism of Kant's first *Critique,* which shows "that no dialectical effort will ever introduce us into the beyond" and "that if metaphysics is possible, it is through a vision and not through a dialectic." [24] The limitations of scientific concepts are peculiarly evident when these concepts are applied to the life and mind; for while life and mind use matter, they also have creative aspects quite foreign to materially oriented scientific concepts.[25] Scientific observations are at best like a series of snapshots to which no motion can be imparted save from another source, and the whole procedure of science is like the use of a net whose meshes are far too coarse to catch mind, movement, or life.

The functioning of instinct, in contrast to that of intelligence, is direct, sharply focused, and narrow in scope. Although instinct develops along an entirely different evolutionary line from that in which intellect emerges, it preserves in itself something of what goes into the making of intellect. It requires division of reality into separate substantial objects and changes of these objects. It needs no spreading out of real duration into a spatially organized mathematical time nor any cutting up of things into measurable units. It isolates no qualities, demands no formal logic, and makes no predictions.[26] Yet it acts always *as if* it knew the eventualities. For example, when a wasp stings its victim in precisely the point to produce paralysis without death and then lays its eggs in its victim, it acts as if, like a skillful surgeon, it knew just what the effect of its action would be.[27] When "the Ammophilia Hirsuta gives nine successive strokes of its sting upon nine nerve centres of its caterpillar, and then seizes the head and squeezes it in its mandibles enough to cause paralysis without

[23] *Creative Evolution,* pp. 308 ff.
[24] *The Creative Mind,* pp. 151, 164.
[25] *Creative Evolution,* pp. 176, 329; *The*

Creative Mind, pp. 33 ff.
[26] *The Creative Mind,* Essay III.
[27] *Creative Evolution,* p. 172.

death," it suggests even greater foresight. Yet the results of its actions can scarcely be said to be *planned* by the stinging insect. Rather there seems to be "a *sympathy* (in the etymological sense of the word) between Ammophilia and its victim, which teaches it from within, so to say, concerning the vulnerability of the caterpillar." [28] If we seek parallels, we must recognize that not in rational processes but "in the phenomena of feeling, in unreflecting sympathy and antipathy, we experience in ourselves . . . something of what must happen in the consciousness of an insect acting by instinct." [29] Instinct operates in some degree in all our life and intercourse to keep us close to the vital forces surging within us. In feelings of moral obligations and in religious rites it acts as a check upon the socially disintegrating influence of intellect.[30]

If, on the one hand, intellect is artificial, indirect, and often misleading, and on the other hand, instinct is narrow, unadaptable, and unreflective, it is evident that for genuine insight into the nature of things we must look to some other source. Such a source Bergson finds in what he calls intuition. Intuition is in general much closer to instinct than to intellect. Like instinct it requires no artificial segmentation of things, no counting, no numbering, no analysis, no symbols, no translation. It is nonlogical and nondiscursive, a kind of "divining sympathy." Nevertheless it is more than instinct. Like intelligence, it rises above the limits of its immediate setting and is genuinely reflective. The instinctive-intuitive penumbra that surrounds intelligence comes to focus in intuition as such; "it is from intelligence that has come the push that has made it rise to the point it has reached." [31] Intuition is thus "instinct that has become disinterested, self-conscious, capable of reflecting upon its object and of enlarging it indefinitely." [32]

In intuition we do not "move round the object" but "enter into it." [33] Intuition is "the kind of *intellectual sympathy* by which one places oneself within an object in order to coincide with what is unique in it and consequently inexpressible." [34] It does not confine itself to snapshots or static cross sections of reality but takes its stand in the midst of life and movement, "in the concrete flow of duration." No mere apprehension of fragments, it grasps totalities in a way quite as unintelligible from the point of view of the parts as a poem is

[28] *Ibid.*, pp. 173 ff.
[29] *Ibid.*, p. 175.
[30] R. A. Audra and Cloudesley Brereton (trans.), Bergson's *The Two Sources of Morality and Religion* (New York: Henry Holt & Co., Inc., 1935), chap. i, esp. pp. 87 ff.; chap. iii, esp. pp. 187 ff.

[31] *Creative Evolution*, p. 178.
[32] *Ibid.*, p. 176.
[33] T. E. Hulme (trans.), Bergson's *An Introduction to Metaphysics* (New York & London: G. P. Putnam's Sons, 1912), p. 1.
[34] *Ibid.*, p. 7.

unintelligible from that of the letters which make up its words.[35] Its transcendence of intellect will seem to some impossible, just as to swim seems impossible save by first learning "to hold ourselves up in the water." But just as in the latter instance one may break the vicious circle by leaping in and struggling, so in the former he may break the circle by frankly accepting the risk. Thus "action" may "cut the knot that reasoning has tied." [36]

Intuition can never be as precise as intellect; nor is it intended as a substitute for intellect. But what it lacks in precision [37] it makes up in immediacy. It comes into play "wherever a vital interest is at stake. On our personality, on our liberty, on the place we occupy in the whole of nature, on our origin and perhaps also our destiny, it throws a light feeble and vacillating, but which none the less pierces the darkness of the night in which the intellect leaves us." [38] It yields in saints the open morality of love, and in mystics an insight into ultimate spiritual reality.[39]

Although for the most part man's intuition is sacrificed to his intellect,[40] intuition is essential to man's mature life. It is not the way of science, but it is the way of metaphysics and of philosophy generally.[41] Upon it depends all genuine insight into mind and the living character of reality.[42] Its results can never be achieved merely by summing up or extending the findings of the sciences, and its natural language is that of images and metaphors.[43] The philosopher needs all that science can give him but must revise the basic assumptions of science. The great philosophers, although often expressing what they saw in the fixed conceptual forms of intellect, have been men of profound intuition,[44] and in the end each has tried to establish a single intuition.[45] The great geniuses of religion and morality have also at their best been led far more by their visions or intuitions than by the calculations of reason.[46] Indeed it is largely to their intuitions that we owe most of what is best in our religious and moral tradition. Even those phases of life which look most to science are indirectly benefited by intuitive insight. The more a philosophy emerges in which intellect is reabsorbed in intuition, the more philosophy and the best in science approximate and supplement one another.[47] Intuitive philosophy "gives us also more power to act and live." For,

[35] Ibid., pp. 29 ff.
[36] Creative Evolution, p. 192.
[37] Ibid., p. 177.
[38] Ibid., pp. 267 f.
[39] The Two Sources of Morality and Religion, chap. iii.
[40] Creative Evolution, p. 267.
[41] An Introduction to Metaphysics, p. 7; The Creative Mind, Essay IV.

[42] Cf. The Creative Mind, p. 48.
[43] Ibid., pp. 48 f.
[44] An Introduction to Metaphysics, p. 92.
[45] The Creative Mind, Essay IV.
[46] The Two Sources of Morality and Religion, esp. chap. iii.
[47] Creative Evolution, pp. 198 f.

with it, we feel ourselves no longer isolated in humanity; humanity no longer seems isolated in the nature that it dominates. As the smallest grain of dust is bound up with our entire solar system, . . . so all organized beings . . . do but evidence a single impulsion. . . . The whole of humanity . . . is one immense army . . . able to beat down every resistance and clear the most formidable obstacles, perhaps even death." [48]

2. BERGSON'S VIEW OF THE OBJECTS OF KNOWLEDGE AND THEIR RELATION TO KNOWING

Since philosophical thought is for Bergson primarily intuitive rather than conceptual, Bergson attempts no definitive conceptual statements concerning the objects of knowledge or their relation to knowing. Yet Bergson recognizes that even intuitions must in some degree be formulated in concepts or at very least in images, if they are to be communicated at all, and his books present imagery and even concepts that suggest a theory of objects in relation to cognition.

In general the objects of intellectual knowing are, as has been observed, material things. But what ultimately are such things and what is their place in reality? Sometimes Bergson writes as though material things constituted an independent kind of objects related only incidentally to minds, but more characteristically he treats matter as a sort of degenerate manifestation of the vital activity which constitutes basic reality. Permanent substance is an illusion, and what we think of as substance is only certain modes of continuous change. It is necessary to suppose "a kind of fusion between . . . substance and movement." [1] One must, as Whitehead has said, "envisage a piece of iron as 'a melodic continuity.' " [2] Even the notion of possibility is misleading—as though future things were shut up to prearranged alternatives and not actually evolving in the course of events. [3] The "immense reservoir of life" is like a great boiler from which a jet of steam gushes out through a crack. Some drops condense and tend to fall back but these are repeatedly lifted again by the emerging steam. The drops that fall back are like matter that tends always to fall back against the flow of life but is ever checked and pushed upward again by that flow. [4] Matter may also be likened to the falling particles of a rocket, ever bearing downward but ever lifted by the continuing force that lifts the rocket. [5] The basic form of matter is that of the geometrical space traced out by movement.

[48] *Ibid.*, pp. 270 f.
[1] *The Creative Mind*, p. 85.
[2] *Ibid.*

[3] *Ibid.*, Essay III.
[4] *Creative Evolution*, p. 247.
[5] *Ibid.*, p. 261.

The basic laws of matter are the laws of this geometrical form and of the logic that grows out of it.

Although the object toward which *instinct* is directed is not dead material but living organisms, apprehension by instinct is so narrow in scope and so low in the scale of consciousness that the propriety of calling it knowledge is doubtful. The deficiencies of both intellect and instinct are overcome in *intuition*, the object of whose apprehension is reality itself. While intuition is difficult to achieve, there are no limits, save those of inattention, to its prospect of apprehension of past and present reality. The entire past is intimately linked with the present and indeed is truly past at all only as attention lapses. That which intuition apprehends is not merely snapshots of reality but the whole living filling, the real duration of which reality is fundamentally constituted. This real duration is best seen in our own, free, creative, ever-changing experience.

Although the metaphorical character of much of Bergson's language makes the discernment of his precise view of the relation between object and knowing peculiarly difficult, one thing seems to be clear, that Bergson wishes to bind these two together much more closely than do most epistemologists. This remains true whether it is intellectual knowledge that is in question or intuitive knowledge.

What Bergson has to say of the relation of knowing and its object in the area of intellectual or scientific knowledge is similar in many ways to the position of the new realists. The observations on which such knowledge rests are not separate representations or sensations that stand between the material object and the perception of it. Rather, these observations are snapshots of reality. Our "present moment is constituted by the quasi-instantaneous section effected by our perception in the flowing mass." [6] Essentially, the material object is independent of being known by any individual. Perception does not add anything to the object. Its activity is for the most part one of selection for practical ends. [7] Brain activities do not produce but only channel the images involved in knowing, and these images are not at all *in* the brain but, insofar as they are spatial, out there where the object is. [8] Even in the case of apprehension of the past, it is no mere symbol that is present to us but the past itself. Nevertheless, "the states of our material world are contemporaneous with the history of our consciousness [and] as the latter endures the former must be bound in some way to real duration." [9] Indeed the states of the world are like an unrolling film which is "attached to consciousness and which regulates its movement." [10]

---

[6] *Matter and Memory*, p. 178.   [9] *The Creative Mind*, p. 20.
[7] *Ibid.*, pp. 27 ff.   [10] *Ibid.*, p. 21.
[8] *Ibid.*, pp. 35 ff.

Some philosophers are puzzled by the fact that there are objects of knowledge at all, and wish to know how we know that anything at all exists. But this is a pseudo-problem. The idea of *nothing* is really quite unintelligible. When we try to think anything away we only succeed in thinking it in another place or in thinking a substitute for it; and when we try to think of nothing, we try to think first of all that is and then to substitute for it.[11] When this fact is made clear the temptation is removed to equate existence with logical existence. Some philosophers have also been concerned to inquire why the object of knowledge should have order, and wonder whether the supposed order is merely the mind's creation. But the fact is that the term "disorder" is really without meaning, represents no idea at all; and when it is used, what we really refer to is only another order than the one anticipated or desired.[12]

The further questions arise why, if primary reality is of the order of life and movement, so much of our cognitive activity should be concerned with the secondary material order, and what consciousness does to pass from the primary to the secondary. The fact is that consciousness needs to do nothing at all to accomplish this passage. Consciousness functions on various levels of tension, a very high degree of tension being necessary to bring the basic living reality into focus. Accordingly, it is no new kind of insight but only an "inversion" or relaxing of the tension of the intuition of life and movement that brings about the intellectual apprehension of matter.[13] The mere suppression of intuition plunges us into static experience of the material world,[14] and the further relaxation of it yields the world of dreams.[15]

When we come to intuitive knowledge, the intimacy of the relation of knower and known is even greater than in the case of intellectual knowledge. Here indeed, except for the fact that the object is not eternal but ever moving and flowing, Bergson writes much like a mystic. As William James has insisted, "we are absolutely sure only of what experience gives us; but we should accept experience wholly, and our feelings are a part of it by the same right as our perceptions."[16] The intuitive knowing attained in pure and whole experience is not confined to apprehending quasi-instantaneous cross sections of reality; it can "grasp change and duration in their original mobility."[17] In intuition the false assumption common to idealism and realism that the brain projects its sensations beyond itself is overcome in apprehension of the "immediately given."[18] In intuition

---

[11] *Creative Evolution*, pp. 272 ff.
[12] *Ibid.*, pp. 220 ff; see also *The Creative Mind*, pp. 72 ff.
[13] *Ibid.*, p. 206.
[14] *Ibid.*, p. 237.
[15] *Ibid.*, p. 238.
[16] *Ibid.*, p. 251.
[17] *The Creative Mind*, p. 167.
[18] *Ibid.*, pp. 90 f.

we attain "direct vision of the mind by the mind—nothing intervening . . . , the indivisible and therefore substantial continuity of the flow of the inner life . . . , a vision which is scarcely distinguishable from the object seen, a knowledge which is contact and almost coincidence." [19] Even in our human intuitions we glimpse the mode of thought of a "perfect being," who is "one who knows all things intuitively without having to go through reasoning, abstraction and generalization." [20]

3. Comments Concerning Bergson's Epistemology

The philosophy of Bergson had at one time a tremendous vogue. It has left a deep impact upon several types of epistemology, especially the pragmatist type, and virtually every type has been at least in some measure influenced by it. The principal achievements of Bergson's thought would seem to be its insights into the phenomenology and the biological and psychological foundations of cognition; and its principal deficiencies, its disparagement of conceptualization and its misguided effort to disclose a kind of cognition below the level of the distinction of subject and object.

A. A very significant contribution to current theory of knowledge in Bergson's thought with reference to the foundations of knowledge is its insistence upon the continuity of human knowing with those more elementary animal efforts to attain successful adaptations to the physical and social environment that may loosely be called instinctive responses. The epistemology of the era of Bergson's early writings was deeply in need of the lesson that his thought had to convey in this connection, and so is some of that even of the present day. Instinctive responses are rooted in basic needs of the organism, are elicited by apprehension of facts, aim at adaptation of the organism to its environment, and sometimes issue in alteration of some aspects of the environment. Cognition springs initially from the same source as instinctive responses, in fact grows out of these responses, and however different from them in some respects, has many of the same characteristics as they. So closely akin are instinct and cognition that the word "know" is sometimes used, at least figuratively, of instinctive responses as well as of cognitions, as when one says that the wasp knows how to paralyze its victims or that the baby knows how to obtain milk. Recent writers have insisted that "knowing how," which includes instinctive and quasi-instinctive knowings as well as genuinely learned ones, is generally speaking basic to "knowing that"; and no instance of knowing can be adequately under-

[19] *Ibid.*, pp. 35 f.   [20] *Ibid.*, p. 155.

stood without being seen in a perspective of biological adaptation which the character of instinctive responses helps to render intelligible.

A second significant contribution to current epistemology in Bergson's thought concerning the foundations of cognition, is an emphasis —neglected by most earlier epistemologists but stressed by the pragmatists as well as Bergson—upon the practical roots of conceptual thinking. Man is in fact a speculating being; but before he can speculate he must survive, and survival depends upon practical adjustment. Hence not only his ways of thinking but the concepts in terms of which he thinks are shaped in part by his practical needs. Every one of his basic concepts, such as *real* and *unreal, physical* and *mental, cause* and *effect, truth* and *falsehood, good* and *evil*, bear upon them the marks of their origin in practical endeavor. Moreover, there are very few, if any, of the multitudes of more specific concepts employed in common-sense and scientific thinking that have not been in some measure selected and molded with the ends of practical judgments in view. To have recognized and driven home this fact is not only to have called attention to an important truth but also to have significantly weakened the hold of the misleading notion of immutably fixed categories upon epistemological thought and to have opened the way for a sanely functional interpretation of the role of concepts in knowledge.

A third contribution to current epistemology of Bergson's thought about the foundations of cognition, one particularly relevant to the phenomenology of cognition, is his ample recognition of the role in cognition of a type of mental activity in which conception plays only a minimal part and which may loosely be called intuition. An almost conceptionless intuition has long been recognized to be present in perception, and perception has itself sometimes been referred to as a mode of intuition. Intuitions have also been felt to operate in personal relations, in some types of moral, esthetic, and religious experiences, and even in elementary logical insights. What was not sufficiently appreciated prior to Bergson, and perhaps still is not, is that intuition plays a substantial part even in what might be called our higher intellectual and speculative activities. Nearly always in attempting to solve a difficult problem we begin to "sense" an answer long before we are able to prove or even to formulate it clearly. Many a scientist after much effort glimpses the desired hypothesis in a kind of intuition before he can prove or formulate it; and even philosophers sometimes gain, in intuitions that follow extensive labors, insights that require weeks or months of new effort to refine and adequately conceptualize. Indeed so common and significant is the phenomenon of indistinctly intuiting truths before one can clearly conceptualize them, that philosophers of science are now very likely to take as initial standards to which their rigidly conceptualized explication—for example of such concepts as probability—must conform, the informed intuitions of ordinary people. To be sure, even our best intuitions need testing and correcting by conceptual procedures; but this does not mean that constructive intellectual effort can ever dispense with intuition. Indeed such effort seems in general to consist of an incessant intertwining of conceptual thought and intuitive insight, each stimulating and checking the other and in turn being stimulated and checked by the other, and each advancing with the other. However impotent intuitions alone may be, they supply in their basic perceptive forms the essential grounds of verification, and in higher forms in which they are informed by concepts, they are fruitful sources of hypotheses and essential guides for the course of inquiry.

B. Nevertheless, Bergson's thought about concepts and intuitions is to a considerable extent dominated by an interpretation of the relation between them as one of conflict, that leads him to depreciate the epistemic role of concepts in favor of intuition and even to claim that concepts falsify reality. This disparagement of concepts is ill-advised, not merely because concepts are in fact important, but because the relation between intuition and conceptualization in cognition is not one of competition or conflict at all. It is rather one of joint operation of different aspects of a single process. Even to ask which yields the better or more basic knowledge is a misleading question. It is a little like asking whether one's eyes or his optic nerve lead to better vision or whether his ears or his auditory sensations yield more accurate hearing. While perceptual intuitions are required for the eventual testing of hypotheses, and higher ones to suggest scientific hypotheses and check metaphysical speculations, it is virtually impossible to form any idea of what intuitive factual knowledge completely devoid of concepts could be like. The most that could be achieved would be a kind of vague feeling for the fact without form or content, and that could scarcely count as knowledge at all. At best it would be no more than a beginning or phase of knowledge. This seems to hold true whether the object alleged to be known be the lowliest physical event or the most impressive human personality or even a divine being. Some sort of encounter there might be, but hardly factual knowledge. In this connection, it ought to be noted that even mystical experiences seem hardly ever to exclude *all* conceptual content, for mystics are able to communicate at least something concerning their experience.

One can of course readily understand why Bergson should have felt a need to place intuition and conceptualization over against one another to the disadvantage of the latter; for the physical science of the period of his youth was drearily mechanistic in such fashion as to rob both nature and human life of most of what was significant, and conceptualization and mechanization seemed to him to go together. But this consideration by no means justifies either the opposing of intuition and conceptualization as competitors or the claim that concepts falsify reality. The trouble with the science of Bergson's day was not that it was conceptual—it could not have been otherwise—but that its concepts were insufficiently developed and inadequate to already achieved intuitions. The truth is that conceptualization never entirely catches up with intuition. If it did intellectual progress would come to a standstill. But the remedy for a serious imbalance between these two sides of cognition is not a condemnation of all concepts as misleading but the development of concepts that are more adequate; and this scientists and mathematicians have been rapidly working toward, for example in modern conceptions of continuity and relativity. Concepts are not prohibited by their nature from applying to dynamic processes; for there can be concepts not only of distinct moments but of continuous processes, and to be a concept of a dynamic process does not demand that the concept itself be dynamic.

C. Insofar as Bergson's philosophy confronts the conflict between idealists and realists concerning the relation of cognitive experience and its object, this philosophy may be regarded as an effort to resolve the problem by disclosing in intuition a level of reality below that of the distinction between cognitive experience and its object. In this effort, however, it can hardly be regarded as successful. One reason is that intuition apart from conception fails to yield factual knowledge; but there is a much simpler and more obvious reason, namely that apart from some distinction between cognitive experience and object there is no knowledge at all. To be sure, there are situations in which the sharpness of the distinction fades into the background, and in such fashion does active cognition sometimes intensify its awareness of its objects that one may say figuratively that the experience is absorbed, as it were, into its object. Thus, for example, a mathematician or a scientist who at first finds his material foreign to him may become so absorbed in it as no longer to be specifically aware of himself or his own efforts. But the absorption is *his* absorption in the mathematical concepts, and the concepts are not exhausted in his thought of them. The metaphor of identity is still only a metaphor. Epistemic distance can be indefinitely diminished in the sense that there can always be further degrees of understanding and appreciation, but apart from some distinction between cognitive experience and object there can be no knowing any more than there can be love without a distinction between loving and the beloved.

CHAPTER 9

Organismic Theories

THE manner in which the type of thought to be considered in this chapter undertakes to mediate the dispute between idealists and realists is quite different from the manner in which that considered in either of the two previous chapters undertakes this task. Instead of attempting simply to select and orient the valid insights of realism and idealism or to discover a level of intuition below the distinction between subject and object, the type of thought now to be considered attempts to unite insights drawn from idealism, realism, intuitionism, and a radical reinterpretation of the presuppositions of modern science, in a fresh synthesis that is both comprehensive and coherent. While a variety of writers have contributed to this type of epistemology, to such an extent has it been dominated by the thought of Alfred North Whitehead (1861–1947) that we shall be content to focus attention in this connection upon the relevant works of Whitehead.[1]

1. WHITEHEAD'S EARLY ACCOUNT OF KNOWLEDGE OF NATURE

The writings of Whitehead fall roughly within three different periods. The works of the first period, from 1888 to 1914, are largely concerned with logic and mathematics and need not directly concern us here. Those of the second period, from 1915 to 1924, present Whitehead's philosophy of scientific knowledge; and those of the

---

[1] Writers whose epistemologies are akin to that of Whitehead and might be appropriately called organismic include Charles Hartshorne (b. 1897), Paul Weiss (b. 1901), and A. C. Garnett (b. 1894).

third, from 1925 to the end of Whitehead's life, give his account of metaphysical knowledge. Because of both its intrinsic importance and its bearing on Whitehead's latest work, we give in this section a brief account of the epistemology of the second stage. But, since only the third stage properly represents Whitehead's final and more comprehensive epistemology, we shall devote the major portion of the chapter to that stage.

The thought of Whitehead's second or middle period is presented in *The Principles of Natural Knowledge, The Concept of Nature, The Principle of Relativity,* and a few supplementary essays. In these writings Whitehead abstracts from metaphysical aspects of epistemological inquiry though without suggesting that these aspects are unimportant.[2] What he attempts to do is to present, in innocence of metaphysical presuppositions, a unified concept of that nature which constitutes the subject matter of physical science.[3]

The primary error to be avoided in this effort, and the principal object of Whitehead's attack, is the "bifurcation of nature." This error consists in one form in thinking that natural reality is composed of substances to which attributes or qualities are attached and in another in supposing that products of mental activity are infused into nature. The one form of the error was begun in the Aristotelian logic of subject and predicate and the other was injected into modern science by Galileo and the seventeenth-century physicists. Both forms of the error were in some degree fastened upon modern philosophical thought by John Locke. Both are serious mistakes. On the one hand, subject-predicate logic, science, and metaphysics are all grossly misleading oversimplifications; and on the other, for purposes of philosophy of science, nature is "closed to mind" [4] and nothing imported by mind belongs to natural knowledge.

The bifurcating missteps of early modern scientific thinking have led to a conceptual framework in terms of which space, consisting of extensionless points; time, consisting of durationless instants; and matter, consisting of point-masses, are mistakenly regarded as ultimate entities. While this pattern of concepts temporarily facilitated the rapid development of mechanics, it was never really satisfactory and has now produced a scientific impasse in which the way to further progress is blocked. Thus, for example, in this pattern, situations of the universe can only be compared at various instants, and such

[2] Cf. A. N. Whitehead, *An Enquiry Concerning The Principles of Natural Knowledge* (Cambridge: Cambridge University Press, 1919), p. vii; Whitehead, *The Concept of Nature* (Cambridge: Cambridge University Press, 1920), pp. 28, 48.

[3] *The Principles of Natural Knowledge,* p. vii; *The Concept of Nature,* pp. 2 f., 48.

[4] *The Concept of Nature,* p. 4.

factors as velocity become mere afterthoughts with little or no meaning.[5] Moreover, since what we know of space is in fact learned from things, no location in space can ever be known, nor can any intelligible account be given of how an idea of such a location can arise. The way out of this impasse is to abandon the false bifurcation that sets sense-data over against things and identifies reality with fictitious points, instants and point-masses; and so to construe nature that basic scientific entities are defined in terms of sense-data and the order of sense-data is explained by the character and functioning of such entities. Indeed, for purposes of natural knowledge, one must recognize that "nature is nothing other than the deliverance of sense-awareness." [6] Such an account of nature will disclose several distinct varieties of relations the discrimination of which will help to reveal the underlying character of natural knowledge. These varieties include "extension," "cogredience," and "ingression."

The primary experiential segments of the first relation, that of extension, are *durations*. A duration may be defined either as "our observational present" or as "the whole of nature apprehended in our immediate experience," the two being essentially the same when the bifurcation of nature is eliminated.[7] A duration is that "slab of nature" disclosed in our specious present. Such a slab includes the whole of nature in the specious present although not all in the whole is equally discriminated. Durations are infinite in their spatial aspects. In their temporal aspects, they so overlap as to give continuity to the resulting time.

The basic elements constituting the stream of durations, and hence all nature in extension, are not separate time, space, and matter but factors from which all these are derivations, namely *events* or occurrences. Events involve wholes and parts, and there is no single way in which they must be divided. An event may be spoken of as "the specific character of a place through a period of time." Hence, for example, all that was going on in the Roman Senate house on the day of the death of Caesar was an event. What was going on in Pompey's statue during this interval was another event and was a part of the first.[8] Events are what we live through. It is they and they alone that we sense.[9] They cannot be defined in terms of space and time; rather it is in terms of them that space and time are defined. The space and time of events are actually inseparably bound together; but when, for purposes of inquiry, they are considered separately, the

---

[5] Whitehead, Time, Space, and the Material" (*Aristotelian Society*, 1919), Supplementary Vol. II, pp. 44 ff.

[6] *The Concept of Nature*, p. 185.

[7] *Ibid.*, p. 186.

[8] "Time, Space, and the Material," p. 47.

[9] Cf. *The Concept of Nature*, p. 15.

division may be made in any one of a variety of ways. The order of simultaneity differs from one time system to another. The totality from which time systems are derivative is the creative advance of nature. The space system of any given moment in a time system is absolute, and so is the time system of a given location of a space system. One must not, accordingly, ask without qualification where an event is, or when, but rather where it is at a given time from a given standpoint, or where it is from a given place and in a given time system.

The second important relation involved in an adequate account of natural knowledge, that of cogredience, is defined by reference to an experiential duration and consists in "the preservation of unbroken quality of standpoint within the duration. It is the continuance of identity of station within the whole of nature which is the terminus of sense-awareness." [10] The special epistemological significance of cogredience lies in the fact that it is the relation of the "percipient event which is 'here' to the duration which is 'now.' " [11] By the percipient event is meant simply that biological event "included in our observational present which we distinguish as being in some peculiar way our standpoint of perception." [12] It is in terms of cogredience of duration and percipient event that notions of motion and rest arise; for motion expresses a comparison of position in one instantaneous space and positions in other instantaneous spaces of the same time system, "and cogredience yields the simplest outcome of such comparison, namely, rest." [13]

The third relation essential to an adequate concept of nature, that of ingression, concerns "the way the character of an event shapes itself in virtue of the being of the object," or more simply, the "modification of the event by the object." [14] By an object is meant not a particular occurrence of a character but a character itself, or what is commonly called a universal. Between objects and the events into which objects have ingression there is a kind of mutual dependence; for "the event is what it is, because the object is what it is," and "objects are what they are because events are what they are." [15] Unlike events, time, and space, objects are by their nature such that the notions of "extending over" and of "whole and part" do not apply to them. Contrary to common opinions, they cannot be readily located. In some instances they are quite remote from the locations assigned them, as for example, in cases such as those of the amputated limb

---

[10] *Ibid.*, p. 110.
[11] *Ibid.*, p. 108.
[12] *Ibid.*, p. 187.

[13] *Ibid.*, p. 192; cf. also p. 188.
[14] *Ibid.*, p. 144.
[15] *Ibid.*

that still seems to hurt and of the tooth that hurts when it is another tooth that is decayed.[16] As a matter of fact, one cannot properly say that objects are located at all. What one should say is that objects are *situated* in the events into which they have ingression, and that these events are located in such and/or such manner. This does not permit even an indirect assignment of location to any object, for the object is never confined to a simple event or a limited series of events. Rather, while the modifications correlated with the object have a "focal" character for "those events which belong to the stream of its situations," [17] the object itself consists of systematically adjusted modifications impressed upon all events. This means that with respect to events the object is a whole systematic assemblage of modifications involving an "unresolvable multiple relation," [18] and that "each object is in some sense ingredient throughout nature." [19]

Objects are of many different kinds, of which three are especially important, namely sense-objects, perceptual objects, and scientific objects. Sense-objects are presupposed in all other kinds of objects and are situated in the events in which they are sensed.[20] Perceptual objects are collections of actually sensed objects and habitually associated ones.[21] They include both illusory objects and physical objects. A physical object is distinguished by the fact that "its situation is an active conditioning event," and that "the same event can be the situation of the perceptual object of a number of possible percipient events." [22] A physical object is one of which the generating source is at the place where it seems to be and one that is publicly observable. For illusory objects these conditions do not hold. Because physical objects do not adequately express the "various *roles* of events as active conditions in the ingression of sense objects into nature," we seek to discover a basic kind of objects, namely scientific objects such as electrons, quanta, and event-particles. These are objects which "embody those aspects of the character of the situations of the physical objects which are most permanent and are expressible without reference to a multiple relation including a percipient event." They are not mere formulas but "the things in nature to which the formulas refer." [23] Unlike physical objects, basic scientific objects seem not to be uniform in the sense that they can intelligibly be said to exist at a moment; they are rather like tunes in requiring a certain duration in order to exist.[24]

[16] *Ibid.*, pp. 146 ff.
[17] *Ibid.*, p. 190.
[18] *Ibid.*
[19] *Ibid.*, p. 145.
[20] *Ibid.*, pp. 149 ff.
[21] *Ibid.*, pp. 153 ff.
[22] *Ibid.*, p. 156.
[23] *Ibid.*, p. 158.
[24] *Ibid.*, p. 162.

If nature involves extension and cogredience of events, and ingression of objects in the manner indicated, the general character of natural knowledge can be sufficiently indicated without recourse to a stultifying bifurcation of nature. Objects of all kinds, being basically universals, are not either abstracted from nature or observed in nature; they are rather *recognized* in the events in which they have ingression. Events on the other hand are not recognized but *observed* in terms of the objects having ingression in them. Sense-objects are directly recognized. The order attaching to the sequence in which they occur is however rather unreliable. Hence they are organized in perception in terms of the selected patterns of perceptual objects, which, when they reflect their generating causes, are veridical. Even the order of perceptual objects remains somewhat unreliable, and modern science has been obliged in formulating its laws to have recourse to simpler entities lying below the threshold of sensory experience. But here a serious epistemological difficulty is encountered. While modern science has been quite successful in deducing sense-data from such basic concepts as those of event-particles, electrons, quanta, and the like, it has not succeeded at all in attaching to these terms any nonfictional meaning that is rooted in actual sensory experiences. One does not and cannot directly experience event-particles, quanta, and electrons, and one has no right simply to assume the existence of extensionless points or durationless instants.

The requisite meanings can, however, be established by defining the basic entities of science through the method of "extensive abstraction." That method hinges upon "the systematic use of abstractive classes" or sets.[25] An abstractive set is one such that "(i) of any two members of the set one contains the other as a part, and (ii) there is no event which is a common part of every member of the set." [26] Thus, for example, insofar as a time sequence can be thought of separately, an instant is a set of progressively brief intervals converging toward, though never arriving at, a limit; and insofar as a space can be thought of separately, a point is a set of progressively small values having nevertheless no smallest member. The procedure is similar for defining lines and planes as well as those "event-particles" and related abstracta which lie at the base of modern scientific theory. In this fashion the method of extensive abstraction is able to define entities having the simplicity required by the equations of modern science and to do so "in terms of the immediate facts of experience." [27] By means of the resulting definitions the whole of scientific knowledge may be rooted in the verifiable actualities of sensation.

[25] *The Principles of Natural Knowledge*, p. 104.

[26] *The Concept of Nature*, p. 79.

[27] *Ibid.*, pp. 85, 173.

2. WHITEHEAD'S SUBSEQUENT ACCOUNT OF KNOWLEDGE OF REALITY

With the publication in 1925 of *Science and the Modern World,* which ushers in the third stage of his epistemology, Whitehead abandons his attempt to discuss knowledge of nature as such without recourse to metaphysical inquiry. In this book and in his subsequent *Religion in the Making; Process and Reality; Symbolism, Its Meaning and Effect; Adventures of Ideas; and Modes of Thought;* Whitehead regards nature as an abstraction, and frankly assumes the role of cosmic metaphysician that he had previously endeavored to avoid. The importations of mind against which nature had formerly been said to be closed are now no longer shunned, and speculation is no longer feared. The subject of epistemological inquiry is not simply knowledge of nature in the scientific sense but knowledge of all of reality. Hence every experiential source of insight and every legitimate type of inference is duly recognized, even when full clarity and rigor cannot be attained. The effort is pressed to restore to the interpretation of our apprehension of reality that wholeness and speculative coherence of which absorption in an excessively abstractive scientific outlook tends to rob it. This endeavor of Whitehead to achieve organismic wholeness in the interpretation of knowledge is now to be followed first with reference to the process of knowing, then with reference to the relations of subject and object, and finally with reference to the nature and function of truth.

A. The fact that Whitehead abandons philosophy of science as such in favor of speculative metaphysics does not mean that he abandons his empirical base. The whole process of knowing continues to rest for him upon experiential foundations. His chief complaint against opposing epistemologies is not that they are too empirical but rather that they are not empirical enough. Focusing attention almost exclusively upon the clear and distinct data with which science is concerned,[1] these epistemologies have lost sight of the breadth and depth of the vast sea of experience of which clear data are only luminous portions at the surface. In doing so they have not only distorted experience and obscured much of reality but they have also broken the vital bond of subject and object and rendered knowledge of reality impossible. The scope of the concept of experience must then be widened to include neglected ranges of feeling, and this widening process will render knowledge more empirical, not less so.

[1] Whitehead, *Adventures of Ideas* (New York: The Macmillan Co., 1933), pp. 171 ff.

As the idealists remind us, any object or concept not in some sense experienced is utterly inconceivable. Not only are we "in the world" but in an important sense "the world is in us," [2] and in the end, "all knowledge is derived from, and verified by, direct intuitive observation." [3]

The connections between conceptual knowledge and the experiences on which they rest are, however, often complicated. Even perceptual experience is complex. In all of its varieties the process of knowing "is constituted by the reception of entities, whose being is antecedent to that process, into the complex fact which is that process itself." [4] The task of the epistemologist who wishes his account of the process of knowing to be both empirical and comprehensive is first to bring to light the character of the basic constituents of knowing events, then progressively to disclose the structure of those precognitive events the understanding of which is essential to a proper appreciation of the character of cognitive events, and only afterward to undertake the analysis of the knowing itself.

(1) The basic components of cognition are "actual occasions" and "eternal objects." Every instance either of knowing or of that rudimentary experience that lies below the level of actual cognition is an "actual occasion." Other actual occasions or entities must be among the constituents of any actual occasion. The whole order of things is such that no actual occasion can exist or be satisfactorily defined apart from predecessors and that each actual occasion affects the nature of all the others. "Actual occasions" are essentially what Whitehead referred to in his earlier writings as events, except in that Whitehead is now concerned not only with relations of events to other events, but also with intrinsic properties of events.

Events are now seen not merely from the outside whence the patterned spatiotemporal relations to which they give rise are most prominent, but also from the inside whence each event begins to disclose its own internal character and significance. Because science and most epistemologies neglect this internal aspect, they never adequately come to know events at all. Basically events are "occasions of experience" to which what may in a broad sense be called "feeling" is fundamental. Of these occasions of experience our conscious human experiences are instances, but they are by no means the only instances. The whole existing order of things consists of such occasions. Actual occasions or entities are "the final real things of which the world is made up." [5] They are, by what Whitehead calls the

---

[2] Whitehead, *Modes of Thought* (New York: The Macmillan Co., 1938), p. 225.
[3] *Adventures of Ideas*, p. 228.
[4] *Ibid.*, p. 229.
[5] Whitehead, *Process and Reality* (New York: The Macmillan Co., 1929), p. 27.

"ontological principle," the only reasons that can be given for the existence of anything. "God is an actual entity, and so is the most trivial puff of existence in far-off empty space." [6] Actual entities constitute the *res vera* of Descartes, the substance of Locke. They do not, however, endure through time and they are immune to change only in that they are forever "passing" over into other occasions. Each occasion emerges from the universe of the past but each by a slightly different "route," so that no two can be precisely alike. Each is fully determinate, yet the becoming of each involves freedom and "creative advance into novelty." [7] Actual occasions are not in time or space; they rather give rise to time and space. They are the drops or buds in which the universe is made and grows.

The other basic components of cognition, "eternal objects," are essentially the "objects" of Whitehead's earlier writings, although somewhat more emphasis is now placed upon ideal possibilities. Eternal objects stand in polar relations to the actual occasions entering into a given occasion in that, though quite different from these occasions, they are equally indispensable to the being of the occasion. They are "pure potentialities for specific determination of fact" and they function as "forms of definiteness." They are similar to the ideas of Plato and the essences of Santayana, but apparently they do not have quite the substantiality of the one or the impotency of the other. Although they lack the ontological completeness of actual occasions, they enter through such occasions into the causal order. They may be appropriately defined in terms of their peculiar epistemological and ontological status. "Any entity whose conceptual recognition does not involve a necessary reference to any definite actual entities of the temporal world is called an eternal object." [8] The term "universals" is near to expressing what is meant by "eternal objects," but this consideration should not be used to justify the erroneous notion that *only* eternal objects can enter the description of particulars. [9] Although eternal objects do not depend on particular temporal occasions, they must exist somewhere. Actually their original situation is in that comprehensive feeling which is "the primordial nature of God," the source of all the novelty in the universe. [10]

(2) The general process by which "actual occasions," whether actually cognitive or below the level of cognition, take form is referred to as "concrescence." The term "is a derivative from the familiar Latin verb, meaning 'grow together,'" and is used to "convey the notion of many things acquiring complete complex unity." [11]

---

[6] *Ibid.*, p. 28.
[7] *Ibid.*, p. 42.
[8] *Ibid.*, p. 70.

[9] Cf. *ibid.*, pp. 76, 226.
[10] Cf. *ibid.*, p. 134.
[11] *Adventures of Ideas*, p. 303.

The concrescence of any given occasion involves, in addition to the occasions and eternal objects that are its data, a general aim and free decision of its own by which it achieves its distinctive character.[12] Since the whole universe enters into the making and the being of a given entity, one may say that "concrescence" is the name for the process "in which the universe of many things acquires an individual unity in a determinate relegation of each item of the 'many' to its subordination in the constitution of the novel 'one.' " [13]

That aspect of concrescence which consists in the reception of previously complete occasions and eternal objects into a new occasion is what Whitehead calls "prehension." Human perception is one variety of prehension but by no means the only one. Every event is in its inwardness a kind of feeling. As Bacon long ago pointed out, physical objects as well as minds have a capacity for *taking account* of things. For example, the weatherglass takes account of cold; and the loadstone, of iron.[14] This basic preconscious kind of prehension underlies all knowing. The subject of the prehension is the actual occasion in which the prehension itself is a "concrete element"; [15] the data are either other occasions or relevant eternal objects; the aim, which brings to focus the relevant eternal objects, is the primordial nature of God; the active ingredient is a feeling; and the resultant is a satisfaction. When the datum of the feeling constituting a given occasion is another actual occasion, the feeling is termed physical, and the process, an objectification of the occasion prehended. When the datum is an eternal object the feeling is called conceptual; and the process, an ingression of the eternal object. Actually, neither of these two situations ever occurs in pure form. Every event and every experience has both physical and mental poles. Accordingly, "the positive prehension of an actual entity by an actual entity is the complete transaction analysable into the ingression, or objectification, of that entity as a datum for feeling, and into the feeling whereby this datum is absorbed into the subjective satisfaction." [16]

Since nothing that has happened is irrelevant to any actual occasion, every such occasion positively prehends all previous occasions; and since no eternal object is completely irrelevant to any occasion, every occasion in some sense prehends every eternal object. But since given previous occasions enter into various present ones by different historic routes, an entity may be prehended in different ways. This difference in historic routes and consequent modes of prehension

[12] Cf. *Adventure of Ideas*, pp. 303; *Modes of Thought*, p. 207; and *Process and Reality*, p. 232.

[13] *Ibid.*, p. 321.

[14] Whitehead, *Science and the Modern World* (New York: New American Library of World Literature, Inc., Mentor Books, 1948), p. 42.

[15] *Process and Reality*, p. 35.

[16] *Ibid.*, p. 82.

gives to prehension a vectorial character and renders the resultant occasions analogous to fields of force. The relevance of many eternal objects to a given occasion, while real enough, is largely negative. Hence not all eternal objects are *positively* prehended by any given occasion. To prehend negatively is to exclude from feeling.[17] Such exclusion from feeling is often epistemologically very significant; for, as Bradley's teachings suggest, it is in the diversification of feeling as positive, negative, physical, cognitive, and otherwise varied that the distinctions in which knowledge consists begin to appear.

(3) When prehensions attain a certain degree of complexity and take on the character of conscious experiences, they often qualify as instances of perception; and perception is the basic variety of that prehension that constitutes knowing. The essential characteristics of prehensions at the level of perception are not essentially different from the characteristics already encountered in more elemental prehensions. The differences consist largely of somewhat increased abstraction and intensification of the mental pole of the prehension. However, perception itself involves at least two distinct modes as well as certain feelings that require further analysis.

One of the basic modes of perception is that of "presentational immediacy," in which perception takes place through sharply focused sense-data. In perceptions of this mode, the part of experience consisting of clear, distinct, and precisely related data [18] identifiable with recognizable eternal objects occupies the foreground of attention. Doubt concerning the data themselves seems impossible; and with respect to them everything is upon the surface to be seen. Presentational immediacy has, ever since Hume, been taken to be the whole perception. But its barrenness was apparent even to Hume. It affords, as he saw, no basis for causal knowledge or even for its own interpretation.[19]

However, underlying the mode of presentational immediacy is another quite different, and for the most part overlooked, mode of perception. To this second mode we owe most of what is significant in our knowledge. It is the mode of causal efficacy. In it we feel the force of events in our own experience; we perceive the conformity of present events to past ones and of future events to present ones. In it we encounter our surest "recognition of other things reacting upon ourselves." [20] Always "the present event issues subject to the limitations laid upon it by the actual nature of the past," and "the complete analysis of the past must disclose in it those factors which

[17] *Ibid.*, p. 66.
[18] Whitehead, *Symbolism, Its Meaning and Effect* (New York: The Macmillan Co., 1927), p. 421.
[19] Cf. *ibid.*, pp. 30 ff., 40 f.; also *Process and Reality*, pp. 187 ff.; and *Adventures of Ideas*, pp. 231 ff., 268 ff.
[20] *Symbolism*, p. 45.

provide the conditions for the present."[21] By comparison with the mode of presentational immediacy, that of causal efficacy is vague and uncertain, at any rate as to its foreground. It is also more primitive. It occurs all the way down the scale of being, whereas the mode of presentational immediacy occurs only in higher organisms.[22] But by the same token, the mode of causal efficacy is far more powerful than that of presentational immediacy. By comparison with presentational immediacy, causal efficacy offers much greater resistance to efforts to control it, and when presentational immediacy has virtually vanished, it lingers on, as do the deep forebodings that often remain with us in the dark.

Actually the two modes never, or almost never, occur in pure isolation from one another. The nearest one ever comes to pure presentational immediacy is in instances of illusion, such as double vision or sensation in the place where an amputated hand used to be.[23] The nearest one comes to pure causal efficacy is in instances of memory and perception of visceral changes. Our actual perceptions normally occur in a compound mode which combines the two simple modes, and it is this that has caused the distinction between presentational immediacy and causal efficacy to be neglected. The compound mode is a symbolic reference which, without in any sense presupposing a vantage point beyond the realm of experience, takes an instance of one mode as a symbol of an instance of the other. Although this process can operate in either direction, its most useful direction is the one from presentational immediacy to causal efficacy, the one in which given present experiences are taken as signs of causal agencies. Symbolism of this sort enormously increases the range of facts to which the organism can respond. Making use of the vectorial character of prehensive feelings, it enables one to trace back from a given experience long chains of causes and causes of causes. But symbolic reference of this sort also opens up very substantial possibilities of error, and it is in wrong symbolic reference that most perceptual errors consist.[24]

Perception in both of its modes is, characteristically, conscious experience, and since consciousness never occurs save when there are alternatives to pressing physical feelings, perception involves at least an awareness of such alternatives, or what may be appropriately called "propositional feelings." The proposition presupposed in a propositional feeling is not exclusively either an actual occasion or an eternal object. Rather, it is a "datum of an impure prehension," an element in a "penumbral complex," a hybrid between pure po-

[21] Ibid., p. 46.
[22] Cf. ibid., p. 23.
[23] Process and Reality, p. 186.
[24] Symbolism, p. 21.

tentialities and actualities." [25] In this respect there is no essential difference between singular, general, and universal propositions. The logical subject of a proposition is a set of actual entities, and the predicate is a set of eternal objects, the latter defining "a potentiality of relatedness" for the former. "The 'locus' of a proposition is those actual occasions whose actual worlds include the logical subjects of the proposition." [26]

Contrary to a common supposition, the same words by no means necessarily express the same propositions. For example, the sentence "Caesar has crossed the Rubicon" will express very different propositions in the mouth of an old soldier of Caesar and in that of a man of the twentieth century.[27] Indeed, no language is ever quite adequate to its propositional purpose and the subjects of propositions remain hazy at their fringes.

Propositions can be related to the actual world in two distinct ways: either in terms of conformity to it or in terms of nonconformity, of truth or of falsity. However, to insist exclusively upon this aspect of the matter, as many logicians do, is to miss the major point about propositions. Propositions are ways of introducing novelty into the universe; and when, in the course of the development of things, a nonconformal proposition has been accepted in feeling, a novelty has been introduced into the universe. This novelty may tend to produce more or less of order and is potential either for evil or for good.[28] But the risk of evil is requisite for good, and "error is the price which we pay for progress." [29]

A proposition does not necessarily enter into feelings. Rather, it is "a datum for feeling, awaiting a subject feeling it." Propositions are quite impartial as to the subjects into whose feelings they enter.[30] They are by no means necessarily judgments, and it is absurd to think, as Bradley did, that most of the time when we are confronting them we are judging.[31] Their role in perception and in knowledge generally is not that of expressing the actual situation but that of formulating the potentialities. They constitute the "lure for feeling." In this capacity they may lead us to new perceptive insights that could never be achieved merely by holding the data of sense before us.

Above the level of perception in the knowing process is the level of judgment. Judgment differs from perception in presupposing the latter and building upon it more complex and correspondingly more precarious conclusions. Its basic variety is intuitive judgment, which,

[25] *Ibid.,* p. 282.
[26] *Ibid.,* p. 283.
[27] *Ibid.,* pp. 297 f.
[28] *Ibid.,* p. 284.

[29] *Ibid.*
[30] *Ibid.,* p. 399.
[31] *Ibid.,* p. 281.

though it involves a critique of perception, is sometimes scarcely distinguishable from perception.[32] Like the propositions with which it operates, judgment does not necessarily involve belief or disbelief.[33] Suspended judgment is in fact the very lifeblood of science,[34] and it occurs far more frequently than "yes" or "no" judgment.[35] When belief does attach to judgment, it consists in the addition of an eternal object which may be referred to as a "belief-character."

"A judgment is a feeling in the 'process' of the judging subject, and it is correct or incorrect respecting *that* subject." It "concerns the universe in process of prehension by the judging subject." [36] At the moment at which it takes place it is invulnerable, and it can only be criticized "by the judgments of actual entities in the future." [37] When error enters into judgment the error is rooted in that aspect of judgment that lies below the threshold of consciousness, but the error is open to the correction and criticism of consciousness. Every judgment involves probability.[38] Plausible probabilities cannot be ascertained with reference to all events, and plausible judgments of natural events are in general limited to the events of the epoch in which these judgments are made.

B. If the *process* of knowing is somewhat as the foregoing account suggests, the character of the subject and the object [39] of knowing and of the relation between them is already suggested and needs only to be made explicit. In this connection, we shall first comment upon Whitehead's idea of the character of each of the terms and then focus upon his conception of the relation between them. With regard to each topic, discussion must begin with levels of concrescence and prehension that lie below that of conscious apprehension.[40]

(1) Basically the subject is neither an inert substance nor a total person nor anything either so static or so complex as either of these. Rather it is the dynamic, emotional, creative and created, and unifying and unified aspect of an actual occasion entity [41] over against which the object or datum aspect is placed. It is both activity and resultant, both forming and formed. In it a datum "is met with feelings and progressively attains the unity of a subject." The subject may be referred to as the "provoked" over against the provoking object, although this phraseology erroneously suggests passivity on

---

[32] *Ibid.*, p. 294.
[33] *Ibid.*, p. 414.
[34] *Ibid.*, p. 419.
[35] *Ibid.*, p. 418.
[36] *Ibid.*, p. 291.
[37] *Ibid.*
[38] *Ibid.*, pp. 408 f.

[39] In this and the succeeding paragraphs the term "object" is used in its usual epistemological sense rather than the special sense in which Whitehead speaks of "eternal objects."
[40] *Adventures of Ideas,* p. 225.
[41] *Process and Reality*, p. 35.

the part of the subject.[42] The subject could at the level of conscious-ness be called thinker as over against thought, but one must recog-nize that "the thinker is the final end whereby there is the thought." [43] The subject is also the feeler over against the felt, but, again, "the feeler is the unity emergent from its own feelings." [44] Thus the subject is "the entity constituted by the process of feeling, and including this process." [45] Everything that is, is at one time or another a subject, for there are no vacuous entities. Those complex subjects that we call persons, which become the subjects in the abstractive process of knowing, are not simple occasions but "per-cipient" *societies* of actual occasions linked by continuous temporal connections along historic routes.[46] These percipient societies owe their perspective character to the negative prehensions of the con-stituent occasions.

(2) The object that stands over against the subject is not a sub-stance, else it could never enter the mind; nor is it a mere universal, else the mind could never apprehend a particular object.[47] The object is the datum from which the occasion starts, the "provoker" over against the "provoked," "an entity which is potentiality for being a com-ponent of feeling." [48] It may consist of either of the two basic kinds of entities or of a combination of these. Thus it may consist either of such actual occasions as make up the existing order of things, of such eternal objects as make up the realm of possibility, of those hybrids of possibility and feeling known as constructable proposi-tions, or of such complex patterns of events as make up what White-head calls "nexus" (plural of nexus).[49] When the object is a physical fact it is made up of occasions which are never merely static but dynamic patterns of living events. Every occasion becomes at some time object,[50] and whether something is regarded as subject or as object depends on its function. Thus "any entity . . . intervening in processes transcending itself, is said to be functioning as an 'ob-ject,' " [51] and to function as an object is "to be a determinant of the definiteness of an actual occurrence." Since each occasion passes into its successors, every object is "enjoying objective immortality in fashioning creative actions." [52] On the abstractive level of knowing, the object first appears as the perceived over against the perceiver, and subsequently it appears in more complex roles.

[42] *Adventures of Ideas*, p. 726.
[43] *Process and Reality*, p. 228.
[44] *Ibid.*, p. 136.
[45] *Ibid.*
[46] Cf. *ibid.*, pp. 162, 182; also *Adventures of Ideas*, pp. 222 ff.
[47] *Process and Reality*, p. 211.
[48] *Ibid.*, p. 136.
[49] *Ibid.*, p. 82.
[50] *Ibid.*, p. 87.
[51] *Ibid.*, p. 336.
[52] *Ibid.*, p. 89.

(3) The subject-object relation is already present in the most elemental relations of the prehending and the prehended, of feeling and data, of eternal objects and satisfactions, and of occasions and concrescences. It becomes the more specifically cognitive relation between knower and known when a relatively high level of consciousness has been attained, and with this more advanced form of the relation we are now principally to be concerned.

Against those critical realists who take the object of knowledge to be a substance only *represented* to the knower and the affirmation of its existence to be dependent in the end on something like animal faith, Whitehead holds, with Alexander, the American new realist, and the idealists, the epistemologically monistic view that the object, even in its particularity, is literally presented to the subject. This view is implicit from the beginning in Whitehead's doctrine that each occasion prehends or receives into itself its predecessors along certain historic routes and is in turn received into its successors. Every perceptive event, no matter how remote its object, takes up into itself all those events that lie between itself and its object. Hence each also prehends whatever objects are prehended by intervening objects. That through which this chain of prehension passes into the knowing mind is the body, and the body is inseparably linked not only with the mind itself but with the whole physical universe.[53] It was because of failure sufficiently to emphasize this link that the British empiricists seemed to face an impassable gap between sensations and things. But even Hume at times recognized that we see *with our eyes* and hear *with our ears,* and in this acknowledgement the gap is in principle filled and the causal and prehensive path linking known and knower indicated. Perception becomes a kind of inheritance in which the ancestral object is imparted into its subject offspring.[54] The unity of subject and object that was already present in aboriginal feeling can now be traced out in the more discriminating inheritance relation of perception, in which "what is inherited" is "feeling-tone with evidence of its origin" or "vector feeling-tone." [55] Thus, in opposition to all representative theories, one may properly insist that "percipient directly integrates antecedent real functionings of object," that in knowing there is a "conflation of real history and not a top-dressing of conjecture," [56] and that no "mere spatio-temporal pattern of sensa . . . but the individual, real facts of the past lie at the base of our immediate experience of the present." [57]

[53] Cf. *ibid.*, pp. 474 ff.; *Adventures of Ideas*, pp. 276 ff.; and *Modes of Thought*, chap. viii.

[54] *Ibid.*, p. 182.

[55] *Ibid.*

[56] *Adventures of Ideas*, p. 338.

[57] *Ibid.*, p. 361.

This monistic aspect of Whitehead's epistemology does not either compromise his realism or prevent the occurrence of a dualistic aspect. However much, in Whitehead's view, certain aspects of the object may be received into the subject, there is always in knowing "a transcendent element characterizing that definiteness to which our 'experience' has to conform," [58] and the transcendent element is not to be completely identified with the experiential one. "The process of experiencing is constituted by the reception of entities, whose being is antecedent to that process, into the complex fact which is that process itself." [59] A whole series of events lies between object and subject and constitutes the route over which the one passes into the other. Hence, provided the terminology is not so used as to suggest an illicit transcendence of experience, the dualistic language of symbolism, in virtue of which a sense-datum is a sign of its cause, remains appropriate to the relation of knower and known.

With the absolute idealists and against all types of logical as well as metaphysical atomists, Whitehead insists that subject and object are inseparably linked both with one another and with the whole universe in organic unity. On the negative side, this organicism involves a rejection of that "simple location" which assumes "the independent individuality of each bit of matter" [60] and attempts unambiguously to locate each in space and time "apart from essential reference to the relations of that bit of matter to other regions of space and to other durations of time." [61] On the positive side, such organicism implies a doctrine of internal relations in which relations and terms are in concrete fact always mutually dependent.[62] Even with reference to the physical aspects of occasions, an interdependence of all occasions is manifest in causal chains linking every event with every other; and with reference to the mental aspects of occasions, an interdependence among occasions is traceable in the vectorial linking of particular feelings each of which bears the marks of its origin. The application of this interdependence to the relation of present and past should be readily apparent to everyone who reflects upon the nature of science and experience, but such interdependence applies also to the relation of present and future, for by anticipation the future influences the present. The relation among contemporary occasions seems to constitute an exception, and indeed there is in this relation a certain fortunate freedom that affords elbow room in the universe; but in the end even contem-

---

[58] *Ibid.*, p. 327.
[59] *Ibid.*, p. 229.
[60] *Ibid.*, p. 200.

[61] *Science and the Modern World*, p. 58.
[62] *Adventures of Ideas*, pp. 144, 201.

porary occasions are at any rate indirectly related to one another through their relations to past and future.[63] There is also a theological aspect of occasions, in which the organic unity of occasions consists in God's bringing to bear upon every occasion those eternal objects that are relevant to it and in this way participating in every act of being and knowing.

C. It is against the background of the doctrine of the reception of actual occasions into subsequent occasions that Whitehead's conception of truth must be considered. If there were static substances with attributes, no truth would be applicable to them, and no "eternal object [is] ever true or false." Unlike eternal objects, "truth and falsehood are always grounded upon a reason, . . . [and] a reason is always a reference to determinate actual entities." [64] Indeed propositions, to which alone the terms "truth" and "falsehood" properly apply, never occur apart from those actual occasions in which entities enter into the making of one another. Hence, "all entities . . . enter into the self-realization of an actual entity in the capacity of determinants of the definiteness of that actuality," and it is "by reason of this objective functioning of entities" that "there is truth and falsehood." [65]

Accordingly, it is to be expected that truth will have at least some of those aspects that pragmatists attribute to it. For one thing, truth is creative. Truth in any occasion is a phase of the formation of that which the occasion becomes. A true proposition (or even a false one) that enters into a noncognitive experience is a "lure for feeling" and serves to lead toward the realization of the experience. At the level of deliberate inquiry, truth is still largely incidental to larger ends including the discovery and creation of beauty.[66] For this reason, as Whitehead repeatedly declares, "it is more important that a proposition be interesting than that it be true." [67] Every disclosure of truth has in it an element of creativity that is more than mere reproduction of physical fact, and in some instances this creativity tends to play a very large role. For example, the truth relation required for the final stretch of beauty is "a discovery and not a recapitulation, . . . that truth relation whereby appearance summons up new resources of feeling from the depths of reality." [68] On more mundane levels also, truth-claims have to be measured in pragmatic terms, and in the end, "the test of justification must always be pragmatic." [69] However, the fact that truth has pragmatic aspects

[63] *Adventures of Ideas*, chap. xii.
[64] *Process and Reality*, p. 392.
[65] *Ibid.*, p. 340.
[66] Cf. *Adventures of Ideas*, p. 342.
[67] *Ibid.*, p. 313.
[68] *Ibid.*, p. 343.
[69] *Process and Reality*, p. 275.

does not warrant a pragmatic definition of truth. For while "it is hardly an exaggeration to say that the very meaning of truth is pragmatic," still "it *is* an exaggeration, for the pragmatic test can never work, unless on some occasion in the future or in the present there is a definite determination of what is true on that occasion." Apart from such nonpragmatic determination one must be "perpetually adjourning decisions of judgment to some later date." [70]

The inadequacy of the pragmatic definition of truth correctly suggests a correspondence theory of truth.[71] Truth is for Whitehead a relation of two objects having different essences but a common pattern. It is "conformation of Appearance to Reality." [72] This relation is to be found principally in the connections of perceptions and their objects and of propositions and their referents.[73] It occurs at the level of immediate apprehension of a feeling, as when the child feels its mother's cheerfulness; at the level of normal perception, as when in given circumstances "we have perceived what well-conditioned individuals of our own type would perceive under those circumstances"; and at the level of conventional responses, as in language and ceremony.[74] The "blunt truth" that we primarily require is, however, the "conformal correspondence of clear and distinct Appearance and Reality." This is achieved primarily in sense perception, where something fundamental in the object may be taken to be veridically received into the subject.[75]

Although as a realist Whitehead adopts a correspondence view of truth, as an *organismic* realist he maintains this view in such a way as to allow room for recognition of substantial elements of the coherence view. Thus, since every event has its inner side, all truth lies in an important sense within experience, being "a conformity of two components within one experience." [76] Again, as the idealists have correctly taught, no proposition and no linguistic statement is ever in itself fully satisfactory.[77] Truth involves a wide variety of degrees. The truth of most factual statements is relative to the observer, and this fact is frequently recognized, as it should be, in the doctrine of the relativity of a probability to the evidence on which the estimate of probability is based.[78] Particularly when one is concerned with the quest for truth in the broad sense in which that quest is linked with man's total interest, "the truth or falsehood of propositions is not directly to the point"; for such truth is only "a comparatively superficial factor affecting the discursive interests

[70] *Ibid.*, p. 275.
[71] Cf. *Science and the Modern World*, pp. 172 f.
[72] *Adventures of Ideas*, p. 309.
[73] *Ibid.*, pp. 361 ff.
[74] *Ibid.*, pp. 316 ff.
[75] *Ibid.*, pp. 321 ff.
[76] *Process and Reality*, p. 290.
[77] *Ibid.*, p. 249.
[78] *Ibid.*, pp. 303 ff.

of the intellect." What is wanted is rather a wider "conformation of Appearance to Reality" in which the occasion, in molding itself to "stubborn fact," also achieves an "adjustment of the Universe by simplification, valuation, transmutation, anticipation." [79] On the negative side truth may be spoken of largely in terms of consistency, as "absence of incompatibility or of any 'material contrast.'" [80] Moreover, the correctness of judgment, which is closely akin to truth, can be measured almost exclusively in terms of coherence. All this, however, should not obscure the fact that with reference both to the wider and the narrower senses of the term, truth itself remains a conformity or correspondence of appearance to reality and is never a mere order either among appearances or among realities. Even correctness of judgment involves such correspondence, being "the subjective form of the integral prehension of the conformity, or non-conformity, of proposition and objectified nexus." [81]

3. Comments Concerning Whitehead's Organismic Epistemology

Of all the theories so far considered Whitehead's is the boldest and the most comprehensive in its approach to epistemological problems. It draws materials from all the physical sciences, from biology, from various branches of psychology, from art, literature, and esthetics, from anthropology, history, social and political theory, and from religion and theology. Almost every significant area of human interest is taken account of in it, and nearly all that can be consistently combined from other epistemologies is included in it. But it is no mere ecleticism. Its author earnestly endeavors to resolve the central conflicts that have divided epistemologies by rethinking categories and placing the whole problem in fresh and enlarged perspectives.

To what extent has this boldly comprehensive approach enabled Whitehead to throw light upon the problem of the relation between cognitive experiences and their objects? In our review of idealist, realist, and mediating theories, this central problem has turned out to include three major issues, first that between idealists and realists, concerning whether the objects of knowledge are experiential or independent of experience; second that between idealists and monistic realists, on the one hand, and dualistic realists, on the other, concerning whether or not apprehending experiences are to be regarded as distinct from objects apprehended; and finally the issue

---

[79] *Adventures of Ideas*, p. 377.   [81] *Ibid.*, p. 290.
[80] *Process and Reality*, p. 414.

that emerges from discussion of the other two, concerning how independent objects can be apprehended through experiences that are distinct from them.

The first thing that must be said concerning the outcome of Whitehead's boldly comprehensive approach to such problems as these is that this approach has not always been enlightening and has sometimes produced unnecessary obscurity and confusion. Like every other writer who has attempted to achieve comprehensiveness, Whitehead has passed over issues of utmost importance all too hastily. He has ignored fundamental distinctions and insisted upon others of doubtful significance. He has invented technical terminological procedures that often have not only failed to clarify what was obscure but obscured what was relatively clear. Nevertheless, the kind of comprehensiveness that Whitehead attempted to achieve can be useful in epistemological inquiry in bringing into focus what has been achieved and in suggesting new lines of inquiry, and Whitehead's own efforts have produced a number of promising suggestions. In the remarks that follow we shall comment briefly upon some of these suggestions concerning each of the three major issues mentioned in the preceding paragraph.

A. Regarding the issue of the extent to which objects of knowledge are experiential or independent of experience, Whitehead is basically a realist. For him, the initial object is as it is, and nothing in the experiential apprehension of it alters that. However, his thought contains at least two significant suggestions indicating how a substantial part of what idealists have contended for can be included within a plausible realism. The first of these suggestions has to do with the role of decision in cognition, and the second with a possible place for feeling in the object itself.

(1) Whereas realists have usually tended to regard cognition as predominately passive reception of what the world presents to experience, idealists have insisted that cognition is by its very nature active. With this idealist claim Whitehead is in full agreement. Indeed, he goes beyond it in claiming that cognitive events, though conditioned by many factors beyond themselves, are not only active but involve at their crucial moments genuine spontaneity or free decision. If this claim (which though not entirely peculiar to Whitehead, is exceptionally clearly developed in his thought and integrated into his system), is essentially correct, it goes a long way toward explaining how, though as realists claim, the object is basically independent of cognitive experience, experience may nevertheless, as the idealists insist, play a vital role in shaping the whole cognitive situation and in molding if not the object itself, at any rate the

object-as-known. Moreover, there do seem to be factors, frequently overlooked but unmistakably present in cognitive experience, which are at very least closely akin to decisions. For example, something like decision appears to be in evidence in our selection of data, in the specific character of the perceptual forms which we give to data, in the acceptance of percepts, in our choices of concepts and conceptual schemes, in our choices of hypotheses for further consideration, and in our willingness or unwillingness to accept data or evidences presented as sufficient for purposes in hand.

(2) Whereas realists have insisted that the object of knowledge must be independent of the apprehending experience, idealists have insisted that at very least the object must have a certain affinity with experience. Some realists have conceded to idealists that experiences are sometimes themselves objects of knowledge. Whitehead has, without abandoning his realism, conceded much more to idealism in insisting that while seen from the outside events are spatio-temporal, seen from the inside they are of the order of feeling. The view that external events are in a literal and ordinary sense basically pure feeling is to be sure a view which though occasionally advocated, has little to commend it. But Whitehead never advocated such a view; and the view that he has advocated has at least this to commend it, that it calls attention to the presumably indubitable fact that knowledge does demand some sort of affinity between object and experience, and that it properly stimulates inquiry concerning what sort of affinity this may be. Moreover, that Whitehead's view, however misleading, is not altogether mistaken is indicated by the consideration that not only esthetic and religious experience but recent scientific inquiry as well tend to suggest that the gap between the organic and the inorganic and perhaps even that that between the sentient and the nonsentient may not be so wide as was formerly supposed.

B. With regard to the conflict of epistemological dualism and epistemological monism, monists contend that unless the object becomes at least momentarily identical with a cognitive experience, it remains separate from cognition and hence cannot be known; and dualists insist that since to know something cannot be to be that thing, a thing can only be known through an experience distinct from itself. Whitehead's mediating suggestion is that cognitive occasions, and indeed all others as well, are such that each occasion receives into itself all previous occasions, especially those upon which its positive prehensions are focused. This means that while the origin of the event or object known retains its own space-time locus, an aspect of that event or object is actually received into the cognitive occasion. To this extent but only to this extent the object is both the same as and different from that through which it is known.

This suggestion is of course open to attack by either dualistic or monistic extremists. The former may insist that it obscures the essential difference between object and experience, and the latter, that it never really brings objects and experiences into the requisite kind of identity. But while such implausible dualistic and monistic extremes as those in which such objections are rooted are scarcely likely to be reconciled, Whitehead's suggestion is by no means implausible and contains some promise of reconciling more moderate versions of epistemological dualism and monism. It is fully in accord with the way we talk about experiencing things that are external to us, about having experiences of such things, and about such things *entering* into our experience. It has the further merit of calling attention to the continuity fully recognized by modern science between the groups of events commonly called objects and their environing events including our sense organs and brains. It also has the sound methodological feature of employing considerations drawn from science to illuminate presuppositions implicit in our ordinary ways of talking about cognitive experiences. Finally, it presents at least one possible way not open to the major objections raised against new realism of showing how an object can retain its distinctive characteristics and yet become in certain of its aspects a part of perceptual experience. The usefulness of this approach is further indicated by the manner in which Russell, Price, and others have employed something like it for similar purposes.

C. With respect to the problem of how independent objects can be apprehended through experiences that are distinct from them, all that Whitehead has said about the entrance of aspects of objects into cognitive events is of course relevant, but in addition Whitehead has offered at least three more specific suggestions, each bearing upon a particular aspect of the problem, that are worthy of further attention. The first concerns the relation of sense-data and scientific concepts; the second, the role of causal inference in cognition; and the third, the role of universals and formal systems in cognition.

(1) One phase of the difficulty of establishing the required links between objects and experiences that has become increasingly disturbing from the early days of modern science until very recently is the gap between scientific concepts and the objects envisaged in them, on the one hand, and sensory and perceptual experiences, on the other. The more refined scientific concepts became the more remote they seemed to be from sensory or perceptual experiences.

A major achievement of Whitehead's middle period was his showing with considerable precision how through his method of extensive abstraction such basic mathematical concepts as point, moment, and line could be interpreted in terms of sense-data without compromising the usefulness of either mathematical or observational concepts. Questions can of course be raised concerning whether or not Whitehead's definitions indicate what we really mean by points, lines, and instants, and in any case his methods encounter difficulties when the attempt is made to apply them to such basic physical concepts as quanta, electrons, and atoms. Indeed most students of recent philosophy of science are inclined to say that it is often impossible to establish definitional connections between concepts of physics and observational experience. Nevertheless, as far as they go, Whitehead's definitions are illuminating, and epistemological inquiry generally, as well as philosophy of science in particular, must repeatedly follow the sort of pattern that Whitehead set in endeavoring to disclose as close and precise links as can be found between scientific concepts and observational experiences. Historically, Whitehead's suggestions concerning the links between science and observations have been extremely influential, and if recent philosophy of science does not refer to them as often as did that of two decades ago, that is not because these concepts are regarded as invalid or useless but in part because they have already been absorbed into the main stream of philosophy of science, and in part because they require more supplementation than was at first thought necessary.

(2) A second phase of the difficulty of establishing the requisite links between apprehended objects and cognitive experiences is represented by the common claims that causal inference is properly applicable only to physical objects and that causal theories of perception already presuppose physical objects. In commenting upon the epistemologies of Russell and Price we have already seen reasons for rejecting these objections to the introduction of causal inference into the solution of the problem in hand. Whitehead goes considerably beyond the reasons offered insisting that causal inference is more primitive than the notion of physical objects, more primitive even than perceptual experience, and capable of leading along vectorial lines as far back as may be required. Moreover, whether or not in fact causal inference is that primitive and cognitively potent, it does seem to be at least as primitive as the notion of physical objects and to be present when the concept of physical objects is as yet undeveloped or inoperative. If this be so, application of the notion of causal inference to the problem of the relation between physical objects and sensory experiences may not be a dubious exten-

sion of the basic notion of causality but a due recognition of a phase of the process by which the developed notions of causality and of physical objects have grown up together; and causal theories of perception, instead of presupposing physical objects, may help to explain how we happen to have concepts of physical objects at all. In any case whether or not perception as such involves causal inference from sensory experience, judgment often does and in doing so seems to constitute inferential apprehension of independent objects. In emphasizing such facts as these Whitehead has given fresh and ponderable grounds for thinking that qualified causal accounts of knowledge may have more value than is commonly credited to them.

(3) A third phase of the difficulty of showing how independent objects can be known through experiences that are distinct from them comes to light in the question how the universals and conceptual systems that are in one way or another involved in the work of all epistemologists can be so interpreted as to be capable of yielding valid propositions and to be applicable to material facts. None of the traditional views seems very promising. Platonism, for example, seems to be both impossible to apply without the threat of infinite regress and incoherent in attempting to combine in its Ideas the incompatibles of universality and causal efficacy. Aristotelianism is applicable and consistent, but incapable of giving any satisfactory account of those phases of conceptual systems that are not directly exemplified. Nominalism yields consistent though clumsy and very restricted formal systems of symbols and rules but is unable to indicate how its symbols can ever yield valid propositions or be applicable save accidentally to anything beyond systems of symbols. On the whole Whitehead's account of universals and conceptual systems is Platonistic and shares the difficulties of that view. Indeed the most conspicuous confusion in Whitehead's thought is his unpromising effort to assign to his eternal objects at the same time universality and the capacity to enter as active ingredients, in a manner parallel to that of preceding events themselves, into the making of new events. However, alongside and within this doubtful Platonism of Whitehead are to be found the outlines of another view, that universals are to be regarded as possibilities that may be fulfilled in whole or in part or in various combinations by actual events and that conceptual schemes are systems or orders of such possibilities. This view is much more plausible and contains suggestions that may prove to be worthy of further study. Indeed even some writers who strongly incline toward nominalism nevertheless regard this view as an attractive approach to the problem of universals. At any rate possibilities and systems of possibilities seem to be discussible, capable of yielding valid proposi-

tions as complex and remote from facts as one pleases, and still applicable in fairly straightforward ways to matters of fact that either realize or fail to realize them.

In concluding the discussion of theories of knowledge that focus upon the problem of the relation between cognitive experiences and their objects, one seems obliged to accept the current view that while these theories yield many interesting and illuminating suggestions, they have by no means resolved the problem or produced a pattern of ideas from which a solution can be drawn. Whether further progress can be made along the same lines remains to be seen. Meanwhile we turn to some theories of knowledge that have focused upon other aspects of the problem of knowledge.

Part IV

PRAGMATIST THEORIES

CHAPTER 10

Empirical Pragmatism

HAVING now considered some major contemporary theories that tend to treat the object of knowledge as dependent upon the subject, some that tend to treat the object as independent of the subject, and some that endeavor to mediate between these extremes, we come now to a group of theories that are concerned not primarily with the theoretical question of the relation of the object of knowledge and the subject at all, but mainly with the more practical problem of how propositions purporting to be knowledge are or can be established. Theories belonging to this group are not, to be sure, unconcerned with the problem of the relation of known and knower, and each of them involves, either explicitly or implicitly, a fairly definite solution for this problem. But the focus of their attention is upon the question of validation. In general their answer is that validation is to be achieved primarily in terms of satisfactory adjustment of one kind or another. For this reason the theories are referred to as "pragmatist" although one must not thereby be led mistakenly to suppose that either external practical adjustment or emotional satisfaction is the only kind of adjustment, or even necessarily the main kind of adjustment, taken into account by these theories.

1. BACKGROUND AND VARIETIES OF PRAGMATIST EPISTEMOLOGY

Although pragmatism in epistemology is comparatively new, some of the major strands of thought that enter into its making are much older. Thus for example the Greek Sophists held that it was the usefulness of beliefs rather than their truth that was important. Plato represented the true as dependent upon the good and in the *The-aetetus* made successful prediction an important part of his refutation of solipsism.[1] The Stoics and the Epicureans sought truth largely for the sake of its guidance of practical life, and some of the medieval thinkers treated knowledge primarily as a means to salvation. The whole trend of British empiricism, from Locke's rejection of innate ideas through Berkeley's renunciation of matter and Hume's denial of a substantial soul to Mill's interpretation of things as permanent possibilities of sensation, represents an effort to exclude from knowledge all that cannot be sustained in such experiential terms as are championed by modern pragmatists. Kant's doctrine of the primacy of the practical reason and the emphasis of Fichte and Schopenhauer upon will foreshadow the volitional and activist strands in pragmatist epistemology. The major impetus to the rise of modern pragmatism was, however, the emergence of the Darwinian theory of organic evolution. The fact that the human body was a product of slow growth presided over by a natural selection that confirmed only those characteristics that were fittest for survival suggested that man's mental powers as well as his body were products of a slow growth oriented to the practical exigencies of life. On this basis Herbert Spencer specifically contended that the categories had arisen within the history of the race because of their survival value.

Apparently the earliest published expressions of the line of thought that directly produced pragmatism as a contemporary movement are to be found in the writings of the eccentric American genius C. S. Peirce (1839–1914). Both the term "pragmatism" and the central idea involved in it, according to Peirce, first came to light in a little Cambridge "Metaphysical Club" of which Peirce was the founder and Chauncey Wright the strongest member. Wright had interested himself in the formulas of science not so much as "summaries of factual truths" but rather as "means through which nature is discovered." [2] Approaching science in the same way Peirce developed a pragmatist view of *meaning* in two now celebrated articles entitled "The Fixation of Belief" (1877) and "How to Make Our Ideas Clear" (1878).

In the first of these articles Peirce contends that "the settlement of opinion is the sole end of inquiry." [3] After examining the often tried method of blind "tenacity," the method of "authority," and "the *a priori method,*" he concludes that the only reliable and self-correcting method is "the method of science." Here an assured "external

[1] Benjamin Jowett (trans.), Plato's "Theaetetus," in *The Dialogues of Plato* (6th pr.; New York: Random House, Inc., 1937), II, 179 ff.

[2] See M. Cohen in C. S. Peirce, *Chance, Love and Logic* (New York: Peter Smith, 1949), pp. xix f.

[3] *Chance, Love and Logic*, p. 16.

permanency" is investigated in such a manner that "the ultimate conclusion of every man shall be the same." [4] In the second article Peirce goes on to suggest that a primary requirement of settling belief in the requisite manner is to interpret meaning solely in terms of effects: "Consider what effects, which might conceivably have practical bearings, we conceive the object of our conception to have. Then, our conception of these effects is the whole of our conception of the object." [5] Thus, for example, "what we mean by calling a thing *hard*" is "that it will not be scratched by many other substances;" [6] and what we mean by saying that "a body is heavy" is that "in the absence of opposing force, it will fall." [7]

However, while Peirce adopted a pragmatist view of meaning, he was unable to be satisfied with a pragmatist view of truth and declined the honor of being regarded as the originator of pragmatism, which William James wished to accord him. As a matter of fact many of Peirce's major contributions, for example in laying foundations of modern symbolic logic and probability theory, are quite irrelevant to the issues of pragmatism, and some of his views on matters to which pragmatism is relevant are rather antipragmatist. For example, with regard to physical objects, he inclines toward the views of modern realists, and concerning universals, toward the views of medieval realists.

For many years the suggestions of Peirce with reference to a pragmatist theory of meaning went unnoticed in the philosophical world. However, at last, in 1898, in an article entitled "Philosophical Conceptions and Practical Results," William James strikingly called attention to the Peirce papers, and with the publication of James's article pragmatism proper may fairly be said to have been launched.

Pragmatism, as it has thus far developed, includes three main varieties each of which has been represented by a single outstanding writer and a number of less significant ones. One such variety, which we refer to as "empirical pragmatism," stresses the central importance of immediate experience and regards knowing as a satisfactory leading of one set of experiences into another set. This is the variety of pragmatism championed by William James (1842–1910). A second variety assigns a larger role to concepts and takes knowledge to consist of patterns of concepts that serve as instruments for the satisfactory resolution of situations involving tension. This is the variety, championed principally by John Dewey, called "instrumentalism." The third main variety of pragmatism distinguishes more sharply than either of the other two between immediate experience and concepts,

---

[4] *Ibid.*, p. 25.   [6] *Ibid.*, pp. 45 f.
[5] *Ibid.*, p. 45.   [7] *Ibid.*, p. 47.

and while regarding the former as fundamental, applies its pragmatic criteria only to the latter. This variety is referred to as conceptual pragmatism and has been advocated principally by C. I. Lewis.

2. James's Account of the Principal Ingredients of Knowing

The characteristic features of James's pragmatism were already in formation during the period of the writing of his monumental *Principles of Psychology* (1890), and some of them were expressed even before the publication of that work, for example, in the essay entitled "The Function of Cognition" (1885). The program of pragmatism was explicitly sketched in the essay on "Philosophical Conceptions and Practical Results" (1898), and in *Pragmatism* its principles were set forth more fully. Various aspects of it were expounded, developed, and defended in the collections of essays under the titles *The Will to Believe and Other Essays* (1896), *The Meaning of Truth* (1909), and *Collected Essays and Reviews* (1920). In James's *Essays in Radical Empiricism* (1912), pragmatism as such was placed in the larger experiential setting in which James wished it placed; and in the two volumes of *A Pluralistic Universe* (1909) and *Some Problems of Philosophy* (1911) certain metaphysical implications and relations of James's empirical pragmatism were suggested. Unfortunately James's death denied him the opportunity to carry out his intention of presenting his philosophy in systematic form. Accordingly, any attempt to sketch James's epistemology systematically must gather its materials as best it can from a wide variety of writings, each having a distinct purpose, and must draw its conclusions with considerable diffidence.

Knowing is not, for James, to be identified with the kind of apprehension of alien substance that some realists take it to be, nor is it simply the immediate intuitive apprehension that Bergson, with whom James agrees at many points, takes it to be. Above all it is not to be identified with that logical necessity with which some idealists tend to identify it. James is a persistent enemy of what he calls intellectualism, and even in his most mature writings he relegates logic to subordinate uses and excludes it altogether from the work of the philosopher. Such are the irreconcilable conflicts to which logic leads that "I have finally found myself compelled to give up logic, fairly, squarely and irrevocably. It has an imperishable use in human life, but that use is not to make us theoretically acquainted with the essential nature of reality." [1]

[1] William James, *A Pluralistic Universe* (New York and London: Longmans, Green and Co., Inc., 1909), p. 212.

Knowing is for James satisfactory anticipation of future experience. So construed it may be regarded from the point of view of content, meaning, verification, or truth, and we shall successively consider James's account of it from each of these points of view.

From the point of view of content, the principal ingredients of knowledge are immediate experience, concepts, and beliefs. Among these the first is by far the most important though the others require more explanation.

A. Immediate experience includes not only sensory experience but also a rich variety of conscious emotional and volitional impulses and many undifferentiated semiconscious and subconscious psychical events. Besides, instead of being made up, as the earlier empiricists thought, of simple and discrete sensations put together from the outside through rational concepts and processes, immediate experience is essentially self-sufficient, containing in itself all the distinctions and joints that are required.[2] Accordingly, genuine empiricism can be established in its own right without recourse to rationalistic supplementation.

Many passages in James's writings seem to suggest not only that reality itself consists essentially of experience and possible experience but also that a purely nonconceptual experience, often even below the perceptual level, has a privileged access to reality by comparison with which conceptual knowledge is a mere shadow and even ordinary perception grossly inadequate. Such, for example, seems to be the suggestion of some of James's statements concerning mysticism.[3] The same suggestion is apparent in many of the things James has said in opposition to abstraction [4] and in others that he has said in defense of the essential completeness of immediate experience.[5] In his essay "Bradley or Bergson" James seems to join hands with Bergson in the claim that "deep knowledge is not of the conceptually mediated, but of the immediate type." [6] However, most experience involves some complexity, and a single experience, if it could exist alone, could not constitute an instance of knowledge.[7] In virtually all knowing there must be at least a leading of one experience into another.

Experiences that are selected out of the vast sea of experience and attain a substantial degree of order—though not the precision of con-

[2] James, *Essays in Radical Empiricism* (New York: Longmans, Green & Co., Inc., 1912), pp. 41 ff.

[3] Cf. James, *The Varieties of Religious Experience* (New York and London: Longmans, Green & Co., Inc., 1902), pp. 422–29; and *Collected Essays and Reviews* (New York: Longmans, Green & Co., Inc., 1920), chap. xxxix.

[4] James, *The Meaning of Truth* (New York: Longmans, Green & Co., Inc., 1909), chap. xxiii.

[5] *Essays in Radical Empiricism*, chap. ii.

[6] *Collected Essays and Reviews*, p. 493.

[7] *The Meaning of Truth*, pp. 2 ff.

cepts—are called percepts.[8] They are segments of experience resembling and otherwise "pointing" toward those fuller experiences which we refer to as realities. They are qualified by past experiences and include anticipations of future ones. My percept of my dog, for example, is that segment of the experience making up the dog which is either suitably similar to the dog or otherwise satisfactorily represents the dog to me.[9]

B. Concepts are more precise, less concrete, and far more dependent on human invention than are percepts. Since concepts are more or less artificial products of man's invention, their employment must be carefully guarded against lapsing into mere verbalism. Concepts are abstract notions selected from the perceptual world, indicating qualities and relations that recur in various settings. Unlike percepts, which are continuous with their contexts, concepts are disjointed. Each means "just what it singly means and nothing else." [10] Thus, for example, *goodness* and *straightness* mean just such pure qualities as they name, whether or not such qualities are ever in experience found in isolation from other qualities and relations or even from their opposites.

Concepts are purely derivative from percepts and serve the ends of percepts. They "flow out of percepts and into them again." [11] Their relation to percepts is similar to the relation sustained by percepts to fuller immediate experiential realities. *"A percept knows whatever reality it directly or indirectly operates on and resembles; a conceptual feeling or thought knows a reality, whenever it actually terminates in a percept that operates on, or resembles that reality, or is otherwise connected with it or with its context."* [12]

Among concepts two somewhat different classes may be distinguished. On the one hand, there are those restricted concepts which we deliberately and specifically apply to particular problems; and on the other hand there are those broad underlying concepts through which we do most of our thinking about anything whatever. The latter are the categories in terms of which our thought takes shape without our specifically attempting to formulate them at all. They include: "thing, the same or different, kinds, minds, bodies, one time, one space, subjects and attributes, causal influences, the fancied, the real." [13]

Classical philosophy, supported by common sense, usually takes the

[8] *Essays in Radical Empiricism*, pp. 197 ff.

[9] *Ibid.*

[10] James, *Some Problem of Philosophy* (New York: Longmans, Green & Co., Inc., 1911), p. 49.

[11] *Ibid.*, p. 47.

[12] *The Meaning of Truth*, p. 32.

[13] James, *Pragmatism* (New York: Longmans, Green, & Co., Inc., 1907), p. 173.

categories to be somehow innate in the mind. But categories, like all other concepts, grow out of the attempt of perceptual experience to regulate itself. Every one of them has a history. Each is an invention of some ancient pioneer of the mind, some forgotten Descartes or Locke of hoary antiquity. While each could have been replaced or done without, each has been confirmed simply by its usefulness to men. Thus while the categories seem, from the point of view of the individual, to be innate and in the main beyond our questioning, they are from the point of view of the race just as much parts of experience and parts of the effort to manage experience as are the most recent concepts of atomic physics.

Concepts are not merely found, they are invented to meet particular needs; they are expressions of man's creative activity. Since they themselves are parts of experience, their coming to be is an enrichment of experience. But, being after all somewhat artificial and fragmentary constructions, their value in themselves is secondary to that of the more immediate experiences which they help to predict and to produce.

The primary function of conceptual beliefs is such anticipation of future experiences as will facilitate the direction of these experiences into desired channels. Sometimes the very fact of the existence of a belief helps to bring about the desired effect quite apart from the deliberate employment of the belief to that end. Thus, for example, one's beliefs about a friend may help to mold the character of the friend and to stimulate responding friendship. Indeed the whole fabric of organized society depends upon the creation of social responses through conceptual beliefs that run ahead of evidence. Similarly, belief in God helps to bring into the world those very divine characters of justice and kindness toward which such belief is directed and which would not exist in the same measure without such belief.[14] Again, one's belief concerning the goodness or evil of the world has a bearing on the nature of the world. If believing the world to be evil, one commits suicide, he helps to make the world evil, whereas, if believing it good, he does his best, he helps to make it better.[15] Even in so directly practical a matter as the attempt to leap over a chasm, the character of one's belief contributes to the consequences. "There are cases where faith creates its own verification. Believe and you shall be right, for you shall save yourself; doubt, and you shall again be right, for you shall perish."[16] The

---

[14] See James, *The Will to Believe* and *Other Essays in Popular Philosophy* (New York & London: Longmans, Green & Co., Inc., 1896), pp. 22 ff.

[15] *Ibid.*, pp. 58 ff.

[16] *Ibid.*, p. 97.

more obvious and characteristic manner in which anticipation in terms of concepts and conceptual beliefs facilitates the satisfactory flow of experience is, however, that of serving as means to deliberate thought and action. Since concepts represent selected aspects of experience and have implications that enable us to relate a wide variety of experiences and possible experiences in orderly fashion without traversing all the intervening links, they permit us to run through reality, as it were, with seven-league boots. They enable us to draw together similar percepts and to separate unlike ones, to classify and predict percepts, and accordingly, by manipulating the conditions of their occurrence, to bring out percepts nearer to the heart's desire.

But just because concepts are so very useful, we must be careful to avoid the temptation to assign them functions that they cannot fulfill. So long as we remember their abstract and instrumental character, they serve us well. But when we forget this, as philosophers often do, and place on them too great a cognitive burden, only chaos and confusion can follow. Concepts are functionally inseparable from the percepts from which for special purposes they are abstracted. They can no more yield independent insights into reality than a single blade of a pair of scissors can cut satisfactorily alone. When we attempt to force them to act in isolation, we falsify reality at least two important ways. In the first place, we endeavor to press the dynamic flow of events into rigid forms into which it will not fit. In the second place, we allow to slip unnoticed between the meshes of our conceptual net some of the most significant aspects of reality, including the continuity given in immediate experience. Because concepts are necessarily disjointed, they can cover continuous reality only "in spots."

C. Both percepts and concepts enter into the knowing process, not primarily, as is often supposed, as bloodless statements or propositions, but as living *beliefs*. Belief is no mere cognitive commitment to an idea. It involves a wide range of interests and dynamic anticipations of further experiences. Only actual beliefs, not mere formal statements or propositions, can properly be said to be verified in terms of immediate experience or indeed be verifiable or true at all. Literally, there is no such entity as a proposition between fact and belief. If a proposition existed at all it could do so only in terms of a "supposal" in somebody's mind, and in fact, no such supposal exists. To the suggestion that some supposal does exist, James replies: "I meet it by asking you squarely whether the supposal of which you make so much be not a purely linguistic entity. . . . '*That*' Caesar existed, *e.g.* is not an intermediary between the objective fact 'Caesar-existed' and the other objective fact 'someone's-belief-that-Caesar-existed,' but a muddle of the two facts." [17]

To the foregoing account of the ingredients of knowing from the standpoint of content must now be added a word about consciousness or mental acts. If the ingredient contents of knowing are immediate experiences, concepts, beliefs, and their combination, what is that consciousness which is commonly supposed to do the knowing? While James sometimes answers in traditional fashion, he more characteristically puts forth a bold suggestion that lies at the root of the account of consciousness offered by new realists and behaviorists, namely, that consciousness is basically not anything at all in addition to its contents, but rather that consciousness simply *is* its contents in certain external relations. *"The peculiarity of our experiences, that they not only are, but are known, which their 'conscious' quality is invoked to explain, is better explained by their relations—these relations themselves being experiences—to one another."* [18]

3. James's View of Meaning

Because James regards all knowing, and indeed all reality, as experience, and reduces consciousness to contents of experience, critics of James sometimes suppose that he confines knowing to the contents of the knowing mind.[1] Such is, however, not the case. All knowing, with the possible exception of some mystical insights, involves, for James, meaning, and it is in the area of meaning that James feels he has most to offer. To be sure, meaning cannot point altogether beyond the realm of experience, but any given experience can point to experiences other than itself, so that while transexperiential meaning is impossible interexperiential meaning is not.

In his first full sketch of his pragmatism, James begins by introducing, with at least general approval, what he takes to be the central doctrine of Peirce's "How to Make Our Ideas Clear," namely, that "to attain perfect clearness in our thoughts of object . . . we need only to consider what effects of a conceivably practical kind the object may involve—what sensations we are to expect from it, and what reactions we must prepare." [2] Not quite satisfied with this formulation, James presents his own account of how to make our ideas clear as follows: "The effective meaning of any philosophic proposition

[17] James, Letter of January 9, 1907 to H. N. Gardiner, in R. B. Perry, *The Thought and Character of William James* (Boston: Little, Brown & Co., 1936), Vol. II, p. 485; see also *The Meaning of Truth*, pp. 282 f.

[18] *Essays in Radical Empiricism*, p. 25.
[1] Cf. *The Meaning of Truth*, pp. xiv ff.
[2] James, "Philosophical Conceptions and Practical Results," in *Collected Essays and Reviews*, p. 411.

can always be brought down to some particular consequence in our future practical experience, whether active or passive, the point lying rather in the fact that the experience must be particular, than in the fact that it must be active." [3] In both statements, and in the thought of the two writers generally, the meaning of an idea lies in anticipated experiences. But on the whole, as the passages quoted suggest, James's emphasis is upon individual sensory experience while that of Peirce is upon activity and upon scientific experiment and generalization.[4] Later on, having become sensitive to criticisms to the effect that pragmatism represented an impossible effort to locate cognitive meanings in practical actions, James endeavors to make it even plainer that in using such terms as "pragmatic" and "practical" he has no intention of excluding genuinely cognitive experiences and indeed that cognitive experiences are epistemologically prior to experiences of activity.[5]

A simple illustration of James's interpretation of meaning in terms of anticipated experiences is suggested, without being fully developed, at the beginning of the second chapter of his *Pragmatism*. A group of campers are quarreling about whether or not the hunter goes around the squirrel that moves around the tree to avoid him. The answer depends, of course, on the meaning of "going around the squirrel," and this in turn depends on the anticipated experiences. If the phrase leads to the expectation that the hunter will have the experience of being first to the north, then successively to the east, south, and west of the squirrel, that is one meaning, and the answer to the question is affirmative. But if the phrase leads to the expectation that the hunter will have the experience of first facing the belly of the squirrel, then one side, then the back, and then the other side, that is another meaning, and the answer to the question is negative, for by the given conditions the hunter, even if he could not see the squirrel all the while, would always be facing the belly of the animal.

Thus for James, the meaning of an idea or belief does not lie in some nonexperiential object that the belief copies, pictures, or describes. It lies rather in the experiences to which belief, if true, will lead. This does not, however, mean that the object believed in must eventually actually be perceived. It is often sufficient that the truth of the belief would make some significant difference in human experience even though a complete perceptive experience is not attained or even possible. A mature formulation of James's concept of meaning that takes account of this qualification is to be found in his "prag-

---

[3] *Ibid.*, p. 412.
[4] Cf. John Dewey, "Supplementary Essay," in *Chance, Love and Logic.*

[5] Cf. *The Meaning of Truth*, pp. 52, 185.

matic rule" and the testing procedure implicit in that rule. "The pragmatic rule is that the meaning of a concept may always be found, if not in some sensible particular which it directly designates, then in some particular difference in the course of human experience which its being true will make. Test every concept by the question 'What sensible difference to anybody will its truth make? . . .' If, questioning whether a certain concept be true or false, you can think of absolutely nothing that would practically differ in the two cases, you may assume that the alternative is meaningless and that your concept is no distinct idea. If two concepts lead you to infer the same particular consequence, then you may assume that they embody the same meaning under different names." [6]

James holds that his account of meaning not only renders the meaning of beliefs about ordinary matters of fact intelligible but throws especially helpful light on metaphysical and theological issues that otherwise remain very obscure. A favorite illustration in this connection is belief in God. In his early essay on "Philosophical Conceptions and Practical Results," for example, James declares that the idea of the existence of God would be "a perfectly idle and insignificant alternative, if the present moment were the absolutely last moment of the world, with bare nonentity beyond it, and no hereafter for either experience or conduct." [7] The idea of God would have no further worth if "his work were accomplished and his world run down." [8] In that case matter and God "mean exactly the same thing—the power, namely, neither more nor less, that can make just this mixed, imperfect, yet completed world." [9] Since, however, the world has a future, the choice between belief and disbelief in God makes a vast deal of difference, namely, that between a life of hope and one of despair. Subsequently, in his *Pragmatism* James reasserts essentially the same position, declaring that "theism and materialism, so indifferent when taken retrospectively, point when we take them prospectively to wholly different outlooks of experience." [10] The real meaning of belief in God lies in all those consequences of it that must find their proper places in the whole of our subsequent experience, especially in those of the preservation of our values and our hopes.

James's treatment of other metaphysical ideas is similar. The meaning of anything depends on what it is "known as." Thus for example, "substance" is not to be interpreted in terms of any such mysterious underlying being as it is often taken to mean. Rather, it

[6] William James, *Some Problems of Philosophy* (New York: Longmans Green & Co., Inc., 1911), p. 60. Reproduced by permission of the publishers.

[7] *Collected Essays and Reviews*, p. 414.
[8] *Ibid.*, p. 415.
[9] *Ibid.*, p. 417.
[10] *Pragmatism*, p. 103.

means the cohesion of just those experienced properties that consti-tute its "cash-value." [11] Hence Berkeley was right in taking substance to be no more than "certain *grouped sensations*." [12]

James's analysis of "soul" is similar to his analysis of "substance." Soul is not soul-substance, but simply what soul is *known as*, namely " 'ideas' and their peculiar connexions with each other." It is "veri-fiable cohesions in our inner life," for here lies the cash value of soul.

"Freedom" is another metaphysical concept that, remaining obscure so long as it is treated nonpragmatically, becomes clear enough in a pragmatic framework. Formerly the problem of freedom hinged upon the "miserable" problems of "merit" and "punishment," but this was irrelevant, for we would punish anyway because of instinct and the social utility of punishment. The real issue is the improve-ment of the world, for it is upon this issue that the concept makes a difference. Thus freedom means possibility of fresh experience, and with this the concept becomes intelligible. "Free-will has no meaning unless it be a doctrine of relief." [13]

4. JAMES'S CONCEPTION OF VERIFICATION

If the meaning of a belief consists in certain experiences that are anticipated in it, then, as is to be expected, verification will consist essentially in the actual occurrence of these experiences. The experi-ences in question are practical in that they are of interest to us, but they are also theoretical in fulfilling cognitive expectations.

Verification tends in most instances to be ambulatory in the sense that the anticipated experiences which would confirm our beliefs are achieved only gradually. Thus, for example, to confirm a conceptual belief about the location of Memorial Hall would be to achieve a succession of experiences each in harmony with the belief at each stage of the journey toward the building. No more than such a suc-cession is meant by verifying the belief. "In this continuing and corroborating . . . , denoting definitely felt transactions, *lies all that the knowing of a percept by an idea can possibly contain or signify*." [1] If the chain of confirmations continues without any "jar" until the requisite percept itself appears, conceptual knowledge becomes com-plete in that that which "terminates that chain was, because it now proves itself to be, what the concept had in mind." [2]

In many instances—indeed in most—it is not necessary or even pos-sible that the ambulatory process of knowledge should be carried all

---

[11] *Pragmatism*, pp. 89 ff.
[12] *Some Problems of Philosophy*, p. 122.
[13] *Pragmatism*, p. 121.

[1] *Essays in Radical Empiricism*, p. 58.
[2] *Ibid.*, p. 61.

the way to its perceptual terminus. In the case of knowing the location of Memorial Hall, *virtual* knowledge was acquired in the early stages of the journey thither. "The immensely greater part of all our knowing never gets beyond this virtual stage." [3] It is enough as a rule that we continue experiencing and "thinking unchallenged." If some serious interruption of expected results occurs, them belief must be either abandoned or suspended. For example, if an object is believed to be heavy but suddenly begins, without apparent reason, to fly upward, the belief is stopped short, and it cannot be resumed until and unless the interruption can be so reconciled with the rest of experience as to harmonize with revised expectations. But, if no serious interruption occurs and the experiences of each stage of inquiry are felt to be fulfillment and if the associated experiences unfold serially, then the beginning of verification may count as verification and virtual knowledge, as knowledge.

The character and tone of the experiences in which verification is sought and found may vary considerably according to the nature of that which is to be verified without in any way affecting the fundamental pragmatic and ambulatory nature of verification. Thus, for example, when that which is to be verified is an ordinary physical object, verification will be a leading toward the percept of the object through a succession of sensory experiences. Verification will be of the same sort when what is to be verified is the bodily aspect of another person. But when that which is to be verified is the inward aspect of another person, verification will also include both a leading toward a terminating experience that can "enter into and figure in two diverse streams of consciousness without turning itself into two units" [4] and a growing satisfaction in "the postulated . . . really existing feeling of another man." [5]

All our cognitive processes are originally set in motion by emotional and volitional needs, and satisfaction of these needs is that for the sake of which in the end cognitive processes operate.[6] Moreover, noncognitive aspects of experience have some evidential weight of their own. Accordingly, it is not surprising that with reference to issues of great importance, such as those of the freedom of the will, the existence of God, the validity of scientific method, and the superiority of truth to falsehood, concerning which purely cognitive evidence is indecisive, the volitional and emotional aspects involved in the verificatory process should become somewhat more prominent than they are with reference to other issues. The direct evidential weight

[3] *Ibid.*, p. 68.
[4] *Ibid.*, p. 127.
[5] *Ibid.*, p. 188.

[6] Cf. *The Will to Believe and Other Essays*, pp. 113 ff.

of these aspects of experience may not be very great, but such is the importance of the issues in question that we must rely upon such evidence as we can get, and since acting upon belief constitutes our only prospect, in these matters, of gaining further evidence, we not only have the right so to act but should be foolish not to do so. Thus, "our Passional nature not only lawfully may, but must, decide an option between propositions, whenever it is a genuine option that cannot by its nature be decided on intellectual grounds; for to say under such circumstances, 'Do not decide, but leave the question open,' is in itself a passional decision—just like deciding yes or no— and is attended with the same risk of losing the truth." [7]

5. James's Account of Truth

Although James's conceptions of meaning and of the process of verification involve some distinctive emphases, they are not nearly so novel as his attempt to equate truth with verification. Writes James: "True ideas are those that we can assimilate, validate, corroborate and verify. False ideas are those that we cannot." [1] Aware of the apparently paradoxical character of this view James is eager that such affinities as his theory of truth retains with common sense and tradition should not be obscured. Hence, he repeatedly insists that for him as for most other philosophers, truth is agreement of idea and object. Indeed, provided the term "agreement" is empirically explained, he has no objection to the intellectual formula that truth "means 'agreement' and agreement means 'truth.' " [2] He is further willing to accept the traditional notion that a true idea must be as reality.

The crucial question is, however, what the relation of *agreeing with* reality or being *as* reality may be. Surely the requisite relation cannot be merely that of copying; for however applicable this relation may be in some cases, as when an idea seems to depict an object, it is totally inadequate in other instances, as when the idea represents a dynamic process like that of erosion. Besides, James queries, what is the use of mere copying? Unless truth adds something, what value does it have? The mere reduplication of all objects achieves nothing. In knowing the truth about me another should *"take account of my presence by reacting on it in such a way that good would accrue to us both."* [3]

What the agreement with, or being as, reality that is truth does consist of is the very same sort of uninterrupted succession of experi-

[7] *The Will to Believe,* p. 11.   [2] *Collected Essays and Reviews,* p. 480
[1] *Pragmatism,* p. 201.   [3] *The Meaning of Truth,* p. 79.

ences leading and guiding toward terminal experiences that constitutes the process of verification. Thus truth becomes itself essentially verification, or at any rate the possibility of verification. This means of course that much of what has been said of verification will become applicable to truth. "Agreement, correspondence, thinking the object as it is all resolve themselves into guidings, into 'getting there' somehow." [4] If agreement be not interpreted in some such fashion, many justifiably accepted truths will be quite unverifiable by virtue of the unattainability of suitable agreements, and the assertion of their truth will become meaningless.[5] Moreover, even where agreement exists, there will often be no more assurance that the idea intends to agree with its object than that one egg intends to agree with a similar one.[6] James does not deny that some other intelligible account of the agreement involved in truth is possible, but he does deny that any other intelligible account has been, or is being, seriously offered.[7]

Not only is the account of truth as verifiability the only available one that renders the concept of truth intelligible, it is also the one that interprets the concept in the simplest terms by reducing the entities involved to the smallest number. Whereas traditional doctrines of truth involve three factors, namely, knowing, reality, and truth, the verification theory requires only two, the reality and knowing or verification, for verification is itself the truth.[8] Between the fact that Caesar died and the verification of this there is no third entity, "that-Caesar-is-dead." [9]

Since truth is essentially verification and verification is satisfactory leading from experience to experience, Dewey and Schiller are right in saying that *"ideas (which themselves are but parts of our experience) become true just in so far as they help us to get into satisfactory relation with other parts of our experience."* [10] Truth is not something intrinsically and eternally attached to an idea; rather "truth *happens* to an idea." [11] Whether or not it happens to a given idea depends on the character of the consequences of holding the idea. Thus "those thoughts are true which guide us to *beneficial interaction* with sensible particulars as they occur, whether they copy these in advance or not." [12] That is to say, " *'the true,' to put it briefly, is only the expedient in the way of our thinking."* [13] It consists in "good consequences." [14]

---

4 *Collected Essays and Reviews*, p. 473.
5 *Ibid.*, p. 483.
6 *Ibid.*, p. 481; see also *The Meaning of Truth*, pp. 237 f.
7 *Collected Essays and Reviews*, p. 473; *Pragmatism*, pp. 235 f.
8 See *The Meaning of Truth*, p. 295.

9 *Ibid.*, p. 283.
10 *Pragmatism*, p. 58.
11 *Ibid.*, p. 201.
12 *The Meaning of Truth*, p. 82.
13 *Pragmatism*, p. 222.
14 *Ibid.*, p. 52.

What is the character of those good or beneficial experiential consequences for which truth is expedient and in terms of which it becomes a satisfactory leading? As is to be expected the consequences include the satisfaction of both cognitive and noncognitive interests. On the cognitive side curiosity and the quest for consistency are among the most persistent of human interests, and consequences satisfying both of these cognitive interests play substantial roles in the constitution of truth. Thus, "a new opinion counts as 'true' just in proportion as it gratifies the individual's desire to assimilate the novel in his experience to his beliefs in stock." [15] And "above all we find *consistency* satisfactory, consistency between present idea and the entire rest of our mental equipment, including the whole order of our sensations, and that of our intuitions of likeness and difference, and our whole stock of previously acquired truths." [16]

However, to treat the satisfaction of cognitive interests as though these were the only consequences that entered into the constitution of truth would be to take such satisfactions out of context and to misconstrue them. Thus to Perry's suggestion that it might be intellectual satisfaction alone that constituted truth, James replied: "You treat it as if it lay apart from all other human urgencies, whereas psychologically it is only one species of the genus human urgency. . . . There are as many ways in which our ideas can fit an object as there are ways in which animals can fit their environment. . . . The truest fit is the *richest* fit." [17] Instead of foolishly supposing with the rationalists that "though neither man nor God should ever ascertain truth, the word would still have to be defined as that which *ought* to be ascertained and recognized"; the pragmatist recognizes that "our obligation to seek truth is part of our general obligation to do what pays," that "truth imposes no other kind of ought than health and wealth do," and that obligation is in terms of "the concrete benefits we gain." [18]

Since the verification which essentially constitutes truth does not require to be carried all the way, it is often sufficient for the truth of a belief that the initial steps of its verification be satisfactorily achieved. These steps "lead us towards direct verification; lead us into the surroundings of the object; and then if everything runs on harmoniously, we are so sure that verification is possible that we omit it, and are usually justified by all that happens." In such cases verifiability "is as good as verification." Thus, in the broad sense that is relevant to truth, to agree with reality is "to be guided either

[15] *Pragmatism*, p. 63.
[16] *The Meaning of Truth*, p. 192.

[17] R. B. Perry, *The Life and Character of William James*, pp. 475 f.
[18] *Pragmatism*, pp. 229 f.

straight up to it or into its surroundings or be put into such working touch with it as to handle either it or something connected with it better than if we disagreed." [19] Actually the process of verification of a belief does not even have to have been specifically begun. A proposition can count as truth if only all the conditions for its being verified are realized save that of the question's having arisen. For example, that a certain constellation of stars consists of just so many can be considered true if all that is wanting is for someone to have inquired about it and counted the stars. Such truth is at least *virtual truth*,[20] and "pragmatically, virtual and actual truth mean the same thing: the possibility of only one answer, *when once the question is raised.*" [21]

The conception of virtual truth helps the pragmatist doctrine of truth to resolve a difficulty with which it is frequently confronted, namely, that concerning truth about the past. In general the answer of pragmatism is that the truth of a belief about a past event lies in leadings that connect a past event with future experiences. The past is "verified indirectly by the present prolongations or effects of what the past harbored," by "its coherence with everything that is present." [22] The truth that "Moses wrote the Pentateuch" rests on the fact that otherwise "our religious habits will have to be undone," and the truth that Julius Caesar was real rests on the fact that otherwise "we can never listen to history again." [23] But, if the objection is raised that propositions about the past were true at the time at which they occurred and hence perhaps long before our present or future experiences, the answer is that of course they were, but only in the sense of being virtually true. All the conditions were there for their being verified; the actual verification was not. But unless at least the possibility of their verification existed no meaning could be attached to the notion of their truth.[24]

Not only is the pragmatist account of the truth of statements about the past reasonably satisfactory, it is vastly superior, James contends, to those of its rivals. Where truth is concerned the problem is not only to show the agreement of the belief and the fact but also to show what fact the belief intended. Upon traditional accounts of truth the requisite connection either cannot be established or must depend upon an unnecessary and essentially incredible concept of an Absolute. For example, when I believe that Caesar existed, if there were two Caesars, the traditional doctrine of truth could supply no criteria for determining which was meant save upon the assumption of an

[19] *The Meaning of Truth*, p. vi.
[20] *Ibid.*, pp. 92 ff.
[21] *Ibid.*, p. 101.

[22] *Pragmatism*, pp. 214 f.
[23] *The Meaning of Truth*, p. 88.
[24] *Ibid.*, pp. 93, 101.

Absolute that decreed that just a certain one was meant. But upor pragmatist principles the concrete leadings that connect the pas event and present and future events are ample designations of jus what Caesar is meant,[25] and no Absolute needs to be postulated.

More basic objections to the pragmatist conception of truth, with reference to which the conception of virtual truth is also useful, are the objections that the pragmatist conception is subjectivistic and even solipsistic. To the charge that the pragmatist account of truth is shut up in solipsism, the answer is that in knowing we are guided toward a reality about which there can always be virtual truth, and that while pragmatism is *"compatible* with solipsism," pragmatism is "epistemological" rather than "metaphysical" and hence "has no special affinity with solipsism." [26] Pragmatism's answer to the charge o subjectivism with reference to truth is to point to the concrete em pirical matrix in terms of which the pragmatist truth seeker searche for truth and to the experiential reality toward which his leading guide him. The pragmatist searches for truth in actual situations and never claims truth when the object is unreal, no matter how satisfac tory the experience seems to be. Indeed he may even call himself an epistemological realist.[27] Any temptation that he might have to force truth to conform to the fluctuations of his subjective feelings i checked by at least three factors that are not within his control namely, what is given in sensation, relations among purely menta ideas, which have their own laws, and the necessity of fitting a new idea to an established body of beliefs.[28]

A final difficulty urged against the pragmatist theory of truth con cerns the *truth* of the theory itself. James's answer is a bold applica tion of the pragmatist conception of satisfactory leadings. The prag matist, James says, takes his own doctrine of truth as a belief o hypothesis which so leads him that "he finds it ultra-satisfactory to accept it." He can also offer it to others in the expectation that the too will find it satisfactory.[29]

6. F. C. S. SCHILLER AND OTHERS

In the thought of the foremost English pragmatist, F. C. S. Schille (1864–1937), most of the central themes encountered in James's prag matism appear, with substantial modifications, in the setting of distinctive *humanism*. Even more given to controversy than James Schiller is the uncompromising foe of an intellectualism which take

[25] *Ibid.*, p. 221.
[26] *Ibid.*, p. 215.
[27] *Ibid.*, pp. 185 f.
[28] Cf. *Pragmatism*, pp. 209 ff.
[29] *Ibid.*, pp. 199 f.

reality and truth to be already fully determinate and the technique of its discovery to be fixed. His special concern in epistemology is the nature of truth and of the logic through which it is discovered. His major writings are devoted in very large measure to the endeavor to work out the main lines of the application of pragmatism to logic.

The humanism which Schiller espouses, especially in his *Humanism* (1903) and in his *Studies in Humanism* (1907), is not so much a philosophical doctrine as it is a frame of mind of which pragmatism is the epistemological expression. It is "the perception that the philosophic problem concerns human beings striving to comprehend a world of human experience by the resources of human minds." [1] It refuses to abstract from actual human purposes and endeavors. Its great spiritual ancestor is not Hegel or even Plato, but Protagoras, for whom man is the measure of all things.[2] It has room neither for an Absolute nor an infallible reason nor an unerring science nor a changeless truth nor eternal being nor transcendental religion. But for reason, truth, science, and even metaphysics and religion, it has ample place so long as these are construed, as they really are, as relative to human purposes and needs.

Concerning meaning, which he regards as "by far the most fundamental of the 'presuppositions' of the theory of knowledge," [3] Schiller directs his attention not primarily to what is meant but to the ascribing of meaning. The point upon which he repeatedly insists is that meaning is to be thought of never in isolation, but always as a psychological fact depending on purpose and use.[4] There is no such thing as "the real meaning of a term" apart from its context. The meaning of such simple expressions as *"it is hot* and *it is two o'clock* flagrantly varies with their use." [5] Verbal meaning is entirely secondary to personal meaning, and "dictionary meanings only offer advice to the uses of a word, and are not *the real and actual meaning* which we attempt to express and understand." [6] The ambiguity of words, instead of being a misfortune, is a great asset, for apart from it the wealth of variety in personal meanings could never be conveyed by words. If we wish to know what a word means in a context we must ask the person who uses it what he intends. So to do would avoid many needless puzzles. For example, it seems pretty clear that Epimenides the Cretan meant in saying that all Cretans were liars only that all other Cretans were liars, and a simple inquiry could

---

[1] F. C. S. Schiller, *Studies in Humanism* (2d ed.; London: Macmillan & Co., 1912), p. 12.

[2] *Ibid.*, chap. ii.

[3] Schiller, *Logic for Use* (New York: Harcourt, Brace & Co., 1930), p. 53.

[4] See *Studies in Humanism*, pp. 9, 95, 149, 171; and *Logic for Use*, pp. 50 ff.

[5] *Ibid.*, p. 118.

[6] *Ibid.*, p. 62.

have saved philosophers much bother over the supposed fallacy involved in his saying.[7]

Truth, for Schiller as for James, always depends on good consequences, and here apparently Schiller has influenced James as much
as James, Schiller. Truth is to be characterized "(1) formally as
logical value; (2) psychologically, as *satisfaction of a cognitive purpose;* (3) materially, as *a truth-claim that works* and is useful; (4)
empirically, as *dependent on the consequences,* of taking it as true."
The fact that *"all truth must work"* does not however mean that all
that works is true. The ascription of this conversion to pragmatists
is an unjustifiable slander by hostile critics. Whatever foundation
there is for it is only in the index of James's *Pragmatism,* not in the
text of any reputable pragmatist work.[8] Truth is a value that we
attach to beliefs and it is entirely relative to the purpose of the inquiry. The purpose in question may of course be primarily cognitive; and, in cases in which it is, any disturbance of the quest by
emotional consideration is harmful. But always the quest takes place
within a total *personal* setting in which emotion is never entirely
irrelevant. A fundamental blunder in most discussions of truth is the
failure to distinguish sufficiently clearly between truth-claims and
truth. The latter includes verification as well as claim, and it is only
those who, with pragmatists, make truth akin to verification who can
do justice to this distinction. Others are all too likely to treat as a
priori true that which only claims to be true, as every judgment
does.[9]

The logic by which men infer truths must, like meaning, be rooted
in psychical fact. Formal logic, which the schools teach—and to the
demolition of which Schiller devotes the whole of his *Formal Logic*
as well as much of his *Logic for Use*—is utterly bankrupt. It absurdly
tries to abstract from actual intentions and merely to manipulate
empty forms. It ignores the quest for genuine truth and prefers to
handle empty assumptions which, having no application, are without
meaning. It endeavors to substitute unreal propositions for actual
judgments. The sound logic which must replace it and which Schiller
tries to begin to build will apply to judgments in their genuine personal settings. Such a logic will follow the threads of meaning through
their actual changes and deal with judgments and chains of reasoning
as they really exist. This does not, however, mean that it will be non-
normative. Rather, standing outside the press of the usual kind of
thinking, it will undertake impartial reflective criticism of such thinking. It will be "the systematic evaluation of actual knowing,"[10] "the

[7] *Ibid.,* pp. 64 f.   [9] *Ibid.,* pp. 28–9, 139, 168 f.
[8] *Ibid.,* p. 157.   [10] *Ibid.,* p. 23.

normative science concerned with cognitive values." [11] Instead of pretending to achieve infallibility, which at best could apply only to empty forms, it will acknowledge, along with all the rest of knowing, its constant risk of error. What the older logic took to be axioms it will regard as only working postulates.[12]

Schiller shares James's conviction that both truths and realities are affected by beliefs. This does not mean that our experience makes all metaphysical reality, for Schiller, like James, claims to retain an element of realism. What it does mean is that the only reality we know, that is, *reality-for-us,* is in substantial measure made by our knowing. The fact is, any reality whatever must be presumed to be in the making, for to identify the actual world with the universe is to ignore the potentiality of the world.[13] Ultimate reality is something to look forward to and not something to be apprehended here and now. Metaphysics as well as any other human discipline must involve a personal element, and it is only a voluntaristic humanism that can do justice to this element.[14]

Schiller emphatically reaffirms James's "right to believe," and on essentially the same grounds. He is, however, somewhat more careful in safeguarding the doctrine and insists that it be followed by expectation of, and responsible effort to achieve, subsequent verification. He holds, for example, that while immortality may be believed in, it should also be scientifically investigated.

Although other British pragmatist writers who may be regarded as closer to James and Schiller than to the pragmatist writers subsequently to be considered have helped to work out and defend the pragmatist tradition, most of their significant pragmatist suggestions are covered in one way or another in the works of James and Schiller. Accordingly we shall be content here with a bare mention of a few of them. Howard V. Knox (b. 1868) was an able pragmatist controversialist who produced a book on *The Philosophy of William James,* another on *The Will to Be Free,* and a book of essays. Alfred Sidgwick (b. 1850) concerned himself especially with the development of a pragmatist logic and in this connection exercised a strong influence upon Schiller. Henry Sturt (b. 1863) produced books on knowledge and ethics from a quasi-pragmatist point of view and edited a book called *Personal Idealism* that presented selected metaphysical convictions of some British pragmatists as well as those of some other allied British writers. The doctrine of truth-claims in D. F. Murry's *Pragmatism* (1912) is very similar to that of Schiller.

---

[11] *Ibid.,* p. 36.
[12] *Ibid.,* p. 160.
[13] *Studies in Humanism,* p. 295.

[14] *Logic for Use,* p. 455.
[15] *Studies in Humanism,* chap. xvii.

While James, Schiller, and their disciples were working out their pragmatism in America and England, other writers working along largely independent lines were developing on the European continent similar but more severely anti-intellectualist types of thought. In Germany, for example, Hans Vaihinger (1852–1933) set forth, under largely Kantian influence, a philosophy of "as if," in which most of our concepts, though useful enough, were fictions that contradicted reality and were indeed themselves often self-contradictory. In France, in the works of E. LeRoy (b. 1870), whose thought resembled that of Bergson, science was merely an instrument of practice, and intuition revealed the secrets of reality; and in Italy, an even more anti-intellectualistic and fideistic type of thought appeared in the work of G. Papini (b. 1881).[16]

7. Comments Concerning James's Empirical Pragmatism

Because James's major philosophical work was done in the early years of the century and its impact has long since been absorbed into the stream of current philosophical thought and because James's expression of the philosophical ideas that he advocates are rarely the most precise expressions of these ideas, James is not frequently cited today as a major source even of the ideas which he was most influential in introducing. But that his work was in fact a major factor in bringing into the stream of contemporary thought some characteristic current themes can scarcely be doubted. Three major features of James's epistemological thought are worthy of special mention in this connection: his verifiability theory of meaning, his pragmatist theory of truth, and his empirical interpretation of certain relations. We shall call attention first to some of the achievements of James's thought with reference to each of these topics and then to some of the deficiencies of his thought concerning each.

A. (*1*) The substance of James's theory of meaning is that the meaning of an idea consists in those experiences that may be anticipated in case the idea is true. The theory in the form given it by James leaves at best many important questions unanswered. Since ideas are only true *of* something rather than simply true, is the theory intended as a theory about meanings of ideas, beliefs, terms, expressions, statements, propositions, or something else? To what extent are emotions, volitions, and actions to count as verifying experiences? Is one to be concerned with experiences actually expected or with those that would, whether expected or not, occur if the idea

[16] Cf. James, *Collected Essays and Reviews*, chap. xxxiv.

or belief were true? To what extent and on what grounds are experiences occurring as a result of having believed or entertained the
idea or belief to count as a part of the meaning? If verifiability in
principle is to be accepted in lieu of actual verification, is technical
achievability demanded, is the physical possibility of verifying events
required or is the logical possibility enough? However, since these
and other questions concerning verifiability theories of meaning
have been discussed at length by subsequent writers, they need not
further concern us for the moment. What does concern us now is the
impact of James's presentation of a verifiability theory of meaning
upon contemporary epistemology.

Although the general idea of meaning as anticipated experience,
being already implicit in suggestions of Berkeley, Mill, Peirce, and
many others with empiricist leanings, was by no means altogether
original with James, never before James had it been specifically isolated and never before or since has it been so persuasively advocated.
Its effect upon contemporary philosophy was widespread and enduring. Not only was the idea taken over by writers of pragmatist bent
but many advocates of rival philosophies as far removed from one
another as Bradley and Royce on the one hand and Perry and Santayana on the other were deeply influenced by it. While those European positivists who were most immediately responsible for the
recent currency of the verifiability theory of meaningfulness largely
drew their direct inspirations from other sources, there can be little
doubt that they themselves have been both directly and indirectly
influenced by James's work and that the philosophical atmosphere
in which their views received ready acceptance, especially in England
and America, was in no small measure prepared by James. One may,
moreover, go on to hazard the evaluative judgments that the net
effect of James's advocacy of a verifiability view of meaning has been
wholesome not only by way of eliminating expressions of doubtful
significance but also by way of encouraging the clarification of expressions the meaningfulness of which could not be doubted but the
meanings of which might otherwise remain needlessly uncertain. In
no small measure as a result of James's work, the whole manner of
the contemporary writings tends to take on, despite considerable
circumlocution, a certain crispness and responsibility to experience
that was all too often missing in the philosophical literature of earlier
periods.

(2) The central feature of James's theory of truth is his claim that
the truth of a belief consists in its leading and guiding without interruption within the area of experience. As in the instance of James's
theory of meaning, such a theory, even if accepted at face value,

leaves unsettled many important questions not unlike the questions
that arise in connection with James's theory of meaning. What is it
precisely that is said to be true? To what extent are actions and
feelings a part of the experiences among which true beliefs are to
lead and guide? Must the leading and guiding be among such experiences as could have occurred without the belief's being held, or
are experiences resulting from the holding of the belief to be counted
also? If so, to what extent?

However, regardless of its indecisiveness upon many such points
as these, James's theory of truth has served an extremely useful purpose in contemporary epistemological thought. This usefulness consists neither in the originality nor the correctness of the theory, for
both are in fact doubtful or at any rate subject to considerable qualification, but in its having forcefully injected into a stalemated controversy a neglected alternative the presence of which rendered the
whole issue more fluid. The argument between advocates of correspondence theories of truth and advocates of coherence theories had
reached an impasse in which each group could refute the view of the
other but neither could substantiate its own view. James's pragmatism placed the issue in broader perspective, and suggested a
number of lines along which progress might be made without abandoning the whole case of any of the rival theories. A few of these
lines may profitably be noted.

In representing truth as a successful leading and guiding among
experiences James was accepting the coherence claim that truth must
be knowable and that more was involved in it than agreement of an
isolated proposition and an isolated fact, but he was also showing
how the implausible coherence claim that the apprehension of truth
demanded reference to the whole of reality could be circumvented.
James's doctrine of truth as a leading and guiding among experience was at the same time an acceptance of the correspondence
claim that truth was an agreement of belief with reality; but it was
also an indication, such as correspondence theories had never been
able to present, of what apprehensible realities there were that true
beliefs should agree with and how one could know what realities
were intended. The realities in question were precisely those experiences toward which certain beliefs led without interruptions, and
one could recognize them by the leading and guiding of beliefs.
Again, in making truth successful leading and guiding among actual
experience, James could both accept the coherence idea of ordered
pattern and the correspondence idea of agreement with reality and
at the same time disclose a dynamic usefulness of truth that was
foreign to the static patterns of pure coherence theories or the mere

copies of pure correspondence theories. Finally, by treating truth as a leading and guiding of the experiences particularly relevant at a given juncture, James's was able to render intelligible, as the purer forms of the older theories could not, the manner in which scientific formulae become outmoded without being simply rejected as false.

(3) A cardinal feature of James's radical empiricism is his insistence that not only sense experiences but also relations, including such basic epistemic ones as those binding sensory experiences together and those uniting cognitive experiences and their objects, were essentially experiential rather than conceptual and inferential. The epistemological significance of this doctrine of James has often not been sufficiently recognized. Earlier empiricists had been inclined to think of sensory experiences as separate impressions that had to be tied together and bound to judgments by logical relations, just as had many rationalists. This had made it relatively easy for such idealists as Green and Bradley to show that pure empiricism leads to skepticism. Assumptions similar to those of the early empiricists were made in the earlier writings of Russell and Wittgenstein, and such assumptions had led these writers themselves to feel that pure empiricism could not be maintained. By contending, however, that not only sense experiences but also the relations uniting and interpreting these were experiential, James felt he had found a way around the difficulty.

Actually we can scarcely accept James's contention quite at face value. In the first place, there seem to be differences between our apprehensions of colors and our comparisons of them, between our sensing of color patterns and our seeing of such patterns as objects, and between our seeing certain surfaces and expecting them to have certain textures. In the second place the notion that the relation between an experience and its object is itself an experience is either nonsense or a reaffirmation of a discredited idealistic notion. However, the ties by which our sensory experiences are bound together in bundles and given objective reference are, as James properly insisted, by no means those of mere logical inference, and these ties much more closely approximate immediate experiences than traditional intellectualist theories are disposed to allow. It is in the light of such considerations as these that empirical theories of knowledge can best be defended. And upon such considerations—in no small part injected into the stream of contemporary epistemology by the work of James—most recent empiricists have built their interpretations of knowledge.

B. The major deficiency in James's epistemological thought is the sort of lack of precision and definiteness already noted in connection with James's accounts of meaning and truth. However, apart from that general deficiency, three more particular deficiencies require special mention. Each consists in the neglect of what might be called the other side of a feature of cognition that it has been James's special merit to call attention to. The deficiencies in question are James's neglect of objective reference, his failure sufficiently to recognize the firmness of the concept of truth, and his unduly minimizing certain nonempirical features of conceptualization.

(1) While what may in a broad sense be called James's theory of meaning provides a virtually limitless range for references to experiences beyond the meaning experience itself, it apparently includes no provision for reference to nonexperiential individuals. Experiences as remote as one pleases may be meant but no provision is made for reference to persons having experiences or things giving rise to them. This is surely a radical departure from what is intended in common discourse, for we want to speak not only of experiences but of particular persons enduring beyond moments of experience and of individual things continuing through space and time even when not tracked by experience. In demanding in general to know what difference something meant would make in experience, James is fighting the battle of common sense and elucidating the actual phenomena of meaning, but in using this weapon to reduce all that is either meant or referred to to experiences and excluding nonexperiential individuals, he is leaving behind common sense and deserting the elucidation of the phenomena to propose a radical theory. That such a radical theory is, despite his protests in the name of common sense, what James does intend to offer is suggested by much that James says about the elimination of consciousness and about limitations on the meanings of a variety of other terms. Such a radical theory he is of course entitled to offer, but hardly without more than the scanty justification he gives, and without more even than the extensive justification that Berkeley attemped for a less radical theory.

(2) Although James's theory of truth injected much-needed elements of flexibility into contemporary discussion of truth and indeed disclosed insufficiently recognized elements of flexibility in the concept of truth itself, the theory also failed adequately to take account of some elements of firmness in the concept of truth that are so basic to the concept that the failure of a theory to recognize them raises grave doubts concerning whether or not the theory is really a theory of truth at all. One such element of firmness is the demand with reference to some statements that such statements conform to objective facts about particular individuals if they are to be considered

true. James's refusals to recognize any such feature of truth is of course implicit in his failure to recognize any references to particular nonexperiential individuals, and that in itself is almost enough to disqualify his theory. In any case, while the uninterrupted leading and guiding of true beliefs among experiences may be an excellent *criterion* of truth about individuals, it is scarcely what anyone means by truth about individuals. Indeed, we commonly allow for an uninterrupted leading a long way by a belief that none the less falls short of truth, and for much blind fumbling and the failing of beliefs that are none the less true. A second element of firmness in the concept of truth never sufficiently grasped by James is the independence of truth of emotional and volitional responses. Emotional and volitional responses may initiate and sustain the quest for truths, and they may follow upon the discernment of truths, but they have no place in the definition of truth. Their achievement may be facilitated by discovery of truth and they may even enter into the meaning of truth in a special esthetic sense, but truth in the usual sense remains quite independent of them. A third element of firmness in the concept of truth partially ignored by James is the independence of any given truth of the impact of belief in that truth upon the relevant facts. To be sure one's believing that a certain thing is going to happen may have an effect on whether or not that thing happens. But if one's belief is about what would happen apart from the belief, then the impact of the belief is irrelevant; and if what one believes is that certain things will happen if one believes that they will, then that is a new complex belief, the truth of which, while depending on the effect of the subordinate belief, is unaffected by the effect of the complex belief itself. A fourth element of firmness in the concept of truth neglected by James is independence of change. To be sure, the truth associated with a sentence may change with the passing of years or indeed of moments, for the meaning of a sentence is dependent upon its context; but given a definite meaning and clear reference the truth value of a statement does not in any ordinary conception of truth change at all, no matter what the changes of circumstances. Again, it is quite evident that some statements fit the facts better than others, and because of this fact old truths are often superseded by new ones. But this does not in any way imply that the advance of science or any other sort of discovery renders any unambiguous statement that once was true untrue.

(3) Although James's recognition that some of the ties among experiences commonly attributed to conceptual inference were actually much closer to immediate experience than was commonly

recognized was a sound and significant contribution to contemporary epistemological thought, his failure sufficiently to recognize that cognition also involves both concepts that can not be said to be mere expansions of immediate experience and deductive logical connections that are in no sense basically empirical, constitutes a serious deficiency in his epistemological thought. However much can be drawn from sensory experience, some of our concepts require something more for their initiation than sense experience. This seems to be true, for example, of such abstract but not logically compound concepts as those of force and justice. It is surely true of most dispositional concepts such as solubility and elasticity, and still more so of concepts involving logical terms such as negation, conditionality, universality, and alternation. Geometrical and arithmetical concepts, such as roundness and number, requiring degrees of precision not encountered in sense experience, would also seem to need some other elements in their origins than sense experiences as such, else the higher nonhuman mammals would also have achieved them. Moreover, however our concepts have been achieved, the deductive relations among them can scarcely be generalizations of perceptions, and James's failure to grasp the distinctive nature and function of deductive systems even in empirical knowledge is one of his most serious shortcomings. It is, however, as we shall see, a deficiency partly made up in the work of James's fellow pragmatist Dewey.

CHAPTER 11

Instrumentalism

THE INSTRUMENTALIST approach to the problem of knowledge, with which this chapter is to be principally concerned, is, like the empirical pragmatism of James, pragmatist in the broad sense that it is concerned primarily not with the relation of the knower and the known, but with the problem of the validation of knowing, and that it attacks the problem mainly from the standpoint of satisfactory adjustment. The thought of the principal advocate of this instrumentalist view, John Dewey, may also be said to be in general agreement with each of what we have called the major themes of James's account of knowing, namely, the ideas of meaning as anticipated experience, of truth as verifiability, and of knowing as satisfactory leading within experience.

Nevertheless there are marked differences between the thought of Dewey and James. Dewey's conception of experience involves much greater emphasis upon objective and outward aspects of experience and less upon the inward feel of experience than does James's. The orientation of Dewey's instrumentalism is primarily biological rather than psychological. Dewey is never disposed, as James is, to find in immediate experience a privileged source of knowledge, and indeed is unwilling to recognize any knowledge at all save as a result of inquiry. He is more interested than James in the special contexts of knowings and less in the general character of knowing. The crucial issues which Dewey takes inquiry concerning knowledge to be designed to illuminate are not, as is sometimes suggested by James, those of religion and metaphysics, but those of science and common sense. The aspect of the knowing process with which Dewey primarily concerns himself is accordingly not the flow of immediacy but the concepts in terms of which this flow can be most usefully anticipated and altered for human ends. Finally, verification is for Dewey primarily in terms of the social responses rather than in terms of the individual ones to which James habitually refers.

The central theme of Dewey's account of knowledge may perhaps appropriately be said to be the instrumental function of experimentally testable concepts in resolving the unsatisfactory features of experienced situations. With remarkable consistency, almost from the beginning of his long philosophical career to its close, Dewey has, in a very substantial series of books and articles from many different approaches, urged this focal idea. The most important of his books concerning knowledge are *Experience and Nature, The Quest for Certainty,* and *Logic: The Theory of Inquiry.* But material may be drawn from almost any of Dewey's philosophical writings without risk of serious inconsistency; for the development of Dewey's thought, after the first few years of his philosophical work, is largely a matter of sharpening and focusing the initial ideas, almost never one of the introduction of radical alteration. For purposes of exposition, Dewey's presentation of his central theme may be organized under the headings of "contextualism," "experimentalism," and "functionalism," and to the exposition of Dewey's account of each of these aspects of his thought we now turn.

1. Dewey's Contextualism

Basic to everything that Dewey writes about knowledge is the conviction that any adequate consideration of knowledge must treat knowings in the setting of inquiry in which they actually occur. This conviction is the central theme of the first essay in Dewey's early *Studies in Logical Theory,* where "the fundamental assumption is *continuity* in and of experience," and "an attempt to discuss the antecedents, data, forms and objective of thought, apart from reference to particular position occupied and particular part played in the growth of experience is to reach results which are not so much true or false as they are radically meaningless." [1] The same idea is repeatedly expressed, for example, in *The Quest for Certainty,* where we know "whenever our inquiry leads to conclusions which settle the problem out of which it grew," [2] and in the *Logic,* where conse-

[1] John Dewey, *Studies in Logical Theory* (Chicago: University of Chicago Press, 1903), p. 10.

[2] Dewey, *The Quest for Certainty* (London: George Allen & Unwin, 1930), p. 189.

quences are "necessary tests of the validity of propositions *provided* these are operationally instituted and are such as to resolve the specific problem evoking the operations."[3] The contextual character of knowing is also one of the principal bulwarks of Dewey's defense against his critics, whose strictures Dewey finds ineffective when knowing is placed in its actual settings.[4]

Theories about knowing that do not consider knowing in its actual biological and psychological setting are referred to by Dewey as "epistemological theories." Endeavoring to abstract from the specific natural and human backgrounds in which thinking processes actually occur, and in which alone these processes are intelligible, such theories vainly try to discuss "the question of the relation of thought at large to reality at large."[5] In so doing, they not only rob particular instances of knowing of the needed checks and balances[6] but also destroy the natural continuity of knowing and known and create artificial gaps between subject and object, mind and matter, and datum and thing. Such gaps once created can never be filled in, so that upon the assumptions of the theories in question knowledge must logically remain forever impossible.[7] This skeptical implication does not mean that traditional epistemologies are entirely useless, for these epistemologies have themselves arisen in particular situations and so, despite their errors, have thrown some light on problems relating to knowledge; it does mean that these epistemologies are inadequate and unpromising as they stand and that the only prospect of substantial progress in theory of knowledge lies in a new contextual logic in which every "act of knowing is treated as an effort to solve a specific problem in a particular situation."

What sort of situations are they in which knowledge occurs? Although the boundaries of such situations can be wide enough to include the far distant in time and space, they must have a certain unity set by the nature of the problem involved.[8] They cannot—as Russell wishes to make Dewey imply—include the whole objective universe,[9] but neither must they be narrowly limited to present subjective experience. Their actual range will vary according to the scope of the particular inquiry. The matrix within which knowing

[3] Dewey, *Logic: The Theory of Inquiry* (New York: Henry Holt & Co., Inc., 1938), p. iv; and John Dewey and J. F. Bentley, *Knowing and the Known* (Boston: Beacon Press, 1949), p. vi; chaps. iv–v.

[4] See Dewey, "Experience, Knowledge and Value," in P. A. Schilpp, *The Philosophy of John Dewey* (Evanston and Chicago: Northwestern University Press, 1939), pp. 548–66 ff., 571; and Dewey, *The Prob-*

lems of Men (New York: Philosophical Library, Inc., 1946), chap. x.

[5] *Studies in Logical Theory*, p. 6.

[6] *Ibid.*, pp. 17 f.

[7] *Ibid.*, pp. 8 f., 21 f; *The Quest for Certainty*, pp. 117 f; *Logic*, pp. 465 f., chap. xxv.

[8] *Knowing and the Known*, p. 315.

[9] "Experience, Knowledge and Value," pp. 545 f.

occurs is in part a biological one in which human organisms exist in environing conditions in such fashion that tensions between contact and distance sensations arise and need to be overcome.[10] The matrix of knowing is also a cultural one in which language and social institutions of all kinds, including science, are important constituents of problems, and elements in their solutions.[11] That within the matrix which gives the situation the special character suited for inquiry and knowledge is its unsatisfactoriness or doubtfulness, and this doubtfulness attaches to the whole situation, not merely to the aspect of it which consists in awareness.[12] Only when "jars, hitches, breaks, blocks, . . . incidents occasioning an interruption of the smooth, straight forward course of behavior" [13] occur, is the inquiry which yields knowing instituted. "There is always as antecedent to thought an experience of some subject-matter of the physical or social world, or organized intellectual world, whose parts are actively at war with each other—so much so that they threaten to disrupt the entire experience, which accordingly for its own maintenance requires deliberate re-definition and re-relation of its tensional parts." [14]

Each problematic knowing situation has of course its own peculiar characteristics and each is partly determined by its own unique problem. Nevertheless certain broad features tend to be common to all such situations. The knowing situation is one with reference to which motor-affective aspects as well as cognitive ones are included in that which prompts the inquiry. It is one in which as a rule the problem initially emerges in the terms and against the background of common sense. It is often a situation in which thinking ranges far from its starting point and employs technical terms and constructs that are remote from everyday life. But however intellectual and technical the logical and scientific constructs of an inquiry may become, the objective and terminus of the inquiry is always in the end a solution in which thought, operating again in the patterns of common sense, re-enters the motor-affective-cognitive stream of human life.

When the false abstractions of epistemological theories are abandoned and knowings are seen in their actual settings, at least four important advances in thought about knowledge follow. In the first place knowing is now seen in its proper relation to inquiry, intelligence, and consciousness. Knowing becomes a product of specific instances of inquiry and a contributor to the growth of intelligence, which is in essence funded meaning based on prior knowing; [15]

---

[10] *Logic*, chap. ii.
[11] *Ibid.*, chap. iii.
[12] See *The Problems of Men*, pp. 348 ff.
[13] *Knowing and the Known*, p. 315.
[14] *Studies in Logical Theory*, pp. 39 f.
[15] "Experience, Knowledge and Value," p. 564.

and consciousness, instead of being an isolated, impotent, and unexplainable entity over against the world, becomes an integral link in that transformation of unsatisfactory situations into satisfactory ones that constitutes knowing.

In the second place, an instance of knowing is no longer regarded as standing over against nature, but is recognized to be an integral part of nature. Thus one may "discern and describe a knowing as one identifies any object, concern, or event." [16] An instance of knowledge in conjunction with its known has the same sort of cosmic status as any fact of nature,[17] and "knowing is an existential overt act." [18] Knowing is not a comparison of natural and nonnatural orders of entities or even a paradoxical interaction between them. It is rather a "transaction" of continually related phases of a single situation.[19] Instead of placing the organism over against his environment and the knower over against the known, one should accordingly speak of a situation involving organic and environmental factors and being progressively organized and transformed in cognitive process.

In the third place, considering knowing in its actual settings enables us to see nature, and, indeed, everything that can be spoken of, as part of experience. Such an achievement is of course precluded if experience is interpreted in the subjectivist manner that has prevailed in empiricist thought since the days of Locke, for the sound naturalism which modern thought must accept is incompatible with subjectivism and could not be reconciled with empiricism at all if empiricism meant subjectivism.[20] However, a situational or contextual account of knowing, recognizing as it does an unbroken continuity between what is immediately given and the remotest conceivable object, is quite unwilling to interpret experience in any sort of subjectivist terms. Experience is not simply a series of mental events; it is rather a chain of facts. It is no longer merely experiencing; it includes also the experienced. Experience "denotes both the field, the sun and the clouds and the rain, seeds, and harvest, and the man who labors, who plans, invents, uses, suffers, and enjoys. Experience denotes what is experienced, the world of events and persons, and it denotes that world caught up with experiencing, the career and destiny of mankind." [21] Upon such an interpretation of experience, naturalism and empiricism are only two aspects of the

---

[16] Dewey, *The Influence of Darwin on Philosophy and Other Essays in Contemporary Thought* (New York: Henry Holt & Co., Inc., 1910), p. 77.
[17] *Knowing and the Known*, p. 56.
[18] *The Quest for Certainty*, p. 233.

[19] *Ibid.*, pp. 67 f.
[20] See "Experience, Knowledge and Value," pp. 586 f.
[21] Dewey, *Experience and Nature* (Chicago and London: The Open Court Publishing Co., 1925), p. 28.

same philosophy, for here "nature's place in man is no less significant than man's place in nature." [22]

The fourth consequence of keeping knowing properly in its context is already implicit in the others. No longer is it necessary to place experience and nature, datum and thing, subject and object, mind and matter, the psychical and the physical over against one another as though they represented opposite kinds of entities, the one kind immediately apprehended and the other known, if at all, only by a kind of inference that can really never be carried through. Rather, in terms of the continuity of actual contexts, the supposedly opposite kinds of entities involved in these dualisms become complementary phases of whole experiences, so that an experience may pass in unbroken movement from the one phase to the other. Thus one may experience not only data, subjects, and psychical facts, but also objects, nature, and material things; and, in appropriate organic conditions, one may immediately apprehend not only sensations and feelings but also books and typewriters.[23]

2. Dewey's Experimentalism

From Dewey's account of the setting of knowing, we turn now to his account of the process, the data, and the instruments of knowing, and to such extent is his account of these aspects of knowing modeled upon the active experimental procedures of modern science that the part of his theory represented by them may most appropriately be called experimentalism. We shall, accordingly, first sketch the general character of Dewey's experimentalist account of the knowing process, and then indicate somewhat more specifically his views concerning the data of knowing, the principal instruments of knowing, and the relations between the knower and the known.

A. The process of coming to know is no mere passive acceptance of something given; nor is it confined to selection and rearrangement of data. It consists rather of active transformation of the ingredients of unsatisfactory situations in the effort to satisfy inquiry. Indispensable to its existence is the performance of operations, and while these operations include mental ones they also include overt ones. To know something is primarily not to discover its antecedents but to discern its consequences.[1] It is to relieve the pressure of an unsatisfactory situation of a certain kind and to transform the situation into a satisfactory one. To do this is not, however, merely, or even mainly, to satisfy noncognitive desire. The operations instituted by

---

[22] *Ibid.*
[23] *Logic*, p. 143.

[1] *The Problems of Men*, pp. 347 f.

the inquiry must be just those required by the conditions that give rise to inquiry if satisfactory results are to be achieved; and if the inquiry is primarily cognitive, its conditions are such that they can never be satisfied by wishful thinking.

A general idea of the pattern of the process by which one comes to know anything is suggested by the character of a five-step procedure for problem-solving outlined in Dewey's little book *How We Think*.[2] An understanding of this procedure will provide a framework within which Dewey's most significant ideas concerning the process of knowing may be seen in appropriate perspective.

(1) Consciousness in general and the inquiring thought in particular in which the knowing process is instituted are, as we have already suggested, not products of the regular, uninterrupted, or habitual flow of events; they occur rather at the growing edges, where strain, tensions, and unsatisfactory situations occur. Thus the knowledge grows out of a break, a jar, "a feeling of discrepancy, or difficulty" in the course of experience. As long as all goes well cognition is quiescent; but upon "the occurrence of a difficulty,"[3] cognition is stirred to activity. The situation requires readjustment, and only because it does is one impelled to initiate the quest for knowledge.

(2) If the quest for knowledge is to achieve any degree of success this first step must yield a second, and, since it is to a specific problem that each inquiry is responsible, this step will be found to consist in "definition of the difficulty."[4] One must suspend judgment and action sufficiently to direct attention upon whatever is relevant to the difficulty and to bring the problem into clear focus. This deferment of action in favor of thought distinguishes human activity from that of the lower animals, and intelligent activity from unintelligent. It permits the direction of attention upon varied features of the situation, the selection of what is significant, and that bringing to bear of past experiences upon present problems that is the root of wisdom.

(3) The third step in a typical process of problem-solving, one that requires special resourcefulness and active ingenuity, is the "occurrence of a suggested explanation or possible solution."[5] This step may employ a kind of inference depending upon past experience, but it also "involves a leap, a jump, the propriety of which cannot be absolutely warranted in advance, no matter what precautions are taken."[6] This is the step that in scientific thought is commonly referred to as the formation of a *hypothesis*. A hypothesis is

[2] Dewey, *How We Think* (New York: D. C. Heath & Co., 1910).
[3] *How We Think*, p. 72.
[4] *Ibid.*, p. 73.
[5] *How We Think*, p. 75.
[6] *Ibid.*

"a suggested or indicated mode of solution . . . formulated as a *possibility,"* and yielding an *"if-then* proposition." [7] The production of hypotheses is scarcely subject to direct control. It depends in part upon "the foundation of habits of mind which are at once enterprising and cautious, . . . and . . . the selection and arrangement of particular facts." [8] Often the first suggestion that occurs will scarcely be sufficient, and the eventual emergence of the most fruitful solution will ordinarily require *"cultivation of a variety of alternative suggestions."* [9]

(4) The next step of inquiry is that of "rational elaboration" [10] or the deduction of the implications of the suggested solution. Once such a solution is indicated one must determine what is implicit in its meaning, and the implications in question will for the most part have the form of operations or experiments to be performed for testing the suggested solution in terms of predictions based upon it. It is primarily at this point that logic in its more restricted sense is included in the knowing process. The problem is to deduce what is involved in the suggested solution sufficiently fully and relevantly to reveal the extent to which such data as are at hand and especially such as may subsequently be disclosed are implied by the suggested solution or hypothesis. The details of this process vary with the type of problem and are often complicated. Generally speaking, what is required is the institution of hypothetical propositions specifying operations to be performed and consequences to be expected if the suggested solution is sound, that is, propositions to the effect that if the suggestion is correct, then if certain things are done certain consequences can be expected. Any number of intermediate operational *if-thens* may of course intervene between the original suggestion and the reference to the final expected consequences. The *if-then* proposition of the suggested solution "must be . . . developed in ordered relation to other propositions of like form . . . , until related contents are obtained forming the special *if-then* proposition that directs experimental observations yielding new data." [11] It should be noted that since any given set of data may be implied by any one of a large or even infinite variety of suggested antecedents, a vast number of alternate hypothetical propositions will often be required.

(5) The final step in problem-solving is that of verification, in which the performance of suggested operations leads to anticipated consequences that tend to confirm one hypothesis and exclude all

[7] *Logic,* p. 427.   [10] *Ibid.*
[8] *How We Think,* p. 75.   [11] *Logic,* p. 427.
[9] *Ibid.*

others. It is "the transformation of data into a unified situation through execution of the operations presented by the hypothetical as a rule of action." [12] In this stage "conditions are deliberately arranged in accord with the requirements of an idea or hypothesis to see if the results theoretically indicated by the idea actually occur." And "if we look and find present all the conditions demanded by the theory, and if we find the characteristic traits called for by rival alternatives to be lacking, the tendency to believe, to accept, is almost irresistible." [13]

The results of verification are, however, for a number of reasons, at best never more than probable. In the first place, the logic on which the hypothetical propositions are based, though suggested by the facts, is formal, postulational, and never fully applicable to facts. In the second place, the number of alternative hypotheticals to be tested is potentially infinite. In traditional terms the affirmation of the consequent of a hypothetical proposition does not warrant the affirmation of the antecedent but at best only contributes to its probability. Finally, the affirmation of expected consequences rests upon empirical data and all such data are subject to further inquiry.

When the tension of an unsatisfactory situation has been resolved, harmony restored, and the problem giving rise to inquiry resolved, it becomes feasible to relinquish the withdrawal of volitional and affective interests in favor of disinterested cognitive ones and to resume the full rounded life which the problem interrupted. Similarly, it is possible to lay aside the technical and scientific notions used as instruments of thought and return to the life of common sense which we ordinarily live and from the interruption of which the problem arose. However, such respite from active inquiry is at best brief, for, as James points out, life is a matter of flights and perches. Every solved problem gives rise to new ones and solutions become data for other inquiries. This does not mean that no progress has been made, for old errors can now be avoided, new adjustments sought on a higher level, and old insights used for new purposes. It does mean that the process of inquiry itself never comes to an end. We are no nearer to the apprehension of ultimate determinate being after inquiry than before, for in this ever-altering world there is no such being.

B. The data upon which the knowing process hinges have been supposed by traditional empirical theories to consist of determinate sets of relatively simple immediately given sensory experiences. But this account of the data of knowing requires considerable modification along a number of lines.

[12] *Logic*, p. 278.   [13] *How We Think*, p. 77.

(*1*) With regard to what kinds of experiences constitute the data of knowing, traditional empirical theories are disposed to limit such experiences to a fairly fixed range of givens. But in fact what constitutes the data of knowing depends upon what experiences are in the instance of each problem, appropriately selected as data. Data are "*taken* rather than given," [14] and what may be appropriately taken varies from one problem to another. Indeed, what is a datum for one inquiry may be a problem for another, and conversely. For example, when we know the size and weight of an object and wish to determine its specific gravity, its size and weight are data and its specific gravity problematic; but when we know its specific gravity and wish to determine its size and weight, its specific gravity is a datum and its size and weight are problems to be resolved by reference to other data.

(*2*) It is true that some types of data are more fundamental than others, and the traditional empirical theories are right in holding that there are immediate experiences which may properly be regarded as the nearest approach we attain to basic data. What we perceive does seem to be more fundamental than what we infer, and what we sense seems to be in some way basic. However, immediate experiences afford no such privileged access to reality as James supposed. They are at best end products of substantial causal chains and, being ontologically secondary, cannot be epistemologically ultimate in any absolute sense. As a matter of fact, immediate experiences do not, strictly speaking, constitute knowledge at all. Instead of being known, such experiences simply occur or are had.[15] Such experiences are, moreover, never beyond further investigation. They help to solve problems, but they solve no problems by themselves, and they create as many problems as they solve.[16] Although, being simply had, they can hardly be in error, judgments based upon them —no matter how directly—are often in error and in need of revision.[17] They are at very best completely lacking in that background of inquiry which is required for "justified assertion." [18] To treat them as if they were knowledge is unwisely to attempt to build scientific methodology upon uncritical notions of sensation instead of properly basing theories of sensation upon scientific knowledge.[19] It is to render reflection superfluous,[20] and to create unnecessary and insoluble epistemological puzzles.[21]

[14] *Logic*, p. 124.
[15] *Experience and Nature*, pp. 18 ff.
[16] "Experience, Knowledge and Value," p. 570.
[17] *Logic*, p. 104.
[18] *Ibid.*, p. 143.

[19] "Experience, Knowledge and Value," p. 11.
[20] Dewey, *Essays in Experimental Logic* (Chicago: University of Chicago Press, 1916).
[21] *Experience and Nature*, pp. 140 ff.

(3) While the elementary data of purely cognitive inquiries are for the most part sensory experiences, there are valuational inquiries that are equally as important, or even more so, and the elemental data of these inquiries include not only sensory factors but emotional and volitional ones as well. To be sure, emotional and volitional factors alone must never be taken to determine even valuational knowledge; but that such factors as likes and dislikes, wishes and desires are relevant to valuation can scarcely be disputed by anyone who considers the matter at all,[22] and valuational knowledge may perhaps well be regarded as a kind of reflective liking.

(4) Since the data of knowing are what are appropriately *taken* as data in terms of the particular problem and since complex experiences are often appropriately so taken, there is no reason why experiences involving considerable interpretative and rational factors cannot be data with reference to some problems. Actually both common-sense inquiry and science constantly employ such data. Thus, for example, most inquiries at the common-sense level involve perceptual data which are by no means pure immediate experiences and already involve substantial interpretative material. Similarly scientific inquiry, instead of beginning again with each investigation, builds upon the findings of previous inquiries. To be sure, such findings are subject to re-examination at any time and even perceptual findings may be questioned and tested, but for purposes in hand perceptions and products of rational inquiry may, and often should, be regarded as data.

C. Since knowing is for Dewey not primarily apprehensional but instrumental, that through which knowing comes to expression consists primarily not of manifestations of reality but of instruments for transforming unsatisfactory situations into satisfactory ones. Among the instruments of knowing are included, accordingly, not only such material instruments as microscopes and balances, but also such intellectual ones as meanings, concepts, terms, propositions, and judgments.

(1) Foremost among the instruments through which cognitive activity begins to transform its initial data, to its ends are *meanings*. Meanings do not consist of "essences or subsistences having some sort of mysterious being apart from qualitative things and changes." [23] They occur wholly in situations in which organisms and environments are inseparably linked, that is to say, as James properly insisted, in experiences. They are, however, as the new

[22] Dewey, *Theory of Valuation* (Chicago: University of Chicago Press, 1939), pp. 6 ff.

[23] *Essays in Experimental Logic*, p. 464.

realists following James properly pointed out, not made up of "mere states of consciousness." [24] While one may be aware that clouds of a certain sort mean rain, such clouds still mean rain when one does not notice the fact. Meanings can never be properly understood save in their functional or instrumental role. Funtionally they consist of operations and associated experiences intended to transform unsatisfactory situations. They are "suggestions" that are linked with, but not dependent upon, data, and tentatively accepted as possible guides to further suggestions and to "physical experimentation." [25] They are plans of action and changes to be wrought, together with experiences anticipated in conjunction with such changes.[26] The experiences anticipated in meanings may be either sensory experiences [27] or more complex cognitions or emotional and volitional responses,[28] depending upon the nature of the inquiry and whether the meaning involved is cognitive or valuational. As significant plans of action, meanings vastly extend the horizon of man beyond that of the beast and that of the intelligent man beyond that of the unintelligent. Serving as "substitutes" for objects of certain kinds they greatly facilitate the process of thought.[29] That to which they attach consists initially of immediate experiences; but since such experiences are unstable, meanings come in time to be organized around linguistic signs which help to render them more manageable and more reliable. The emergence and development of linguistically oriented meanings is in fact a continuous process of fruitful social experiment in nature,[30] and as it matures clear-cut concepts begin to be formed.

(2) *Concepts* are patterns of meaning usually built around significant terms. Often theoretically regarded as apprehended ideas or eternal objects, these concepts are actually fundamental tools of knowing. They have frequently been thought to yield "a picture of the independent and fixed essence of the universe," [31] but such a view of them is entirely misleading. Concepts are definable instruments or modes of operation for the achieving of certain transformations of presented material. Thus, "yard and mile, ounce and pound, gill and gallon, are . . . means of facilitating and executing all kinds of social transactions with reference to use and enjoyment," and so also are "conceptions and principles that serve to measure or

[24] *Ibid.*
[25] *Ibid.*, p. 49.
[26] *Logic,* pp. 351 ff. and *Experience and Nature,* p. 129.
[27] *Ibid.*
[28] See *Logic,* p. 115; *Experience and Nature,* p. 11; and Dewey, *Theory of*

Valuation (Chicago: University of Chicago Press, 1939), pp. 19 ff.
[29] *Essays in Experimental Logic,* pp. 431 f.
[30] *Logic,* pp. 46 ff.
[31] *The Quest for Certainty,* p. 132.

evaluate moral conduct and relations." [32] It would be absurd to suppose that the conceptions of modern science in order "to be valid must correspond to antecedent intrinsic properties resident in the objects dealt with." [33] Instead, as P. W. Bridgman puts it, "the concept is synonymous with the corresponding set of operations," [34] and in fact all "our conceptions and ideas are designations of operations to be performed or already performed." [35] Concepts arise out of particular situations and their value is determined by the extent to which "the operations they direct give us the results which are required." [36]

(3) The *terms,* through which both things and concepts are referred to in discourse, are not, as some logicians suppose, distinct entities standing between things or concepts on the one hand and names on the other.[37] Rather, they are simply inseparable aspects of the naming-named relation, and, when they are of the conceptual variety, their referents are mainly operations to whose performance they lead.

(4) Upon the basis of immediate experiences and concepts, *propositions* are formed as more complex instruments of inquiry. Although they are often confused with judgments, they differ from the latter in being merely suppositional. They formulate possibilities and so give range and power to the endeavor of thought to formulate and elucidate hypotheses. Like meanings and concepts, propositions are often assigned an ontological status they do not properly possess. They are not mental entities but symbolizations of "actual conditions," and "the operations they represent as possibilities." [38] As the logical positivists properly remind us, they are for the most part linguistic, but, as these thinkers fail to notice, they are never merely formal but always deeply rooted in material considerations.[39] That they should *correspond* to their subject matter is of no special importance, for their role is not the passive one of description but the functional one of "transforming an unsettled and doubtful existential situation into a resolved determinate one." [40] They must be treated always as relative to a given situation, for propositions that are suited to one situation often require revision in order to be applicable to another. For example, the propositions of mechanics had to be drastically altered before being applied to "extremely minute bodies of high velocity." [41] Propositions are quite

[32] *Logic,* p. 216.
[33] *The Quest for Certainty,* p. 122.
[34] *Ibid.,* p. 107.
[35] *Ibid.,* p. 132.
[36] *Ibid.*

[37] *Knowing and the Known,* pp. 22, 33, 209.
[38] *Logic,* p. 283.
[39] *Ibid.,* p. 784.
[40] *Ibid.,* p. 198.
[41] *Logic,* p. 141.

as strictly instrumental as the judgments they are capable of formulating.[42] They may in fact be taken to be doubly instrumental, being the instruments of judgments which are themselves the instruments of existential decisions.[43]

It is especially in connection with propositions that deductive logic comes into play. Although such logic is more important than James realized, it must be developed within the framework of a more broadly conceived logic. Logic in this broader sense is identical with the method of inquiry as a whole. It is neither "purely formal" nor an account of the "thought structures of the universe."[44] Rather, both psychological and regulative, it endeavors to criticize and improve the procedures of inquiry by reference to actual cases of successful and unsuccessful inquiry.[45] Its ultimate aim, like that of inquiry of which it is the theory, is "deliberate reconstruction of experience."[46] It is in fact "such clarified and systematized formulations of the procedures of thinking as will enable the desired reconstruction to go on more economically and efficiently."[47] In every case its orientation is to actual problem situations and its principles are as deeply rooted in material as in formal considerations. This empirical situational character and ultimately practical orientation attach in one way or another to every part of logic, including the principles of identity, contradiction and the excluded middle, and the laws of deductive and inductive reasoning.[48] No part of logic is in the end to be viewed in isolation. However, apart from the setting of material inquiry, it is legitimate, in order to sharpen the tools of inquiry, to abstract certain terms and elaborate the implications involved in their meanings, in temporary isolation from particular applications. This is what the deductive sciences of mathematics and formal logic do and these sciences constitute the core of the deductive phase of reasoning. Such formal analysis of logical meanings has the merit of disclosing necessity in the resulting implications[49] and of vastly increasing both the scope and precision of the applicability of concepts. Indeed, generally speaking, the greater the degree of abstraction the greater the degree of applicability. The only test required in analysis of logical meanings is that of facility in transformation.[50] Nevertheless mathematics and the more formal part of logic refer not to a mysterious ontological realm of possibility, but to actually realizable modes of experiment; and mathe-

---

[42] Cf. ibid., pp. 216–19.
[43] Ibid., pp. 166–67.
[44] Dewey, Reconstruction in Philosophy (New York: New American Library of World Literature, Mentor Books, 1953), p. 114.

[45] Ibid., pp. 115 f; Logic, pp. 373 ff.
[46] Reconstruction in Philosophy, p. 117.
[47] Ibid., pp. 114 f.
[48] Cf. Logic, pp. 343 ff.
[49] Ibid., p. 279.
[50] Ibid., p. 399.

matical relations must in the end be operationally defined in terms of "further operations of transformation." [51] Moreover, the roots of deductive logic and mathematics are not intuitions but practical postulations, and the goal of these sciences is not the achievement of a formal science but the solution of material problems. [52]

The universal propositions, in terms of which formal logic or "discourse" proceed, are radically different in kind from generic ones through which existential inference operates. [53] The former are hypothetical, necessary, and relatively independent of actual conditions. The latter are general, probable, and contingent upon brute facts. Hypothetical or universal propositions are essentially definitional, categorical, and operational. They state that if something is of such and such kind and if such and such actions are performed, such and such consequences may be expected. In themselves they tell us nothing of the facts. General or generic propositions inform us of the actual characteristics which may be regularly expected to appear. The *selection* of the hypothetical propositions that are chosen for consideration in discourse depends on previously established generic propositions; otherwise discourse would be irrelevant and useless. But the *establishment* of generic propositions depends on hypothetical ones; otherwise there would be no sufficient guide for testing operations, nor would one know when consequences were actually confirmatory.

(5) The instruments of knowing in which meanings, concepts, terms, and propositions tend to eventuate are *judgments*. Whereas propositions are only suppositional, judgments are decisional. Propositions are "affirmed but not asserted"; judgments are asserted as well as affirmed. [54] Like all other instruments of inquiry, judgments are functional through and through. Traditionally judgments have been thought to consist of psychological processes of a purely mentalistic kind. Such an interpretation, however, not only fails to describe the specific character of judgments but almost completely obscures their functional role in human life. All judgment is activity. Much of it involves overt bodily activity, and some of it demands the use of material instruments. This latter requirement is conspicuous in the case of scientific experimentation but it is often evident enough in common-sense inquiry. The subject of judgment is the confused situation in which judgment occurs. The purpose is the clarifying and harmonizing of the situation, and the success or failure of the judgment must be measured by its contribution to the fulfillment of this purpose. Judgment is "a continuous process of

[51] *Ibid.*, p. 402.
[52] *Ibid.*, pp. 404 ff.
[53] *Ibid.*, chap. xiv.
[54] *The Problems of Men*, p. 339.

resolving an indeterminate, unsettled situation into a determinate, unified one, through operations which transform subject-matter originally given." [55]

D. Since knowing is for Dewey primarily instrumental rather than apprehensional, Dewey does not concern himself very much with the problem of the nature of the object of knowledge as such. However, from the character of such other features of his view of knowledge as have been discussed, it is possible to gain at least a general idea of the drift of his thought with reference to this problem. The objects of knowledge are for Dewey neither, as some idealists hold, mental entities; nor, as the new realists suppose, things that appear at the beginning of inquiry; nor, as some critical realists think, hidden substances that never really appear at all. Rather, they are "subject-matter so far as it has been produced and ordered in settled form by means of inquiry, . . . objectives of inquiry." [56] Objects resulting from old inquiries can of course be used in entering upon new ones—and it is this that gives the new realism its apparent strength. But objects themselves are never merely given, and they appear in experience only as a result of inquiry at some earlier point.[57] Objects are never apprehended in isolation. They are always parts of total situations embracing apprehending organisms and immediate experiences as well as objects.[58] An object is selected and shaped out of a whole situation in the process of transforming the situation; it is never merely placed over against an opposing mind. Failure to see this has misled dualistic realists and created for them impassable gaps between knower and known. The mode in which objects finally occur is not merely that of a group of presented qualities but rather largely that of anticipated experiences. "An object, in other words, is a set of qualities treated as *potentialities* for specified existential consequences." [59] Thus, for example, "powder is what will explode under certain conditions; water is . . . that group of connected qualities which will quench thirst and so on." [60]

That some aspects of what we call objects antedate inquiry into them, Dewey seems on the whole to have no doubt, but that we cannot know these aspects he seems also convinced. The whole process of inquiry is one of transforming situations, and what is there at the beginning can scarcely be what emerges at the end. This consideration may be abundantly illustrated in connection with psychological and sociological inquiries. It applies also to physical ones

[55] *Logic*, p. 21.
[56] *Logic*, p. 119.
[57] *Ibid.*, pp. 520 ff.

[58] *Ibid.*, pp. 66 ff.
[59] *Ibid.*, p. 129.
[60] *Ibid.*

with reference both to macroscopic objects and to submicroscopic ones. The known star is very different from the tiny speck of light that first appeared, and the Heisenberg principle, according to which the light rays necessary to visibility always alter the event, discloses the fact that our eventual conceptions of basic physical events must always be different from anything we can possibly observe.[61] In any case, since the process of inquiry is an attempt to alter unsatisfactory situations, for knowing merely to *reveal* what was there at the start would be useless.

3. DEWEY'S FUNCTIONALISM

As Dewey's conception of the setting of knowing may be appropriately referred to as "contextualism" and his conception of the process of knowing as "experimentalism," his conception of the nature of truth may be appropriately referred to as "functionalism." Since knowing consists in transforming an indeterminate and unsatisfactory situation into a determinate and satisfactory one, to say that a judgment is known to be true is to say that the judgment has warranted assertability. Indeed truth in the sense of being known as fully as conditions permit may be taken to be essentially equivalent with warranted assertability.[1] Thus for any judgment to be true is for it to stand in the dual functional role of satisfying the conditions of present or past inquiry and promising to be useful in satisfying future inquiries.

As warranted assertability, truth consists not of a single fixed and eternal truth,[2] but of a collection of truths.[3] The truth in truths is, as James pointed out, "the guiding or leading power of ideas by which we 'dip into the particulars of experience again.' "[4] Thus truth may be said to be an idea's *working* in its situation. "The idea is true which works in leading us to what it purports."[5] The true is the reliable, and "if ideas, meanings, conceptions, notions, theories, systems are instrumental to an active reorganization of the given environment, to a removal of some specific trouble and perplexity, . . . they are reliable."[6] One can speak much more appropriately of judging truly than of true propositions, and when one uses the latter type of expression one should recognize that he does so somewhat metaphorically.

[61] *Quest for Certainty*, pp. 192 ff.
[1] See "Experience, Knowledge and Value," p. 603; and *Knowing and the Known*, p. 304.
[2] *Ibid.*, p. 121; *Experience and Nature*, p. 172.
[3] *Ibid.*, p. 410.
[4] *Essays in Experimental Logic*, p. 304.
[5] *Ibid.*
[6] *Reconstruction in Philosophy*, p. 128.

Instead of being in situations from the outset, truths have to be made. Their relation to reality is not like that between a photograph and an object but rather like "that between invention and the conditions which the invention was intended to meet." [7] Error is indeed the rule, and truth the exception which must be fashioned out of the vast sea of experience.[8] If I hear a rumbling noise in the street, the truth that the noise is that of a streetcar is "made" only when I go to the window and transform the doubtful situation of which my vague apprehension of a passing streetcar is a part.[9]

Some caution is, however, necessary in interpreting truth as *working* and as being *made*. That truth *works* does not mean simply that anything that works in any sense whatever is true; rather, that only is true which satisfies the specific cognitive conditions involved in the inquiry giving rise to the truth-claim. Indeed it is only as these cognitive conditions are adequately met that the truth-claims will be sufficiently reliable to be satisfactorily put to use in the attainment of those noncognitive satisfactions which are often the ultimate sources of the quest for truth. In like manner that truth is *made* does not mean that one can make true anything one pleases. Conditions and limits of the making of truth are laid down in the special conditions of each inquiry, and general conditions are being progressively discovered in the methodology of science. Truth may properly be said to consist of that which an unbiased "scientific man" would assert, that in the discovery of which scientific method is supreme, "that which is accepted upon adequate evidence," such evidence being determined by "observation and experiment." [10] Accordingly, the manner of the determination of truth is both rigorous and subject to social scrutiny. "Truth and falsity depend upon what others find when they warily perform the experiment of observing reflective events"; and "to convince of error as well as to lead to truth is to assist another to see and find something which he has failed to find and recognize." [11]

Without abandoning the concept of truth as verifiability or warranted assertability, truth can, as James showed, be interpreted as a kind of correspondence; and indeed Dewey, like James, believes that the verifiability view is the only intelligible correspondence view. The correspondence in question does not consist in copying as a photograph copies an object, for in that case either the copy would be of no use or the object would be inaccessible. Rather, the

---

[7] *Essays in Experimental Logic*, pp. 24 f.

[8] *Experience and Nature*, p. 310.

[9] *The Influence of Darwin on Philosophy*, pp. 140 f.

[10] *Essays in Experimental Logic*, pp. 63 f.

[11] *Experience and Nature*, p. 37.

correspondence in question is an "answering, as a key answers the conditions imposed by a lock, or as two correspondents answer each other, . . . as, in short, a *solution* answers the requirements of a problem." [12] It is not indeed a corerspondence to antecedents at all but "a relation which *propositions,* as means of inquiry, have . . . to those existential consequences which, in virtue of operations existentially performed satisfy (meet, fulfill) conditions set by occurrences that constitute a problem." [13]

In addition to the concept of truth in the sense thus far discussed, namely, as that which is as near truth as present conditions permit, there is a concept of truth in a more ultimate sense in which the limitations of present conditions are removed. And despite our present inability to remove these conditions, truth in this more ultimate sense may still be defined and thought about in terms of ultimate discovery provided the definition adequately recognizes the tentativeness of discoveries to date. Concerning truth in this sense Dewey follows Peirce, writing as following: "The best definition of *truth* from the logical standpoint which is known to me is that of Peirce: 'The opinion which is fated to be ultimately agreed to by all who investigate is what we mean by truth. . . . Truth is that concordance of an abstract statement with the ideal limit towards which endless investiagtion would tend to bring scientific belief, which concordance the abstract statement may possess by virtue of the confession of its inaccuracy and one-sidedness, and this confession is an essential ingredient of the truth.' " [14]

4. Other Broadly Contextualistic Versions of Instrumentalism

Among philosophers who have accepted instrumentalist epistemologies akin to that of Dewey, some have, like Dewey, adopted views that place knowing in broad biological contexts without giving major emphasis to any single feature of that context. Others, while recognizing the wider context, have been especially concerned with the social setting of cognition. Still others have been primarily interested in the instrumental role of concepts in scientific theory. The present section is designed to illustrate the work of writers of the first group, and the next two sections, that of the other two groups.

The various writings of Addison W. Moore (b. 1866) on the problem of knowledge have stressed the experiential continuity of the knowing process, the social orientation of that process, and the element of objectivity retained within pragmatist doctrines of truth.

[12] *The Problems of Men,* p. 343.   [14] *Logic,* p. 345 n.
[13] *Ibid.,* p. 348.

One phase of Moore's pragmatist insistence upon continuity in the knowing process is to be found in what he has to say about the relation of the logical and the nonlogical ingredients of knowledge. This relation involves, Moore holds, both distinguishability and continuity. Theories that minimize or obscure the distinction between the logical and the nonlogical by attempting to "make all perceptions, anticipations and even instincts and habits" logical accomplish only verbal results in that the distinction between the implicitly logical and the explicitly logical must in any case be retained.[1] Such theories are also inadequate in presuming the ultimate dispensability of perception and memory,[2] unscientific in excluding hypotheses from inquiry, and self-defeating in destroying any "basis for the distinction between logical and non-logical results."[3] But theories which deny the continuity of cognitive and noncognitive elements in knowing, or "refuse to give the operations of perception, memory, etc., any place in logic"[4] condemn thought in general and logic in particular to a barren intellectualism that is never able "to thrust its hands into the vitals of nature," or "to acquire a real control over nature."[5] They are able to "make no connections between logical and non-logical conduct" or "to distinguish in a specific case truth from error."[6] Accordingly, the only plausible account of knowing must be one in which logical and nonlogical factors, though distinguishable, are functionally continuous. The precise point at which nonlogical factors in knowing are linked with and begin to give rise to logical ones is "the point where non-logical processes instead of operating as direct unambiguous stimuli and response become ambiguous with consequent inhibition of conduct."[7] But the nonlogical factors do not now drop out of the process. Rather, they "take on the form of sensations and universals, terms and relations, data and hypotheses,"[8] of logical conduct, and logical conduct "aims to remove ambiguity and inhibition in unreflective conduct."[9]

In view of Moore's stress upon the continuity of the logical and nonlogical elements in knowing, it is not surprising to find him also insisting upon the continuity of knowing and object. The situation in which inquiry occurs is never merely a psychological one, and the problem or ambiguity to be resolved is never "for a merely onlooking, beholding psychical mind."[10] Every activity, including cognitive

[1] A. W. Moore, "Reformation of Logic," in John Dewey and Others, *Creative Intelligence* (New York: Henry Holt & Co., Inc., 1917), p. 80.
[2] *Ibid.*, p. 81.
[3] *Ibid.*, p. 87.
[4] *Ibid.*, p. 87.
[5] *Ibid.*, p. 73.
[6] *Ibid.*, p. 87.
[7] *Ibid.*, p. 83.
[8] *Ibid.*
[9] *Ibid.*, p. 86.
[10] *Ibid.*, p. 84.

activity, involves interaction. "That there is such a thing as conduct at all means that there are certain beings who have acquired definite ways of responding to one another," and forms of interaction in "perceptions, memory, etc.—are not to be located in either of the interacting beings but are functions of both." [11] No subject can exist save in continuity with objects and no thought without things. The datum of science is not a mere found sense-datum but "the result of operations," [12] and the object is not something there at the start but something emerging in the process of knowing. Universality means "*continuity* of experience" and the "concrete" is "the test of the universal." [13] Even the sandwich resting upon the mantel and its alteration in being eaten are continuous with the thought of the sandwich in that the eating *begins* with the thinking. At least in the sense of "assisting to remake," "knowledge *helps* to make . . . the world." [14]

A third phase of Moore's emphasis upon continuity is his insistence upon the continuity and even partial identity of the knowing mind and its social setting. To say that the knowing self is placed among other human beings is not enough to break the strangle hold of solipsism. One must recognize that the knowing self involves the social setting in its own constitution. It was because of failure to see this fact that philosophy was, from the time of the Sophists until recently, unable to answer the challenge of the individualistic psychology of the Sophists, and compelled, in its effort to avoid skepticism, to resort to all sorts of strained metaphysical devices such as the Platonic hypostatizing of universals.[15] It was also because of failure to recognize the pragmatist doctrine of the involvement of society in the structure of the self that critics of pragmatism mistakenly accused pragmatists of a solipsism which is as far as possible from their thought.[16] Pragmatists insist upon "the social origin and function of consciousness." "*Not only in its origin, but in its continued development and operation must it* [consciousness] *always be a function of the whole social situation of which it is born.*" [17] Indeed, the whole of the readjustment achieved through thought, of which consciousness is a part, is "always in and of a 'social situation.' " [18] The concepts in terms of which thought proceeds, the hypotheses which it formulates, and even the data at which its preliminary operations arrive are all so thoroughly socially conditioned that to regard them as mere products of individual minds is hopelessly to misrepresent them.

[11] *Ibid.,* p. 84.
[12] *Ibid.,* p. 90.
[13] Moore, *Pragmatism and Its Critics* (Chicago: University of Chicago Press, 1910), p. 186.
[14] *Ibid.,* p. 219.
[15] *Ibid.,* chap. ii.
[16] *Ibid.,* chap. x.
[17] *Ibid.,* p. 230.
[18] *Ibid.,* p. 232.

Although Moore, like other pragmatists, regards truth as a working resultant of satisfactory situational adjustments achieved in the continuum of our varied instincts and impulses in their social and physical settings, his presentation of the pragmatist doctrine of truth cautiously preserves as much as possible of the traditional idea of truth. Thus for example, true ideas are ideas which not only work, but "which work in the way they set out to work." The idea that an ache is caused by a certain tooth is not true if the pulling of the tooth merely brings some other satisfaction but only if the extraction stops this specific ache. Similarly, Saul's idea of where his father's asses are is not true if he does not find them where he seeks them, even if there he finds a kingdom.[19] Again, truth is responsible to a certain grain in nature which cannot be ignored if truth is to be ascertained. Unless some prior connection existed between the tooth and the ache the idea that the ache is caused by the tooth will not work.[20] Furthermore, instead of being fully identified with the consequences of a true proposition, the truth of an idea is often sufficiently indicated by saying that the consequences of the idea are *initiated* in the idea, as for example the appropriate tooth extraction is *begun* in the idea that it is that tooth which is aching.[21] Finally, it is not directly with the attainment of satisfaction that the quest for truth is concerned but rather with "the removal of ambiguity, and inhibition" that stand in the way.[22]

Stephen C. Pepper has over a long period continued to call attention to the strands by which cognition is linked directly to its immediate situation and indirectly to wider contexts in society and nature in ways that disclose its kinship with ethical choices and esthetic appreciations.[23] Despite a tolerance that recognizes the defensibility of other world views, Pepper himself believes that basic realities, including cognitive ones, are of the order of vital historical events each involving its own qualities, having textures that reach out in all directions, and leading where blockage occurs to new instruments.[24] Pepper contends that truth is "the result of an instrumental texture which removes a blocking and integrates a terminal texture." [25]

[19] *Ibid.*, p. 87.
[20] *Ibid.*, p. 90.
[21] *Ibid.*, p. 91.
[22] "Reformation of Logic," p. 98.
[23] S. C. Pepper, "Transcendence," *University of California Publications in Philosophy*, VIII (1926), 51–69; Pepper, "A Contextualistic Theory of the Possible," *Ibid.*, XVII (1934), 179–97; Pepper, "Categories: Studies in the Problem of Relations," *Ibid.*, XIII (1930), 73–98; Pepper, "The Order of Time," *Ibid.*, XVIII (1935),

3–20; Pepper, "The Individuality of a Work of Art," *Ibid.*, XX (1937), 81–97; Pepper, *The Source of Value* (Berkeley: University of California Press, 1958).

[24] *World Hypotheses* (Berkeley: University of California Press, 1942), especially chap. x.

[25] *Ibid.*, p. 269; cf. also Pepper, "Truth by Continuity," *University of California Publications in Philosophy*, X (1928), 27–59.

Acknowledging that there may well be fully determinate facts, he denies that any of them can be known with certainty; [26] and he further insists in thoroughgoing empirical fashion that even the alleged universality of the categories must be subjected to examination in terms of evidence.[27] Works of art, like moments of cognition, he holds, are to be tested not by their character alone or by their coherence in an absolute whole but by their qualities in contexts.[28]

Arthur E. Murphy finds in Dewey's view of knowledge, and indeed also in that of Whitehead, the roots of an "objective relativism" that resolves the conflict of epistemological monism and epistemological dualism by combining heretofore supposedly incompatible elements of objectivity and relativity.[29] "The objective facts of the world of nature and of reality are the very 'apparent' and relative happenings disclosed to us in perception," [30] and "what we experience *also* belongs to and is, under the special but entirely natural conditions of organic interaction, a sample of the nature to which we claim to refer." [31] Murphy believes, however, that Dewey was not always true to his own contextualism and that the objective relativism implicit in Dewey's contextualism requires to be purified and kept distinct from the thinner strand, in some of his works, of reliance upon future social consequences.[32] Murphy has become increasingly dissatisfied with the traditional type of philosophical criticism which tends to reject all that is not indubitable and so subject to modes of confirmation totally different from those implicit in it. He takes a proper criticism of knowledge to be one which "specifies the context in which various types of statements have a significant use, in order that we may judge their meaning and truth in that context . . . [and studies] the ways in which men do in fact communicate and get information about the world and each other." [33]

Other significant contributions to an instrumentalism with a broad contextualistic base include J. Loewenberg, Lewis E. Hahn, A. F. Bentley, and Paul Marhenke. Loewenberg has emphasized the pri-

[26] Pepper, "The Issue Over the Facts," *University of California Publications in Philosophy*, XXV (1950), 121–39.

[27] Pepper, "What Are Categories For?" *Journal of Philosophy*, XLIV (1947), 546–56.

[28] Pepper, "Some Questions on Dewey's Aesthetics," in P. A. Schilpp, *The Philosophy of John Dewey* (Evanston, Ill.: Northwestern University Press, Library of Living Philosophers, 1939, 1951), pp. 371–89.

[29] Murphy, A. E., "Objective Relativism in Dewey and Whitehead," *Philosophical Review* XXXVI (1927), 121–44.

[30] *Ibid.*, p. 122.

[31] Murphy, "Dewey's Epistemology and Metaphysics," in Schilpp, *The Philosophy of John Dewey* (Evanston, Ill: Northwestern University Press, The Library of Living Philosophers, 1939, 1952), p. 220.

[32] *Ibid.*, pp. 193–225.

[33] Murphy, "Two Versions of Critical Philosophy," *Proceedings of the Aristotelian Society*, XXXVIII (1937–38), 145, 159; cf. also, Murphy, *The Uses of Reason* (New York: The Macmillan Co., 1943).

ority assigned by contextualism to a kind of datum very different from that with which most current epistemologies begin. The sense-data with which many epistemological analyses have begun cannot properly be taken as starting points at all, for instead of being "pre-analytic," they are at best altogether "post-analytic" features of cognitive situations discovered at the end of analysis, not present at the start of analysis.[34] Hahn has undertaken to work out a detailed theory of perception on contextualistic lines. Like Loewenberg he protests against what he regards as a metaphysically biased attempt to ground perception in sense-data, and contends that the proper starting point for studies of perception is the kinds of macrocosmic observations of physical objects we actually make.[35] Perception has, Hahn believes, both practical and esthetic foundations, but the basic reality is the patterned event and the object of knowledge standard operations.[36] Bentley's approach to contextualistic epistemology stresses behavioristic and biologically interactional aspects of cognitive responses.[37] Marhenke indicates other reasons for misgivings concerning the attempt to ground the interpretation of perception in the notion of sense-data,[38] and attempts to show that virtually all thinking is discursive, and understanding, interpretable in terms of dispositional properties.[39]

5. INSTRUMENTALIST THEORIES EMPHASIZING SOCIAL CONTEXT

One of the most penetrating and influential of all pragmatist accounts of knowledge is that of G. H. Mead (1863–1931). Like Dewey, Mead regards the epistemological problem in its traditional forms as relatively unimportant and prefers to concentrate upon the problem of the proper procedures for scientific discovery. The usual version of the epistemological problem is, he thinks, originally that of "getting

[34] J. Lowenberg, "Pre-Analytic and Post-Analytic Data," Journal of Philosophy, XXIV (1927), 5–14; and "The Futile Flight from Interpretations," University of California Publications in Philosophy, XXV (1950), 169–97.

[35] Lewis E. Hahn, "Neutral and Indubitable Sense-Data as the Starting Point for Theories of Perception," Journal of Philosophy, XXXVI (1939), 589–600; and Hahn, "Psychological Data and Philosophical Theory of Perception," Ibid., XXXIX (1942), 296–301.

[36] Hahn, "A Contextualistic Theory of Perception," University of California Pub-

lications in Philosophy, XXII (1942), 1–205.

[37] A. F. Bentley, Behavior, Knowledge and Fact (Bloomington, Ind.: The Principia Press, Inc., 1935); and John Dewey and A. F. Bentley, Knowing and the Known.

[38] Paul Marhenke, "Moore's Analysis of Sense Perception," in Schilpp, The Philosophy of G. E. Moore (Evanston, Ill.: Northwestern University Press, Library of Living Philosophers, 1942, 1952), pp. 255–80.

[39] Marhenke, "Propositions and Sentences," University of California Publications in Philosophy, XXV (1950), 273–98.

from an experienced effect to a world that is responsible for the effect," and more recently, that of "relating our immediate perceptual world with an atomic and subatomic world that is not and cannot be perceptual." [1] But with neither of these problems does or need the working scientist concern himself, and it is the presuppositions and procedures of the working scientist that give the philosopher his problem. These presuppositions contain at least two ideas that science cannot itself establish, namely that of "the systematic and uniform character of natural processes" and that of "the integral part which those individual experiences, within which appear the problems of science and their hypothetical solutions, occupy in nature." [2] Philosophical inquiry concerning knowledge is thus properly occupied not primarily with the problems of knower and known or of sensory objects versus scientific objects, but with such problems as those of the uniformity of nature and the place of individual experience in nature. In this sense "the epistemological problem, having seemingly died of inanition, has been found to be at bottom a problem of method or logic." [3]

What Mead has to say concerning the relation of knowing to its situation agrees with, and perhaps goes even beyond, the contextualism of Dewey. Knowing occurs only in a situation, and the meaning and truth of any piece of knowledge is dependent upon the situation in which it occurs in such fashion that what is true and known in one situation may be untrue or not known in another. Indeed, it is only as placed in particular contexts that anything can properly be spoken of at all. "The reflective experience, the world, and things within it exist in the form of situations." [4] In such situations nothing is to be taken as absolute or independent. The organism depends upon its environment, but the environment also depends upon the organism. Concepts that are pertinent are pertinent to *this* situation, and the procedures that are relevant are relevant to *this* situation. Even things perceived are what they are in terms of the situation in which they are perceived. They might well have been quite other than they are if their situations had been different. It was failure to see this, coupled with an attempt to force all data into the rigid patterns of Greek society, that ruined the science of the Greeks.[5] Russell seems to make a similar mistake in demanding "hard facts." [6]

[1] G. H. Mead, *The Philosophy of the Act* (Chicago: University of Chicago Press, (1938), p. 27.

[2] *Ibid.*, p. 29.

[3] G. H. Mead, "Scientific Method and the Individual Thinker," in John Dewey and Others, *Critical Intelligence* (New York: Henry Holt & Co., Inc., 1917), p. 226.

[4] *The Philosophy of the Act*, p. 215.

ual Thinker," pp. 198 ff.

[5] "Scientific Method and the Individ-

[6] *Ibid.*, p. 206.

For Mead as for Dewey, the particular feature of a situation that calls forth a knowing process is its problematic character. Inquiry begins when there is "lack of adjustment between the individual and his world," when what was an object for the individual is no longer so,[7] when the object has been swallowed up in doubt and uncertainty that inhibit action. What has to be achieved in face of a problematic situation is not merely satisfactory adjustment but the ongoing of an *activity*. Always where there is knowing, there was an activity going on before the inquiry began. The problematic phase of the situation has interrupted the activity, and the quest for knowledge becomes a search for a way of resuming the interrupted activity. Even the "perception of physical things presupposes an act that is already going on in advance of perception and is a process within which perception lies."[8] The data that are given with reference to any given problem consist for Mead not merely of a few selected and especially pertinent previously ascertained facts, but of a vast sea of assured fact upon which the present doubt is merely a small island.[9] The problematic is but a gap, a hole to be filled up in the immeasurably greater area of the unproblematic in which it arises. Mead is indeed willing to acknowledge the existence of a realm of subjectivity to which belong both unestablished hypotheses and many varieties of errors and illusions, but he insists that insofar as we follow the procedure of science this subjective realm can never swallow up the far larger expanse of assured fact within which it occurs as a temporary aberration.[10]

The most distinctive feature of Mead's thought about knowledge appears in the role it assigns to the concept of sociality. While this concept is present and indeed important in the thought of Dewey, Moore, and many other instrumentalists, it is in Mead's thought the keystone of the whole system. Only in terms of it do most of the other significant features of Mead's account of knowing become adequately intelligible at all. Sociality does not begin upon the human, or even upon the animal level, but is present throughout nature, as for example in the relation of the earth and the sun. It may be defined as the property of the act that "calls out an activity in objects which is of a like character with its own."[11] In it lies the only satisfactory account of the origin and nature of the knowing self, for an organism becomes and remains a self only in a setting in which it is placed over against similarly reacting organisms. "We appear as selves in our conduct in so far as we ourselves take the attitude that

---

[7] *The Philosophy of the Act*, p. 6.
[8] *Ibid.*, p. 149.
[9] *Ibid.*, chap. ii.

[10] *Ibid.*, pp. 32 ff.
[11] *Ibid.*, p. 150.

others take towards us." [12] This forever precludes solipsism, at any rate from the point of view of scientific procedure. "The individual himself is, after all, there only in so far as he arises in the community." [13] The concepts in terms of which we think are social instruments, and the character of accepted objects on which further inquiry must operate varies according to the society in which such objects occur. The objects that emerge as the fruits of complete inquiry are so much social achievements that an object not arrived at and sustained by a community of thought is scarcely thinkable. A common world is presupposed in a private one. To be sure we see things in terms of individual perspectives, but always "in experience the individual perspectives arise out of a common perspective, the common perspective is not built up of individual perspectives." [14] The social world is the one in which we live and move. It is only as this world breaks down at one point or another that problems arise, or that sound hypotheses on the one hand or errors on the other emerge. Hence it is in the terms of sociality, as its sometimes useful suspension, that even doubt, suggestion, error, and subjective experience generally are to be explained.[15]

The kind of preoccupation with the social aspect of knowledge that is found in America in Mead, to a lesser degree in Dewey, and in Europe in a variety of other writers has given rise in recent years to a new discipline often referred to as "the sociology of knowledge." This discipline for the most part abandons as impossible any attempt to justify the objectivity of knowledge, and focuses attention upon a social conditioning that determines the character of all our thinking from political slogans to the basic propositions of our logic and mathematics. The leading European exponent of this discipline is Karl Mannheim.[16]

Other writers who have placed special emphasis upon the social context of cognition include Charles W. Morris and Sidney Hook. After examining five other leading types of theory of mind, Morris concludes that Dewey's functionalist type of thought is capable not only of avoiding the errors that are fatal to the other types but also of embracing all of the best insights of the others in a comprehensive objective relativism in which what appears is also an event of nature. His own most significant contribution to instrumentalism and indeed to philosophy in general is an analysis of the nature and function of

[12] Mead, *The Philosophy of the Present* (Chicago: The Open Court Publishing Co., 1932), p. 185.

[13] *The Philosophy of the Act*, p. 413.

[14] *Ibid.*, p. 140.

[15] *Ibid.*, pp. 46 ff.

[16] Louis Worth and E. Shils (trans.), Karl Mannheim's *Ideology and Utopia, An Introduction to the Sociology of Knowledge* (New York & London: Harcourt, Brace & Co., & Kegan Paul, Trench, Trubner & Co., Ltd., 1936).

signs that has laid down, especially in its distinction between syntax, semantics and pragmatics, the broad outlines of a large part of recent discussion of signs. Hook stresses the dynamic objective and transactional character of concepts as instruments.[17] For him "the logic of demonstration is the logic of discovery grown cold," [18] and the instruments of thought are not unlike the coins of exchange. He has added to his study of the theoretical foundations of pragmatism a substantial series of books and articles from a pragmatist point of view on current social issues.[19] Other writers emphasizing social aspects of instrumentalism include H. C. Brown, J. H. Tufts, Horace Kallen, and B. H. Bode.

6. OPERATIONALISM, P. W. BRIDGMAN

By far the most significant of those writers who have concentrated upon the application of broadly instrumental ideas to specific problems of the interpretation and methodology of modern physical science is P. W. Bridgman (b. 1882), whose approach to knowledge has come to be referred to as "operationalism."

Like most other thinkers of the broadly pragmatist type Bridgman's emphasis is throughout basically empirical. Nothing is ever to be presumed known save through experience. A term can be meaningful only as what is expressed by it can be tested by experience. A verification can be achieved only through an experience, and *"for the experience itself there can be no substitute."* [1] Always in the end "the only appeal is to experiment," [2] and from first to last, thought is held in check by a basic "inability of our minds to transcend experience." [3] With reference to present events we simply "have to accept the experience," [4] and "the only possible attitude toward the future is one of unreserved acceptance, no matter how distasteful or contrary to expectations." [5] Somewhat to the chagrin of many of his empiricist, instrumentalist, and operationalist friends, instead of interpreting experience in quasi-objective terms as Dewey often does, Bridgman insists that the experience upon which science in the end

[17] Sidney Hook, *The Metaphysics of Pragmatism* (Chicago: The Open Court Publishing Co., 1927).

[18] *Ibid.*, p. 88.

[19] Hook, *Reason Social Myths and Democracy* (New York: Humanistic Press, Inc., 1940); *Towards the Understanding of Karl Marx* (New York: The John Day Co., 1933); *From Hegel to Marx* (New York: Humanities Press, Inc., 1950).

[1] P. W. Bridgman, *The Intelligent In-*dividual and Society (New York: The Macmillan Co., 1938), p. 38.

[2] Bridgman, *The Logic of Modern Physics* (New York: The Macmillan Co., 1927), p. 51.

[3] Bridgman, *The Nature of Physical Theory* (New York: Vanuxam Press, 1936) p. 27.

[4] *Ibid.*, p. 28.

[5] *Ibid.*, p. 30.

rests is always basically personal and private. It is of that impenetrable kind with reference to which one person can never be sure that the qualities in his experience are the same as the supposedly corresponding ones in the experience of another in case the other chooses to hide his experiences.[6] In this sense at any rate science has at its foundations to be solipsistic,[7] and "public science" becomes a particular kind of "private science." [8]

However, the most significant part of Bridgman's account of knowledge is what he has to say about concepts. Although all scientific thought must be grounded in immediate experience, a way has been found in concepts to transcend immediate experience; and since through concepts all manner of avoidable misconceptions have crept into scientific thought, careful analysis of scientific concepts can do much to clarify the foundations of science.

Concepts are, as Einstein has rightly insisted, not inevitable forms of our thought but purely human inventions. Their purpose is ultimately "intelligent" adaption to our situation. Accordingly they are not, as Einstein thought, to be evaluated in terms of their degree of simplicity,[9] but rather in terms of their yielding the cognitive results that are wanted. The supposition that nature is essentially simple and rational has nothing to support it; and that mathematics should apply to nature is not in the least marvelous since mathematics was invented to this very end.[10]

The primary method by which the *meanings* of concepts are to be determined is that of noticing the *operations* involved in their employment. Thus, "the true meaning of a term is found by observing what a man does with it, not what he says about it." [11] A concept may be said to be "synonymous with the corresponding set of operations." [12] Thus, for example, "to find length, we have to perform certain physical operations," and "the concept of length involves as much as and nothing more than the set of operations by which length is determined." [13] Similarly, *simultaneity* has, since Einstein, been defined not as absolute but as a relative temporal property of events that "depends on their relation to the observer, and in particular on their velocity." [14] The concept of *velocity* in its ordinary sense is to be interpreted in terms of the operations by which we "observe the time at which the object is in one position, and then later observe the time at which it is at a second position, divide the distance between the two positions by the time interval, and if necessary, when

---

[6] *The Intelligent Individual and Society*, pp. 148 ff.
[7] *Ibid.*, p. 153.
[8] *Ibid.*, p. 158.
[9] *Ibid.*, pp. 90 f.

[10] *Ibid.*, pp. 60 ff.
[11] *Ibid.*, p. 7.
[12] *Ibid.*, p. 5.
[13] *Ibid.*
[14] *Ibid.*, p. 8.

the velocity is variable take the limit." [15] Even logical and mathematical concepts, if they are to be more than empty forms, must be interpreted in terms of the operations by which they are employed and tested in experience.[16] For example, *identity* is "determined by the operations by which we make the judgment that this object is the *same* as that one of my past experience." [17]

Operational analysis is not by any means a mere technical procedure remote from everyday life. It applies to common-sense statements as well as to scientific ones. Whenever one "wants to assure himself that he understands the meaning of a term or wants to discover what a question means, he makes an analysis of what he does in using the term or answering the question." [18]

Ideally the operations governing the interpretation of a term should be unique, for otherwise one will not be sure how to apply the term and some ambiguity will be inevitable. Thus "in *principle* the operations by which length is measured should be uniquely specified," for "if we have more than one set of operations, we have more than one concept." [19] Since contradictions do not occur within physical operations, it is also desirable that the operations defining a concept should be "physical operations actually carried out." [20] Such operations may include pencil-and-paper operations, but no reference to mentally conceived *properties* can ever be an adequate substitute for reference to actual operations. To speak in terms of properties is to speak in a potentially self-contradictory manner that is almost sure to demand new, drastic changes in science of the sort that Einstein had to undertake in his special theory of relativity. But if we speak "in terms of actual operations, we need run no danger of having to revise our attitude toward nature." [21]

If the operational method of determining meaning is adhered to, many of our questions come to be "without meaning," for it is plain that concerning many of these questions we cannot "find operations by which one answer may be given." [22] This is true, for example, of such questions as "whether a star is at rest or not," and "whether the absolute scale of magnitude may be changing, but in such a way as to affect all things equally." [23] We inquire without meaning when we ask: "May space be bounded?" "Are there parts of nature forever beyond our detection?" "Is the sensation which I call blue really the

[15] *Ibid.*, p. 97.
[16] *The Nature of Physical Theory,* chaps. iv-vi; *The Intelligent Individual and Society,* chap. iii.
[17] *Ibid.*, p. 92.
[18] *Ibid.*, p. 20; see also *ibid.*, p. 43.
[19] *The Logic of Modern Physics,* p. 10;

see also *The Intelligent Individual and Society,* pp. 22 f.
[20] *The Nature of Physical Theory,* p. 8.
[21] *The Logic of Modern Physics,* p. 6.
[22] *Ibid.*, p. 28.
[23] *Ibid.*

same as that which my neighbor calls blue?" and "Is a universe possible in which the laws are different?" [24] The meaninglessness that characterizes such questions about matters of fact also infects some questions about logic and mathematics, such as, "May there be missing integers in the series of natural numbers as we know them?" and "Is a universe possible in which $2 + 2 \neq 4$?" [25] Questions relating to such concepts as those of absolute time and freedom of the will are unspecifiable in terms of physical operations and therefore fundamentally meaningless.[26] Even if one grants that some concepts not specifiable in terms of physical operations have some nonphysical meaning, and indeed involve operations, one would still have to insist that since the operations in question lead back only to other words rather than to actual operations, they are, if not meaningless, at least "footless" and that the operations that are involved are merely verbal.[27]

Although the rejection of some alleged concepts on the ground of their lack of operational interpretability has been perhaps the most debated aspect of Bridgman's operationalism, what Bridgman in *The Logic of Modern Physics* and elsewhere is especially concerned to show regarding meaning is not merely that some commonly accepted concepts and questions are meaningless or even footless but that some concepts that are quite meaningful in some contexts become first vague and then meaningless when transferred to other contexts. Thus, for example, the basic concepts of classical physics, such as those of velocity, time, space, force, mass, and the like, while clear enough in the settings of ordinary large-scale events, lose much of their meaning when applied either to very great velocities, to the universe as a whole, or to subatomic events. This sort of relativity of meaning applies not only to the concepts of physics but also to the more basic ones of logic and mathematics. Thus while the law of the excluded middle is sufficiently applicable to some kinds of cases, it becomes operationally inapplicable, and hence essentially meaningless, with regard to others; [28] and even the principles of identity and enumeration are inapplicable to certain aspects of wave mechanics.[29]

Other writers who adopt an operationalist type of instrumentalism include S. S. Stevens, B. F. Skinner, C. C. Pratt, and (with qualifications) A. C. Benjamin. Stevens holds that while all scientific propositions, including those of psychology, require conceptual frames, such propositions *"have empirical significance* only when their truth can

[24] *Ibid.,* pp. 30 f.
[25] *Ibid.*
[26] See *The Intelligent Individual and Society,* pp. 24, 116 f.
[27] *Ibid.,* pp. 77 ff.
[28] *The Nature of Physical Theory,* chap. iv.
[29] See *ibid.,* chap. viii.

be demonstrated by a set of concrete operations." [30] C. C. Pratt, in his book *The Logic of Modern Psychology* recommends a moderate version of operationalism that instead of either accepting observations at face value or confining itself to operations, "follows the development of concepts from the starting-point of observations," [31] and asks of any observation where, when, and under precisely what conditions it was made. Instead of throwing out all concepts that are not purely operational, such an operationalism accepts such nonoperational concepts as current science may require for purposes of convenience [32] and even retains a limited place in psychology for subjective experiences. Benjamin, while opposing most of the older forms of operationalism as entirely too restrictive to be useful, suggests that operationalism can nevertheless be generalized to become a useful method for determining what concepts may and what may not significantly be admitted into the conceptual frames of scientific thought.[33]

7. COMMENTS CONCERNING INSTRUMENTALISM

Although the sort of instrumentalism initiated by Dewey has, as we have seen, been more or less specifically adopted by a number of able philosophers, the impact of that way of thinking has reached far beyond these philosophers and, in fact, been felt throughout the whole range of contemporary thought. The focal points of the impact of instrumentalism on contemporary epistemological thought are the central emphases of instrumentalism upon the relativity of cognitions to their situations and upon the role of bodily activity in the acquisition of knowledge. A variety of specific instrumentalist suggestions in theory of knowledge are rooted in these central emphases. We shall notice first the contributions involved in the central emphases as such, then those involved in the more specific suggestions, and finally some of the deficiencies of instrumentalist theories.

[30] S. S. Stevens, "Psychology and the Science of Science," *Psychological Bulletin*, XXXVI (1939), 222; see also Stevens, "Psychology: The Propaedeutic Science," *Philosophy of Science*, III (1936), 90–103; Stevens, "The Operational Basis of Psychology," *American Journal of Psychology*, XLVII (1935), 323–30; S. S. Stevens, "The Operational Definition of Psychological Concepts," *Psychological Review*, XLII (1935), 517–27; S. S. Stevens (ed.), *Handbook of Experimental Psychology* (New York: John Wiley & Sons, Inc., 1951); B. F. Skinner, *Behavior of the Organism* (New York: Appleton-Century Co., 1938);

and *Science and Human Behavior* (New York: The Macmillan Co., 1953).

[31] C. C. Pratt, *The Logic of Modern Psychology* (New York: The Macmillan Co., 1939), p. 81.

[32] *Ibid.*, p. 8.

[33] A. C. Benjamin, *Operationalism* (Springfield, Ill.: Charles C. Thomas, 1955); see also Benjamin, "Operationalism—A Critical Evaluation," *Journal of Philosophy*, XLVII (1936), 394–44; and Benjamin, "The Operational Theory of Meaning," *Philosophical Review*, XVI (1937), 644–49.

A. Dewey's emphasis on the relativity of cognition to situations has at least three different facets. The first two concern general biological and social settings, and the third, particular situations.

(*1*) Ever since Aristotle, writers on theory of knowledge have recognized that man was an animal, but they have also been inclined to keep his rationality distinct from his animality and to attribute all or nearly all of his cognition to his rationality. To be sure, a variety of philosophers have drawn some basic biological factors into the analysis of cognition. For example, Hume attributed the supposed necessity of causal inferrence to a kind of instinctively supported custom and habit. Santayana made knowledge of fact dependent on animal faith, and James and Bergson linked ideas with organic needs; but for all three of these writers, the crucial phases of cognition lay not so much in organic responses as in distinctively psychical processes. Similarly, Spencer and Nietzsche both grasped something of the significance of evolutionary process but the work of both of these philosophers lay largely outside the main stream of philosophic thought. Biologists had indeed long interpreted the whole of human activity in evolutionary terms but the leading epistemologists were slow to follow their lead. Dewey and his associates were the first major group of philosophers to place cognitive processes squarely in the midst of the evolutionary struggle and to treat them unequivocally as moments in the ongoing endeavor of intelligent organisms to adapt to dynamic physical and biological settings. In so doing they brought epistemological thought into line with the best insights of biologists and gave to it a new note of practical seriousness.

(*2*) Ever since Aristotle, philosophers have recognized that man is a social animal, but curiously enough when they have come to write of his cognition, they have written almost as though this phase of his life occurred in complete isolation from his social setting, as though each man faced his cognitive situations alone. To be sure, some sociologists and social psychologists have written in another vein, but philosophers have been slow in seeing the point. Dewey and those who have adopted his type of approach to the problems of knowledge have for the first time within the main stream of Western philosophy adequately insisted not only that the cognitive efforts of men are the efforts of social beings to adjust to other social beings but that to such an extent are man's language, concepts, and basic categories formulated in social contexts that he, as it were, carries his social environment with him even when he is alone. In so doing they have in some degree brought epistemology into line with the best insights of sociologists and social psychologists and given it new depth of perspective.

(3) Throughout the history of epistemological thought, philosophers have been inclined to write about knowledge in general and cognitive situations in general as though there were a single kind of knowledge and a single context of knowledge, or at most not more than two or three kinds of knowledge and of cognitive situations. Instrumentalists have, however, properly insisted not only that cognition is relative to biological and social backgrounds in general but that each instance of cognition is relative to its own particular context and that there are multitudes of different contexts each with its own distinctive or even unique features, so that no instance of knowing is properly characterized without reference to its time, place, physical, cultural, and social setting, unique circumstances, and particular intent. In so doing instrumentalists have disclosed more adequately than any of their predecessors the full richness of the variety in man's cognitive efforts.

B. Closely associated with the instrumentalists' emphasis upon situation, and perhaps even more distinctive, is their sound insistence that knowledge of fact always depends upon activity, including bodily activity. Ancient and medieval philosophers had spoken (though in somewhat equivocal fashion) of active intellect, and idealists had stressed the active side of knowing; but the activity in question was always mental rather than physical. Expermentalists in physical science had long been well aware that physical objects must be altered by physical bodies in order to yield the fullest scientific results, but the implications of modern experimental methods were not adequately reflected in what philosophers said about science. It remained for the instrumentalists sufficiently to see the significance of modern scientific experimentalism and to project what they saw into the midst of contemporary philosophical thought about knowledge. What they saw and said not only reflected the actual practice of scientists but also called attention to neglected aspects of common-sense cognition. The man of common sense as well as the scientist employs all manner of manipulations and movements to facilitate his inquiries. Even when there is nothing else to be done he looks, listens, feels, tastes, and smells; and these are not merely mental operations, for one must look with his eyes, hear with his ears, feel with his hands and other parts of his body, taste with his tongue, and smell with his nose. To be sure, one can also remember, reflect, and imagine, but even the products of our knowing in these ways rest back upon apprehensions achieved through activities of the body.

C. Since the intention of instrumentalists is, generally speaking, to disclose the conditions of validity at the levels of common-sense and scientific inquiry, it is to be expected that their most fruitful suggestion in theory of knowledge would concern inquiry at these levels, and this is indeed the case. The first four suggestions of theirs that we shall mention are at these levels. A fifth suggestion, however, is at the level of a type of philosophical inquiry somewhat beyond these levels.

(1) In the light of their sound emphases upon context and experiment, instrumentalists have been able to give due recognition to previously neglected responsibilities of philosophers to elucidate and evaluate the procedures in terms of which people actually endeavor in common-sense and scientific inquiry to justify their judgments of matters of fact. Indeed, instrumentalists go much farther and describe as deplorable "epistemology" any effort on the part of philosophers of knowledge to go beyond the methods of common-sense and scientific inquiry to examine an alleged ultimate validity of knowledge claims. But whether or not this latter more radical position is solid, at least the former more modest one is. Human beings are constantly engaged in knowledge quests of utmost importance to them both practically and theoretically, and the philosopher of knowledge may not justifiably excuse himself from the less adventurous task of careful elucidation and evaluation of these actual inquiries in the interest of a possibly more exciting attempt to lay bare the ultimate foundations of knowledge. The very great importance of the more modest type of philosophical examination of knowledge claims is significantly indicated both by the enormous growth of recent interest in philosophy of science in America and by the emergence in Great Britain of a school of philosophy that elucidates common-sense knowledge claims in terms of ordinary language.

(2) The instrumentalists' insistence upon context and experiment has enabled them to arrive at an interpretation of meaning in terms of operations that can be specifically defined and actually carried through. A legitimate complaint against older accounts of meanings is that they involve implications that either exclude the possibility of confirmation altogether or make complex demands concerning confirmation that are remote from the meanings in question.[1] The force of this objection is obvious in the case of such a view as that of Locke which found in thing-statements a reference to an unknowable substance. But the objection also applies in the case of many more strictly empirical theories including some verifiability theories and even perhaps the verificatibility theory of the empirical pragmatist James, for such theories often require confirmation in terms of "post-analytic" sense-data. The contextual and experimental account of meaning advocated by instrumentalists, especially in its operation-

[1] See esp. A. E. Murphy, "Two Versions of Critical Philosophy."

alist form, avoid these difficulties. No veil of sense hides an inscrutable thing. No precarious attempt to isolate pure sense-data or to carry through dubious reductionist logic is demanded. The plain man, when asked what he means, can reply straightforwardly in terms of what he thinks he and others can do if his statement is true and his concept applicable. The scientist can lay down quite precise descriptions of the operations that must be performable if his concept applies and, what is even more important, he can introduce new concepts whose meaning can be made quite definite from the outset. It is accordingly not surprising that many scientists have enthusiastically embraced the operationalist theory of meaning as indicating just what their clearest concepts do and as containing the promise of the clarification or replacement of their more obscure concepts.

(3) A further significant suggestion growing out of the instrumentalists' insistence upon context and experiment is their recognition of the creative role of conceptual thought as an instrument of cognition at both the common-sense and the scientific levels. Most philosophers of an empirical turn of mind have been disposed to minimize the importance of conceptual thought as somewhat remote from actual facts and most philosophers of a rational turn of mind have been disposed to think of such thought as in favorable circumstances a literal transcript of reality. Even James, who shared many of the same pragmatist presuppositions as the instrumentalists, was disposed to look with suspicion upon conceptual thought and to reject formal logic altogether. The instrumentalists were never tempted to make this sort of mistake. Not only do they recognize the basic importance of concepts and formal systems but they assign to concepts and systems constructive functions far beyond the merely transcriptive ones given to them by rationalists. Concepts are, they rightly contended, the most important tools of cognition, and formal deductive systems are required for maximum facility in passing from one experience to another. No context can be adequately coped with apart from intellectual constructs carried over from previous situations and qualified to meet the needs of present ones, and no activity can be enlightened apart from conceptual frames constructed with creative imagination to meet actual needs. The plain man confronted with novel situations—and every situation is in some degree novel—chooses concepts from an enormous range of concepts embedded in previously achieved systems, and is inventive in the peculiar turns he gives his concepts in order to deal with his special situations. By just such selections and inventions commonly accepted conceptual frames have been achieved and come to be altered. The scientific discoverer not

only uses a wide variety of conceptual tools in old and new ways, but devises new concepts and whole systems of concepts that can by no means be merely abstracted from the facts or constructed as literal transcriptions of these but render facts intelligible and manageable. Such a pragmatic view of the conceptual instruments of science is, through the influence of instrumentalists and others, coming increasingly to be a part of a widely accepted tradition both in philosophy of science and in philosophy generally.

(4) A fourth significant suggestion concerning the validation of common-sense and scientific cognition growing out of the instrumentalists' emphasis upon context and experimental activity is their introduction of the concept of warranted assertability. On the one hand to assert in the most literal sense that a statement is true is to make no allowance even for excusable mistakes. But on the other hand when all appropriate tests have been made, merely to say that the statement is assertable or credible hardly seems adequate. Both the plain man and the scientist may sometimes need a term to indicate what he has in mind when, having every reason to be confident of what he says, he wishes neither to be held accountable for strict finality in his assertions nor to understate his case. For this important purpose the instrumentalists' term "warranted assertability" is admirably suited. Indeed, the term has already come fairly widely into use for this purpose and may become a significant part of our language. But whether or not it does, the clarification of the concept with its emphasis on probabilism and relevant tests is significantly useful in the interpretation of scientific statements, for such statements at any given stage in scientific development are not put forth as ultimate descriptions of the universe but as statements precise enough for present purposes, and justifiable in the light of the tests that are relevant to those purposes and open to modification and revision in the light of further inquiry.

(5) One significant suggestion concerning theory of knowledge prompted by the instrumentalists' contextualism and experimentalism is concerned, as previously indicated, not so much with the validation of cognition at the level of common sense and science as with a metaphysical phase of theory of knowledge. Generally speaking, instrumentalists have been disposed to condemn inquiries of this latter sort as mere "epistemology" or theory of knowledge in the bad sense. However, their special emphases seem to throw light on at least one problem in this area, and they have not been hesitant to press the metaphysical suggestion involved in this fact. The suggestion in question, present in some degree throughout Dewey's work and explicitly developed in Murphy's objective relativism, is that since

the products of cognitive activity are always achieved as responses of living organisms in natural environments, they cannot be, on the one hand, identical with known objects, as epistemological monists hold, nor on the other hand, outside of or distinct from nature, as epistemological dualists sometimes hold. The products of cognitive activity are rather distinct events *in* nature that may properly serve as representative samples *of* nature. Moreover, this suggestion, which we have previously encountered in the works of Whitehead, whether or not it resolves the issue between epistemological monists and epistemological dualists, is undoubtedly a real contribution to the solution of the problem. It gives due recognition to the facts obscured by epistemological monists of epistemological distance and of the physics and physiology of perception. It also rejects the extreme dualist view that makes the observer an outside spectator endeavoring, as it were, to look in upon nature but forever prevented by a screen of sense. It places cognition squarely within the causal means as caused by natural events and in turn causing such events, and as so much a part of nature as to embrace some aspects of nature within itself.

D. Since instrumentalists have offered their theories principally as interpretation or validation of judgments at the scientific and common-sense levels, it is principally at these levels that their deficiencies as well as their merits should be noted. Three such deficiencies are to be noted here, having to do with the object of knowledge, meaning, and truth.

(*1*) Throughout his writings Dewey has insisted that the object of knowledge is something that does not exist prior to inquiry but is a product of the resolution of the unsatisfactory situation leading to inquiry. The object comes at the end of the process rather than at the beginning. Now, such an account surely stands for a significant fact, for the fully developed object is indeed not there *for the inquirer* at the start, and the *object-as-known* does occur only at the end of the process. But Dewey's way of putting the matter is, to say the least, misleading, for the object or fact that scientific inquiry is about is there at the start and what the inquirer wants to know is what that object or fact was before he intervened, how it would have been apart from his activity, his activity having been injected only to disclose what potentialities were there all the while. Otherwise the findings of the scientist become only a sort of subjectivistic narrative of his own experiments. In the end Dewey seems to acknowledge this when, in reply to Murphy's criticism on this score [2] and apparently unmindful of some things he has written, he denies ever intending to say that

[2] See A. E. Murphy, "Dewey's Epistemology and Metaphysics," in Schilpp, *The Philosophy of John Dewey*, pp. 193–225.

the scientist does not investigate objects prior to his own inquiries.[3]

(2) While the instrumentalists have properly recognized the role of activity in cognition in general and that of an operational element in meaning in particular they have tended often to overplay their hands in these matters. This tendency is of course most pronounced in the writings of operationalists as such but it appears throughout the works of instrumentalists. What must be done in order to verify a statement to be sure is implicit in the meaning of the statement, but simply to equate the meaning of the statement with the operations relevant in its verification, as many operationalists have been inclined to do, is to leave undetermined what is to be tested by operations. Moreover, even as a statement of test conditions, pure operationalism is inadequate; for at least as important as confirmatory operations are the observations that are made in the process of and at the end of the operations. The forms of pragmatism advocated by James and Lewis have adequately recognized this fact. Perhaps some operationalists would be disposed to say that they have taken such observations for granted all the while, but if so, much of the distinctiveness of their operationalism is lost. Changes are of course in progress in operationalist theory, and it seems likely that the eventual form of the theory will be one in which operations themselves will be taken to be only one among a variety of factors involved in determining scientific meanings.

(3) Instrumentalists have not as a rule tried to *equate* truth with warranted assertability or to define the one in terms of the other. What they have often done is to offer the concept of warranted assertability as a substitute notion, which, as it gradually comes into use, will permit the less useful notion of truth, like the state in Marxist theory, to wither away. This program will, however, not do. Even if truth were never attainable the concept of truth would still be required to indicate the target of all cognitive activity, apart from which such activity loses its direction and becomes aimless. Abandonment of the concept of truth would require drastic alteration of the concept of knowledge and of many related concepts in such fashion as to lead to serious confusion. Even the concept of warranted assertability itself can hardly be adequately defined apart from some such concept as that of truth, for what assertions are warranted depends in part upon what the relevant tests are, and that can scarcely be determined apart from reference to truth objectives of cognitive activity.

E. Although instrumentalist accounts of knowledge must be criticized primarily in the light of their bearings upon that common-sense

---

[3] Dewey, "Experience, Knowledge, and Value," in *ibid.*, pp. 556 ff.

and scientific inquiry upon which they are focused, criticism in the light of their bearings upon more distinctively philosophical issues cannot be entirely ignored. For one thing, instrumentalists themselves have not been content to let such problems alone, and for another thing such questions cannot be considered to be unimportant. Serious deficiencies of instrumentalist theories in this larger setting include the following:

(1) The troublesome problem of sense-data cannot be gotten rid of, as most instrumentalists seem to think, simply by insisting that philosophical inquiry begins as common sense begins with observations of physical objects and operations. If philosophical inquiry begins with observations and overt operations, it cannot be content to stop with them. Sometimes, as in the case of the painter or the physician seeking to interpret symptoms or the bewildered drinker or sleepwalker seeking to determine whether or not he is sober or awake, we need even for practical purposes to go behind observations to note the order of a sensory given. At other times, as in the case of the philosopher who wants to understand, we cannot but inquire for theoretical purposes what, if anything, lies behind and supports our observations. Indeed it is somewhat surprising that philosophers of such critical spirit as instrumentalists should be ready to cut inquiry short at the point of observation of external fact and not wish to consider possible data of more elemental kinds. Even if the sensory given turns out, as is scarcely likely to be the case, to be always "post-analytic," it still may occupy a place of considerable importance in the order of the eventual justification of cognitive claims.

(2) Although instrumentalists have a great deal to say about the logic of inquiry and in their later works recognize the legitimacy of formal systems of logic and mathematics, they have curiously little to say about the internal character and validity of formal systems. One cannot but feel that this is because formal systems, unlike more directly practical concepts, are somewhat alien to the general tenor of their thought and are only recognized somewhat reluctantly and tardily in response to current philosophical trends. In any case the lack of a satisfactory interpretation of formal systems must be regarded as a serious deficiency in most instrumentalists' writings. It is of course true that Morris' work on signs is a significant contribution, but that is fairly recent and isolated as far as instrumentalism is concerned. Moreover, Morris belongs almost as much to the group of physicalistic logical positions as to that of instrumentalists. Perhaps it was in some measure on account of the failure of instrumentalists to take formal systems sufficiently seriously that philosophical leadership passed quickly from them for a time to logical positivists.

(3) Valuable as is the instrumentalists' application of the notion of man's involvement in nature to the issue between epistemological monisms and epistemological dualism, neither that hint nor anything else in objective relativism even approximates a resolution of this issue. One may indeed and must cheerfully acknowledge that human cognitions are genuine samples of nature, but the crucial question still remains, whether such cognitions are at all adequately representative either of nature as a whole or of the parts of it that especially interest us. Moreover, being primarily prospective rather than retrospective in outlook, instrumentalists can scarcely rely, as Whitehead who advances the same suggestion can, upon the tracing back of vectoral lines. Instead, objective relationists, especially in Dewey's *Experience and Nature* and in some of Murphy's writings, offer the much bolder suggestion that after all in a broad sense nature just *is* experience, and experience, nature. But this sort of suggestion depends upon well-known ambiguities in the word experience and reintroduces confessions repeatedly encountered in various forms of idealism.

CHAPTER 12

Conceptual Pragmatism

As we have now had occasion to see, James placed his major emphasis upon the role of immediate experiences in knowing, and Dewey placed his major emphasis upon conceptual reconstruction. Neither writer was always able to avoid confusion between these two aspects of knowing. There is, however, a kind of pragmatism which draws a sharper distinction than did either James or Dewey between immediate experience and concepts and, while recognizing the importance of immediate experience, confines its specifically pragmatist doctrine largely to the general orientation of the knowing process and the conceptual aspects of that process. The principal proponent of this sort of pragmatism is C. I. Lewis (b. 1883), who refers to his own manner of thinking as "conceptual pragmatism."

A student under the idealist Royce, the realist Perry, and the pragmatist James, and steeped in the thought of Kant and Peirce, Lewis has achieved his philosophical development in intimate contact with the major trends of the epistemological thought of the first quarter of the century. Himself one of the principal contributors to the growth of modern symbolic logic and, without being a positivist, one of the important influences upon many logical positivists, Lewis has also been directly involved in the development of some principal trends bearing upon epistemological questions in the second quarter of the century. Beginning with a pragmatism closer perhaps to the thought of Peirce than to that of any other writer, Lewis has worked out a brand of pragmatism that is clearer and more rigorous than any previously developed.

1. LEWIS' CONCEPTION OF THE GENERAL ORIENTATION OF KNOWLEDGE

Lewis is quite as strongly convinced as either James or Dewey that knowing has its origin and retains its general orientation in the demands of man's practical experience. "Thought is continuous with action,"[1] and were it not that man must act he would not have begun to think. A "cognitively guided behavior is merely the farthest reach of adaptive response"; and "without this function of appropriate guidance of action, our complex modes of knowledge would not have come to be."[2] Thus "knowledge is pragmatic, utilitarian, and its value, like that of the activity it immediately subserves is extrinsic."[3] The function of knowledge is such prediction of future experiences as facilitates the control of these experiences for the attainment of what is valued. "To know is to apprehend the future as qualified by values which action may realize," and "the utility of knowledge lies in the control it gives us, through appropriate action, over the quality of our future experience."[4]

This conception of the essentially practical function of knowledge is of course reflected in the way in which the term "knowledge" is used. Good usage demands of that which is called knowledge that it be true, significant of something beyond the cognitive experience itself, grounded upon reasons, and certain. Unfortunately all these characteristics can scarcely be realized simultaneously, so that in fact not one but perhaps several varieties of knowledge must be recognized.[5] At least three major kinds of apprehensions have been placed by philosophers among such varieties, namely, immediate experiences, analytic judgments, and empirical judgments of matters of fact. Immediate experiences yield certainty but, having no grounds or reasons and being incapable of falsity and therefore also of truth, they are not really appropriately regarded as knowledge at all. Analytic judgments are essentially certain, may have sufficient grounds, and are capable of being either correct or incorrect; but "they can scarcely be said to mean or point to anything beyond and independent of the cognitive experience itself," and are therefore to be regarded as knowledge in only a qualified sense.[6] Empirical judgments of matters of fact are lacking in certainty but have all the other marks of knowl-

---

[1] C. I. Lewis, *Mind and the World Order* (New York: Charles Scribner's Sons, 1929), p. 34.
[2] Lewis, *An Analysis of Knowledge and Valuation* (La Salle, Ill.: The Open Court Publishing Co., 1946), p. 12.

[3] *Mind and the World Order,* p. 145.
[4] *An Analysis of Knowledge and Valuation,* p. 4.
[5] *Ibid.,* p. 27.
[6] *An Analysis of Knowledge and Valuation,* p. 29.

edge. Accordingly these judgments, on which our practical decisions are normally based, are the most promising claimants to the term "knowledge."

Although the immediate experiences and analytic judgments that fail fully to satisfy the criteria of knowledge have a certainty that the empirical judgments of matters of fact that are characteristically called knowledge lack, empirical judgments of matters of fact have as their two primary foundations immediate experiences and analytic judgments and are sustained by the certainties in these foundations. Before attempting to characterize empirical knowledge, one must, accordingly, first consider the character of those immediate experiences and analytic judgments in which empirical knowledge is grounded.

2. Lewis' Account of the Immediate Experience

That in immediate experience which constitutes one of the primary foundations of empirical knowledge is what Lewis calls "the given." The given, in contradistinction to all conceptual and interpretative elements in knowing, is immediate and incorrigible. It is neither object nor sensation, nor nerve path, for the idea of each of these presupposes the given and at the same time involves interpretative elements.[1] The given lies within the area of the awareness I should have if, lacking interpretative capacities, "I were an infant or an ignorant savage,"[2] that which "no activity of thought can create or alter."[3] It "remains unaltered, no matter what our interests,"[4] and constitutes the "brute fact element in perception, illusion and dream."[5]

The given is not, however, the whole of that in experience which is immediate and incorrigible, and it should be carefully distinguished from the related aspects of immediate experience. The requisite distinction can best be clarified by reference to an unpublished letter by Lewis to the author (March 28, 1953) in which Lewis located the given in the larger area of what he calls the "found." The found embraces not only the given, but "anything phenomenologically capable of being discovered directly in experience." It includes not only "visual redness" and "tactual hardness," but also "pain or angriness, or feeling of conation," or "my morning feeling of irascibility or euphoria, or my afternoon feeling of letdown-ness," and indeed a virtually infinite variety of direct experiences as yet unassigned either

[1]Cf. *Mind and the World Order*, p. 55.
[2]*Ibid.*, p. 50.
[3]*Ibid.*, p. 53.
[4]*Ibid.*, p. 52.
[5]*Ibid.*, p. 57.

to physical objects, bodily conditions, imagination, memory, or anything else.

To point out the specific criteria that distinguish the given or
presentational from the remainder of the found is by no means easy.
These criteria are not sufficiently suggested by saying that the given
is what is actually sensed, for what is and is not so sensed must be
determined by fallible judgment. Nor, since immediate experiences
of kinds used in cognitive reference sometimes occur without being
sensed at all, can the criteria of the given be indicated in terms of
the use that is actually made of the found. The only satisfactory
basis of the needed distinction is in fact the phenomenological one
which describes the given as "the sort of found item likely to be
assigned cognitive significance." Thus the given is "that which
directly exhibits the phenomenological qualities usually accepted as
sanctioning objective reference, marking those experiences to which
cognitive significance is normally assigned." This definition, of
course, leaves entirely open the question whether or not this assignment, or any resulting empirical judgment, is in any particular instance correct.

Although the given is an "identifiable constituent" in every instance of empirical knowledge, it is not "to be discovered in isolation," but "is admittedly an excised element or abstraction." [6] Since
it is a basic constituent of apprehension of physical objects, the given
may be said to consist of "sense-data"; but if such language is used,
the suppositions sometimes connected with such language, that sense-
data necessarily depend on the senses and that sense-data can contain
elements not directly presented should be avoided.[7] Since it presents
itself in qualitative terms, the given may also be said to consist of
presentations of qualia or essences, but this must not lead to an
identification of the given with qualia, or essences, as such. Unlike
the properties denoted by concepts, which always have a time span
and can never be given all at once, the qualia intuitively presented
in instances of the given are immediately present, repeatable, and
"recognizable from one to another experience." [8] Accordingly they
constitute something like universals.[9] A presentation of qualia, in
which an instance of the given consists, is neither named, enduring,
nor repeatable, but is a "unique event." [10]

Every attempt to arrive at a precise verbal formulation of the
given is foredoomed to failure, for the given being immediate is
"ineffable." [11] The best we can do by way of conveying the impression

[6] *Ibid.*, p. 66.   [9] *Ibid.*
[7] *Ibid.*, p. 61.   [10] *Ibid.*, pp. 60 f., 121 f.
[8] *Ibid.*, p. 60.   [11] *Ibid.*, p. 53.

of a given is to qualify an object-statement regarding that to which the given in question would normally refer, by using such terms as "looks like" "sounds like," etc. Thus, in attempting to express what is given when one sees a familiar flight of steps, one might say, "I see what *looks like* granite steps." [12] But even such an expressive statement as this leaves out much of the richness of the detail of the given and imposes upon the rest categorical distinctions that are alien to it. Indeed, every attempt to express the given "imports concepts which are *not* given." [13] Nevertheless, the given, like the found of which it is a part, remains "incorrigible and indubitable." [14] It remains unaltered, no matter how we think or conceive.[15] "Subtract, in what we say that we see, or hear, or otherwise learn from direct experience, *all that conceivably could be mistaken;* the remainder is the given content of the experience inducing this belief." [16] Insofar as statements purporting to express the given are correctly formulated and understood, the only doubt that can arise concerning them is whether or not the person who makes them is telling the truth.[17] Apart from the indubitability of the given, empirical knowledge vanishes in an indefinite regress of probabilities and becomes in fact quite impossible.[18]

3. Lewis' Conception of Meaning and Analytic Judgments

The second of the two foundations on which empirical knowledge rests consists, as has been indicated, of analytic judgments. Problems concerning such judgments are intimately interwoven with problems concerning meaning, and the solution of the former must be preceded by consideration of the latter.

While the question of the nature of meaning was of vital importance to James, even James's fellow pragmatist, Dewey, felt obliged to complain that James had failed to make explicit the distinctions between meanings of things, meanings of ideas, and meanings of truth. Dewey is more careful than James, but on the whole tends himself to remain somewhat hazy concerning the precise character of the various types of meaning. Lewis, however, building upon the work of earlier pragmatists and oriented to recent analytic trends in

[12] *An Analysis of Knowledge and Valuation,* p. 179.
[13] *Mind and the World Order,* p. 62.
[14] Lewis, "The Given Element in Empirical Knowledge," *Philosophical Review,* LXI (1952), 168–75.

[15] *Ibid.,* p. 52.
[16] *An Analysis of Knowledge and Valuation,* pp. 182 f.
[17] *Ibid.,* p. 179.
[18] *Ibid.,* pp. 185 ff.; "The Given Element in Empirical Knowledge," p. 169.

philosophy, has carried through a meticulously careful analysis of the varieties of meaning.

Meaning is prior to language and is to be found wherever one thing is sign of something else. It takes on linguistic forms when people come to depend for survival on "cooperation with others." [1] A linguistic symbol involves (1) a mark or sound, (2) "a recognizable pattern of marks or sounds used for purposes of expression and communication," (3) "a word or expression" including both symbol and meaning and (4) "the meaning which is expressed." [2] Meanings may apply either to terms, propositional functions and/or propositions. Primarily it is terms which mean, and, contrary to a common view, every term in an intelligible proposition must have a meaning.[3] The meanings with which knowing is most directly concerned are those of propositions. Every term, propositional function, or proposition has a meaning in each of four distinct modes.

Lewis' definitions of the modes of meaning of terms are as follows: (1) "The *denotation* of a term is the class of all actual things to which the term applies. (2) The *comprehension* of a term is the classification of all possible or consistently thinkable things to which the term would be correctly applicable. (3) The *signification* of a term is that property in things the presence of which indicates that the term correctly applies and the absence of which indicates that it does not apply. (4) Formally considered, the *intension* of a term is to be identified with the conjunction of all other terms each of which must be applicable to anything to which the given term would be correctly applicable." [4]

The corresponding definitions of the modes of meaning of propositions are these: (1) The *denotation* or "extension" of a proposition is "a class of one—the actual world—in case it is true, and is an empty class in case it is false." [5] (2) "A proposition *comprehends* any consistently thinkable world which would incorporate the state of affairs it signifies." [6] (3) The *signification* of a proposition is "the state of affairs referred to." [7] (4) "The *intension* of a proposition comprises whatever the proposition entails," or "whatever must be true of any possible world in order that this proposition should be true of or apply to it." [8]

It is primarily upon the intensional mode of meaning that the analytic judgments forming the framework of empirical knowledge

[1] *An Analysis of Knowledge and Valuation*, p. 72.
[2] *Ibid.*, pp. 73 f.
[3] *Ibid.*, p. 79.
[4] C. I. Lewis, *An Analysis of Knowledge and Valuation* (LaSalle, Ill.: Open Court Publishing Co., 1946), p. 39. Reproduced by permission of the publishers.
[5] *Ibid.*, p. 57.
[6] *Ibid.*
[7] *Ibid.*, p. 51.
[8] *Ibid.*, pp. 55 f.

depends, but this mode of meaning involves contrasting linguistic and nonlinguistic varieties and accordingly requires further refinement. "The linguistic meaning of an expression is the intension of it as that property which is common to all expressions which could be substituted for the one in question without altering the truth or falsity of any statement, or altering the signification of any other context in which this expression in question should be constituent." [9] This linguistic variety of intensional meaning can in itself yield nothing of any considerable importance, for one could learn all that is involved in verbal expressions, all that is in any dictionary and vastly more, without having the least idea how to apply anything that he had learned.[10] The nonlinguistic variety of the intensional meaning of an expression referred to as "sense meaning" in contrast to "verbal meaning" may be defined as a *"criterion* in mind, by reference to which one is able to apply or refuse to apply the expression in question in the case of presented, or imagined, things or situations." [11] Such meaning often involves, but is not confined to, imagery. It consists of that which is before the mind to determine the applicability of a concept and, when precise, is "a scheme, a rule or prescribed routine and an imagined result of it which will determine the applicability of the expressions in question." [12] In this connection one may note in passing that while sense meaning involves, as Bridgman suggested for scientific concepts, specific operations, it also involves imagined sensory results, else the meaning would remain inapplicable to actual experience.

By reference to that aspect of the intensional mode of meaning which consists of sense meaning or criteria in mind, it is possible to indicate the ground of the essential certainty of analytic judgments in general, and of those in particular on which empirical knowledge rests. Basically the traditional doctrine that the truth of analytic judgments is determined solely by the meanings of such judgments is essentially sound, but it needs some further refinement.

Examination of the intensions and comprehensions of various expressions reveals that meanings in either mode may range in value all the way from zero to universality and that meanings in the two modes vary inversely to one another, as meanings in intension and extension are often supposed to do but in fact do not. Thus, for example, the term "round square" has zero comprehension and universal intension, and conversely the term "being" has universal comprehension and zero intension. This inverse variation suggests that analytic propositions, being basically dependent on their meanings

[9] *Ibid.*, p. 132.
[10] Cf. *ibid.*
[11] *Ibid.*, p. 133.
[12] *Ibid.*, p. 134.

alone, may properly be taken to be those having zero intension and universal comprehension. Thus, "an analytic proposition is one which would apply to or hold of every possible world; one, therefore, whose comprehension is universal, and correlatively, one which has zero intension." [13] By the same token "a self-contradictory or self-inconsistent proposition is one which has zero comprehension, and could apply to or hold of no world which is consistently thinkable." [14] Synthetic propositions lie of course between analytic ones and self-contradictory ones, having intensions and comprehensions that are neither zero nor universal.

The fact that analytic propositions have zero intensions and accordingly place no limits upon any thinkable world is the essential ground of their certitude. Their truth, being independent of all the contingencies of fact or experience, can never be refuted by any experience and continues to hold no matter what.[15] The analytic and the a priori are thus identical [16] and indubitable. However, while recognition of the zero intension of analytic propositions sustains the certainty of such propositions, it fails in at least two respects to afford an adequate account of such propositions. First, since it shows all analytic statements to be alike in intension, it can scarcely explain how analytic statements can differ from one another, as they obviously do. And second, since it refers only to intensions and says nothing further about kinds of propositions, it is of little help in determining what propositions are in fact analytic.[17] Both of these considerations demand the recognition of a more specific kind of meaning for propositions having zero intension.

The requisite kind of meaning may be distinguished by attending to the intensional meaning of the *terms* constituting an analytic proposition and the order in which these terms occur, and the resulting species of intensional meaning may be appropriately referred to as "analytic meaning." Thus the analytic meaning of propositions may be said to be "their meaning as complex expressions whose intension is constituted by the intensional meaning of their constituents and the syntactic order of these." [18] The discrimination of such a species of meaning avoids the paradoxical supposition that all analytic propositions are the same in intensional meaning. Accordingly, instead of having paradoxically to say that two such analytic statements as "iron is a heavy metal" and "2 + 2 = 4," being alike in having zero intension, simply have the same meaning; we can now

---

[13] *Ibid.*, p. 57.
[14] *Ibid.*
[15] Cf. *ibid.*, pp. 29, 57, 93; and *Mind and the World Order*, pp. 217 f.

[16] *An Analysis of Knowledge and Valuation*, p. 35.
[17] *Ibid.*, p. 155.
[18] *Ibid.*, p. 85.

point out that the analytic meanings of these statements are quite different. The discrimination of analytic meaning also yields a criterion, and the only satisfactory criterion, for the determination of whether or not a proposition is analytic; for by consideration of the intensions of the terms involved and their order, experiments in thought are now possible to determine whether or not a proposition holds independently of the nature of the facts of the world.

That the truth and analytic meanings of analytic propositions depend respectively upon the zero intentionality and the order and meanings of the terms of these propositions implies that statements expressing analytic propositions involve conventional elements but by no means justifies the suggestion sometimes offered that such statements are purely conventional. So long as relations among symbols are undetermined, one may attach to any intentional meaning any symbol one pleases. And so long as relations between symbols and meanings are undetermined, one may set up any relations one chooses among symbols. But, because of the restrictions involved in the relations of meanings to one another, once relations among symbols are determined, symbols can no longer be arbitrarily assigned to meanings. For the same reason, once symbols have been assigned to meanings, relations among symbols can no longer be arbitrarily arranged.[19] Accordingly, some statements come to be analytically true and others false in a sense that, though involving conventions, is basically nonconventional.

Among the various kinds of propositions whose truth depends solely on the meanings of the expression involved, one of the most important is made up of the principles of logic, on the basis of which inference proceeds. For the most part these are broad principles that "everybody knows upon reflection," and much of the rest that goes by the name of logic is only "logomachy." [20] Some philosophers suppose that logic can be grounded solely in the character and rules of linguistic signs; but while logic can, of course, substitute variables for nonlogical terms, the truth of the propositions of logic continues to be dependent upon the meanings of such *logical* terms as "all," "some," "if then," "and," "or," and the like. The apprehension of logical truths, like that of all other analytic truths, is attributable in the end to thought experiments concerning nonlinguistic meanings.[21] Precisely what concepts are selected as basic in logic and what sort of corresponding logical system is adopted is

19 *Ibid.*, pp. 107 ff.
20 *Ibid.*, p. 36 n.
21 Cf. Lewis, "Some Suggestions Concerning Metaphysics of Logic," in Sidney

Hook, *American Philosophers at Work* (New York: Criterion Books, Inc., 1956), pp. 93–105.

partly a matter of choice to be pragmatically settled by reference to the demands of inference, but once logical concepts are chosen, the associated logical propositions are intensional and depend upon relations of meanings involved.[22] Indeed, since the intensional meaning of any proposition includes all that is implied in the proposition, the logic which helps to unfold the meaning is already in this sense a part of what is meant, and logic may accordingly be thought of as "a heuristic device for ameliorating our universal human stupidity." [23]

Analytic propositions include, in addition to logic, all the truths of mathematics, which Whitehead and Russell have undertaken to show to be extensions of those of logic. They include also all manner of explicative statements that are neither logic nor mathematics, such statements, for example, as "All birds are bipeds," "If an eagle is a bird then an eagle is a biped," [24] "Monday follows Sunday," and numerous statements explicating the meanings of moral and esthetic concepts.

The class of analytic propositions that is most relevant in the attainment of empirical knowledge consists of propositions revealing the meanings of statements referring to matters of empirical fact, especially those referring to physical objects. About statements of this kind much more remains to be said.

4. Lewis' Conception of the Meaning and Confirmation of Empirical Judgments

When the general character of the given and of analytic judgments has been clarified, two major problems remain with reference to objective empirical knowledge of physical objects. One concerns the specific meaning or conceptual analysis of statements formulating such knowledge. The other is the problem of the verification or confirmation of such statements.

The mode of meaning that is essential to understanding of empirical knowledge is not the denotative or extensional one; for while that mode of meaning is presupposed in our apprehensions of real connections and is sometimes important for emotional reasons, it affords no basis for useful anticipations of future experiences. The essential mode is also not either that of comprehension or that of signification, for the one refers merely to possibilities regardless of exemplifications and the other only to properties regardless of association with terms or expressions.[1] The mode of meaning that is

---

[22] *An Analysis of Knowledge and Valuation*, pp. 111 ff.; cf. also *ibid.*, p. 91.
[23] *Ibid.*, p. 113.
[24] *Ibid.*, pp. 127 f.
[1] *Ibid.*, pp. 39 ff., 133 n.

essential for the understanding of empirical knowledge is rather the intensional one, and the crucial aspect of intensional meaning is not the linguistic one but the conceptual one referred to as "sense meaning" and indicating a criterion in mind or test scheme.

The judgments that are primarily relevant to the understanding of empirical knowledge are synthetic judgments of two different varieties referred to respectively as "terminating" and "nonterminating judgments." The first or terminating variety is made up of judgments having the following pattern, that if, in the presence of a certain sensum *S*, a certain act *A* seems to be performed, a certain sensum *E* will result. Such judgments are fully verified if the appropriate sensory resultant *E* occurs under the specified conditions. They are accordingly appropriately called terminating judgments and since they may be well-grounded and yet are also capable of error prior to verification, they can also be regarded as instances of genuine empirical knowledge though they are scarcely what we characteristically refer to as instances of empirical knowledge. In any case, the usefulness of terminating judgments consists largely in their role in the testing of nonterminating judgments, and it is upon these latter that one's interest tends to focus. Nonterminating judgments include all sorts of judgments of matters of fact about physical objects, from "the simplest assertion of perceived fact—'There is a piece of white paper before me'—to the most impressive of scientific generalizations—'The universe is expanding.' "[2] They are appropriately called nonterminating judgments for the reason that no finite set of observations or terminating judgments can fully verify them or exhaust their meaning.

In terms of the distinction between terminating and nonterminating judgments it becomes possible to give a specific account of the sense meaning of empirical judgments about matters of objective fact or physical object judgments. Thus, "the sense meaning of any verifiable statement of objective fact, is exhibitable in some set of terminating judgments each of which is hypothetical in form; it is a judgment that a certain empirical eventuation will ensue if a certain mode of action be adopted."[3] The set of terminating judgments in question will have to include all judgments such that the truth of any one of them would tend further to confirm the object judgment and the falsity of any would tend to disconfirm it; and the range of such judgments is inexhaustible, if not in variety, at any rate in the time span of the possible experiences which they could express. Excluding a qualification subsequently to be indicated, the sense meaning of a judgment about a physical object can be formulated in an

---

[2] *Ibid.,* p. 185. [3] *Ibid.,* p. 211.

analytic judgment to the effect that the original judgment implies that if certain sense-data are present and a certain act is performed, certain sense-data will eventuate. Thus, letting P stand for the judgment about the physical object, S for the data present, A for the act performed, and E for a resulting sensory effect, the sense meaning of a physical object statement may (subject to subsequent correction) be symbolized in the following formulation:

$$\text{"P.} < : S_1 A_1 \to E_1$$
$$\text{P.} < : S_1 A_2 \to E_2$$
$$\text{P.} < : S_2 A_1 \to E_3 \text{"} \, ^4$$

At least three problems come immediately to mind concerning this formulation: that of the character of the primary relation "$<$," that of the character of the secondary relation "$\to$," and that of the manner in which the judgments we make about physical objects come to be such as to involve the meanings that are implied in them.

(*1*) Since an inexhaustible series of terminating judgments has the same meaning as the object statement *P*, one could properly say that the primary relation of the formula under consideration was one of logical equivalence. However, since an inexhaustible series can never be sustained in experience, or even imagined in detail, one may more significantly say that each of the terminating judgments on the right-hand side of the relation is simply a part of what the statement on the left "means." [5] The formula as a whole represents an analytic judgment explicating the intensional meaning of a physical object judgment, and the primary relation is an instance of the relation that Lewis in his symbolic logic called "strict implication." [6] This relation is one such that if the antecedent is true, it would be not only false but inconsistent or unthinkable to say that the consequent is false, one such that from the truth of the antecedent, that of the consequent follows without further reference to empirical fact. Thus, for example, that there is a piece of paper before me means or strictly implies that if I should seem to write upon what seems to be before me, certain marks would appear, that if I should seem to tear what seems to be before me, it would appear torn, and so on.

(*2*) The subordinate relation of the formula, symbolized by "$\to$" and connecting the initial datum and the act with the expected result, is of a rather different kind. On the one hand, it can scarcely be so strong a relation as strict implication, for one does not consider it unthinkable that the expected result should fail to follow and it is

[4] *Ibid.*, pp. 248 f.
[5] *Ibid.*, pp. 208, 236.

[6] Lewis, *Symbolic Logic* (New York: The Century Co., 1932), chap. viii.

not possible to deduce the expected result from the antecedent conditions.[7] On the other hand, it can scarcely be so weak a relation as the material implication developed by Russell and commonly found in current textbooks of logic; for one intends to say more than that the truth of the antecedent is not in fact followed by the falsity of the consequent, and one would surely not want to say that the falsity of the antecedent invariably assured the truth of a proposition involving the relation.[8] Instances of the relation in question are rather instances of what Hume called "necessary connections of matters of fact." [9] And a proposition based on one of them is often somewhat misleadingly referred to as a "contrary-to-fact-hypothesis." [10] Concerning such propositions, what one should say is not that the antecedent must be untrue but rather that the truth or falsity of the antecedent does not determine that of the proposition.

(3) How do the judgments that we make about physical objects come to be such as to imply or mean the terminating judgments that explicate them? In the light of what has been said about meaning, the answer might seem to be simply that the terminating judgments in question are implicit in physical object statements by virtue of the connections of meanings involved, and indeed these terminating judgments are so implicit. This, however, does not entirely solve the problem, for not only implications of meaning but also initial choices of concept and propositions are involved. The range of possible concepts and propositions is virtually infinite, and concepts and propositions might have been chosen which had little connection with experience and little chance of being confirmed. Our actual choices of physical object concepts and propositions are so guided by past experience that we select such concepts and propositions as can imply terminating judgments likely to be exemplified or, at any rate, capable of being exemplified.[11] Not only is our selection of concepts and propositions so made as to conform in general to experience, it is also so shaped as to direct attention to those aspects of reality that have some prospect of being useful for the direction of action. Thus, without in any way necessarily distorting reality, we choose our concepts and propositions at least partly upon the basis of pragmatic considerations, and "the classification of phenomena and the discovery of law . . . grow up together." [12]

In the light of the foregoing comments on the meaning of physical object judgments and on the structure of the analytic judgments that explicate such judgments, it is now possible to indicate just how the

[7] Cf. *ibid.*, pp. 212 f.
[8] Cf. *ibid.*, pp. 213 ff.
[9] *Ibid.*, p. 212.
[10] Cf. *ibid.*, p. 220.
[11] Cf. *ibid.*, p. 236.
[12] *Mind and the World Order*, p. 263.

conjunction of analytic judgments and givens can yield empirical knowledge. The substance of the matter is this: By means of appropriate analytic judgments we explicate the meanings of our pragmatically and experimentally oriented nonterminating empirical judgments in terms of open series of terminating judgments, the fulfillment of which is anticipated. When the given conforms to some of these terminating judgments, our objective empirical judgments are thereby supported in some degree. When the support becomes sufficient to render acceptance of these judgments amply rational, they are said to be known to be true, or at any rate probable.

But what specifically is the character and degree of the support required? Some philosophers are disposed to think that what is required is full verification. Such verification of an objective empirical judgment refers to the full disclosure of the truth of the judgment, "the determination of it as true" [13] through the actual presentation of all that was anticipated in the explication of its meaning. But full verification can scarcely be the degree of support demanded for empirical knowledge. An objective empirical judgment can never attain that degree of support; for such a judgment means or implies an infinite series of terminating judgments, and no series of that kind can ever be completely exemplified. Never does one reach a point at which no further evidence could be relevant to the determination of the truth of an objective empirical judgment.[14] Moreover, if an objective empirical judgment could be completely verified it would not then qualify as empirical *knowledge;* for a judgment that is fully verified lacks that ingredient of anticipation that is essential to empirical knowledge, and any judgment that will be verified in the future will come to lack that essential ingredient.

One might be inclined to suppose that if full verification of an objective empirical judgment is impossible, at any rate full proof of the falsity of such a judgment is possible. The analytic judgments explicating an objective empirical judgment was said to assert the strict implication of a series of terminating judgments, so that if any one of the implied terminating judgments failed, the objective empirical judgment would necessarily fail also. However, examination of the actual process of inquiry shows that inquiry does not always move in this way. Some objective empirical judgments are so strongly believed and so well-grounded that when their implications fail, instead of withdrawing them, one re-examines the situation in search of some other explanation; and this consideration calls for a qualification of the earlier account of objective empirical judgments.

[13] *An Analysis of Knowledge and Valuation,* p. 254.   [14] Cf. *ibid.,* pp. 254 ff.

Thus, if I seem to take two steps and reach out, then I shall seem to feel a doorknob, but if when I have performed the act the sensation expected does not follow, instead of withdrawing the statement that a doorknob was there, I am likely to say that I misjudged the distance or lost the sensation in my hand, or something else of that sort. Accordingly, it seems best to qualify the interpretation of such an objective empirical statement as the one about the knob by saying that the statement implies that if I seem to take two steps and reach out, certain sensations will result if I have judged the distance correctly and my sensations operate normally and so on. But since I cannot possibly cover all the conditions for correctness and normalcy that might be relevant, I had better add a probability clause to the interpretation, saying that the original statement means that if certain acts seem to be performed under certain circumstances, certain sensations will "in all probability" follow. Thus, the earlier general account of objective empirical judgments must now be qualified to indicate that such judgments imply that if certain acts seem to be performed in certain sensory circumstances, certain sensations will in all probability follow.[15]

Since neither full verification nor full falsification of empirical judgments of matters of fact is possible, the process by which such judgments receive sufficient support to be regarded as knowledge is more appropriately referred to as one of "confirmation" than as one of "verification." The confirmation of an objective empirical belief is a *partial* verification that sufficiently warrants the maintenance of the belief; it is the justification of the belief or "the determination of it as rationally credible."[16] Such justification has various degrees, is marked by no hard and fast line between what does and what does not constitute knowledge, and is never complete.

The incompleteness of the justification even of beliefs properly said to constitute knowledge involves the difficulty of implying that one may know what is in fact false, but this difficulty is not solved by saying—as is obviously not the case—that what one knows is a mere mathematical probability formula. Hence it seems best to embrace the difficulty and continue to say that what one knows is a physical object even though his knowing is no more than confirmed belief, "justified belief, warranted belief, rational belief,"[17] or probable belief. So long as one knows what he is doing no serious confusion need result from this manner of speaking.

Although the probabilities involved in the confirmatory process may be defined in terms of an exact set of a priori principles, the

[15] *An Analysis of Knowledge and Valuation*, pp. 236 ff.

[16] *Ibid.*, p. 254.

[17] *Ibid.*, p. 323.

probabilities actually arrived at in empirical confirmation can never be formulated with mathematical precision. They must remain approximations dependent upon rough estimates and pragmatically determined selections of reference and quaesitum classes.[18]

Every given that exemplifies one of the terminating judgments involved in the meaning of an objective empirical judgment contributes at least a little in its own right to the confirmation or probability of that empirical judgment. The degree of its contribution depends upon the degree of the improbability of the original judgment in case the given anticipated in the terminating judgment fails to occur.[19] Accordingly, in addition to its own direct contribution to the knowability of the objective judgment, each sustaining of any of the terminating judgments involved helps to render all the other terminating judgments initially more probable by rendering the objective judgment itself more probable; and so each may contribute to the total confirmation far more than its place in the series of terminating judgments would suggest. Moreover, just as the convergence of the testimony of several independent but not very reliable witnesses may build a far stronger case than that of any one of the witnesses could sustain, so the congruence of the exemplifications of a number of terminating judgments interdependently implied by an objective empirical judgment may facilitate far stronger confirmation of that judgment than could any single piece of evidence.[20]

Since knowing involves probability one might be disposed to think that the base could have somewhat less certainty than the given or that the given itself might be uncertain. However, that the given on which the knowing process is based is certain has already been seen, and that nothing less than the certainty of the given will do becomes apparent upon reflection. If one says that the given is only probable, he is then called upon to furnish grounds for this probability, and if these grounds themselves are not indubitable givens but only further probabilities, then further grounds must be furnished and so on until all appreciable probability is lost in infinite regress of probabilities of probabilities.[21] In this insistence upon an indubitable given, Lewis goes far beyond the claims of his fellow pragmatists Dewey and Bridgman and probably beyond those of James. Lewis is in this connection specifically critical of operationalism, which, he thinks, properly insists upon the operational character of concepts but does not sufficiently recognize the immediately experiential character of the criteria of their applicability.[22] For similar reasons Lewis

[18] *Ibid.*, p. 237; chap. x.
[19] *Ibid.*, p. 237.
[20] *Ibid.*, p. 239.

[21] *Ibid.*, pp. 332 f.
[22] *Ibid.*, pp. 195 ff., 242 ff.

rejects that current "physicalism" which endeavors to translate all statements into the language of physical objects and fails to give adequate attention to the immediate experiential base of physical object statements themselves.

Nevertheless it must be acknowledged, Lewis thinks, that the material directly supplied by the given is not sufficient to fill in what is required by the sense meaning of objective empirical judgments. Also demanded are memories, belief in general reliability of memory, and a principle of induction. Past givens are at best only represented by present ones, but the confirmatory process cannot proceed without past givens as represented in memory. Apart from past remembered givens the generalizations represented in the terminating judgments that interpret our objective empirical judgments would never be thought of; and even if they were, they could never be confirmed. The present occurrence of a given only confirms the fact that the generalization holds in the present instance, and it could never do more than that save for its association with memories. Indeed, apart from a general reliability of memory, "the question of the past" could probably never have arisen at all.

The inductive principle required for objective empirical knowledge is closely related to the reliability of memory, for it assumes a relevance of past experience in the future.[23] The principle is that "the incidence of any property in a well-defined class, as found for a sufficiently large number of past observed cases, will be approximately indicative of the incidence of that property amongst instances of that class in general." [24] The grounds for insisting upon the presupposition of such a principle are similar to those for insisting upon the reliability of memory, namely that apart from the reliability of induction as well as of memory, we can have no "criterion of the empirically real" and that "to repudiate this belief is to repudiate all thought and action." [25]

The attempt is sometimes made to maintain empirical knowledge without reference to the reliability of memory or induction or, for that matter, of the given, solely on the basis of congruence or coherence; but while congruence may add enormously to the weight of evidence, it can never alone yield empirical knowledge. Whole systems of propositions can be completely coherent without containing a single truth, and unless alleged evidences have at least some initial credibility none can be conferred upon them by their congruence.[26]

23 *Ibid.*, p. 362.   26 See *ibid.*, pp. 338 ff.; see also *Symbolic*
24 *Ibid.*, p. 273.   *Logic*, pp. 335 ff.
25 Cf. *ibid.*, p. 362.

Lewis does not directly discuss at any considerable length the problem of the ultimate character of the objects of knowledge and of their relation to the known, partly because he does not think that much can be significantly said about this problem and partly because he is much more concerned about the structure of the actually encountered process of knowing. What Lewis has had to say that is relevant to the problem appears to carry some phenomenalistic overtones. For example, it is the experimentally given rather than the physical that is epistemologically fundamental. Reality is encountered only in the clothing of conceptual schemes, which, while setting no limits to experience, determine limits of various kinds of reality. And the mode of meaning that is crucial is the intensional one, in which universals play a significant part, rather than the denotative one, in which particularity is crucial.

For such reasons as these, some interpreters of Lewis regard his system as basically phenomenalistic. However, he himself repudiates such an interpretation as an unjustifiable misunderstanding,[27] and there is much in what he has written to suggest fairly substantial realist leanings in his views. Lewis invariably represents the given as quite independent of our thought or interest and insists that coherence yields no knowledge without a given. The connections discovered among givens are, for him, "real connections quite independent of our ideas and continuing to hold regardless of whether or not we ever actually encounter them.[28] It is in terms of our experience of these real connections that we build our concepts, and in doing so we at the same time "establish the actuality of things seen, learn that real objects exist, and apprehend the basic probabilities by which our experienceable world of objects is recognized to exist.[29] Moreover, while the intensional mode is epistemologically basic, it need not be regarded as metaphysically so; in any case the extensional or denotational mode is quite as genuine and refers from the outset to real objects and to an independently existing world.

While Caesar's death means in the intensional mode certain future verifying experiences, no one should be so foolish as to suppose that this, rather than a past "chunk of reality" is what is denoted or referred to.[30] That objective empirical statements are "logically equivalent" to open series of terminating judgments does not imply "identity of things referred to in them." [31] Lewis has sometimes gone so far as to say that he is a "primitive Kantian," being obliged

[27] Cf. Lewis, "A Comment," *The Philosophical Review*, LXIII (1954), 193–96; and *An Analysis of Knowledge and Valuation*, pp. 223 ff.

[28] *Ibid.*, pp. 223 ff., 227 ff., 187 n.
[29] *Ibid.*, p. 236.
[30] *Ibid.*, pp. 197 ff.
[31] *Ibid.*, p. 202.

in some sense to acknowledge some sort of thing-in-itself as "that which" manifests itself in our knowing. But then he continues to insist that he is unable to say anything further about such a thing-in-itself save in terms of those of our experiences that are reliably connected with it.

Although most of what Lewis has written upon the subject of knowledge has dealt with empirical knowledge of physical objects, Lewis has also been very much concerned with valuational knowledge.[32] Indeed there are indications that valuational knowledge is the more vital of the two interests and that what Lewis has had to say about empirical knowledge of physical objects is to a considerable extent preliminary to his account of valuational knowledge. Valuational knowledge is for Lewis a good deal more closely akin to empirical knowledge of physical objects than it is for most recent writers. In fundamental structure these two modes of knowledge are essentially of the same kind. The primary difference is that the data of valuational knowledge lie in a different area of immediate experience than do those of knowledge of objects. Whereas the data of the latter type of knowledge consist of sensory givens those of the former consist of more emotionally toned immediate experiences, and these latter may appropriately be referred to as experience of "satisfaction." Thus, when one says, for example, that a certain object is valuable, his statement is interpretable as predicting that under certain specified conditions certain experiences of satisfaction will occur; and when such experiences do in fact occur, the original valuational statement is in some degree confirmed much in the same manner as an objective empirical judgment is confirmed by the occurrence of certain sensory experiences. Accordingly, although the data are somewhat different, essentially the same sort of validity may be claimed for valuational judgments as for objective empirical ones.

5. COMMENTS CONCERNING THE CONCEPTUAL PRAGMATISM OF C. I. LEWIS

The problem concerning knowledge upon which pragmatist theories of knowledge have for the most part focused is, as we have seen, not either the problem of the nature of knowledge or that of the relation of knower and known, but that of the validation or justification of knowledge claims. In commenting upon the empirical pragmatism of James and the instrumentalist pragmatism of Dewey, we have seen how James, while grounding cognition in sensory givens, fails sufficiently to appreciate the role of concepts and con-

[32] *Ibid.*, Pt. III.

ceptual schemes in knowledge, and how Dewey, while more fully aware of the latter aspect of knowledge, neglects the former. In commenting upon the conceptual pragmatism of Lewis we shall inquire concerning the extent to which Lewis is able so to relate these two aspects of cognition as adequately to represent the basic modes of the justification of knowledge claims. In the light of the manner in which Lewis has approached the issues three topics principally require comment, namely Lewis' view of the given, his account of conceptual schemes and analytic judgments, and his account of the meaning of physical object statements. We shall touch first upon some significant suggestions of Lewis concerning each of these three topics and then upon some apparent deficiencies in Lewis' thought concerning each.

A. (1) As the preceding expositions and comments have indicated, any account of cognition that is to penetrate beneath the surface of what is simply assumed in common sense and scientific inquiry must find a place for some sort of sensory given; but most accounts of such givens have been open to very damaging criticisms. One of the principal merits of Lewis' conceptual pragmatism is that of presenting an account of sensory givens that is at the same time modest enough to be free from most of the criticisms that have undermined most other such accounts and clear enough to be illuminating. Thus Lewis has never claimed for his givens that they were public or physical or quasi-physical or distinguishable prior to analysis or perceived or known or substitutions for knowledge or barriers to knowledge. Yet he has, at any rate in general, supplied sufficient directions to enable one to identify instances of his givens and significant grounds for holding that adequate cognition required such givens. He has moreover linked his givens in interesting fashion with the validation of objective judgments as well as with those feelings in which he finds value judgments rooted.

(2) Although Dewey's appreciation of the role of conceptual schemes in cognition was superior to that of James, his understanding of the character of such schemes and of the analytic judgments involved in them remained, as we have suggested, quite inadequate. A second important achievement of Lewis' conceptual pragmatism consists in combining a balanced insight into the role of conceptual schemes and analytic judgment in cognition with a much more satisfactory account of the origin, foundation, and confirmation of such schemes and judgments than had previously occurred in pragmatist epistemology or perhaps in any other.

In *Mind and the World Order*, Lewis has presented one of the clearest and most convincing formulations yet given of the manner in which we choose our concepts and conceptual schemes. As the development of alternative geometries and even logics, not to speak of systems of scientific laws, has abundantly shown in recent years, one is by no means shut up to any single pattern of concepts and deductive relations; and intelligent inquiry remains free to choose, in the light of the data and of practical considerations, those systems that best suit the purposes of such inquiry. Not only does the scientist make relatively free conceptual choices, but the growth of language itself represents a series of such choices, and even within a given language at a given time groups and individuals continue to exercise such choices. To be sure, the individual does not usually make his major conceptual choices in the moment of problem-solving, for without some prior commitments he cannot even raise questions; but throughout the history of his race and even his own history, conceptual choices have been made and in the light of changing situations will continue to need to be made.

All this Lewis has amply pointed out long in advance of its more common recognition in recent years. But in showing this element of selectivity concerning concepts and conceptual schemes Lewis has not, even in *Mind and the World Order,* lost sight of the aspects of conceptual schemes and analytic judgments that are not subject to volitional selection. In *An Analysis of Knowledge and Valuation* he has, at a time when such an emphasis was much needed to stem a rising tide of excessive conventionalism, stressed the considerations that once the meanings of a deductive system are determined its entailments are no longer a matter of choice; that however free our choices of systems, the entailments within a system rest upon an order that for the most part precludes further choice; and that the grounds of such orders lie in relations among meanings. Apart from some such orders, conceptual schemes would be arbitrary analytic truths, sheer inventions, and that part of the validation of empirical knowledge that depends upon them, unreliable. The whole development of mathematics, modern logic, and a large part of that of the physical sciences strongly sustains the recognition of orders of concepts that are largely fixed when the character of the concepts is determined, and so also does the widespread refusal of philosophers to be satisfied with either purely empirical or purely conventional accounts of mathematics and logic.

Not only does Lewis' account of conceptual schemes and analytic judgments successfully combine the elements of free choice and determinate order recognizable in our actual use of such schemes and judgments, it also suitably calls attention to at least one important way in which the formulation and justification of analytic judgments takes place. When an individual considers two terms and wishes to know whether the applicability of the one entails that of the other, at least one way in which he may proceed is to inquire in an "experiment in thought" whether or not the conditions of the applicability of the one term include or exclude those of the applicability of the other. There is, moreover, ample evidence to support the claim that such experiments in thought repeatedly enter into both the building and the application of conceptual schemes. Indeed, it is difficult to see how in the end even purely logical truths can be arrived at or tested apart from such experiments, for logical truths seem ultimately to rest upon the very same kinds of foundations in relations among meaning as do other analytic truths. The whole matter of meanings and the foundations of analytic judgments will, however, require further comment later on.

(3) Whatever may be the truth about the meanings that one ordinarily attributes to physical object statements, it is apparent that, as an account of meanings that one may plausibly attribute to physical object statements when one is pressed for eventual grounds for affirming such statements, Lewis' interpretation of such statements has much to commend it. Thus, if, having already interpreted a statement attributing a certain property to a physical object in such a way as to be able to confirm the statement by his own and other people's observations, one is asked for a further interpretation that will also confirm the implied observation statements, the only really promising recourse would be an interpretation of the statement in terms of connotative meanings indicating patterns of sensory givens to be anticipated in case the statement was true. The logical relation between the original statement and the indicated patterns of sensory givens would apparently have to be of the order of analytic truth; for it is a relation of inclusion of meaning, and such inclusion seems, as has been previously suggested, to be the root of analytic truth. The analytic truth in question would, however, have to be an implication concerning what givens would probably, rather than certainly, ensue upon a possible sensory situation; for if the anticipated pattern fails, one does not necessarily withdraw the original physical object statement. Formulations of the anticipated sensory patterns presumably have to take some such form as that of the subjunctive conditionals; for, on the one hand, no specific occurrence of any sensory datum is unconditionally entailed by any physical object statement and, on the other hand, the connection between the conditions and the occurrence of the experience cannot be merely one of material implication in which the nonoccurrence of the condition implies anything whatever. Moreover, the set of subjunctive conditionals

relevant to the meaning of any physical object statement seems, as Lewis holds, to be inexhaustible; for it appears to be impossible to place any temporal limit upon the range of the experiences that might prove relevant to the confirmation of any physical object statement. Finally, the attributing of probability to physical object statements only in proportion to the improbability of the implied sensory patterns in case the physical object statements are false and the demand for systematic order among the implied sensory patterns are, as Lewis insists, important features of the kind of interpretation of physical object statements in question; for only in case the sensory experiences implied by the truth of a physical object statement are relatively unlikely to occur either by accident or for reasons unconnected with the physical object statement is the physical object statement appreciably supported by sensory experiences, and only when anticipated sensory patterns acquire considerable complexity do they become sufficiently improbable in case a given physical object statement is false to render that statement plausible.

B. However, despite the suggestive and philosophically significant features of Lewis' accounts of the given, analytic judgments, and the meanings of physical object statements, his accounts of these subjects involve enough deficiencies to remind us that the quest for an adequate philosophical theory of the justification of knowledge claims remains far from complete in the work of the pragmatists.

(1) The sort of account of the given presented in Lewis' writings would seem to require further development along at least four lines. First, the distinction between the given and those feelings and other experiences that constitute the remainder of the found needs to be more sharply drawn. In his published writings Lewis has said very little about this distinction; and while his suggestion that the distinction must be worked out in terms of the phenomenological feel of those experiences that ordinarily enter into the confirmation of empirical judgments may be sound as far as it goes, it has surely as yet not been adequately developed, and serious questions may still arise concerning just what kinds of experiences ought to enter into the confirmation of empirical judgments. Second, the distinction between the given and the interpretative elements that admittedly enter into nearly all of our actual experiences needs to be more sharply drawn. Granted that we never can get our givens pure, if verification is to hinge upon givens, we must at least know how to get them purer than Lewis has thus far shown us how to get them; and, as recent studies in perception reveal, that is a much more difficult task than is likely to be supposed. Third, even if the givens were sharply distinguished from associated factors, the relation of

the given to those statements that purport to express it would require considerable further elucidation. Only through such statements can the given be satisfactorily linked with the physical object statements of science and common sense. But having freely acknowledged that the given is never entirely adequately put into words, Lewis has told us all too little concerning just how the given *is* connected with its verbal expressions. Finally, Lewis' demand for an incorrigible base for empirical knowledge would seem to require some modification; for in view of the difficulty of sharply distinguishing the given, no such base would seem in practice to be quite attainable, and in view of the initial plausibility of statements that approximate the given, no such base would seem to be required. Actually Lewis' own rejection of the need for, or possibility of, mathematical probabilities for empirical statements would seem to suggest the acceptabiilty of something short of complete incorrigibility as a base for knowledge; for provided the statements taken as basic are initially plausible, complete incorrigibility is no longer required when the quest for mathematically exact probabilities is abandoned.

(2) Despite the illuminating character of much that Lewis has said concerning analytic judgments, and apart from other difficulties in his account of such judgments, one must resist the suggestion—if such a suggestion be present in the thought of Lewis—that interpretation in terms of sense meanings and experiments in thought supplies the *only* satisfactory philosophical accounts of such judgments. Numerous extensional interpretations have been attempted and while none have been very successful, some have been illuminating and others may prove more so. Moreover, although the truth of supposedly analytic statements is often tested by "experiments in thought," such experiments are by no means the only tests so employed. For example, if I wish to know whether or not a particular statement by a given individual is analytically true, I may inquire whether or not under any circumstances he would have said anything incompatible with the statement. Even when I wish to make sure whether or not a statement of my own was analytically true, I may attempt to do so by asking what else I would have said under different circumstances. And certainly when one wishes to know whether or not a statement as commonly made in a given language is analytic, one may well seek to find out by inquiring what other things people do or might say. To be sure, such inquiries can be extended to yield criteria of applicability, but sometimes they are used instead to yield rules of language that in turn disclose analytic truth and sometimes they are used to disclose analytic truth more directly. To be sure, Lewis has to some extent recognized the existence of other

approaches than the one he stresses to the vindication of analytic statements, but what he apparently fails adequately to emphasize is the consideration that for the clarification of the logic in use in social communication and in science, inquiries concerning not simply meanings and criteria in mind but what people *say* or might say is of very great importance. This does not exclude the possibility that the analytic statements of common discourse may be subject to philosophical criticism in terms of the very sort of examination of criteria in mind that Lewis advocates, or that the analyticity of which he speaks is of a different and more fundamental kind than the analyticity determined by forms of speech, but it surely does suggest that the examination of forms of speech is at least a necessary preliminary to further philosophical inquiries in the area of analytic truth and an essential guide to modes of expressions of whatever it is that the philosopher uncovers.

(3) If the meaning of physical object statements with which one is concerned is the meaning of such statements that is ordinarily most directly relevant to confirmation in common sense and science, Lewis' account of the meaning of such statements surely misses the mark. Moreover, this ordinary meaning is surely the meaning with which one is most often concerned and its elucidation is, as instrumentalists and ordinary language philosophers repeatedly point out, at least one important part of the job of the philosopher. The ingredients of this meaning are not sensory givens but anticipated observations of things, events, and persons, and their reactions; and only when serious doubts arise do more subtle elements of meaning come into play. Even where grounds for doubt occur, the meaning that is relevant to confirmation usually hinges upon more careful observation and better controlled conditions and not as a rule upon immediate givens. Only under very special circumstances do meanings in terms of anticipated sense-data underlying observations come to be relevant to confirmation.

It is of course with reference to these special situations in which philosophers' questions arise, that Lewis' account of the meaning of physical object statements is especially pertinent. However, even when what is being inquired into is this sort of eventual meaning, it seems doubtful that Lewis' account can be regarded as entirely satisfactory. In the first place, it seems very doubtful that Lewis' account of the mode of meaning most relevant to the confirmation of physical object statements can yield patterns of sense statements logically equivalent to physical object statements. Apart from prior reference to a physical object it is difficult to see how patterns of sense statements relevant to the confirmation of a physical object statement can be selected out and organized.[1] Apart from reference to other physical objects it seems equally difficult adequately to describe the conditions that are to be expected to obtain when required sensory conditions are expected to occur.[2] Moreover, since the subjunctive conditions entailed by physical object statements are only probabilities, the conditions under which the presence or absence of sensory experience demands the withdrawal of a physical object statement must remain vague. In any case, the required chain of confirmation experiences is said to be infinite and is therefore not traversable.

In the second place, even supposing Lewis' account of the mode of meaning of physical object statements in question to be capable of producing the patterns of sense statements equivalent to physical object statements, one would still be compelled to doubt that this account could express adequately what one eventually meant by physical object statements. When, for example, I say that a physical object of a certain sort is before me, I seem at very least to mean that *something* having capacities to produce certain perceptual or sensory effects is before me, and my attempted reference to a particular individual—not to a featureless one but one having the capacities in question—is just as integral a part of my meaning as is my allusion to anticipated sensory effects. Lewis comes at times close to recognizing just this fact, for he has a substantial place in his system for extensional modes of meaning. But his sharp separation of extension and intension, with a vast preponderance of emphasis on the latter, and his notion that the extension of a physical object statement is the whole world and not a particular part of it have obscured the conjunction of reference and sense meaning. What would seem to be needed is an interpretation of physical object statements that not only recognizes both extensional and intensional modes of meaning but holds the two together in such fashion that each illuminates the other and both together conform to our actual meanings and serve as useful guides to confirmation.

Thus, despite substantial progress, the most illuminating of the pragmatist theories has left some crucial problems concerning the validation of knowledge claims unsolved. Whether or not the analytic theories now to be considered have been able to contribute further to the solution of these problems as well as to that of their own special problems we shall presently endeavor to see.

[1] See E. J. Nelson, "The Verification Theory of Meaning," *Philosophical Review*, LXIII (1954) 182–92.

[2] See Roderick Chisholm, "The Problem of Empiricism," *Journal of Philosophy*, XLV (1948), 512–17.

Part V
ANALYTIC THEORIES

CHAPTER 13

Phenomenalistic Analysis

WHEREAS ancient and medieval philosophy concerned themselves primarily with the problem of being and modern philosophy with that of knowledge, recent philosophy has become increasingly preoccupied with the problem of meaning. Thus, insofar as the most recent phase of philosophy concerns itself with the problem of knowledge at all, it approaches the problem primarily neither from the standpoint of inquiry into the relation of the knower and the known nor from that of the justification of hypotheses but from that of the discernment of meanings or the analysis of linguistic expressions. The expressions analyzed are primarily those containing such terms as "know," "believe," "think," "perceive," "understand," "true," "valid," and related terms referring to instances of cognition, and secondarily expressions containing such terms as "table," "chair," "apple," "earth," "above," "around," "eat," "oxidize," and other terms through which representative instances of knowing are formulated.

1. BACKGROUND AND PRINCIPAL BRANCHES OF ANALYTIC PHILOSOPHY

The classical and medieval philosophers and the early modern rationalists all devoted considerable attention to the discernment of meanings, but this enterprise consumed at best only a fraction of the philosophical efforts of these thinkers and in any case was likely to be regarded by them not as a distinct discipline, but as an aspect of discovery of the structure of reality. The British empiricists from Bacon through Mill resolutely undertook the analysis of some linguistic expressions but tended to regard this work as preliminary to philosophy rather than as philosophy proper. Analytic philosophy as it has developed in recent years differs from earlier philosophies involving analysis in regarding inquiry concerning meaning as its main business, in being for the most part anti-metaphysical, and in making substantial use of the techniques of modern logic. In the direct intellectual heritage of recent analytic philosophy are the British empiricists; certain recent continental scientists and interpreters of science including Helmholz, Poincaré, Duhem, Bolzman, Mach, and Einstein; and the leaders of recent logical inquiry including Peano, Hilbert, Schroeder, and especially Frege,[1] Russell, and Whitehead.

The first clear expressions of the contemporary analytic movement are to be found in the early writings of G. E. Moore and Bertrand Russell, which also, as we have had occasion to see, manifested other philosophical interests that were not primarily analytic. Other significant expressions of the movement emerged at the beginning of the third decade of the present century in the thought of the members of a group of Viennese philosophers and scientists commonly referred to as the Vienna Circle. Deeply influenced by the study of continental scientists and by the logical writings of Bertrand Russell and Ludwig Wittgenstein, the members of this circle undertook to show that meaningful expressions could invariably be reduced to either empirical statements or tautologies, though they differed considerably among themselves concerning the character and end products of the reductive process. At first nearly all of them, following Russell, took sentences expressing sensory experiences to be basic, but subsequently most of them came to regard sentences reporting observations of physical objects as basic. Further expressions of analytic philosophy came from the pens of the members of a group of German philosophers and scientists often called the Berlin Group. The thought of most members of this group resembled that of the members of the Vienna Circle, but was in general somewhat less rigid in its requirements for meaningful language and somewhat more favorably disposed toward realist epistemology. Many of the members of both the Vienna Circle and the Berlin Group migrated to America at the time of the rise of the Nazis in Germany. Meanwhile the British analytic movement was placing its emphasis more upon ordinary language

[1] In recent years the influence of Frege's works, at any rate upon British analytic philosophers, has come to be greater than that of Russell. Of Frege's works two volumes have thus far appeared in translation: J. L. Austin (trans.), Frege's *The Foundation of Arithmetic* (2d ed.; Oxford: Basil Blackwell, 1953); and Peter Geach and Max Black (trans.), *Translations from the Philosophical Writings of Gottlob Frege* (Oxford: Basil Blackwell, 1952).

than upon logic, and other analytic movements were beginning to appear elsewhere.

Contemporary analytic philosophies can for our purposes be conveniently classified under four main types referred to respectively as "phenomenalistic analysis," "physicalistic analysis," "pragmatic analysis," and "ordinary-language analysis." The first two types are varieties of "logical positivism" or "logical empiricism." Both varieties of logical positivism take scientific knowledge as the norm of all knowledge, regard empirical statements and tautologies as the only meaningful expressions, and look to artificial languages to correct the ambiguities of ordinary language. The two varieties of logical positivism differ from one another, however, concerning the nature of the basic empirical statements that analysis yields. Phenomenalistic theories, at first advocated by nearly all of the members of the Vienna Circle, take basic empirical statements to be statements expressing sensory experiences. Physicalistic theories, advocated at the outset by several members of the Berlin Group and now advocated by most members of the Vienna Circle as well, take basic empirical statements to be statements expressing observations of physical objects. The third type of theory, pragmatic analysis, which has developed largely in America, while following the other theories in making extensive use of artificial languages, takes no decisive stand on the issue of phenomenalistic versus physicalistic analysis and even abandons the sharp distinction between analytic and synthetic statements. Instead, it places its emphasis upon the relativity of meanings to the practical purpose of particular discourses. The fourth type, ordinary-language analysis, which has developed mostly in England, differs from all of the other recent analytic theories in attempting to steer clear of artificial languages. It also reduces science to the status of one among a variety of significant modes of human inquiry, and focuses attention upon the meaning of ordinary expressions.

In passing, one may note interesting parallels between phenomenalistic analysis, physicalistic analysis, and pragmatic analysis on the one hand and more traditional forms of idealism, realism, and pragmatism on the other. But the analytic philosophies are, as we shall see, very different from their earlier counterparts, and the parallels must not be pressed too far.

2. The Phenomenalistic Analysis of Moritz Schlick

Members of the Vienna Circle, which began to function in the early twenties and was discontinued in the mid-thirties, included among others Philipp Frank, Otto Neurath, Hans Hahn, Gustav Bergmann,

Rudolf Carnap, Kurt Gödel, Friedrich Waismann, and Herbert Feigl. The recognized leader of the group was Moritz Schlick, with whose work we begin our account of logical positivism in general and of phenomenalistic analysis in particular. Although Schlick's systematic work on epistemology, *Allgemeine Erkenntnislehre* (1918), dates from a period prior to his association with the Vienna Circle, it already contains much that came to be characteristic of logical positivism as well as a good deal of discussion of epistemological themes that is of general interest quite apart from logical positivism. The remainder of Schlick's writings belong for the most part to the period of his association with the Vienna Circle and consist mainly of a succession of essays that illuminate basic ideas of the logical positivist movement, and a posthumous book on philosophy of science entitled *Philosophy of Nature*.

Schlick's *Allgemeine Erkenntnislehre* presents among other things the following contentions. Philosophy in general is not a superior science governing the other sciences but an inquiry concerning the general principles of the sciences, and epistemology in particular is not a precondition of the sciences though it may be helpful in interpreting them.[1] Knowing at the level of everyday life is recognition of an object as a certain kind of object.[2] Such knowledge is ordinarily achieved through remembered representations.[3] Scientific judgments link concepts with facts by logical connections that lead back to experiences.[4] The conceptual ties involved are saved from the indefiniteness of immediate experience by being introduced in terms of axiomatic systems designed at the same time to fit the facts and to facilitate deduction.[5] The bonds between concepts are thus purely analytic, and there is no a priori knowledge that is not analytic.[6] We have then so to order the relations of our signs that they correspond unambiguously to the relations of facts though the system adopted does not have to be the only one that could correctly represent the facts.[7] Knowing requires a general reliability of memory as well as a certain unity of experience, but it has no need of "inner perception." Verification of a factual hypothesis is possible, as James saw, in that such an hypothesis together with auxiliary assumptions implies certain consequences, and these in turn imply further consequences until the level of immediate experience is reached. But the inductive process in terms of which such experience confirms the original hypothesis yields no more than a probability supported by habit and

[1] Moritz Schlick, *Allgemeine Erkenntnislehre* (2d ed.; Berlin: Springer-Verlag, 1925), pp. 1–4.
[2] *Ibid.*, p. 6.
[3] *Ibid.*, pp. 14 ff.
[4] *Ibid.*, pp. 19–28.
[5] *Ibid.*, pp. 29 f.
[6] *Ibid.*, pp. 131 ff.
[7] *Ibid.*, pp. 55 ff.

the necessities of practical life. Verification of analytic statements is far more reliable and can be achieved through understanding of meanings without further reference to facts. The criterion of truth is the unambiguous ordering of judgments to facts,[8] and causal law represents a kind of reality independent of knowing mind.

In the essays of the period of his close association with the Vienna Circle and in his posthumous *Philosophy of Nature* Schlick goes beyond his earlier views concerning the function of philosophy to urge in characteristic analytic fashion that whereas the task of science is "pursuit of truth," that of philosophy is "pursuit of meaning." There are no specific "philosophical" problems, but philosophy has the task of finding the meaning of *all* problems and their solutions. It must be defined as the activity of *finding meaning*.[9]

Not only does Schlick adopt the characteristic analytic view of philosophy as quest for meaning, he also wholeheartedly embraces the logical-positivist thesis that meaning is to be equated with verifiability. This thesis he feels, however, must be formulated with care. Some members of the Vienna Circle have written as though meaning were to be equated with actual verification, and they have been properly taken to task by C. I. Lewis on the ground that such a theory would prelude certain clearly meaningful statements, for example about the other side of the moon and about a life after death. Schlick contends that he has never intended to confine meaning to verification but has all along intended to identify the meaningful with that which *can be* verified or the verifiable.[10] Moreover, that which determines the limits of possibility he holds, is not present physical achievability, for no one knows when the boundaries of such achievability may be enlarged. The only limits of verifiability are those set by "logical possibility." Thus, since conditions under which statements about the other side of the moon or about the immortality of the soul could be established can quite readily be conceived, such propositions are genuinely meaningful regardless of their truth or falsity.

In another important essay, entitled "Is There a Factual A Priori," Schlick directs a concerted attack against recent advocates of the synthetic a priori, insisting more emphatically than ever that all a priori statements are analytic and nonfactual. Edmund Husserl and Max Scheler and their followers have supposed that such propositions as "every tone has a determinate pitch" and "a green spot is not also red" are both factual and a priori. However, while all such proposi-

[8] *Ibid.*, pp. 148 ff.
[9] Schlick, "The Future of Philosophy," *College of the Pacific, Publications in Philosophy*, I (1932), 58.
[10] Schlick, "Meaning and Verifications," *Philosophical Review*, XLV (1936), in Feigl and Sellars, *Readings in Analytic Philosophy* (New York: Appleton-Century-Crofts, Inc., 1949), pp. 146–49.

tions can be seen to be a priori, or knowable without specific reference to experience, that they are *factual* cannot be successfully maintained. They are really trivialities determined solely by the rules of the use of the words involved. "Given the meanings of the words, they are *a priori*, but purely formal—tautological, as indeed are all other *a priori* propositions. As expressions which have nothing to say, they bring no knowledge." [11]

When the majority of the members of the Vienna Circle abandoned their appeal to sentences expressing immediate sensory experiences as the ultimate justification of all factual statements and became physicalists, Schlick remained at first unconvinced and in 1934, in the official journal of the Circle, protested against physicalism and defended the phenomenalistic analysis that he himself as well as other members of the group had previously adhered to.[12] In the attempt to secure solid objective foundations for science, physicalism takes as its basic protocols such statements as that N. N. has observed such an object at such and such a time and place. But, protests Schlick, between the object itself and the statement is room for all manner of lies and mistakes. In the end the N. N. must be oneself if the report is to be the most reliable, and even so there remains room for illusions and the possibility of slips between the moment of the actual event and the subsequent moment of the protocol. Whereas the whole purpose of referring to protocols was to gain a starting point that was certain, what is a protocol becomes in physicalism a matter of choice. Defenders of physicalism fall back at this point upon the coherence of protocols with sentences already established in science, regarding those protocols as reliable which demand the least revision of established sentences. But coherence is of no value unless something is already established; there can be whole systems of coherent falsehoods. Besides, truth cannot be established by counting the sentences that need correcting; where sentences are firmly established no such economy principle is needed, and of course, sentences precisely describing immediate experience are difficult to formulate for the reason, among others, that by the time they are formulated the experience has already passed. Nevertheless, what they describe can be the complete fulfillment of predictions about experience, and they themselves come as near as any sentences can to stating what is given and certain. Whatever else may be the case I feel what I feel. Unlike other synthetic sentences, all of which are questionable, sentences

[11] Schlick, "Is There a Factual A Priori," *Wissenachaftlichen Jahresbericht der Philosophischen Gesellschaft an der Universitaet zu Wein fuer das Vereinsjahr 1930/31;* W. S. Sellars (trans.), in Herbert Feigl and W. S. Sellars, *Readings in Philosophical Analysis* (New York: Appleton-Century-Crofts, Inc., 1949), p. 285.

[12] Schlick, *"Uber das Fundament der Erkenntnis,"* Erkenntnis IV (1934), 79–99.

describing immediate experiences are virtually beyond question. Accordingly, it is ultimately upon such sentences as "here and now lines intersect," and "here and now red and blue meet," rather than upon such sentences as "so and so observes such and such [physical object]" that the structure of science must be built.

By 1935 Schlick was willing to acknowledge that physicalistic language represented at any rate one very useful way in which the findings of science might be experienced.[13] Physicalism is capable, he now thinks, of giving a complete picture of the world, and even psychological facts could be expressed in its language. Even so, Schlick's approval of physicalism is cautious and qualified. He emphasizes what Carnap only concedes, that the expressibility of experiential phenomena in physicalistic terminology is simply a fortunate fact of nature and not a necessary characteristic of reality, and he seems to retain the conviction that experiential statements are in the end epistemologically more fundamental than physicalistic ones.[14]

In the light of Schlick's views concerning the character of philosophy, meaning, the a priori, and protocols during the period of his association with the Vienna Circle, it is hardly surprising that in that period his opposition to dogmatic metaphysics became stronger even than in the earlier years, and that even the modest place that he had earlier retained for a qualified realism was now somewhat diminished. No statement can be meaningful, he contends, that is not in principle verifiable in terms of sensory experience, and the a priori offers no avenue of insight into *nonsensible reality*. The business of science is descriptive generalization,[15] and the universe requires no causal "glue" to hold it together.[16] Neither vitalism nor mechanistic determinism can be successfully maintained,[17] and scientific laws are largely matters of successful predictions. Schlick even at times flatly denies that there are any metaphysical questions and affirms in characteristic logical-positivist fashion that all questions are in principle answerable.[18]

Nevertheless Schlick did not on the whole go quite so far as other logical positivists in rejecting metaphysics, and a kind of realism that affirms a stubbornness in facts resisting all the manipulation of our

[13] Schlick, "On the Relations between Psychological and Physical Concepts," *Revue de Synthese*, 1935; W. S. Sellars (trans.), in Feigl and Sellars, *Readings in Analytic Philosophy*, pp. 393–407.

[14] *Ibid.*, pp. 399 ff.

[15] Amethe von Zeppelin (trans.), Schlick's *The Philosophy of Nature* (New York: Philosophical Library, Inc., 1949), pp. 17 ff.

[16] Cf. Schlick, "Causality in Everyday Life," *University of California, Publications in Philosophy*, XV (1932), 522.

[17] Schlick, "A New Philosophy of Experience," *College of the Pacific, Publications in Philosophy*, Vol. I (1932).

[18] Cf. "Causality in Everyday Life," pp. 1920).

conceptual scheme and demanding that such schemes must be oriented to it remains in his writings to the end. In an essay on "Space and Time in Contemporary Physics" [19] written shortly before he came to Vienna, Schlick raises the question whether molecules, electromagnetic fields, and other supposed nonsensible entities referred to in science really exist or are only convenient fictions, and he expresses a clear preference for the former view. While he infrequently qualifies this position and recognizes fully that in "contrast to mechanical theory electroatomism is concerned with basic concepts which are non perceptual . . . of a totally non-pictorial nature," [20] he continues to hold science responsible to encountered fact. Thus, for example, in reply to the charge of a fellow positivist, who leans toward a coherence account of scientific truth, that Schlick is trying to compare facts with sentences, Schlick replies that this is precisely what he is trying to do.[21] Schlick steadfastly resists such conventionalism as he finds, for example, in the physicist Eddington, and holds that the formulas of physics, instead of being purely formal, always imply unspecified rules of application to reality that prevent our free manipulation of them.[22]

3. INITIAL PHENOMENALISTIC ANALYSIS OF RUDOLF CARNAP

Although the view, initially adopted by nearly all members of the Vienna Circle and characteristic of what we have called "phenomenalistic analysis," that all meaningful object statements can be reduced to statements expressing the immediate experiences in terms of which object statements are verified or falsified, was admirably stated and long adhered to by Schlick, Schlick's version of the theory was never fully or systematically developed, and has been thought by some advocates of this view a little extreme. A more moderate and more ample and systematic presentation of the theory by a writer who later abandoned it, is to be found in Rudolf Carnap's *Der Logische Aufbau der Welt*, which was published in 1928 and supplemented in the same year by the same writer's *Scheinprobleme in der Philosophie*.

The central problem of *Der Logische Aufbau der Welt*, and of epistemology generally, is not, Carnap holds, a spurious metaphysical

[19] F. A. Broxe (trans.), Schlick's "Space and Time in Contemporary Physics" (New York: Oxford University Press, (1920).

[20] *The Philosophy of Nature*, p. 119; cf. also pp. 27 ff.

[21] "Facts and Propositions," *Analysis*, II (1935), 65–70.

[22] Herbert Feigl and May Brodbeck (trans.), Schlick's "Are Natural Laws Conventions?" in Feigl and Brodbeck, *Readings in the Philosophy of Science* (New York: Prentice-Hall, Inc., 1953), pp. 181–88; and Schlick, *The Philosophy of Nature*, chap. viii.

problem such as that of the reality of various kinds of objects or that of the conflict of idealism and realism.[1] Nor, despite the fact that epistemology must trace knowing back to its roots, is the central problem the psychological one of indicating chronologically the successive stages in the knowing process.[2] Nor indeed, though epistemology must consider logical implications at every stage, is the principal problem the logical one of the character of the implicative relation.[3] The problem is rather that of setting forth a justifying analysis that, beginning with objects we claim to know, traces back the significance of our statements step by step in such fashion as ultimately to ground these statements securely upon epistemologically elementary factors,[4] as for example my statement about the mind of another person may be traced back through statements about my observation of his behavior and grounded ultimately in statements about my immediate experience. Accordingly, the problem of epistemology involves, on the one hand, an inquiry concerning the character of the relation by which our statements about objects lead back to more elemental statements, and on the other hand, an indication of the principal stages in this process.

The relation with which epistemology is principally concerned is a definitional one in terms of which our complex statements about objects are linked by a chain of definitions with epistemologically elemental statements. At each step an object or type of object is defined, in accord with appropriate rules of translation,[5] in terms of something more basic. For example, fractions can be defined in terms of whole numbers; prime numbers in terms of natural numbers having only one and themselves as parts,[6] and anger in terms of physical reactions.[7] The equivalence involved in the definitions employed is extensional in the sense that two statement fuctions are considered equivalent if the same terms satisfy both,[8] so that the fact that the two parts of the definition are not equivalent in intension is irrelevant. The logical basis for the required chain of extensional definitions has been admirably worked out in the *Principia Mathematica* of Whitehead and Russell.

More, however, is involved in the epistemological relation of leading back to elemental factors than extensional definition, for whereas a definitional chain may lead in either direction [9] one needs a criterion for the epistemologically more fundamental. In general an object is

[1] Rudolf Carnap, *Der Logische Aufbau der Welt* (Berlin-Schlachtensee: Weltkreis-Verlag, 1928), pp. 72, 250.
[2] *Ibid.*, pp. 202 ff.
[3] *Ibid.*, pp. 172, 250.
[4] *Ibid.*

[5] *Ibid.*, p. 143.
[6] *Ibid.*, p. 47.
[7] *Ibid.*, p. 71.
[8] *Ibid.*, pp. 61 f.
[9] *Ibid.*, p. 74.

epistemologically primary in relation to another which is episte-mologically secondary, if the second is known through the mediation of the first.[10] Thus, in terms of a previous example, the bodily reactions of another person are from my point of view epistemologically prior to his anger, although chronologically his anger may be prior to his bodily reactions.[11] More specific tests of epistemological priority may be formulated in terms of levels of justification and freedom from error. A statement by which another statement is justified is episte-mologically more basic than the statement so justified, and a statement that can be seen to be free from errors that remain possible for an equivalent statement is epistemologically more basic than the equivalent statement.[12] Thus, for example, since my statement about another's anger is justified by a statement about his behavior and since the former statement may result from errors that are precluded from the latter, my statement about another's behavior is episte-mologically more basic than the statement about another's anger that is known by it.

What now are the principal stages in the justificatory chain of definitions by which our complex statements are traced back to their epistemological foundations? Or, to begin at the other end: What are the principal stages by which our complex statements are built up or constituted by justifying definitions based on epistemologically elemental materials?

The foundation upon which the whole structure of knowledge must rest is not, as some would suppose, general psychological facts common to all human beings, for the affirmation of such facts must itself rest upon less objective foundations. The basic elements are rather immediate experiences in their individual unity.[13] Although such experiences are subjective they cannot be ruled out as solipsistic or confined within the *I;* for the conception of the *I* is a class concept which arises only at a much later stage, and the experiences in question are "givens" that depend upon no such sophisticated concept. Experiences themselves cannot, however, be taken up into the logical system,[14] so that a relation expressive of them and at the same time suited to the purposes of logic must be discovered. Such a relation is that of memory-similarity, which consists of either identity or close resemblance of remembered elements of experience. Upon this relation, the whole structure of knowledge and of justifying analysis must rest.[15] From this point on, all that is needed is a logical chain of

[10] *Ibid.*
[11] *Ibid.,* sections 51, 52.
[12] Carnap, *Scheinprobleme in der Philosophie* (Berlin-Schlachtensee: Weltkreis-Verlag, 1928), pp. 15 f.
[13] *Der Logische Aufbau der Welt,* p. 91.
[14] *Ibid.,* p. 140.
[15] *Ibid.,* p. 110.

definitions in which each more complex term is introduced by a definition through more elemental terms resting ultimately upon the ground relation of memory similarity, or in which each more complex statement is analyzed in terms of more elemental ones until the ground relation of memory similarity is reached.

On the basic level of experience memory similarities yield the following constructions, each of which is grounded upon the preceding one: circles of qualities, classes of qualities, similarities of qualities, classes of sensations such as visual sensations, the discrimination of individual and general components in experience, visual perspective, order of colors, and temporal order.[16] In this chain of elements of experience, the constructions of visual perspective and temporal succession have already laid the foundation for material objects, for such objects may be constituted by adding color to moving world points. Visual things are definite parts of the resulting visual world though each such thing can be reduced to its more basic experiential elements.[17]

Above the level of statements about the physical world, and ultimately translatable into terms of such statements, is the level of statements about the experiences of other people. Statements on this level are built upon observation of other people's behavior in conjunction with analogies drawn from our own experience, and they are always reducible to statements in physical terms about behavior.

Above the level of statements about other minds, and reducible in turn to such statements, are statements about cultural and social relations. Such statements, like all the others, rest in the end upon statements about immediate experience, and they are accordingly in the end fully definable in terms of statements about immediate experience. Thus physical objects, other minds, and societies are not really objects in the full sense but what may be called "quasi-objects," introduced by definition in order to help us organize our experience. Such an account does not of course describe the manner in which we actually come to think of things, but it does describe the interpretation to which our attempt to achieve a justificatory analysis brings us.

Philosophers have persisted in asking whether or not objects were real in some sense other than the one indicated here, and thus the quarrel between realism, idealism, and phenomenalism has developed. But to be concerned with such spurious problems is to be lost in the mist of metaphysics. To trace a statement about an object back to its experiential roots is all that can be done by way of revealing the meaning of the statement or the reality of the object. This is not to say that every meaningful statement is a verified one, but it is

---

[16] *Ibid.,* pp. 110 ff.   [17] *Ibid.,* pp. 165 ff.

to say that every meaningful statement must be such that some mode of empirical verification is at least thinkable concerning it. The quest for meaning is thus a quest for those definitions which mark out the path of verification, and the quest for reality can have no significance beyond the tracing out of such a path.

4. The Phenomenalistic Analysis of A. J. Ayer

Although the English philosopher A. J. Ayer (b. 1910) was not a member of the Vienna Circle, his first book, *Language, Truth and Logic,* is one of the most clearly formulated and provocative expressions both of logical positivism in general and of the phenomenalistic variety of that movement in particular. In the present section we shall be concerned solely with the relatively pure phenomenalistic logical-positivist thought presented in the original edition of that book and in the main body of the second edition. We shall reserve for later consideration those modifications of this type of thought introduced in Ayer's subsequent work.[1]

The business of philosophy, Ayer contends, is not to compete with empirical science, for the philosopher neither is nor can be in a position to furnish speculative truths which would compete with the hypotheses of science.[2] The attainment of supersensible truth is ruled out, not indeed as Kant thought by limitations of man's rational capacities, but rather by the literal meaninglessness of any such truth.[3] Hence the sole business to which philosophy can significantly give itself is the clarification of meaning. Since all of the propositions of philosophy are accordingly analytic, there is no real reason for quarrels or the existence of schools of thought among philosophers.[4] Most of the problems of meaning connected with common sense have already at one time or another been settled, so that for the most part the task of the philosopher now consists in an enlightened analysis of the basic concepts of science by men trained both in philosophy and in science.[5] That branch of philosophy which purports to disclose the nature and validity of knowledge, so-called "epistemology," is for the most part a false discipline. The philosopher can properly show whether or not one's beliefs are such that "experience can justify

---

[1] Since the main text of the conveniently available second edition of *Language, Truth and Logic* is exactly the same as that of the original edition, the page references in our presentation even of the earliest phase of Ayer's thought will be to the second edition. The references in our presentation of subsequent stages of Ayer's thought will be to the new introduction and the footnotes added in the second edition of *Language, Truth and Logic* and to Ayer's later works.

[2] A. J. Ayer, *Language, Truth and Logic* (2d ed.; London and New York: Victor-Gollancz, Ltd. and Dover Publications, Inc., 1946), pp. 31 f.

[3] *Ibid.,* pp. 34 f.

[4] *Ibid.,* pp. 34, 133 ff.

[5] *Ibid.,* pp. 152 f.

them," but philosophy itself justifies no belief. Scientific beliefs can stand upon their own feet, for "the only sort of justification that is necessary or possible for self-consistent empirical propositions is empirical verification.[6] Moreover, there is no field of experience which cannot, in principle, be brought under some form of scientific law." [7] The primary task of philosophy with reference to knowledge is then not to justify knowledge, but to work out an analysis both of epistemological terms and of those propositions which purport to formulate knowledge. The analysis involved is not mere "empirical study of the linguistic habits or any group of people." [8] It is rather a more fundamental logical "deduction of relations of equivalence from the rules of entailment" involved in the language under consideration. Its method for the most part consists not in furnishing *explicit* definitions such as that "an oculist is an eye doctor," but rather in producing definitions *in use* in which whole sentences are recast in such ways that neither the term to be defined nor any of its synonyms is included in the rephrased version.[9] Thus, for example, following Russell, "the round square cannot exist" is translated "no one thing can be both round and square," and "the author of *Waverley* was Scotch" becomes "One person and one person only, wrote *Waverley*." [10]

If the task of philosophical inquiry is analysis that brings the meanings of factual statements more clearly to light and rules out metaphysics, what is the criterion of meaningfulness in statements that such analysis employs? Leaving out of account for the moment statements of logic and mathematics and other apparently a priori statements, the only plausible criterion of meaningfulness in factual statements is that of verifiability. This need not suggest that every meaningful statement must in fact be verified,[11] or even that a statement be "strongly" verifiable or falsifiable, in the sense of being "established with certainty." Actually many meaningful statements are not sufficiently important to cause one to take the trouble to verify them, and no factual statement can ever be *fully* either verified or falsified.[12] However, if a statement is to be considered factually meaningful it must be verifiable at least in the weak sense that *some* "observations" would be "relevant to the determination of its truth or falsity." [13] More precisely, a factual proposition is meaningful if and only if "some experiential propositions can be deduced from it in conjunction with certain other premises without being deducible from those

[6] *Ibid.*, p. 49.
[7] *Ibid.*, p. 48.
[8] *Ibid.*, p. 70.
[9] *Ibid.*, p. 60.

[10] *Ibid.*, p. 61.
[11] *Ibid.*, p. 36.
[12] *Ibid.*, pp. 37 f.
[13] *Ibid.*, p. 38.

other premises alone." [14] Thus to explicate the meaning of any empirical statement is so to rephrase it by a suitable definition in use that its sensible verifiability is adequately revealed. If this cannot be done the statement is literally nonsense. The required rephrasing need not represent the meaning of the terms involved in the intensional or connotative sense, but should represent the significance of the sentence in the only sense that is important for scientific or common-sense knowledge, namely the denotative or extensional one.

As a matter of fact, the intensional sense of meaning represents mainly a psychological reference to the thoughts of the speaker rather than a logical reference to the implications of his statement. It has accordingly no serious cognitive significance. [15]

Statements a priori, or necessary truths, such as those of logic and mathematics, may seem at first to constitute exceptions to the basic rule that no factual proposition is significant save as it is verifiable in terms of sense experience. This difficulty could be met either by showing that such statements instead of being necessary a priori are really after all only empirical statements subject to the same verifiability test as any other factual statements. This way out was tried by J. S. Mill, who undertook to show that the statements of logic and mathematics were only very reliable factual statements subject to the usual empirical tests. But Mill's effort failed; for in fact no matter what empirical evidence is presented, we always manage to save the truth of logic and mathematics. Thus, for example, if in a given case five pairs of objects did not seem to be equal to ten objects, what we should doubt would not be that $2 \times 5 = 10$, but rather that we had five pairs to start with or that all the original objects and no more were involved throughout the process. [16]

This determination to preserve logic and mathematics at all costs gives us the clue to the correct solution of the problem of a priori necessary truths. Such truths are really not factual at all but represent decisions to use language in certain ways. That is to say, a necessary truth is analytic in Kant's sense of the term, in that its predicate belongs already to its subject. The truth involved in this suggestion is better expressed by saying of any necessary statement that "its validity depends solely on the definition of the symbols it contains." [17] It explicates meanings but tells us nothing about the world. In this sense it is purely tautological though, owing to the slowness of human wit, it may when linked with other tautologies yield surprising results. It is not only the statements of deductive logic and arithmetic that have this verbal and tautological character; so also do the statements of

[14] *Ibid.,* p. 39.   [16] *Ibid.,* p. 75.
[15] *Ibid.,* pp. 68 f.   [17] *Ibid.,* p. 78.

geometry, of mathematical induction, and those in terms of which philosophical analysis is carried out. Indeed all meaningful propositions whatever fall either in the class of propositions that are in principle empirically verifiable or in that of those that are analytic and tautological. A metaphysical sentence is literally nonsensical and may be defined as "a sentence which purports to express a genuine proposition, but does, in fact, express neither a tautology nor an empirical hypothesis." [18] If one asks why, in the light of so simple and obvious a criterion of meaningfulness, people persist in asking and trying to answer meaningless metaphysical and ethical questions, the answer is that people are deceived by the forms of language and the superstition that to every word some existent entity must correspond. Thus, for example, the problem of substance arises because "we cannot, in our language, refer to the sensible properties of a thing without introducing a word or phrase which appears to stand for the thing itself"; [19] and the problem of being occurs because the term "existence" is taken to stand for an attribute.[20] The problems of normative ethics are in similar fashion rooted in the fact that such purely emotive terms as "good," "right," and "ought" are mistakenly supposed to represent descriptive properties.[21] What then, for Ayer, can the nature of the objects of knowledge be? In general such objects must be regarded as constructions of sense experiences. They are one and all "definable" in terms of "sensible manifestations." [22] This view does not imply either that a material object literally is "a collection, or system, of sense-contents," [23] or that a meaningful sentence about a material object must contain no reference to anything not a sensory experience. The one interpretation would itself be metaphysical and the other would illegitimately rule out all reference to atoms, electrons, and other useful constructs as well as to chairs, tables, and other familiar objects. Nor again does the theory of constructions mean that the material objects of scientific concepts are *fictions*, for surely tables and atoms are not fictions in the sense in which "Hamlet or a mirage is." [24] What the theory of constructions in logical empiricism does indicate is that every sentence about an object *can be translated* into a sentence that refers to nothing but sense experiences and their relations. Sense experiences related to one another by way of certain precisely definable patterns of resemblance and continuity give rise to the constructions known as material objects,[25] and such experiences related in various other ways give rise to the constructions known

[18] *Ibid.*, p. 41.
[19] *Ibid.*, p. 42.
[20] *Ibid.*, pp. 42 f.
[21] *Ibid.*, pp. 102–13.

[22] *Ibid.*, p. 49.
[23] *Ibid.*, p. 63.
[24] *Ibid.*, p. 63.
[25] *Ibid.*, pp. 65 f.

respectively as ourselves, other minds, past events, future events, and laws of nature. However, all statements involving constructions are alike in being either empirical hypotheses subject to testing by subsequent sensory experience, or rules for guiding anticipations of future experience.

Are the objects of knowledge then independent of the knowing mind or are they not? If the question is, are sensory experiences independent of sensing, the answer must be, of course, in the negative; for the *esse* of sense-data is their *percipi*, and a sense content is a part rather than an object of a sense experience.[26] However, if one asks whether the constructions known as material objects, selves, laws of nature, and past events are independent of knowing minds, the answer is in the affirmative; for all such constructions represent not merely sensations but relatively permanent possibilities of sensations, and sentences about them must be analyzed in terms not only of actually occurring sensations, but also in terms of sensations that would occur under certain circumstances.[27]

The problem of the nature of truth is really a pseudo-problem, for to say that a proposition is true is to do no more than to assert the proposition, and no empirical test could possibly be devised for a theory of the nature of truth.[28] The *criterion* of the truth of a proposition is simply the actual occurrence of the experiences whose prediction is implied in the truth. Actually, however, we never fully achieve truth; for every empirical statement, whether about a material thing, a law of nature, a mind, or even a past event, implies an infinite chain of experiences such that the requirements of its truth can never be completely fulfilled. So-called "ostensive" propositions directly recording immediate experiences might involve their own complete verification if there were any, but in fact there are none. While sensory experience itself is immediately given and unmistakable, any attempt to put such experience into words already involves descriptive as well as demonstrative elements and is therefore corrigible and never completely verifiable. Since we can never be certain of the truth of any empirical proposition, the practically important questions in the area of knowledge concern probabilities of future experiences. The probability of an hypothesis measures "the degree of confidence with which it is rational to entertain the hypothesis." [29] The degree of rationality of a belief depends on the extent to which it is "arrived at by the methods which we now consider reliable." [30] Such methods at present include all that we mean by scientific method. They in-

26 *Ibid.*, p. 140.   29 *Ibid.*, p. 101.
27 *Ibid.*, pp. 140 f.   30 *Ibid.*, p. 100.
28 *Ibid.*, pp. 87 ff.

volve not only ways of testing individual hypotheses but ways of testing whole systematic orders of hypotheses in which the confirmation of any part tends to confirm the whole. However, no set of procedures or hypotheses is necessarily final, and from the standpoint of logic any hypothesis can be saved if we are willing to sacrifice enough others. In answer to the question why our quest for knowledge should proceed as it does, some philosophers have suggested that such procedure is demanded in the interest of economy, but economy could be achieved simply by ignoring inconvenient observations. Actually, the ultimate ground of our procedure is the practical need to be successful in predicting experiences, and the degree of success is in the end the test of such empirical knowledge as we attain, whether of things, selves, the past, or the future.

5. Subsequent Developments in Ayer's Thought

Although Ayer's thought about knowledge has so changed since the first publication of *Language, Truth and Logic* as to be scarcely any longer regarded as a form of logical positivism, the later phases of Ayer's epistemology may profitably be considered here as illustrative of some changes that a phenomenalistic type of logical positivism began to undergo soon after it was brought to England. In this connection we shall first note some modifications of Ayer's earlier position included in his *Foundations of Empirical Knowledge* (1940), his new introduction to the second edition of *Language, Truth and Logic* (1946), and his *Philosophical Essays*. These modifications concern especially Ayer's views of the nature of philosophy, the verifiability criterion, the nature of meaning, the character of analytic statements, and the nature of ethical and metaphysical statements. Next we shall observe the manner of Ayer's continuation of his phenomenalistic type of analysis in the same three volumes. Finally we shall call attention to a few salient features of Ayer's recent volume, *The Problem of Knowledge* (1956).

A. Although Ayer had been inclined in *Language, Truth and Logic* to agree with those who claimed that "there are no philosophical propositions" and that philosophy must be content to "make other propositions clear," [1] he now thinks that to say that philosophical propositions are "about the usage of words is . . . inadequate." [2] The fact is that philosophical propositions, insofar as they are about usage at all, are not about words but about classes of words; and the philosophical propositions, if true, are not, like those of the lexicog-

---

[1] *Ibid.*, p. 26.   [2] *Ibid.*

rapher, empirical but, like those of the logician, analytic.[3] Philosophical analysis does not consist primarily of "definitions in use" or for that matter necessarily of definitions at all.[4] For example, philosophical statements interpreting material objects in terms of sense-data do not succeed in *defining* or *translating* physical object statements in terms of sense-data, "for no finite set of observation statements is ever equivalent to a statement about a material thing." [5] Moreover, some instances of genuine philosophical analysis do not even have forms approximating that of a definition. For example, Moore's demonstration that while it makes sense to say that "all tame tigers growl," it does not make sense to say that "all tame tigers exist," is not at all like a definition.[6]

While Ayer's more mature works by no means abandon the verification criterion of meaningfulness, they place the principle in a setting somewhat different from that of *Language, Truth and Logic,* and they suggest some significant qualifications. The principle is now explicitly said to be not itself a verifiable fact or an "empirical hypothesis" but simply a "definition" presumably indicating the range of literal meaningfulness with reference to which "truth" and "falsity" are applicable and common-sense and scientific understanding are achievable.[7] Moreover, the possibility is now cheerfully acknowledged that alternative definitions may quite plausibly represent other senses of meaning, and advocates of such definitions are asked only to supply definite criteria.[8] Even concerning statements that are meaningful, not all of the evidence for their truth is said to be contained in their meaning. Moreover, the criterion of meaningfulness that requires that from a meaningful statement together with other premises must follow an observation statement is now said to be in one respect too broad. On the basis of that criterion "the Absolute is lazy" is literally meaningful. In order to exclude such statements, which of course he does not wish to regard as meaningful, Ayer now insists that the "other" premises be either analytic or empirically verifiable. Thus the criterion of verifiability, and hence also of meaningfulness, now reads as follows:

A statement is directly verifiable if it is either itself an observation-statement, or is such that in conjunction with one or more observation-statements it entails at least one observation-statement which is not deducible from these other premises alone; and . . . a statement is indirectly veri-

---

[3] *Ibid.,* p. 26 n.
[4] *Ibid.,* p. 24.
[5] *Ibid.*
[6] *Ibid.,* p. 24.
[7] *Ibid.,* p. 16; and Ayer, "The Vienna

Circle," in A. J. Ayer and Others, *The Revolution in Philosophy* (London: Macmillan & Co., Ltd., 1956), p. 75.
[8] *Ibid.,* pp. 75 f.; and *Language, Truth and Logic,* pp. 15 f.

fiable if it satisfies the following conditions; first, that in conjunction with certain other premises it entails one or more directly verifiable statements which are not deducible from these other premises alone; and secondly, that these other premises do not include any statement that is not either analytic, or directly verifiable, or capable of being independently established as indirectly verifiable. . . . A literally meaningful statement, which is not analytic, . . . should be either directly or indirectly verifiable.[9]

Ayer is, however, ready to concede that perhaps when all the plausible qualifications that have been offered are duly considered, no really adequate criterion of verifiability has yet been worked out.[10]

Ayer's account of what various kinds of statements mean has been somewhat more drastically altered than his account of the verifiability criterion of meaningfulness. Thus, whereas he had formerly said that statements concerning sensory experiences "define" or "translate" statements about physical objects, he now declares that such "translations . . . are not forthcoming," that there are good reasons for supposing that they cannot be made,[11] and that the meaning of physical object statements must remain somewhat vague. Although "every statement about a material thing entails some set of statements or other about sense data, . . . there is no set of statements about the occurrence of particular sense-data of which it can be truly said that precisely this is entailed by a given statement about a material thing. . . . Not only can we go on testing a statement as long as we like without being able to arrive at a formal demonstration of its truth, but for any test that we actually do carry out there are always an indefinite number of other tests, differing to some extent . . . which would have done just as well." [12] Hence "every significant statement about a material thing can be represented as entailing a disjunction of observation-statements, although the terms of this disjunction, being infinite, can not be enumerated in detail." [13] Similar considerations hold regarding statements about other minds and about past events; but about both, special qualifications of the original doctrine of *Language, Truth and Logic* are also required. Statements concerning the past had in the first edition of *Language, Truth and Logic* been thought of as being translatable into propositions about "present or future experiences." [14] But in fact while such state-

[9] A. J. Ayer, *Language Truth & Logic*, 2d. ed. (London and New York: Victor Gollancz Ltd. and Dover Publications, Inc., 1946), p 13. Reproduced by permission of the publishers.

[10] "The Vienna Circle," p. 74.

[11] Ayer, "Philosophical Skepticism," in H. D. Lewis' *Contemporary British Phi-*

losophy, 3d series (London & New York: George Allen & Unwin, & The Macmillan Co., 1956), p. 61.

[12] Ayer, *Foundations of Empirical Knowledge* (London: Macmillan & Co., Ltd., 1947), pp. 240 f.

[13] *Language, Truth and Logic*, pp. 12 f.

[14] *Ibid.*, pp. 19, 102.

ments are indeed verifiable in terms of implied observation-statements, the observation-statements in question may refer to experiences that would be *possible* if one were observing at the past time involved as well as to actual experiences in the present or the future. The present impossibility of observing past experiences is simply a contingent fact rather than a logical impossibility which would rule out the meaningfulness of statements about the past that can no longer be tested.[15] Statements about other people's experience are not to be so simply interpreted in terms of one's own observations of their behavior as Ayer had at first thought. On this point, however, Ayer is hesitant. In the *Foundations of Empirical Knowledge* he argues extensively to the effect that since our inabilty to enter directly into the experiences of another is only a contingent fact, statements about other people's inner experiences are verifiable in principle and can be supported by arguments from analogy.[16] In the introduction to the second edition of *Language, Truth and Logic,* he is inclined to return to the behavioristic position of the original text of that book, to the effect that the meaning of statements about other people's experiences lies wholly in our own observations. In his *Philosophical Essays,* Ayer returns once more to the more liberal position of his *Foundations of Empirical Knowledge.* After considering the various linguistic conventions that would or would not make the sharing of the experiences of others impossible, Ayer concludes that insofar as one is considering only the descriptive content of an experience, the question whose experience it is is essentially arbitrary, so that for example in establishing correlations of properties one need not be prevented from crossing boundaries between the experiences of various persons. "The inference is not from my experience as such to his experience as such, but from the fact that certain properties have been found conjoined in various contexts to the conclusion that in a further context the conjunction will still hold. This is a normal type of inductive argument." [17]

The most significant modification that Ayer has found to be required with reference to analytic statements alters the status of such statements but retains a rootage for them in language. Analytic statements, instead of being "themselves linguistic rules" and hence only doubtfully either true or false, ought properly to be regarded rather as statements *grounded in* rules of language and therefore "necessarily true." Thus, for example, "it is a contingent empirical fact that the word 'earlier' is said in English to mean earlier, and it is an arbitrary . . . rule of language that words that stand for temporal

[15] *Ibid.,* p. 19; see also Ayer, *Philosophical Essays* (London: Macmillan & Co., Ltd., 1954).

[16] *Foundations of Empirical Knowledge,* chap. iii.

[17] *Philosophical Essays,* p. 214.

relations are to be used transitively; given this rule, the proposition that if A is earlier than B and B is earlier than C, A is earlier than C becomes a necessary truth." [18]

On the matter of ethical statements, and indeed on that of what he had called metaphysical statements generally, Ayer is also now more cautious than in his earlier work.[19] While the distinctly normative aspects of ethical statements continue to be expressions of emotional and volitional commitment, still much in such judgments may be regarded as classification of facts under descriptive types, and a reference to facts in the attempt to achieve persuasive results. Accordingly, although ethical statements can be shown to have emotive roots, to call them purely emotive and meaningless is not in accord with good English usage. What one must do is rather to recognize that such statements function quite differently from most statements, in that with reference to them "we cannot distinguish between pointing to the evidence itself and pointing to that for which it is supposed to be evidence." [20] Moreover, concerning metaphysical statements generally, instead of saying flatly that all of them are meaningless and so giving the erroneous impression that they are merely a purposeless collection of sounds one should regard them as quasi-symbols [21] each of which requires "detailed analysis." [22]

B. Whereas the tendency of Ayer's more recent writings is in most respects to qualify and liberalize his earlier position, his recent attitude with reference to the phenomenalist basis of knowledge remains as firm as ever, and even more explicit despite the defection of many of his earlier associates in this view. Ayer is, to be sure, quite ready to acknowledge with the later Carnap that we ordinarily speak in a material object language and indeed that nearly all that we need to say could be expressed in physicalistic terms, so that the sense-datum language and the physicalistic one become alternate languages either of which is satisfactory. However, Ayer explicitly resists the suggestion of recent physicalists that "the conception of sense-data is not precise or even clear . . . [or] that [sense-data] are mythical entities imposed upon us through philosophical confusion." [23] He insists with Schlick that the expressibility of significant truths in physicalistic terms is merely a contingent fact, and he goes on to assert that the sense-datum language is epistemologically more basic than material object language in that "while referring to sense-data is not necessarily a way of referring to physical objects, referring to physical objects is neces-

---

[18] *Language, Truth and Logic*, p. 17.
[19] Cf. *Language, Truth and Logic*, pp. 20 ff.; and *Philosophical Essays*, pp. 231, 249.
[20] *Ibid.*, p. 237.

[21] Ayer, *Thinking and Meaning* (London: H. K. Lewis & Co., Ltd., 1947), pp. 12 f.
[22] *Language, Truth and Logic*, p. 16.
[23] "Philosophical Skepticism," p. 61.

sarily a way of referring to sense-data." [24] Thus the language of sense-data can explicate what is involved in the language of material objects while the converse of this is not true.

Certainly it is not possible literally to translate the language of material objects into that of the senses, but since the reasons for this fact lie largely in the vagueness of physical object language, the untranslatability of physical object language need not entirely forbid us to speak of physical objects in the language of sense or prevent us from approximating every physical object statement in the language of sense or hinder our formulation of suitable translation rules. Indeed, Ayer now contends, the impossibility of stating all of the sensory implications involved in a material object statement need no longer be regarded as a barrier to our attaining certainty with reference to material object statements as verified through their sense language implications.[25]

The supposition that verification can ever be adequately achieved within a merely linguistic system having sufficiently coherent formation and transformation rules is a serious mistake to which logical empiricists are often tempted. If consistency were the only test, then "two mutually exclusive sets of propositions each of which is internally self-consistent" might be encountered, and one would have the hopeless task of deciding between them on the basis of consistency alone.[26] An adequate language requires in addition to formation and transformation rules semantic rules that "correlate certain signs in the language with actual situations," [27] and in the end "we verify the proposition not by describing but by having an experience." [28]

Experiences had can themselves be tied into the language system and give validity to claims made in it in a way previously rejected, but now recognized, in that recognition of essentially incorrigible ostensive propositions linking actual experiences with a phenomenalist linguistic system are after all achievable. We do express our immediate experiences and essentially the only mistakes we can make in expressing these experiences are verbal ones.[29]

C. Although Ayer's recent book *The Problem of Knowledge* is not so distinctively analytic as some of his earlier works, it is his one book that is focused most specifically on epistemological issues as such. Its leading ideas include the following. A verifications criterion of mean-

[24] *Philosophical Essays*, p. 104; see also "Philosophical Skepticism," p. 61.

[25] See *Foundations of Empirical Knowledge*, pp. 729 ff.; *Philosophical Essays*, pp. 133 ff.; and *Language, Truth and Logic*, p. 24.

[26] *Foundations of Empirical Knowledge*, p. 91.

[27] *Philosophical Essays*, p. 120.

[28] *Thinking and Meaning*, p. 28.

[29] *Language, Truth and Logic*, pp. 10 f., and *Foundations of Empirical Knowledge*, pp. 80 ff.

ingfulness—though not directly advocated—remains the test of significance in statements.[30] To know is not merely to be sure but to have *"the right to be sure"* in the light of the facts.[31] The skeptic directs his doubts against alleged knowledge of physical objects, the past, and other minds, and these doubts cannot be answered merely by pointing out the meaning of the term "know." [32] If one demands absolute certainty and a kind of inference that turns induction into deduction, then no knowledge is to be had. Even statements formulating immediate experiences can be mistaken and in other than verbal ways, for we can be in doubt about the comparative lengths, for example, of two phenomenally given lines.[33] Mistakes are easily made in analytic judgments, and the demand for deductively provable induction is one that by its nature cannot be met.[34]

However, our doubts tend naturally to come to rest after the evidences have been traced back to certain lengths; and if we are willing to accept such evidences as are available to us, we can in a legitimate sense be said to have genuine knowledge in all three of the areas against which the skeptic directs his attack. Concerning physical objects, it is conceivable that such objects are as we see them, though evidence for this is hardly to be had, and abundant evidence is at hand to show that with respect to some of their characteristics physical objects are not as we see them. The problem of sense-data can be avoided, but then it can also be intelligibly put and must be faced.[35] Physical objects cannot reasonably be reduced to sense-data, for they endure when there are no sense-data and no such infinite chains of data as phenomenalism would require are demanded for the existence of physical objects.[36] Nevertheless we can, through approved inductive procedures, know something about physical objects in terms of sense-data for the reason that the concept of a physical object is so framed that sensory experiences are evidential with reference to such objects.[37] The situation with reference to knowledge of the past is similar. Past events are neither directly perceived nor reducible to present experiences.[38] Memory gives no infallible or even highly reliable apprehension of them. Indeed, the reliability of memory depends more on inductive inferences than they upon it. But by following the best authenticated inductive procedures we can both know the past and support our own memories.[39] Knowledge of other minds may seem to be in a different situation owing to the fact

[30] Ayer, *The Problem of Knowledge* (London & Baltimore: Penguin Books, Ltd., 1956), pp. 184 f., 190 f.
[31] *Ibid.*, pp. 31 ff.
[32] *Ibid.*, pp. 34 ff.
[33] *Ibid.*, pp. 61 ff.
[34] *Ibid.*, pp. 71 ff.
[35] *Ibid.*, pp. 105 ff.
[36] *Ibid.*, pp. 118 ff.
[37] *Ibid.*, pp. 130 ff.
[38] *Ibid.*, pp. 154 ff.
[39] *Ibid.*, pp. 161 ff.

that other minds seem to be *other* by definition, and we certainly cannot reduce other minds to our own experiences. But the term "other" is systematically ambiguous, and there is no distinct class of other minds as such. Accordingly, we may legitimately make reasonable inferences concerning other minds upon the basis of the analogy of our own experiences together with a variety of indirect evidences.[40]

6. Gustav Bergmann

Our exposition of phenomenalistic analytic theories may appropriately be concluded with a brief account of the thought of Gustav Bergmann (b. 1906) who, though a member of the Vienna Circle from its inception, has written his more significant essays relative to theory of knowledge only in recent years and whose works represent an interesting compromise between the outlook of those logical positivists who stress the importance of artificial language and that of those who do not. Bergmann's principal essays on theory of knowledge are collected in his book, *The Metaphysics of Logical Positivism,* published in 1954, and some further indications of his views on this subject are contained in his subsequent book *Philosophy of Science.*

Like Carnap and unlike Schlick and Ayer, Bergmann contends that the best method in philosophy is "reconstructionist," in formulating an ideal language and then commenting upon it,[1] but unlike Carnap he also finds a very important place for ordinary language. The ideal language, Bergmann holds, should be capable in principle of saying all that can be said in ordinary language and at the same time of dissolving or resolving the special problems of philosophy [2] and avoiding the traditional snares of metaphysics. For the purpose of such language, schema that show how what we want to say could be expressed are quite sufficient and no working out of all propositions in detail is necessary. The essential features of the required linguistic framework are already furnished for us in the *Principia Mathematica* of Russell and Whitehead.[3] The task of the philosopher is not to formulate in terms of his ideal language materially correct propositions about the world; that is the job of the scientist. The task of the philosopher is rather to determine the scope of the language and to discuss the problem of its adequacy to common

[40] *Ibid.,* pp. 214 ff.

[1] Gustav Bergmann, *The Metaphysics of Logical Positivism* (New York: Longmans, Green & Co., Inc., 1954), pp. 32 ff.

[2] Cf. Bergmann, *Philosophy of Science* (Madison: University of Wisconsin Press, 1959), p. 39.

[3] *The Metaphysics of Logical Positivism,* p. 37.

sense, science, and the resolution of philosophical problems. The form which his basic inquiry should take is not that of the traditional epistemology, which asks, "What is real?" or that proposed by W. V. Quine which inquires concerning "what is to serve as an instance of a quantified variable." His basic question is rather what undefined descriptive terms can be admitted into an adequate ideal language system.[4] The language in which the ideal language is to be discussed is the ordinary language of common sense.[5] For while the philosopher's terms need not be those of common sense, it is in the terms of common sense that everything ultimately must be made intelligible.

Concerning analytic statements, Bergmann is in general agreement with other writers considered in this chapter, but the emphasis is less on the formal character of analytic truth, and Bergmann pays more attention to the difficulties that have recently been urged against the distinction between analytic and synthetic statements. All meaningful statements, Bergmann believes, in orthodox logical-positivist fashion, must be either analytic or factual and empirical. There are no a priori truths about matters of fact. All a priori statements are analytic, and all analytic statements are tautological or empty. Indeed, such statements "say nothing about the world." [6] But the fact that analytic statements are tautological does not, Bergmann thinks, imply that the distinction between analytic and synthetic is merely definitional or conventional. Instead of being invented or created by philosophers this distinction is intuitively felt; it is explicated by philosophers.[7] The distinction rests upon logic rather than merely upon verbal definitions. To say that it is merely conventional is to confuse grammar and logic.[8] Analytic truth also depends upon logic. It is not to be distinguished by its certainty, for although it does in fact afford the best examples of certainty, its certainty is incidental rather than essential to its definition.[9] Characteristic of analytic statements is the "vacuous occurrence of the descriptive signs in them," [10] a vacuous occurrence being one such that any other descriptive sign could be substituted without altering the truth value of the statement in which the sign occurs. Thus "when a descriptive sign occurs in any analytic sentence, the sentence obtained by replacing it with another descriptive sign of the same category is also analytic." [11] The nature of analytic statements is

[4] *Ibid.*, pp. 120 ff., 238 f.
[5] *Ibid.*, pp. 74 ff.
[6] *Ibid.*, p. 45; cf. also *Philosophy of Science*, pp. 24 ff.
[7] Cf. *The Metaphysics of Logical Positivism*, pp. 25 or/and 45 ff.

[8] *Ibid.*, pp. 14, 188.
[9] *Ibid.*, p. 46.
[10] *Ibid.*, pp. 292 f.; cf. also *Philosophy of Science*, p. 27.
[11] *The Metaphysics of Logical Positivism*, p. 38.

also appropriately indicated by saying that " 'p' implies 'q' if and only if 'if p then q' is analytic." [12]

The kind of examples often cited as possible exceptions to the principle that analytic truth is tautological include such facts as the transitivity of time, and the extensity of colors. If such statements were analytic, as Wittgenstein, for example, seemed to think them, serious difficulties would be involved for the tautology interpretation. In fact, however, such statements attempt to relate undefined descriptive terms and so are not analytic at all.[13]

Although Bergmann is as fully convinced as either Carnap or Ayer of the empirical character of factually meaningful statements he is perhaps even more mindful than they of the difficulties that have been disclosed in attempts to formulate criteria of meaning in terms of empirical verifiability. For one thing, the meanings of statements need to be known before verifications can be undertaken.[14] Besides, what requires empirical connections is not a statement as a whole but the descriptive terms involved in it. Hence, instead of furnishing a verifiability criterion of meaningfulness, Bergmann undertakes to indicate the bounds of meaningfulness in terms of a principle of acquaintance that requires: "(1) that a particular is to occur in a statement only if its referent is immediately apprehended —in perception, memory, or imagination—by the speaker; and (2) that an undefined predicate is to occur in a statement only if at least one exemplification of it is known to the speaker." [15]

That the data, in terms of which meaningful factual statements must in the end be interpretable, are those of immediate sensory experience, Bergmann stoutly contends against all supporters of current physicalism. The attempt to reduce all statements to physical terms is an "implicit materialism" utterly unwarranted by the character of experience, and it should be a "closed" phase of logical positivism.[16] What we call physical objects are never apprehended save in terms of experience, and it is experience that must be treated as basic. This consideration must not, however, be taken as implying a metaphysical phenomenalism that pronounces phenomena alone real. Such a view would raise again the spurious metaphysical issue between realism and idealism and violates the principle of the logic

---

[12] Ibid.

[13] Cf. ibid., pp. 50, 94, 228 ff.; and Philosophy of Science, p. 77.

[14] Cf. The Metaphysics of Logical Positivism, pp. 156 f.

[15] Ibid., p. 158; see also Bergmann, "Comments on Professor Hempel's 'The Concept of Cognitive Significance,'" Pro-

ceedings of the American Academy of Arts and Sciences, LXXX (1951), 78–88.

[16] The Metaphysics of Logical Positivism, pp. 4, 6, 8, 65; and Bergmann, "An Empiricist Philosophy of Physics," in Herbert Feigl and May Broadbeck, Readings in the Philosophy of Science, p. 266.

of *Principia Mathematica* which forbids the ascription of existence to an unqualified entity. One must remain a linguistic phenomenalist. No other equally adequate method is available for the philosophical interpretation of factual statements, and no other non-analytical statements are irrevocable as are those of the phenomenalist language.[17]

On two important points Bergmann differs from most other analytic philosophers except Moore, to whom he acknowledges considerable indebtedness. An adequate ideal language, Bergmann contends, must include at least one term to represent mental acts. Only a language that includes reference to mental acts as such can either do justice to the phenomena, or dispel *metaphysically* "phenomenalistic implications of a consistent empiricism," or give promise of that completedness in "description of the world" at which a satisfactory philosophy aims.[18] Such reference need involve nothing about a metaphysical self, but it will properly distinguish between objects and reasonings.[19] Considerations similar to those that demand terms for mental acts also require recognition that "the ideal language contains at least one undefined descriptive term whose interpretation is the relevant root meaning of one of the English words that occur characteristically in ethical or esthetic judgments." [20]

7. Comments Concerning Phenomenalistic Analysis

The group of thinkers who initiated logical positivism in the early decades of the present century were convinced that they were giving a new direction to philosophy. If the philosophy of the subsequent decades is indicative of the future, they were in part right; for while recent philosophy has broken with them at some points, it has followed them in focusing upon analysis of meanings and uses rather than upon speculation concerning properties and existences. Accordingly, the major features of the epistemological thought of both types of logical positivism require careful critical scrutiny. The first two features of phenomenalistic analysis to be considered in the comments that follow, namely the doctrines of the divisibility of all significant cognitive statements into analytic ones and empirical ones and that of the empirical testability of all significant empirical statements, are common to both types of logical positivism. A third feature of phenomenalistic analysis to be discussed here, the doctrine

---

[17] Cf. *The Metaphysics of Logical Positivism*, p. 104; and *Philosophy of Science*, p. 83.

[18] *The Metaphysics of Logical Positivism*, p. 16.
[19] *Ibid.*, pp. 54 ff.
[20] *Ibid.*, pp. 243–44.

of the reducibility of all empirical statements to the language of immediate experience, is characteristic of phenomenalistic analysis and antithetical to physicalistic analysis.

A. The doctrine that all significant cognitive statements are either analytic (i.e. analytic or self-contradictory) or empirical, or, to put the crucial point more sharply, the doctrine that all significant cognitive nonanalytic statements are empirical, was suggested in the writings of Locke and Hume but was first explicitly worked out and effectively projected into contemporary thought by the logical positivists. Logical positivists of all types have agreed upon it, and it has always been a characteristic mark of their thought.

Now apparently at least three suggestions implicit in this doctrine can be readily accepted even by philosophers who are not positivists. One is the suggestion that we do in fact, at least in intension, distinguish between analytic and synthetic statements, between statements whose truth or falsity is in some sense determinable solely in terms of logic or language and those whose truth or falsity is not so determinable. The second is that, whatever the difficulties of determining the analytic or synthetic character of some borderline statements, a great many statements seem rather plainly to be analytic and a great many others to be plainly synthetic. For example, elementary laws of logic are clearly analytic, and most statements descriptive of ordinary matters of fact are clearly synthetic. The third suggestion is that the vast majority of synthetic statements are empirical statements. For example, all descriptions of particular past or present physical events and all statements describing our own or other people's experiences are plainly empirical.

Logical positivists and most nonpositivists may further agree that if it be true that at least an intensional distinction can be drawn between analytic and nonanalytic or synthetic statements and that most statements of the latter sort are empirical statements of matters of fact, these considerations are important for theory of knowledge. These considerations suggest, for example, that such epistemic terms as "true" and "known" have greater complexity of application and possibly of meaning than might otherwise have been supposed, and that the epistemologist has special responsibilities for elucidating these complexities. They also suggest that the modes of verification applicable to the one class of statements will be very different from those applicable to the other and that the epistemologist must endeavor to clarify these different modes and their relations to one another.

The crucial question is not, however, whether or not some or even most nonanalytic statements are empirical but whether or not all of them are. Concerning this question, the appropriate reply at present would seem to be a cautious negative, or at very least not a confident affirmative; for many statements, particularly statements formulating various basic principles of our reasoning, are now seen not to fit neatly into the analytic-empirical dichotomy. Thus, while most of the descriptive statements that we make about matters of fact are empirical, some of the principles by virtue of which we pass from one type of statement to another do not appear to be simply classifiable as either analytic or empirical. For example, those principles by virtue of which we pass from statements about our immediate experiences to statements about physical objects, those through which we pass from statements about observed behavior to statements about other minds, and those by which we pass from statements about particular objects or events to predictions concerning the future or to scientific generalizations, are scarcely to be construed as analytic statements, and clearly they are not empirical either. The same considerations hold with reference to the statement itself that all nonanalytic statements are empirical. It would seem also that statements to the effect that certain broad types of action are right or that certain broad types of objects are beautiful are also not readily classifiable as either analytic or empirical. Indeed it is no longer entirely clear that statements of arithmetic and geometry can be altogether unambiguously classified as either analytic or empirical. For while purely formal systems that are analytic can surely be established for each, it is, on the one hand, by no means so certain as it once seemed that arithmetical and geometrical statements interpreted in such a way as to be applicable are true solely by virtue of logic or the meanings involved, and, on the other hand, it would be very odd to regard the statements of arithmetic and geometry as statements of empirical facts.

B. In their affirmation of the verifiability theory of meaning, the logical positivists go beyond the claim that all significant nonanalytic cognitive statements are empirical to claim that all such statements are in principle empirically testable. Such a verifiability theory of meaningfulness was implicit in the works of Berkeley, more nearly explicit in the works of James, and also present in the works of instrumentalists and operationalists. However, while other philosophers had a part in bringing the theory into its recent vogue, logical positivism—especially in its phenomenological phase—played the dominant role in bringing about this result.

Interpreted in any sort of strict way, the verifiability theory has on the whole, after a period of wide acceptance, fared not too well in very recent philosophy. Two basic difficulties have been encountered: that of finding any quite satisfactory formulation of the verifiability requirement, and that of verifying the requirement itself.

The first difficulty, to put it more specifically, is that it has thus far proved impossible to find any precise formulation of the verifiability criterion of meaningfulness that is satisfactory even to those "tough-minded" philosophers who would like to confine the empirically meaningful largely to scientific statements. This difficulty has been most convincingly worked out by logical positivists themselves. Thus for example, Carl Hempel, whose thought we shall consider more fully in the next chapter, sketches the difficulty somewhat as follows.[1] If the verifiability criterion is put in the form that a meaningful sentence must be such as to be deducible from a finite set of observation sentences, then it is too wide in failing to eliminate nonsensical sentences formed by conjunctions, and alternations of nonsensical sentences with significant ones, also too narrow in excluding generalizations, and at the same time inconsistent in not excluding falsifications of generalizations. If the criterion is taken to be the falsifiability of empirically significant sentences, some of the same problems recur in another form. Moreover, all thus far presented refinements of these types of criteria have been shown to be inadequate. A different type of approach to the problem is one which attempts to define the verifiability of a statement merely by showing the empirical applicability of all of its nonvacuous terms. But now the apparently insoluble problem is how the nonvacuous terms are to be distinguished. All this does not lead Hempel to reject the verifiability principle outright, but it does lead him to distrust that principle save in relation to a specific system. Considerations of a similar sort lead Israel Sheffler, after a detailed examination of the matter, to regard attempts to apply a verifiability criterion as "a hope for a clarification and a challenge to constructive investigation rather than a well-grounded doctrine."[2]

The second difficulty in attempting to establish a criterion of meaningfulness in terms of empirical testability is that even if such a criterion could be satisfactorily formulated, there would apparently still be no way either of justifying it as a *general* criterion or of showing that some *special* realm of discourse to which it was relevant should be given preferred status. The major obstacle to the establish-

[1] Carl Hempel, "Problems and Changes in the Empirical Criterion of Meaning," *Review International de Philosophie*, IV (1950), 41-62, reprinted in Leonard Linsky, *Semantics and the Philosophy of Language* (Urbana: University of Illinois Press, 1952), pp. 163-85; and Hempel, "The Concept of Cognitive Significance, a Reconsideration," *Proceedings of the American Academy of Arts and Sciences*, LXXX (1951), 61-77.

[2] Israel Sheffler, "Prospects of a Modest Empiricism," *Review of Metaphysics*, X (1956-57), 383-400, 602-25.

ment of a general criterion is not that no such criterion can be deduced from other principles, for perhaps deduction is not in place in such matters, but that it does not seem possible to abstract any common characteristic of significant statements. The major obstacle to claiming exclusive rights for a criterion arrived at by analysis of significant statements in a special realm of discourse is that the criteria arrived at by analysis of significant statements in other realms of discourse seem to have equally valid claims within their own realms. To be sure the alternative is always open of laying down criteria by decree. But in order to do this, one seems obligated to accord the same privilege to all others who wish to issue decrees; and while the generosity of such tolerance would be commendable, it could hardly accomplish much toward the clarification of the issue.

However, to say that the attempt to achieve and justify a formulation of a verifiability criterion of meaningfulness has failed is not to say that the verifiability theory has accomplished nothing or is of no current use. Actually the theory has prevented philosophers and others influenced by them from making a great many vague and irresponsible statements they otherwise would almost certainly have made, and caused them to consider carefully just what their statements did mean. Even the failure of advocates of the theory to disclose any general criterion of meaningfulness has proved useful in stimulating intensified inquiry concerning the relations between significant statements and empirical tests and between the tests appropriate to discourse. Regarded not as a rigid standard to be uniformly applied but as an adaptable demand for responsibility to the type of experience relevant to the realm of discourse under consideration in any given inquiry, the verifiability theory may continue to serve a useful purpose.

C. The claim that all significant empirical statements, including physical object statements, can be reduced to the phenomenalistic language of immediate experience is a bold step beyond the claim that all significant cognitive nonanalytic statements are empirical and that all empirical statements are empirically testable. Previously put forward in one way or another by Hume, Mill, Mach, James, and Russell, and with very important qualifications by Price and Lewis, this claim was never before pressed with such explicitness and thoroughness as in some of the works of the phenomenalistic analysts. If it can be established it will in a single stroke eliminate the most difficult of the traditional epistemological problems. Can this bold claim in fact be established or even made to appear highly plausible? And if not, what significant facts, if any, were its advocates getting at?

Since the reduction of all significant empirical statements to phenomenalistic language is a further step beyond the reduction of all significant nonanalytic statements to empirical ones and of empirical ones to empirically testable ones, and since it is largely dependent upon these other reductions for its own plausibility, it ceases to be plausible when the implausibility of those other reductions becomes apparent. Besides, there are other serious objections to the reduction in question. As has been pointed out by phenomenalistic analysts themselves, no physical object statement unconditionally either entails or is entailed by any phenomenalistic statement, and the conditions requisite for any sort of entailment linking such statements are far too complex to be completely formulated. Logical equivalence between a physical object statement and a phenomenalistic statement can be at best achieved only in terms of an infinite series of phenomenalistic statements, and no such series can be carried through. Actually, few phenomenalistic analysts have ever attempted to proceed much beyond the first few steps in working out a phenomenalistic analysis of any physical object statement.

Even if a formal equivalence could be established between a physical object statement and a series of phenomenalistic statements, such a series of phenomenalistic statements could scarcely be said adequately to represent either the manner in which terms for physical objects are actually used or the intentions of a person who makes a physical object statement in the sort of circumstances in which such statements are ordinarily made. The first of these points has been, as we shall presently see, amply elucidated and emphasized by ordinary language philosophers. Concerning the second a few reminders of certain aspects of the manner of our speech and thought may be helpful. When, for example, an ordinary person speaks of a physical object before him, he commonly intends much more than is actually given or ever can be given in his experience. He *refers to* what is not and cannot be an experience, and he continues quite unwilling to be assured that all he has in mind is anticipated experience. Again, when one speaks of a thing as enduring unobserved through a period of time, he ordinarily seems to intend to say more than that possibilities of experiences are there all the while, and he would be greatly perplexed if told that nothing else was or had been there. Once more, when one speaks of recognizing an individual after the lapse of an interval of time, he commonly wants to convey a good deal more than that he now has experiences similar to experiences he had on previous occasions or will have on subsequent occasions. Rather, he insists that in a literal sense the same individual is present again. What is true of the intentions of the common man in these matters seems to be true of those of scientists as well. While what is intended in some scientific concepts can be directly indicated in terms of the operations and observations needed to verify them, what is intended in others, as is now being increasingly recognized, cannot. The scientist requires, in order to express what he is getting at, whole systems of constructs that are not reducible to phenomenalistic or even to observational terms, and while some of his constructs represent merely convenient modes of transition within his system, others represent what he takes to be irreducible ingredients of his system. Beyond such suggestions as these, however, the case against phenomenalistic reductionism need hardly be pressed; for while a number of writers have quite properly argued that the issue of phenomenalism is philosophically formulable and discussible, few, if any, at the present time any longer hold that the reduction of all physical object statements to phenomenalistic language is in practice either feasible or desirable.

This breakdown of phenomenalistic reductionism does not, however, mean that all that the phenomenalistic analysts have said about a phenomenalistic language is mistaken. Implicit in the comprehensive claim that *all* significant empirical statements can be reduced to the phenomenalistic language of immediate experience are the more modest claims that a restricted phenomenalistic language is possible, useful, and in an important sense even epistemologically basic. There are good reasons for thinking that in these more modest claims, despite such objections as the foregoing to comprehensive phenomenalistic reductionism and other objections to phenomenalistic language itself, the phenomenalistic analysts are essentially correct.

Against phenomenalistic language as such have been brought the objections that it is not the language that we learn to speak or do speak, that it is not the language of scientific discovery or proof, that when we attempt to speak it we are obliged to draw much of our terminology from the language of physical objects, that at best it is not incorrigible, and that since such terms as "looks," "appears," and "seems" already have ordinary uses in the language of physical objects, there is not even any clear-cut logical device for "introducing" phenomenalistic language. However, while each of these objections asserts a fact that ought certainly to be recognized and each constitutes a valid objection against claims that have sometimes been made for phenomenalistic language, neither any one of them nor all of them together yields any adequate reason for thinking phenomenalistic language either not possible or not useful or not in some way epistemologically basic.

The possibility of phenomenalistic language does not require any special logical devices or any technical vindication. All that is needed is that people should in fact have sensory and perceptual experiences distinguishable from the physical objects to which they refer, and be able to talk in a terminology appropriate to these experiences. That people do in fact have such experiences we have repeatedly argued, though the fact scarcely seems to require argument. That people can talk in a terminology appropriate to these experiences is sufficiently evident in the fact that they do sometimes talk in this way, and that their language is at such times partly derivative matters not at all. For one thing, philosophers talk in such language when they discuss given experiences, and their talk is not necessarily more stupid or confused than that of ordinary people. For another thing, ordinary people use such language when for any one of many possible reasons their experiences as such take on special interest. As for the "introduction" of phenomenalistic language, what is required is not a clear-cut logical device—at best such devices can yield misunderstandings—but simply a variety of informal ways of drawing attention to the relevant experiences in conjunction with an appropriate terminology. Of such ways there are many, and each may be used to rectify misunderstandings that may remain when another has done its work. Such ways include not only special uses, not too difficult to explain, of such terms as "looks," "appears," and "seems," but also a variety of other less formal devices for calling attention to experiences in abstraction from the existence of any physical object to which they might refer. The availability of these informal procedures obviates any need for a clear-cut logical device.

That phenomenalistic language should be not only possible but useful requires not that such language be prior to any other language but only that there be facts of some kind that it describes and that these facts be interesting to someone. Such facts are to be found in abundance both in experiences in abstraction from their objects and in experiences that have no objects. Sometimes philosophers are interested in experiences as such for no other reason than that they occur, and more often philosophers are interested because experiences seem to have a bearing on the foundation of empirical knowledge. In any case talk about such experiences seems to many philosophers, as it does to Firth, to be essential to the raising of a question that unavoidable, however obvious the answer, namely the question of whether or not reality consists only of phenomena. But experiences as such may also become matters of intense interest even to the common man, when for example, he becomes suspicious of his observations and wishes to confirm them, when he talks with his oculist and his psychiatrist, or even when he wishes to express some aspects of his love and his religion.

That phenomenalistic language should be not only possible and useful but also epistemologically basic requires not that such language should be chronologically or in general logically prior to any other language, or even that it should be incorrigible, but only that in an eventual order of justification, it should play a basic role. To be sure, in common sense and science, justification is in the main sought on the basis of observations of physical objects; and although justification of observations is not usually required, when it is, it is usually sought in terms of further observations. However, the question can still be intelligibly put as to what is the justification of the knowledge claim of observations themselves. In order to put this question, one must use such terms as "knowledge" in somewhat unusual senses, for what is observed and backed by other observations is usually said already to be known. But such knowledge claims are sometimes mistaken, and some philosophers wish while recognizing the legitimacy of the usual sense of such terms as "knowledge" also to employ these terms in more demanding specialized senses. To such a procedure common sense lends some support, for when what was said to be known as observed turns out in fact to be false, the ordinary man will say not that he knew what was false but that he only thought he knew something and didn't. For purposes of discussing the justification of possible knowledge of observation statements in the suggested technical sense of the term "knowledge," phenomenalistic language seems to be essential. Indeed, the most important philosophical use of phenomenalistic language would seem to be just the use in which it is employed to discuss the structure of the foundations of knowledge in the elemental justification of the observation statements on which the superstructure of knowledge is built. Such employment of phenomenalistic language may throw significant light not only upon general epistemological problems but also upon the relations of various specific kinds of knowledge to one another and of epistemology to the foundations of ethics, esthetics, and logic.

CHAPTER 14

Physicalistic Analysis

As LOGICAL postivists or logical empiricists, the philosophers considered in this chapter are in basic agreement with those considered in the preceding chapter in nearly all important respects. Both groups insist upon a verifiability criterion of meaning. Both make a sharp distinction between empirical synthetic statements and a priori analytic ones and regard all other statements as meaningless. Both take the analysis and clarification of the language of science to be the chief business of philosophy and both are inclined to regard the construction and examination of ideal languages as the best method of clarification. Both are also vigorously anti-metaphysical.

While various differences distinguish the views of individual writers within each group, one major difference distinguishes the two groups from each other. Whereas writers advocating phenomenalistic analysis insist that sense experiences are epistemologically basic and that statements expressing them constitute the fundamental language to which all intelligible expressions lead back, physicalists believe that observations of material things are basic to all knowledge and that observation statements constitute the core of the language of cognitively meaningful discourse.

1. THE PHYSICALISTIC ANALYSIS OF RUDOLF CARNAP

Although Rudolf Carnap at first advocated a phenomenalistic type of analysis and did not adopt the physicalistic point of view as early as some other members of the Vienna Circle, he has been widely acknowledged almost from the time of his adoption of that point of view as the outstanding exponent of the physicalistic type of logical positivism. However, even after his adoption of physicalism, and within its framework, Carnap's position has shifted considerably, and the major shifts of his position have usually been accompanied by corresponding adjustments in the views of most of the other representatives of the physicalistic branch of logical positivism. Accordingly Carnap's thought, following its earliest period, may well be regarded as representative not only of some claims common to nearly all logical positivists and of further claims common to nearly all physicalists, but also of the principal changes in physicalistic analysis since the early thirties. In summarizing here Carnap's thought since the early thirties, we shall be concerned successively with his ideas of metaphysics and the nature of philosophical inquiry, the criterion of meaningfulness and the formal and material modes of language, the structure of knowledge, probability, and truth.

A. As a consistent logical empiricist Carnap continues in the period of his physicalist thought, as in the earlier one, to hold as a central conviction that the only nontautological statements that are cognitively meaningful are empirical ones. Accordingly his opposition to all forms of metaphysics is as severe as ever. At about the time of his shift to physicalism, he writes in an essay that "the logical analysis of the pretended propositions of metaphysics has shown that they are not propositions at all, but empty word arrays, which on account of notational and emotive connections arouse the false appearance of being propositions." [1] In *The Logical Syntax of Language* he declares in similar fashion: "The sentences of metaphysics are pseudo-sentences which are on logical analysis found to be either empty phrases or phrases which violate the rules of syntax." [2] In the *Unity of Science* Carnap says: "Concerning the essence of the Universe, of the Real, of Nature, of History, etc. we supply no new answers but reject the questions themselves as questions in appearance only." [3] In his *Philosophy and Logical Syntax,* Carnap treats metaphysics as a kind of deceptive poetry that "gives the illusion of knowledge without actually giving any knowledge." [4] In his more recent wrtings, Carnap has not found it necessary to resume the attack against metaphysics, but that the same objections remain ready

---

[1] W. M. Malesoff (trans.), Rudolf Carnap's "On the Character of Philosophic Problems," *Philosophy of Science,* I (1934), 5.

[2] Rudolf Carnap, *The Logical Syntax of Language* (New York & London: Harcourt, Brace & Co., & Kegan Paul, Trench, Trubner & Co., Ltd., 1937), p. 8.

[3] M. Black (trans.), Carnap's *The Unity of Science* (London: Kegan Paul, Trench, Trubner & Co., Ltd., 1934), pp. 22 f.

[4] Carnap, *Philosophy and Logical Syntax* (London: Kegan Paul, Trench, Trubner & Co., Ltd., 1935), p. 31.

to be brought forth if needed is sufficiently apparent,[5] for "the usual ontological questions about 'reality' (in an alleged metaphysical sense) " remain "pseudo questions without cognitive content." [6]

The rejection of metaphysics does not, however, mean for Carnap, as it almost does for Wittgenstein, a rejection of philosophy. Quite apart from an alleged metaphysics with which it has been too often confused, philosophy has a job to do. That job is primarily the analysis of the language of science. The job is most satisfactorily done through the construction of ideal languages in terms of which the findings of science can be so formalized that their logical character is adequately disclosed; even natural languages are "best represented and investigated by comparison with a constructed language which serves as a system of reference!" [7] At first Carnap was disposed to devote his efforts almost exclusively to the development and defense of constructed languages. Even at the present time when many analytic philosophers are turning to other methods, Carnap, while now acknowledging the legitimacy and usefulness of such other methods,[8] continues to think that an artificial language of science, so complete that the meaning of every symbol in it would be unambiguously clear even apart from consideration of the context, can be constructed.[9]

The particular form which the philosophical problem of analysis of the language of science took in Carnap's mind at the beginning of the period under consideration was that of the *syntax* of scientific language. Since empirical fact is the domain of science, the philosopher's business is not to discover facts. His concern is rather with logic than with facts, and in particular with the logic of science. But since logic is basically the syntax of language, the philosopher is to study "the syntax of the language of science." Since philosophy is often thought to include metaphysics, one had perhaps better say that *"the logic of science takes the place of the inextricable tangle of problems which is known as philosophy,* [and that] . . . all philosophical problems that have any meaning belong to syntax." [10] The philosopher must formalize and explicate the formation and transformation rules of the language of science, including not only the

[5] Cf. Carnap, *Meaning and Necessity* (Chicago: University of Chicago Press, 1947), pp. 43, 71; and Carnap, "The Methodological Character of Theoretical Concepts," in Herbert Feigl and Michael Scriven, *The Foundations of Science and the Concepts of Psychology and Psychoanalysis* ("Minnesota Studies in the Philosophy of Science," I [Minneapolis: University of Minnesota Press, 1956]), pp. 39, 54–56.
[6] *Ibid.,* pp. 44 f.
[7] *The Logical Syntax of Language,* p. 8.
[8] Carnap, *Meaning and Necessity* (2d ed.; Chicago: University of Chicago Press, 1956), p. 250.
[9] *Ibid.,* p. 232.
[10] *The Logical Syntax of Language,* pp. 279 f.

initial logical rules of science but also those rules that science has adopted in the light of its discoveries of empirical facts.[11] The resulting system will primarily be a sound postulational one in which both the terms and the sentences are taken extensionally, that is with reference to objects and truth functions respectively, rather than with reference to properties and propositions.

Some philosophers object to the conception of philosophy indicated here on the grounds that a purely syntactical and extensional logic is inadequate and that logic requires consideration of the meanings of terms. But Carnap is unwilling at first to agree. To be sure, "if the meanings of two sentences are given, the question of whether one is the consequence of the other or not is settled," but *"in order to determine whether or not one sentence is a consequence of another, no reference need be made to the meaning of the sentences. . . . It is sufficient that the syntactical design of the sentences be given.* All questions in the field of logic . . . are then resolved into syntactical questions. A special logic of meaning is superfluous." [12] Other philosophers are inclined to doubt the validity of the whole effort to formulate a syntax of language on the ground that in view of Russell's theory of types no language can express its own syntactical rules, but Carnap believes that his *Logical Syntax of Language* demonstrates the possibility of just such expression. Carnap's own formulation of certain elemental languages for the expression of scientific fact are not, however, presented as the only acceptable patterns of formal language. Even in the early thirties Carnap insisted upon a principle of tolerance to the effect that "everyone is entitled to build up his own logic, i.e. his own language as he wishes. All that is required of him is . . . that he must state his methods clearly, and give syntactical rules." [13] Subsequently, in the spirit of a then recently acquired interest in the pragmatic aspects of language, Carnap went on to say: "Let us grant to those who work in any special field of investigation the freedom to use any form of expression which seems useful to them; the work in the field will sooner or later lead to the elimination of those forms which have no useful function. Let us be cautious in making assertions and critical in examining them, but tolerant in permitting linguistic forms." [14]

In the late thirties the logician Tarski was able to persuade Carnap that syntax was not the whole basis of logic and that in order to

[11] *Philosophy and Logical Syntax,* chap. ii.

[12] *The Logical Syntax of Language,* pp. 258 f.

[13] *Ibid.,* p. 52.

[14] Carnap, "Empiricism, Semantics and Ontology," from *Revue Internationale de Philosophie,* II (1950), in L. Linsky, *Semantics and the Philosophy of Language* (Urbana: University of Illinois Press, 1952), p. 228.

disclose logical connections fully one must refer to meanings also. This did not by any means cause Carnap to abandon the effort to lay the foundations of a formalized language of science, but it did cause him to add to formation and transformation rules, rules governing the meanings of terms, and to make other requisite adjustments in his system. Thus in Carnap's *Introduction to Semantics* (1942) and *Formalization of Logic* (1943) an altered perspective comes to light. Instead of being entirely free, the construction of a language system is somewhat limited by the meanings to be assigned to its terms, and the range of meanings that can be assigned to an already constructed system is limited by the character of that system. The formation and transformation rules of Carnap's system remain, however, essentially extensional in the sense that any intensional expressions that may occur are translatable into extensional ones. With regard to the basis of the rules on which logic rests, the shift of emphasis from syntax to semantics makes a rather considerable difference, for logical truth is now seen to rest mainly upon semantic rather than syntactic concepts; but with regard to the formal analytic character of the language in terms of which the logic of science is thought to be best explicated, no appreciable change is involved. Indeed even comparatively recently Carnap has argued, against Quine, who doubts the validity of the distinction between analytic and synthetic statements, that whatever the situation may be concerning natural languages, the "meaning postulates" of formal systems are sufficient to distinguish and validate analytic statements in such systems.

Following the publication of *Introduction to Semantics*, Carnap's conception of the formal language system in terms of which philosophy is to clarify and explicate the language of science is further liberalized by the assignment of a significant role to the intensional mode of meaning. Carnap now finds both extensions and intensions in all kinds of linguistic expressions. Intensions are needed, among other things, to provide for logical modalities such as necessity and impossibility. The extension of a name or definite description is the individual named or described, and the intension is an individual concept. The extension of a sentence is the truth value of the sentence, and the intension is the proposition expressed. The extension of a predicate is the class designated, and the intension is the property that distinguishes the class.[15] Every extension can be translated in terms of an intension, but the converse may not be true. Even better than translating either into the other is, however, to translate both intensions and extensions into a neutral language, for this

---

[15] *Meaning and Necessity*, pp. 16–46.

brings to focus the fact that no metaphysical implications are involved and at the same time gets rid of many complicating aspects of logic and language. In a subsequent article Carnap goes a step further and insists that while intensional meaning has no implications regarding consciousness and could be determined even for a robot, it is indispensable to the understanding and use of the languages both of common sense and science.[16]

Having gone so far as to affirm the indispensability not only of semantics but also of intensional meaning, Carnap is now ready also to insist upon a philosophic concern with pragmatics or the *uses* of language, and this in turn leads away from exclusive preoccupation with formal languages and toward consideration of natural languages. Thus the recent article referred to above undertakes to show among other things that the intensional concepts of synonymy and analyticity apply to natural languages and need to be pointed out as explicanda of the corresponding formal concepts. A subsequent article contends that while pragmatics is not essential to the justification of such semantic concepts as analyticity and synonymy, it may greatly facilitate their justification. The article closes with an appeal for further inquiry in pragmatics: "There is an urgent need for a system of theoretical pragmatics, not only for psychology and linguistics, but also for analytic philosophy." [17]

B. Even though many logical empiricists have now come to doubt the possibility of formulating a satisfactory verifiability criterion of empirical meaningfulness, Carnap continues to believe that such a criterion is one of the principal tools of philosophical inquiry, although his understanding of just what constitutes the criterion has undergone considerable change. Carnap's earliest view of the matter was that only those sentences are empirically significant which are actually "translatable into the observation language." [18] Subsequently, in the early thirties, he held that a statement was empirically meaningful if and only if one could deduce observation statements from it. A little later, in "Testability and Meaning," Carnap held that a statement's connectibility through material implication by reduction chains to observation statements was enough to assure for it empirical significance. Finally, in recent writings he further liberalizes the criterion to the extent that a statement may be considered empirically meaningful if it is properly formed by the rules of its language and each of its descriptive terms is such that a

[16] "Meaning and Synonyms in Natural Language," Appendix D of the 2d ed. of *Meaning and Necessity*, pp. 233–45.

[17] "On Some Concepts of Pragmatics,"

Appendix E of *Meaning and Necessity*, p. 250.

[18] "The Methodological Character of Theoretical Concepts," p. 39.

sentence containing it "makes a difference for the prediction of an observable event." Such a criterion holds good even of some sentences that cannot be tested by observation, but is none the less definite and not a mere matter of degree.[19]

Although Carnap's conceptions of philosophical inquiry and of the verifiability criterion have frequently served as instruments for the elimination of metaphysical and other meaningless terms and sentences, their function is by no means exclusively destructive. One significant constructive function, particularly emphasized in the earlier years of the period under consideration, was the implementation of a suggestion that not all sentences that failed to pass the test of empirical significance were utterly devoid of any kind of cognitive meaning but that some of them were in fact disguised syntactical statements that served purposes not unlike those of philosophical statements themselves. Such sentences, referred to by Carnap as pseudo-object sentences, "are formulated as though they refer to . . . objects, while in reality they refer to syntactical forms, and specifically, to the forms of the designation of those objects with which they appear to deal." [20] The test for such sentences is that while they are expressed in sentences in the material mode of genuine empirical statements, they can be translated into sentences in the formal mode of statements about syntax. Thus, for example, such sentences as "the rose is a thing," "this book treats of Africa," and "the evening star and the morning star are identical," read as though they were straightforward object sentences similar to "the rose is red," "Mr. A visited Africa," and "the evening star and the earth are about the same size." Actually, however, each can be expressed in the formal mode as a statement about syntax as follows: The first sentence becomes "the word 'rose' is a thing word"; the second, "this book contains the word 'Africa' "; and the third, "the words 'evening star' and 'morning star' are synonymous." [21] Statements that cannot be expressed in the formal mode are either genuine empirical statements or else nonsense.[22]

C. We turn now to Carnap's conception of the structure of knowledge. Primarily, three problems are involved: that of the observation statements upon which the structure rests, the character of the logic employed, and the meaning and mode of confirmation of statements that are not directly observational. Regarding the second of these problems enough has already been said in exposition of Car-

[19] "The Methodological Character of Theoretical Concepts," pp. 49, 59 ff., 31 f.

[20] *The Logical Syntax of Language*, p. 285.

[21] *Philosophy and Logical Syntax*, pp. 60 ff.

[22] Whether Carnap would now go quite this far is doubtful, but this at any rate was his position in the mid-thirties.

nap's view of the nature of philosophical inquiry; we shall accordingly concentrate upon the other two.

(1) Knowledge no longer rests for Carnap, as it formerly did, upon a basis of indubitable sentences, but there is a kind of sentence which expresses the data of the scientist, which is psychologically basic for all of us, and to which alone all other kinds of sentences can be connected intersubjectively. The sentences in question are simple observation sentences regarding physical objects, such as, "the temperature here is between 5 and 10 degrees centigrade." [23] The thesis of physicalism is that all intelligible statements can be intelligibly connected with such sentences, and this thesis is strongly advocated by Carnap. That the data on which such sciences as physics and chemistry, geology, and astronomy rest are intersubjectively expressed in physicalistic sentences goes without saying, for "it is clear that every determination arising can be reduced to physical determination." [24] The case of biology is clouded by the current controversy over vitalism, but biological concepts can quite readily be reduced to physical ones without deciding the character of biological laws. For example, the concept of fertilization may be regarded as a concept of union of sperm and ovum with "redistribution of parts," while the precise character of the laws involved remains an open question. Similarly, "the definition of any psychological term reduces it to physical terms" without prejudicing the question of the laws concerned, and the same is true of sociology. Thus "at ten o'clock Mr. A was angry" is to be translated "at ten o'clock Mr. A was in a certain bodily condition which is characterized by the acceleration of breathing and pulsation, by the tension of certain muscles, by the tendency to certain violent behavior and so on." [25] To the objection that we cannot know the inner states of another person the reply may be made that we can at any rate apprehend verbal behavior in terms of which states are signified, and if such a reply is not acceptable then in any case intersubjective discourse is ruled out.

Concerning the question how one knows the correctness of basic observation sentences, Carnap's answer is to the effect that if the various senses of each of several observers agree in interpreting the readings of properly situated apparatus the basic sentences necessary for scientific construction can be authenticated. Thus, the sort of sentence in question can be amply, though not indubitably, confirmed "under suitable circumstances . . . with the help of a few observations." [26] However, while the intersubjective observability

[23] The Unity of Science, p. 53.
[24] Ibid., p. 67.
[25] Philosophy and Logical Syntax, pp. 89–90.

[26] Carnap, "Testability and Meaning," The Philosophy of Science, III (1936), 455.

of physical objects gives to physical object language certain logical and psychological advantages over phenomenalistic language, it is worthy of note that an even stronger physicalistic thesis may some day take the basic language to be that of microphysics; and Carnap seems to regard as increasingly plausible the "possibility of constructing all of science, including psychology, on the basis of physics, so that all theoretical terms are definable by those of physics and all laws derivable from those of physics." [27]

(2) The character of the development of Carnap's thought concerning the relation between scientific statements and the basic sentences on which they rest has been suggested in a general way in what has been said about Carnap's idea of the verifiability criterion. We must now consider the relation in more detail.

In the earliest period of Carnap's thought the relation between the statements of science and the phenomenalistically conceived basic sentences to which they led back was one of logical equivalence or intertranslatability. In the beginning of the physicalistic period now under consideration Carnap took the relation between scientific statements and the physicalistically conceived observation statements on which they were based to be such that definitive observation statements were deducible from scientific statements with the help of the syntactically conceived laws of logic and formally defined principles of science. The requirements involved in this view, however, also turned out to be too stringent. The deducible observation statements in terms of which a scientific statement would have to be interpreted might well be infinite in number and so unexemplifiable in any finite time. Moreover, the deduced observation statements would be conditional statements such that if the conditions indicated were never achieved, the conditional statements, and accordingly the initial scientific statements, would paradoxically have to be said to be true when in fact they were not. For example, "x is soluble in water" may be said, according to the view in question, to mean "whenever x is put into water, x dissolved." [28] But if x is never put into water, the hypothetical statement is true no matter what x is, so that the absurd conclusion would have to be drawn that x is soluble in water even if x is a match or some other insoluble object. In view of difficulties of this latter sort, Carnap abandoned the idea of the interpretation of scientific expressions solely in terms of observation statements deducible from them and presented instead in his "Testability and Meaning" an indirect mode of introducing scientific expressions through what he called "reduction sentences." In such

[27] "The Methodological Character of Theoretical Concepts," pp. 74 f.   [28] "Testability and Meaning," p. 440.

a sentence the expression to be introduced appears neither as the defiendum of a defining statement nor as the major antecedent of an implication, but as a link in a chain of conditional statements whose other members are observation statements. A sentence introducing the expression "soluble in water" should read not "if x is soluble in water, then . . . ," but "if any thing x is put into water at any time t, then, if x is soluble in water, x dissolves at time t, and if x is not soluble in water, it does not." [29] Some terms may of course be introduced directly by definition, as when whales are defined as a species of mammals, but as a rule the introduction of terms through reduction sentences is not only less liable to absurdity but also more convenient in that it enables one to build up scientific concepts gradually as new evidence is accumulated. In this view scientific statements may be said to be testable if a way is known to establish the observational conditionals involved. Even if a scientific statement is not testable in that no way is now known to establish its observation conditionals, it may still be confirmable in the sense that the predicates involved in those conditionals belong to the "class of observable predicates," [30] and it may be said to be meaningful if it is even partially confirmable. The confirmation of a scientific sentence consists of course in the exemplification of its conditional observation sentences in actual observations, and its partial confirmation consists in the exemplification of some of these sentences.

In Carnap's recent writings even the moderately liberal account of the relation between scientific expressions and observation statements is regarded as somewhat too rigid to conform to the actual procedures of scientific inquiry. While some scientific expressions can be appropriately treated as dispositional terms to be interpreted through either reduction chains or operational definitions, most scientific expressions must be interpreted in such a way that probability relations rather than deductive ones come to play the leading role. To this end Carnap has developed a distinction between "dispositional predicates" and "theoretical constructs" paralleling a distinction of Kenneth MacCorquodale and Paul Meehl between "intervening variables" and "hypothetical constructs." [31] The principal differences between dispositional predicates and theoretical constructs are the following: (1) Whereas a dispositional term "can be reached from predicates of observable properties by one or more steps," theoretical terms are reached much less directly. (2) Whereas a

[29] *Ibid.*, pp. 440 f.
[30] *Ibid.*, p. 456.
[31] See Kenneth MacCorquodale and Paul Meehl, "Hypothetical Constructs and Intervening Variables," in Herbert Feigl and May Brodbeck, *Readings in the Philosophy of Science* (New York: Appleton-Century-Crofts, Inc., 1953), pp. 596–611.

"specified relation" between a certain condition and an anticipated result "constitutes the whole meaning" of a dispositional term, a theoretical construct retains considerable "incompleteness of interpretation." (3) Whereas with reference to a dispositional term the regularity of the relation between the condition and the anticipated result "is meant as universal, i.e. holding without exception; with reference to theoretical constructs the parallel relation admits of exceptions." [32] The tests for the applicability of theoretical constructs make ample allowance for disturbing factors and can never produce "absolutely conclusive evidence but at best evidence yielding a higher probability." [33] Most of the theoretical part of science, Carnap now believes, is better constructed in terms of theoretical constructs than in terms of dispositional or operational predicates.[34]

D. Since most scientific knowledge is formulated in terms of theortical constructs connected with observation sentences by probabilities, the structure of scientific knowledge involves a logic of probability. In awareness of this consideration, Carnap has devoted much of his effort during the past ten years to the problem of probability. To some of his conclusions in this area we now turn.

That which thories of probability attempt to explicate is not, as is commonly thought, a single concept but two quite distinct concepts.[35] One is the concept of the degree of confirmation of a statement and the other is that of the relative frequency of a property or event in the long run. Accordingly, the widely divergent theories of probability often encountered need not be, as they appear, conflicting interpretations of a single concept, but may be parallel accounts of quite different concepts each of which serves a useful purpose. However, there remains a close correspondence between the two concepts, so that nearly all that can be significantly said in terms of relative frequency can be adequately translated into the language of degree of confirmation.[36]

Of the two kinds of probability, the one with which Carnap primarily concerns himself is degree of confirmation. Probability of this sort depends on a logic of probability and, despite differences, the inductive logic involved resembles deductive logic in a number of important respects. Both are genuine instances of logic. Both are purely a priori relations independent of facts and independent of the

[32] "The Methodological Character of Theoretical Concepts," pp. 66 f.

[33] Ibid., p. 69.

[34] Ibid., pp. 66, 68.

[35] Carnap, "The Two Concepts of Probability," Philosophy and Phenomenological Research, V (1944–45), 513–32; and

Carnap, The Logical Foundations of Probability (Chicago: University of Chicago Press, 1950), pp. 23 ff.

[36] See ibid., pp. 41 ff., 550 ff.; and Carnap, The Continuum of Inductive Methods (Chicago: University of Chicago Press, 1952), pp. 1, 30.

ruth or falsity of the premises that enter into them.[37] For both, the
·elation of premises and conclusion is "purely logical in the sense
hat it depends merely upon the meanings of the sentences or more
·xactly upon their ranges."[38] Indeed, inductive logic could be said
·o be an extension of deductive logic by the addition of a new con-
irmation function.[39] The significant difference lies in the fact that
)nly the less extensive deductive logic yields conclusive results while
.he more extensive inductive or probability logic yields confirmations
n varying degrees.

Probabilities in the sense in which Carnap is primarily concerned
.vith them are always relative to evidence, and the principal problem
)f the logic of probability is to find a way of formulating the extent
)f the confirmation of a hypothesis upon given evidence that will at
he same time be numerically precise (varying from 0 to 1) and con-
:orm to our intuitions and the actual practice of scientists. Thus far
iuch formulations have been achieved at most only for the first two
)f five major kinds of inductive inference. The five kinds include
'direct inference, . . . from the population to a sample; . . . pre-
·lictive inference, . . . from one sample to another; . . . inference
From analogy, . . . from one individual to another; . . . inverse in-
Ference, . . . from a sample to the population; and universal infer-
·nce, . . . from a sample to a hypothesis of universal form."[40] Even
For the two kinds concerning which substantial progress has been
made, precision can be attained only in terms of a highly simplified
language in which the elements are individuals and qualitative predi-
:ates. As yet no satisfactory probability logic for statements concerning continuous quantities has been achieved. Where numerically
precise probability statements cannot be arrived at, classificatory
probability statements indicating that a hypothesis is confirmed by the
evidence, and comparative probability statements indicating that an
hypothesis is confirmed by the evidence as much as or more or less
than another, may sometimes be formulated. Carnap firmly believes,
however, that numerically precise statements of probability can eventually be achieved for virtually every sort of situation.[41]

The quest for numerical measures for probabilities may well begin
with possibilities. The sum of all possibilities is the sum of all state
descriptions. A state description is a conjunction of sentences stating
"for every individual . . . and for every property designated by a
primitive predicate . . . whether or not this individual has this

---

[37] "Remarks on Induction and Truth," *Philosophy and Phenomenological Research*, VI, 595.

[38] *Ibid.*, p. 596.

[39] *The Logical Foundations of Probability*, pp. 199 ff.

[40] *Ibid.*, pp. 207 f.

[41] *Ibid.*, pp. 21 ff.

property." [42] The range of a sentence consists of those state descrip tions in which it holds.

The probability of an hypothesis upon given evidence is in gen eral a ratio of the evidence to the range of the hypothesis and the evidence, but just how the ratio is to be determined is a difficult mat ter. When the hypothesis holds for all state descriptions, as in the case of a tautology the probability is clearly 1. Conversely when the hypothesis is false for all state descriptions, as in the case of a self contradiction, the probability is equally clearly 0. Such probability propositions hold regardless of whether or not factual evidence i available.[43] But when the hypothesis is neither tautologous nor self contradictory the determination of the requisite ratio is not so simple and methods must be derived for determining ratios that accord as fully as possible with intuitive insights and scientific procedures. So long as no factual evidence is available, it might seem plausible for this purpose simply to count every state description as initially equi probable. But as soon as factual evidence comes into the picture such a procedure is seen to be highly implausible, failing to allow for learning from experience. Since the determination of probabilities in terms of the state descriptions in the ranges of the sentences con cerned gives no more weight to recurrence of predicates than to the number of individuals to which these predicates apply, this procedure makes no such provision as intuition and scientific method make for learning from experience.

A procedure that is plausible alike for cases in which factual evi dence does not exist and cases in which it does exist is as follows First, a structure is defined as a disjunction of all those state descrip tions that are alike in everything except the pattern of individuals involved or as a disjunction of all state descriptions that could be made alike simply by shifting the individuals involved; and all struc tures are regarded initially as equi-probable.[44] Then within each structure equal weight must be given to each state description. Thus the place of each state description in the whole will be represented by a fraction determined by multiplying its ratio to its own structure by the ratio of its structure to the whole. On this basis the recurrence of predicates can be given due weight, and learning from experience can be adequately allowed for. For example, if three blue balls have been drawn from a bag whose contents are unknown save for the fact that it contains some blue or white balls, if all state descriptions are counted alike the probability of drawing another blue ball is only $\frac{1}{2}$ whereas if structure descriptions are first counted as equi-probable

[42] *Ibid.*, p. 71.
[43] Cf. *ibid.*, pp. 557 ff.
[44] Cf. *ibid.*, pp. 108 ff., 114 ff.

he probability turns out to be ⅗, which approximates more nearly what intuition would suggest and takes experience into account.[45]

Although the procedure outlined is designed largely to facilitate direct inductive inference, i.e. inferences from population to sample, by suitable qualifications similar formulae could be worked out to fulfill the requirements of predictive inference, inference by analogy, inverse inference, and even universal inference.[46] In order to confirm probabilities involving future events, it is not necessary, as is commonly thought, to proceed through a universal law. In practical matters, such as the building of bridges, people are interested in results, not everywhere and in all time, but here and in the near future or at most during the next few hundred years.[47] Thus, even without unlimited confirmation of universal laws, degrees of confirmation concerning the future can by rational reconstruction be properly brought into line with our probability intuitions, in a manner similar to that in which Euclid by rational reconstruction worked out a system of geometry in line with our spatial intuitions.

All this is not to say that there can exist only one way of explicating the probabilities of events. Actually a continuum of inductive methods is possible. This continuum ranges all the way from systems which, like that of Reichenbach, tend to attribute directly to an infinite universe the frequencies found in a sample, to those which, like that of Peirce, refuse to attribute anything to an infinite universe on the basis of a finite sample on the ground that in such a universe no sample is large enough to be significant. Systems leaning toward the first of these extremes give considerable weight to empirical evidence and are well suited to large and clearly defined samples; systems leaning toward the second give more weight to coherence [48] and are safe even when samples are small or ill-defined. The best system, Carnap believes, will mediate between the extremes and while, generally speaking, giving substantial weight to evidence, will avoid the "straight rule" which attributes directly to the universe the characteristics found in the sample.[49]

E. In view of Carnap's early identification of philosophy with logical syntax, his subsequent rejection of incorrigible protocol sentences, and the present claim shared by him and most other members of his group that it is rather systems than separate statements that are in the end to be tested, one might well expect that Carnap would adopt a version of the coherence theory of truth. But while there are hints of

[45] Carnap, "What is Probability?" *Scientific American*, CLXXXIX (1953), 134 f.
[46] *Ibid.*, pp. 562–67.
[47] *Ibid.*, pp. 572 ff.

[48] Carnap, *The Continuum of Inductive Methods* (Chicago: University of Chicago Press, 1952), pp. 1 f., 5 ff.
[49] *Ibid.*, pp. 2, 79.

such a theory in his writings, the theory to which Carnap explicitly commits himself is rather a version of the correspondence theory.[50]

However rigorous and formal the system in terms of which science is justified, science remains in the end responsible to observations and depends for its truth upon the occurrence of the properties designated by its basic terms. To attempt, as Reichenbach and others have done, to merge the concept of truth with that of probability is to deny the principle of the excluded middle, to confuse knowledge with truth, and to involve one's self in other insoluble paradoxes.[51] Whereas verification and confirmation are pragmatic concepts, truth is a semantic concept [52] whose character is indicated by saying that "to assert a sentence is true means the same as to assert the sentence itself." [53] That truth is such a semantic characteristic is not, however, all that is to be said about truth. Underlying the semantic concept of truth is an absolute concept of truth, in terms of which truth applies not to sentences but to propositions, and propositions are linked not with nonsemantic sentences but with facts.[54] In the end truth depends on individuals having or not having the properties designated by the sentences referring to them,[55] and the truth of a statement having a time reference does not change with changes in the facts to which the statement refers.[56]

2. OTHER PHYSICALISTS OF THE VIENNA CIRCLE: HERBERT FEIGL AND PHILIPP FRANK

A. In very considerable part, the other members of the Vienna Circle have tended to follow the lead of Carnap, but often they have developed significant insights of their own and sometimes they have differed substantially with Carnap. The first of the two philosophers to be considered as representative of these other members of the Vienna Circle is Herbert Feigl (b. 1902) of the University of Minnesota. The thought of Feigl has both influenced and been deeply influenced by that of Carnap. The principal matters concerning which Feigl's thought differs from that of Carnap are his less extensive use of artificial languages, his somewhat more liberal accounts of meaning and induction, and his stronger inclination toward a cautious realism.

[50] Cf. *Introduction to Semantics*, p. 29.
[51] Carnap, "Truth and Confirmation," in Herbert Feigl and Wilfrid Sellars, *Readings in Philosophical Analysis* (New York: Appleton-Century-Crofts, Inc., 1949), p. 119; *Logical Foundations of Probability*, p. 177; and "Remarks on Induction and Truth," p. 60.

[52] Cf. *Introduction to Semantics*, p. 28.
[53] *Ibid.*, p. 26.
[54] *Ibid.*, pp. 240 ff.
[55] *Logical Foundations of Probability*, p. 69.
[56] *Remarks on Induction and Truth*, p. 601.

The general logical-empiricist doctrine that all cognitively meaningful statements are basically either formal or subject to empirical confirmation is embraced at the outset and repeatedly reaffirmed by Feigl, and that all formal statements, including all statements of logic and mathematics, are analytic and tautological Feigl steadfastly maintins. Thus, in an early essay Feigl endorses the view that the foundation of logic lies in "the stipulation that we adhere to conventions agreed upon," [1] and in a recent article he argues that "it is a matter of purely terminological decision whether we choose to characterize analytic propositions as factually meaningless or as the null case . . . of factual content." [2] Even the suggestion that analytic truth may sometimes be sufficiently grounded in meanings as represented by implicit definitions is rejected by Feigl, who persists in holding that "analytic propositions are true by virtue of meanings stipulated by explicit definitions." [3] To the strictures of Quine, White, and others against a sharp distinction between analytic and synthetic judgments, Feigl replies that while these strictures may have some weight in the area of methodology, they have none in that area of logical structure which is the principal domain of the philosophy of science,[4] and further that "intelligible and responsible communication is impossible without adherence to rules of inference which presuppose, at least, contextually and temporally fixed meanings." [5] Feigl does, however, concede that the *ultimate* justification of the linguistic rules themselves in which logical truth is grounded is pragmatic.[6]

Feigl's doctrine of the empirical criteria of meaningfulness is more flexible and more liberal than his account of the tautological character of analytic statements and indeed than the accounts of meaning criteria of most logical empiricists. While insisting upon the ultimate responsibility of factually meaningful statements to experience, Feigl is critical of all extremely narrow empirical and operational accounts of meaningfulness. "No scientist restricts factual meaningfulness to testability within the bounds of the technical facilities of the moment," and any attempt to restrain theoretical constructions unduly

[1] Herbert Feigl, "Logical Positivism, a New Movement in European Philosophy," *Journal of Philosophy*, XXVIII (1931), 284.

[2] Feigl, "Confirmability and Confirmation," *Revue Internationale de Philosophie*, V (1951), 270.

[3] Feigl, "Notes on Causality," in Feigl and Brodbeck, *Readings in the Philosophy of Science*, p. 416.

[4] "Confirmability and Confirmation," p. 275.

[5] Feigl, "Some Major Issues and Developments in the Philosophy of Science of Logical Empiricism," in Feigl and Scriven, *The Foundations of Science and the Concepts of Psychology and Psychoanalysis*, p. 8.

[6] Feigl, "*De Principiis Non-Disputandum*," in Max Black, *Philosophical Analysis* (Ithaca, N.Y.: Cornell University Press, 1950), p. 152.

is likely to yield recurrences of such misguided efforts as the attempts of Mach and Oswald to eliminate from science references to atoms.[7] Indeed, Feigl has now so far liberalized the criteria of meaningfulness that "factual meaninglessness can be charged against any assertion only if the premises of the hypothetico-deductive system stand in contradiction with the very idea of a test which would either confirm or disconfirm the assertion in question." Thus meaningfulness is measured against the idea of a test, not the existing means of testing.

Concerning the type of language, to which the justification of science leads back, Feigl seems at the period of Carnap's *Aufbau* to have approved the attempt to build upon a phenomenalistic language.[8] This attitude was soon replaced by an adoption of physicalism as decidedly preferable for the purpose of revealing the justificatory structure of science. Nevertheless, Feigl, unlike Carnap, continues to regard phenomenal language as not only possible but epistemologically basic at least in the sense that "knowledge by acquaintance . . . remains in any case the ultimate confirmation base of *all* knowledge claims." [9]

Concerning the structure of scientific justification Feigl rejects every effort to confine scientific language to terms that can be dispositionally or operationally defined. Instead he advocates a free construction of new hypotheses from which new data as well as old can be deduced. Such construction must of course retain at least some contact with observation. Einstein's thought is a model of the proper "middle of the road position" in making "the formation of scientific theories . . . a matter of free constructions, a matter of casting a net of concepts and laws, tied only in a relatively small number of points to the ground of experience." [10] It is moreover only in terms of such a network of concepts and laws that the recently much discussed problem of counterfactual conditionals is to be resolved, for while the necessity of recognizing such conditionals by no means removes the need for empirical connections, it does reveal the inadequacy of the logic of material implication for the purposes of science and requires the acknowledgment of a texture of laws that remain in force even when test conditions do not exist.[11] Concerning the problem of in-

[7] Feigl, "Operationalism and Scientific Method," *Psychological Review*, LII–LIII (1945–46) 253 f.

[8] "Logical Positivism," p. 393.

[9] Feigl, "The Mental and the Physical," in *Concepts Theories and the Mind-Body Problem* ("Minnesota Studies in the Philosophy of Science," Vol. II [Minneapolis: University of Minnesota Press, 1958]), p. 435.

[10] Feigl, "Principles and Problems of Theory Construction in Psychology," in Wayne Demmis and Others, *Current Trends in Psychological Theory* (Pittsburgh, Pa.: University of Pittsburgh Press, 1951), p. 203.

[11] Cf. "Notes on Causality," p. 18, and "Some Major Issues and Development in the Philosophy of Science of Logical Empiricism," p. 18.

duction, Feigl adopts a pragmatic justification similar to the one worked out more elaborately by Reichenbach.[12] Not content with the adoption of a physicalistic language basis for a science consisting essentially of a nomological network, Feigl has gradually moved toward a genuine critical realism built around the idea of the nomological network. In a paper published in 1935, while continuing to reject metaphysical realism as such, Feigl finds an implicit realism in the failure of complete verification and in the epistemological recognition that the "knowing mind or . . . organism is a part of that spatio-temporal-causal structure called a physical world."[13] More recently in his "Existential Hypotheses," Feigl insists that he has all the while sought "to formulate and vindicate an Empirical Realism" and that a rapprochment between phenomenalism and realism is now more than ever in prospect. The meaning of a physical object statement can never be adequately translated in terms of phenomena and "the surplus meaning is understood to consist in *the factual reference* of the constructs employed in theoretical laws . . . and the existential hypotheses."[14] Such factual reference must of course be understood not in terms of isolated objects but in the context of a whole semantic system. It is also inevitably involved in all scientific inquiry. All "attempts at 'reduction' " of "such unobservables as electro-magnetic fields, atomic and subatomic particles, photons, etc." are "complete failures," and the theoretical entities in question properly claim reality in nomological networks. Feigl says, "If this be metaphysics, make the most of it!"[15] The distinction between evidence and reference is and must remain, in all instances, save those of elemental data, inevitable and fundamental.[16]

Feigl applies his critical or "semantic" realism to minds as well as bodies. At first he was inclined to think statements concerning the mental and the physical to be simply two different kinds of languages referring to the same facts,[17] but he now thinks this monistic double language theory misleading and prefers a monistic double knowledge theory in which experiential data and certain inferred concepts of neurophysiological patterns have the same reference but are different

[12] Cf. "The Logical Character of Induction," in Herbert Feigl and Wilfrid Sellars, *Readings in Analytic Philosophy* (New York: Appleton-Century-Crofts, Inc., 1949), pp. 297–304; and "Some Major Issues and Developments in the Philosophy of Science of Logical Empiricism," p. 29.

[13] Feigl, "Sense and Nonsense in Scientific Realism," *Actes Du Congres Internationale De Philosophie Scientifique*, Herrmann, Cie. Editeura, III (1935), 54.

[14] Feigl, "Existential Hypotheses," *Philosophy of Science*, XVII (1950), 48.

[15] "Some Major Issues and Developments in the Philosophy of Science of Logical Empiricism," p. 17.

[16] Cf. "The Mental and the Physical," p. 32.

[17] Feigl, "Logical Analysis of the Psychophysical Problem," *Philosophy of Science*, I (1934), 425–45.

ways of attaining knowledge of the same thing.[18] Such identity of the mental and the physical involves no logically necessary identity of mind and body, and the synthetic parallelism between the two, upon which recognition of their identity depends, must be established by science rather than philosophy. However, much progress toward the establishment of the requisite parallelism has already been made, and Feigl is convinced that the process will continue. Once the parallelism is duly granted, sound philosophical analysis leaves no adequate ground for insisting upon the existence of two distinct entities, and strongly suggests that the referents of mental terms may be identified with those of physical terms. "The raw feels of direct experience, as we 'have' them, are empirically identifiable with the referents of certain specifiable concepts of molar behavior theory, and these in turn . . . are empirically identifiable with the referents of some neurophysiological concepts." [19]

B. Philipp Frank (b. 1884) differs from most of the other members of the Vienna Circle in two important respects, in being himself a physicist as well as a philosopher, and in devoting more attention to the broaden relations between scientific knowledge and other human achievements and activities.[20] His conclusions concerning the character of scientific knowledge itself are very similar to some of those already discussed, and need not be dwelt upon here. Thus, all knowing consists of tautologies and empirical statements. Operational testability is in general the criterion of empirical meaningfulness,[21] and confirmation is in terms of observation. The function of science is largely that of leading successfully from one experience to another,[22] and philosophical debates, for example between idealism and realism, cannot be adjudicated on scientific grounds. Even such cautious realism as that suggested by Feigl cannot be sustained.[23] As to the character of the basic sentences on which scientific knowledge must rest, Frank's earlier writings tend to be phenomenalistic; even in his latest work he speaks on occasions of the basic data of science as "dancing spots." [24] However, in view of the actual procedures of scientists and the tendency of some writers to seek support in phenomenalistic lan-

[18] Feigl, "The Mind-Body Problem in the Development of Logical Empiricism," in Feigl and Brodbeck, *Readings in the Philosophy of Science,* pp. 612–26; and "The Mental and the Physical."

[19] *Ibid.,* p. 445.

[20] Philipp Frank, *Between Physics and Philosophy* (Cambridge: Harvard University Press, 1941); Frank, *Modern Science and Its Philosophy* (Cambridge: Harvard University Press, 1949); Frank, *Relativity,*

A Richer Truth (London: Jonathan Coke, 1951); Frank, *Philosophy of Science* (Englewood Cliffs, N.J.: Prentice Hall, 1957).

[21] *Between Physics and Philosophy,* p. 9.

[22] *Modern Science and Its Philosophy,* p. 278.

[23] Frank, "Comments on Realistic versus Phenomenalistic Interpretations," *Philosophy of Science,* XVII (1950), 166–69.

[24] *Philosophy of Science,* p. 6.

guage for idealistic metaphysics, Frank is favorably inclined toward the physicalistic point of view of Carnap and Feigl.[25]

A large part of what Frank has written has been concerned with the relation between science and philosophy. Much of what he has had to say on this subject consists in pouring scorn upon traditional philosophies for attempting to produce knowledge apart from experience. However, more recently Frank has come to believe that even metaphysical systems have positive functions to perform, and his latest book attempts to disclose the nature of those functions. Despite the fact that in ancient times experiential apprehension of reality lay largely in the province of the artisan and philosophical apprehension in that of the aristocrat, science and philosophy were able in those periods to maintain a fairly unified front, for the reason that science lacked the precision needed to bring it into conflict with philosophy.[26] When in the sixteenth century science began to take on mathematical forms, a radical rift between science and philosophy became inevitable and has continued ever since.[27] Scientific data could be deduced from middle axioms, which such data in turn supported, but the allegedly intuitive deliverances of philosophy remained in intellectual isolation. Such a rift is, however, intolerable. On the one hand the high-level theories of science cannot be sustained on purely scientific grounds and are in need of other considerations to render them plausible and useful, and on the other hand philosophical ideas may often perform these very tasks.[28] Unfortunately the philosophical ideas that have usually been offered, whether in traditional philosophies or in "spiritualistic" interpretations of modern science, have been largely out of keeping with the actual achievements of science.[29] The philosophies of pragmatism and positivism are proving more successful, and the kind of desirable unified science embracing the social as well as the physical sciences that grows out of them may be able not only to render the products of science more plausible to common sense but also to show what kinds of high-level theories are most likely to lead to the best social results.[30]

3. Some Representatives of the Berlin Group: Hans Reichenbach and Carl Hempel

Members of the Berlin Group, which worked independently of the Vienna Circle but in general accord with the objectives of that association, included among others Hans Reichenbach, Walter Dubislov,

[25] *Modern Science and Its Philosophy*, pp. 35, 86, 98, 171.
[26] *Philosophy of Science*, chap. i.
[27] *Ibid.*, chap. ii.
[28] *Ibid.*, pp. 17–20.
[29] *Ibid.*, chaps. vii, x.
[30] *Ibid.*, chap. xv.

A. Hertzberg, Kurt Grelling, and Carl Hempel. Of these the most influential was Reichenbach, whose thought, together with some phases of that of Hempel, will be considered here.

A. From the beginning of his career onward Hans Reichenbach followed with keen interest and genuine insight the developments of modern physical science, and labored incessantly to interpret these developments in a philosophical frame of reference. This intense preoccupation with the methodology and achievements of modern science led to the production of an impressive succession of scientifically oriented books including *Atom and Cosmos,*[1] *Experience and Prediction,*[2] *The Philosophic Foundations of Quantum Mechanics,*[3] *From Copernicus to Einstein,*[4] *The Direction of Time,*[5] *Theory of Probability,*[6] and *Philosophy of Space and Time.*[7] It also led Reichenbach to reject a large part of traditional philosophy—especially the rationalistic part—and to put most of his own thinking into a probability frame of reference that seemed to him to be required by the character of recent physics. We shall consider successively Reichenbach's attack upon rationalism, his view of meaning, his accounts of possible modes of construction of knowledge and types of objects of knowledge, and his interpretation of the key concepts of probability and induction.

(*1*) Not content simply to condemn rationalism in terms of a general theory of meaning, Reichenbach undertook to disclose the specific weaknesses of the basic roots of the rationalistic approach to philosophy.[8] The foundations of rationalism lie, he thought, in an unwarranted attempt to extend the useful discoveries of mathematics beyond their own proper domain. In Plato, mathematics is confused with ethics; and in Aristotle, it controls instead of serving physics. Kant pretended to bring rationalism and empiricism together but only succeeded in infecting the concept of experience with rational elements. Unfortunately the rationalists were able to persuade the empiricists to adopt their ideal of perfect demonstration, so that consistent empiricism was brought in Hume to inevitable skepticism.

[1] Hans Reichenbach, *Atom and Cosmos* (New York: The Macmillan Co., 1933).

[2] Reichenbach, *Experience and Prediction* (Chicago: University of Chicago Press, 1938).

[3] Reichenbach, *The Philosophic Foundations of Quantum Mechanics* (Berkeley and Los Angeles: University of California Press, 1944).

[4] Reichenbach, *From Copernicus to Einstein* (New York: Philosophical Library, Inc., 1942).

[5] Reichenbach, *The Direction of Time* (Berkeley and Los Angeles: University of California Press, 1956).

[6] Reichenbach, *Theory of Probability* (Berkeley: University of California Press, 1949).

[7] Reichenbach, *Philosophy of Space and Time* (New York: Dover Publications, Inc., forthcoming).

[8] Reichenbach, "Rationalism and Empiricism: An Inquiry into the Roots of Philosophic Error," *Philosophical Review,* LVII (1948), 330–46.

The liberation of thought from the clutches of rationalism has, however, at last been well begun by a series of brilliant discoveries. First the discovery, within a few years after the death of Kant, of non-Euclidean systems of geometry, compelled recognition that the geometry supposed to be imposed by reason had alternatives and that the question of the geometry of the actual world had to be decided by empirical tests.[9] Then, the development of logistics revealed that the whole of the apparatus of logic and mathematics, which rationalism had tried to read into reality, was in fact tautologous and devoid of factual content.[10] Finally, scientific thought itself discovered, through such developments as the theories of organic evolution, relativity, and quantum mechanics, the implausibility of the rigorous determinism that rationalism long endeavored to impose upon science.[11] Together these discoveries have made possible a new knowledge in which science, delivered from the demand for full demonstration, can yield probabilities that not only serve the ends of practical achievement but also facilitate the advance of scientific theory.

(2) The selection of a criterion of meaningfulness is not, Reichenbach thought, a matter for proof but rather one for decision. "Meaning is a function which symbols acquire by being put into a certain correspondence with the facts,"[12] and what kind of correspondence with what kinds of facts is taken to yield meaningful statements may, within limits, be determined by the choice of those who use symbols. However, some choices are much less useful, illuminating, and harmonious with the processes of common sense and science than others. Thus, for example, while people may legitimately choose to interpret meanings in terms of subjective feelings and inner convictions, such an interpretation can scarcely be rendered "consistent with their behavior" and is likely to be "an empty system unrelated to the world of experience."[13]

What is wanted is a theory in terms of which "there is as much meaning in a proposition as can be utilized for action,"[14] and accordingly a satisfactory theory of meaning must be grounded not in people's subjective feelings and images[15] but in physical facts. Thus "signs are physical things . . . [and] meaning is a property of signs, and not something added to them."[16] Bearing in mind that it is propositions and not isolated words that have meaning, one may as a

[9] See *The Rise of Scientific Philosophy* (Berkeley & Los Angeles: University of California Press, 1951), pp. 125 ff.
[10] *Ibid.*, pp. 215 ff.
[11] *Ibid.*, pp. 157 ff., also see *Philosophic Foundations of Quantum Mechanics.*
[12] *Experience and Prediction*, p. 17.

[13] *The Rise of Scientific Philosophy*, p. 258.
[14] *Experience and Prediction*, p. 80.
[15] Cf. *ibid.*, p. 159.
[16] *The Rise of Scientific Philosophy*, pp. 256 f.

first approximation of a theory of meaning adopt a verifiability view to the effect that *"a proposition has meaning if, and only if, it is verifiable as true or false* . . . [and that] *two sentences have the same meaning if they obtain the same determination as true or false by every possible observation."* [17] Such a criterion would, however, eventually eliminate all factual statements, for no factual statement can be fully verified. What is needed is a criterion in which the concept of verifiability is replaced by that of applicability of probability weight. Thus, *"a proposition has meaning if it is possible to determine a weight, i.e. a degree of probability, for the proposition; [and] two sentences have the same meaning if they obtain the same weight, or degree of probability, by every possible observation."* [18]

(3) Concerning the basis upon which an epistemological construction of the world is to be achieved, Reichenbach considers four alternatives including an *"impression basis,"* a *"concreta basis,"* a *"proposition basis,"* and an *"atom basis."* [19] From the point of view of logic there are no compelling reasons for preferring one of these bases to another; "logic does not distinguish one basis as the necessary one." [20] However, from the point of view of psychology and of conformity to "the actual performance of knowledge," [21] one basis may be decidedly preferable to another, and with this fact in mind the four bases must be examined.

Construction upon an impression basis represents an effort to "reduce knowledge to an absolutely certain basis." [22] It presupposes nothing about physical objects and reduces all statements about such objects to such phenomenalistic statements as "I had the impression of a flash of light as is produced by the beam of a lighthouse, *or* by a flash of lightning, *or* by a blow with the fist on my eye." [23] This basis has the advantage that its elemental statements are more certain than those of any other basis, but this superior sense of certainty is grounded merely in the fact that statements on the impression basis are really logical alternations whose truth demands are less than those of statements on other bases.[24] Impression statements are psychologically secondary,[25] not intuitive,[26] and they can ordinarily be formulated as in the above sentence only by making use of *concreta* statements. In any case, however more certain than *concreta* statements they may be, they are at best not completely certain. They always involve fallible memory,[27] and we stand ready to withdraw them when

[17] *Experience and Prediction*, pp. 30–31.
[18] *Ibid.*, p. 54.
[19] *Ibid.*, p. 263.
[20] *Ibid.*, p. 203.
[21] *Ibid.*, p. 204.
[22] *Ibid.*, p. 90.

[23] *Ibid.*, p. 170.
[24] *Ibid.*, p. 173.
[25] *Ibid.*, pp. 140 ff.
[26] *Ibid.*, p. 177.
[27] *Ibid.*, pp. 179 ff.

they conflict with systems of established facts.[28] If we begin with them even ordinary physical object statements must be arrived at indirectly and by projection or extension rules not provided for in their terminology.[29]

The atom basis starts with statements concerning atoms, electrons, and related scientific objects having a low degree of initial certainty but substantial inductive support. It has the advantage of requiring no extensions or projections beyond itself and for this reason is most used by physicists. However, this basis has the very great disadvantage of being quite unintuitive and building upon the result of considerable chains of inference, at any point of which mistakes can be made. The ordinary objects of the physical world are arrived at in this terminology only by reduction, and reference to impressions requires further reductions.

The concreta or physical object basis for most purposes is preferable to the others. Characteristic statements on this basis are such ordinary statements as "there is a table," "this steamer has two funnels," "the thermometer indicates 15° centigrade," and "there is a flash of lightning." [30] They consist primarily of "reports about the objects of our personal macrocosmic environment (concreta) at a certain moment." [31] The *concreta* basis represents the mode of construction that is most intuitive and most natural to man, for it is in the ordinary world of houses, books, and other macrocosmic objects that our daily lives are lived, and most of what we say either of impressions or of scientific objects is inferred from observations of physical objects.[32] The fact that on the concreta basis statements involving scientific objects and even impressions must be arrived at by inference through extension rules is of course a disadvantage, but no basis is fully satisfactory for all purposes and the other advantages of the concreta basis are generally sufficient to offset this disadvantage.

The proposition basis is quite different from the other three in that it builds not directly upon any kind of nonlinguistic fact but upon sentences. This basis, attributed to Carnap by Reichenbach, has the advantage of being "more closely related to knowledge than the object basis" in that "the system of knowledge" is "composed of sentences." [33] It also has the advantage of enabling one to distinguish strict implications from material implications as no object basis does. But it tends to obscure the consideration that science is in quest for

[28] Reichenbach, "The Experimental Element in Knowledge." *Philosophical Review* LXI (1952), 155.
[29] *Experience and Prediction*, p. 264.
[30] *Ibid.*, p. 34.
[31] Reichenbach, "The Verifiability The-
ory of Meaning," *Proceedings of the American Academy of Arts and Sciences,* LXXX (1951), 95.
[32] *Experience and Prediction*, p. 289.
[33] *Ibid.*, p. 268.

connections among facts, not for connections among sentences. It tends to lead to an overemphasis upon the conventional aspects of language and to obscure the consideration that "there are some essential features of language which are not arbitrary but which are due to the correspondence of language with facts."[34] The choice of geometrical principles, for example, is no longer arbitrary when certain "definitions of co-ordination" have been formulated.[35] Thus while the proposition basis is not wrong and may be used for certain purposes, it must for most purposes be treated as secondary to the concreta basis, which grounds itself in observations of macrocosmic objects and events.

In line with his account of the four bases for the construction of knowledge, Reichenbach writes of at least four different types of objects of knowledge. One consists of impressions; another of concreta, which may be either subjective or objective; another of abstracta, which language distinguishes for purposes of convenience, and the other of scientific objects. Reichenbach also often speaks of "illata," or inferred objects, which include nearly all scientific objects and also, oddly enough, most impressions.[36] Abstracta do not constitute an independent type of object, for in fact they are reducible to concreta in much the sense in which a brick wall is reducible to a pattern of individual bricks.[37] In this connection the relation of abstracta and concreta contrasts sharply with that of external things and impressions, for while abstracta are reducible to concreta, external things are by no means reducible to impressions.[38]

The problem of the existence of an external world is, according to Reichenbach, a real one not to be "cut short . . . by sophistical remarks."[39] Actually, physical objects are ordinarily presented to us in our observations of concreta; and while valid observations must be confirmed by inference, the objective reality of these objects is not precluded by that requirement. The real world of waking life differs from that of dreams by its coherent causal connections.[40] One could indeed begin with a positivistic language and in it express the results of actual observations, but only if he adopted rules of language which by probability inference enabled him to project such a language to cover independently real objects could he properly say what we ordinarily intend to say.[41] Far better, then, as a rule, is to begin with a normal system that includes reference to inferred objects. It is true of course that we cannot adequately speak of quantum phenomena

[34] Ibid., p. 271.
[35] Ibid.
[36] Experience and Prediction, p. 266.
[37] Cf. ibid., pp. 105 ff.
[38] Cf. ibid., pp. 129 ff.
[39] Ibid., pp. 92 f.
[40] Ibid., p. 139.
[41] Ibid., pp. 114 ff.

in the normal language of ordinary objects, for our instruments inevitably interfere with our observations and normal language leads to causal anomalies.[42] One could use this fact as a reason for confining his language to the positivist level, on which causal anomalies do not arise; but such limitation would preclude important questions. The best course would then seem to be to begin with a normal system built on a concreta basis, and then to adopt in terms of probability inference further extension rules whereby basic issues concerning quantum phenomena can be raised and one can speak "about an atomic world as real as the ordinary physical world."[43]

The knowledge with which science is primarily concerned consists in large part of nomological or lawlike statements, the logical character of some of which has in recent years been seen to involve serious problems. Among nomological statements the analytic ones pose no special problems. They represent limits of probability statements and constitute tautological means of translating one set of statements into another at a given level of language without themselves adding anything to knowledge. Much more difficult to characterize are synthetic nomological statements, which yield information concerning regularities among facts and constitute what are often called laws of nature. Such statements are certainly not material implications, for we should not be willing to affirm the truth of a lawlike statement merely because its antecedent was false. Nor are nomological statements generalized implications, for even the falsity of an antecedent in all cases would not be a sufficient reason for affirming a lawlike statement.[44] The major requirements for nomological statements are actually as follows: that they be *general* in the sense of being "all-statements,"[45] that they be *exhaustive* in the sense that "all the possibilities opened up by the statement are exhausted by the objects of the physical world,"[46] that the contradictories of their antecedents be not implied, that they be *universal* and not restricted "to certain times and places,"[47] that they be exhaustive and contain no reference "to a particular space-time region," and finally that they be verifiable in the sense of being capable of being shown to have a high degree of probability.[48]

The logic through which knowledge, whether formulated in nomological statements or not, is best achieved and sustained is primarily neither deductive proof, nor confirmation by the establishment of the

[42] *Philosophic Foundations of Quantum Mechanics,* pp. 20 ff.
[43] *Ibid.,* p. vii.
[44] Reichenbach, *Nomological Statements and Admissible Operations* (Amsterdam: North-Holland Pub. Co., 1954), p. 9.

[45] *Ibid.,* pp. 8 f.
[46] *Ibid.,* p. 29.
[47] *Ibid.,* p. 9.
[48] *Ibid.,* pp. 10 ff.

consequents of conditions,[49] nor demonstration by special methods of induction. It is rather, as the preceding account has essentially suggested, a logic of probabilities, with reference to which deductive logic is simply the limiting case, and the special methods of induction supplementary aids. Accordingly, one may appropriately affirm that "the problem of probability . . . contains the nucleus of every theory of knowledge." [50]

The most satisfactory approach to the problem of probability is to begin with a purely formal calculus in which an entire system is built upon postulated axioms in accord with stipulated rules. Fortunately such a calculus has already been for the most part worked out by mathematicians in the form of a widely accepted system of rules that would enable one to pass from one set of probability statements to another without further recourse to facts. Gathering up the essential features of this calculus in the first eight chapters of his *Theory of Probability*, Reichenbach addresses himself in the remaining chapters of that book to the more philosophical problems of the interpretation of the formal calculus and of the assertability of the calculus with reference to physical objects. Both problems are somewhat complicated by the fact that that to which the term "probability" is intended to refer is sometimes "*sequences of events* or other physical objects" and sometimes "*single events* or other single physical objects." [51]

If an interpretation of the calculus of probability is to serve as an illuminating instrument without unwarranted assumptions the whole calculus must be shown to follow tautologically from the interpretation adopted. The interpretation that fulfills this requirement as far as the probability of sequences of events is concerned is clearly a relative frequency one. Such an interpretation takes the probability of a certain kind of event to be the limit of the frequency with which that kind of event is encountered in its sequence. The existence of the limit for any sequence involving a certain frequency is taken to mean that for any difference, however small, there is a number of cases such that the total relative frequency encountered from that number of cases onward will not deviate from the relative frequency in question by more than that difference.[52] That such an interpretation fulfills the requirement of entailing all of the rules of the calculus is implicit in the fact that the calculus, despite being purely formal, was designed for the very purpose of fulfilling the demands of this interpretation.

[49] Reichenbach, *The Theory of Probability* (Berkeley & Los Angeles: University of California Press, 1949), pp. 95–96, 431.
[50] *Ibid.*, p. v.
[51] *Ibid.*, p. 338.

[52] See *ibid.*, p. 338; cf. also Reichenbach, *The Direction of Time* (Berkeley & Los Angeles: University of California Press, 1956), pp. 96 ff.

The interpretation does, however, involve some difficulties. For one thing, if a sequence is infinite, a given finite segment places no restrictions upon the eventual frequency. Fortunately, however, the series that we have to deal with are all finite and we need to deal with none that cannot be finitized or brought within manageable bounds.[53] A second difficulty, growing out of the answer to this one, lies in the fact that the concept of the limit applies, strictly speaking, only ot infinite series, in that deviations from a given frequency can be reduced indefinitely only if the series continues indefinitely. The answer to this difficulty lies in the fact that the limit concept is, like most of the laws of physics, a useful idealization, and that if it does not operate perfectly, it is nevertheless a sufficient approximation where the very large numbers with which we have to deal are concerned.[54]

Concerning the assertability of probability statements about physical objects, two kinds of theories present themselves. A priori theories endeavor to establish among events at least some connections independent of actually encountered frequencies, by assuming in one way or another that certain unknown factors are equipossible.[55] However, such theories are in fact built upon mechanisms of games of chance upon which certain already established but insufficiently recognized considerations have significant bearings. When these considerations are duly acknowledged, every reliable factor reduces to an encountered frequency.[56] Thus we are brought back to an a posteriori basis to which only observed frequencies and the formal calculus are relevant.

When we come to the probabilities not of sequences but of single events, such as the probability that it will rain today or that Julius Caesar was in Britain, we seem to be dealing with a different probability concept altogether.[57] Sometimes the alleged new concept is interpreted as a degree of expectation and sometimes as a unique characteristic. But the first of these accounts obscures the fact that probabilities are thought to be objective rather than subjective, and the other would afford no basis for action or indeed for that establishment of probability in terms of which meaning is assured. Actually, what is significant in the alleged probability of single events can be reduced to relative frequencies by discovering larger sequences and counting the frequencies of the kinds of events in question in them.[58] Thus, for example, one can interpret the probability of rain today in terms of the relative frequency of rain in the class of days

---

[53] *The Theory of Probability*, p. 348.
[54] *Ibid.*, p. 349.
[55] *Ibid.*, pp. 352 ff.

[56] *Ibid.*, pp. 355 ff.
[57] *Ibid.*, p. 366.
[58] *Ibid.*, pp. 71 ff.

resembling today in certain relevant respects. A better way of achieving a similar result is to transfer the inquiry to a metalinguistic basis and to regard the probability as the relative frequency of the reliability of the statement describing the event in question in a class of related statements. Thus the reliability of a statement to the effect that Caesar was in Britain would be measured by the number of chroniclers who report such an event and the relative number of reports of each that is "corroborated by the reports of other writers." [59]

Since our statements even about the events in terms of which one determines relative frequencies are only probable, the full execution of probability determination requires, instead of the ordinary two-valued logic, a multivalued one, in which truth and falsity are only limiting values of a scale that ranges between 0 and 1. Both for general probability purposes and for the interpretation of quantum mechanics Reichenbach has outlined such probalility logic. [60]

The problem of the justification of induction is basically that of the justification of the method of simple enumeration involved in the frequency interpretation of probability. In this connection it becomes apparent at the outset that if the frequencies encountered in series could be assumed to have limits the method could in fact be justified. Plainly, if one takes a frequency encountered up to a given point as an initial posit and then corrects his posit with each substantial accession of new data, his posit will eventually fall within any allowable difference, however small, provided there is a limit. If corroborating evidence is available, as is nearly always the case in scientific procedure, the required posit may be reached far more quickly in terms of concatenated probabilities. In some cases initial experiments may even permit a correct estimate upon the basis of only a single instance. Moreover, while in each case in which corroborating evidence is not available the initial posit is, as it were, blind in the sense of having no specific "weight" attached to it, a weight can be attached by a subsequent secondary posit referring to the first in a metalanguage; and this posit may in turn be weighted in a new metalanguage in such fashion that the proper posit may be approached with considerable assurance, and only the last posit need remain blind. [61]

However, the assumption that sequences encountered have limits is in fact one that we are not entitled to make. This assumption, which is a form of the doctrine of the uniformity of nature, could be

[59] *Ibid.*, p. 379.
[60] *Ibid.*, chap. x; and *Philosophic*

Foundations of Quantum Mechanics, pp. 150–66.
[61] *The Theory of Probability*, pp. 465 ff.

rationally justified only by induction and is therefore not available for the justification of induction itself. The alternative of acceptance of a synthetic a priori is even less promising. Accordingly, if justifying induction means justifying *belief* in induction, there is no justification for induction. Actually, however, justification does not mean establishing belief but giving adequate grounds for action, and in this sense an inductive rule that bids us posit successively encountered frequencies can be justified in that if there is a limit of a frequency it can be found by this method.[62] Being a sufficient condition for the discovery of the limit, if there is one, the method is at least a necessary condition for the discovery of such a limit. In following it we may be wrong if there is no limit, but it is our only chance. Hence our actions are justifiable in following it. There may even be specific procedures that improve upon this method, but if there are better methods that fact can only be discovered by following this method.

B. Although Carl G. Hempel (b. 1905), now of Princeton University, was a member of Reichenbach's Berlin Group and continues to represent some of the special emphases of that group, he also studied in Vienna under Schlick, continues to maintain close contact with members of the Vienna Circle, and fuses in his thought aspects of the thought of both groups.

In 1935 Hempel seems to have been in almost every respect an orthodox physicalistic logical positivist. He then held that a physical object statement was "nothing but an abbreviated formulation of . . . test sentences," [63] that even psychological statements could be translated into physical object statements, which in turn could be translated into observation sentences,[64] and that the only meaningful statements not so translatable, those of logic and mathematics, were purely analytic and without empirical content.[65] Soon afterward, however, Hempel began to have serious misgivings, especially about the verification criterion of meaning and the translatability of meaningful sentences in terms of observation sentences.[66] At first he adopted Carnap's liberalization of the translatability thesis through reduction chains that connected physical object statements with observation statements without defining the former in terms of the latter, but subsequently he came to feel that the liberalization must be extended by means of the concept of connectibility with coherent scientific systems. In 1945 and 1946 in his "Studies in the Logic of Confirmation," and in "A Definition of 'Degree of Confirmation'"

---

[62] *Ibid.*, pp. 469 ff.
[63] Carl Hempel, "The Logical Analysis of Psychology," in Feigl and Sellars, *Readings in Philosophical Analysis*, p. 376.
[64] *Ibid.*, pp. 377 ff.

[65] Cf. Hempel, "On the Nature of Mathematical Truth," and "Geometry and Empirical Science," in *op. cit.*, pp. 222–49.
[66] *Op. cit.*, p. 373.

written jointly with Paul Oppenheim, Hempel undertook to work out in terms of a carefully defined artificial language a precise account of the sort of confirmation, short of verification, by which meaningful empirical statements can be linked with observation bases. Five years later he subjected the meaning criteria that had been proposed up to that time to severe scrutiny, concluding that every one of those criteria would either undermine science or open the door to an unwanted metaphysics, and that empirical philosophers had best abandon the quest for a meaning criterion suitable for natural language and direct their efforts toward the achievement of an unambiguous artificial language in which all empirical terms are defined ostensively.[67] The following year Hempel sharpened his attack upon attempted meaning criteria for isolated sentences and offered his own criteria for meaningful systems.[68]

No scientific statement, Hempel thinks, can be tested by itself, but each is an integral part of a whole and must be tested in terms of its place in a whole, which itself must be tested as a whole. Scientific systems are interpreted axiom systems connected at various points with observation and conforming to observational fact in varying degrees. The confirmation and meaningfulness of systems and theories come to be matters not of absolutes but of degrees, depending upon: "a. the clarity and precision with which the theories are formulated, . . . b. the systematic, ie. explanatory and predictive power of the systems . . . , c. the formal simplicity of the theoretical system, d. the extent to which the theories have been confirmed by evidential experience." [69] If a system corresponded perfectly with the observation it would be replaceable by observation sentences and therefore, by the "theoretician's dilemma," useless, but in point of fact a scientific system can never be more than an approximation which conforms to observation in high degree and in which even the distinction between analytic and synthetic is no longer perfectly sharp.[70] However, the inevitable gap between theoretical systems of science and observational data does not, in Hempel's opinion, justify the sort of leap to realist reference that Feigl and some other analytic philosophers are now proposing.[71]

[67] Hempel, "Problems and Changes in the Empirical Criterion of Meaning," in Leonard Linsky, *Semantics and the Philosophy of Language* (Urbana: University of Illinois Press, 1952), pp. 163–85.

[68] Hempel, "The Concept of Cognitive Significance: A Reconsideration," *Proceedings of the American Academy of Arts and Sciences*, LXXX (1951), 61–77.

[69] *Ibid.*, p. 74.

[70] Hempel, "The Theoretician's Dilemma," in Herbert Feigl and Michael Scriven, *Minnesota Studies in the Philosophy of Science*, Vol. II.

[71] Hempel, "A Note on Semantic Realism," *Philosophy of Science*, XVII (1950), 169–73.

4. Some Independent Physicalists: Karl Popper, Ernest Nagel, and Wilfrid Sellars

The three philosophers to be considered in this final section of the present chapter are not to be specifically connected with either of the two groups thus far considered in this chapter though they have had frequent contacts with members of both groups. They also do not form any close-knit group of their own. They are rather to be thought of as representing a large number of philosophers who are, or have been fairly close to being, logical positivists without adhering to any specific group within logical positivism or even confining themselves to its general tenets. The first is a native of Vienna who has spent a large part of his mature philosophical life in various parts of the British Commonwealth. The second is a native of Czechoslovakia who spent most of his life in the United States. The third is a native of the United States.

A. Karl R. Popper (b. 1902) is convinced that sound philosophical inquiry needs to be related to the history of the subject,[1] and he has been much more interested than most of the analytic philosophers thus far considered in relating his own views to those of earlier philosophers. He takes the business of philosophy to be primarily that of the study of *"the growth of the scientific knowledge"* with special reference to its cosmology.[2] Two contrasting concepts of science held by other philosophers Popper rejects as extreme and mistaken. One is an "essentialism" that takes scientific theories to "describe the 'essences' or the 'essential natures' of things."[3] The other is an "instrumentalism" that holds "that a universal law or a theory is not a proper statement but rather 'a rule, or set of instructions, for the derivation of singular statements from other singular statements."[4] With the instrumentalists and against the essentialists, Popper rejects the view that essences are discoverable,[5] but with the essentialists and against the instrumentalists, he holds that science is *"capable of real discoveries."*[6] Regarding the social sciences, he is especially hostile to a "historicism" that seeks to explain events in history by some determining principle, and insists that our knowledge of laws of human events must be achieved in terms of limited hypotheses that can be

[1] K. R. Popper, *The Logic of Scientific Discovery* (London: Hutchinson & Co., Ltd., 1959), p. 16.
[2] *Ibid.*, p. 15.
[3] Popper, "Three Views Concerning Human Knowledge," in H. D. Lewis (ed.), *Contemporary British Philosophy* (London & New York: George Allen & Unwin, &

The Macmillan Co., 1956), 3d series, p. 366.
[4] *Ibid.*, p. 373; see also *The Logic of Scientific Discovery*, p. 37 n.
[5] "Three Views Concerning Human Knowledge," pp. 365–72.
[6] *Ibid.*, p. 385.

individually tested.[7] In its inquiry concerning the growth of scientific knowledge, philosophy has, Popper believes, no peculiar method. Its method is rather that of all "rational discussion," namely, that of "stating one's problem clearly and of examining its various proposed solutions critically."

Unlike most contemporary philosophers of science, Popper rejects what he takes to be inductive reasoning, the sort of reasoning that proceeds from particular cases to general laws. The major difficulty of induction is that it can never yield the kind of laws that science needs. Science requires universal laws that are more than mere inference licenses and more than mere enumerations.[8] But since all possible cases can never be examined and no *general principle* of induction can be rendered plausible, induction is unable to do the job. Universal propositions are conclusively falsifiable, and particular ones, verifiable; but particular ones are not falsifiable and neither are universal ones verifiable.

Since the universal propositions required by science are not verifiable, verifiability cannot be the criterion, insofar as a criterion is wanted, of significance. Actually, attempted criteria of significance are of little use in any case; for at best they only set aside certain statements as not "belonging to empirical science" [9] without in any way showing them to be meaningless. Moreover even metaphysics may not be without "value for empirical science." [10] What is required is not so much a criterion of significance as a method of demarcation, distinguishing science from metaphysics. This is the problem of Kant as contrasted with that of Hume. Since the universal law statements that interest the scientist are conclusively falsifiable though not verifiable, the required criterion is not verifiability but falsifiability. Genuine scientific statements are those that are falsifiable by experience.[11]

The method by which science has progressed has never been that of mere generalization from particulars but always that of forming bold hypotheses and then trying one's best to refute them.[12] The more specific a hypothesis is, in the sense of yielding a wealth of deductions that expose it to falsification by experience, the more content it has. The trouble with such theories as those of Marx and Freud is that they presume to explain everything and leave no way open in which they could be refuted. In this they are in marked contrast to the

[7] See Popper, *The Open Society and Its Enemies* (Princeton, N.J.: Princeton University Press, 1950); and "The Poverty of Historicism," *Economica*, n.s., XI (1944–45).

[8] *The Logic of Scientific Discovery*, pp. 37, 62 ff.
[9] *Ibid.*, p. 35.
[10] *Ibid.*, p. 38.
[11] *Ibid.*, pp. 40 ff.
[12] *Ibid.*, pp. 278 ff.

genuinely scientific theory of Einstein, which can be put to risky tests at many points.[13] The same sort of difficulty affords ample reason for rejecting various conventionalist theories, for such theories are designed to be saved at all costs. They cannot be refuted and hence tell us nothing.[14]

The sentences in which scientific inquiry comes to rest are not irrefutable protocol sentences either of the phenomenalistic kind or of the physicalistic kind.[15] Efforts to build upon such sentences are really in the end psychologistic in relying upon a mere feeling of certainty. No empirical sentence is ever beyond the possibility of further testing. Basic sentences are those concerning which competent observers agree that they are so grounded in observation that no further testing is needed. We drive our stakes down, as it were, not until we reach bedrock, but until there is no need to drive them any further. To this extent science depends upon decisions.

Scientific statements attain, at best, not certainty but probability, and the probability logic involved is that of a modified frequency theory. The formal logic needed in the quest for scientific knowledge is essentially that which has been worked out in traditional and modern systems, but the theory on which it rests is not that of formalized system of axioms and theorems but rather that of a trivialization in terms of a theory of deducibility in which "an inference is valid if every interpretation—which makes the premises true also makes the conclusion true." [16]

B. Although the work of Ernest Nagel (b. 1901) has been devoted principally to the philosophy of science, and most of his comments on theory of knowledge have occurred in the course of criticisms of the work of other writers, what he has had to say about theory of knowledge amounts to at least an outline of a coherent and significant theory to the main features of which a considerable number of recent philosophers of science would be ready to subscribe. The theory is especially interesting for the conections it tends to establish between the ways of thinking of Dewey, especially those expressed in his later writings, and contemporary physicalistic analysis.

Like all of the other philosophers thus far considered in the present chapter, Nagel construes the meaningfulness of empirical statements in terms of ties with observations, and takes the logical links between statements to be formal and largely linguistic. Thus, he contends that if any theory is to be meaningful, "propositions

[13] Popper, "Philosophy of Science, a Personal Report," in C. A. Mace, *British Philosophy in the Mid-Century* (London: George Allen & Unwin, 1957), pp. 155 ff.

[14] *The Logic of Scientific Discovery*, pp. 78 ff.

[15] *Ibid.*, pp. 43 ff., 93–111.

[16] Popper, "New Foundations for Logic," *Mind*, LVI (1947), 193–235.

about possibly observable states of affairs must be specifiable which would contradict the theory," [17] and he is unwilling to accept as meaningful any alleged factual statements for which no empirical evidence could be supplied. He rejects as impossible Mill's empirical logic and all other attempts to ground logic in observation,[18] and he consistently takes logic and mathematics to consist of formal regulative rules of meaningful language.[19] While he is not willing to go all the way with a purely conventionalist view of logic, he is as firmly convinced as any conventionalist of the possibility and intertranslability of alternative logical and mathematical systems, and he holds that which of these systems is to be used "clearly is a matter of choice not controlled by the traits of some subject-matter." [20] Data, and observational and formal statements, according to Nagel, have their proper roles in knowledge, but the role of the former is material, while that of the latter is instrumental only.[21]

The attempt to build knowledge of physical facts upon indubitable knowledge of sense-data is, Nagel thinks, bankrupt. If the structure of knowledge is begun with the immediate it can never rise above the immediate; in any case we have no warrant for such a beginning. We do indeed sometimes obtain knowledge, for "unless we did possess knowledge of true propositions at *some* time, we could not intelligibly assert that we are ever in error"; but this consideration in no way justifies the suggestions often confused with it, that "some propositions are self-evident and that some propositions must be known immediately." [22] The assumption underlying the insistence upon indubitable sense-data, namely that "the conclusion of a non-demonstrative inference cannot be more certain than any of its premises is a mistake,[23] and knowledge is an achievement at the end of a process of inquiry rather than a given with which inquiry begins. As a matter of fact, even on the showing of some of the most ardent advocates of sense-datum foundations for knowledge, sense-data can hardly be logically admitted as premises on which the

[17] Ernest Nagel, "The Meaning of Probability," *Journal of American Statistical Association*, XXXI (1936), pp. 13 f.

[18] See Ernest Nagel (ed.), *John Stuart Mill's Philosophy of Scientific Method* (New York: Hafner Publishing Co., Inc., 1950), p. xlvi; and "Logic Without Ontology," in Feigl and Sellars, *Readings in Philosophical Analysis*, pp. 198 ff.

[19] *Ibid.*, p. 203; see also Morris R. Cohen and Ernest Nagel, *An Introduction to Logic*, in Feigl and Brodbeck, *Readings in the Philosophy of Science*, pp. 119–47.

[20] Nagel, "The Formation of Modern Conceptions of Formal Logic in the Development of Geometry," *Osiris*, VII (1939), 221.

[21] Cf. Nagel, "A Budget of Problems in the Philosophy of Science," *Philosophical Review*, LXVI (1957), 206.

[22] Nagel, "Truth and Knowledge of the Truth," *Philosophy and Phenomenological Research*, V (1944), 56; see also Nagel, "Probability and Theory of Knowledge," in Nagel, *Sovereign Reason* (Glencoe, Ill.: The Free Press, 1954), pp. 262 ff.

[23] Nagel, *Sovereign Reason*, p. 175.

structure of knowledge can be built; for, as these same advocates admit, sense-data do not present themselves as such but must be disclosed by a process of analysis that already involves "cognitive commitments."[24]

What we know consists not of simple sense-data nor indeed of more complex concreta in immediate experience[25] but of objective facts. Its arena is, as Reichenbach at his best has seen, "the objective common-sense world of houses and trees and wars," and " 'immediate existents' are not objects but instrumentalities of . . . knowledge."[26] Thus while prior to inquiry we cannot properly be said to know any sense-datum, most of us do know following inquiry "that the earth is spherical in shape, that Roosevelt [was] in office longer than any previous president, or that ice floats on water."[27]

The objectivity of what we know is not, however, to be taken to imply a metaphysical realism regarding scientific statements, even though that realism be a semantic realism. Thus Nagel rejects Feigl's contention that the view that "all the statements of science are 'translatable' . . . into the statements formulating matters of direct observation, . . . into the so-called physicalistic language," should be replaced by a semantic realism in which nonobservable things are "designated" in terms of lawlike networks.[28] Such a thesis, Nagel thinks, begs the crucial question by its use of the ambiguous term "designated." It also overlooks a plausible operationalist alternative which, without attempting to "translate" statements of science in terms of operations, insists "that the function of [scientific] theories can be adequately understood and described in terms of the observable connections their use establishes between classes of observation statements."[29] Scientists themselves are hesitant about "claiming 'factual reference' for all elements that appear in their intellectual constructions. . . . Why should philosophies of science be less circumspect?"[30]

The phase of Nagel's account of knowledge that most closely resembles the views of Dewey is his persistent insistence upon adequate regard for the contexts and actual procedures of inquiry. No statement can be properly understood at all apart from the kind of context in which it emerges, and no statement can be thought of as verified save in terms of methods appropriate to the purpose for

---

[24] See Nagel, "Mr. Russell on Meaning and Truth," in *op. cit.*, pp. 190–210, esp. p. 201; see also Nagel, "Probability and Theory of Knowledge," in *op. cit.*, pp. 248 ff., 257 ff.

[25] *Ibid.*, pp. 257 ff.

[26] *Ibid.*, p. 264.

[27] "Truth and Knowledge of the Truth," p. 56.

[28] Nagel, "Science and Semantic Realism," *Philosophy of Science*, XVII (1950), 174 ff.

[29] *Ibid.*, p. 176.

[30] *Ibid.*, p. 181.

which it is made. The reason that most scientific statements are best understood in the context of observation is that scientific statements arise in that context. Thus criticisms of science based on the remoteness of science from common experience for the most part become pointless when one takes seriously Dewey's reminder that "scientific objects are formulations of complex relations of dependence between things in gross experience."[31] However, the extension of language, by means of scientific theory, beyond the observational level may lead to pseudo-questions if one reads into the scientific theory meanings appropriate only to the observational level. The danger of such confusion is already evident even in classical physics, when for example one refers to "a force of attraction."[32] The risk is accentuated in quantum mechanics, where, for example, reference to the indeterminacy either of velocities or positions may, by association of quantum uses of the terms with ordinary uses, lead erroneously to the impression that there are gaps in the causal principle.[33]

Philosophical statements, like scientific ones, lend themselves to confusion when one interprets their theoretical constructs as though they were special apprehensions of entities independent of the methods of inquiry. One must not "suppose that philosophers can advance a knowledge of the world they inhabit by methods essentially different from those which the ordinary skilled worker in field, factory, or laboratory employs,"[34] and it is "an integral character of skilled workmanship to insist upon the fact that no statement or proposal has any meaning apart from the methods which are or may be employed to establish or execute them."[35] If one is to avoid the confusions so often engendered by extensions of language beyond the ordinary contexts of its origin into the domains of scientific and philosophical theory, one must keep clearly in mind the initial and terminal observational setting of inquiry and interpret the terms of science and philosophy as instruments of inquiry rather than as categories of reality. Thus, although it is often thought that scientific terms clarify scientific procedures, the fact is that "the procedures which are involved in using them, instead of being clarified by means of allegedly ultimate categories of science or philosophy, themselves clarify and make intelligible everything else."[36]

[31] Nagel, "Dewey's Theory of Natural Science," in Sovereign Reason, p. 106.
[32] Nagel, "Some Reflections on the Use of Language in the Natural Sciences," Journal of Philosophy, XLII (1945), 627.
[33] Nagel, "The Causal Character of Modern Physical Theory," in Feigl and Brodbeck, Readings in the Philosophy of Science, pp. 419–37.
[34] Nagel, "Some Theses in the Philosophy of Logic," Philosophy of Science, V (1938), 46.
[35] Ibid., p. 46.
[36] "The Formation of Modern Conceptions of Formal Logic in the Development of Geometry," p. 222.

Scientific statements must often, according to Nagel, be interpreted as probability statements, and the question of the meaning of such statements is one to which Nagel has devoted a great deal of attention. The Laplacean or classical theory, according to which a probability is measured by "the ratio of the numbers of members in classes of equiprobable alternatives," must be rejected because, among other things, it fails to provide a logical bridge for predictions.[37] The intuitionist theory of Keynes is equally untenable, for the reason that it lacks adequate objective controls.[38] The most plausible interpretation of probability statements of the variety that indicate that a certain kind of event is likely to be followed by a certain kind of result is an interpretation in terms of relative frequency.[39] The frequency interpretation itself may be conceived in terms of either finite reference classes, or limits of infinite reference classes, or a "set-theoretical approach, . . . which takes probability to be a theoretical parameter associated with classes of elements and which provides rules . . . for the acceptance or rejection of probability of hypotheses on the basis of observable relative frequencies in finite classes." [40] Whatever the interpretation, probability theory, like most of the theories of science, provides at best a theoretical framework which requires for its application the adoption of pragmatic rules.[41] Probability statements that do not directly refer to the incidence of kinds of events in reference classes can sometimes nevertheless be construed in terms of relative frequencies; but in the matter of probability statements, as elsewhere, meaning depends on context," [42] and it must be acknowledged that the term "probability" cannot always be readily construed as relative frequency. For one thing it seems clear that the probability of a scientific theory can scarcely be interpreted as a frequency,[43] and the probability of a specific event on the basis of specific evidence is also scarcely to be interpreted in frequency terms.[44]

C. Wilfrid Sellars (b. 1912) of Minnesota has endeavored more seriously than any other philosopher of the group now under con-

[37] See Nagel, "Is the Laplacean Theory of Probability Tenable?" *Philosophy and Phenomenological Research*, VI (1946), 614–18; and *Principles of the Theory of Probability* (Chicago: University of Chicago Press, 1939), pp. 44 ff.

[38] *Op. cit.*, pp. 48 ff.

[39] "The Meaning of Probability," pp. 10–30; "Principles of the Theory of Probability," pp. 17 ff.; and "Probability and Non-Demonstrative Inference," *Philosophy and Phenomenological Research*, V (1945), 486 ff.

[40] "A Budget of Problems in the Philosophy of Science," p. 212.

[41] *Ibid.*, pp. 212 ff.; and "Probability and Non-Demonstrative Inference," pp. 489 ff.

[42] "The Meaning of Probability," pp. 10 ff.

[43] Cf. "The Meaning of Probability," p. 16; and "Principles of the Theory of Probability," pp. 60 ff.

[44] "Probability and Non-Demonstrative Inference," pp. 494 ff.

sideration to do full justice to the insights of the major schools of traditional philosophy. Brought up in the critical realism of his father, R. W. Sellars, immersed in the traditions of rationalism and ethical intuitionism by his work at Oxford, and subsequently deeply influenced by the logical empiricism of Carnap, Sellars has labored hard to achieve on a realistic basis a tenable reconciliation of rationalism and empiricism within the framework of analytic thought.[45]

The criterion of meaningfulness that Sellars initially presents and continues to adhere to with some modifications involves two distinct aspects. One is concerned with the verification base and the other with the connecting links of an empirical language system. Verification depends on the experiencing of sentence tokens and their designata together: *"A verified sentence is a sentence, a token of which is co-experienced with its designatum."* [46] Sentences are linked together by conformation rules, and such rules, instead of including only the tautologous connections of formal logic, include many restrictions rooted in fact and embodied in the syntax of the language.[47] Thus a meaningful descriptive predicate is one either belonging to a verified sentence or connected with such a sentence by conformation rules.[48] In Sellars' more recent writings the problem of the criterion of meaningfulness drops into the background; but in view of his increased insistence upon the priority of a coherent conceptual system over any alleged independent given experience and of his present belief that the demands of empiricism are sufficiently met if such a system makes contact with reality only at certain crucial points, it may safely be assumed that Sellars' present criterion of meaningfulness would assign a relatively larger role to the lawlike coherence of the conformation rules of the language and a relatively smaller role to the coexperiencing of tokens and their designata than did his earlier criterion.

Although it is largely in terms of intentionality or meaning that the mental is to be distinguished from the nonmental,[49] meaning is not a relation of a physical sign and a mental content. Nor indeed,

---

[45] Cf. Wilfrid Sellars, "Language, Rules and Behavior," in Sydney Hook (ed.), *John Dewey, Philosopher of Science and Freedom* (New York: Dial Press, Inc., 1950); "Epistemology and the Way of Words," *Journal of Philosophy*, XLIV (1947), 645; and "Acquaintance Description Again," *Journal of Philosophy*, XLVI (1949), 496.

[46] Wilfrid Sellars, "Realism and the New Way of Words," in Feigl and Sellars, *Readings in Philosophical Analysis*, p. 435.

[47] *Ibid.*, p. 439.

[48] *Ibid.*, p. 441.

[49] Wilfrid Sellars, "Mind, Meaning and Behavior," *Philosophical Studies*, III (1952), 83–94; "A Semantical Solution of the Mind Body Problem," *Methodos*, V (1953), 45–84; and "Empiricism and the Philosophy of Mind," in *The Foundations of Science and the Concepts of Psychology and Psychoanalysis* (Minneapolis: University of Minnesota Press, 1956), pp. 253–329.

in any usual sense of the term "relation," is meaning a relation at all. The term "meaning" belongs rather to a distinctive semantic level of discourse. To be sure, meaning involves private mental episodes, and when people accustomed to use the language of objects have learned to use the language of meaning they can employ the latter language as a model in learning to recognize and speak about private episodes; but people can use the language of meaning without even being aware that they experience any private mental episodes.[50] The language of meaning is sufficiently grounded in mastery of the systems of rules of languages. For example a person understanding both German and English can intelligibly state that " 'Rot' in German means red" without thinking of any private mental episode. In doing so he would be conveying the information that the word "Rot" plays in German the same role that the word "red" plays in English. It should, however, be noted that while such information is what the statement conveys, what the statement *says* is something more.[51] The statement says that " 'Rot' means red," and saying this presupposes that the hearer understands "red." Just as the universe could be adequately described without any references save indirect ones to the language of ethics, so the universe could be described without reference to the language of meaning; but both the language of ethics and the language of meaning are significant, and neither need be regarded as secondary or subordinate to the language of fact.

Because acceptance of abstract entities such as universals and propositions seems to them to lead to an objectionable Platonism in which universals are taken to be intuited, most nominalistically inclined philosophers tend to reject abstract entities altogether; [52] and if such Platonism were presupposed in acceptance of abstract entities, these philosophers would be right. In fact, however, acceptance of abstract entities does not in any sense imply the objectionable Platonist thesis that universals are intuited; and in a wholesome psychological nominalism, once this fact is acknowledged, no good reason remains for declining to accept abstract entities.[53] Indeed, such entities are needed alike in logic, in ordinary discourse, and in mathematics; and their existence in the sense in which a psychological nominalism can accept them may as well be assumed. Universals are apprehended not then as intuited contents but as concepts. Their definitions are rooted in the systems of laws of their respective languages, which they in turn help to make; for laws are as essential

---

[50] *Op. cit.*
[51] Cf. "A Semantical Solution of the Mind Body Problem," p. 81.

[52] Wilfrid Sellars, "Language, Rules and Behavior," pp. 289–315.
[53] *Ibid.*

to concepts as concepts are to laws.[54] As to *what* universals are to be accepted, one must not suppose that these are to be limited to the predicates that seem to be required at the present juncture of scientific development, but room must be made for "the predicates it will be reasonable to *introduce* (or to *discard*)." [55]

The central core of a language system consists of a network of logical and physical laws that are a priori in the system to which they belong. The truth of these laws is implicit in the rules that give meaning to the terms of the language, and for this reason the laws are often said to be analytic. Whether or not they are in fact analytic depends on whether the term "analytic" is used in an inclusive sense to refer to any proposition that is true by virtue of its meaning, or in a narrower sense, to refer only to propositions of logic, in which descriptive terms appear "vacuously." [56] When the term "analytic" is used, as it more commonly is, in the narrower sense, most non-logical a priori statements may appropriately be said in a restricted sense to be not analytic but synthetic, so that there are in fact synthetic a priori statements within any given language system. Although the laws of a language system are a priori within that system, such a system itself is pragmatically oriented to experience, and is constantly being modified to meet the demands of its points of contact with experience.[57]

Although knowledge must be built upon experience, the view, common to many empiricists, that primary knowledge is immediately given sensory experience and that all other knowledge is a secondary development built upon such knowledge as its data is a misleading myth. The myth springs from "a mismating of the idea that there are certain 'inner episodes' which occur . . . without any previous process of learning . . . [and] the idea that there are certain 'inner episodes' which are non-inferential knowing." [58] Although there are in fact inner episodes indispensable to knowing, such episodes are not knowings, nor are they data of knowing. Objects are known and spoken of before sense-data can be distinguished, and one can—as has been noted—learn to use the language of intentionality or meaning without becoming aware at all that there are any inner episodes. That concept formation on which all knowledge depends

[54] See Wilfrid Sellars, "Concepts as Involving Laws and Inconceivable Without Them," *Philosophy of Science*, XV (1948), sections IV, V, and IX.

[55] "Counterfactuals, Dispositions, and the Causal Modalities," in *Minnesota Studies in the Philosophy of Science* (Minneapolis: University of Minnesota Press, 1958), II, 305.

[56] Wilfrid Sellars, "Is There a Synthetic A Priori," in Sidney Hook, *American Philosophers at Work* (New York: Criterion Books, Inc., 1956), pp. 136 ff.

[57] *Ibid.*, pp. 155 ff.

[58] "Empiricism and the Philosophy of Mind," p. 267.

is inseparably bound up with the process of learning a language, and it is within the framework of object language that the knowing process begins. Although sensory experience is involved in observing, such observing does not occur apart from concepts framed in dealing with objects.

The primary objects of our knowledge are accordingly not mere sense-data, to which physical objects are secondary, but physical objects themselves and real connections between such objects. Whatever may be the causal prerequisites of our knowledge, it is physical objects that we know.[59] This does not of course mean that we intuit physical objects. That in terms of which we apprehend the real connections that constitute and connect physical objects is primarily a conceptual or linguistic scheme whose links are not mere constant conjunctions but genuine entailments permitting us to say, for example, that it is highly probable that such and such entailments of a scientific system hold.[60]

Even the problem of induction is in principle solved in the character of the language systems in which the problem is raised, for such systems involve the probability of the entailments built into the network of observationally grounded laws that constitute the systems. Language systems must of course remain flexible if they are to continue useful. The laws of nature are not either rational intuitions, observed regularities, or mere promises of discoverable regularities, but "inference tickets" on the basis of which description and explanation may proceed. The most general of these laws, such as the principle of causality, are not parts of a "super-description of the world" to be verified by data, but principles of the language system without which inquiry could not be initiated at all.

5. Critical Remarks Concerning Physicalistic Analysis

At the close of the preceding chapter we discussed two doctrines common to all logical positivists, those of the dichotomy of analytic and empirical statements and of the verifiability of criteria of significant empirical statements, and one doctrine especially characteristic of phenomenalistic logical positivists, the reducibility of all significant empirical statements to phenomenalistic ones. We shall here discuss two further doctrines more or less common to all logical positivists, those of philosophy as the logic of science and of logic as

[59] Wilfrid Sellars, "Physical Realism," *Philosophy and Phenomenological Research,* XV (1954), 19 ff.

[60] Wilfrid Sellars, "Counterfactuals, Dispositions, and Causal Modalities," Pt. III.

a system of tautologies; and one doctrine especially characteristic of physicalistic logical positivists, the translatability of significant statements into physicalistic language.

A. With the exception of instrumentalists, the logical positivists have been among the few contemporary philosophers adequately to recognize that, whatever may be the philosopher's task regarding ultimate foundations of knowledge, the philosopher has a responsibility to elucidate the logic by which scientific knowledge is actually justified. Moreover, in calling attention to and discharging this responsibility, logical positivists have generally had considerable advantage over instrumentalists, for whereas Dewey and his close associates had for the most part relatively little firsthand acquaintance with science, many positivists have been themselves able scientists. Some of the members of the Vienna Circle were physicists and mathematicians. Scientists of many types have been interested in and often ready to adopt conclusions of logical positivists, and logical positivists have kept in close touch with the work of scientists. Some of them have ventured scientific suggestions of their own, and a number of them have done extensive studies in the logic of probability, which is intimately related to scientific work in mathematics, social science, and physics. A liberal and active cooperation continues between scientists and logical positivists, for example in the unity of science movement and in such joint efforts as have produced the recent *Minnesota Studies in Philosophy of Science*. All this has been to the good, for on the one hand, science rests upon philosophical presuppositions and at its growing edges becomes peculiarly aware of the need for philosophical orientation, and on the other hand, philosophy focuses upon methods and concepts supplied by science and can scarcely be relevant to current issues apart from considerable insights into scientific methods and achievements. One may well hope that a lasting benefit of logical positivism will be a continuing recognition of the need for philosophical training for scientists, for scientific training for philosophers, and for mutual cooperation between scientists and philosophers.

Nevertheless, the claims and performances of logical positivists with respect to the relation between philosophy and science are open to criticism in at least two respects. In the first place, even if the terms "logic" and "science" be more generously conceived than the logical positivists conceive them, to represent philosophy as the logic of science and no more is to take too narrow a view of philosophy. Philosophy has always endeavored to interpret not one aspect only of human experience but all aspects, and human experience includes much besides science. It includes purposes and feelings that are not mainly cognitive, and even on its cognitive side it includes historical and biographical facts that can scarcely be reduced to scientific formulae, and political and social facts that can be compressed into no rigid scientific patterns. It also includes ethical, esthetic, and religious experiences that philosophers have always supposed it their duty to try to elucidate. The philosophy of science may possibly be limited to the logic of science—though even that is doubtful—but philosophy itself can scarcely be so limited.

In the second place, one cannot but have serious misgivings about the extent to which logical positivists have adhered to their own program of elucidating the actual justificatory procedures of science. Certainly in the beginning their major weapon against the high-handed and unempirical procedures of idealist metaphysics was an emphasis upon the empirical methods of working scientists. However, having come upon the initially fruitful techniques of dividing significant statements into analytic and empirical ones and applying a testability criterion of significance; they came, at any rate until very recently, to be somewhat rigidly disposed to press all scientific logic into molds conformable to those principles rather than more flexibly ready to give due consideration to such varied forms of actual scientific inference lying outside the range of those principles as informal inferences from particulars to particulars, free use of analogies, construction of models, and a wide range of other informal appeals to reasonableness found in the procedures of working scientists. As a reason for their unwillingness to take more serious account of actual procedures of scientists, logical positivists have repeatedly offered the consideration that as philosophers of science, they were interested not so much in how the scientist got his ideas as in how these ideas could be logically justified. But it may well be that logical justification is much closer to actual confirmatory procedures than logical positivists realize, and that the failure of logical positivists to pay closer attention to the actual procedures of scientists is an important part of the explanation for the fact that, despite commendable efforts, logical positivists have not yet achieved the sort of results that might have been expected by way either of facilitating scientific work or of elucidating scientific methods and findings.

B. Provided one does not insist too exclusively upon an extensional account of logic, at least this much in the characteristic logical positivist interpretation of logic as a system of tautologies seems to be sound, that a very substantial part of what may broadly be called logic, including not only logic proper but also much of mathematics and a wide range of other conceptual truths, are tautologous in the sense that the truth involved in them is dependent not upon facts but upon meanings and uses. Alternative claims are to the effect that logic is grounded in unanalyzable essences, that it is rooted in a metaphysical order of cosmic reality, and that it consists of empirical generalizations. Neither of the first two alternatives, even if true, would yield significant clues concerning how logical patterns could in practice be discovered, and the third leaves altogether unexplained the apparently significant difference in kind between the assurances and modes of verification attaching to empirical truths, on the one hand, and logical truths, on the other. The suggestion that logical truth is rooted not in facts about the world but in considerations concerning meaning and use fulfills both types of requirements. It suggests the sort of inquiry needed to discern logical truths and indicates why we should be as certain as we are concerning logical truths even when we are doubtful about facts.

The logical-positivist treatment of logical truth as tautologous seems also to be sound in its due recognition of the value of formal systems that explicitly express certain logical patterns in specific symbols with rules. The working out of such systems is a useful undertaking that can often illuminate logical structures, rule out errors, and sometimes facilitate thinking. It is an undertaking in which logicians, mathematicians, and others have long been more or less successively engaged. Its recent fruits speak for themselves and owe much to the contributions of logical positivists.

However, the logical-positivist interpretation of logic as tautologous has not been confined to linking logic with meaning and uses and the construction of formal systems of symbols with rules for their manipulation. It has also, at least in some of its earlier syntactic versions, tended to confine logic to the construction and rigorous employment of formal systems. That logical positivists have intended their syntactic systems to be taken as actually identifiable with or substitutable for the logic of common sense and science is not indeed entirely clear; but since their pronouncements have sometimes been interpreted to that effect, it seems worth-while to suggest that insofar as they have meant any such thing they seem to have been mistaken.

In the first place, there can scarcely be any question of literally reducing the logic involved in actual scientific and other reasonings to any formal system of physical signs and accompanying rules. The logic of such actual reasonings consists of relatively informal conceptual and linguistic procedures having such distinctive characters of their own that, however like them formal patterns of symbols may be, formal patterns can never be regarded either as quite identical with them or as adequate reductions of them. The methods by which these informal procedures must be discerned include conceptual and linguistic analyses that are very different from the methods of constructing and analyzing artificial symbolic systems, and the methods for employing these procedures are also different from methods of employing formal systems. Moreover, the construction and use of significant formal symbolic systems is itself by no means as free as was once supposed, but presupposes, as Carnap has come in part to realize, some of the very semantic and pragmatic factors that enter into the informal logic that formal systems are supposed to reduce. At very best the sort of formal systems offered by early versions of logical positivism as reductions of informal logic can only be useful representations of that logic that help to clarify the characters of some of its transitions and to facilitate the elimination of some types of error.

In the second place even if systems of symbols with rules are regarded only as representations designed to elucidate logical relations that are themselves of another order, the representations remain entirely too limited for the job assigned to them. No system of symbols yet offered even approximates the richness of actually encountered logical relations. The area of relations that are essentially logical in being largely independent of nonlinguistic facts embraces, as we have tried to indicate, far more than science. For example, implicative relations are to be found in political, personal, historical, ethical, religious, esthetic, and other types of discourse that can scarcely be construed as scientific. Besides, even the variety and complexity of the nonempirical relations involved in scientific discourse are by no means adequately suggested in current symbolic systems. One very obvious deficiency in such systems is their inability to cope with the subjunctive conditionals that seem to be involved in most scientific generalizations, and many other deficiencies in such systems could be pointed out with reference to the widely varied modes of reasoning to be found in scientific documents. The richness of logic, in its broadest sense, is as great as that of language itself, and any attempt to force all nonempirical relations into any such narrow molds as the systems of symbols offered by logical positivists is sure to involve the obscuring of distinctions that may turn out to be very important. In recent years, leaders of logical positivism, recognizing the inadequacy of their own earlier systems, have enlarged the scope of these systems to include semantics and pragmatics as well as syntactics, but their statements of pragmatics and semantics define even these topics in such highly formalized fashion as to remain remote from and inadequate to actual discourse.

In the third place, even if a formal system of symbols with rules adequately representing the logic of common-sense and scientific discourse were at hand, there would scarcely be any point in attempting to substitute that system for the logic of such discourse. It would still be necessary on each occasion to understand the logic of such discourse in order to know how to fit it into the symbolic system, and the more a symbolic system becomes independent of the patterns of purposes and meanings it elucidates the more it must embody similar purposes and meanings in itself.

C. The physicalists' claim that the language of observable physical objects is not only natural and intersubjective but also a language into which all other languages can be translated and the one that is preferable to all others as the basic language for the confirmation of significant cognitive statements, clearly contains some important insights, especially with reference to the philosophy of science. The language of observable physical objects is in fact in considerable measure the language that we first learn and speak and from which much of the vocabulary of other ways of speaking is drawn. It is also in fact intersubjective in a way that phenomenalistic language is not. Accordingly, it has become for the most part the language of confirmation in science and therefore the most appropriate language for the philosopher of science who attempts to elucidate the structure of the actual confirmatory procedures of science.

Nevertheless, one can by no means accept all that is involved in the claim in question, and however useful the basic assumptions of this claim may be in philosophy of science as such, these assumptions are scarcely adequate for the purposes of general epistemology.

In the first place it is to be doubted that the occurrence of language other than physicalistic language is anything like so rare as the physicalists insistence upon the naturalness of physicalistic language would lead one to suppose. For example, there is language involving various kinds of abstractions, such as states, communities, governments, wars, courage, justice, beauty, and the like. Then there is language of what might be called intermediate entities, such as shadows, the sky and rainbows; language of fantasy and fiction; language of sensory experiences, such as sensations of colors, sounds, and smells; and language of emotions and of moral, religious, and esthetic experiences. There is also language of microphysics, which, though sometimes thought of as another version of physicalistic language, is very different from the language of observable physical objects. The fact that some of the terms of some of these languages are drawn from the language of physical objects is interesting but by no means undermines the distinctness of these other languages, for the references and the intensions of such terms are quite different in their uses in these other language forms from those of their uses in physical object language.

In the second place, the claim that the language of observable physical objects is our natural language seems to rest upon an assumption that, though rarely if ever actually stated by logical positivists themselves, apparently lies at the root of the prima-facie reasonableness of the suggestion that physicalistic language be treated as the basic language of confirmation of all cognitively significant statements. This assumption is that since the language of physical objects is in considerable measure the language that we learn and use, the mode of experience which it expresses is somehow chronologically, psychologically, or even logically prior to the mode of experience which other types of language, especially phenomenalistic language, express. Apart from some such assumption as this a large part of the reason for translating other languages into physicalistic languages would be removed. But the assumption is patently false. To be sure, the experiences which a large part of the speech of the normal adult expresses are experiences of physical objects. But the experiences which the language of the young child expresses are by no means so clearly experiences of physical objects. Not only are they often experiences of images, dreams, and fantasies, but even when they are experiences for the most part of physical objects, the boundary between what is physical object and what is not becomes hazy. The farther back we trace the child the less distinct does the experience of physical objects as such become. If we may extrapolate to the experiences of the infant we may be reasonably sure that his experiences are by no means experiences of distinct physical objects but experiences of something like the "buzzing blooming confusion" of which James spoke, and such that if they could be expressed they would have to be expressed in some sort of quasi-phenomenalistic language. The situation seems to be similar as one traces back the experiences of persons in deepening stages of intoxication, or the modes of thought of less and less developed races. The farther languages and experiences are traced back the less distinct does the physical object concept become and the more prominent do more primitive undiscriminating modes of language and experience become. The achievement of experiences of physical objects is natural and once achieved is an exceedingly convenient base for normal inquiry and speech, but it does indeed seem to be an achievement, and to be preceded both in the history of the race and in that of the individual by more primitive undifferentiated experiences. Even the well-integrated adult, when confronted by bewildering experiences which he is unable to compare with observations, is sometimes obliged to focus attention upon the patterns of his more primitive experiences in order to find his way through his confusion. That the child uses from the start apparently physicalistic terms is due to the influence of his more practical teachers and to the fact that by the time he learns to talk he is beginning to clarify physical concepts; but even so, the terms become physicalistic for him only as his concepts also become really physicalistic, and that takes considerable time even after he has learned to talk.

In the third place, insistence upon the intersubjectivity of physicalistic language misleadingly suggests the existence of a kind of ground of intersubjective assurance which, if it could be produced by physicalistic language, would tend to render physicalistic language basic to empirical confirmation; but it cannot in fact be so produced. Physicalistic language does of course yield intersubjective assurance in the important senses that its reference is not to abstracted sense-data or even to percepts but to publicly observable objects, and that the observations involved are generally adequate for purposes of science. Such considerations as these tempt one to take the unqualified assertion of the intersubjectivity of the language of observable physical objects to mean that not only the observed objects referred to are intersubjective, but also that the observations that apprehend such objects are intersubjectively assured. But this sort of intersubjectivity can scarcely be attained, and neither the perceptual character of the objects in question, nor their physical existence, nor the sufficiency of observations for scientific purposes has any tendency to show that observations themselves are intersubjective or can ever be considered final when the issues are basically epistemological. Observations, no matter how complete their content or how objective their reference, remain experiences of individuals, and for basic epistemological purposes—indeed sometimes even for practical purposes—subject to further review. Physicalists in some measure recognize this fact and sometimes take it seriously, but are all too likely to brush aside its implications with such dubious remarks as that at any rate a few observations will do.

If the language of physical objects is a smaller part of the whole of our language than physicalists claim, if the experiences which it expresses are no more fundamental than those expressed by phenomenalistic language—indeed in crucial respects less so—and if physicalistic language is incapable of yielding intersubjective assurances in any fundamental epistemological sense, then most of the reasons that would make one wish to translate all other language into physicalistic language tend to disappear. We must now go on to suggest that such translation is in any case impossible. As we endeavored to say in speaking of phenomenalistic languages, while the language of physical objects is connectible with that of immediate experience, it is not translatable into the languages of physical objects. The converse seems to be equally true. While the language of immediate experience is connectible with that of physical objects, it can never be completely adequately reformulated in terms of the language of physical objects. That is to say, while one can by speaking of physical objects suggest to a sensitive listener the character of his experiences so that the listener may get what he means, he can never fully say in that terminology what the character of his experience is. The two ways of speaking move on two different levels and there is no way of making a literal translation. Even where the vocabularies of the languages are similar their logics are very different from one another. Each has its own function to perform that cannot be performed by the other. The lover, the poet, the psychologist, the philosopher, and often even the physician have occasion to speak a language which, whatever terms it may borrow by way of metaphysical uses, cannot be crammed into the molds of physical object language. It may also be noted in this connection that even the language of microphysics, which logical positivists recognize as another possible version of physicalistic language, while of course connectible with the language of observable things, can never be entirely adequately translated in that language; and as Bridgman and other physicists have repeatedly pointed out, much of the current confusion in the interpretation of modern physics results from misguided attempts to press the results of the new physics into the ready-made patterns of a prevailing object language. Again two languages operate on different levels, and though connectible are not fully intertranslatable.

CHAPTER 15

Pragmatic Analysis

THE WRITERS now to be considered are, like those considered in the two preceding chapters, in the main empirically oriented and primarily concerned with the philosophical interpretation of scientific inquiry. They are, however, unlike their previously considered fellow analysts in rejecting the sharp dichotomy of analytic and synthetic statements and in insisting upon a pragmatically oriented continuum of statements ranging between analytic and synthetic limits. None of these writers is committed either to physicalism or phenomenalism, and each tends to choose his language base according to the character of the problem in hand and to treat scientific knowledge as pragmatic guidance rather than literal description. The first three of these writers, Willard Quine, Nelson Goodman, and Morton White, are in essential agreement on most major issues. The fourth differs radically from the others in some significant matters but agrees with them in rejecting a dichotomy of analytic and synthetic statements in favor of a more flexible gradualism.

1. WILLARD VAN ORMAN QUINE

Although Willard Quine (b. 1908) of Harvard has been preoccupied during much of his philosophical career with technical problems of formal logic, he has also been alert to epistemological and ontological bearings of logical inquiries. With reference to his work in logic as such, Quine's major objectives have included rigor in logical proofs and tests, the unification and simplification of logical notation, and the elimination of unnecessary entities and assumptions. Thus Quine has tirelessly endeavored to disclose improved mechanical decision procedures for those parts of logic that permit such procedures.[1] He is disturbed by the failure of quantification theory to yield mechanical test procedures for all its phases, and even more deeply by Gödel's proof of the impossibility of even half-mechanical proof procedures for elementary number theory.[2] He finds compensating satisfaction, however, in the fact that some parts of mathematics do admit of decision procedures and that methods are available all along the line for determining whether or not proofs are possible.[3] Quine's quest for uniformity in logical notation is manifested in his insistence that the existential quantifier be interpreted always in the same way,[4] in his attempts to discover plausible ways of reformulating modal statements and statements involving propositional attitudes, such as striving and believing in quantifiable terms,[5] and even more significantly in the attempt to overcome the notational complexity of Russell's theory of types that he first offered in his "New Foundations for Mathematical Logic"[6] and subsequently refined in the successive editions of his *Mathematical Logic* in 1940 and 1951.[7] Quine proposes ways of replacing the attributes that he finds even in *principia Mathematica* and the works of Carnap by conceptual classes.[8] Indeed he would prefer to go further and to place logic on a nominalistic basis if that could be conveniently done.[9] However, he admits that a purely nominalistic logic would be very inconvenient even if achievable, and that important parts of mathematics are not possible apart from a minimal admission of classes.[10]

Quine has great confidence in the power of modern logical procedures to throw light upon philosophical issues including not only

[1] Cf. Willard Quine, *Mathematical Logic* (rev. ed.; Cambridge: Harvard University Press, 1951), sec. 10, 19–20, 33–34; Quine, *Methods of Logic* (New York: Henry Holt & Co., Inc., 1950), esp. sec. 5–7, 9–11, 18–21, 27, 28; and Quine, "A Proof Procedure for Quantification Theory," *Journal of Symbolic Logic*, XX (1955), 141–49.

[2] *Methods of Logic*, pp. 244 f.

[3] *Ibid.*, pp. 247 f.

[4] Cf. Quine, *From a Logical Point of View* (Cambridge: Harvard University Press, 1953), pp. 3 ff.

[5] Quine, "The Problem of Interpreting Modal Logic," *Journal of Symbolic Logic*, XII (1947), 43–48; "Three Grades of Modal Involvement," *Proceedings of the Eleventh International Congress of Philosophy*, XIV, 65–91; and "Quantifiers and

Propositional Attitudes," *Journal of Philosophy*, LIII (1956), 177–87.

[6] See *From a Logical Point of View*, chap. v.

[7] *Mathematical Logic*, chap. iv; see also *Methods of Logic*, Sec. 42; and "On Frege's Way Out," *Mind*, LXIV (1955), 143–59.

[8] *From a Logical Point of View*, pp. 122 f.; Quine, "On Carnap's Views on Ontology," *Philosophical Studies*, XII (1951), 65–72; cf. also *Methods of Logic*, p. 132; and *Mathematical Logic*, p. 121.

[9] Willard Quine and Nelson Goodman, "Steps Toward a Constructive Nominalism," *Journal of Symbolic Logic*, XII (1947), 105–22.

[10] See *ibid.*; and *Methods of Logic*, sec. 41.

semantic and logical ones [11] but also even traditional ontological ones. It is true of course that "ordinary language remains . . . fundamental . . . as a medium of ultimate clarification," but for purposes of the "creative aspect" of "philosophical analysis" ordinary language lacks the precision and freedom from misleading suggestion that are attainable along modern "quantificational lines." [12] Among the philosophical problems to which Quine addresses his logical point of view are those of analyticity, ontology, and truth, and to his suggestions concerning each of these problems we now turn.

A. Although the distinction between analytic statements and synthetic ones has long been widely, though not universally, accepted as epistemologically basic and regarded as virtually axiomatic by most modern empirical philosophers, the distinction turns out upon examination to have, Quine thinks, very little foundation. It is true of course that such substitution instances of laws of logic as "no unmarried man is married," can generally be accepted without regard to particular facts, but then what is involved here is rather primarily logical truth than analyticity.[13] The crucial question concerns alleged analytic statements that though not logical truths can supposedly be turned into such truths by substituting synonyms for synonyms as in the instance of "no bachelor is married." [14] The basic difficulty lies in the "notion of 'synonymy' which is no less in need of clarification than analyticity itself." [15] For purposes of the clarification of the notions of synonymy and analyticity appeal to the procedures of definition is of no use, for definition itself depends upon synonymy.[16] Interchangeability *salva veritate* is also of little use for in " 'Bachelor' has less than ten letters" one could surely not substitute "unmarried man" for "bachelor" without altering truth values. Perhaps the requisite substitutions could be made in the case of "necessarily all and only bachelors are unmarried men," but here notions of cognitive synonymy and analyticity are presupposed. Certainly in an extensional language, one in which "any two predicates which . . . are true of the same objects . . . are interchangeable *salva veritate,* interchangeability, *salva veritate* is no assurance of cognitive synonymy"; nor is there any "assurance . . . that the extensional agreement of 'bachelors' and 'unmarried men' rests on meaning rather than on accidental matters of fact, as does the extensional agreement of 'creature with a heart' and 'creature with kid-

---

[11] Cf. Quine, Preface to J. T. Clark, *Conventional Logic and Modern Logic* (Woodstock, Md.: Woodstock College Press, 1952).

[12] *From a Logical Point of View,* pp. 106 f.

[13] *Ibid.,* pp. 22 f.

[14] *Ibid.,* p. 23.

[15] *Ibid.*

[16] *Ibid.,* pp. 24 ff.

neys.' " [17] The attempt is sometimes made to rescue synonymy and analyticity by appeal to the semantic rules of artificial languages, but such an appeal treats these concepts as irreducible for its special uses and is of little value with reference to actual linguistic behavior.[18]

The attempt is often made to define an analytic statement in terms of the verifiability theory of meaning, as a statement that "is confirmed no matter what," [19] and this view is rendered plausible by the fact that the truth of statements depends apparently on separable linguistic and nonlinguistic components. But the fact is that the full confirmation of any individual statement is impossible, and "it is nonsense, and the root of much nonsense, to speak of a linguistic component and a factual component in the truth of any individual statement." [20]

B. Prerequisite, Quine thinks, to any satisfactory discussion of what exists or even of how one is to determine what exists, is clarification concerning how one commits oneself to the existence of anything. Philosophers often suppose that the use of singular terms commits one to the existence of something named by such terms. Thus when one speaks of John, or a lion, or even Pegasus, it is said that one presupposes the existence of something spoken about. Thus the claim may be made that in statements such as "Pegasus does not exist," at least an idea of Pegasus or a nonexistent but subsistent Pegasus is implied. But the fact is that the existence of an idea is not what is in question, and the acceptance of subsistences leads to all sorts of embarrassing questions about their size, location, similarities and so on.[21] One may of course still claim that Pegasus exists at least in meaning, but while one may need to refer to meaningfulness and sameness of meaning, even this implies nothing concerning "intermediary entities called meanings." [22] The confusion involved in the use of singular terms for which no corresponding reality is discoverable can in large part be avoided by Russell's theory of descriptions, which first translates sentences containing proper names into sentences containing definite descriptions, and these in turn into quantificational sentences containing neither names nor definite descriptions. Indeed, by an extension of this procedure, which unfortunately Russell himself is unwilling to accept, it is possible to get rid of singular terms altogether and thus to demonstrate the fact that the use of such terms need carry no ontological commitment.[23] When the con-

[17] *Ibid.,* pp. 30 f.
[18] *Ibid.,* pp. 32 ff.
[19] *Ibid.,* p. 37.
[20] *Ibid.,* p. 42.
[21] *From a Logical Point of View,* pp. 1 ff.

[22] *Ibid.*
[23] *Mathematical Logic,* pp. 146 ff.; *From a Logical Point of View,* pp. 7 ff.; "Rejoinder to Mr. Geach on What There Is," p. 153; and *Methods of Logic,* sec. 37.

fusion involved in singular terms is removed, an unambiguous and entirely neutral criterion of ontological commitment is available in terms of the use of quantified variables. Thus, as Quine repeatedly insists, "a theory is committed to those and only those entities to which the bound variables of the theory must be capable of referring in order that the affirmations made in the theory be true." [24] Some philosophers, including Carnap, think that quantification involves no ontological commitment. But whereas one can "at the drop of a hat" get rid of the suggestion of ontology involved in using names by simply rephrasing in line with the theory of descriptions, no comparable method for eliminating the ontological commitments involved in taking something to be a value of a bound variable in a true statement is available, and one can scarcely avoid responsibility for assuming the existence of "the several species" if he says for example that "some zoölogical species cross fertilize." [25]

Much more important than how commitments occur is of course the very different question how ontological commitments are justified. Concerning this question, Carnap and other logical empiricists hold that two quite distinct groups of questions are involved. One consists of external questions, or questions concerning the conceptual scheme; the other consists of internal questions, or questions concerning what the facts are within the conceptual scheme . The first group of questions is answered pragmatically in terms of linguistic decisions; the second, scientifically, in terms of observational inquiries. Actually, however, in view of the difficulty of establishing any sort of satisfactory distinction between the analytic and the synthetic, no such dichotomy of internal and external questions can be sustained. Carnap's device for maintaining the dichotomy, the use of different styles of symbols, is nothing more than a technical procedure without adequate foundation in fact or logic; and so-called external questions belong to the same "continuum" that embraces internal questions.[26] If Martians were to confront us with a language of science claiming fully to represent the facts of science without using the metaphysical terms involved in our science, we should rightly demand that such a language include statements of all the truths formulated in our scientific language, but we should have no right to demand that their language place the boundaries between conceptual frame and fact or between analytic and synthetic as our language does.[27]

[24] From a Logical Point of View, pp. 13 f.; cf. also "Rejoinder to Mr. Geach on What There Is," pp. 153, 159.
[25] From a Logical Point of View, p. 13.
[26] "On Carnap's Views on Ontology," Philosophical Studies, II, 65–72.

[27] Quine, "Logical Truth," in Sydney Hook (ed.), American Philosophers at Work (New York: Criterion Books, Inc., 1956), p. 131.

How then are ontological statements, or indeed any other statements, justified? Quine's answer involves three major contentions: first, that all kinds of statements are to be justified in basically the same way; second, that it is not really individual statements but whole systems of statements that are to be justified; and third, that justification is always at bottom pragmatic. With reference to the first of these contentions the underlying ideas have already been sufficiently indicated. No clear distinction can be made between analytic and synthetic, external and internal, or linguistic and nonlinguistic statements; and no fundamental distinction can be made among kinds of tests to which different statements are to be subjected.

Turning to the second contention, to speak of "the empirical content of an individual statement" at all is at best "misleading," for "our statements about the external world face the tribunal of sense experience not individually but as a corporate body." [28] Indeed, "our whole body of affirmations . . . is a devious but convenient system for relating experiences to experiences." [29] The system contains many gaps and "impinges on experience only along the edges." [30] When discrepancies come in "we retain a wide latitude of choice as to what statements of the system to preserve and what ones to revise." [31] Naturally we prefer to revise what will upset the system least and so tend to give priority on the one hand to those statements that are closest to experience and on the other hand to those general logical and mathematical principles that are most fundamental to the system.[32]

The test in terms of which the system must justify itself is a pragmatic one. Some philosophers, including Lewis in *Mind and the World Order,* and Carnap in "Empiricism, Semantics and Ontology," apply pragmatic tests to the conceptual frame and not to the content; but actually all of our concepts are grounded in pragmatic considerations. "Physical objects are conceptually imported into the situation as convenient intermediaries . . . comparable, epistemologically, to the gods of Homer, [and] in point of epistemological footing the physical objects and the gods differ only in degree and not in kind." [33] The situation is similar with reference to "atomic and subatomic entities," forces, matter, and energy; and the "classes and classes of classes" of mathematics are also "epistemologically . . . myths on the same footing with physical objects and gods." [34] Just what in detail the pragmatic test recommended is, Quine has yet not spelled out,

[28] *From a Logical Point of View,* p. 41.
[29] *Ibid.,* p. 42.
[30] *Ibid.,* p. 42.
[31] *Methods of Logic,* p. xii.

[32] *From a Logical Point of View,* pp. 42 ff.
[33] *Ibid.,* p. 44.
[34] *Ibid.,* pp. 44 f.

but presumably he has in mind the fulfillment of objectives of science in leading inquiry in each instance successfully from one set of experiences to another.

C. If justification is essentially pragmatic, what kinds of entities are in fact justified? To begin with the negative side, Quine's pet aversions are so-called meanings. It is true that expressions are *meaningful* and that they *mean*,[35] but to go on to say that therefore expressions have meaning is to multiply entities beyond necessity. Much of one's "felt need for meant entities" is due to failure to make the sort of distinction between meaning and reference [36] that is suggested, for example, by the fact that though "evening star" and "morning star" are by no means *alike in meaning* they refer to the same star. Indeed, a large part of what is important concerning meaning as distinct from reference is involved in the context "alike in meaning," and most of the rest is contained in such terms as "significant" and "meaningful." There is no need for supposititious "intermediary entities" called "meanings," [37] and the alleged "explanatory value" of such entities is surely illusory.[38] Meanings as ideas are "worse than useless for linguistic science," and to say that meanings subsist rather than exist is to introduce intolerable complexity and confusion into logical notation and ontological discourse.

As a matter of fact, Quine thinks, there is very little point in ascribing being either to any sort of universal or even to mental entities. While one commonly says that there are red houses, roses, and sunsets, and while the general predicate "red" is surely *true of* each of these and many other objects, there is no need to say that there is an entity "redness" which these objects have in common.[39] Moreover, if one must speak of red in substantive terms, there is no reason why one should not think of it simply as an individual embracing all the red things in the universe without itself being any more a universal or less a thing than a river.[40] It is only as a manner of speaking that we need the language of universals; and if convenience in mathematical notation seems to require abstract entities at all, classes would seem to be enough to fill the need without reference to attributes.[41] Regarding mental entities, one must not of course deny either that we sense or that we are conscious, but one can, and probably should, deny that "it is efficacious so to frame our conceptual scheme as to mark out a range of entities or units of a so-called mental kind in

---

[35] Cf. *From a Logical Point of View*, p. 163.

[36] *Ibid.*, p. 22.

[37] *Ibid.*, p. 48.

[38] *Ibid.*, p. 22.

[39] *Ibid.*, p. 10.

[40] *Ibid.*, p. 72.

[41] *Ibid.*, p. 122; cf. also *Methods of Logic*, pp. 225 ff.

addition to the physical ones." [42] The trouble with "the idea is that its use . . . engenders an illusion of having explained something." [43]

On the positive side, the kinds of entities that do seem to be pragmatically justified include ordinary physical objects which, though not entirely unlike Homer's gods, have far greater explanatory power.[44] Also to be included are scientific objects at the atomic and subatomic levels, such levels being "posited to make the laws of macroscopic objects, and ultimately the laws of experience, simpler and more manageable." [45] Mathematical objects may be posited in the same spirit though the abstract entities allowed should be kept to a minimum.[46] Physical objects need not be continuous either in space or in time but consist of "sums of particle movements." [47] Experience itself is that to which the whole conceptual frame must conform, and language is the indispensable instrument of experience.

D. Implicit in what has been said concerning Quine's views on analyticity and ontology is an interpretation of truth that, while recognizing a very considerable conventional element in truth, rejects the attempt of Carnap and others to make a very large class of truths purely conventional. Repeatedly suggested in other writings of Quine, this interpretation is more explicitly sketched in "Truth by Convention." [48]

In a broad sense truth must be defined in a common-sense way as a sort of correspondence to reality or mirroring of the world [49] such that " 'James smokes' would be said to be true . . . [under] precisely the circumstances under which James would be said to smoke." [50] Unfortunately, however, "utterances about physical objects are not verifiable or refutable by direct comparison with experience," and the statements to which we attribute truth or falsity are for the most part intricately interwoven with elaborate conceptual schemes with which they stand or fall. In order to place certain crucial parts of a conceptual scheme at least temporarily beyond dispute and to facilitate ready transition from one part of the system to another, it is often feasible to formalize the crucial parts in terms of patterns of postulates and definitions; and the progress of science has often been

---

[42] Quine, "On Mental Entities," *Proceedings of the American Academy of Arts and Sciences*, LXXX; *Contributions to the Analysis and Synthesis of Knowledge*, p. 5.

[43] *From a Logical Point of View*, p. 48.

[44] *Ibid.*, p. 44.

[45] *Ibid.*

[46] *Ibid.*

[47] *Methods of Logic*, p. 210; see also *From a Logical Point of View*, p. 72.

[48] Quine, "Truth by Convention," in Herbert Feigl and Wilfrid Sellars, *Readings in Philosophical Analysis* (New York: Appleton-Century-Crofts, Inc., 1949); cf. "Logical Truth."

[49] *Methods of Logic*, p. xi.

[50] *Mathematical Logic*, p. 4.

facilitated through such formalization.[51] In this manner most of the truths of mathematics can be regarded as definitional abbreviations of truths of logic, and those that resist such treatment can readily be brought into the system by the use of a few additional postulates.[52] Much of physics can likewise be regarded as a formal system, and modern philosophy tends increasingly to stress the conventional element at the expense of the interpretive one in a wide variety of sciences.

However, there are limits to the usefulness of formalization. Any conceptual scheme has to be oriented to observation in order to be of any use. Certainly physical conventions have to be selected in conformity to observational experience and are subject to change when observation seems to require such change. Elementary logic itself can scarcely be reduced to pure convention, for "if logic is to proceed *mediately* from conventions, logic is needed for inferring logic from conventions." [53] Indeed "it is impossible in principle . . . to get even the most elementary part of logic exclusively by the explicit applications of conventions stated in advance"; for "the logical truths, being infinite in number, must be given by general conventions rather than singly, and logic is needed . . . to begin with . . . in order to apply the general conventions to individual cases." [54] The products of *legislative* postulation being "always postulates by fiat, are not *therefore* true by fiat," [55] and when postulates have once been laid down, however arbitrarily, further employment of them is in terms of *discursive* postulation, which "fixes . . . not truth but only some particular ordering of truths." [56] None of the truths that we apprehend is either pure convention or pure fact. Together they constitute "a pale gray lore, black with fact, and white with convention," and there do not seem to be "any quite black threads in it, nor any white ones." [57]

2. NELSON GOODMAN

Somewhat less explicitly pragmatic and more systematic than the epistemology of Quine is the epistemology implicit in the writings of Nelson Goodman (b. 1906) of the University of Pennsylvania. Like most of the analytic philosophers so far considered, Goodman attempts to produce neither a systematic epistemology, nor a description of an independently existing cosmic order, nor an analysis of ordinary

---

[51] "Truth by Convention," p. 250.
[52] *Ibid.*, p. 254.
[53] *Ibid.*, pp. 271 f.
[54] "Logical Truth," p. 124.

[55] *Ibid.*, pp. 127, 132.
[56] *Ibid.*, p. 127.
[57] *Ibid.*, p. 133.

language. Foregoing all endeavor to portray either "the process of acquiring knowledge" or "the genesis . . . of ideas," Goodman attempts, rather, like Carnap in *Der Logische Aufbau der Welt,* to achieve a "rational reconstruction" of the "process of acquiring knowledge." What concerns him most is not "primacy in the cognitive process, but serviceability as a basis for an economical, perspicuous and integrated system." [1] While the attempted rational reconstruction allows considerable freedom, its purpose, its choice of basic elements, and its method of construction are not altogether unlike those of common discourse, for it is, after all, explanatory. In it "the definiens is a complex of interpreted terms and the definiendum a familiar meaningful term, and the accuracy of the definition depends upon the relation between the two." [2]

With regard to what is to count as an explanation, the limits that Goodman sets for himself are rather stringent. He will have nothing to do with meanings, attributes, intensions, classes, powers, dispositions, counterfactual assertions, possibilities, necessities, or any other such suppositious abstractions. His principal grounds for rejecting all such abstractions are "a philosophical intuition that cannot be based on anything more ultimate," the fact that such abstractions lead to "paradoxes," [3] and the fact that appeal to such abstractions only reformulates problems of philosophy rather than resolving them. In the end whether such abstractions are to be accepted by anyone or not comes to be a matter of philosophic conscience. Some philosophic consciences are less puritanical; they can endure a good deal of obscurity. Goodman's philosophic conscience cannot.[4]

The rejection of meanings and modalities, however, confronts philosophical construction with very serious difficulties, and among the principal merits of Goodman's thought is a candid recognition of the gravity of some of these difficulties.

The most obvious difficulty is that of finding a way of expressing both the basic truths of logic and the facts and laws of common sense and science in terms of a nominalism in which all predicates are predicates of individuals and no abstraction is treated as a value of a quantified variable.[5] This difficulty can be overcome, Goodman believes, by supplying some sample nominalistic translations and fur-

---

[1] Nelson Goodman, "The Revision of Philosophy," in Sidney Hook (ed.), *American Philosophers at Work* (New York: Criterion Books, Inc., 1956), p. 80.
[2] Goodman, *The Structure of Appearance* (Cambridge: Harvard University Press, 1951), p. 3.
[3] Nelson Goodman and W. V. Quine,

"Steps toward a Constructive Nominalism," in *Journal of Symbolic Logic,* XII (1947), 105.
[4] Goodman, *Fact, Fiction and Forecast* (Cambridge: Harvard University Press, 1955), pp. 37 f.
[5] "Steps toward a Constructive Nominalism," pp. 106 f.

nishing rules by which the other requisite translations could be made.[6] Such samples and rules Goodman and Quine have endeavored to supply in a previously mentioned article; what sort of system Goodman attempts to build in the light of these earlier efforts we are presently to see.

A second difficulty, one that applies especially to the deductive phases of philosophical construction, is that of clarifying the conception of "likeness of meaning" without venturing beyond the intel-
to Platonic Ideas is ruled out by the nature of the problem, and at
ligible realm of extensions into the chaotic one of intensions. Appeal
best there is no way "to find out whether two terms stand for the
same Platonic Idea."[7] Reliance on the notion of "mental idea or image" is no more useful, for we do not know "what we can and what we cannot imagine," and many predicates "have no corresponding image."[8] Attempts to explain likeness of meaning in terms of concepts and possibilities are also futile, for all manner of self-contradictions are conceivable and the notion of possibility is notoriously ambiguous. At the same time, efforts to explicate likeness of meaning directly in terms of the extensions involved will not do, for many terms that are alike in extension are not alike in meaning. Thus, for example, the terms "centaur" and "unicorn" have "the same null extension," but do not "have the same meaning." Nevertheless, there is a way of distinguishing, for while unicorn and centaur have the same extension, unicorn-feet and centaur-feet do not have the same extension, nor do unicorn-picture and centaur-picture or unicorn-description and centaur-description. Generalizing, one may formulate a test of difference of meaning in extensional terms as follows: "For every two words that differ in meaning either their extensions or the extensions of some corresponding compounds of them are different."[9] The unfortunate consequence of this criterion is that *"no two different words have the same meaning."*[10] The only way around this difficulty that Goodman has so far found is to qualify the criterion so as to "exclude every compound for which the corresponding compounds of every two terms have differing extensions," and to focus attention upon the kinds of compounds that show some words to be different in meaning and some alike.[11] At best, however, likeness of meaning must probably be recognized to be a matter of degree and relative to "the purposes of the immediate discourse."[12]

[6] *Ibid.*, pp. 111 ff.
[7] Goodman, "On Likeness of Meaning," in Margaret Macdonald (ed.), *Philosophy and Analysis* (Oxford: Basil Blackwell, 1954), p. 55.
[8] *Ibid.*, pp. 55 f.

[9] *Ibid.*, p. 60.
[10] *Ibid.*, p. 61.
[11] Goodman, "On Some Differences About Meaning," in Macdonald (ed.), *op. cit.*, p. 69.
[12] "On Likeness of Meaning," p. 62.

Another more serious difficulty, affecting primarily empirical phases of philosophical construction, is that of counterfactual conditionals. Such statements as "if that piece of butter had been heated to 150° F., it would have melted," and "had the match been scratched it would have lighted," are invariably true, but so also are all other statements in which both antecedent and consequent are false. The significant formulation of scientific inferences depends upon our finding a reliable way of distinguishing conditional sentences that warrant factual inferences from those that are merely true by virtue of the falsity of their antecedents.[13] Two fundamental problems are involved: that of defining "relevant conditions" or specifying "what sentences are meant to be taken in conjunction with an antecedent as supplementary grounds for inferring the consequent," and that of defining the laws on which the inference is based.[14] No satisfactory solution of the first problem seems to be in prospect, for the reason that any sentences used to specify the required conditions seem themselves to involve counterfactual sentences and so to lead to an infinite regress.[15] The problem of defining laws is even more serious, for whereas law-likeness seems to depend upon confirmability prior to the determination of all instances, we do not yet know how such confirmability can be recognized.[16] What specific ways of overcoming these difficulties Goodman proposes, we shall see in the concluding paragraphs of this section. Meanwhile, we shall outline the sort of constructional system that Goodman attempts to set up within the limits of his self-imposed restrictions and in the light of the difficulties that he perceives.

A constructionist system that undertakes to render the structure of knowledge intelligible may be built either on physicalistic or phenomenalistic foundations. The type of system chosen by Goodman, but without attempted proof, is a phenomenalistic one. Against phenomenalism the argument is often offered that the phenomenalistic program cannot be completed as the physicalistic one can, but the truth is that intelligibility is much more important in a system than is completeness.[17] A further argument against phenomenalism is that "the units in which experience is actually given" are observations of physical objects, but such is the intervention of the descriptive process that no one can really know what units are actually given.[18] A more important objection to phenomenalism is that the purposes of ordinary inquiry and science are better served by a physicalistic system,

[13] *Fact, Fiction and Forecast,* pp. 13 ff.
[14] *Ibid.,* p. 17.
[15] *Ibid.,* p. 23.
[16] *Ibid.,* pp. 24 ff.

[17] See "The Revision of Philosophy," pp. 77 f.
[18] *Ibid.,* pp. 79 f.

but in fact the attempt to construe science solely in terms of thing-language confronts difficulties at least as great as those involved in the attempt to construe it in sense-language.[19] Without claiming any essential superiority for a phenomenalistic system, one may say that such a system is sufficiently justified by the fact that it "provides an orderly and connected description of its subject-matter in terms of perceptible individuals."[20] It is also capable of yielding a "finite ontology" suited to our powers of perception and construction and capable of being "discussed and tested quite as intersubjectively as those of any other system."[21]

Phenomenalistic systems may be distinguished from one another in two different ways. They include on the one hand a Platonism that "admits nonindividuals as entities" and a nominalism that does not, and on the other hand a realism that "admits nonparticulars as individuals" and a particularism that does not.[22] Thus phenomenalistic systems may be "platonistic and realistic, or nominalistic and realistic, or platonistic and particularistic, or nominalistic and particularistic." Professor Carnap's *Aufbau*, which has set an admirable example of the general sort of construction likely to prove illuminating,[23] is a system of the Platonistic particularistic kind, but lacks a satisfactory account of the similarities that bind together the various instances constituting, for example, a color.[24] The sort of system that Goodman prefers is the realistic-nominalistic variety which "admits qualitative non-concrete individuals . . . though it excludes all non-individuals."[25] The leading principles of the system are not, however, adaptable to other foundations and could be translated, for example, into the terminology of a Platonism that recognizes non-individuals.

A constructional system requires as its essential instruments definitions, a logical order, and primitives. The definitions involved need not be grounded in synonymy, which has been seen to be virtually unascertainable, nor indeed even in extensional identity. Sufficient grounds for working definitions can be achieved when "the extension of the definiens is isomorphic to the extension of the definiendum,"[26] that is, when the definiens is obtainable by "consistently replacing the ultimate factors" of the definiendum. What is wanted is "a system framed in the language of individuals" such that "the truth value of every sentence consisting solely of logical signs and extralogical defined terms of the system remains unchanged when all the extra-

[19] *Ibid.*, pp. 80 ff.
[20] *Ibid.*, p. 105.
[21] *The Structure of Appearance*, p. 107.
[22] *Ibid.*
[23] See *The Structure of Appearance*,

chap. v; and "The Revision of Philosophy," pp. 75 ff.
[24] *Ibid.*, pp. 123 ff.
[25] *Ibid.*, p. 107.
[26] *Ibid.*, p. 11.

logical defined terms are replaced by their respective definientia in the system." [27]

Turning now to the logical order requisite to a constructional system, one will need to take over from the usual calculus of modern logic "the stroke ('|') of truth-functional incompatibility, . . . the individual variables, the quantifiers, the truth-functional connectives, and the marks of punctuation." [28] The logical system will, however, require reinterpretation so as to yield in place of a calculus of classes a suitable calculus of individuals.[29] The distinctive primitive of the logical calculus of individuals is "overlaps," the character of which may be indicated by saying that "two individuals overlap if they have some common content." [30] With the help of this primitive one may go on to define a variety of other terms appropriate to individuals, such as "discrete," "part," "proper part," "product," "negate," "collective," "dissective," "pervasive," and "cumulative." [31] Thus for example, "one thing is part of another if and only if whatever overlaps the former also overlaps the latter." [32]

The extralogical primitives of a constructional system are not to be chosen for their inherent indefinability; for "no term is absolutely indefinable," and any indefinable is indefinable only relative to a given system.[33] Extralogical primitives are rather to be chosen for their usefulness in rendering experience intelligible. Although, as primitives, such primitives are not formally defined, they should of course be such as can be made clear by unofficial explanation. The list of extralogical primitives must be adequate to the purpose in hand, but since adequacy could be secured "by adopting as primitives all predicates not excluded by the conditions of the problem at hand," [34] another consideration becomes crucial in the choice of primitives, namely, *simplicity*. "The minimum or simplest adequate basis is wanted." [35] The criteria for the measurement of simplicity can, Goodman thinks, be accurately formulated in terms of an axiomatic system, which—though too complex to be detailed here—assigns complexity values in terms of numbers of predicate places, segments, and joints, with due regard to the effects of reflexivity and symmetry.[36]

[27] *Ibid.*, p. 28.
[28] *Ibid.*, p. 30.
[29] *Ibid.*, pp. 42 ff.
[30] *The Structure of Appearance*, p. 43.
[31] *Ibid.*, pp. 43 ff.
[32] *Ibid.*, p. 44.
[33] *Ibid.*, p. 57.
[34] *Ibid.*, p. 59.
[35] *Ibid.*
[36] Goodman, "On the Simplicity of Ideas," *Journal of Symbolic Logic*, VIII (1943), 107–21; "The Logical Simplicity of Predicates," *Ibid.*, XIV (1949), 32–41; "An Improvement in Theory of Simplicity," *Ibid.*, XIV (1949), 228–29; *The Structure of Appearance*, chap. iii; "New Notes on Simplicity," *Journal of Symbolic Logic*, XVII (1952), 189–91; and "Axiomatic Measurement of Simplicity," *Journal of Philosophy*, LII (1955), 709–22.

In a realistic nominalistic system of the phenomenalistic type the kind of individual units required by the simplicity criterion are arrived at by dividing "the stream of experience into its smallest concreta and these concreta into sense qualia." [37] Thus qualia or "presented characters" are the atomic individuals of the system.[38] Such characters consist of "colors, lines, visual-field places, and various nonvisual qualia." Sizes and shapes are secondary and reducible.[39] One need not say that "any quale is literally separable from the rest of experience" [40] or that qualia are "the units in which experience is originally given"; [41] qualia need only "be found within the whole . . . and be distinguished from other qualia." [42] Division into qualia is not "a spatial division"; [43] and gaps between segments of a quale are no barrier to its being an individual. As in the case of any other kind of individual the "boundaries [of a quality] may be complex to any degree." [44] Qualia are not to be confused with properties. The former come and go while the latter remain relatively constant. For example the *presented* colors of an object vary while what is thought of as the color of the object remains the same. The properties of a thing are determined by changes or "its appearance under all those sorts of conditions that are regarded as critical or standard"; the qualia associated with the thing are all of the appearance of the thing.[45] Qualia are thus not subject to error and verification in the sense in which properties are, though they are subject to comparison with one another. Qualia are by their primitive nature untestable. They cannot be "*both* unreliable and untestable, for an unreliable judgment, after all, is one that is frequently found to be false *when tested.*" [46] Since qualia are untestable and presentation of them cannot be revived, comparisons of two or more of them must be based on a "decree" grounded in experience; and it is in this fact that the immunity of such comparison from being false consists.[47] However, a comparison of qualia can, contrary to Lewis' opinion, be withdrawn. This follows from its basis in a decree, for a decree "is vulnerable to cancellation by another decree. The untestable is not irrevocable." [48] Thus, for example, "suppose (perversely) I decree that the quale presented by a (red) apple now is the same as that presented by the (blue) sky yesterday noon. Then I cannot very well also maintain both . . . that the quale now presented by the sky is the same as that presented by it yesterday noon, and . . . that the quale pre-

[37] *The Structure of Appearance,* p. 147.
[38] *Ibid.,* p. 176.
[39] *Ibid.,* p. 156.
[40] *Ibid.,* p. 148.
[41] *Ibid.,* p. 151.
[42] *Ibid.,* p. 148.
[43] *Ibid.*
[44] *Ibid.,* p. 43.
[45] *Ibid.,* p. 99.
[46] *Ibid.*
[47] *Ibid.,* pp. 99 f.
[48] *Ibid.,* p. 100.

sented by the apple now is very different from the quale presented by the sky now." [49] Similarly, "the judgment I made a little while ago that a reddish patch occupied the center of my visual field at that moment will be dropped if it conflicts with other judgments having a stronger combined claim to preservation . . . , for example . . . that the patch occupying the same region an instant later was blue and also that the apparent color was constant over a period covering the two instants." [50] In these cases a judgment about qualia is revoked, but the revocation does not involve testing the qualia.

When qualia are chosen as the basic individual units, the central problem of construction is that of showing what *things* and *qualities in the ordinary sense* are. The first step is to explain informally a new primitive W and to show its relation to associated terms. The primitive in question is "symmetrical, irreflexive, and nontransitive," [51] and may be "read as 'is with' or 'is at.' " [52] Any pair which it connects "belong to different categories of some one sense realm," so that it cannot connect, for example, two colors or two places or a color and a sound. It is rather the sort of relation that holds between "a color and a place at which the color occurs, between a place and a time at which the place occurs, and between a color-spot and a time at which the color-spot occurs." [53] In a realistic system a *concretum* is taken to be "a *fully* concrete entity that has among its qualities at least one member of every category within some sense realm." [54] The relation W "obtains between every two discrete parts of a concretum." [55] A *complex* is such that "an individual is a complex if and only if every two discrete parts of it bear the relation W to each other," [56] and since a quale has no discrete parts, any individual that is either discrete or "the sum of individuals that are together" is a complex.[57] Thus a concretum is "a complex that bears the relation W to no other individual"; [58] it is "an individual of which every two discrete parts are together but which is not with any individual." [59] Concreta are thus the molecules of the system. They are proper parts (i.e. parts less than wholes) of no complex and all their parts are complexes.

In the light of such an account of being with and of concreta, the distinction between qualities, things, and instances begins to come to focus. Qualities are certainly neither things nor concreta, but they also need not be mere qualia. They are "just those complexes which

---

[49] *Ibid.*
[50] Goodman, "Sense and Certainty," *Philosophical Review*, IV (1952), 160.
[51] *Ibid.*, p. 165.
[52] *Ibid.*, p. 173.
[53] *Ibid.*

[54] *Ibid.*, p. 160.
[55] *Ibid.*, p. 164.
[56] *Ibid.*, p. 166.
[57] *Ibid.*, p. 166 f.
[58] *Ibid.*, p. 167.
[59] *Ibid.*, p. 183.

are not qualia." [60] The converse of the relation "is a quality of" is the relation "is an instance of." Accordingly, "instances are just those complexes which are not qualia." [61] One may then say that "concreta are instances but never qualities," and that "complexes that are neither qualia nor concreta . . . are both instances (of their proper parts) and qualities (of more comprehensive complexes that contain them)." [62]

Suitable interpretations for such terms as "abstraction," "concretion," "particularity," and "universality" now begin to emerge. Thus on the one hand *an individual is concrete* if and only if it is exhaustively divisible into concreta," [63] so that sums of concreta as well as a concretum are concrete. On the other hand, "an individual *is abstract* if and only if it contains no concretum," so that "qualia and all other proper parts of concreta, [and] certain compounds . . . for example the sum of several colors or lines or of a place, time and color that are not all together" are all abstract.[64] The contrast between particular and universal may be formulated in parallel fashion. *"An individual is particular if and only if it is exhaustively dividible into unrepeatable complexes;* while *an individual is universal if and only if it contains no unrepeatable complex."* Thus all qualia and all sums of several qualia of one kind are universal; all concreta and all sums of concreta are particular; and such individuals as are the sum of a concretum and a quality foreign to it are neither universal nor particular." [65]

Having in this fashion fixed the fundamental terms of his system, Goodman searches in the fourth part of his *Structure of Appearance* for a predicate in terms of which the order of the world can be construed. He considers the choice of a "similarity predicate," but finds similarity as "part identity" unsatisfactory and similarity interpreted in any other way unduly vague.[66] Also considered is the predicate "is just noticeably different from." However, such a predicate presupposes a map of qualities, in that two qualities are just noticeably different only if no noticeably different quality is between them, whereas such a map is just what one is trying to construct.[67] The predicate that Goodman chooses is "matches," in the sense in which one quality may match each of two others though the other two do not match one another and in which qualities are identical *"if and only if they match all the same qualia."* [68]

[60] *Ibid.*, p. 186.
[61] *Ibid.*
[62] *Ibid.*
[63] *Ibid.*, p. 200.
[64] *Ibid.*

[65] *Ibid.*, p. 201.
[66] *Ibid.*, pp. 119 f.
[67] *Ibid.*, p. 222.
[68] *Ibid.*, p. 221.

By the use of his basic constructional apparatus and the predicate "matches," Goodman is now able to interpret sense categories in terms of continuous paths of matching qualia,[69] spatial relations in terms of spans of matching qualia,[70] and time as an ingredient of each concretum.[71] While Goodman freely acknowledges the elementary character of the realistic-nominalistic-phenomenalistic constructions sketched in *The Structure of Appearance*, he believes that upon the elemental foundations he has laid, the whole edifice of knowledge can, despite the difficulties indicated in his earlier writings, be built.

In his recent *Fact, Fiction, and Forecast* Goodman returns to the group of problems with which his article on counterfactuals was concerned. Since little or no progress has been made on the resolution of the problem of counterfactuals since the 1946 publication of the article,[72] Goodman thinks it wise to approach the problem from a fresh standpoint. Accordingly, the new chapters of his *Fact, Fiction and Forecast* begin with the problem of dispositions, which is both simpler and less linguistic in orientation than the problem of counterfactuals.

Dispositions are not to be explained in terms of possibilities, for possibilities, like classes and attributes, are among the dubious extravagances of non-nominalistic ontology. Rather, dispositions are to be explained in terms of the kind of projection which links as a single individual a complex belonging to one time and place and a complex belonging to another. In terms of such projection, a place in a visual field that at present lacks a certain color that is present at another time and place may be said to be colorable with reference to that color, and a stick that is not at present under pressure may be said to be flexible.[73] The crucial problem is to justify such projections in terms of lawlike statements, and this problem is essentially the problem of induction.

The old problem of induction, concerning how in general we can know the future on the basis of past evidence, has been, by more or less common consent, solved or at any rate dissolved. The basic solution is as old as Hume.[74] The quest for deductive proof of the future on the basis of the past and present is vain in principle, and induction has such general justification as it needs in the actual habits of our common-sense and scientific inquiries.[75] A new problem of induction, however, continues to confront us, namely what specifically are the confirmatory processes in terms of which common-sense and

[69] *Ibid.,* pp. 233 ff.
[70] *Ibid.,* pp. 241 ff.
[71] *Ibid.,* pp. 283 ff.
[72] *Fact, Fiction and Forecast,* pp. 42, 59 n.

[73] *Ibid.,* pp. 44 ff.
[74] *Ibid.,* pp. 63 ff.
[75] *Ibid.,* pp. 65 ff.

scientific inquiry operate.[76] In the search for a solution the best way to proceed is to begin with the projections actually made, that is, with those accepted upon evidence but not yet fully examined, and then to resolve conflicts. Excluded from the outset will be both violated and exhausted hypotheses. Remaining hypotheses will be supported by evidence in varying degrees, depending upon circum-stances and previous information.[77] In formulating lawlike state-ments, better entrenched predicates are to be preferred to less en-trenched ones, and in case of conflict the latter must give way to the former.[78] Specific rules can be laid down for determining preferences and such rules can progressively approximate a formalization of those habits by which confirmation is achieved.

Goodman does not feel that rules that he lays down for legitimate projections and lawlike statements have as yet supplied an adequate formula. He does feel that a satisfactory solution of the problem of projection can be achieved, and that it will furnish at the same time a solution of the problems of counterfactuals, dispositions, kinds, sim-plicity, and randomness.[79]

3. MORTON G. WHITE

The epistemological thought of Morton White (b. 1917) is similar to that of his Harvard colleague Quine. However, White's thought differs from that of Quine in being somewhat less preoccupied with implications of formal logic and in being more directly and deeply influenced by John Dewey and other pragmatically and socially ori-ented philosophers [1] on the one hand and by recent British analysts of ordinary language on the other. White is also in one respect more radically pragmatic than is Quine and in another respect less radically so. We shall consider first White's rejection of abstract entities and the distinction between analytic and synthetic, and then his more constructive account of knowing.

A. Like Quine and Goodman, White persistently refuses to accept any such alleged abstract entities as meanings, attributes, or classes. Not satisfied simply to attack the notion of meanings, White under-takes so to expose the roots of the error as to hinder its recurrence. In the early years of the present century meanings were thought to exist somewhat as the world was thought to exist. Russell, for exam-ple, held that the term "philosopher" in "Socrates is a philosopher"

[76] *Ibid.*, pp. 73 ff.
[77] *Ibid.*, pp. 90 ff.
[78] *Ibid.*, pp. 96 f.
[79] *Ibid.*, pp. 117 ff.

[1] See Morton G. White, *The Origin of Dewey's Instrumentalism* (New York: Co-lumbia University Press, 1943); and *Social Thought in America* (New York: The Viking Press, Inc., 1949).

denoted the meaning of the word "philosopher." [2] His principal basis for this position was that since one understands the word "philosopher," the attribute of being a philosopher must exist as a meaning for the term.[3] Russell's line of thought was not unlike that of Moore's argument for the existence of an external world on the basis of the implication of the existence of such a world in the admitted existence of his own hand. Actually, Russell rejected Moore's argument for the existence of the external world on account of its failure to lead to something with which we are acquainted; but he thought that, being acquainted with meanings as well as requiring them to explain our understandings, we must accept the existence of meanings. However, Russell's thought about meanings was confused and mistaken. To begin with, if he were going to speak of meanings at all, he should have recognized with Mill that what is *denoted* by such a term as "philosopher" is a subject, not an attribute, and that "the attribute of being a philosopher" is at most only *connoted*, not denoted, by the term "philosopher." [4] The argument from understanding to meanings is a *non sequitur,* for the existence of meanings follows from my understanding a term only on the doubtful assumption that in understanding I *grasp* the meaning. In any case the term "meaning" is so much more obscure than the term "understanding" that the former term has little or no explanatory value.[5] Even Moore's argument for the existence of an external world, inadequate though it be, is more plausible than Russell's argument for meanings, for at least it leads to phenomenal facts whereas Russell's attempted defense of meanings leads only to ghosts.[6]

Attempts are sometimes made to rehabilitate abstract entities by distinguishing between different senses of "exists," between categorical and noncategorical relations, and between external and internal questions. The first of these distinctions ascribes ordinary existence to physical objects and subsistence to universals. Such procedure, however, not only introduces needless complication into logic, but overlooks the fact that there must be a basic sense of "exists" if one is even to say that there are different senses of the term.[7] Such procedure is also quite unnecessary since one can avoid both "queer" entities and an undesirable multivocalism with reference to "exists" by comparatively simple rephrasings of misleading sentences. For example, instead of saying "there is a difference in age between John and Tom," one may well say simply "it is not the case that John is

---

[2] White, *Toward Reunion in Philosophy* (Cambridge: Harvard University Press, 1956), pp. 31 f.

[3] *Ibid.,* pp. 33 ff.

[4] *Ibid.,* p. 32.

[5] *Ibid.,* pp. 37 f.

[6] *Ibid.,* pp. 55 ff.

[7] *Ibid.,* pp. 76 f.

as old as Tom.[8] As for so-called categorical distinctions, they are in no fundamental respect different from other distinctions. One has in any case first to know something about a subject matter before he can distinguish it from other subject matters, and there are no "intrinsically categorical and intrinsically noncategorical predicates." [9] Carnap has suggested that the problem of the existence of meaning does not belong among the internal questions of fact within a given system but among the external questions of the frame of reference of the system itself, but if meanings should be established along the lines of this distinction they would be virtually devoid of ontological or epistemological significance.[10]

While some philosophers who have grave doubts about the existence of meanings or any other abstract entities seem to be not in the least uneasy about the distinction between analytic and synthetic statements, White, like Goodman and Quine, regards this distinction as extremely dubious. Even in his articles in the forties concerning the paradox of analysis, White showed signs of misgivings about the synonymy on which the distinction between analytic and synthetic rests.[11] In his writings in the fifties he has produced a polemic against the distinction that is even more intense than that of Quine or Goodman.

The analytic statements with which White is concerned are not primarily truths of logic, such as "P is P," or their substitution instances, such as "every man is a man," but rather those analytic statements derived from truths of logic or their substitution instances by putting synonyms for synonyms, such as "Every man is a rational animal." [12] The basic difficulty lies in the notion of synonymy on which such analytic statements rest. Even if one's philosophy gains in "ontological clarity" by excluding such doubtful entities as attributes, the gain may be purchased at the cost of "semantic obscurity" if it depends, as is often the case, upon substituting synonymy of predicates for identity of attributes, for the former concept is scarcely clearer than the latter.[13]

One type of defense of synonymy and analyticity, that of C. I. Lewis' recent work, depends upon "going behind language . . . to

[8] *Ibid.*, p. 68.
[9] *Ibid.*, p. 96.
[10] *Ibid.*, chap. vi.
[11] See White, "Analysis and Identity: a Rejoinder," *Mind*, LIII (1944); "A Note on the Paradox of Analysis," *Mind*, LIV (1945), pp. 71–72; "On the Church–Frege Solution of the Paradox of Analysis," *Philosophy and Phenomenological Research* (1948), pp. 305–8.

[12] White, "The Analytic and the Synthetic: An Untenable Dualism," in Leonard Linsky (ed.), *Semantics and the Philosophy of Language* (Urbana: University of Illinois Press, 1952), p. 275; see also *Toward Reunion in Philosophy*, pp. 128 f.
[13] White, "Ontological Clarity and Semantic Obscurity," *Journal of Philosophy*, XLVIII (1951), 373–77.

meanings whose identity we must see."[14] But even if the implied ontology could be accepted, the intuition in terms of which we must see relations of meanings would either be so difficult or so obvious as to be relatively useless. The attempt to explain likeness or difference of meaning by reference to insight into meanings, is like Molière's physician's explanation of why a drug puts people to sleep by reference to the "dormitive virtue" of the drug.[15] The extensionalist treatment of analytic statements as those the contradictories of which are self-contradictory is scarcely more revealing than the intensionalist treatment of meanings as discoveries of special insights. Recognition of the relevant contradictories depends on prior recognition of synonymies.[16] A related defense of synonymy and analyticity depends on the linguistic test that, for example, "if *we were presented with something which wasn't a rational animal we would not call it a man.*[17] However, many people would also not call a thing a man if it were not a featherless biped; and even if the reasons for the denial in the one case are different from those in the other, the sort of test in question would at best show synonymy to be no more than a matter of degree. Further defenses of synonymy by appeal to artificial languages are quite besides the point, for they reveal nothing concerning terms in actual use and involve no such knowledge of the world as the kind of analytic statements under consideration purport to formulate.[18] We may, if we wish, regard such terms as "analytic" as what John Austin calls performative phrases akin to "I promise," or we may use such terms as a kind of ritual. But to treat them in this manner is to leave entirely open the crucial questions when or by what justification the performance or ritual is to be undertaken.[19]

B. The constructive part of White's epistemological thought may be appropriately thought of as an analytic neopragmatism that is in one respect more radical and in another more conciliatory than the older pragmatisms. This neopragmatism is radical in the sense that it demands the application of practical tests to every aspect of knowledge. Unlike the conceptual pragmatism of Lewis' earlier writings it declines to limit pragmatic tests to the area of basic concepts; and unlike Carnap's recent thought it refuses to restrict them to the external questions of frames of reference.[20] With Quine it holds that scientific questions, such as those of "the existence of electrons or

[14] *Toward Reunion in Philosophy*, p. 139; see also "The Analytic and the Synthetic: An Untenable Dualism," p. 323.
[15] *Toward Reunion in Philosophy*, pp. 139 ff.
[16] *Ibid.*, pp. 143 ff.; and "The Analytic and the Synthetic: An Untenable Dualism," pp. 324 ff.
[17] *Ibid.*, p. 282.
[18] *Ibid.*, p. 321; *Toward Reunion in Philosophy*, pp. 122 ff., 148 ff.
[19] *Ibid.*, pp. 152 ff.
[20] *Ibid.*, pp. 18 ff.

bacteria," are just as surely subject to considerations of a practical kind as are those of the existence of "categories like events, numbers, attributes or physical objects." [21] But whereas Quine treats sensory reports as "feelers that make contact with experience in some non-pragmatic way," [22] seems to recognize nonpragmatic elements in knowledge, and digs a "great ditch" between *singular* statements *of fact*" and *"sensory reports,"* [23] White's pragmatism subjects even reports of sensation to pragmatic tests.

In opposition to all who set limits to the range of statements which may be regarded as hypothetical and subject to broadly pragmatic tests, White insists "that the class of categorically acceptable statements is at any given moment heterogeneous with respect to traditional classifications of statements," [24] and refuses to say that "all or only so-called sensory reports are terminal," [25] or indeed that any others are. To be sure, for purposes of any given discourse, some sentences must be regarded as "pinned down"; but no sentence is irrevocably pinned down, and sentences of any system may or may not at a given time be treated as pinned down.[26]

However, while White's pragmatism is radical in refusing to set any fixed limits to the range of applicability of practical considerations, it is moderate in insisting that the applicable tests are not all practical and that even the practical tests are not mere matters of expediency. James was wrong in saying that "that which we ought to believe is that which it is expedient to believe." [27] Quine has properly emphasized the importance of simplicity and of prediction of experience, and Goodman, that of philosophic conscience.[28] No genuine issues of knowledge are "creatures of convenience." [29] Not even ontology is to be altogether "left at the mercy of pragmatic considerations. Like some of one's moral beliefs, one's basic philosophical commitments are not easily surrendered in exchange for pragmatic success." [30] Due weight must always be given not only to practical considerations akin to those of ethics and to successful prediction but also to "respect for old truths, simplicity, . . . clarity." [31] No such irresponsibility and haziness as the older pragmatism tended to sustain can any longer be permitted, and the new friends in the house of pragmatism must help "to start draining its swampy foundations and blocking its metaphors." [32]

[21] *Ibid.,* p. 18.
[22] *Ibid.,* p. 274.
[23] *Ibid.,* pp. 275 f.
[24] *Ibid.,* p. 284.
[25] *Ibid.*
[26] *Ibid.,* p. 281.
[27] *Ibid.,* p. 274.

[28] *Ibid.,* pp. 276 ff.
[29] *Ibid.,* p. 280.
[30] *Ibid.,* pp. 280 f.
[31] *Ibid.,* p. 284.
[32] White, review of Leon Cheswistek's *The Limits of Science,* in *Philosophical Review,* LX (1951), 124.

Eventual appeal to ethically oriented broadly pragmatic criteria is the common bond that unites the three different philosophical inquiries with which *Toward Reunion in Philosophy* is concerned, namely ontology, logic, and ethics. In ontology, the thought of the present century at first rooted itself in reification of meanings, and when this rootage failed, it grounded itself in verbal conventions.[33] When this procedure also proved unsatisfactory, it turned to ontological decisions. But such decisions have themselves somehow to be justified, and justification is always akin to ethics. Thus "we set up a rule which allows us to give a reason for calling an expression meaningful . . . , just as a moral rule allows us to give a reason for saying that something ought not to be done." [34]

In the logical theory of the early part of the century, the attempt was to build upon an analyticity grounded in meaning.[35] When this failed, an analyticity of artificially defined terms was worked out.[36] But while some statements must indeed be accepted as a basis of further inquiry, the crucial question is how to justify one's choices of such statements, and here again the question comes to be one of ethically oriented pragmatic considerations. The choices of the philosopher in this area are somewhat like those of the judge, who also must make justifiable decisions, except that in the choice of basic statements "such factual considerations" as guide the judge are often lacking.[37]

Finally, ethics itself began in the present century by reliance upon meanings, which Moore, for example, took to be distinctively ethical, and perhaps some terms are to be so taken. But the important fact is that such terms must be so *taken,* and which ones are to be so taken is a problem, answers to which can themselves only be evaluated upon ethicopragmatic grounds. No part of philosophical inquiry or indeed of any sort of knowing can in the end remain completely isolated from the broadly pragmatic ethical considerations. "All statements which express knowledge are connected with each other," [38] and "describing, doing, and evaluating are all of them . . . connected parts of the enterprise" of "reunion in philosophy." [39] Practical and theoretical considerations must always be kept in perspective, and pragmatic considerations tempered by other equally important ones. At the present juncture of philosophical development, accordingly "nothing could be more important than reuniting . . . the analytic, pragmatic, linguistic concern of the recent Anglo-American tradition

[33] *Ibid.,* pp. 9 ff.
[34] *Ibid.,* p. 109.
[35] *Ibid.,* pp. 113 ff.
[36] *Ibid.,* pp. 148 ff.
[37] *Ibid.,* pp. 162 f.

[38] Note White, *The Age of Analysis* (New York: New American Library of World Literature, Inc., 1955), p. 242.
[39] *Ibid.,* p. 299.

and the more humane, cultivated concerns of the predominantly continental tradition." [40]

4. ARTHUR PAP

Arthur Pap (b. 1921) of Yale University differs from Quine, Goodman, and White in regarding such abstract entities as meanings, concepts, and propositions, as well as intuitions, not as liabilities to philosophical inquiry but as indispensable factors in that process. He does, however, agree with these other pragmatic analysts in being distrustful of metaphysics, in rejecting the sharp dichotomy of analytic and synthetic, and in insisting upon treating scientific statements within a framework of flexible conceptual systems. He also presses his positive inquiry into the character of necessary statements that are not strictly either analytic or empirical much further than any of the other pragmatic analysts, and it is mainly with his account of necessary statements that we shall be concerned here.

Although, like Quine, Goodman, and White, Pap has shown strong tendencies toward a severe nominalism,[1] and although he continues to insist that the metaphysical implications of his assumptions about abstract entities are zero, unlike these other writers, Pap believes that a nominalism that excludes meanings, propositions, and concepts would exclude certain genuinely significant and important types of statements.[2] Apart from the recognition of propositions as distinct from sentences, statements to the effect that something is believed or known can never be adequately expressed,[3] and modal statements come to be contingent upon language habits in ways that are quite contrary to the intention of such statements.[4] Even truth-claims are compromised, for generally speaking, truth is not a semantic concept referring to sentences but a relation between propositions and facts.[5] In like fashion, apart from recognition of meanings and concepts, the foundations of many necessary truths, such as that "nothing which is round is square," and that if B is darker in color than A, and C than B, then C is darker than A, are destroyed.[6]

Meanings are not, Pap thinks, to be identified with the introspectable images and feelings accompanying the use of words, for such

[40] *The Age of Analysis,* p. 242.

[1] Arthur Pap, *Elements of Analytic Philosophy* (New York: The Macmillan Co., 1949), pp. 87 ff.

[2] Pap, *Semantics and Necessary Truth* (New Haven, Conn.: Yale University Press, 1958), pp. 50 ff.

[3] *Ibid.*

[4] Cf. *ibid.*, pp. 127 ff., 163 ff.

[5] Cf. Pap, "Propositions Sentences and the Semantic Definitions of Truth," *Theoria,* XXVII (1954), 23–35; "Note on the Semantic and the 'Absolute' Conception of Truth," *Philosophical Studies,* III (1952), 1–8.

[6] *Semantics and Necessary Truth,* p. 53.

images and feelings are highly variable and unreliable.[7] Nor are meanings primarily to be discerned by asking people what they intend in the use of certain terms, for people are often quite seriously lacking in insight concerning what is involved in what they say. Methods of verification are significant checks on meaningfulness and are useful guides to meaning.[8] But they cannot be identified with meanings. It is often merely because of a "belief in an empirical law" rather than a logical entailment that a person accepts certain evidences as validating a given statement.[9] Moreover, some clearly meaningful statements cannot be verified, e.g. statements to the effect that the qualities of the experiences of two people are exactly alike.[10] Meaning is, generally speaking, to be identified with use, and the content of any given concept depends upon the range of the application that one who employs it would be willing to give it.[11]

The currently orthodox doctrine concerning a priori or necessary truths is that they are invariably analytic. The claim is that all statements are either empirical or analytic, that there are no synthetic a priori truths.[12] Whether or not this doctrine can be sustained and what its significance is depends upon how "analytic" is interpreted. One of the two major alternatives is to regard analytic statements, along lines suggested by Leibnitz and Quine, as statements whose contradictories are self-contradictory, or statements derivable from truths of logic by placing synonyms for synonyms. This view is beset from the outset by difficulties in defining logical truth and synonymy.[13] However, even if these difficulties are waived, this narrow view of necessary truth is altogether incapable of explaining such elementary necessary truths as that two straight lines never enclose an area in Euclidean space, that all colored objects are extended, that nothing is both red and green all over, and that whatever has pitch has loudness.[14]

[7] Ibid., pp. 397 ff.

[8] Elements of Analytic Philosophy, pp. 315, 322; cf. Semantics and Necessary Truth, pp. 400 f.

[9] Ibid., p. 403.

[10] Pap, "The Philosophical Analysis of Material Language," Methodos, I (1949), pp. 362 ff.

[11] Elements of Analytic Philosophy, pp. 455, 458; Semantics and Necessary Truth, pp. 393 ff.

[12] Semantics and Necessary Truth, chap. v.

[13] Pap, "Logic and the Concept of Entailment," Journal of Philosophy, L (1947), 348–87; Pap, "Synonymity and Logical Equivalence," Analysis, IX (1949), 51–57; Pap, "Logic and the Synthetic A Priori," Philosophy and Phenomenological Research, X (1949–50), 500–14; Pap, "Are All Necessary Propositions Analytic?" Philosophical Review, LIII (1949), 299–320; and Semantics and Necessary Truth, chap. vi.

[14] Pap, "Logical Nonsense, Philosophy and Phenomenological Research," IX (1948–49), "Logic and the Synthetic A Priori," pp. 500–14; "Are All Necessary Propositions Analytic?" pp. 299–320, Semantics and Necessary Truth, pp. 17, 35 ff; and "Once More Colors and the Synthetic A Priori," Philosophical Review, LXVI (1957), 94–99.

The other major alternative is to define analytic statements, along lines suggested by Kant and more specifically worked out by Lewis, as statements whose truth is dependent on the meanings of the terms involved. Unfortunately, however, this view takes so much into its definition of the analytic as to allow no possibility of a necessary truth that is not analytic and no opportunity for discussion of the issue or even stating it. As an argument to show that all necessary truth is analytic, this procedure is accordingly circular and relatively useless.[15] The orthodox claim that all necessary truths are analytic is either false or trivial; false if analyticity is interpreted narrowly in terms of placing synonyms for synonyms in logical truths, and trivial if analyticity is interpreted broadly in terms of relations of meanings.[16] Similarly, sharp dichotomy of analytic and empirical is either not exhaustive or not exclusive; not exhaustive if analyticity is interpreted narrowly and not exclusive if it is interpreted broadly.[17] Such writers as Carnap have sought a way out of this dilemma by making analyticity wholly relative to artificial language systems, but such a course, whatever its other merits, tends to cut off the conception of necessary truth from all significant use in connection with scientific knowledge and common discourse.[18]

Necessary truth may appropriately be said to embrace two distinct varieties. The first and more formal variety includes truths of logic, substitution instances of truths of logic, and truths derived by putting synonyms for synonyms in truths of logic. The second and more material or *loosely* analytic variety consists of statements that are true by virtue of the meanings of the terms involved but not on the basis of logic and definitions alone. Whether the second variety is referred to as either broadly analytic or as synthetic a priori is largely a matter of verbal preference. Any materially necessary statement may be turned into a formally necessary one by stipulating suitable definitions, and it often turns out to be convenient to treat empirical generalizations as functional formal truths for purposes of certain scientific inquiries.[19] This latter consideration should not, however, lead one to think that the distinction between propositions that are necessary and those that are not is either on the one hand merely arbitrary or on the other hand capable of being altogether sharply drawn. The necessity of statements is basically determined by the entailments of actual usage rather than by functional conventions. But between statements that are quite clearly necessary and others that are clearly

---

[15] *Semantics and Necessary Truth,* pp. 94–108.

[16] *Ibid.,* pp. 108 ff.

[17] *Ibid.,* pp. 210–18.

[18] *Ibid.,* chap. xiv.

[19] Pap, "The Different Kinds of *A Priori,*" *Philosophical Review,* LIII (1944), 465–84; cf. also *Semantics and Necessary Truth,* pp. 229–36.

not are still others whose status is by no means so clear. One must accordingly be willing to accept a gradualism that acknowledges degrees of necessity, the degree of the necessity of any proposition depending upon the tenacity with which one would adhere to it despite complicating evidence.[20] At the foundations of most sciences are to be found both necessary and nonnecessary statements, but it is often difficult to say which is which. The linkage of scientific statements to observation statements is not nearly so likely to be fully necessary as is commonly supposed, for most of the concepts of science are now regarded as open concepts, whose definitions may be progressively modified.[21]

How are necessary truths apprehended? A currently popular view is that necessary truths are grounded solely in linguistic rules and that they are apprehended in the recognition of such rules. However, such a view leaves the rules themselves unexplained and fails to account for the fact that changes in the meanings of terms leave altogether unaltered the necessary relations of the underlying propositions.[22]

A view which most champions of the orthodox dichotomy of analytic and empirical are especially anxious to avoid is the view that intuition is required for the apprehension of necessary truths. However, the essential correctness of this view is apparently inescapable.[23] With regard to the necessary connections that are discerned between such simples as colors, between color and specific colors, and between pitches and tones, it is difficult to see how any other mode of apprehension could be applicable than intuition. Surely these connections are not empirical. No logical implication is involved in saying that the same space cannot be both red and green at the same time, nor is any formal contradiction involved in denying such a relation. What is not nearly so often recognized is that many entailments even among more complex concepts which are explicated by philosophical analyses are in like manner discerned by intuition. If intuition did not first discern entailments that set the criteria for formal analysis, then there would be nothing by which the correctness of an analysis could be tested, and analysis would be only an interesting game with no relevance for significant human discourse.[24] These considerations may be notably exemplified in

[20] *Ibid.,* pp. 344–55.

[21] Pap, "Reduction Sentences and Open Concepts," *Methodos,* V (1951), 328; *Semantics and Necessary Truth,* chap. xi.

[22] Pap, "Are All Necessary Propositions Analytic?" *Philosophical Review,* pp. 315 ff.; "Synonymy, Identity and the Paradox of Analysis," p. 122.

[23] Pap, "Reduction Sentences and Open Concepts," *Methodos,* V (1951), 328; *Semantics and Necessary Truth,* chap. xii.

[24] Pap, "The Philosophical Analysis of Natural Language," *Methodos,* I (1949), 344–69; *Semantics and Necessary Truth,* chap. xiii.

current analyses of such basic notions as those of probability and lawlike statements. One may go a step further and say that even those statements whose necessity seems to depend upon definitions are rooted in intuition. A definition never creates necessity; it only transfers necessity. Thus, for example, the necessity of a father's being a male parent is not created by the definition of a father as a male parent; necessity is only transferred by that definition from the logical truth that a father is a father to the nonlogical truth that a father is a male parent; and the plausibility of the definition itself rests on the preanalytic intuition of the entailment of the concept of a male parent in that of a father.[25] Moreover, even the truths of logic themselves, if they are to be more than formal devices of irrelevant constructed languages, must be grounded in intuitional insights.[26]

The psychological character of the intuitional foundation of necessary truths does not, however, in any sense discredit or render these truths mysterious or metaphysical. Intuition is a natural way of knowing, and after all, science as well as logic and philosophical analysis rest in the end upon it.[27] Moreover, it is the psychological character of the intuitional base of necessary truths that permits avoidance of the paradox of analysis and so prevents the shipwreck of the philosophical venture. If analysis did no more than to disclose identities with reference to which complete substitutivity was required, attempted analyses would have to be either inconsequential or false. However, since the insights on which the criteria of analysis rest are psychological and intuitional, they involve degrees of necessity and so rule out the demand for complete substitutivity and enable analysis to be informative without being false.[28]

5. COMMENTS CONCERNING PRAGMATIC ANALYSIS

The writings of the pragmatic analysts have, despite their relatively limited extent, begun to produce considerable readjustment in contemporary epistemological thought both by their attack upon strongly entrenched empirical doctrines and by their own constructive suggestions. The main features of these writings leading to such results are the attempt to exclude abstract entities, the repudiation of the dichotomy of the analytic and the synthetic, and the pragmatic account of the confirmation of knowledge claims.

[25] "The Philosophical Analysis of Natural Language," pp. 344–69; cf. Semantics and Necessary Truth, pp. 163–70.

[26] "The Philosophical Analysis of Natural Language," pp. 358 ff.; cf. Semantics and Necessary Truth, pp. 182 ff.

[27] "The Philosophical Analysis of Natural Language," pp. 358 ff.; Semantics and Necessary Truth, pp. 419–22.

[28] Ibid., pp. 290–301, 344–55, 400–404.

A. Although other philosophers have attempted to get rid of abstract entities, none have done so with such thoroughness and logical acumen as some of the pragmatist analysts, especially Quine. The grounds of the pragmatic analysts' attempt to achieve this result—which we shall consider in its general form as an attempt to get rid of universals—are, apart from what Goodman has called "philosophic conscience," somewhat as follows: The acceptance of meanings as universals rests upon the false assumption that every word names a meaning and that to understand a term is to intuit its meaning. The term "exists" has but a single sense which precludes the existence of universals, and to say that there are universals leads to all manner of embarrassing questions about their sizes, shapes, and locations. All that is expressed by sentences having as their subjects terms for universals can be better expressed by sentences in which such terms are confined to predicates. Indeed, it is desirable that not only terms for universals but all singular terms be eliminated from a purified type of discourse.

Certainly much of what is contended here is sound and still insufficiently recognized by other philosophers. Many terms with which notions of universals are commonly connected, such as adjectives and verbs, do not even purport to name anything, and to say that they have denotations may be misleading. If the substantive terms corresponding to them, such as courage and tallness, do name anything, they surely do so in a manner very different from that in which proper names name individuals. To say that understanding a sentence demands an intuiting of a universal as its meaning goes far beyond anything normally required for understanding a sentence, and perhaps in the wrong direction. Certainly to say that universals exist alongside other things or that they enter as forces into the determining of the vectorial lines of events would be to be guilty of a fairly obvious category mistake. Moreover, for sentences having universals as their subjects it is in fact often possible to find approximate equivalents in which what was expressed in the subject is included in the predicate. For example, "the house is red" approximates in meaning "red is the color of the house."

Nevertheless, certain considerations continue to demand attention that seem to render the entire exclusion of universals inadvisable and perhaps even impossible. Some of these are as follows. For one thing, we continue to use multitudes of abstract terms in substantival forms and in straightforward subject positions in sentences; and apparently our language and thought would be seriously impoverished if this practice were prevented. Even if we could rephrase all sentences in which this occurs so that the terms for universals occurred only in the predicates, the question would persist why we keep using this allegedly misleading form of expression. Besides, in actual fact the rephrased sentences rarely if ever succeed in expressing just what is expressed in the original sentences having terms for universals as their subjects. Even when the translations are made with moderate success, questions keep pressing concerning the predicates that presuppose universals. But in addition to the fact that we persist in talking the language of universals, we seem actually to require such language for a number of important purposes. For one thing, we need to talk about properties that things have or that we mean to ascribe to them when we say certain things about them, and to most people it would seem absurd to deny the existence of such properties. For another, we need to talk about the relation of properties to one another, as when we say that red is a color, or courage is a virtue. More especially, we need to talk about the relations of extremely abstract concepts such as we employ in mathematics, and regarding this point even Quine admits that the abandonment of universals would mean the abandonment of much of the most useful part of mathematics. Only by surrendering very large segments not only of human language but of human thought can universals be entirely gotten rid of.

Some sort of compromise would, accordingly, seem to be required. Actually, it is possible to admit and even insist upon most of the objections of pragmatic analysts against traditional accounts of universals without any very radical abandonment of universals. This suggests the essential soundness of the sort of procedure adopted in this matter by some of the ordinary language analysts; [1] of not rejecting the language of universals but endeavoring to discover how that language is actually used, of pruning away needless entities but assigning to universals essentially the kinds of reality and function that our common ways of thinking and talking actually for the most part do assign to them. This would presumably mean that one would deny that there are things or causal forces or namable entities called universals. But it would also mean that one could well continue to say that things have properties, that these properties have certain relations to one another and may be apprehended by us, that there are multitudes of possibilities related to one another in many different ways and sometimes realized in things and sometimes not, and that many of these possibilities even among those that are never realized in things can be apprehended by us. A very great deal would remain to be worked out concerning universals and their relations to one another, to things, and to our minds; but their existence in a properly restricted sense could be affirmed and we should

[1] Especially in Strawson's *Individuals*.

have avoided the major peril of being pushed at the outset into either of the extremes of making universals eternal objects or of ruling universals out altogether.

Two objections raised by pragmatic analysts would to be sure not be met by such an account of universals, namely, the objection that the one sense of "exists" precludes the existence of universals and that all singular terms including abstract ones are best eliminated. But the insistence upon a single sense of "exists" is wrong from the start. The sense of "exists" in which a nation exists is not the same as that in which its citizens exist. Nor is the sense in which rainbows exist the same as that in which the drops of water composing it exist. Things and solutions of mathematical problems do not exist in the same sense. Nor do things and universals. But failure to exist as material individuals exist affords no ground for comprehensive denial of existence to nations, rainbows, mathematical solutions, or universals. Apparently a basic reason, apart from its bearing on the problem of universals, for the insistence of pragmatic analysts upon a single sense of "exists" is that a variety of senses of this term is incompatible with the smooth operation of the standard system of symbolic logic in which " $\exists$ " plays a cardinal role. But whatever the force of this reason for logicians, it has little force for the common man or for most philosophers. One would suppose that formal systems should be adapted to what we think and say rather than the converse.

Concerning the proposal that universals be eliminated as members of the logically undesirable class of singulars, the appropriate reply would seem to be similar to the suggested reply to the proposal that all but the one preferred sense of "exists" be eliminated, a reply to the effect that while the acceptance of such a proposal might make for logical elegance, it would be inimical to ontological and epistemological relevance. Surely it is initially and perhaps even eventually toward singulars as individuals that the quest for knowledge is directed, and any proposed logical system that in the interest of the exclusion of universals excludes the whole class to which they belong, including even individuals, would surely seem to have lost its bearings and indeed to have become in the most significant sense unpragmatic. In any case the attempt to get rid of singulars can scarcely claim to have been successful, but turns out, as in the case of the substitution of the awkward expression "the x that pegasizes" for "Pegasus," to be an extremely artificial and ineffective expedient that not only fails in the end to exclude reference to individuals but tends to obscure rather than disclose the kinds of conceptual schemes through which human inquiry does and presumably must operate.

B. The argument of pragmatic analysts against the analytic-synthetic dichotomy is, it will be recalled, somewhat as follows. The notion of analyticity involves that substitution of synonyms in logical truths and cannot be extensionally defined without referring to the notion of synonymy (either directly or indirectly through such notions as those of self-contradiction and definition), and the notion of synonymy itself is not extensionally definable. Such intensional concepts as meaning and possibility are too vague to be of any help. Actual usage leaves necessity in doubt, and the notion of necessity itself depends upon that of analyticity.

There can be little doubt that the pragmatic analysts' insistence upon such doubts as these has rendered valuable service to contemporary philosophy by demanding a re-examination of the whole notion of a dichotomy of analytic and synthetic. That dichotomy had come to be in recent philosophy so readily and easily accepted that both the theoretical difficulties involved in accepting it and the practical problems flowing from the apparent impossibility of carrying it through were all too easily glossed over. The pragmatic analysts' contention that one can draw no sharp line between those sentences that are synthetic and those that are analytic is entirely sound. It may well be that far more sentences are indeterminate in terms of such a dichotomy than are determinate or perhaps that none at all are fully determinate. Even if one is dealing with statements rather than sentences, it may well be that many of them cannot be placed in terms of this dichotomy. Such questions as what precisely is meant by a statement's being analytic or synthetic, and whether or not the distinction between analytic and synthetic is exhaustive and its terms mutually exclusive need to be thoroughly re-examined, and the doubts of the pragmatic analysts have stirred fruitful discussion of these issues. These doubts have also stimulated interesting discussion of the related questions of the possibility of a synthetic a priori and of degrees of necessity.

However, none of these facts should be taken to mean that the pragmatic analysts have accomplished the overthrow of the notion of analyticity. The dichotomy of analytic and synthetic has long served a very useful purpose and certainly ought not to be abandoned without considerably more of a hearing than pragmatic analysts have so far given it. Indeed, there are good reasons for thinking that a carefully guarded version of it may be in a good deal less hopeless state of health than pragmatic analysts' writings would lead one to think. To begin with, even if one approaches the subject in the pragmatic analysts' preferred extensional way, in terms of logical truths and the substitution of synonyms for synonyms, the possibility of finding marks of synonymy that if not definitive are at least illuminating has scarcely been as yet fully explored. For the most part Quine and White assume rather than seek to prove the unintelligibility of synonymy, and Goodman, on whom they rely at this point, can scarcely be said, in the relatively little that he has written on the subject, to have exhausted the topic. Indeed, at the end of his main essay on the subject he seems himself almost to be on the trail of a possibly useful mode of distinction.

However, one does not need to confine oneself to extensional definition of analyticity as substitution of synonyms for synonyms in logical truths. One can, for example, describe analyticity by reference to linguistic behavior,[1] i.e. by reference to acceptances and rejections of certain types of sentences without a notion of synonymy at all. Such an approach need not depend upon reference to observations of nonlinguistic facts. By taking into consideration physical, social, behavioral, and linguistic contexts, it substantially increases its chances of success, for sentences as such are notoriously likely to shift their meanings when used in different situations. Indeed, a good deal could presumably be achieved by philosophers endeavoring to work out in what sort of contexts various kinds of expressions were likely to be treated as true or false without regard to confirmatory or disconfirmatory observations, and such inquiry need have none of the vagueness that pragmatic analysts are disposed to ascribe to inquiries of this type.

Actually, it is not necessary to confine discussion of analyticity to the levels of extensional substitution of synonyms and linguistic behavior. A distinction between analytic and synthetic has long been made with some degree of success in intensional terms, and the notion of meaning to which Quine, Goodman, and White so strongly object has in this connection, as we have seen, a good deal more promise than their treatment would indicate. Lewis and others have developed illuminating interpretations of analyticity in terms of inclusions and exclusions of meaning criteria which, despite their failure to fit into preferred extensional schemata, are not at all analogous to the stupid remark of Molière's physician. In fact, it would seem to be the case that a major function of extensional accounts of analyticity is the explication rather than the elimination of intensional ones, and if so, clarification of the explicanda may contribute to rather than hinder that of the explicata. Moreover, even if experiments in thought come to be involved, this need not be reason for condemnation of an initial intensional approach to the

---

[1] For an interesting account of analyticity in such terms see Bennett, *Proceedings of the Aristotelian Society*, LIX (1958–59), 163–88.

subject. Private experiences seem in the end in any case to be involved in the observations, and recognitions included in empirical verifications. They may very well be involved also in the basic foundations of the logical truths with which pragmatic analysts initiate their discussion of analyticity; and Pap for one has begun to recognize that something of this sort is so. Indeed it may be that logical truths themselves are instances of a wider range of analytic truths that are basically dependent upon relations of meanings and recognizable by recognition of such relations. However imprecise, then, the notion of analyticity may be, it surely need not be altogether abandoned or regarded as unimportant.

C. The pragmatic view of confirmation now to be briefly commented upon is in general to the effect that both logical and empirical sentences are to be tested not one by one on the basis of fixed theoretical considerations but as parts of whole systems and relatively to the purposes for which the systems are constructed and used. Such a pragmatism has most of the merits of the older pragmatisms as well as some further merits of its own. It rightly recognizes with the older pragmatisms a practical orientation of cognition. It is more thorough than the older pragmatisms in making itself responsible for the application of pragmatic tests to every aspect of cognition and deliberately renouncing reservations that appear in some other pragmatic systems. It consistently insists that all sentences be held open to revision. It is more philosophically and less situationally oriented than, for example, the instrumentalism of Dewey, in being concerned less with the pragmatic resolution of particular practical problems than with the clarification of conceptual schemes. Its methods are more rigorously analytic than those of any of the older pragmatisms. It recognizes more fully than any significant nonidealistic approach to problems of confirmation the manner in which the meaning of any particular sentence is intricately interwoven with whole systems of meanings. It is more closely related to the actual procedures of scientific confirmation than the older pragmatisms, and accurately reflects a strong tendency of scientists to test their conceptual schemes as wholes. Indeed, the claim of the pragmatic analysts that every sentence belongs to a system that is subject to pragmatic tests as a whole is in general scarcely contradictable and in some of its specific applications sound and illuminating.

Nevertheless, the doctrine of pragmatic systemic confirmation has not yet been spelled out in very great detail by pragmatic analysts, and when it is simply asserted without considerable qualifications it fails to exclude unfortunate interpretations and indeed tends sometimes to encourage them. For example, while the pragmatic analysts probably do not intend their doctrine so to be used, that doctrine can be used in support of extensive applications of emotional and volitional tests of scientific systems. In any case it fails to indicate in what sense basic choices in the confirmatory process are pragmatic. It carries the suggestion that not only sentences but everything whatever in the cognitive situation is revisable; and this suggestion seems, to say the least, doubtful with reference to immediate sensory experiences and some analytic insights as distinct from their expressions in sentences. Within the province of pragmatically testable sentences themselves, the doctrine tends, for example in its comparison of the sentences of science and those of mythology, to obscure certain basic differences. It is, to be sure, true that the testing of the sentences of science, like that of the sentences of mythology, is in an important sense ultimately pragmatic; but there is a world of difference, as Quine well knows but does not sufficiently indicate, between the logically and empirically responsible methods built into the one set of sentences and the relatively irresponsible methods involved in the other. The doctrine in question also tends to obscure rather radical differences in kind among various phases of even the most adequate types of inquiry, for example between logical analysis, empirical observation, and inductive inference, which however interdependent they may be, must simply not be run together. The idea of degrees of truth associated with the doctrine seems to suggest a confusion of truth and closeness of fit, for while no sentence may be known to be true, some statements may presumably nevertheless be completely true. Finally, the claim in question may in some respects be too rigid, and in that sense not quite pragmatic enough; for it envisages apparently only comparatively rigid formal systems, whereas for many purposes more illuminating statements may be relatively informal ones which, while still retaining systemic relations, are of a different order.

CHAPTER 16

Ordinary-Language Analysis

By THE early thirties there had already emerged in England, in opposition alike to traditional technical philosophies and to the formalized analysis of both phenomenalistic and physicalistic analysts, a type of philosophical analysis that focused upon ordinary modes of discourse. Although this type of analysis is sometimes directed toward the specialized language of mathematics and the physical sciences, its primary subject matter is ordinary language. The instrument in terms of which its analyses are conducted is also largely ordinary language, and so is the language in which its results are formulated. It often undertakes to press its quest beyond language toward an understanding of underlying concepts, but its attention is nearly always specifically directed toward expressions in common use.

Analysis of and in terms of ordinary language is of course not altogether new in Western philosophy. It was already in evidence in the Socratic dialogues, and it has repeatedly reasserted itself in various revolts—such as those led by Hobbes, Locke, and James—against the technical jargon of established philosophical schools. However, most revolts against technical philosophy have developed in protest against one brand of technical philosophy in the interest of another brand and so have involved technical terminologies of their own. Contemporary ordinary-language analysis is different from its predecessors in being a protest not against a particular brand of technical philosophy but against philosophical technicality itself. It is set forth not in the interest of a particular brand of philosophy but in the interest of excluding philosophical confusion and facilitating understanding through comparative study of forms of common speech.

The earlier phases of contemporary ordinary-language analysis were deeply influenced by the common-sense aspect of G. E. Moore's philosophy, especially by Moore's insistence that such terms as "man," "world," "self," "external world," "know," and "perceive" be taken in their ordinary senses. Indeed, some of Moore's earlier works are as notable for their methods of ordinary-language analysis as they are for their realist conclusions. However, more recent phases of ordinary-language analysis have been dominated by the thought of a writer whose conclusions display no such connection with traditional epistemological problems as do those involved in Moore's works, and whose devotion to ordinary language, though slow in arriving, was more thorough than that of Moore—namely, Ludwig Wittgenstein (1889–1951).

Accordingly, since the main features of Moore's work have been indicated in another connection, we shall, in examining ordinary-language analysis, begin with Wittgenstein. We shall subsequently consider some writers who, like Wittgenstein, were at first inclined toward logical atomism and subsequently turned to ordinary-language analysis, then some younger writers who began their productive philosophical careers in the practice of ordinary-language analysis, and finally some who, being primarily concerned with philosophy of science, have brought even to that discipline significant aspects of the ordinary-language approach. As a preliminary to sketching Wittgenstein's ordinary-language analysis, we shall indicate the character of the logical atomism that marked Wittgenstein's earlier work and helped significantly to shape the whole conemporary analytic movement.

1. Ludwig Wittgenstein

A. Wittgenstein's *Tractatus Logico-Philosophicus* has exercised an influence second to none over the entire literature of the philosophy of the past three decades. The fact that its author subsequently abandoned many of its characteristic claims did not prevent its serving as a foundation for other types of philosophical analysis, and the fact that he later became the leading exponent of ordinary-language analysis makes it an invaluable source of insight concerning both the roots of ordinary-language analysis and the points at which such analysis differs from other types of analysis that have been built upon its basic ideas.

"The world," according to the *Tractatus*, "is everything that is the case," [1] and whatever is the case is a fact. "An atomic fact is a combination of objects," [2] and "it is essential to a thing that it can be a constituent part of an atomic fact." [3] Atomic facts are bound together neither by logical necessity nor by causal necessity but are "independent of one another." [4] When objects are given, "*possible* atomic facts are also given." [5] Thus, "the totality of existent atomic facts is the world," and "the existence and nonexistence of atomic facts is the reality." [6]

The propositional signs of language are facts [7] through which we "make to ourselves pictures of facts." [8] "Colloquial language," however, tends to "disguise . . . thought and requires enormously complicated" procedures for its understanding, so that it is "impossible immediately to gather the logic of language." [9] Moreover, "most propositions . . . about philosophical matters are not false, but senseless," and most of them "result from the fact that we do not understand the logic of our language." [10] What is needed, accordingly, is a simplified language which depicts facts and reveals logical relations in the character of its symbols. The language of *Principia Mathematica* approximates such a language but remains defective at various points.[11]

The basic terms of the requisite language are names whose sole meaning is to be found in objects to which they refer.[12] The elementary propositions of the language depict atomic facts, and complex propositions depict complex facts. "The proposition is a picture of reality." [13] As the "gramophone record, the universal thought, the score, the waves of sound" all resemble one another in structure, so the proposition resembles the state of affairs which it depicts.[14] Elementary propositions are basically neither affirmative nor negative but involve the possibility of either.[15] All propositions are truth

[1] Ludwig Wittgenstein, *Tractatus Logico-Philosophicus* (New York & London: Harcourt, Brace & Co., & Kegan Paul, Trench, Trubner & Co., Ltd., 1922 & 1933). The numerals in reference to the *Tractatus* are those assigned by Wittgenstein to paragraphs of the book. The best available exposition of the teachings of the *Tractatus* is G. E. M. Anscombe's *An Introduction to Wittgenstein's Tractatus* (London: Hutchinson's University Library, 1959), which unfortunately appeared too late to be taken into account in the sketch that follows.
[2] *Ibid.*, 2.01.
[3] *Ibid.*, 2.011.

[4] *Ibid.*, 2.061.
[5] *Ibid.*, 2.0124.
[6] *Ibid.*, 2.04, 2.06.
[7] *Ibid.*, 3.14.
[8] *Ibid.*, 2.1.
[9] *Ibid.*, 4.002.
[10] *Ibid.*, 4.003.
[11] *Ibid.*, 3.325.
[12] *Ibid.*, 3.203.
[13] *Ibid.*, 4.021.
[14] *Ibid.*, 4.0141.
[15] Cf. *Ibid.*, 4.0621, 5.43–5.44; see also Wittgenstein, "Notes on Logic," September 1913, *Journal of Philosophy*, LIV (1957), 239 f.

functions of elementary propositions. That is to say their character is completely given in the patterns of truth and falsity involved in the elementary propositions composing them. Thus, for example, every elementary proposition is a truth function of itself, and that combination of two elementary propositions which is true only in case both elementary propositions are true is a truth function of the two and is commonly referred to as conjunction. Similarly that combination of elementary propositions which is false only in case the first is true and the second false is another truth function of the elementary propositions and is commonly called material implication.[16]

In view of this truth-functional character of all propositions, the propositions of logic, which are designed to show the necessary relations among propositions, are neither truths about the world nor products of a supersensible world. Rather, "the propositions of logic are tautologies." [17] They provide useful devices for helping to overcome human inability to survey large patterns of propositions, but they add nothing to what is already given in elementary propositions. Logic stands in no need either of principles of inference or of logical constants.[18] Its symbols are self-sufficient, and their significance is amply displayed in truth tables. Being wholly analytic, logic tells us nothing about the world. "Logic *precedes* every experience—that something is *so*," [19] but "all propositions of logic say the same thing. That is, nothing." [20] Since logical syntax makes no mention of its symbols, no theory of types is needed.[21] The structures of logic are not to be talked about; [22] they are to be shown in the character of symbols.[23]

Atomic facts are never knowable a priori, and accordingly they cannot "give elementary propositions *a priori*." [24] The truth of any proposition depends upon the agreement or disagreement of its sense with reality.[25] Since elementary propositions bring together names, they must picture atomic facts in order to be true, and complex propositions must combine pictures in such a way as to mirror complex facts. To apprehend the truth of an elementary proposition we compare its sense with the facts. To apprehend the truth of a more complex fact we follow through the truth-functional patterns involved. The coordinated patterns of a propositional picture are "the feelers of its elements with which the picture touches reality." [26] The

---

16 Cf. *Tractatus*, 5.513.
17 *Ibid.*, 6.17.
18 Cf. *ibid.*, 5.4.
19 *Ibid.*, 5.552.
20 *Ibid.*, 5.43.
21 *Ibid.*, 3.33, 3.331.

22 *Ibid.*, 4.0312.
23 *Ibid.*, 3.3421.
24 *Ibid.*, 5.5571.
25 *Ibid.*, 2.222.
26 *Ibid.*, 2.1515.

truth of elementary propositions can be ascertained with a high degree of reliability through observation of atomic facts. We need make no mistakes in logic as such, for "it is the characteristic mark of logical propositions that one can perceive in the symbol alone that they are true." [27] Probability sentences have no special objects; they result from combinations of elementary propositions grounded in acquaintance and other propositions not so grounded.[28] Scientific theories are neither elemental propositions nor combinations of them. They represent rather a kind of linguistic net in which we endeavor always with only incomplete success to catch reality.

Philosophical inquiry has no special object, and accordingly when philosophy has performed its clarifying mission it must step aside in favor of empirical observation. "The right method of philosophy would be this. To say nothing except what can be said, *i.e.* the propositions of natural science, *i.e.* something that has nothing to do with philosophy: and then always, when someone wished to say something metaphysical, to demonstrate to him that he had given no meaning to certain signs in his propositions." [29] By this principle most of the statements Wittgenstein himself has made will of course be ruled out. "He who understands me finally recognizes them as senseless, when he has climbed out through them, on them, over them." (He must so to speak throw away the ladder, after he has climbed up on it.)

"He must surmount these propositions; then he sees the world rightly.

Whereof one cannot speak, thereof one must be silent." [30]

"What can be said at all can be said clearly; and whereof one cannot speak, therefor one must be silent." [31]

B. In the later phases of Wittgenstein's thought,[32] as represented in his *Remarks on the Foundation of Mathematics* and his *Philosophical Investigations,* certain characteristic attitudes remain much the same as in the *Tractatus.* For example, in both the *Tractatus* and the later writings, Wittgenstein depreciates universals, mental

[27] *Ibid.,* 6.113.
[28] *Ibid.,* 5.1511 ff.
[29] *Ibid.,* 6.54.
[30] *Ibid.,* 6.54–7.
[31] *Ibid.,* Preface, p. 7.
[32] Among the various available expositions and comments upon Wittgenstein's later work the following are worthy of special note: G. E. Moore, "Wittgenstein's Lectures in 1930–33," *Mind,* LXIII (1954), 289–316, and LXIV (1955), 1–37; Norman Malcolm, "Wittgenstein's *Philosophical Investigations,*" *Philosophical Review,*

LXIII (1954), 530–59; P. F. Strawson, review of Wittgenstein's *Philosophical Investigations,*" *Mind,* LXIII (1954), 70–99; J. N. Findlay, review of Wittgenstein's "Philosophical Investigations," *Philosophy,* XXX (1955), 173–79; P. L. Heath, "Wittgenstein Investigated," *Philosophical Quarterly,* VI (1956), 66–71; David Pole, *The Later Philosophy of Wittgenstein* (London: University of London Press, Ltd., 1958); and Norman Malcolm, *Ludwig Wittgenstein, A Memoir* (London: Oxford University Press, 1958).

entities types, logical constants, infinites, body-mind dichotomies, and all such logical and metaphysical paraphernalia; he prefers objects, concrete facts, actually encountered logical structures, and behavioral patterns. However, in his later writings, Wittgenstein's views of the function of ordinary language, the task of philosophy, and the nature of meaning are very different from the views of the *Tractatus* concerning these subjects, and the later views have been especially influential in shaping current ordinary-language analysis.

Both in the *Tractatus* and in the later writings Wittgenstein fully recognized the great complexity of ordinary language. His attitudes toward this complexity were, however, very different in the two sets of writings. In the *Tractatus* Wittgenstein found in the complexity of ordinary language a challenge to display the structure of language in a perfect language in which all complex statements were reduced through tautologies to elementary statements picturing atomic facts. In the later writings he came to regard the attempt to achieve such a perfect language as useless and misleading, and preferred to unravel the complexities of ordinary language by direct piecemeal attack upon specific problems in the terms of that ordinary language in which in the end all explanations must be expressed. Thus, "when I want to talk about language . . . I must speak the language of every day. Is this language somehow too coarse and material for what we want to say? *Then how is another one to be constructed?* . . . Philosophy may in no way interfere with actual use of language; it can in the end only describe it." [33] The kind of inquiry that seeks to analyze statements into simple ones may serve a useful purpose; but this fact must not be allowed to seduce us into thinking that an "analyzed form" is a "more fundamental form" than an unanalyzed one,[34] for we could not imagine people who had names for . . . combinations of colour but not for the individual colours?" [35] Actually atomic facts are not in any case isolable, and elementary sentences referring to them cannot really be distinguished.[36] "It makes no sense at all to speak absolutely of the simple parts of a chair," and whether or not anything is composite depends upon the "particular language game" one is involved in.[37] Pure tautologies hardly have any actual linguistic use, and while the statements of mathematics are different from ordinary factual statements they differ among themselves and are embedded in a setting of richly varied linguistic forms. Indeed of language generally, one must say that

---

[33] Ludwig Wittgenstein, *Philosophical Investigations* (New York: The Macmillan Co., 1953), pp. 48 f.
[34] *Ibid.*, p. 30.

[35] *Ibid.*, p. 31.
[36] "Wittgenstein's Lectures in 1930–33," pp. 1 f.
[37] *Philosophical Investigations*, pp. 21 f.

instead of being designed for the single purpose of picturing reality or stating "how things are," it is intended to be instrumental to the varied purposes of the human organism. It is more like a chest of tools than a photographic film. Among the many language games involved in it are "giving orders and obeying them, describing the appearance of an object, or giving its measurements, constructing an object from a description . . . , reporting on events, speculating about an event, forming and testing a hypothesis, presenting the results of an experiment in tables and diagrams, making up a story and reading it, play acting, solving a problem in practical arithmetic, translating from one language to another, asking, thanking, cursing, greeting, praying." [38] It would be impossible to name one single characteristic of all language games. Such games crisscross in all manner of ways. They form a family rather than an individual, and are related by overlapping rather than by homogeneity.[39] The investigation of language is therefore not a uniform logical procedure but a varied reflective inquiry into actual linguistic experiences adapted in each instance to the kind of language game under consideration.

The drastic change in Wittgenstein's later attitude toward the function of ordinary language led to a change in his view of the nature and function of philosophy. Traditional philosophical problems, Wittgenstein came to believe, are not, as he had formerly thought, direct results of the complexity of ordinary language; they are rather products of special ways of regarding language. One does not get involved in them so long as he uses language in the usual ways. Thus, for example, in ordinary discourse we have no difficulty in connecting names and things; but when "the philosopher tries to bring out *the* relation between name and thing by staring at an object in front of him and repeating a name . . . innumerable times," [40] naming begins to look like a queer business. Thus "philosophical problems arise when language *goes on holiday*." Such problems occur "when language is like an engine idling, not when it is doing work." [41] Accordingly, a sound contemporary philosophy will deal with problems of traditional philosophy neither "by showing that a particular question is not permitted nor by answering it," but by showing how traditional puzzles can be properly avoided. A sound philosophy will clear away traditional puzzles. Thus philosophy becomes "a battle against betwitchment of our intelligence by means of language." [42] Its task is "to bring words back from their metaphysical to their everyday use," [43] "to shew the fly the way out

[38] *Ibid.*, p. 12.
[39] *Ibid.*, pp. 31 ff.
[40] *Ibid.*, p. 19.

[41] *Ibid.*, p. 51.
[42] *Ibid.*, p. 47.
[43] *Ibid.*, p. 48.

of the fly-bottle."[44] As a physician engaged in "the treatment of our illness," the philosopher must first "cure himself of many sicknesses of the understanding before he can arrive at the notions of sound human understanding."[45] His effort will be by varied "therapies"[46] so to disclose the circumstances of our confusions that "since everything lies open to view there is nothing to explain."[47] He approaches his task not in the ambitious manner of the building of a house but rather in the more modest manner of "the tidying up of a room."[48]

Whereas in the *Tractatus* Wittgenstein identified the meaning of a basic term with the object named by it, he subsequently specifically repudiated this view and came to distinguish sharply between the bearer and the meaning of a name. Thus, for example, "when Mr. N. N. dies one says that the bearer of the name dies, not that the meaning dies."[49] No term means save in a general context of more or less established linguistic habit and particular circumstance of utterance. Significant expressions do not emerge suddenly or in solitude; they depend on training in specific social settings and on the establishment of customs. Neither naming nor meaning has to be fully precise, and a certain amount of vagueness is often advantageous.[50] The meaning of a term is neither a queer kind of subsisting entity nor an image nor a feeling in consciousness. Pictures are often involved in meaning, but pictures, feelings, and other "inner states"[51] may vary independently of meanings. One can of course calculate in his head, but usually he learns to do so on paper first.[52]

The rules of language obviously have a very important bearing upon the meanings of terms but even such rules do not constitute or necessarily disclose the meaning of a term.[53] One may quite well know the rules and even observe someone pointing at an instance of what is meant without grasping what is meant.

The fact is that the meaning of a term is for the most part given in the use of the term, or perhaps better, it is the use of a term rather than its meaning that is important. If, for example, someone says "I am here," what we should ask is "how, on what occasions, this sentence is used."[54] Such a question would suffice to prune away the queer aspects of statements and bring linguistic inquiry into its normal setting. In endeavoring to understand any sentence one

[44] *Ibid.,* p. 103.
[45] G. E. M. Anscombe (trans.), Ludwig Wittgenstein's *Remarks on the Foundations of Mathematics* (Oxford: Basil Blackwell, 1956).
[46] *Ibid.,* p. 51.
[47] *Philosophical Investigations,* p. 50.

[48] "Wittgenstein's Lectures in 1930–33," p. 27.
[49] *Ibid.,* p. 20.
[50] *Ibid.,* pp. 33 ff.
[51] *Ibid.,* p. 181.
[52] *Ibid.,* p. 220.
[53] *Ibid.,* p. 17.
[54] *Ibid.,* p. 141.

should ask "in what special circumstance this sentence is actually used." [55] Indeed, for a very large class of cases, a sufficient definition of meaning is given by saying that "the meaning of a word is its use in the language." [56] A term becomes meaningful for us when we learn its use in the language, and when we forget the use of a term, that term "loses its meaning for us." [57]

Like most other significant expressions, expressions relating to knowing cannot be reduced to any simple pattern but have a wide variety of uses. A few of Wittgenstein's remarks concerning some of the more important uses of some of these terms, including those associated with understanding words, sensing, seeing, and predicting, are now to be noted.

Since meaning is largely use, the criterion of that knowing, or preliminary to knowing, that consists in understanding verbal expressions is the ability to apply the expression. Thus, for example, one's grasp of a mathematical series is his capacity to "go on" with the series.[58] Understanding of a word is of course compatible with some doubts concerning the application of the word, and no rules of usage can guarantee understanding. Rules are helpful signs. One must first learn "to follow a rule" before he can apprehend "what it means to follow a rule." [59]

The knowing involved in logic is, as was observed in the *Tractatus*, rooted in linguistic usage. Such is the importance of this method of knowing that one is inclined to think of logic as something sublime and of its subject matter as "something that lies beneath the surface," [60] as "a pure intermediary between propositional signs and facts." [61] The real importance of logic, however, implies no such sublimity in the subject matter of logic. "We must stick to the subject of our every-day thinking." [62] The concepts with which logic is concerned have a use that is "as humble a one as that of the words 'table,' 'lamp,' 'door.' " [63] However, no good purpose is served by trying, as was done in *Principia Mathematica* and in the *Tractatus*, to formalize logic, for one must in any case learn to use the forms.[64] Logical patterns are indeed rooted in language but they are not by any means as rigid or simple as was assumed in the *Tractatus*.

Mathematics, instead of simply belonging, as in the *Tractatus*, along with logic in the broad class of tautologies, is to be distin-

[55] *Ibid.,* p. 48.
[56] *Ibid.,* p. 20.
[57] *Ibid.,* p. 28.
[58] *Ibid.,* pp. 73 f.
[59] *Remarks on the Foundations of Mathematics,* p. 184.

[60] *Ibid.,* p. 43.
[61] *Ibid.,* p. 44.
[62] *Ibid.,* p. 46.
[63] *Ibid.,* p. 44.
[64] *Remarks on the Foundations of Mathematics,* p. 9.

guished from logic. It is, like logic, rooted in language, but it is not identifiable with logic or derivable from logic. Logical proofs are only general whereas mathematical ones are specific.[65] To be sure, mathematical proofs are not factual ones, but neither are they logical ones. They have their own peculiar character which is by no means easy to delineate. Whether proofs can be said to exist at all respecting those parts of series beyond which operations have been or readily can be carried is to be doubted,[66] and it is hardly sensible to say that even God knows the answer in such cases. Calculation does not have to be invariable, but when it becomes quite irregular one is no longer said to calculate. Mathematics, like logic, says nothing material about the world. If you know the results of a calculation "that is not to say you know anything," for the "mathematical proposition is only supposed to supply a framework for a description." [67] Other mathematical and conceptual systems quite different from the accepted ones would have been possible under other conditions.[68] The correctness of a mathematical proposition is implicit in the symbols, but the justification of the system of symbols lies elsewhere than in the symbols.[69]

Although one's sensations may play a significant role in his knowing, sensations are not themselves instances of knowing. The reason is not that there are no sensations but simply that in terms of our language we can scarcely intelligibly speak of knowing our own sensations. "It cannot be said of me that I *know* I am in pain"; and "*I* cannot be said to learn" of my sensations. "I *have* them." [70] No light is thrown upon "the philosophical problem of sensation" by an attempt "to study the headache I now have."[71]

We learn the use of terms for pains and other sensations through the outward manifestations of these experiences, and indeed if there were no such manifestations, pains and other sensations could not be spoken of at all.[72] Even if a person privately invented something like a name for his private pains, the application of the alleged name would "have no criterion of correctness." [73] Through the external signs of pain other people can often know that I am in pain, and I can know that they are.

What is commonly called seeing involves two quite distinct uses of the term "see," as for example, in the contrasting statements "I

---

[65] *Ibid.*, pp. 145 ff.
[66] *Ibid.*, pp. 67 f., 72 f.
[67] *Ibid.*, p. 160.
[68] Cf. *ibid.*, p. 38.
[69] *Ibid.*, p. 82.
[70] *Philosophical Investigations*, p. 89.

[71] *Ibid.*, p. 104.
[72] *Ibid.*, p. 92.
[73] *Ibid.*, p. 92; see also Leonard Linsky, "Wittgenstein on Language and Some Problems of Philosophy," *Journal of Philosophy*, LIV (1957), 285–93.

see *this*" (accompanied by a drawing) and "I see a likeness between these two faces." [74] The second of these uses refers to what may be called a "seeing as." Thus, for example, a certain kind of drawing may be seen as either "a glass cube, . . . an inverted open box, . . . a wire frame . . . or three boards forming a solid angle"; [75] another as either a rabbit or a duck; a third as either a wedge, a geometrical figure, or a triangular hole; a fourth as either an inverted staircase or a noninverted one; and a fifth as a white cross, a black cross, or a double cross. Since in all these instances of *seeing as,* the drawing remains unchanged while the way of seeing changes, one is tempted to think of the seeing as interpretation. But *seeing as* differs from interpretation in that, unlike interpretation, it involves no possibility of either error or verification. [76]

Matters of prospective fact, such as that "this book will drop to the ground when let go, . . ." [77] and that "I shall get burnt if I put my hand in the fire," [78] may be known with "certainty"; and such certainty is sufficiently justified by its success. [79] One does not indeed need to reason that similar experiences have often occurred in the past, and one does not "infer that a chair is there from sense-data." [80] But if a ground is requested for believing that something will happen in the future, a statement that a certain event has occurred in the past "is simply what we call a ground for assuming that this will happen in the future." [81] One must not say merely that such a ground "makes the occurrence of an event probable," for "to say that this ground makes the occurrence probable is to say nothing except that this ground comes up to a particular standard of good grounds—but the standard has no grounds." [82]

2. Early Converts to Ordinary-Language Analysis

The writers now to be considered are writers who, like Wittgenstein, adhered in the initial phases of their philosophical work to other approaches to philosophy (in most instances to some sort of logical atomism) and only against the background of these other orientations came to adopt the ordinary-language approach. The most eminent writers of this group are John Wisdom of Cambridge and Gilbert Ryle of Oxford. These two writers will be treated as representative of the group, and the work of some other related writers will be briefly touched upon as space permits.

[74] *Philosophical Investigations,* p. 193.
[75] *Ibid.*
[76] *Ibid.,* p. 212.
[77] *Ibid.,* p. 106.
[78] *Ibid.,* p. 135.
[79] *Ibid.,* p. 106.
[80] *Ibid.,* p. 136.
[81] *Ibid.,* p. 135.
[82] *Ibid.,* p. 136.

A. The development of the philosophical thought of John Wisdom (b. 1904) closely parallels that of Wittgenstein to whom Wisdom acknowledges very substantial indebtedness. Both writers were strongly inclined in their earlier years toward logical atomism and pictorial interpretations of language, and both subsequently rejected these earlier positions in favor of ordinary-language analysis. However, Wisdom's thought is all the while less rigidly tied to linguistic analysis than is that of Wittgenstein, and Wisdom's manner of presentation of his thought is more systematic and less linguistic than that of Wittgenstein.

In the stage of his thought represented by Wisdom's earliest essays, the world is taken to consist of facts reducible to simple facts and ultimately to elemental ones, and facts are disclosed by analysis of the sentences that picture them. Material analysis is regarded as a scientific defining of terms upon a single level of abstraction, as when a psychologist who says " 'I am in awe of you' means 'I fear and admire you.' " ¹ Formal analysis is the logical clarification of the structure of a statement upon a single level of abstraction, as when a logician explains that "every dog is dangerous" can be translated into "something is a dog and dangerous and it is not the case that something is a dog and not dangerous." ² Philosophical analysis takes one from an initial level of abstraction toward a deeper level locating facts more directly, as when a philosopher analyzes the statement *"every nation invaded France"* as *"every group of individuals with common ancestors, traditions and governors forcibly entered the land owned by Frenchmen."* ³ Such analysis proceeds from more to less abstract sentences, and elements referred to in the analysans are more individual and less abstract than those in the analysandum. Eventually analysis arrives at ultimate "elements," and the basic facts which less basic sentences display are "displayed" in basic sentences.⁴ The basic facts are referred to both by the sentences with which philosophical analysis begins and/or those in which such analysis eventuates, though the latter display terms more directly than the former, and what the two say of the facts is not the same.

In the later stages of Wisdom's thought linguistic inquiry is still the method of the philosophical quest, and understanding of reality is the goal of the quest. However, reality no longer consists of a fixed hierarchy of facts eventuating in elementary facts, and linguistic inquiry is no longer precise logical analysis leading to basic sentences. The philosophical quest is now a free use of ordinary language to dis-

¹ John Wisdom, *Philosophy and Psycho-Analysis* (Oxford: Basil Blackwell, 1933–1953), p. 17.

² *Ibid.*, p. 18.
³ *Ibid.*, p. 30.
⁴ Cf. *ibid.*, p. 32.

solve puzzles created by the traditional use of philosophical language. "Philosophy is not only less like discovery of natural fact than people once supposed, it is also less like the discovery of logical fact than they next supposed, and more like literature." [5]

That philosophical statements of the traditional kind are often puzzling is not, however, to be taken to mean that such statements are misbegotten or useless. Such statements are the meeting place of analysis and hypothesis.[6] They are indeed mainly verbal but they reveal a great deal that is not merely verbal. Taken literally, such philosophical statements as that "nothing is really good or bad" and that "mind is an illusion" [7] are false, but they reveal profound truths hinted at even in ordinary language.[8] Taken in their purely logical sense, philosophical sentences are rather boring tautologies, but to dismiss them as pure tautologies is to lose the insight achievable through the strain of their paradoxes.[9] They are a little like the statements of the neurotic, which are acted upon but not quite believed, and like those of the psychotic, which are neither acted upon nor quite believed.[10] The kind of analysis required to unravel them is not formal logical analysis but stories that in plain language disclose those factors that incline us to say "yes to these," and those that incline us to say "no." [11] They bring no news but they illuminate known facts. "They reveal what lies not behind or beyond but in the obvious." [12] They are like the words of a man who, in the presence of a lady trying on a new hat, says "Taj Mahal," and in so doing enables the lady to see what she saw before in a new light.[13] Sometimes, as in the case of some of the words of Nietzsche or Jesus, they drastically and permanently alter the sense of words and recast language in new molds.[14]

Among the most puzzling of all philosophical statements are statements to the effect that we really don't know the past, the future, material objects, or others' minds. Yet no satisfactory answer seems to be forthcoming to philosophical objections to such knowledge. No adequate defense of such knowledge can be grounded upon analogy; for whereas a present experience of lights across the street may indicate a party there by analogy with previous *experiences* of parties there when the lights were on, we can have had no experience of past or future *events* or *material objects* which may by analogy be connected with our present experience. The reductionist contends that since " to know that in every way a thing seems so is to know that it is so, . . . to say 'it is so' is to say no more than 'It seems

<hr />

5 *Ibid.*, p. 242.
6 *Ibid.*, pp. 125 ff.
7 *Ibid.*, p. 227.
8 *Ibid.*, p. 50.
9 *Ibid.*, pp. 116 ff., 228.

10 *Ibid.*, p. 174.
11 Cf. *ibid.*, p. 178.
12 *Ibid.*, p. 228.
13 *Ibid.*, p. 248.
14 *Ibid.*, p. 225.

so.' " [15] But the skeptic may properly point out that seeming so in every way and being so do not mean the same and that the relation between the former and the latter is not deductive. The skeptic goes on to argue that since "no one . . . has reason to say that a thing is so beyond the reason he has for saying that then and there to him it seems so. Therefore no one . . . has for what he says as to what is so the reason another could have. . . . Therefore no one . . . has for what he says as to what is so all the reason one could have. Therefore no one . . . really knows that a thing is so." [16] But, in this argument the skeptic tends to contradict himself; for insofar as knowledge of other minds is impossible, their reason for what one says does not represent a reason that one could have.

The truth about the paradox of knowledge appears to be similar to that concerning other philosophical puzzles and to be somewhat as follows. In the ordinary sense of the term "know" we certainly do know the past, the future, things, and other minds; and to say we do not is either false or a gross distortion of language. Nevertheless, there is a logical sense of "know" in which we do not and cannot know anything but the immediately present—if indeed we may properly be said to know even that. We never can directly apprehend what is already past or not yet, and we cannot directly apprehend *things* apart from their manifestations or know other minds as they know themselves. That such knowledge is impossible is a fact of logic. Yet one must be wary of too easy solutions of epistemological problems. The logical approach reveals something hidden in the ordinary approach, and ordinary usage affords some grounds for the logical approach. One only begins to gain insight into reality when one unravels the whole story of the considerations that make him wish to agree with the skeptic and those that make him wish to agree with the nonskeptic.

In addition to the difficulties which the quest for knowledge of other minds shares with the quest for knowledge of past and future events and material objects, it involves the special difficulty that whereas no one directly apprehends the past or future or a material object, someone knows the mind of another better than I do. Hence the skeptic can press his argument with telling effect, to say that I cannot have all the evidence that could be had regarding another mind. Even proof of telepathy could not remove this barrier, for sensations received through telepathy would still be my sensations. Thus, while in the ordinary sense of the term we certainly do know other minds and would be absurd in denying this fact, and while telepathy might give us a knowledge of other minds "comparable to

[15] John Wisdom, *Other Minds* (Oxford: [16] *Ibid.*, p. 238.
Basil Blackwell, 1952), p. 240.

our own knowledge in memory," there is a sense of the term "know" in which necessarily knowledge of other minds is precluded.[17] This consideration may represent in the end a real "isolation which we may defeat but cannot vanquish, . . . a conflict in the human heart which dreads yet demands the otherness of others." [18]

B. Although Gilbert Ryle (b. 1900) of Oxford did not, like Wittgenstein and Wisdom, produce influential early works in a philosophical vein quite different from that of his subsequent works, his philosophical thought does seem to have passed through a series of stages before arriving at the point of view which he has rather consistently maintained throughout most of his philosophical writings. The earliest period was apparently an Aristotelian one shaped by his initial training at Oxford.[19] The second was a more or less phenomenological period reflected in an essay entitled "Phenomenology," [20] in which, though written at a time when phenomenology no longer particularly appealed to him, Ryle regarded phenomenologists as right in taking philosophical propositions to be a priori and in taking phenomenology to be a part of philosophy. It is perhaps to some of his earlier Aristotelian and phenomenological views that Ryle refers when he subsequently writes, in *The Concept of Mind*, that "the assumptions against which I exhibit most heat are assumptions of which I have been a victim." [21] A third stage seems to have involved the adoption of a picture theory of language akin to that of Wittgenstein's *Tractatus*. This stage is represented in an early article, "Negation," where Ryle regards statements as conforming to facts, including "negative facts"; [22] in a subsequent article, "Are There Propositions?" where Ryle contends that "there is a relation between the grammatical structure of a statement and the logical structure of the fact that it states"; [23] and even in "Systematically Misleading Expressions," where while Ryle is inclined to reject the picture theory as such, he holds the function of illuminating statements to be to exhibit "the real form of the fact . . . in a new form of words." [24]

Ryle's present philosophy remains Aristotelian in its emphasis upon individuals and in some phases of its logic. It shows marks of the

[17] *Ibid.*, p. 208.

[18] *Ibid.*, p. 217; cf. John Wisdom, "The Concept of Mind," *Proceedings of the Aristotelian Society*, L (1949–50), 189–204.

[19] Cf. John Passmore, *A Hundred Years of Philosophy* (London: Gerald Duckworth & Co., Ltd., 1957), p. 440.

[20] Gilbert Ryle, "Phenomenology," *Proceedings of the Aristotelian Society, Supplementary Vol. XI* (1932), 68–83.

[21] Ryle, *The Concept of Mind* (New York: Barnes & Noble, Inc., 1949), p. 97.

[22] Ryle, "Negation," *Proceedings of the Aristotelian Society, Supplementary Vol. IX*, 80.

[23] Ryle, "Are There Propositions?" *Proceedings of the Aristotelian Society*, XXX (1927–30), 125.

[24] J. O. Urmson, *Philosophical Analysis* (Oxford: Clarendon Press, 1956), pp. 141 ff.; Ryle, "Systematically Misleading Expressions," in Antony Flew, *Logic and Language* (Oxford: Basil Blackwell, 1952), 1st series, p. 36.

influence of phenomenology as well as of Frege in its insistence upon the a priori character of philosophical statements, in its retention of the notion of conceptual analysis as opposed to purely linguistic analysis, and indirectly in its insistence on analysis of use rather than of usage only. It also retains closer affinities with the philosophy of Wittgenstein's *Tractatus*, especially the doctrine of showing, than do some other ordinary-language philosophies. Nevertheless its major affinities are with ordinary-language philosophy.

While philosophers have always been engaged in philosophical inquiry, along with other types of inquiry, it was only, Ryle thinks, with Russell's "distinction between the true-or-false, on the one side, and the meaningless or nonsensical, on the other," that the modern understanding of the distinctive character of philosophical inquiry began to come clearly to light.[25] Scientific inquiry is concerned with the distinction between truth and falsehood; philosophy, with that between sense and nonsense. The attempt in the light of this distinction to equate the meaning of a statement with its mode of verification did not succeed—to equate "the meaning of a law-statement" with "the method of its application" would have been more enlightening— but the use of the distinction in the verifiability theory did help to bring to light the rich variety of types of statements.[26] In terms of the distinction in question the philosopher can, however, map out a geography of concepts. His method is principally that of a *reductio ad absurdum* that deduces "from a proposition . . . consequences which are inconsistent with each other or with the original proposition." [27] The operation of this method can be seen admirably at work already in Plato's *Parmenides* where, without benefit of notions of types or categories, Plato is using *reductio* arguments in just such ways as tend to lead to theories of types and categories.[28] Although the methods of the philosopher are largely negative they yield positive results by marking out the boundaries of purified concepts, "charting the logical powers of ideas, . . . determining with method and definitive check the rules governing the correct manipulation of concepts." [29] In this production of positive results by negative means, they are like threshing operations or the testing of metals by strains.[30] The work of the philosopher is not, however, that of the logician—though some

---

[25] Ryle, "The Verification Principle," *Revue Internationale de Philosophie*, V (1951), 245; and "Thinking Language," *Proceedings of the Aristotelian Society*, Supplementary Vol. XXV (1951), 81.
[26] "The Verification Principle," pp. 748 f.
[27] Ryle, *Philosophical Arguments*, p. 6; see also *The Concept of Mind*, p. 8.

[28] Ryle, "Plato's Parmenides," *Mind*, XLVIII (1939), 304 f.
[29] *Philosophical Arguments*, p. 10; cf. Ryle, "Categories," *Proceedings of the Aristotelian Society*, XXXVIII (1937–38), 189–90.
[30] *Philosophical Arguments*, pp. 6 ff., 19 f.

philosophers are also logicians—for unlike the demonstrations of logicians the philosopher's argument can never become proofs and are not designed to be proofs.[31] Unlike proofs they have no premises. Insofar as the work of the philosopher is positive, it is somewhat like the efforts of the surgeon to describe his procedures to a student and then to check his descriptions of them against a slower rehearsal of his procedures.[32] The work of the philosopher cannot be done piecemeal, for "it is the foreign relations, not the domestic constitution, of sayables that engender logical troubles." [33] The aspect of language that gives the philosopher his leads for the analysis of concepts is not mere usage, the investigation of which is largely a philological problem, but use, what language is used for, and that aspect of language requires *logical* investigation. That philosophers are mainly concerned with more or less standard uses of terms does not mean that they are not concerned with technical terms.[34] The language in which philosophers formulate their own conclusions is, however, mainly ordinary language, for "to replace the infant's fingers and feet by pliers and pedals would not be a good plan." [35]

The focus of the philosopher's inquiry is not upon words, for words vary from one language to another. Nor is it upon sentences, for to say that a sentence has a use is at least doubtful. The focus is rather upon terms, a term being an element common to a variety of propositions. To mean is not the same as to imply, and what a statement "signifies is not to be equated with any or all of the consequences which can be inferred from the statement. . . . Deducing is not translating." [36] Still less is the meaning of a term to be equated with anything allegedly named by the term. Indeed, because of the temptation to adopt such a view and the consequent puzzles concerning universals which it engenders, one would generally do better to speak not of the meaning of an expression but of "the rules of employment of that expression." [37] The mistake of equating meaning with naming has almost invariably been made by philosophers in the past. Even Frege did not quite shake himself from it, and Carnap's insistence in *Meaning and Necessity* that every term has an extension as well as an intension is a notorious case of it.[38] While there are, of course, proper names that mention individuals, most terms are not used mention-

[31] Ryle, "Proofs in Philosophy," *Revue Internationale de Philosophie*, VI (1954), 150 f.

[32] *Ibid.*, p. 156.

[33] Ryle, "The Theory of Meaning," in C. A. Mace, *British Philosophy in Mid-Century* (London: George Allen & Unwin, 1957), p. 264; cf. also Ryle, *Dilemmas*

(Cambridge: Cambridge University Press, 1954), pp. 128 ff.

[34] Ryle, "Ordinary Language," *Philosophical Review*, LXII (1953), 167–86.

[35] *Dilemmas*, p. 35.

[36] "The Theory of Meaning," p. 250.

[37] *Ibid.*, p. 254.

[38] Ryle, "Meaning and Necessity," *Philosophy*, XXIV (1949), 69–76.

ingly at all. They name nothing and are not such that anything, even characteristics allegedly mentioned by them, can be predicated of them.[39] Thus "circular" and "large" name nothing and cannot be said to have characteristics. If we did wish to name anything in such connections we would speak of "circularity" and "largeness," not "large" and "circular"; but even that way of speaking is at best misleading. Most terms are predicative and not at all substantive. Some terms, such as "unity," "plurality," "all," "some," "not," and the like, represent a special class of formal concepts that cannot be properly characterized as elements of language and thought at all, but are only shown in the structure of our statements.[40]

The term "know" does not refer to any sort of occult mental or conscious happening in the private theater of one's mind, for "there are no such happenings"; [41] and the whole idea of a private theater belongs to an untenable Cartesian "Ghost in the Machine" dualism.[42] Knowing is of two kinds, "knowing how" and "knowing that." [43] Of these two the former is the more basic. One does not have to plan his actions first and then act. Apart from knowing how, the effort either to attain or to apply knowledge would involve infinite regress.[44] Even understanding the acts of another person is a mode of knowing how.[45] Knowledge is basically dispositional in consisting not in internal images of present events but in capacities to do certain things. One's knowledge or ignorance is almost invariably determined by what he would do in a variety of circumstances.[46] The term "know" differs from the term "believe" in referring to a capacity rather than a mere tendency.[47] Unlike such terms as "seek," it is an achievement word rather than a process word. That is to say it refers to the completion of a process rather than to a process itself, and this is the reason that one cannot know erroneously.[48] Unlike the term "belief," which belongs to the family of "motive words," "knowledge" is of the family of skill words; and skill words have methods rather than sources only.[49]

The term "sensation," as it is ordinarily used, refers sometimes to such uncomfortable feelings as pains, itches, nausea, suffocation, thirst, and the like,[50] and sometimes to feeling things with hands, lips, tongue, or knees.[51] The awkwardness of using the term "sensation,"

[39] "Plato's Parmenides," pp. 138 ff.
[40] Ibid., pp. 312 ff.
[41] The Concept of Mind, p. 161.
[42] Ibid., pp. 15 f.
[43] Ibid., pp. 27 ff.
[44] The Concept of Mind, pp. 30 f.
[45] Ibid., pp. 52 ff.
[46] Ibid., p. 44.
[47] Ibid., p. 123.

[48] Ibid., p. 152.
[49] Ibid., p. 134.
[50] Ibid., p. 243; Ryle, "Sensation," in H. D. Lewis (ed.), Contemporary British Philosophy (New York: The Macmillan Co., 1956), p. 429.
[51] The Concept of Mind, p. 241; see also "Sensation," p. 431.

as philosophers often do to refer to less tangible elements in perceptions, is seen in the fact that philosophers seem unable even to describe sensations save by referring to something physical. Thus, for example, even a glimpse is a glimpse of something and a pain is described as "a stabbing a grinding or a burning pain." [52]

However, the view that sensation is an ingredient in sense perception has become the "official view" in many philosophical circles, and while this view is artificial and misleading, one may say in terms of it without distorting language too seriously that to perceive something entails having at least one sensation,[53] and that "sensing" is an achievement word as "observing" (in one of its senses) is not. These considerations afford no justification for the prevalent idea that sensation is distinctively mental and occurs within a private theater. The reason that other people cannot observe my sensations is not that my sensations occur inside me but that sensations cannot be observed at all; [54] and the reason that sensations cannot be observed is deeper than a mere lack of instruments with which to observe them, for "we cannot think what it would be like to apply instruments to our sensations." [55] The sense-datum theory, which postulates private objects of sensation, "rests upon a logical howler, the howler, namely, of assimilating the concept of sensations to the concept of observation." [56] Since observing entails sensations, if sensations themselves were observed, then observing them would involve having other sensations and so on in infinite regress.[57] Moreover, instances of sense-data turn out upon inspection to be only special kinds of perceiving. Thus, for example, when a person "looks at a round plate tilted away from him," he is not "seeing an elliptical look of a round plate" but a plate which "looks as an elliptical but untilted plate would look." [58]

Perceiving involves, as the "sensation" of the official view does not, recognition and expectation. It needs no addition of intellectual action to constitute its knowledge, for it already involves intelligence. One may not however, properly ask what must be *added* to sensation in order to yield perception. Perception is simply sensing in the perspective of a perceptive recipe, and in perceiving one is not doing two things but only one. Verbs referring to perceptions "such as 'see,' 'hear,' 'detect,' 'discriminate' and many others" are, like sensation words, success or achievement words.[59] The supposition that sensing is like a prison wall around us from which we must in perception escape by some inferential act or causal process is altogether without

[52] *The Concept of Mind*, p. 203.
[53] Cf. *ibid.*, p. 200.
[54] *Ibid.*, p. 309.
[55] *Ibid.*, p. 206.
[56] *Ibid.*, p. 213.
[57] *Ibid.*
[58] *Ibid.*, pp. 216 ff.
[59] *Ibid.*, p. 222.

justification.[60] The question how we pass from sensations to external objects is a spurious question,[61] but if it be asked how we learn about physical objects (i.e. learn perception recipes), the answer is simply that we learn by practice. We learn as we learn what comes next in a tune and as we learn what color a given object is likely to appear to an observer under standard light. Errors occur when we misapply perception recipes, but unless we had learned perception recipes and were capable of veridical perception there could be no perceptual errors.[62]

Thinking, which is already present in perception, is no more an inner process than is sensation or perception. One may do his "calculating aloud, or on paper" [63] and in sorting things with his hands one may be thinking. To learn to calculate with one's lips closed or in one's head is a special technique that has to be acquired.[64] When one performs a manual operation skillfully he performs one thing and not two, and normally he has no occasion to formulate rules and then follow them. Thinking is never to be equated merely with being guided by symbols or even with talking. One can talk parrotlike in response to symbols without thinking, and one can think, in working with things, without symbols.[65] Thinking is always more than merely successful manipulations or even talking, but the *more*, instead of being an inward process, is simply knowing what one is doing, paying heed, trying, acting from motives, being careful.[66] Thinking occurs on two distinct levels. One is that of ordinary action and conversation, and the other is that of deliberate, studied, or didactic discourse. Deception is more likely to occur on the second than on the first level, and it is also on the second level that constructive achievement and cultural advancement are attained.[67] However, the second is no more inward than the first.

The term "thinking" and related words have both process and achievement senses. Clear-cut categories and concepts belong mainly to the product and not to the process. In the actual process of thinking we are constantly fumbling and have to make use of such tools of thought as we can find. Logic is not either a part of the real world or an ideal achievement. It may be developed either by substitution or by the use of logical operations, and neither of these is description of fact.[68] Logical principles formulate those procedures which have

[60] *Ibid.*, pp. 223 f.
[61] *Ibid.*, p. 224.
[62] *Ibid.*, pp. 224 ff.
[63] *Ibid.*, p. 234; see also *Dilemmas*, pp. 94 ff.
[64] *The Concept of Mind*, p. 34.
[65] *Ibid.*, pp. 282 ff.

[66] *Ibid.*, p. 32, 143–44.
[67] *Ibid.*, pp. 309 ff.
[68] Ryle, "Why Are the Calculuses of Logic and Arithmetic Applicable to Reality?" *Proceedings of the Aristotelian Society, Supplementary Vol. XX* (1946), 20–29.

been found to be requisite in successful inferences.[69] In this sense they are prescriptions of performatory rules that may be violated by human beings, never by nature.[70] They give us, however, no more than broad schemata that have already been carefully worked out. Many relations among concepts that are involved in satisfactory inference have not been successfully charted and need to be worked through by the philosopher or informal logician, whose business it is to explore the yet unbroken territory.[71] Whatever our formal logical principles may be, applications must at some time be made without recourse to further principles, else inference is lost in infinite regress. "So" and "because" statements are applications of principles. "If . . . then" statements are inference licenses or tickets.[72]

C. Among other writers who came to ordinary-language analysis after previous orientation in different methods, one of the most interesting is Friedrich Waismann (b. 1896), now of Oxford, who was a member of the Vienna Circle before its dissolution in the early thirties and presumably shared the rather rigid logical position prevalent in the group at that time. In the mid-thirties Waismann's thought began to take on a coloring closely akin to some aspects of the second period of Wittgenstein's thought. Thus, while Waismann continued, in his *Introduction to Mathematical Thinking,* to hold to a verification theory of meaning and a conventionalist account of mathematics, he insisted that "mathematics does not consist of tautologies, . . . is not a branch of logic," [73] and that the subject matter of mathematics is not a single concept called "number" but a whole "family" of concepts varying in meaning according to applications.[74] At the same time, Waismann emphatically contended that since to doubt an experience "doesn't make sense," it also makes no sense to say that there is "indubitable knowledge of immediate experience." [75] Subsequently Waismann specifically repudiated the doctrine that "the meaning of a statement is the method of its verification." [76] This he did on the grounds of an "essential incompleteness of an em-

[69] *Ibid.*
[70] *Ibid.*
[71] *Dilemmas,* pp. 111 ff.
[72] Ryle, "If, So, and Because," in Max Black (ed.), *Philosophical Analysis* (Ithaca, N.Y.: Cornell University Press, 1950), pp. 323–40.
[73] Friedrich Waismann, *Introduction to Mathematical Thinking* (New York: Ungar Publishing Co., 1951). For an excellent summary of the crucial issues in Waismann's book, see Ernest Nagel's review of the original German edition, in *Journal of Philosophy,* XXXIV (1937), 693–95.

[74] See *ibid.;* and *Introduction to Mathematical Philosophy,* p. 234.
[75] Waismann, "The Relevance of Psychology to Logic," *Proceedings of the Aristotelian Society, Supplementary Vol. XV* (1936), in Feigl and Sellars, *Readings in Philosophical Analysis* (New York: Appleton-Century-Crofts, Inc., 1947), pp. 211, 215.
[76] Waismann, "Verifiability," *Proceedings of the Aristotelian Society, Supplementary Vol. XIX* (1945).

pirical description" [77] by virtue of which both foreseen and unforeseen elements can always be added.[78] He replaced the verifiability theory of meaning with an emphasis upon the wide diversity of possible meanings rooted in actual usage. For example, when I know French, or sweetness, or misery, or a man, or his writings, or his motives, Waismann contends, I know in at least six different senses of the term "know" and there are many more possibilities. Logic itself represents no single calculus but varies from language to language and even within a single language when the usage of some such crucial terms as "if . . . then" varies, as is often the case within a language! [79] Waismann also substitutes for the sharp analytic-synthetic dichotomy of the early positivist period a more tolerant view, similar to that of Wisdom, in which such statements as "time is measurable," "space has three dimensions," "I have one body," and "I can't feel another's pain" are seen from one point of view to be factual and from another to be quite distinct from all factual statements, and in which such statements, though rooted in language, disclose more than linguistic facts.[80] Waismann now believes that every sort of minute analytical inquiry, and every particular philosophical argument, is secondary to the major business of philosophy, which is vision, the seeing, not indeed of new facts, but of significance in facts such as was not seen before.[81]

A philosopher whose intellectual pilgrimage has covered somewhat more territory than that of most exponents of ordinary-language analysis is J. N. Findlay (b. 1903) of the University of London. Findlay began his philosophical work under the influence of Hegel and Bergson, and the influence of Hegel has continued through all the subsequent phases of Findlay's thought.[82] Thus in his presidential address before the Aristotelian Society, Findlay praised Hegel's thought for its concentration upon the here and now, its emphasis upon fluidity in reality, its insistence on ideal potentiality in the world, and its recognition of the profound significance of ordinary language.[83] Findlay's initial Hegelian phase was according to his own account followed by phases of "Russellian realism, of Meinongian *Gegenstandstheorie*,[84]

[77] *Ibid.*, p. 121.
[78] *Ibid.*, p. 123.
[79] Waismann, "Are There Alternative Logics?" *Proceedings of the Aristotelian Society*, XLVI (1945–46), 77–104.
[80] Waismann, "Analytic-Synthetic," *Analysis*, XI (1951), 53 ff.
[81] Waismann, "How I See Philosophy," in H. D. Lewis (ed.), *Contemporary British Philosophy* (London & New York: George Allen & Unwin, Ltd., & The Macmillan Co., 1956), pp. 482 ff.

[82] See J. N. Findlay, "An Examination of Tenses," in H. D. Lewis (ed.), *Contemporary British Philosophy*, p. 167; and "Some Merits of Hegelianism," *Proceedings of the Aristotelian Society*, LVI (1955–56), 1 ff.
[83] *Ibid.*, pp. 1–24.
[84] See Findlay, *Meinong's Theory of Objects* (London: Oxford University Press, 1933).

and Husserlian phenomenology."[85] Subsequently Findlay was deeply influenced by Wittgenstein's ordinary-language approach to philosophy, and during most of the forties his thoughts were largely dominated by that point of view. Philosophy he took to be an "attempt . . . to discover *the best ways of speaking* in the familiar fields in which we work and live, . . . to *talk well* of the facts of everyday experience."[86] The objective of this philosophical effort was to restore the good sense of which traditional philosophy tended to rob ordinary language. Thus, for example, whereas no confusion had been involved in ordinary ways of speaking of time, when traditional philosophy began to press such language with the twin clubs of strictness and consistency, such puzzles as how moments that could occupy no interval could yield finite temporal expanses and how one could measure a past that was no longer present began to emerge. A sound contemporary philosophy would restore sanity to talk about time by proposing linguistic conventions in which the artificial puzzles no longer appeared.[87] It would in doing so also achieve at least some clarification of ordinary language itself.[88]

By the end of the forties Findlay had come to have somewhat less confidence in ordinary language than previously. Thus he thought that the philosopher must "develop into more considered and consistent forms, the implications of . . . ordinary ways of speaking."[89] In the fifties Findlay's conception of philosophy is still broader. He "attaches rather more importance to . . . metaphysical perplexities and problems" than he formerly did;[90] and no longer confirms philosophical inquiry to linguistic analysis; he is now "concerned with concepts or modes of conceiving rather than with words." He thinks that concepts are revealed not by language alone but alike "in verbal expressions, in the performance of acts, and in the undergoing of inner life occurrences."[91]

Findlay regards the verification principle as a "great divide" in philosophy in the sense that once a sound version of this principle has been acquired, many previously insolvable puzzles in philosophy can be successfully handled.[92] He is also inclined to think that Russell's principle of acquaintance can be philosophically illuminating

---

[85] "An Examination of Tenses," p. 167.
[86] Findlay, "Dr. Joad and the Verification Principle," *Hibbert Journal*, XLVIII (1949–50), 125; cf. "Linguistic Approach to Psycho-Physics," *Proceedings of the Aristotelian Society*, L (1949–50), 42–64.
[87] Findlay, "A Treatment of Some Puzzles," in Antony Flew (ed.), *Logic and Language* (Oxford: Basil Blackwell, 1951), 1st series, pp. 37–54.

[88] Cf. Findlay, "Morality by Convention," *Mind*, LIII (1944), 169.
[89] Findlay, "Can God's Existence Be Disproved?" *Mind*, LVII (1948), 178.
[90] "Time: A Treatment of Some Problems," Introductory note.
[91] "An Examination of Tenses," p. 169.
[92] See "Dr. Joad and the Verification Principle."

if not pressed too far.[93] Findlay is, however, quite unwilling to make a sharp distinction between factual and nonfactual inquiries, but he finds "an extraordinary analogy between our reasoned problemative attitudes and our moral estimates such that both may very properly be regarded as branches of a single faculty of reason." [94] Moral insights are, as the emotivists have correctly shown, grounded neither in purely intellectual judgments of matters of fact nor in intuitions of non-natural properties, but in emotionally oriented attitudes expressed by common moral judgments.[95] Accordingly, moral insights will always vary somewhat concerning what is just and good. But these considerations do not imply either that moral judgments are neither true nor false, or that such judgments are merely persuasive, or that they can apply indiscriminately to anything one pleases. Human attitudes in general are normal only as they are rooted in human nature and connected in definite ways with specific types of physical objects, and moral attitudes in particular are so restricted by principles of public approvability, reflective testability, and impartiality that "we should simply not *call* a set of feelings ethical in which . . . these principles were not followed or approved." [96]

A writer who, as both a philosopher of the type under consideration and a psychologist, has produced a series of articles illuminating certain special phases of the growth of ordinary-language analysis, is C. A. Mace (b. 1894) of the University of London. Some of Mace's earlier pronouncements reflect a Platonism akin to that of the earlier writings of Russell and Moore. For example, an essay entitled "Beliefs" declares that "the sort of objects which participate in perception may participate also in beliefs," [97] and another essay entitled "The Nature of Formal Validity" contends that "the course of thought is determined in large measure by its objective content." [98] In 1934 Mace set forth the thesis somewhat reminiscent of Wittgenstein's *Tractatus*, "that facts and propositions attain to a representation only in sentences which also express a state of mind; and that all assertions which also express a state of mind exhibit reference to a fact or proposition." [99] When his thought took on, as it did in the late thirties, something of the flavor of ordinary-language analysis, Mace continued to be interested, as he had always been, in keeping in sight the dis-

[93] "Knowledge by Acquaintance."
[94] Findlay, "Probability without Nonsense," *Philosophical Quarterly*, II (1952), 238 f.
[95] Findlay, "The Justification of Attitudes," *Mind*, LXIII (1954), 145–61; "Morality by Convention."
[96] *Ibid.*, p. 161.
[97] C. A. Mace, "Beliefs," *Proceedings of the Aristotelian Society*, XXVIII (1928–29), 227–50.
[98] Mace, "The Nature of Formal Logic," *Proceedings of the Aristotelian Society*, Supplementary Vol. X (1931), 27–42.
[99] Mace, "Representation and Expression," in Margaret MacDonald (ed.), *Philosophy and Analysis* (Oxford: Basil Blackwell, 1954), p. 18.

tinctively mental. Accordingly, in the style of the ordinary-language analysts he now contends that it is less misleading to say that psychology studies mental acts than to deny that psychology studies such acts.[100] Introspection is, Mace holds, an indisputable fact. For example, one can discover in himself the feeling that he has a cold or is going to sneeze before the diagnostician can tell that he has a cold.[101] What may be debated regarding introspection is how to interpret or describe the facts. For example, on the basis of the same data the existence of mental acts and images of abstract ideas has been affirmed and denied.[102] The difficulty is to say what you see—to say it in a clear, correct, and illuminating way.[103] The fact of introspection is probably more interesting than significant in philosophy, but recognition of this fact at least helps to rule out crude behaviorism.[104]

The earliest period of the philosophical writing of Austin Duncan-Jones (b. 1908), who preceded Margaret Macdonald as editor of *Analysis*, shares in large part the logical atomism and picture theory of language found in Wittgenstein's *Tractatus*. For example, in this period Mr. Duncan-Jones is much concerned to clarify the notion of identity of structure, upon which the picture theory rests,[105] as well as the notion of entailment, in which logico-mathematical relations are rooted.[106] He wishes even to find facts corresponding to ethical terms and is perplexed when he is unable to find such facts in the case of the term "intrinsically good."[107] Perhaps his most interesting suggestions in this period are that since all complexes can be broken down no complex can be a universal of which a simple element is an instance, and that in fact only simples can be universals or have instances.[108] Subsequently, Duncan-Jones has become intensely interested in the implications of common speech. Inquiring, for example, whether or not philosophy analyzes common sense, he suggests that so long as the philosopher is doing what Wisdom called "same-level analysis," he is in fact clarifying what people mean by ordinary expressions, but that when the philosopher launches into what Wisdom called "new-level analysis" he may be doing something more

[100] Mace, "Does Psychology Study Mental Acts or Dispositions?" *Proceedings of the Aristotelian Society, Supplementary Vol. XXVII* (1947), 164–74.

[101] See Mace, "Abstract Ideas and Images," *Proceedings of the Aristotelian Society, Supplementary Vol. XXVII* (1953), 148; and Mace, *Some Trends in the Philosophy of Mind* (London: George Allen & Unwin, 1957), p. 108.

[102] *Ibid.*, pp. 236 ff.

[103] *Ibid.*, p. 242.

[104] "Abstract Ideas and Images," p. 148.

[105] Austin Duncan-Jones, "Definition of Identity of Structure," *Analysis*, II (1934), 14–18.

[106] Duncan-Jones, "Is Strict Implication the Same As Entailment?" *Analysis*, II (1935), 70–78.

[107] Duncan-Jones, "Ethical Words and Ethical Facts," *Mind*, XXXII (1933), 473–500.

[108] Duncan-Jones, "Universals and Particulars," *Proceedings of the Aristotelian Society*, XXXIV (1933–34), 62–86.

though just what he is doing is difficult to say.[109] Ten years later, although Duncan-Jones does not think that the proposition that "all philosophical questions [are] questions of language" can be proved, he thinks that questions of usage may be very significant in discussing philosophical issues.[110] With more specific reference to the relations of two modes of expression bearing upon ethical problems, Duncan-Jones now holds that while commands and assertions can be converted into one another, commands are often directed to individuals whereas assertions are not, that the premises of arguments issuing in commands must contain commands, and that commands require no support of factual statements whereas ought statements do require such support.[111]

Margaret Macdonald began her philosophical writing just at the time of the beginning of the transition from the logical atomism and the picture theory of language to ordinary-language analysis. An early essay (1934), entitled "Verification and Understanding," while repudiating the verification theory of meaning as such, presents a view of meaning very like the picture theory. To know what a proposition means is to know what it is "used to represent," [112] and "I understand propositions when I am acquainted with those objects . . . which enable me to 'construct' the set which would make the proposition true." [113] Three years later, however, Miss Macdonald was committed to ordinary-language analysis, of which she has remained one of the most thoroughgoing practitioners and ardent advocates.[114]

Most of the traditional philosophical problems, according to Miss Macdonald, are not real problems at all. Having stretched ordinary terms far beyond the usual boundaries,[115] the philosopher produces puzzles that are, to say the least, queer and often seem "to be concerned with a logical impossibility." [116]

[109] Duncan-Jones, "Does Philosophy Analyze Common Sense?" *Proceedings of the Aristotelian Society, Supplementary Vol. XVI* (1937), 159 ff.

[110] Duncan-Jones, "Are All Philosophical Questions, Questions of Language?" *Proceedings of the Aristotelian Society, Supplementary Vol. XXII* (1948), 49–62.

[111] Duncan-Jones, *Proceedings of the Aristotelian Society*, LII (1951–52), 189–206.

[112] Margaret Macdonald, "Verification and Understanding," *Proceedings of the Aristotelian Society*, XXXIV (1933–34), pp. 144 f.

[113] *Ibid.*, p. 145.

[114] See Macdonald, "Induction and Hypotheses," *Proceedings of the Aristotelian Society, Supplementary Vol. XVI* (1937), 20–35; and Macdonald, "The Philosopher's Use of Analogy," in Antony Flew (ed.), *Logic and Language* (Oxford: Basil Blackwell, 1952), 1st series, pp. 80–100.

[115] MacDonald, "The Philosopher's Use of Analogy."

[116] "Induction and Hypothesis," p. 28; see also "The Philosopher's Use of Analogy," pp. 81 ff.; "The Language of Political Theory," in Antony Flew (ed.), *Logic and Language*, pp. 167 ff.

The proper task of the philosopher today is neither to try to solve philosophical problems as Moore did,[117] nor to disintegrate the ordinary terms appropriate to them as Russell did when he tried to reduce all meaningful propositions to "propositions composed wholly of logically proper names" and to make even John Smith and this apple logical constructions.[118] The proper business of the contemporary philosopher is rather to dissolve traditional philosophical problems by showing how they arise from an improper extension of ordinary usage. The criterion of such usage is "the actual use by a sufficient number, over a long enough period, of serious and responsible users of a language who know the field of study or relevant circumstances." [119] Philosophical work is not to be done in large chunks, as Ryle contends, but in small, relatively isolated segments, in accord with the policy of the periodical *Analysis,* which Macdonald edited. Even with the reference to a sufficiently specific problem, an analysis adequate to dispel the haze of traditional philosophy cannot be achieved simply by assimilating the questionable term to one or a few ordinary expressions, as in Ryle's attempt to show that the use of the term "mind" for an entity is like mistaking a collection of students and teachers for an entity called a *"university"* or certain facts about particular men for an entity called *"the average man."* [120] Rather, any suitable analysis must consist of a whole series of fairly complex "stories" which compare puzzling expressions both internally with other terms belonging to the same area of experience and externally with terms belonging to other areas of experience.[121] Such an analysis will display the same theme in many lights, somewhat as one might see "the same scene painted by Constable, Cézanne and Picasso, or the character of Hamlet portrayed from Burgage to Olivier. The term "know" is used in a wide variety of senses and the task of the philosopher relative to it is not to try to force it into a unified pattern or to inquire concerning knowing in general but to explore the varied ramifications and relations of the actual usage of the term. Very roughly, the propositions purporting to express knowledge may be said to include "analytical propositions," "empirical propositions," and "assertions or expressions of value." [122] Of these the first, which include logical, mathematical, and other linguistic propositions "state rules for the uses of symbols or . . . follow from such rules within a

[117] Cf. Macdonald, *Philosophy and Analysis* (Oxford: Basil Blackwell, 1954), p. 12.
[118] *Ibid.,* p. 8 f.
[119] *Ibid.,* p. 6.
[120] Macdonald, "Professor Ryle on the Concept of Mind," *Philosophical Review,* LX (1951), 86 f.

[121] Macdonald, "Ethics and the Ceremonial Use of Language," in Max Black (ed.), *Philosophical Analysis* (Ithaca, N.Y.: Cornell University Press, 1950), pp. 211 ff.
[122] Macdonald, "Natural Rights," *Proceedings of the Aristotelian Society,* XLVII (1946–47), 228.

linguistic or logical system."[123] The second, empirical propositions, depend for the most part on inductive inference and can often be known with certainty to be true.[124] The rationalists' contention that apart from logical necessity causal connections of facts would be merely accidental rests upon an abuse of the term "accident" which in plain English refers simply to "something which we did not fore-see,[125] and the contention of Ayer and others that all empirical statements are mere hypotheses disregards the fact that the term "hypothesis" has a perfectly good use of its own.[126] There is no general problem of induction any more than there is a general problem of knowledge. That an assertion of causal connection passes the appropriate inductive tests is enough to warrant the affirmation of the connection, for the inductive tests in question are the criteria of such a connection.[127] To allege that one may be always dreaming is no plausible objection; for there is no general problem of dreaming, and whether or not one is in a particular instance dreaming is not difficult to ascertain.[128] Value judgments are neither wholly factual nor wholly emotive; they depend upon prior decisions, which in turn are influenced by a variety of both factual and emotional considerations.[129] They have normative and authoritative characteristics that assimilate them more nearly to the language of religious rites than to that of either narrative statements or expressions of personal feeling.[130]

3. Younger Exponents of Ordinary-Language Analysis

It is to be expected that writers who begin their philosophical work in a new movement without previous commitment to any earlier movement will work out the major themes of the movement with more thoroughness and fewer restraints than those who have come into the movement from other backgrounds. In general—though not invariably—this expectation is borne out in the instance of ordinary-language analysis in Great Britain. The number of significant younger British contributors to the achievements of the movement is, moreover, already quite large. While the movement has exercised considerable influence in America, the number of thoroughgoing adherents

[123] *Ibid.*
[124] "Induction and Hypothesis," p. 34.
[125] *Ibid.*, p. 24.
[126] *Ibid.*, p. 28.
[127] Cf. *ibid.*, p. 33.
[128] MacDonald, "Sleeping and Waking," *Mind*, LXII (1953), 202–15.

[129] See "Natural Rights"; and MacDonald, "Distinctive Features in Criticisms of Arts," *Proceedings of the Aristotelian Society, Supplementary Vol. XXIII* (1949), pp. 183 f., 190 ff.
[130] "Ethics and Ceremonial Language," pp. 222 ff.

there is still small. In the endeavor to give some idea of the thought of the younger philosophers of the movement in the space available, we shall briefly sketch the main ideas concerning knowledge of four such philosophers and mention in passing one or two notable contributions of four others.

A. Since much of the work of ordinary-language analysis is done in discussion rather than in writing, it is not surprising that some of the most influential philosophers of the group now under consideration are philosophers who have written comparatively little. Such a philosopher is J. L. Austin (b. 1911) of Oxford. Austin believes that it is the business of philosophy both to trace out in detail our ordinary uses of words [and] to clarify them out to some extent.[1] Although in an early essay he discussed the error of endeavoring to establish universals on the basis of the use of common names and supported the claim that relations can be sensed,[2] Austin's main contributions have taken the form of a series of astute though unsystematic comments upon the uses of such terms as "know" and "true."

To say that one knows something is more than merely to assert something, Austin thinks. Merely to assert something is strictly to imply only that one believes it, not that he knows it, so that one who has asserted something may appropriately be asked whether or not he knows it.[3] Saying that one believes something differs from saying that one knows it in that it is always appropriate to ask "why do you believe and how do you know?" but not to ask "how do you believe or why do you know." [4]

The specific character of knowledge is suggested by the kind of challenges with which a claim to know may be confronted. To begin with, one's previous experiences and present opportunities may be questioned. For example, if someone says that he knows that "there's a bittern at the bottom of the garden," he may appropriately be asked how he came "to be in a position to know about bitterns," how he came "to be in a position to say there's a bittern here and now," how he can "tell bitterns," or "how he can tell the thing here and now is a bittern." [5] But in addition, one's facts may be questioned.[6] Thus one who claims that here is a goldfinch, may be asked, "But do you know it's a real goldfinch?" or, "Are you certain it's the right red for a goldfinch?" [7] However, apart from such specific questions, merely

[1] See J. L. Austin, "Other Minds," in Antony Flew, ed., Logic and Language, 2d series (Oxford: Basil Blackwell, 1953); "A Plea for Excuses," Proceedings of the Aristotelian Society, LVII (1956–57), 1–30; Austin, "Ifs and Cans," (London: Oxford University Press, 1956).

[2] Austin, "Are There A Priori Con-

cepts," Proceedings of the Aristotelian Society, Supplementary Vol. XVIII (1939), 83–105.

[3] "Other Minds," p. 124.
[4] Ibid., pp. 124 f.
[5] Ibid., p. 126.
[6] Ibid., p. 132.
[7] Ibid.

general questions that suggest no particular reason for doubt but imply the impossibility of all knowing are metaphysician's wiles not unlike those of the conjurer who stimulates suspicion without giving any idea what one should guard against.[8]

A general philosophical challenge to knowledge of the feelings of others sometimes takes the form of questions concerning degrees of assurance. Thus it is alleged that one may know his own feelings but not those of another in that a degree of assurance attaches to the first that cannot possibly attach to the second. This sort of distinction is "the 'original sin' by which the philosopher cast himself out from the garden of the world we live in."[9] One cannot in fact always be sure of his own feelings. Not only may he misname or misrefer them,[10] he may also be uncertain in more basic ways.[11] For example, one may simply lack sufficient experience of a sensation to permit assured judgment concerning it,[12] or he may try to "savour" the current experience more fully. Besides, the term "know" is ordinarily followed not by a direct object at all but by a "that" clause, and when this fact becomes clear, the distinction between allegedly known sensations and other kinds of knowledge loses its plausibility.[13]

A general philosophical challenge to all knowledge claims is involved in the suggestion that whereas we can't be wrong if we know, "we seem always, or practically always liable to be mistaken."[14] But this sort of challenge brings to light an intimate connection between the verb "know" and such "performatory" words as "promise" that removes its sting. While I certainly should not say "I know" if I am aware of some special reason for doubt, or say "I promise" if I have some special reason to think I cannot do what I promise, human ignorance and weakness in general are not sufficient grounds for refusing to say either "I know" or "I promise," and to suppose that they are is only a philosopher's obsession.[15] It is of course true that when I say "I know" or "I promise" I take a "new plunge" beyond the one I take when I say "I am quite sure" or "I fully intend," but the new plunge is not in affirming greater assurance or fuller intentions, for there is nothing in the one scale "superior to being quite sure" or in the other scale "superior to fully intending."[16] The new plunge consists rather in each case in self-commitment or the assuming of special responsibility for the truth of the statement or the fulfillment of the promise. In the case of saying one is quite sure or fully in-

[8] *Ibid.*, p. 135.
[9] *Ibid.*, p. 136.
[10] *Ibid.*, p. 135; cf. also Austin, "How to Talk," *Proceedings of the Aristotelian Society*, LIII (1952–53), 230 ff.
[11] "Other Minds," p. 135.

[12] *Ibid.*, p. 137.
[13] *Ibid.*, pp. 140 ff.
[14] *Ibid.*, p. 142.
[15] *Ibid.*, p. 145.
[16] *Ibid.*, p. 144.

tends, a take-it-or-leave-it attitude is implied that is no longer implied in saying that one knows, or in promising.[17] The objection may be raised against the analogy between knowing and promising that when "things turn out badly . . . we say in the one instance, "You're proved wrong so you *didn't* know," and in the other instance, "You've failed to perform, although you *did* promise." [18] But even here the difference is not as great as may appear. If one never intended to perform one may say in one sense that he *"didn't* promise." [19] And in some cases in which one is proved wrong, instead of saying "you didn't know," one would be inclined to say in analogy to appropriate statements about a failing promise, "You can't have known or you had no right to say you knew." [20] "I know" is not simply a "descriptive phrase"; it is in important respects a ritual phrase similar to "I promise," "I do," "I warn" and the like.[21]

Knowing another mind involves some special problems, but like all other knowing it depends upon previous experience and present observation. To suppose that such knowing proceeds from physical symptoms to mental facts is a mistake.[22] Angry looks and actions are not mere symptoms of anger; they are ways of venting it. There are many grounds upon which a claim to know the mind of another may be doubted, but to suggest that one may never know the mind of another is a philosopher's artificial doubt and need not be taken too seriously. Defense of knowledge of other minds on the analogy of one's own experience only invites further doubts.[23] Believing in other minds is natural; it is doubt that must be justified. To be in doubt merely because we are unable to "introspect" the feelings of others is to bark up the wrong tree, for the simple fact is that we don't introspect the feelings of others but that we often do know them.[24]

The adjective "true," according to Austin, does not apply primarily either to sentences, propositions, or words. For one would not say either that something was true in English, or that the meaning of a sentence was true, or that an isolated word was true. It is rather statements that are true.[25] The condition of their being true is somewhat misleadingly said to be correspondence with facts. A fact may itself be taken to be a "true statement," but this leads to the errors of the coherence theory. A one-to-one correspondence between facts and statements may be assumed, but this leads to the perplexities of the correspondence theory.[26] Actually, "a statement is said to be true

[17] *Ibid.*
[18] *Ibid.,* p. 145.
[19] *Ibid.*
[20] *Ibid.,* p. 146.
[21] *Ibid.,* pp. 146 f.
[22] *Ibid.,* pp. 147 ff.

[23] *Ibid.,* p. 137.
[24] *Ibid.,* p. 158.
[25] Austin, "Truth," *Proceedings of the Aristotelian Society, Supplementary Vol. XXIV* (1950), 111 ff.
[26] *Ibid.,* pp. 116 f.

when the historic state of affairs to which it is correlated by the demonstrative conventions . . . is of a type with which the sentence used in making it is correlated by the descriptive conventions.[27] Any attempt to establish a picture theory of truth is vitiated by the purely conventional character of the relation between symbols and their referents and by the considerations that no picture or recording, however "accurate," can ever be "true (of)" any event [28] but many different statements can be. A statement that a statement is true involves more than the original statement in that it refers to the relation of the original statement to the world as the original statement cannot. In analogous fashion, negation differs from falsehood in that whereas a language could be framed so as to get along without an expression for falsehood, none could get along without an expression for negation.[29] The usefulness of a statement varies with the tightness with which it fits the situation, but the truth of a statemen does not so vary.[30] Many utterances often taken to be statements are not intended to be regarded as true or false at all, for example, "a formula in a calculus . . . , a performatory utterance, . . . a value judgment, . . . a definition, . . . [or] a part of a work of fiction" [31] and some of the perplexities of truth theory would be avoided if this fact were fully recognized.

B. The thought of Stuart Hampshire (b. 1914) displays perhaps a little less confidence in ordinary language than does that of his Oxford colleague Austin. Hampshire's thought also represents, within the framework of ordinary-language analysis, a somewhat less physicalistic and behavioristic and a slightly more mentalistic and introspectionist perspective than does the thought of either Wittgenstein or Ryle. In this respect Hampshire's thought is more like that of Wisdom than like that of any of the other three. Hampshire is also more favorably disposed toward the verification theory of meaning than are most recent British analysts and at the same time more open-minded with reference to the possibility of metaphysics than are most of the earlier analysts.

Philosophy has been from the Socratic dialogues onward, according to Hampshire, in persistent search for a sure method of verification, and its history has in no small part consisted of the substitution of new methods for old ones that have lost their usefulness.[32] The distinctive characteristic of recent British philosophy is that, following the lead of G. E. Moore, it has largely dropped the quest for a single

---

[27] *Ibid.*, p. 116.
[28] *Ibid.*, p. 120.
[29] *Ibid.*, pp. 121 ff.
[30] *Ibid.*, p. 124.

[31] *Ibid.*, p. 125.
[32] Stuart Hampshire, "Changing Methods in Philosophy," *Philosophy*, XXVI (1951), 142.

method and adopted the view that "all devices are justified insofar as they in effect make several distinctions clearer which were not clear before." [33] It has tended to become pure description of ordinary language, involving little attempt at explanation. But while such description can be extremely illuminating, it can hardly constitute quite the whole job of philosophy. A concept may indeed be sketched by indicating the specific conditions of applications of the terms that express it, but philosophical inquiry actually begins only when "a weighted comparison between the conditions of certainty attached to expressions of different types" is initiated.[34] On the basis of such a comparison the philosopher selects a standard of certainty and attempts to show how "conventions of application of different types conform . . . to the standard." [35] Thus a "philosophical thesis . . . consists in the assimilations of the different methods of confirmation in actual use to some single explanatory pattern." [36] The plotting of actual usage is "a necessary check upon philosophy," but philosophy must "go beyond the mere plotting of the ordinary uses of words." [37] Theory of knowledge in particular "is concerned with the logical relations between statements in which perceiving knowing and believing are mentioned," [38] i.e. with "the conditions for the proper use of 'know' and 'certain' in conjunction with sentences of different types (and) how these sentences are typically used." [39]

Significant logical patterns are not, as Quine seems to think, primarily to be found in formal logical systems or indeed in any sort of sentences as such. However useful formal systems may be, they have, in order to be significant, to be translatable into ordinary terminology, and the meaning of any sort of sentence depends upon its context. The most significant logical patterns are to be found in the actual uses of ordinary language, and the most important task of the logician is to search out these patterns.[40] With regard to the character of sentences involved in logic, one may well follow the lead of Strawson in regarding entailment sentences as not themselves necessary but contingently true or false because grounded in use. But one needs also to make clear a sharp three-fold distinction, at which Strawson hints but sometimes obscures, between "true-or-false ordinary statements about the non-linguistic world (and [people's] linguistic habits . . .); true-or-false intensional meta-statements to the effect that particular

[33] Ibid., p. 144.
[34] Hampshire, "The Interpretation of Language," in C. A. Mace, British Philosophy in the Mid-Century, pp. 274 ff.
[35] Ibid., p. 278.
[36] Ibid., p. 275.
[37] Ibid., p. 279.

[38] Hampshire, "Logical Form," Proceedings of the Aristotelian Society, XLVIII (1947–48), 42.
[39] Hampshire, "Self-Knowledge and the Will," Revue Internationale de Philosophie, VII (1953), p. 230.
[40] "Logical Form," pp. 37–58.

mentioned expressions are necessary or impossible . . . ; [and] rules . . . , which are not true or false, but are observed or not observed." [41] The basis of logical necessity and impossibility is always linguistic, so that, for example, that " 'p and not q is impossible' means . . . , that 'p and not q' is not a significant statement in (either my or most people's or these scientists' or . . .) use of language." [42]

Despite the serious criticisms repeatedly launched against the verifiability theory of meaning, Hampshire has insisted that basic ideas involved in that theory were indispensable to a fruitful interpretation of meaning. Thus, both in his earlier essays and in more recent ones, he holds that "to understand a sentence which expresses an empirical proposition is to be able to imagine and to recognize situations to which the sentence can properly be used to refer." [43] He makes the method of verification rather than any more formal property the test of logical form,[44] and continues to take "methods of application in actual use to be the clue to meaning." [45] The indispensable truths involved in the verification theory he takes to be the substance of the meaning of any term. Nevertheless, he insists upon ample qualifications.[46] Intending and referring, both of which are included in meaning, unavoidably involve subjective aspects. Although meaning ordinarily points to something in the external world, "in reporting what our intentions were on a particular occasion, and also in stating which of two objects we were referring to when we made a particular statement, we can in the last resort confirm our statements only by our own introspection and reflection.[47] Accordingly, it is not possible to indicate "a general criterion or set of decisive tests" governing the intending or referring of an expression, in the sense of showing how "*anyone* . . . can make sure that the expression has been correctly applied on a given occasion." [48]

What knowledge is attainable by human beings and in what ways depends upon what the subject of inquiry is. With reference to "what goes on in the mind or in the consciousness of the speaker," there are expressions such that "any affirmative categorical statement in which they occur can only be finally and conclusively confirmed . . . by the designated subject of the statement, and must always be a matter of

[41] Hampshire, "Mr. Strawson on Necessary Propositions and Entailment Statements," *Mind*, LVII (1948), 356.

[42] *Ibid.*, p. 356.

[43] Hampshire, "Ideas, Propositions and Signs," *Proceedings of the Aristotelian Society*, XL (1939–40), p. 16; cf. also "Self-Knowledge and the Will," *Revue Internationale de Philosophie*, VII (1953), 230.

[44] Hampshire, "Logical Form," pp. 40 ff.

[45] *Ibid.*, pp. 38–58.

[46] "Self-Knowledge and the Will," pp. 230 f.

[47] Hampshire, "Referring and Intending," *Philosophical Review*, Vol. LXV (1956).

[48] *Ibid.*, p. 7.

indirect inference to anyone else." [49] Direct or immediate confirmation is attainable regarding to subjective aspects of meaning and reference and also regarding to all manner of statements concerning sensations and feelings, such as the statement "I feel giddy." [50] It is also attainable in certain instances of awareness of freedom, for no matter how hemmed in a person is by heredity, circumstances, habit, or ill-health, he may be at times aware as no one else can be with reference to him that he could try to do better.[51] With reference to "what goes on in the external world," the experience of the subject of the statement has no such finality, and one must depend on induction and the coordination of indirect evidences.

Concerning knowledge of other minds, the argument based on analogy has often been criticized on the ground that since no member of the class of other minds has ever been known, the generalization upon which the argument proceeds is without foundation. This objection, however, is based upon a logical blunder. Since every human individual is in some settings another mind to some persons, there is in fact no fixed class of other minds, and no basic reason why argument concerning other minds cannot proceed on a sound analogy. The analogy that is wanted is not an analogy between my feelings and the symptoms of my feelings on the one hand and your feelings and the symptoms of your feelings on the other but analogy between different uses of the same methods of argument by different people on different occasions." [52] Knowing my own feelings, I can always check your methods of argument concerning my mind against my own feelings. Hearing your reports of your feelings, I can check my methods of argument concerning your mind against these reports. And in these ways each of us can and does develop self-correcting methods of argument with reference to other minds that are quite adequate to human needs apart from any direct insight into the minds of others.

The quest for metaphysical knowledge is by no means, Hampshire thinks, the senseless search many recent philosophers have supposed. Thus Hampshire treats some metaphysical questions as unavoidable, and in his *Spinoza* protests that "we cannot lay down the limits of intelligibility until we have explored beyond these limits." [53] Subsequently in *The Age of Reason* he defines philosophy itself as "a free inquiry into the limits of human knowledge and into the most general

[49] *Ibid.*
[50] Hampshire, "The Analogy of Feeling," *Mind*, LXI (1952), pp. 1 f.
[51] Hampshire, "Freedom of the Will," *Proceedings of the Aristotelian Society,*
Supplementary Vol. XXV (1951), pp. 161–78.
[52] "The Analogy of Feeling," p. 5.
[53] Hampshire, *Spinoza* (Baltimore: Penguin Books, Inc., 1951), p. 216.

categories applicable to experience and reality." [54] More specifically, in his essay "Identification and Existence" he contends that metaphysical statements and even existential ones can be rendered plausible on grounds that are not merely linguistic by re-examining the relations between such basic concepts as "existence, knowledge, identity, and truth." [55] This sort of achievement is possible in the following manner. One may consider the "conventionally accepted criteria of application" attached, for example, to such subject-terms as "God" or "vast and impersonal forces in history." [56] One may then compare these criteria with "more general requirements which any such criteria of application should satisfy." If then the conventionally acceptable criteria of the term "God" or the term "vast impersonal forces in history" turn out to be incompatible with these more general requirements, then one must either recognize that in the ordinary sense the referent of the terms in question may not properly be said to exist, or else, if there remain compelling grounds for making such statements, one must revise his general criteria for the application of subject-terms. [57] In passing it should be noted that Hampshire's own criteria for the application of subject-terms include the demand that the reference of the term "must be understood, and if necessary explained, as a reference to something present and noticeable in the environment of the speaker." [58]

C. Although the ordinary-language movement is primarily British, some American philosophers have been deeply influenced by it, and a few are fully committed to its procedures and perspectives. Of these latter Norman Malcolm (b. 1911) of Cornell is a notable example. His work is the more interesting from our point of view because most of his analyses have been directly concerned with what may be called epistemological terms.

Ordinary language, Malcolm holds, is never self-contradictory, for even when what such language states is false the language has an application. [59] Traditional philosophical statements tend to abuse ordinary language and as a result are likely to be either false [60] or at any rate paradoxical. [61] The proper task of philosophical analysis is

[54] Hampshire, *The Age of Reason* (New York: New American Library of World Literature, Inc., 1956), p. 12.
[55] Hampshire, "Identification and Existence," in H. D. Lewis (ed.), *Contemporary British Philosophy* (London: George Allen & Unwin, 1956), pp. 193 f.; cf. also "The Interpretation of Language," pp. 278 f. 278 f.
[56] *Ibid.*, p. 197.
[57] *Ibid.*, pp. 195 f.

[58] *Ibid.*, p. 208.
[59] Norman Malcolm, "Moore and Ordinary Language," in P. A. Schilpp (ed.), *The Philosophy of G. E. Moore* (Evanston and Chicago: Northwestern University Press, 1942), pp. 343–68.
[60] *Ibid.*
[61] Malcolm, "Philosophy for Philosophers," *Philosophical Review*, LX (1951), 329.

not only to show the traditional philosopher that his paradoxes are an abuse of ordinary language but also to point out for him precisely where he goes wrong and what tempts him to make statements that reject common sense without disagreeing with common sense concerning empirical facts.[62] In the performance of this analytic task the most illuminating mode of inquiry deals not with meanings, thoughts, or propositions, but as Wittgenstein repeatedly showed, with uses, modes of verification, and methods of learning expressions.[63]

Although sensory experiences, including afterimages, are incorrigible, they are not to be thought of as instances of knowing. So to think of them is not only an abuse of language but a fatal step in the direction of skepticism, for if knowing consists of immediate sensory experiences it can scarcely also include the very different experiences of perceiving objects.[64] That which can be known is that which it is possible " 'to find out,' 'establish,' 'make sure,' 'determine that it is true' ";[65] but sensory experiences are such that we can do none of these things with reference to them. I can find out whether or not I am hot by using a thermometer, but I cannot *find out* whether or not I *feel* hot at all. Such a sentence as "I know that I feel hot" simply has no normal use.[66] If one must speak in epistemological terms of immediate experiences he had better, instead of using an ordinary word such as "known," use a philosopher's expression such as "directly apprehended," which Moore correctly explains as appropriate to afterimages. Since no apprehension of a physical object is incorrigible in the sense in which the apprehension of an afterimage is, the term "directly apprehended" is not, as Moore was sometimes inclined to think, applicable to the apprehension of the surface of physical objects.[67]

At one point in his career Malcolm argued, in opposition to Moore, that one ought not to say that he knows a fact that is before him such as that here is a hand. The reason is not that such a proposition is not certain but rather that it is so certain that there has been no "question at issue" or "doubt to be removed," and no such occasion "to give a reason" or to conduct an "investigation" as is normally present when the term "know" is appropriate.[68]

[62] Cf. *ibid.*, pp. 329–340.

[63] Cf. Malcolm, "Are Necessary Propositions Really Verbal?" *Mind*, XLIX (1940), 191 ff.; cf. also "The Nature of Entailment," *Ibid.*, pp. 333 ff.; and "Dreaming and Skepticism," *Philosophical Review*, LXV (1956), 23, 30.

[64] Cf. Malcolm, "Russell's Human Knowledge," *Philosophical Review*, V (1950), 94–106.

[65] "Philosophy for Philosophers," p. 330.

[66] *Ibid.*, p. 335; cf. also "Knowledge of Other Minds," *Journal of Philosophy*, LV (1958), 976 ff.

[67] Malcolm, "Direct Perception," *Philosophical Quarterly*, III (1953), 301–16.

[68] Malcolm, "Defending Common Sense," *Philosophical Review*, LVIII (1949), 203 ff.

However, for the most part Malcolm's efforts with reference to the problems of knowledge have been devoted to the more basic thesis that such terms as "certainty" and "know" are properly used concerning at least some empirical matters of fact. His central contention is that in ordinary discourse we repeatedly say of some empirical statements that they are certain [69] and known and of others that they are not. While it is always possible to be wrong about the truth of a particular statement, to refuse to use the terms "certain" and "known" with reference to *any* such statements is to deprive the terms "certain" and "known" and their opposites of any ordinary use; for if no empirical statements are certain, one can scarcely see how anyone could come to think of any as uncertain. In defense of his thesis against the claim of Lewis and others that no empirical statement can be fully verified because of infinite possibilities of the falsification of some consequences of such a statement, Malcolm contends that such an argument presupposes the certainty of some empirical statements, that neither infinity of consequences not logical possibility of refutation is relevant to the certainty of a proposition, and that with reference to some empirical statements, such as that I am now reading a certain line, nothing can add to their certainty.[70] Subsequently, in an article entitled "Knowledge and Belief," Malcolm makes a significant distinction between a strong and a weak sense of "know," and contends that empirical statements of matters of fact are included under each. The term "know" is used in the weak sense when one says that he knows some empirical fact, such as that there is water in the gorge, but would be willing to admit that he could be wrong. In this sense many empirical statements are obviously said to be known. The term "know" is used in the strong sense when one says that he knows something and there is nothing that he would count as evidence against the truth of his statement. In this sense some of the propositions of mathematics, such as $2 \times 2 = 4$, are known to be true, but others, such as $92 \times 16 = 1472$, requiring calculations are not so known to be true. Nevertheless such an empirical statement as "here is an ink bottle" is known in the strong sense in that "I do not now admit that certain future occurrences would disprove it." [71] That some such empirical statements are known to be true should, moreover, be apparent in the fact that "in order for it to be possible that any statements about physical things should *turn out to be false,* it is necessary that some statements about physical things cannot turn out

[69] Cf. "Are Necessary Propositions Really Verbal?" p. 195; and Norman Malcolm, "Certainty and Empirical Statements," *Mind,* LI (1942), 20 ff., 36 ff.

[70] Malcolm, "The Verification Argu-

ment," in Max Black (ed.), *Philosophical Analysis,* pp. 244–98.

[71] Malcolm, "Knowledge and Belief," *Mind,* LXI (1952), 186.

to be false.[72] It is true that the strong sense of "know" is not quite like "directly apprehended," for in the case of the directly apprehended not only is there nothing that I would now recognize as evidence against the statement in question but there is nothing at all that could in any sense count as evidence against it. Even the sort of Cartesian doubt that is based upon the suspicion that one may be dreaming is incapable of undermining one's ordinary knowledge of the physical world, for whatever serves as a criterion for thinking, wondering, inquiring, fearing, or suspecting is a criterion for one's not being in deep sleep; and while one may be deceived when he is half-asleep, one does not in such a case have to be deceived.[73]

D. P. F. Strawson (b. 1919) of Oxford has offered interesting suggestions concerning theory of logic, meaning and reference, truth, and the metaphysics of the conceptual frame in which cognition ordinarily occurs. Logic, according to Strawson, is "internal criticism . . . of discourse."[74] Its principal instrument is the concept of inconsistency, which is applicable not to sentences but to statements such as may be expressed by sentences.[75] The statements of a system of logic are grounded in the most general tautologous "rules about words."[76] Being generalized and formalized, all systems of logic to some extent misrepresent ordinary language, and it is a task of theory of logic to bridge the gap between logic and ordinary language. For example, truth-functional logic misrepresents ordinary language by treating "if . . . then" expressions as nonimplicative;[77] the calculus of classes deviates from ordinary language by building generalizations upon empty classes;[78] and even the modern predicative logic, which reduces all other statements to positive or existential ones, conflicts with ordinary language in its failure to do justice to the variety of possible subjects of statements or to the time references of verbs.[79] The expedients necessary to bridge these gaps between logic and ordinary language include such a distinction between meaning and reference as will, for example, remove the temptation to force fictional statements and descriptions into the artificial molds of existential language,[80] such an elimination of the trichotomy, truth, falsehood, and meaninglessness as will permit an ample recognition that many fully meaning-

[72] Ibid., p. 187.
[73] Malcolm, "Dreaming and Skepticism," Philosophical Review, LXV (1956), 14–37; cf. Dreaming (London & New York: Routledge & Kegan Paul, Ltd., & Humanities Press, Inc., 1959).
[74] P. F. Strawson, Introduction to Logical Theory (London & New York: Methuen & Co., Ltd., & John Wiley & Sons, Inc., 1952), p. 2.

[75] Cf. ibid., pp. 189 f., 211 f.
[76] Ibid., p. 12.
[77] Ibid., pp. 82 ff.
[78] Ibid., pp. 109 ff.
[79] Ibid., pp. 143 ff., 150 f.
[80] Ibid., pp. 184 ff.; cf. also Strawson, "A Reply to Mr. Sellars," Philosophical Review, LXIII (1954), 221 f.; and "On Referring," Mind, LIX (1950), 320 ff.

ful sentences do not purport to make either true or false statements,[81] and such a recognition that entailment statements are not themselves necessary statements as will exclude the apparent conflict of extensional and intensional logic.[82]

Russell's theory of descriptions, Strawson contends, involves errors of "major philosophical importance," [83] and lies at the root of crucial mistakes in the whole way of thinking represented by Russell's type of philosophy. In Russell's own thought, it represents a false assumption that the subject of a significant sentence cannot fail to name something. Hence it leads him first to the implausible theory that what is properly named is always a sense-datum [84] and then to the even less plausible Platonic view that what is properly named is only qualities.[85] By distinguishing between a sentence, its use, and an utterance of it, one may avoid Russell's root confusion of meaning and reference and see that it is a sentence that is significant, that only in certain of its uses does an utterance of a sentence refer, and that when a sentence is not used to refer, the question of its truth or falsity simply does not arise.[86] Even Russell's effort to confine the reference of uniquely referring sentences to sense-data is, however, preferable to Quine's attempt to eliminate singular statements altogether, for at least it preserves a sound awareness that "quantified sentences presuppose unquantified sentences." [87]

The "philosophical problem of truth" is taken by Strawson to be essentially identical with the problem of "the actual use of the word 'true.' " [88] The current semantic thesis to the effect that "to say that any assertion is true is not to make any further assertions at all" [89] is correct, Strawson thinks, in its "denial that the phrase 'is true' has any assertive or descriptive function" [90] but inadequate in failing to recognize that the phrase has a "performatory" function signifying "agreement or disagreement" with utterances that have been or may be made.[91] The somewhat different semantic thesis to the effect that "to say that a statement is true is to make a statement about a sentence in a given language" [92] is wrong in asserting that "the phrase '. . . is true' is used to talk *about sentences*," [93] but right in implying that to say that a statement is true is to do something different from just

[81] Cf. *Introduction to Logical Theory*, pp. 170 ff.

[82] Strawson, "Necessary Propositions and Entailment Statements," *Mind*, LVII (1948), 184–200.

[83] Strawson, review of Bertrand Russell's "Logic and Knowledge," *Philosophical Quarterly*, VII (1957), 376.

[84] *Ibid.*, pp. 374–76.

[85] *Ibid.*, p. 378.

[86] "On Referring," pp. 27–40.

[87] "Logic and Knowledge," p. 378.

[88] Strawson, "Truth," in MacDonald, *Philosophy and Analysis*, pp. 260 f.

[89] *Ibid.*, p. 261.

[90] *Ibid.*, p. 273.

[91] *Ibid.*, p. 274.

[92] *Ibid.*, p. 261.

[93] *Ibid.*, p. 262.

making the statement.[94] However, it would be a mistake to think of truth statements as purely performatory. Insofar as statements containing "is true" are about statements at all, they are not, as Austin thinks, about statements in the sense of what statements state.[95] Logically true statements are distinguishable from true statements of matters of contingent fact by virtue of their continuing to hold no matter what legitimate substitutions are made in their extralogical terms, but it should be noticed that the conditions of legitimacy for such substitutions can scarcely be specified without reference to the acceptance of such notions as synonymy, which such writers as Quine seek to exclude.[96] Entailment statements are not themselves necessary statements but are really contingent statements based upon linguistic usage.[97]

In his recent book entitled *Individuals*, Strawson has sketched a "descriptive metaphysics" which, in contrast to a "revisionary metaphysics," attempts to "describe the actual structure of our thought about the world." [98] Since talk of metaphysical entities that are not knowable is pointless, particulars must be recognizable or reidentifiable. Such reidentifiability seems to be fundamentally rooted in a spatiotemporal frame of reference.[99] Since sense-data do not themselves possess the requisite spatiotemporal characteristics for reidentification, but can be identified only by reference to already identified persons, they cannot be basic particulars.[100] The most convincing candidates for the status of basic particulars are material bodies, for such bodies clearly have the requisite spatiotemporal characters and are inconceivable without them.[101] Persons are, however, also to be regarded as basic particulars of a special kind, to which the predicates of both body and mind are applicable.[102] Ascription of awareness to others is a condition of ascription of it to oneself.[103] The distinction between particulars and universals may be approached either through grammatical styles, through categorial modes of collecting terms, or through degrees of completeness.[104] The first approach calls attention to differences between the "singular grammatically substantival" type of expression used to introduce particulars into propositions, and the

[94] *Ibid.*, p. 261.

[95] Strawson, "Truth," *Proceedings of the Aristotelian Society, Supplementary Vol. XXIV* (1950), 129 ff.

[96] Strawson, "Propositions, Concepts and Logical Truths," *Philosophical Quarterly*, VII (1957), 15-25.

[97] "Necessary Propositions and Entailment Statements," pp. 184 ff.

[98] Strawson, *Individuals* (London: Methuen & Co., Ltd., 1959), p. 9.

[99] *Ibid.*, pp. 23 ff.

[100] *Ibid.*, p. 41.

[101] *Ibid.*, pp. 38 ff.

[102] *Ibid.*, p. 103.

[103] *Ibid.*, pp. 94 ff.

[104] See Strawson, "Particulars and General," *Proceedings of the Aristotelian Society*, LIV (1953-54), 231-60; "Proper Names," *Proceedings of the Aristotelian Society, Supplementary Vol. XXXI* (1957), 191-228; and esp. *Individuals*, Pt. II.

type of expression that "contains at least one finite form of verb in the indicative mood" used to introduce universals.[105] The second, or categorial approach stresses the differences between being "an instance of" and being "characterized by," the first being appropriate to particulars and the second to universals.[106] The third approach mediates between the other two calling attention to the fact that particulars have a kind of completeness that universals lack.[107] The introduction of particulars into discourse begins with basic feature-placing statements to which the subject predicate distinction is inapplicable, such as "snow is here," [108] and proceeds through analogy to genuine references to particulars.[109] Satisfactory discourse can never achieve such exclusion of singular statements as Quine wishes to achieve.[110] But neither can it get along without nonparticulars. Indeed, once the basic character of particulars and the nature of the distinctions between modes of introducing particulars and universals are understood, it is unnecessary and unnatural to decline to place universal terms in subject positions or to refuse to accord to them such secondary degrees of reality as our actual ways of thinking do accord them.[111]

The contributions of J. O. Urmson (b. 1915) of Oxford to ordinary-language analysis include an attempt to explain and refute the logical atomism and the logical positivism that preceded ordinary-language analysis, some suggestions concerning the superiority of such analysis over the earlier methods, and some significant specimens of such analysis. Logical atomism, despite its commendably analytic and anti-metaphysical slant, rests, Urmson thinks, upon a metaphysics that can claim the support neither of common sense, nor of ordinary language, nor of any exclusively tenable conventional language.[112] It leads inevitably to solipsism,[113] is unable to produce instances of its atomic sentences, underestimates the nonpictorial and conventional aspects of language, and is completely incapable of carrying through its reductive analysis.[114] Logical positivism makes no pretence of revealing "the structure of the world," but involves difficulties, such as its loss of contact with the world through excessive formalism,[115] almost as serious as those of logical atomism. What is needed in place of these earlier systematized efforts to overcome the mistakes

[105] *Ibid.*, p. 147.
[106] *Ibid.*, p. 172.
[107] *Ibid.*, pp. 180–89.
[108] *Ibid.*, p. 202.
[109] *Ibid.*, pp. 214 ff.
[110] See *ibid.*, pp. 214–21; and Strawson, "Singular Terms, Ontology and Identity," *Minds*, LXV (1956), 433–54.
[111] *Individuals*, chap. viii; Strawson,

"Proper Names," *Proceedings of the Aristotelian Society, Supplementary Vol. XXXI* (1957), 228.
[112] J. O. Urmson, *Philosophical Analysis* (Oxford: Clarendon Press, 1956), pp. 25 ff., 102 ff., 130 ff.
[113] *Ibid.*, pp. 134 ff.
[114] *Ibid.*, pp. 146 ff.
[115] *Ibid.*, pp. 117 ff.

of traditional philosophies is a much more humble and direct attempt to clear away particular linguistically initiated misunderstandings. The slogans of the new approach are: "Don't ask for the meaning, ask for the use," and "Every statement has its own logic." [116] Specimens of Urmson's own efforts to produce analyses of the requisite kind include the following suggestions: that the verb "know" belongs, along with such verbs as "believe," "deduce," "rejoice," "regret," and "conclude," to a class of verbs that have no present continuous forms and can be placed anywhere within the sentences to which they are attached without altering the meanings of the sentences; [117] that although so-called necessary truths may be conventional, it is a non-conventional fact that there must be *some* rules of language if there is to be communication; [118] that probabilities concerning inductive generalization cannot be formulated in numerical terms; [119] that the term "good" is similar to terms used in grading and like them includes among its criteria both factual and emotional considerations; [120] that "motive" is very different from cause; [121] and that recognition of kinds is dependent, if not upon the language we use, at any rate upon those rules of language by which kinds are distinguished.[122]

Without discussing at any considerable length the question of what philosophical analysis is, D. F. Pears (b. 1921) of Oxford has done a number of significant analyses that bear upon epistemological problems. One such study stresses the unavoidability of tensed verbs and hence the "categorial nature of time." [123] Another attempts to compromise the conflict between those who accept and those who reject the dichotomy of analytic and synthetic statements by suggesting that such facts as the impossibility of an object's being two different colors all over at the same time are really due to a discerned incompatibility of classes but that this incompatibility depends in part upon our having picked the classes in the way we have.[124] Other articles suggest that careful scrutiny of meaning, which is presupposed both in real-

---

[116] *Ibid.*, p. 179.

[117] J. O. Urmson, "Parenthetical Verbs," *Mind*, LXI (1952), 480–96.

[118] Urmson, "Are Necessary Truths Truths of Convention?" *Proceedings of the Aristotelian Society, Supplementary Vol. XXI* (1947), 104–17.

[119] Urmson, "Two Senses of Probable," in MacDonald, *Philosophy and Analysis* (Oxford: Basil Blackwell, 1954), pp. 191–98.

[120] Urmson, "On Grading," in Antony Flew (ed.), *Logic and Language*, 2d series, pp. 159–86.

[121] Urmson, "Motives and Causes," *Proceedings of the Aristotelian Society, Supplementary Vol. XXVI* (1953), 179–94.

[122] Urmson, "Recognition," *Proceedings of the Aristotelian Society, LVI* (1955–56), pp. 259–80.

[123] D. F. Pears, "Time, Truth and Inference," in Antony Flew, *Essays in Conceptual Analysis* (London: Macmillan & Co., Ltd., 1956), p. 251.

[124] Pears, "Incompatibilities of Colors," in Antony Flew (ed.), *Logic and Language* (Oxford: Basil Blackwell, 1955), 2d series, pp. 112–22.

ism and in nominalism, would help to remove the temptation to affirm the existence of universals [125] and also to overthrow the mistaken rejection of individuals implicit in acceptance of the identity of indiscernibles.[126] Pears contends that although the hypothethical statements of phenomenalism are peculiar and cause considerable discomfort, they remain intelligible and have proved very effective in eliminating some unwanted unknowables.[127] Concerning the problem of counterfactuals Pears suggests that our preference, in common sense and science, for hypothetical statements of which the antecedents hold is due simply to the fact that such hypotheticals facilitate quicker falsifiability and firmer confirmation rather than to any inherent want of significance in statements whose antecedents are false.[128]

In a frequently referred-to essay G. A. Paul has discussed some basic problems involved in sense-datum language.[129] The term "sense-datum" is not, he holds, objectionable on the ground of its newness, for new words can be and are often intelligibly introduced into language. The difficulty is rather that this term has certain features peculiarly likely to render it misleading. Sense-data cannot, like the referents of other terms, be located by any sort of experiment. One is unable to tell what it would be like for there to be no sense-data. Nor is there any objective test for the shape of a sense-datum. Sense-datum language is peculiarly liable to lead us to talk as though there existed a queer kind of entity to which the term "sense-datum" referred. This temptation may be avoided by the language of "looking" and "appearing," which can serve all of the purposes of sense-datum language. There is no English usage for expressions referring to sense-data continuing to exist when no one is aware of them. Tests for the having of the same data can best be worked out in behavioral terms; the introduction of imagery is pointless.[130] Paul has also commented illuminatingly upon Lenin's theory of perception, which as a representation theory is, he finds, quite remote from the manner of our actual perception.[131]

G. J. Warnock (b. 1923) is the author of a number of publications that contribute to the history of philosophy and to current philosoph-

[125] Pears, "Universals," in *ibid.*, pp. 51–64.

[126] Pears, "The Identity of Indiscernibles," *Mind*, LXIV (1955), 522–27.

[127] Pears, "The Logical Status of Supposition," *Proceedings of the Aristotelian Society, Supplementary Vol.* XXV (1951), 83–98.

[128] Pears, "Hypotheticals," in MacDonald (ed.), *Philosophy and Analysis*, pp. 210–26.

[129] G. A. Paul, "Is There a Problem about Sense-Data?" in Antony Flew (ed.), *Logic and Language* (Oxford: Basil Blackwell, 1952), 1st series, pp. 101–16.

[130] *Ibid.*, p. 115.

[131] Paul, "Lenin's Theory of Perception," in MacDonald (ed.), *Philosophy and Analysis*, pp. 278–86.

ical discussion.[132] One of the most interesting features of his thought as reflected in his book on Berkeley is his willingness to take much more seriously than most ordinary-language philosophers the traditional problems of perception. Berkeley was wrong, Warnock holds, in saying without qualification that we perceive our own ideas; but had he said instead that we *"immediately* perceive" our own sensations, he would have said something essentially sound and significant, for there is indeed a sense in which "I am, as it were, the authority on my own sensations . . . —on the question how things now appear to me." [133] It is also correct to say, Warnock suggests, that a number of statements about sensory experiences may make acceptance of a material-object statement reasonable but that since no inference is involved here and no specified number of sensation statements is required, what in fact we do is this: at some point finding further quest for sensory grounding for our material-object statements not worthwhile, we drop all reference to sensations and speak simply of material objects as such.[134] However, whatever light may be thrown upon philosophical problems by attempting to translate ordinary language into the language of sense-data, Warnock believes that clearer light is to be had if we "instead examine directly the use of the puzzling locutions themselves . . . , finding out exactly how they and related expressions are actually used." [135]

4. Ordinary Language and the Philosophy of Science

Among those writers who have adopted the essential features of ordinary-language analysis are some who have devoted substantial portions of their work to the philosophy of science. Since the major epistemological problems of philosophy of science are different both from those of traditional epistemology and from those of the main stream of ordinary-language analysis, it is to be expected that fresh suggestions would emerge from this confluence of interests in ordinary-language analysis and philosophy of science. We shall consider here very briefly some suggestions of five writers. Three are British

[132] G. J. Warnock, "Verification and the Use of Language," *Revue Internationale de Philosophie,* V (1951), 307–22; "Metaphysics in Logic," *Proceedings of the Aristotelian Society* LI (1950–51), 197–222; "Reducibility," *Proceedings of the Aristotelian Society, Supplementary Vol. XXVI* (1952); Warnock, "Every Event Has a Cause," in Antony Flew (ed.), *Logic and Language,* 2d series (1953), pp. 95–111;

Warnock, "Seeing," *Proceedings of the Aristotelian Society,* LV (1954–55), 201–18; Warnock, *Berkeley* (London: Penguin Books, Ltd., 1953); Warnock, *English Philosophy Since 1900* (London: Oxford University Press, 1958).
[133] *Berkeley,* p. 161.
[134] *Ibid.,* pp. 182 ff.
[135] *Ibid.,* p. 244.

philosophers who have been in direct contact with the ordinary-language movement. One is a British-educated American and one a native of Finland who taught for a number of years at Cambridge. *A. R. B. Braithwaite* (b. 1900) of Cambridge, who acknowledges special indebtedness to Moore, Wittgenstein, Ramsey, and J. M. Keynes, has endeavored in characterizing the logic of science to do justice alike to the insights of Hume, the actual procedures of scientists, and the claims of common sense. The basis on which science rests, Braithwaite holds, is experience, not in the subjective or phenomenalistic sense, but, generally speaking, in the ordinary sense in which physical objects are said to be observed. This is the basis upon which scientific discoveries proceed, and the conflict between phenomenalism and realism need not be injected into the philosophy of science.[1] Acceptance of an observational basis is not, however, to be so construed as to exclude such "private data of immediate experience" as may be found useful in psychology or economics. Such data are in certain cases "deducible from general hypotheses," and "the publicity of its data is . . . not the hallmark of a science." [2]

In addition to basic experience a scientific system requires a formal calculus consisting of marks with rules and an eventual interpretation. The more general hypotheses of the system will constitute its apex, and observation-statements its base. If a set of observations is entailed by an hypothesis the failure of any one of the observations involved will falsify the hypothesis; but since most of the observation-statements with which science is concerned are entailed not by single hypotheses but by a group of them, a given hypothesis threatened by the failure of an observation may be saved by relinquishing some other hypothesis in the group. A given hypothesis tends to be confirmed not only by those observations which it generalizes but also by all other observations that strengthen other hypotheses with which it is linked in the deductive system of science. One must not suppose, as Russell did, that the theoretical concepts of science, such as those of atoms and electrons, are "logically constructed out of observable entities," for to do so is to render these concepts "incapable of being modified to explain new sorts of facts." [3] Implicit definitions of the theoretical terms of a scientific theory can be satisfactorily given by "reciting the initial formulae of the theory's calculus." [4] Scientific insight is often facilitated by the use of models in which the basic definitions become not only logically but also epis-

[1] R. B. Braithwaite, *Scientific Explanations* (Cambridge: Cambridge University Press, 1953), pp. 2 ff.; cf. also "Propositions about Material Objects," *Proceedings of the Aristotelian Society*, XXXVIII (1939–40), 268–90.

[2] *Scientific Explanations*, p. 8.

[3] *Ibid.*, p. 53.

[4] *Ibid.*, p. 78.

temologically prior to observations, but models are dangerous in that they may tempt one to attribute to the model empirical character-istics "other than those which made the model an appropriate one." [5]

In view of the difficulties of sustaining empirical generalizations, philosophers of science have in recent decades increasingly looked to theory of probability for support for induction.[6] Genuine statistical probability statements such as that "the probability of a radium atom disintegrating within 1,700 years is approximately $\frac{1}{2}$" must be carefully distinguished from so-called probability statements that attempt to attach probability to theories, such as that the probability of the theory that "influenza is . . . a virus disease," is represented by a certain fraction.[7] The characteristic attributed in the latter sort of instances is better referred to as "reasonableness of belief" than as "probability." [8] Genuine probability statements come to be applicable and hence empirically meaningful only when some rule is adopted in terms of which they are to be rejected, but the degree of stringency of the rejection rule must depend upon the purpose of the investigation, and each rejection must be subject to further rein-forcement or subsequent retraction by further tests.[9] Induction can be assimilated to deduction neither by assuming a major premise, nor by stressing the mere probability of the conclusion, nor by any other method. Its justification, insofar as it needs one, must consist rather, as Peirce pointed out, in its success in yielding true predic-tions.[10] By simple enumeration one may assay the success of various more refined inductive policies, and if induction itself is involved in this process it enters rather as a principle of inference than as a premise. If a given inductive policy frequently yields successful pre-dictions, it is already sufficiently justified;[11] for only inductive pol-icies regularly yield such results, and to demand more is to demand what is not possible.

Scientific laws are, as Hume pointed out, constant conjunctions, requiring no added principle of necessity. This does not mean that they involve no more than the conditional of the usual propositional calculus, in terms of which every conditional having a false ante-cedent is thereby confirmed. They are rather correctly said to in-volve subjunctive conditionals such as would hold if the antecedent were true. However, what makes the subjunctive appropriate and distinguishes scientific laws from accidental conjunctions is neither logical nor natural necessity but the fact that scientific laws are not

[5] *Ibid.*, p. 93.

[6] Braithwaite, "Probability and Induc-tion," in C. A. Mace, *British Philosophy in the Mid-Century*, p. 135.

[7] *Ibid.*, p. 136.

[8] *Ibid.*, pp. 136 f.; cf. also *Scientific Ex-planation*, pp. 118 ff.

[9] *Ibid.*, chaps. vi–vii.

[10] *Ibid.*, pp. 264 ff.

[11] *Ibid.*, pp. 267 ff.

only true conditionals but also belong to deductive systems whereas accidental connections do not.[12] Teleological explanation may not be as fundamental as causal explanation, but, like the latter, it involves deductive links and successful prediction. Moreover, it may be quite useful when causal explanation cannot be achieved.[13] In passing it should also be noted that formal calculi may, according to Braithwaite, go a long way toward resolving ethical differences even when agreement concerning ends cannot be achieved.[14]

B. Stephen E. Toulmin (b. 1922) of the University of Leeds has brought basic insights of the ordinary-language approach to philosophy to bear upon a number of important issues in philosophy of science, ethics, and epistemology.

Inquiry into the foundations of scientific knowledge must at the outset, Toulmin thinks, distinguish carefully between empirical or natural history generalizations on the one hand and scientific theories, principles, laws, and models on the other. Empirical generalizations are deeply rooted in the classifications of ordinary language.[15] Their logic is the traditional logic and they are linked with their instances by deductive ties that require the rejection of a generalization in case of the failure of an instance. Considerable progress in achieving empirical generalizations must be made before science can begin, but such generalizations are not themselves science. They tabulate without explaining and they lack that specific and systematic order that is characteristic of genuine scientific statements.[16] In contrast to empirical generalizations, scientific theories and laws, though "drawing their life from the phenomena they are used to explain," [17] are products of controlled imagination.[18] Apparent exceptions to a theory or law can either be explained by other laws or ruled out by limiting the range of the theory or law. Scientific theories and laws are not so much true or false statements as guides to experience having wider or narrower fields of application.[19] They are not premises but principles of inference.[20] They function somewhat as do maps that guide one through a territory without strictly implying anything concerning that territory.[21]

Inductive inference requires no metaphysical principle of uniformity of nature but is sufficiently supported by a methodological

[12] Ibid., pp. 295 ff.
[13] Ibid., pp. 339 ff.
[14] Braithwaite, "Common Action Toward Different Moral Ends," Proceedings of the Aristotelian Society, LIII (1952–53), 29–46; Braithwaite, Theory of Games as a Tool for the Moral Philosopher (Cambridge: Cambridge University Press, 1955).
[15] Stephen Toulmin, The Philosophy of Science (London: Hutchinson's University Library, 1953), pp. 50 ff.
[16] Ibid., pp. 52 f.
[17] Ibid., p. 39.
[18] Ibid., pp. 43 ff.
[19] Ibid., pp. 79 ff.
[20] Ibid., p. 102.
[21] Ibid., pp. 105 ff.

assumption that inductive problems can be solved.[22] The basic term in probability theory is not the substantive "probability" but the adverb "probably," which is rather an indication of a way of speaking than a description of a situation. Adequate recognition of this fact would tend to eliminate the temptation either to transform probability into relative frequency, or to make paradoxical claims to the effect that a statement can be probable but untrue, or to distinguish between probabilities of facts and probabilities of statements.[23]

The necessary statements used in science and elsewhere are not, Toulmin contends, to be so sharply separated from empirical statements as is commonly thought. Advocates of a synthetic theory of necessary statements must of course admit that one does not "see" the truth of such statements in the same way that one sees empirical facts, but advocates of an analytic theory of necessary statements must admit that recognition of the truth of such statements does not depend solely upon definition. What is required for recognition of the truth of many necessary statements, such as that both of the starting contestants in a "knock-down" regatta cannot enter the finals, or that a thing cannot be both of two colors all over, is understanding of the situations on which the statements are made.[24] In any case it would be a mistake to think that the "only statements representing genuine propositions are those which are straightforwardly classifiable either as necessary or as contingent." [25]

The error of forcing judgments into rigid patterns and failing to recognize the flexibility of ordinary language is especially apparent in the sphere of moral judgments. Both objective and subjective ethical theorists have mistakenly supposed that reasons could be given in support of moral judgments only in case some property or process could be found to correspond to ethical concepts. Finding no such concepts, both have been unable to account for the fact that "there may yet be ethical differences, even when all sources of factual disagreement have been ruled out." [26] Assuming, as has been commonly done since the days of Pearson and Mach, that cognitive statements are descriptive only, emotivists in ethics have reasoned that since ethical language is not descriptive, it must be mere emotion or persuasion.[27] But the fact is that decription is only one

[22] *Ibid.*, pp. 104 ff.

[23] Toulmin, "Probability," in Antony Flew (ed.), *Essays in Conceptual Analysis* (London: Macmillan & Co., Ltd., 1956), pp. 157–91.

[24] Toulmin, "A Defense of Synthetic Necessary Truths," *Mind*, LVIII (1949), 164–77.

[25] *The Philosophy of Science*, p. 103.

[26] Toulmin, *An Examination of the Place of Reason in Ethics* (Cambridge: Cambridge University Press, 1950), p. 44.

[27] Stephen Toulmin and Kurt Baier, "On Describing," *Mind*, LXV (1956), 13–18.

special mode of expression in a sphere of language that has room for many modes of expression. A considerable variety of reasons can be given in support of an ethical judgment, depending, for example, upon whether or not the judgment is made within a context of accepted moral rules.[28]

A major mistake that has haunted epistemology in all areas from the beginning is the futile endeavor to assimilate all knowledge to analytic knowledge and to regard all statements that are not analytic as deficient. Actually, analytic knowledge covers a relatively narrow range of arguments, and arguments as actually used can be logical, deductive, and even necessary without being analytic.[29] Much of the temptation to assimilate all valid arguments to analytic statements would disappear if one would look at arguments in their actual contexts and distinguish the warrant which connects data and conclusions from the backing by which warrants are supported. Thus, for example, from the datum that Peterson is a Swede, one may infer the conclusion that Peterson is probably not a Roman Catholic by the warrant that "a Swede can be taken to be almost certainly not a Roman Catholic," with the backing that "the proportion of Roman Catholic Swedes is less than 2%"; but, in this instance as in many others, while the data and the warrant entail the conclusion, the data and the backing do not.[30] The task of the epistemologist, who must work hand in hand with the practically oriented logician,[31] is not indeed to press all judgments into a single analytic mold but to discern what in the actual process of inquiry is common to various fields of knowledge and what is peculiar to each, not to demand that knowledge claims in a given field "measure up against analytic standards" but to discern "whatever sort of cogency or well-foundedness can relevantly be asked for in that field."[32] Thus, "the absence of entailments from substantial arguments . . . is nothing to regret, or to apologize for, or to try to change." It is "characteristic . . . of our very fields of argument."[33]

C. J. O. Wisdom of the London School of Economics has presented, along with some interesting suggestions concerning the nature of philosophical inquiry, a view of scientific knowledge similar in important respects to views of Reichenbach and Popper. After surveying the historical transition from speculative to analytic philosophy, Wisdom concludes that philosophy is a shadow cast upon

[28] *An Examination of the Place of Reason in Ethics*, pp. 150 ff.; cf. also Toulmin, "Knowledge of Right and Wrong," *Proceedings of the Aristotelian Society*, L (1949–50), 139–56.

[29] Toulmin, *The Uses of Argument* (Cambridge: Cambridge University Press, 1958), pp. 135 ff.

[30] *Ibid.*, pp. 209 ff.

[31] *Ibid.*, pp. 254 ff.

[32] *Ibid.*, p. 248.

[33] *Ibid.*, p. 250.

the "wall of reality" by the falling of the light of "the unconscious energy and desires" of the philosopher on the philosopher himself.[34] Philosophy involves speculation—which reveals the nature not of reality but of the philosopher—logical analysis, which is essentially logic, and psychocentrics, which discloses the philosophical form of "the way in which man reacts to his environment." [35] A sample of psychocentrics is Wisdom's study of Berkeley, in which he traces the leading ideas of Berkeley's philosophy to childhood complexes and points out that while "the analysis of a philosophy does not itself refute the philosophy" it does afford "a good practical indication of whether or not there is something objective present." [36]

An example of logical analysis is Wisdom's study of scientific inference. Wisdom rejects induction in favor of hypothetico-deductive inference whose validity rests upon a kind of bet on the nature of the universe. Induction, which Wisdom takes to consist strictly of generalizations based upon instances, fails to sustain either noninstantial concepts, such as gravitation,[37] or the interpolations and extrapolations of instantial generalization.[38] Induction can be justified neither as deduction from general principles, nor as sheer descriptive fact,[39] nor as probable inference.[40] The problem of the justification of induction is not indeed a pseudo-problem, but it is a problem that has no solution.[41] The successor to the problem of the justification of induction is the problem of the reasonableness of the adoption of "unfalsified hypotheses." [42] Such an adoption is deductively valid provided the universe is favorable toward unfalsified hypotheses, although it is always possible that the universe is not. "Thus our real hope of success is to gamble on the universe being favorable." [43] This account, Wisdom suggests, differs from Reichenbach's solution of the problem of induction mainly in not being tied to a frequency view of probability and in vindicating not induction as such but the hypothetico-deductive method actually practiced by modern scientists.[44]

D. The topics with which the epistemologically oriented essays of Max Black of Cornell (b. 1909) have been concerned include the character of philosophical inquiry, the nature of logical and mathe-

[34] J. O. Wisdom, *The Metamorphosis of Philosophy* (Càiro: Al Maaref Press, 1947), p. 207.

[35] *Ibid.*, p. 218.

[36] J. O. Wisdom, *The Unconscious Roots of Berkeley's Philosophy* (London: Hogarth Press & Institute of Psychoanalysis, 1953), p. 230.

[37] J. O. Wisdom, *Foundations of Infer-* *ence in Natural Science* (London: Methuen & Co., Ltd., 1952), Pt. I.

[38] *Ibid.*, Pt. II.

[39] *Ibid.*

[40] *Ibid.*, Pt. III.

[41] *Ibid.*, Pt. II.

[42] *Ibid.*, p. 223.

[43] *Ibid.*, p. 229.

[44] *Ibid.*, pp. 231 f.

matical necessity, the problem of basic sentences of empirical knowledge, and the problem òf induction.

Philosophical inquiry, Black holds, is not metaphysics, but neither is it science [45] nor the investigation of artificial languages.[46] Rather, philosophical inquiry is a mode of linguistic analysis. Sometimes Black seems to suggest that the analysis is mainly concerned with concepts, and a conceptual aspect of analysis is never entirely lost sight of, but for the most part Black's analysis seems to be concerned with natural linguistic expressions. Among the primary tasks of analysis are the discernment of the types, levels, and degrees of complexity of linguistic expressions.[47] The notion of analysis seems to involve a paradox noticed by Moore in that, for example, whereas to say that "being a brother is identical with being a male sibling" would seem to be to say the same thing as "being a brother = being a brother," the two statements do not by any means say the same thing.[48] But this paradox can be resolved by keeping in mind that one cannot assimilate "a mere identity with a proposition in which a non-identical relation is a component." [49] Analysis is in general "clarification of meaning," but there is no simple "analysis of analysis," and it is a mark of living analysis "to resist arbitrary confinement." [50] Attempts to say what we mean seem inevitably to involve irreducible metaphors. While some metaphors are such that literal language can be substituted for them, others are not.[51] These latter gain their expressive force from interactions of the systems of meaning that they bring together, and they are often more satisfactory than literal statements in allowing the experienced interpreter to achieve a proper distribution of emphasis that could not be achieved by literal expressions.[52]

Although a priori or necessary statements differ from ordinary factual ones in being in general formal, they are not separated from factual statements by any hard and fast barriers, for formal statements seem to involve factual connections and any factual statement can by appropriate stipulations be transformed into a formal one.[53]

[45] Max Black, *Philosophical Analysis* (Ithaca, N.Y.: Cornell University Press, 1950), pp. 5 ff.

[46] Black, *Problems of Analysis* (Ithaca, N.Y.: Cornell University Press, 1954), chap. xiv.

[47] Black, "Philosophical Analysis," *Proceedings of the Aristotelian Society,* XXXIII (1932–33), 237–58.

[48] Black, "The Paradox of Analysis," *Mind,* LIII (1944), 263 ff.

[49] *Ibid.,* p. 265; see also Black, "The Paradox of Analysis Again," *Mind,* LIV

(1945), 272–73; and "How Can Analysis Be Informative?" *Philosophy and Phenomenological Research,* VI (1946), 628–31.

[50] *Philosophical Analysis,* p. 14.

[51] Black, "Metaphors," *Proceedings of the Aristotelian Society,* LV (1954–55), 278.

[52] *Ibid.,* pp. 258 ff.

[53] Black, "Conventionalism in Geometry and Necessary Statements," *Philosophy of Science,* IX (1942), 335–49; and *Problems of Analysis,* pp. 172–290, 298–99; cf. "Necessary Statements and Rules," *Philosophical Review,* LXVII (1958), 313–41.

Even such statements as are clearly necessary cannot be said to depend for their necessity merely upon linguistic conventions.[54] At very least their necessity depends upon *prior* acceptance of linguistic rules,[55] and for the most part the relation of implicans and implicate seems at any rate to involve a demand that one *"see* that it is impossible for the one to be true and the other false."[56] The necessity involved in mathematics is much like that in logic, but the logistic thesis that absorbs mathematics into logic or deduces mathematics from logic cannot be carried through. Whereas "logic is syntax of possible states of affairs," mathematics is the syntax of *all* organized systems.[57]

Concerning the sort of basic statements on which knowing is often supposed to rest, Black rejects the view that scientific statements about elementary particles such as electrons are basic, on the ground that such statements already involve substantial interpretation.[58] He is equally hostile to the logical atomism of Wittgenstein and Russell for the reason that such atomism mistakenly oversimplifies language and depends upon an untenable principle of acquaintance.[59] The sense-datum theory fares no better at Black's hands, for no communicative use is possible for terms referring to what is by definition entirely private.[60] This does not, however, mean that Black takes some physical object statements to be known.[61] Indeed, from the beginning Black has been inclined to oppose the adoption of all manner of primitives and to regard the growth of knowledge as coherently cumulative rather than as linearly deductive.[62]

The insuperable difficulty encountered by attempts to justify induction is, Black thinks, that the problem is so formulated that no justification is possible.[63] By common consent induction is argument "permitting the negation of the conclusion to be consistent with the joint assertion of all the premises." [64] Accordingly the sort of deductive justification of induction often demanded is logically impossible. The addition of a necessary premise can make no difference, and neither can the attempt to inject a probability calculus.[65] Attempts, like that of Reichenbach, to justify induction on pragmatic grounds

[54] *Ibid.*

[55] Black, "The Analysis of a Simple Necessary Statement," *Journal of Philosophy,* XL (1943), 39–46.

[56] *Ibid.,* p. 279.

[57] *The Nature of Mathematics,* p. 144.

[58] Black, *Language and Philosophy* (Ithaca, N.Y.: Cornell University Press, 1949), pp. 234 ff.

[59] *Ibid.,* pp. 152 ff., 122 ff.

[60] *Ibid.,* 18 ff.; *Problems of Analysis,* pp. 58–79.

[61] Black, "Certainty and Empirical Statements," *Mind,* LI (1942), 361–67; "Problems of Analysis," p. 36.

[62] Cf. *The Nature of Mathematics,* pp. 140 ff.

[63] *Language and Philosophy,* pp. 66 ff; *Problems of Analysis,* pp. 187 ff.

[64] *Language and Philosophy,* p. 67.

[65] *Ibid.,* pp. 67 ff.

are also of no avail, for being infinitely flexible they afford no criteria, and to claim that induction is self-correcting only begs the question.[66] In the case of particular inductive rules there can be excellent reasons for acceptance,[67] but the possibility and indeed the likelihood remains—Lewis and other to the contrary notwithstanding —that there are series concerning which it is quite "impossible to make probability judgments." [68]

E. Although G. H. von Wright (b. 1916), formerly of Cambridge and now of Helsinki, is principally a logician and philosopher of science, he has long been closely associated with British philosophers of ordinary language and has consistently endeavored to work out his constructions with due regard to the claims of common usage. The topics that have principally concerned him are those of induction and modal logic.

By inductive inference is meant, von Wright holds, the following: "from the fact that something is true of a certain number of members of a class we conclude that the same thing will be true of unknown members of that class." [69] No attempts to validate this principle upon a priori grounds can, von Wright thinks, in the nature of the case succeed. Hume has shown that there can be no synthetic a priori vindication of it,[70] and Kant was never able to indicate how his synthetic a priori could be applied.[71] Attempts to deduce inductive statements from more general laws always fall back in the end upon analytic statements and so assume what was to be proved, as do all other attempts to establish induction deductively. Either we define things so that all A's are B's or else we say when an apparent failure occurs that A only appears to be present or B to fail.[72] The attempt to reduce inductive relations to mere conventions succeeds only in pushing the problem back into the area of the coordination of facts to conventions.[73]

Attempts to justify induction upon a posteriori grounds fare little better. Mere deduction of data affords no basis for prediction unless alternative hypotheses can be eliminated; [74] and since it is in the nature of the case impossible to examine all relevant alternatives, such elimination can never be carried through. Hence Mill's methods are no better than heuristic devices.[75] Indeed, not even a

---

[66] Problems of Analysis, pp. 157–87.
[67] Ibid., pp. 191–208.
[68] Ibid., p. 225.
[69] Cf. G. H. von Wright, A Treatise on Induction and Probability (London: Routledge & Kegan Paul, Ltd., 1951), pp. 13 f.; also von Wright, The Logical Problem of Induction (Oxford: Basil Blackwell, 1957), p. 1.

[70] The Logical Problem of Induction, pp. 18 ff.
[71] Ibid., pp. 22 ff.
[72] Ibid., pp. 38 f.
[73] Ibid., pp. 40 ff.
[74] Ibid., pp. 59 f.
[75] Ibid., pp. 76 ff.; cf. A Treatise on Induction and Probability, chap. iv.

probability of inductive inference can be established, for while a fairly satisfactory calculus of probability can be set up, attempts to tie facts to the calculus must vindicate inductive inference either analytically or not at all.[76] Thus, if by a guarantee of induction is meant conclusive verification of inductive predictions or generalizations, no such guarantee is possible. Indeed, that negative conclusion is a kind of disguised tautology implicit in the formulation of the problem itself. Since the problem concerns inference to unknown members of a class, to claim to know the members in question would be a kind of contradiction. Our failure to see this fact at once is due simply to our not being clear as to the kind of vindication of induction we seek.[77] Accordingly, that we cannot justify induction in the sense of proving it ought not to disturb us. For science and common sense it is enough that we do think inductions made in accord with certain principles probable and rational. The task of philosophy with reference to induction is simply the critical one of bringing to light the impossibility of finding a proof of induction and accordingly freeing thought for the constructive task of building a calculus of probability that accords with our intuitions concerning observed occurrences and yields satisfactory scientific results. In this connection it is worthy of note that what renders our actual inductions plausible and interests the scientist is not merely "observation of a *regularity* of a certain kind but observation of *changes* of a certain kind." [78]

The major objective of most of von Wright's various studies of *formal* logic is that of setting up rigorous formal calculi subject to definite decision procedures and in accord with our intuitions concerning quantifications and modalities. Thus he undertakes to show how mechanical decision procedures in terms of truth functions and normal forms can be achieved, not only for ordinary truth-functional statements, but also for the kinds of generalizations involved in syllogisms and even for modal statements referring to possibilities, necessities, and contingencies.[79] Von Wright believes that a rigorous logic of epistemic statements or statements containing such words as "know" can be developed parallel to the logic of ordinary modal statements. He undertakes to sketch a similar logic for "ought" statements.[80]

[76] See *The Logical Problem of Induction*, pp. 54, 176–82.

[77] *Ibid.*, pp. 178 ff.; cf. *A Treatise on Induction and Probability*, pp. 20 ff.

[78] Von Wright, *Logical Studies* (London: Routledge and Kegan Paul, Ltd., 1957), p. 157.

[79] Von Wright, *An Essay in Modal Logic* (Amsterdam: North-Holland Pub. Co., 1951); and *Logical Studies*.

[80] See *Essays in Modal Logic*, chaps. iv–v; and *Logical Studies*, chap. iv.

5. COMMENTS CONCERNING ORDINARY-LANGUAGE ANALYSIS

Although the theory and practice of ordinary-language analysis varies considerably among advocates of this way of doing philosophy, such analysis may be said, broadly speaking, to consist of an attempt to map the logic of the common ways of correct expression in a given language by disclosing significant patterns in what informed users of the language are inclined to say in varied circumstances. In commenting upon the application of this method to epistemological problems, we shall first focus attention briefly on four representative suggestions of ordinary-language analysts and then turn to the more general problem of the usefulness of the method of ordinary-language analysis in further epistemological inquiry. The four representative suggestions to be considered are ordinary-language interpretations of epistemic terms as having paradigm cases, and as achievement, dispositional, and performatory terms.

A. (*1*) Against the claim that we cannot know any matter of material fact, ordinary-language analysts have sometimes argued to the effect that the use of such terms as "know" as applicable to material objects would be meaningless if there were no instances of knowledge of material objects, and that since such usage evidently is not meaningless, there must be some matters of material fact that we know. This sort of argument has attractive simplicity and, whether valid or not, calls attention to some important considerations relating to knowledge. It reminds us that the meanings of some terms are learned largely through acquaintance with their instances and could be gotten at best only with great difficulty if there were no instances. It also properly recognizes that responsible people repeatedly use the term "know" of all manner of material facts with such complete confidence that something seems to have gone wrong when philosophers begin to assert that we can know no matters of material fact, and that these philosophers' assertions are to say the least highly misleading.

Nevertheless the paradigm-case argument cannot be accepted at face value. To begin with, the argument that in order to be meaningful a term has to have instances is applicable, if at all, only to simple ostensively defined terms. If a term is complex, it is always possible that while its ingredient elements may be simple and have each its instances, the complex term itself may have been artificially compounded so as to correspond to nothing at all in the material world. Actually, it is not even certain that simple terms always have applications, for what is intended in a simple term may sometimes be suggested in other ways than by direct encounter. In any case, the term "know" in the sense in question is evidently complex, and accordingly such that the nonoccurrence of an instance of its application remains at least conceivable, however unlikely. A basic difficulty in the paradigm-case argument is, as Wittgenstein has properly noted, that it is built from the start upon the mistaken notion that every meaningful term must designate something.[1] The argument has also, of course, no bearing at all upon the sort of question that some philosophers raise when they ask whether or not in some special philosophical sense we know matters of material fact. The most that can be claimed along the lines indicated by the argument is something like what Moore properly claimed, namely that in the ordinary sense of the term "know" we do in fact (not in logical necessity) know some matters of material fact.

(2) Ordinary-language analysis has, in the work of Ryle, produced the significant suggestion that certain key epistemic words such as "know," "perceive," "see," and "hear" are not, as often supposed, process words like "run," "travel," and "seek" but rather achievement words like "win," "arrive," and "find." This suggestion is said to have the advantage of avoiding the temptations, on the one hand, to say that one can "know what is not the case" or see what is not there, and on the other hand, to suppose that the observable processes of looking and listening require other supplementation by other processes, especially by inward processes of seeing, hearing, and perhaps intuition.

Certainly one cannot long consider the actual uses of the terms in question without recognizing that these terms are in fact achievement terms at least in the sense that they refer to completed operations. To know or see or perceive something at all is already to have apprehended that thing. Hence, not only is Ryle's suggestion that key epistemic terms are achievement terms essentially sound, but the first advantage claimed for that suggestion clearly holds. Once it is recognized that knowing, perceiving, seeing, and hearing are achievements and not merely processes, the inclination to speak of knowing, perceiving, seeing, or hearing unsuccessfully or erroneously disappears in that when relevant success has not been achieved the terms in question are simply inapplicable.

The other advantage sometimes claimed for the recognition of the achievement character of key epistemic terms—that it avoids the need to inject other processes, especially inward ones, in addition to the observable processes of looking and listening and the like, into

[1] See Strawson, review of Wittgenstein's *Philosophical Investigations*, *Mind*, LXIII (1954).

cognition—is much more doubtful in at least three ways. First, it must be seriously doubted that looking and listening are themselves quite properly characterized as observable processes; for what can be observed about these processes is at best only one aspect of what is characteristic of them, and one might have ample opportunity to observe another person and yet be altogether mistaken concerning whether or not that person was looking or listening. Second, whether or not seeing and hearing involve inward processes, something seems to be going on in seeing and hearing that is not present in looking and listening; and whatever this is that is going on cannot be gotten rid of by distinguishing between processes and achievements. Third, whether or not seeing and hearing are themselves inward processes, they seem at least to imply something very like inward process that cannot be excluded by distinguishing between process and achievement words, for seeing or hearing is normally at least being literally aware of something over an appreciable interval of time.

(3) One of the most widely acclaimed products of ordinary-language analysis is the view, again of which Ryle has been the principal exponent, that knowledge is dispositional. According to this view, an instance of knowledge is neither an event nor a habit, neither a process nor a structure, but a disposition consisting of a set of facts to the effect that the person said to possess the knowledge would respond to certain situations in certain ways.

This dispositional account of knowledge involves a number of wholesome correctives of mistaken trends in epistemology. To begin with, it properly points out, against epistemologists who have over-emphasized cognitive acts, that instances of knowledge are not necessarily cognitive occurrences and that they can exist in the absence of such occurrences. Aristotle was well aware that one can know many things to which his attention is at the moment in no sense directed, and so may anyone else be aware who unambiguously raises the question. We know the alphabet, the multiplication tables, and multitudes of facts that we have previously learned, not only when we are thinking of them but also when we are thinking of other things or not thinking of anything at all. The dispositional view of knowledge also correctly points out against epistemologists who are too much inclined to think of knowledge as copying facts, that even an instance of awareness of a fact can scarcely count as an instance of knowledge apart from a capacity to continue to respond appropriately in a variety of circumstances. For example, even if one looks directly at an automobile parked in front of his house, he can scarcely be said to know that automobile is there unless he is capable of identifying locations and recognizing automobiles; and one can scarcely be said to know the sum of two numbers if he can give the correct answer only when he is adding numbers of oranges. Again, the dispositional account of knowledge properly points out, against those who confine discussion of knowledge to private theaters of cognitive experience, that instances of knowledge manifest themselves in both nonverbal and verbal behavior. Whatever may go on in private consciousness, what counts as knowledge in public communication is what is manifested by words and deeds. The schoolboy who says he knows the answer but can't give it has a poor case, and as for the farmer who is said to have a percept of a ditch across his path and straightway walks into the ditch, we are inclined to doubt if he knew that a ditch was across his path even if he says he knew. Finally, against epistemologists who become prematurely bogged down in discussion of the internal structure of knowledge, the dispositional account of knowledge usefully reminds us that discourse concerning knowledge can be carried a long way in terms of description of what would be said or done under certain circumstances without raising disturbing questions concerning epistemological structures or processes.

Nevertheless, dispositional accounts of knowledge are inadequate and misleading in several important respects. In part these infelicities seem to be due to failure of what advocates of the dispositional view wish to say about knowledge to square with some persistent connotations of the term "dispositional," and in part they seem to be due to failure of what these philosophers wish to say about knowledge in accord with the conotations of "dispositional" to square with plausible description or explanation of what is commonly called knowledge.

One misleading feature of dispositional accounts of knowledge is that they tend to obscure a multiplicity and diversity in knowledge that are not to be found in dispositions in the usual sense. A disposition in the usual sense is, generally speaking, a pattern of tendencies so broad that the number of terms available to characterize dispositions is for the most part limited to a few dozen words. Moreover, a disposition in the usual sense is like a character, and unlike a trait or a mood, in being something that a person has, generally speaking, only one of at any given period of his life. But the number and variety of the pieces of knowledge that are possible may approach the virtually limitless number and variety of the things that there are, and the number and variety of those that one might at any time properly be said to have could well be far greater than that of the whole vocabulary of rich language. To be sure, advocates of dispositional accounts of knowledge are to some extent aware of these considerations, and they sometimes point out that they are using the term "disposition" in a specialized (extraordinary) sense; but the term does not lend itself readily to such stretching as they impose upon it, and its common connotations keep coming back to obscure both for them and for those that follow them the richness and variety of our knowledge.

Another closely related misleading feature of dispositional accounts of knowledge is their tendency to obscure a certain relevance to particular facts that is required of manifestations of instances of knowledge but not of manifestations of dispositions. In order to count as a manifestation of a disposition an occurrence need only belong to a broad class of occurrences in keeping with the character of the disposition ascribed. For example, to count as a manifestation of a calm disposition an action need only be calm, and to count as a manifestation of an irascible disposition a response need only be irascible. But in order to count as a manifestation of knowledge, a response must be relevant to the particular fact or set of facts said to be known. For example, to count as a manifestation of my knowing that five plus seven is twelve, my words or actions must be either a statement or an action that in some sense implies, or has reference to, just that fact. Similarly, if I am said to know that a friend is dead, the action or words that manifest this fact must be relevant to this particular fact, as, for example, my not going at the usual time to the place at which I was accustomed to meet him or my visiting his grave.

A further misleading feature of dispositional accounts of knowledge is that their usual behavioristic slant obscures the cardinal role of conscious experience in the occurrences into which knowings are for the most part felt to be cashable. Thus, for example, while my knowing that five times eight equals forty or that an old friend is now in town need not require that I be thinking of these facts but does require that I normally be prepared to respond with appropriate words or deeds when occasion arises, it surely seems also to require that I be capable upon appropriate occasions of awareness of the facts in question. So deeply imbedded is this sort of consideration in our ways of thought and language that to call anything that could never issue in awareness or anything "knowledge" would appear to be an outrageous abuse of language. Moreover, the best basis for saying that one knows a certain fact is often not that he behaves in a certain way but that he is having or has had certain conscious experiences. "How do I know that the apple is red? Well, I see it." Or, "How do I know he has gone? I saw him leave." In such knowledge claims the reports may be verbal behavior, but what is reported as a primary manifestation of knowledge is not behavior at all but experience.

A final objection to predominately depositional accounts of knowledge is that by describing knowledge largely in terms of certain responses under the impact of certain stimuli, they tend to mask our ignorance of what lies between stimulus and response and to cut off psychological and epistemological inquiry prematurely. To focus attention with reference to knowledge upon the question of what emerges in what situations can indeed be helpful by way of postponing difficult questions and even gaining constructive insights, but the whole area between stimulus and response, or situation and reaction, is surely not a blank, and problems concerning its structures and operations are not only crucial to the psychologist but also basic to the epistemologist. The analogy of dispositional accounts of physical properties is in this respect illuminating. While to speak of a physical property such as solubility in terms of what happens when certain things are done can often be illuminating, but to regard such an account as the whole story about such properties would tend to obscure basic questions concerning what lies between the initial situation and the resulting outcome and so to cut out much of the very heart of a scientific inquiry that refuses to stop with gross situations and results and thrives upon the quest for minute intervening structures and events.

(4) Austin's suggestion that such terms as "know," especially when used in the first person present singular, are not merely descriptive terms but performatory ones akin to "promise" has, like the dispositional account of knowledge, come to be widely accepted. Moreover, it accurately reflects some significant features of actual usage. Certainly in prefacing statements by "I know," we are doing something more than simply making the statements, else we should not persist in using the preface. While the something more may often involve other features, such as resistance to questions or doubts that have been raised, it seems nearly always to involve the sort of performatory commitment of which Austin writes. Austin's suggestion also seems to have most of the significant uses that he claims for it and some others besides. It links the term "know" with multitudes of terms that are not purely descriptive and stimulates consideration of the interesting suggestion that all expressions have nondescriptive aspects. It helps us to see hitherto unnoticed ways in which statements can go wrong, why it sometimes happens that one can legitimately say that he knows what in actuality is false and why one may decline to say that he knew what in fact he does know. More specifically it enables us to explain the plausibility of the paradoxical

formula "if I know I can't be wrong" without accepting that formula; it shows why one should never say he knows when he is aware of any special reason for thinking he might be wrong though in fact he might be wrong.

However, while epistemic terms often have performatory functions they also nearly always, as Austin would be among the first to acknowledge, have descriptive functions, and it is with the descriptive functions that epistemologists are primarily concerned. Unfortunately the analysis of the performatory functions of epistemic terms throws relatively little light upon these descriptive functions save by way of disclosing that they may claim no exclusive rights. Moreover, concerning the traditional problems of cognitive relations and the justification of knowledge claims, the analysis of performatory functions accomplishes little besides making philosophers a little less uncomfortable in their failure to solve these problems, and this may turn out to be a dubious blessing.

B. The foregoing comments concerning four suggestions selected from a wide range of significant suggestions by ordinary-language analysts should be sufficient to indicate that ordinary-language analysis is on the one hand capable of penetrating insights into matters relating to theory of knowledge but has thus far in the main dealt with problems upon the periphery of the subject and sometimes presented ill-balanced views of cognitive situations. However, ordinary-language analysis is relatively new and the deficiencies in question could be due to other factors than the character of such analysis itself. What we have now to ask is then what in general are the prospects for fruitful contributions to epistemological inquiry through ordinary-language analysis.

Just by virtue of what ordinary-language analysis for the most part is, as detailed inquiry into the logic of ordinary language and endeavor to straighten it out a little, a number of significant gains in epistemology may be expected through such analysis. First, philosophers may be expected more than ever to unlock and bring to light the treasures of epistemological wisdom lying ready in the modes of our common speech. And that wisdom is far greater than is likely to be supposed; for many a shade of difference between uses of words contains, unnoticed by most current speakers of the language, gems of unpretentious insight of countless generations. Second, some of the confusion concerning knowledge in which ordinary people and philosophers alike are often trapped by the overlappings and ambiguities sometimes involved in ordinary language itself may be expected gradually to give way before patient analyses pointing out the perils and modest proposals leading to occasional improvements. Third, those confusions concerning knowledge that result from indiscriminate intermingling of ordinary language and philosophical language may be expected to be somewhat diminished as philosophers learn increasingly either to express their insights in a refined ordinary language or else to make clear in such language what sort of technical language they are using. Fourth, the removal of linguistic confusions together with the achievement of constructive insights into the logic of the relations among epistemic and associated expressions may be expected to prepare the way for progress in theory of knowledge by clarifying the issues and presenting fruitful suggestions for their solution. Fifth, these same processes may be expected to make available to philosophers an increasingly well-understood and unambiguous linguistic instrument for the formulation and expression of whatever they are able to discern concerning knowledge. The value of this aspect of the work of linguistic analysts would, moreover, be difficult to exaggerate; for no matter what technical devices a philosopher may employ he must be prepared to explain his findings in ordinary language, and current analyses of ordinary language begin to have a precision far surpassing that of most traditional philosophers and a breadth and openness to all the forms of speech and thought that comes as a welcome relief from the narrowness of the prescriptions of earlier forms of philosophical analysis. Finally, some of the clarifications and constructive suggestions resulting from ordinary-language analysis may be expected to contribute not only to useful preparation and methodology for epistemological inquiry but also directly to the discernment of epistemological truths. The truth of a statement depends not upon the facts alone but upon agreement between the facts and what the statement means; so that, as ordinary-language philosophers themselves note, the discernment of the meaning of the statement as well as the discovery of the facts is involved in the discernment of truth. Moreover, especially in such a subject as epistemology, where a large part of the issue hinges upon what is meant, discernment of use and meaning may be a prominent part of the discernment of truth.

But however useful ordinary language analysis may be and however large the task it has yet to perform, such analysis can scarcely by itself constitute a sufficient method of epistemological inquiry. To begin with, such analysis deliberately deprives itself of the use of vast ranges of significant phenomenologically explorable experiential data to which any adequate theory of knowledge would seem to be responsible. In the second place, by confining itself to the forms of ordinary language—and even to those of a single tongue—, ordinary-language analysis renounces the use of significant findings in the physiological, psychological, sociological, anthropological, and even philological sciences that epistemology can ill-afford to ignore, and tends to ground its own findings too much in that faith and science of the past out of which the language of the present has grown. In the third place, ordinary-language analysis deprives itself of that development and refinement of new concepts and terms that has always seemed indispensable not only for the adequate expression of achieved philosophical insights but also for the achievement of new ones. In the fourth place, whereas the development and refinement of initially artificial and extraordinary deductive conceptual schemes has proved essential to clarity, ready reference, reliable transition, satisfactory comprehension, and growing insight in every particular area of knowledge from physics to jurisprudence and would seem to be even more so with reference to theory of knowledge itself, ordinary-language analysis specifically forbids its own participation in the development of any conceptual schemes which are not already implicit in ordinary language. Finally, by limiting itself to language in general and in particular to use rather than meaning, ordinary-language analysis precludes itself from any direct attack upon the basic epistemological problems of the structure of knowledge and the justification of knowledge claims from full-scale attack even upon the problem of the meaning of epistemic terms.

Index